SYSTEMATIC THEOLOGY.

Wm. B. Eerdmans ——————— Company
Grand Rapids, Michigan

SYSTEMATIC THEOLOGY

by

CHARLES HODGE

IN THREE VOLUMES

Volume I

Wm. B. Eerdmans Publishing Company
Grand Rapids, Michigan

Reprinted, October 1981

ISBN 0-8028-8135-1

PHOTOLITHOPRINTED BY EERDMANS PRINTING COMPANY
GRAND RAPIDS, MICHIGAN, UNITED STATES OF AMERICA

CONTENTS OF THE FIRST VOLUME.

INTRODUCTION.

CHAPTER I.

ON METHOD.

CHAPTER II.

THEOLOGY.

CHAPTER III.

RATIONALISM.

CHAPTER IV.

MYSTICISM.

PART I.

THEOLOGY PROPER.

CHAPTER I.

ORIGIN OF THE IDEA OF GOD.

CHAPTER II.

THEISM.

CHAPTER VI.

THE TRINITY.

CHAPTER VII.

THE DIVINITY OF CHRIST.

xiv CONTENTS OF THE FIRST VOLUME.

CHAPTER XIII.

ANGELS.

INDEX FOR THE THREE VOLUMES

A.

INDEX. 5

16 INDEX.

Ewald, Professor, John Ludwig (d. 1822),
admits that reconciliation to God must precede reformation, iii. 197.

Exaltation of Christ,
what it includes, ii. 626; Lutheran doctrine of ii. 631 ; the doctrine of some modern theologians, ii. 633.

"Exercise Scheme," ii. 282, iii. 7.

Existence of God,
in what sense a matter of intuition, i. 194 ; in what sense a matter of proof, i. 202 ; the proof of, i. 204 ff.

Expiation,
meaning of the word ii. 478; effected by vicarious punishment, symbolically by the sacrifices of the Old Testament, really by the death of Christ, ii. 478, 501, 507, 509.

Extreme Unction,
one of the seven sacraments of the Romish Church, iii. 495.

F.

Facts,
of theology found in the Bible, i. 10, 15 ; full induction needed, i. 12 ; principles to be inferred from them, i. 13 ; their authority admitted, i. 57 ; scientific men often invest their theories or conjectures with the authority due only to facts, ii. 20, 21, 27, 28.

Fairbairn, Principal Patrick (Glasgow),
on expiatory sacrifices, ii. 501.

Faith,
etymology of the Hebrew, Greek, and Latin words by which it is expressed, iii. 42 ; its generic idea is trust, iii. 43 ; the general and limited senses of the word, iii. 44 ; not to be considered simply in relation to religious truth, iii. 45 ; definitions of, founded on its subjective nature, iii. 45 ; definition founded on the nature of its object, iii.

53 ; definitions founded on the nature of the evidence on which it rests, iii. 57 ; it is a conviction founded on testimony or authority, iii. 60 ; proof of that position, iii. 63 ff ; religious faith, different kinds of, historical, temporary, and saving, their specific difference, iii. 67 ff. ; what is meant by the testimony of the Spirit which is the foundation of saving faith, iii. 69 ff.

Faith and Knowledge,
the difference between the two, iii. 46, 75, i. 353 ; knowledge essential to faith, i. 353, iii. 84 ; the impossible and the irrational cannot be believed, i. 352 f., iii. 83 ; what is true in religion cannot be false in philosophy, iii. 78 ; Lutheran doctrine on that point, iii. 79 ; the incomprehensible or what is above reason may be believed, iii. 81 ; Romish distinction between explicit and implicit faith, iii. 86.

Faith and Feeling,
faith is not founded on feeling, iii. 49, 88 ; it is not determined by the will, iii. 49 ; religious, however, not mere assent, iii. 89 ; it includes knowledge, assent, and trust, iii. 91.

Faith and Love,
Protestant doctrine that true faith is always attended by love, iii. 93 ; the Romish doctrine of " fides informis et fides formata," which makes love the essence of faith, iii. 94.

The Object of Faith,
distinction between " fides generalis" and " fides specialis," iii. 95 ; the special object of saving faith is Christ, *i. e.*, receiving the testimony of God concerning Him, iii. 96 ; Christ in all his offices the object of faith, iii. 99 ; is the sinner required to believe that Christ loves him ? iii. 99 ff.

of God," i. 364 ; definitions of God, i. 366 ff. ; divine attributes, nature of, i. 368 ff. ; classification of, i. 374 ; God's relation to the universe, i. 591 ff., ii. 22 ; his personality, i. 216, 238, 239, 379.

Gomarus (a leader in the Synod of Dort), taught a two-fold covenant, one with the visible, the other with the invisible Church: the sacraments belong to the former, iii. 564.

Goodness of God, includes benevolence, love, mercy, and grace: the difference between them, i. 427 ; relation of the goodness of God to the existence of evil, i. 429 ; different theories on the subject, i. 430 ff.

Good Works, their nature, iii. 231, 236 ; Romish doctrine, 233 ; works of supererogation, iii. 234 ; distinction between precepts and counsels, iii. 235 ; necessity of good works, iii. 238 ; controversy in the Lutheran Church on this subject, iii. 238 f. ; antinomianism, iii. 241 ; relation of good works to rewards, iii. 241 ; Romish doctrine, iii. 241 ; Protestant doctrine, iii. 243 f.

Gospel. See *Call.*

Gottschalk (d. 867), condemned by the Latin Church in the ninth century for teaching the doctrines of Augustine, ii. 168.

Gousset, Cardinal, the Eucharist produces grace by its inherent virtue, iii. 677 ; the eating of Christ's flesh (John vi. 48-65) is not spiritual but by the mouth, iii. 682 ; participation of the Lord's Supper not necessary to salvation, iii. 683 ; the Eucharist a sacrifice, iii. 687 ; on the state of unbaptized infants after death,

iii. 745, 746 ; the future punishment of the wicked everlasting, iii. 748 ; he admits that the general belief of the Romanists is that the fire which is everlasting is material, iii. 748 ; on purgatory, iii. 750.

Government, of God extends over all his creatures and all their actions, i. 575 ; the doctrine stated, i. 581 ; proof of it, i. 583 ff. ; its relation to the free acts of men, i. 588 ; to sin, i. 589 ; different theories concerning its nature, deistical theory, i. 591 ; theory of entire dependence, i. 592 ; of no efficiency in second causes, i. 595 ; of preëstablished harmony, i. 597; of " concursus," i. 598 ; the Scriptural doctrine, i. 605 ff ; distinction between the providential efficiency of God and the operation of the Spirit, i. 614, ii. 665.

Grace, meaning of the word, ii. 654; why the supernatural influence of the Spirit is called grace, ii. 654 ; distinct from the moral influence of the truth, ii. 655, 660 ff. ; common grace granted to all men, ii. 654, 668 ff.; Lutheran doctrine on that subject, ii. 656 ; rationalistic doctrine, ii. 657 ; effects of common grace, ii. 670 ; Wesleyan doctrine of sufficient grace, ii. 329 ; Remonstrant doctrine, ii. 327 ; Semi-Pelagian doctrine, ii. 712; scholastic distinction between preventing, coöperating, and sanctifying, and habitual grace, ii. 716 ; Tridentine doctrine, ii. 717 ; the synergistic controversy, ii. 720 ; Arminian controversy and action of the Synod of Dort, ii. 724.

Grace, Efficacious, why so called ; different answers

Hahn, Doctor Augustus,
on the doctrine of impanation, iii. 649.

Half-way Covenant,
controversy on the subject, iii. 567.

Hamilton, Sir William (d. 1856),
on Cousin's philosophy, i. 304; on the veracity of consciousness, i. 340; invincibility of belief involves the truth of the thing believed, i. 340; his arguments against transcendentalism, or the philosophy of the Infinite, i. 346 ff.; God, because infinite, cannot be known, cannot be conscious, cannot know, cannot be cause, cannot be a person, i. 347 ff.; makes God an object of faith but not of knowledge, i. 352; the Bible, he says, gives regulative, not absolute, knowledge of God, i. 354; arguments against his whole theory, i. 356 ff.

Harmony, Preëstablished,
theory of, i. 597.

Hartley, Doctor David (d. 1757),
a disciple of Locke, i. 249; his explanation of sensation and thought, i. 250.

Hase, Doctor Charles Augustus (Jena),
on Monism, ii. 731; on the nature of faith, iii. 57; definition of implicit faith, iii. 87; the Lutheran doctrine of justification, iii. 115.

Hasse, J. A.,
his exposition of Anselm's doctrine of grace, ii. 715.

Heathen,
the rule by which they are to be judged, i. 27, 28; they are to be converted to the faith of Christ, iii. 800; and by the ministry of the church, iii. 804; no Scriptural doctrine derived from a heathen source, iii. 785.

Heaven,
usage of the word in Scripture, ii. 630; designates a place as well as a state, ii. 630; Scriptural doctrine of, iii. 855, 859; is the consummation of the kingdom of Christ, iii. 859; recognition of friends in, iii. 781; Romish doctrine of, iii. 748.

Hebrews,
analysis of the epistle to the, ii. 496.

Heidegger, John Henry (d. 1698),
confounds power and knowledge in God, i. 395.

Heidelberg Catechism,
on original sin, ii. 229; the satisfaction of Christ, ii. 481; definition of saving faith, iii. 90; its special object, iii. 101; definition of justification, iii. 114; on the use of images in churches, iii. 304; definition of the sacraments, iii. 487; on the efficacy of baptism, iii. 580; on the Lord's Supper, iii. 633.

Heine, Heinrich,
his avowal of Hegelianism, iii. 430.

Hell,
meaning of the word, ii. 616; Scriptural doctrine of, iii. 875; objections to that doctrine answered, iii. 878; Romish doctrine of, iii. 747.

Helvetic Confession, First,
on the efficacy of the sacraments, iii. 501; on the Lord's Supper, iii. 627.

Helvetic Confession, Second,
on original sin, ii. 228; inability, ii. 258, 259; person of Christ, ii. 405; satisfaction of Christ, ii. 481; divine nature impassible, ii. 483; efficacious grace, ii. 681; justification, iii. 114; against the use of images, iii. 304; the sense in which the knowledge of the Scriptures is necessary to salvation, iii. 469; nature of the sacraments, iii. 487; the administrator of the sacraments, iii. 514; proper subjects of infant baptism, iii.

of Damascus, 97 ; Lamarck, 11 ; Limborch, 97 ; Livingstone, 39 ; Lubbock, 94 f. ; Luther, 98, 103 ; Lyell, 31–37 ; Mares, 98 ; Mivart, 5, 8, 32 ; Morell, 58 ; Morlot, 35 ; Morton, 63, 81 ; Müller, 90 ; Murchison, 31 ; Murphy, 20, 24 ; Nevin, 58 ; Olshausen, 51, 57 ; Origen, 66 f. ; Owen, 25 ; Pasteur, 8 ; Pelagius, 67 ; Pictet, 31 ; Prestwich, 39 ; Prichard, 80 ; Schemrling, 37 ; Sedgwick, 31, 36 ; Shedd, 52, 53, 59, 71, 74 ; St. Hilaire, 31 ; Strauss, 4 ; Tertullian, 67 ; Thomson, 20 ; Turrettin, 67 ; Tyndall, 8 ff. ; Usher, 40 ; Wallace, 9, 17, 18, 33 ; Whately, 94 ; Wilberforce, 68.

Man of Sin, iii. 812–823.

Manducation,
according to the Reformed (and to Augustine) it is by faith (to believe is to eat), iii. 640, 643 ; Calvin's view, iii. 644 ; Lutheran doctrine, iii. 667 ; doctrine of the Church of England, iii. 640.

Manichæans,
doctrine on the origin of evil, ii. 132.

Mansel, Dean Henry Longueville,
his " Limits of Religious Thought," i. 342 ; his definition of the Absolute and Infinite, i. 347 ; his conclusions from that definition : the Infinite cannot be known, must include all being, cannot know, cannot be cause, cannot have moral attributes, cannot be a person, i. 342, 347, 349, 351, 362 ; nevertheless our nature demands a personal God, i. 341, 342, 343 ; God not an object of knowledge, but of faith, i. 352 ; regulative knowledge, i. 354 ff. ; his use of the words " conception " and " knowledge," i. 336, 358 ; on the authority of consciousness, i. 361 ; on our consciousness

of self, i. 377, 378 ; anthropomorphism admitted to be the condition of all human theology, i. 343.

Marcionites,
their doctrine of the origin of evil, ii. 132.

Marck, John,
on the doctrine of mediate imputation, ii. 211 ; on the theory of a two-fold (half-way) covenant, iii. 563.

Mares, Samuel (d. 1675),
on divine concursus, i. 598 ; on the image of God, ii. 98.

Marheinecke, Philip Conrad (d. 1846),
makes the Bible teach the Hegelian philosophy, i. 6.

Maria Francisca,
miracles of, iii. 456.

Mariolatry, iii. 285 ff.

Marshall, Doctor John,
essential difference between physical and vital force, i. 266.

Marriage,
its nature, iii. 376 ; it must be between one man and one woman and for life, iii. 380, 380 ; proof of this, iii. 380 ff. ; polygamy tolerated by the law of Moses, iii. 381 ; forbidden by Christ, iii. 382 ff. ; a heathen man, if a polygamist, must renounce his polygamy before his admission to the Christian Church, iii. 387 ; in what sense marriage is a religious institution to be religiously solemnized, iii. 376 ; marriage as a civil contract, iii. 377 ; bishops not forbidden in 1 Timothy iii. 2 to marry a second time, iii. 388 ; marriage cannot be dissolved by the will of the parties or by the power of the State, iii. 378, 379 ; a higher state than celibacy, iii. 389 ; the analogue of the relation between Christ and his Church, iii. 370 ; Paul's doctrine on the subject, i'i 370, 373,

edge of God, i. 365 ; on the specific difference between knowledge and faith, iii. 55.

McIlvaine, Doctor Joshua Hall, "A Nation's Right to worship God," iii. 347.

McNeile, Doctor Hugh, the world not to be converted before the second coming of Christ, iii. 864.

Means of Grace, why so called? iii. 466 ; to what their efficacy is due, iii. 470, 501 ; the Word, iii. 466 ; the sacraments, iii. 485 ; baptism, iii. 526 ; the Lord's Supper, iii. 611 ; prayer, iii. 692.

Mediate Creation, i. 556.

Mediate Imputation. (See *Imputation.*)

Mediator, the Scriptural usage of the word, ii. 456 ; the sense in which the Church of Rome makes saints and angels mediators, ii. 456 ; Christ the only mediator between God and man, ii. 455 f.; the necessary qualifications for the work, ii. 456 f.; his threefold office as mediator, ii. 459.

Melancthon, Philip (d. 1560), explanation of the Trinity, i. 479 ; creation out of nothing, i. 556 ; definition of sin, ii. 180 ; his synergistic doctrine, ii. 324, 720 ; on the relation of good works to justification, iii. 238 ; the celibacy of the clergy insisted upon by the Church of Rome for the sake of power, iii. 375 ; the sacraments signs and seals, iii. 504.

Mental Reservation, iii. 445.

Merati (Romanist), on mixing wine and water in the Eucharist, iii. 617.

Mercy, a special form of goodness, i. 427.

Method, theology a science, i. 1 ; need of system, i. 2 ; nature of method and its importance as applied to theology, i. 3 ; the specula-

tive method, i. 4 ; the mystical method, i. 6 ; the inductive method, i. 9 ; the proper office of the Christian theologian, i. 10 ; necessity of the teaching of the Holy Spirit, i. 16.

Meyer, Henry Augustus William, on Ephesians v. 2, ii. 509 ; on our Lord's command "Swear not at all," iii. 309 ; on Ephesians vi. 4, iii. 353; on desertion as a ground of divorce, iii. 395 ; the "end" (finis hujus sæculi) contemporaneous with the second advent of Christ, iii. 839.

Michaelis, John David (d. 1791), denies all supernatural influence in the conversion of men, ii. 730 ; on the ground of the Levitical prohibitions as to marriage, iii. 408.

Michaelis, John Henry (d. 1738), on Leviticus xvii. 10, ii. 501 ; on Isaiah liii. 10, ii. 508 ; the literal meaning of the third commandment, iii. 305.

Middle Ages, theological characteristics of, i. 73.

Mill, John Stuart, his definition of a cause, i. 208 ; denial of final causes or design, i. 228.

Millennium, Jewish doctrine of, iii. 862 ; the patristic doctrine, iii. 863 ; the doctrine which makes the millennium subsequent to the second advent, iii. 843 ; the modern doctrine, iii. 858.

Miller, Hugh (d. 1856), on the unequal distribution of property in England, iii. 427.

Mind, its existence as a substance revealed in consciousness, i. 276, 277 ; its existence the most certain fact of knowledge, i. 277, 377 ; its essential attributes, i. 378 ; the existence of finite minds necessitates the belief in an Infinite Mind, i. 234 ; mind-force not the only

defines species "a primordial organic form," ii. 81.

Morus, Samuel Frederick Nathaniel (d. 1792),
on conversion, ii. 730.

Mosaic Economy,
included the covenant of grace, ii. 375; considered as a national covenant: a revelation of the law as a covenant of works: Moses taught what Paul taught of the plan of salvation, ii. 375; hence the different modes in which it is represented in the New Testament, ii. 375, 376; contrasted with the New Dispensation, ii. 376, 377.

Mosheim, John Lorenz (d. 1755), pious frauds of heathen origin, iii. 448; on the claim of different orders of monks of power over purgatory, iii. 770.

Motive,
meaning of the word, ii. 289; criterion of the relative strength of motives, ii. 289; in what sense the will is determined by the strongest motive, ii. 289.

Mozley, J. B.,
Bampton Lectures for 1865, on miracles; discussion of the theory of the intelligence of nature, i. 611; his definition of a miracle, i. 625.

Müller, Doctor Julius (Halle),
"every attempt to spiritualize matter ends in materializing spirit," i. 273; on Schleiermacher's theory of sin, ii. 140; alienation from God the essence of sin, ii. 148; on Augustine's doctrine of sin, ii. 159; his definition of free agency, ii. 292; the resurrection of the body not due to a participation of the Lord's Supper, iii. 677; comparison of the doctrines of Luther and Calvin on the Lord's Supper, iii. 667; against the ubiquity of Christ's body, iii. 671; a vital organizing force continues in the soul, but not operative between death and the resurrection, iii. 778; the general resurrection contemporaneous with the second coming of Christ, iii. 841.

Müller, Max,
on the Hindu religion and its effect on the Hindu character, i. 316, 317; on the unity of the human race, ii. 90.

Münzer,
his doctrine of community of goods, one of the causes of the "peasant war," iii. 430.

Murphy, John Joseph,
his works on "Habit and Intelligence in their Connection with the Laws of Matter and Force," his doctrine is that intelligence (not always conscious, but sometimes merely organizing) is inseparable from life, ii. 24.

Musculus,
on the omnipotence of God, i. 409.

Μυ rτήριον,
rendered "sacramentum," in the Vulgate, iii. 486.

Mysticism,
meaning of the word, i. 61; its philosophical use, i. 61; the sense in which evangelical Christians are called Mystics, i. 63; applied to all systems which exalt the feelings above reason, or the inward teaching of the Spirit above the Scriptures, i. 64; in this sense Schleiermacher's system is mystical, i. 65; mysticism is distinguished from spiritual illumination and the leading of the Spirit, i. 67, 68; in the early church, i. 69; in the Middle Ages, i. 73; the "Theologia Mystica" of the so-called Dionysius, the Areopagite, i. 70; character and influence of that work, i. 71 ff.; different classes of mediæval mystics, i. 74 ff.; mysticism at the time of the Reformation, i. 79; the Refor-

P.

Paley,
the Sabbath of perpetual obligation if given at the beginning, iii. 329 ; teaches that the right of property is founded on the law of the land, iii. 423.

Palfrey, John Gorham, D. D.,
his " History of New England " : the half-way covenant, iii. 567, 569.

Palmer, C. (in Herzog's Encyclopädie),
denies the divine, but asserts the moral, obligation of the Sabbath, iii. 324, 334.

Palmer, William (of the Oxford School),
denies that any moral qualification is requisite for admission to the rite of baptism, iii. 543.

Pandiabolism, i. 307 f.

Pangenesis, ii. 32.

Pantænus,
one of the heads of the catechist school of Alexandria, iii. 542.

Pantheism,
meaning of the term, i. 299 ; the three forms in which the theory is presented, i. 300 ; the principles which are involved in all the forms, i. 300 ff. ; Brahminical pantheism, i. 309 ff. ; Grecian pantheism, i. 318 ff. ; Mediæval pantheism, i. 328 ff. ; Modern pantheism, i. 330 ff. ; practical effects of the system, i. 332. *Authors referred to* (all in vol. i.) : Aristotle, 326 ff. ; Baur, 305 ; Bischer, 308 ; Calderwood, 301 ; Colebrooke, 318 ; Cousin, 300, 306, 309, 319 ; Döllinger, 319 ff. ; Duff, 318 ; Erigena, 329 ; Fichte, 301 ; Hamilton, 301, 304 ; Hegel, 302 ; Hunt, 302 f., 306 ; Jones, 318 ; Leo, 308 ; Michelet, 302 ; Morell, 304 ; Müller, 316 ff. ; Plato, 322 ff. ; Renan, 301 ; Ritter, 329 ; Rosenkranz,

307 ; Schwegler, 328 ; Schleiermacher, 302 ; Spinoza, 301, 303, 305, 330 ; Strauss, 301, 307 ; Tholuck, 308 ; Wegscheider, 299 ; Wilson, 313.

Pantheistical Christology, ii. 429.

Papacy,
the Antichrist of 2 Thessalonians ii. 3–10, iii. 813.

Paracelsus (d. 1541),
alchemist and theosophist, i. 83.

Paraclete,
the claims of the Montanists concerning, i. 69.

Paradise,
Scriptural usage of the word, iii. 727.

Parents,
their duties, iii. 352; their special obligation to secure a Christian education for their children, iii. 353.

Park, Professor Edwards A. (Andover),
his work on the atonement, ii. 578.

Parmenides,
Greek philosopher of the Eleatic School, i. 319.

Partial Inspiration, i. 181.

Pascal, Blaise (d. 1662),
on the imperfection of our knowledge of God, i. 350 ; on the Jesuit system of morals, iii. 445.

Pearson, Bishop John (d. 1686),
on the subordination of the Son and Spirit to the Father, i. 465 ; on the " descensus ad inferos," ii. 621 ; on the proper notion of faith, iii. 62.

Peccatum,
the distinction sometimes made between " peccatum " and " vitium," ii. 230.

Peck, George, D. D.,
on Christian perfection, iii. 192, 254.

Pelagius,
his profession and character, ii. 152 ; the fundamental principle of his system is that a man is responsible for nothing which is not within the power of his

doctrine of "concursus," i. 598
ff.; Scriptural principles: the
real existence of matter, i. 605
f.; the efficiency of physical
forces, i. 606; these uniformly
acting forces, or laws of nature,
always controlled by God, i.
607; the divine efficiency in
relation to vital processes, i.
610; over mind, i. 614; distinction between the providential
efficiency of God, and the operations of the Spirit, i. 614.

Prudentius,
on the intermediate state, iii.
739.

Psalter of Mary, iii. 286.

Punishment,
the primary ground of its infliction is not the reformation of
the offender, or the prevention
of crime, but the satisfaction of
justice, i. 417 ff.; punishment
not merely. a natural consequence, i. 426, iii. 197; capital
punishment, iii. 363; future
punishment, iii. 868 ff.

Purgatory,
the Romish doctrine, iii. 749;
arguments urged by Romanists
in support of the doctrine, iii.
751 ff.; arguments against it,
iii. 757 ff.; under the power
of the keys, iii. 750, 758; this
doctrine the great engine of
priestly power, iii. 751; its
history, iii. 766 ff.

Puritan,
historical use of the word: the
broader and the more restricted
sense of the term, iii. 544; the
Puritan theory of the Church,
iii. 544 f.; principles regulating
admission to Church privileges,
iii. 569, 571.

Pusey, Doctor, Edward Bouverie
(Oxford),
on prayers for the dead, iii. 752;
his denunciation of the doctrine of purgatory, iii. 752,
756.

Q.

Quakers,
their origin, i. 88; their peculiar religious system a form of
mysticism, i. 92; Barclay's
views, i. 93; doctrine of the
orthodox Quakers, i. 90; different views as to the nature
and authority of the "inward
light" given to all men, i. 92
f., 95; what is meant by the
leading of the Spirit, i. 96 f.;
many called Quakers are really
Deists, i. 92.

Quenstedt (Lutheran theologian, A.
D. 1617–1688),
on the distinction between revelation and inspiration, i. 156;
the attributes of God differ
from each other only in our
conceptions, i. 370; he teaches
however that they are not all
to be resolved into causality, i.
373; nature of God's omnipresence, i. 384; his idea of
the divine immutability, i. 391;
defines the will of God "the
essence of the Deity considered as inclined to good," i.
402; "concursus" he understands to be the influx of the
divine efficiency into that of
the creature, so that the two
are one, i. 599; the difference
of God's coöperation with necessary and free causes, i. 601;
in sinful acts: the effect is
from God, the defect from
the creature, i. 602; common
grace is the grace common to
all who hear the gospel, not to
all mankind, ii. 656, 657; the
Word of God has inherent,
supernatural, divine power,
which is always savingly efficacious unless resisted, ii. 656,
657, iii. 480, 481; the Spirit
only acts in and through the
Word: the action or efficiency
of the two are one and inseparable, iii. 481; the world is to
be annihilated, iii. 853.

deny the inability of fallen men to do what is spiritually good, ii. 327; this ability however is "gracious," *i. e.*, due to the grace of God, ii. 327, 675; this grace granted in sufficient measure to all men, ii. 328, 675; those who improve this grace are converted or saved, ii. 328; those whom God foresees will thus believe and persevere in faith, He elects and determines to save, ii. 328; grace is called efficacious "ab eventu," ii. 676; justification, with them, is simply pardon, iii. 190; the ground of it faith, or evangelical obedience, iii. 167, 190 ff.; the work of Christ not a satisfaction to justice, ii. 575; the works which are declared not to be the ground of justification are the perfect works of the Adamic law, iii. 136 f.; on perfection in this life, iii. 253 f.; on the sacraments, iii. 490.

Renan,
defines pantheism as materialism or the denial of a living God, i. 301.

Representation,
the principle of, everywhere recognized in Scripture, ii. 198.

Reprobation,
how far sovereign and how far judicial, ii. 320, 321.

Reservation, Mental, iii. 445.

Reserve,
in teaching, iii. 87.

Resurrection,
of Christ, the certainty of, ii. 626; the importance of, ii. 627; of men, the doctrine of, iii. 771; the identity of the present and future bodies, iii. 774; wherein that identity consists, iii. 775; nature of the resurrection body, iii. 780; in what sense it is to be spiritual, iii. 783; the general resurrection coincident with the second advent of Christ,

iii. 838; of the martyrs, iii 841; the doctrine not borrowed by the Hebrews from the heathen, iii. 785; history of the doctrine, iii. 785.

Reubelt, J. A.,
a translator of "Gess: The Scriptural Doctrine of the Person of Christ," ii. 431.

Revelation,
supernatural, possibility of, i. 35; necessity of, i. 36, 364, iii. 75; evidences of, i. 53; its relation to philosophy, i. 55, iii. 76, 78; to science, i. 57; the progressive character of the revelations contained in the Bible, i. 446; revelation distinguished from inspiration, i. 155.

Revelation, the book of, iii. 826.

Reward,
relation to works, iii. 243 f.; Romish doctrine on the subject, iii. 241; merit of congruity and of condignity, iii. 241.

Richard, of St. Victor (d. 1173),
held that the truths of faith should be sustained by rational demonstration, i. 74; he belonged to the class of evangelical mystics, i. 79.

Righteousness,
original: wherein it consisted, ii. 99; Romish doctrine on the subject, ii. 103; Pelagian doctrine, ii. 106; arguments to prove, against the Pelagian doctrine, that moral character may precede moral action, ii. 107 ff.; the two distinct meanings, the moral and the forensic, of the word righteousness, iii. 119, 141; the righteousness of Christ: wherein it consists, iii. 142; in what sense is it the righteousness of God? iii. 143; the sense in which it is imputed to the believer, iii. 144;

Ritter,
his exposition of the philosophy of Scotus Erigena, i. 329; on Anselm's doctrine of the relation of faith and reason, i

75; on the philosophy and theology of Duns Scotus, ii. 717; on the world-period, of Brahmins, Stoics, and Plato, iii. 787.

Ritualism,
the theory that grace and the benefits of redemption are conveyed only through the sacraments; opposed to the Scriptures and to the whole spirit of Christianity, iii. 520 f.

Rivet, Andrew,
his work against the doctrine of mediate imputation and in support of the decision of the French Synod against Placeus, ii. 206.

Robinson, Doctor Edward (d. 1863),
his refutation of the legend of the discovery of the true cross, iii. 461; his arguments to show that, from the scarcity of water, the baptism of the multitudes of the early Christians, by immersion, was well nigh impossible, iii. 534 f.

Romanists,
their doctrine as to the rule of faith, i. 104; incompleteness and obscurity of the Scriptures, i. 105 f.; on tradition, i. 108 ff.; their theory of the Church, i. 129 ff.; the organ of its infallibility, i. 112; their doctrine on the original state of man, ii. 103; on sin, ii. 164; on original sin, ii. 174 ff.; on the imputation of Adam's sin, ii. 175; on the person of Christ and the Trinity they teach the doctrine of the Church universal: see those subjects; on Christ's descent into hell, ii. 621; on the satisfaction of Christ, ii. 484; on the doctrine of grace or influence of the Spirit, ii. 717; on regeneration, iii. 27; on faith, iii. 89; their distinction between explicit and implicit faith, iii. 86; between faith as formed and unformed,

iii. 94; relation of faith to justification, iii. 165; their doctrine on justification, iii. 166; on good works, iii. 135, 233, works of supererogation, iii. 234; precepts and counsels, iii. 235; on perfectionism, iii. 251; on the decalogue, iii. 273; invocation of saints and angels, iii. 281; idolatrous worship of the Virgin Mary, iii. 285; worship of images, iii. 296; marriage a sacrament, iii. 398; on divorce, iii. 397; on the sacraments, iii. 489; their number, iii. 492; their efficacy, iii. 508; on baptism, iii. 609; on the Eucharist, iii. 677; transubstantiation, iii. 678; adoration of the host, iii. 681; the state of the dead, iii. 743; the "limbus patrum" iii. 744; "limbus infantum:" no unbaptized infant is a partaker of the redemption of Christ, iii. 745; hell, iii. 747; heaven, iii. 748; purgatory, iii. 749; satisfactions for sin, iii. 753; the power of absolution, iii. 494, 753, 758; on Antichrist, iii. 831.

Romans,
epistle to the, the positions which it assumes or asserts, ii. 494.

Rosa Maria,
of Lima: miracles ascribed to her, iii. 456.

Rosenkranz,
the identity of God and man, the fundamental principle of religion and philosophy, i. 6; avowed deification of evil, i. 307.

Rosenmüller, John George (d. 1815),
literal meaning of the Third Commandment, iii. 305; Genesis ix. 6, enjoins death as the punishment of murder, iii. 363; the law in Leviticus xviii. 18 does not forbid the marriage of a deceased wife's sister, iii. 416; marriage constitutes the

S.

niary and penal satisfaction, ii. 470 ff. ; the Protestant doctrine as presented in the symbols of the Lutheran and Reformed churches, ii. 480 ff. ; its intrinsic worth, ii. 482 ; the Romish doctrine on that point, ii. 484 ; the doctrine of the Scotists and Remonstrants denying the intrinsic worth of Christ's satisfaction, ii. 485 ; Christ's satisfaction rendered to justice, ii. 489 ; rendered to the law, ii. 493 ; proof of the Protestant doctrine from the priestly office of Christ, ii. 496 ; because He was a sacrifice for our sins, ii. 498 ff., 508 ff. ; and bare our sins, ii. 504 ; He saves us by his death, by his blood, ii. 514 ; He was made a curse for us, ii. 516 ; He redeems us from the law as a covenant of works, ii. 517 ; the Protestant doctrine concerning satisfaction, involved in what the Bible teaches of the believer's union with Christ, and other doctrines, ii. 520 ; the doctrine is implied (and therefore proved) in the religious experience of believers in all ages, ii. 523 ; objections urged against the doctrine : the only legitimate objections must be those founded on Scripture, ii. 527 ; it is said that the innocent cannot be treated as guilty, or the guilty as innocent, ii. 530 ff. ; the modern substitute for the Protestant doctrine unsatisfactory, ii. 533 ff. ; it is denied that there is any such attribute in God as vindicatory justice, which calls for satisfaction on account of sin, ii. 539 ; the common doctrine assumes an antagonism in God between love and justice, ii. 540 ; satisfaction unnecessary if the sinner repents, ii. 541 ; the concise statement given by Delitzsch

of the essential elements of the church doctrine, ii. 543 ; the satisfaction of Christ rendered specially for those given to him by the Father, ii. 544 ff. ; but as it is infinitely meritorious and as well suited to one man as to another, it is an adequate ground for the offer of salvation of men, ii. 557 ; the Romish doctrine of satisfaction as a part of repentance, iii. 493, 753. *Authors referred to* (all volume ii.) : Alexander, 508 ; Anselm, 486 ; Bähr, 498 ; Bretschneider, 484, 513 ; Calvin, 513 ; Curcellæus, 486 ; Delitzsch, 498 ; 507, 512, 543 ; Dorner, 538 ; Ebrard, 496, 533 ; Eisenmenger, 500 ; Emmons, 484 ; Fairbairn, 501 ; Harbaugh, 533 ; Hofmann, 498 ; Keil, 498 ; Limborch, 486 ; Meyer, 509 , Michaelis, 498, 501, 508 ; Outram, 500 ; Robinson, 512 ; Schoettgen, 500 ; Schmidt, 512 ; Scotus, Duns, 486 ; Sykes, 498 ; Toplady, 526 ; Wahl, 512 ; Wegscheider, 513 ; Wesley, 526 ; Young, 498.

Saving Faith,
founded on the testimony of the Spirit with and by the truth, iii. 68 ; proof of that doctrine from Scripture and from experience, iii. 70 ff. ; it is not mere assent, but includes trust, iii. 90 f. ; its special object is Christ, iii. 96 ; and consists in the act of receiving him, in all his offices, as our God and Saviour, iii. 97, 99 ; how far must the sinner believe that God, for Christ's sake, is reconciled to him personally, iii. 99 ff. ; assurance not necessary to saving faith, iii. 106 ; the grounds of the assurance of salvation as presented in Romans viii., iii. 110 ; this faith works by love and purifies the heart, iii. 93.

knowledge, i. 25, ii. 646 ff.; parents are bound to see that they are made part of the education afforded to their children, iii. 353 ff.

Scudamore, W. E., formerly Fellow of St. John's College, " Eucharistica, a commentary on the order for the Administration of the Lord's Supper " : on the kind of bread used in that ordinance, iii. 615 ; on mixing water with the wine in the Eucharist, iii. 617 ; on mixing bread and wine together and the Syrian practice of dipping the bread into the wine, iii. 620 ; on withholding the cup from the laity: enjoined by the Council of Constance, iii. 621.

Second Advent. See *Advent*, iii. 790 ff.

Second Canon, as some Romanists call the Apocryphal books of the Old Testament, i. 105.

Second Commandment, iii. 290 ff.

Seiss, Doctor Joseph Augustus, his book, entitled " The Last Times," teaches that the 'final judgment is to be a protracted administration, iii. 845 ; men and nations are to survive the end of the world as described by St. Peter, iii. 864 ; this earth freed from the curse is to be the future heaven of the redeemed, iii. 866.

Selden, John (d. 1654), " De Legibus Hebræorum," teaches that the Jewish Sabbath was simply a day of relaxation, iii. 337.

Seleucia, Council of (A. D. 359), adopted a Semi-Arian Creed, i. 144.

Self-Defence, the right of, iii. 364, 365.

Self Determination, distinguished from self-determination of the will, ii. 294.

Selfishness, the theory which makes all sin

to consist therein, ii. 144; objections to it, ii. 145.

Semi-Arians, their doctrine concerning Christ, i. 455 f., 459.

Semi-Pelagianism, arose principally from the opposition of the monks to Augustine's denial of the merit of good works, and his doctrine of predestination, ii. 165 ; the principal leaders of the movement were Cassian, Vincent of Lerins, and Faustus of Rhegium, ii. 165; they taught that men are enfeebled, but not spiritually dead, since the fall of Adam, ii. 166, 712 f.; they need the assistance of divine grace, ii. 166, 712 f.; this assistance is moral suasion as to its nature and mode of action, ii. 167, 714 ; the sinner begins the work of turning to God (he does not need the " gratia præveniens "), ii. 167 ; God aids the efforts of the returning sinner, and the sinner coöperates with the aid or grace afforded, ii. 167 ; of course there is no sovereignty in election or predestination, ii. 165, 712 ; this system sanctioned by the Synod of Arles, A. D. 475, ii. 166 ; condemned by the councils of Orange and Valence, A. D. 529, ii. 167 f. ; in the Latin Church the Dominicans were inclined to Augustinianism, the Franciscans to Semi-Pelagianism, ii. 715 f.; the Council of Trent took a middle ground between these parties, ii. 717.

Semler, John Solomon (d. 1791), " Historia descensus Christi ad inferos," ii. 621.

Senses, the, we are compelled by a law of our nature to confide in their testimony within their legitimate sphere, i. 60: they give us immediate knowledge of the ob-

jective reality of their objects,
i. 192 ; Romanists deny their
authority in matters of faith,
i. 59 f.

Separation,
causes which Romanists admit,
justify the separation of hus-
band and wife, iii. 400.

Serpent, the, ii. 127.

Seven Sacraments,
of the Church of Rome, iii. 492 ff.

Seventh Commandment, iii. 368.

Shedd, Doctor W. G. T. (New
York),
philosophical explanation of the
doctrine of the Trinity, i. 481 ;
his exposition of realism, ii.
52 ; on the mediæval mystics,
i. 76 ; on the Romish doctrine
of original sin, ii. 177 ; Anselm's doctrine of sin and grace,
ii. 715 ; on the difference between the soteriology of Anselm and that of Protestants,
iii. 149.

Sheol, ii. 616 ; iii. 717, 734, 738.

Shields, Professor Charles Wood-
ruff (Princeton),
on the philosophy of the Absolute, i. 365.

Sin,
the nature of the question concerning it, ii. 130 ; its psychological, as distinguished from its
moral nature, ii. 131 ; metaphysical theories : (1) the
dualistic theory, ii. 132 ; (2)
that sin is merely limitation, ii.
133 ; (3) Leibnitz's doctrine
that sin is a necessary consequence of the imperfection of
the creature, ii. 134 ; (4) Antagonism, ii. 137 ; (5) Schleiermacher's doctrine, ii. 138 ; (6)
Sensuous theory, ii. 140 ; (7)
that all sin consists in selfishness,
ii. 144 ; doctrine of the early
Church, ii. 149 ; Pelagian doctrine, ii. 152 ff. ; Augustine's
doctrine, ii. 157 ; the philosophical element of his doctrine, ii. 157 ; the sense in
which he made sin a negation,

ii. 158 ; why he so represented
it, ii. 159 ; moral element of
his doctrine, ii. 159 ; connection of his doctrine on sin
with his religious experience,
ii. 160 ff. ; in what sense he
makes all sin voluntary, ii.
161 ; his whole system of doctrine the logical, and Scrip-
turally sustained, consequence
of what the Spirit taught him
of his own sinfulness, 160 f.

Doctrine of the Latin Church,
great diversity of views in that
Church, on the nature of sin,
ii. 164 ; Semi-Pelagian doctrine, ii. 165 ; doctrine of Anselm, ii. 169 ; doctrine of Abelard, ii. 169 ; doctrine of
Thomas Aquinas, ii. 171 ;
doctrine of the Scotists, ii.
173 ; Tridentine doctrine, ii.
174.

Protestant Doctrine,
sin defined by Protestants as
want of conformity in act, disposition or state, to the divine
law, ii. 180, 187 ; sin is a specific evil, ii. 181 ; it has a relation to law : not of expediency,
or of reason, but of God, ii.
182 ; that law requires perfect
conformity to its demands, so
that everything short of moral
perfection in a rational creature is of the nature of sin, ii.
184 ; it does not, therefore,
consist exclusively in acts of
the will, ii. 186 ; sin includes
guilt and pollution, *i. e.*, it is
related both to the justice and
holiness of God, ii. 188. *Authors referred to* (all vol. ii.) :
Abelard, 169, f. ; Ambrose,
151 ; Amyrant, 205 ; Andra-
dius, 178 ; Anselm, 169 ; Aquinas, 171 ; Athanasius, 151 ;
Augustine, 132 f., 154, 157 ff. ;
Baier, 180 ; Baur, 132 f., 177
f. ; Bellarmin, 178 f. ; Beza,
209 ; Bretschneider, 140, 143 ;
Calvin, 209 ; Cappel, 205

his providence, ii. 337 ; and in the dispensations of his grace, ii. 339, iii. 475.

Speaker's Commentary,
the idolatry introduced by Jeroboam consisted in the worship of the true God by idols, iii. 293.

Species,
meaning of the word, ii. 78 ; definitions of, ii. 79 ff. ; evidence of the identity of species, ii. 82 ff. ; proof that the human race are of one species, ii. 86 ff.; species immutable, ii. 79 ; on the different theories of the evolution of species, see *Development. Authors referred to* (all volume ii.) : Agassiz, 80 ; Bachman, 79 ; Candolle, de, 80 ; Cuvier, 80 ; Dana, 81 ; Flourens, 79 ; Morton, 81 ; Prichard, 80.

Speculative Philosophy,
the name given to the system which assumes that all truth is to be deduced from certain postulates of nature and of the laws of being, i. 4 f. ; modifications which in modern times this philosophy has induced in the doctrine concerning God and his relation to the world, i. 6, 300 ; see also under the heads of the several attributes of God ; on the nature of man, ii. 62, 447 ff. ; on sin, ii. 133–149 ; on the person of Christ, ii. 429–447 ; on his work, ii. 450, 589 ; on regeneration, iii. 18–27 ; on justification, iii. 196, –212 ; on the sacraments and the Church, iii. 650–661.

Spencer, Herbert,
" First Principles of a New Philosophy " : he teaches that the unity of religion and science consists in both admitting that the power manifested in the universe is inscrutable, i. 42 ; inscrutable force, without consciousness, or intelligence, or will, is God, i. 241 ; asserts the correlation of physical and mental forces, but admits that it is mysterious how light becomes a mode of consciousness. i. 273.

Spinoza (b. 1632),
admitted the existence of only one substance of which the attributes are thought and extension, i. 331 ; the infinite alone is real, all else is phenomenal or apparent, i. 331 ; hence finite minds are transient manifestations of the infinite mind, i. 301 ; human thoughts or acts are simply forms of God's activity, i. 303 ; there is no freedom of action in God or man, i. 303 ; sin not a moral evil, it is simply limitation of being : power and goodness are identical, i. 305, ii. 133 ; we can have as clear an idea of God as we have of a triangle, i. 338 ; intelligence and will in God are no more like intelligence and will in us than " canis, signum cœleste " is like " canis, animal latrans," i. 394 ; a miracle is declared to be an event the cause of which is unknown, i. 627.

Spirit, The Holy,
meaning of the word " spirit," i. 376 ; the essential attributes of a spirit, i. 377 f. ; why the third person of the Trinity is called " The Spirit," i. 522 ; his personality, i. 522 ff. ; his divinity, i. 527 ; his relation to the Father and the Son, i. 528 ; his work in nature, i. 529 ; the giver of intellectual gifts, i. 530 ; his office in the economy of redemption, i. 531 ; history of the doctrine, i. 532 ; the Spirit the author of revelation and inspiration, i. 531, 532 ; his influence on the minds of men in the form of common grace, ii. 654 ff. ; distinct from the providential efficiency of

God, ii. 665 ; the effects of this common influence of the Spirit, ii. 670 ; his certainly efficacious influence, ii. 675 ff. ; history of the doctrine, ii. 710 ff. ; effects of the saving influences of the Spirit : conviction of sin, ii. 273, 672 ; regeneration, iii. 3, 29 ff. ; spiritual illumination, i. 67, 179 ; his guidance, i. 98 ; his indwelling in believers, i. 532, iii. 105, 227, 228 ; sanctification and all its fruits, iii. 216, 229 ; his testimony to and with the truth, iii. 69 ff. ; his inward witness to the sonship of believers, iii. 107.

Spiritual Death,
involves entire destitution of holiness, or the absence of spiritual life, and all ability to do what is spiritually good, in 244.

Spiritual Discernment, ii. 261.
explained by the Apostle in First Corinthians ii. 14, ii. 262.

Spirituality of God,
we get the idea of spirit from self-consciousness, i. 376 ; in assuming that God is a Spirit we affirm that He has all the attributes which belong essentially to our spiritual nature, namely, self-consciousness, personality, intelligence, will and power, and moral nature, i. 379 ; the Scriptures teach that He possesses all these attributes, i. 380.

Spontaneity,
often used as antithetical to necessity, for voluntary action : in this sense, materialists deny that there is any evidence of spontaneity in nature, i. 271, 278, iii. 696 ; sometimes the word is used as antithetical to reflection or deliberation : in this sense, any feeling or act is spontaneous which reveals itself in the consciousness by a law of our nature or from the habitual state of the mind, as

pity, a sense of justice, etc., ii. 286.

Stahl, Frederick Julius,
his " Philosophie des Rechts " · ethics and jurisprudence founded on theism, iii. 260 ; the canon law wrong in making error as to the condition of one of the parties, as bond or free, a ground for annulling the marriage contract, iii. 379 ; the state bound to conform to the divine law in its legislation concerning marriage, iii. 404 ; on the foundation of the right of property, iii. 425 ; on Communism, iii. 432.

Stancarus, Franz (d. 1574),
contemporary of the Reformers, in opposition to Osiander, who held that justifying righteousness is the divine essence, taught that the righteousness of Christ was the work of his human nature exclusively, iii. 182.

Stapfer, Professor John Frederick (d. 1775).
" Institutiones Theologiæ Polemicæ " : resolves justice into wisdom and benevolence, i. 419; adopted the theory of mediate imputation, ii. 207.

Stapleton, Thomas (Romanist : d. 1598),
state of the Church in the time of Antichrist, iii. 835.

State, the,
a divine institution, iii. 357 ; limits of its authority, iii. 341, 358, 359 ; its relation to the Church, ii. 605 ; in England, iii. 544.

Stephen,
" Thesaurus " : on the word βαπτίζω, iii. 527.

Steudlin,
" Dogmatik " : teaches that justification by faith means that men are made righteous or upright by faith in the great principles of moral and religious truth, iii. 135.

necessary belief involved in self-consciousness, i. 277, 378, ii. 387 ; it has objective existence, continued identity, and power : it acts, i. 606 ; the existence of substance denied by Hume, i. 214; by Comte, i. 254 f. ; by the advocates of the doctrine of continued creation (so far as creatures are concerned), i. 579 ; by President Edwards in his theory of identity, ii. 217 ; by those who resolve all matter into force, i. 606 ; this denial subverts the foundation of all knowledge, inasmuch as it involves the denial of the veracity of consciousness, i. 214.

Sufficient Grace,
the doctrine of, as held by the Remonstrants and Wesleyan Arminians, i. 31, ii. 327, 329.

Suicer,
on the word βάπτισμα, iii. 536 ; on the early sect (Aquarii) who used water instead of wine in the Lord's Supper, iii. 616 ; on the Oriental custom of mixing the bread and wine in the Eucharist, iii. 620.

Suicide, iii. 367.

Sunday Laws, iii. 340.

Supererogation, Works of, iii. 234.

Supernatural,
meaning of the word, i. 19, 154, 623, iii. 37, 214.

Supernaturalists,
those who, in opposition to Rationalists, admit a supernatural divine revelation, ii. 729.

" Suppositum,"
meaning of the word, i. 454.

Supralapsarianism,
the theory of, ii. 316; objections to, ii. 318.

Swearing, False, iii. 305.

Swedenborg, Emanuel (b. 1688),
on the person of Christ, ii. 421 ; his doctrines as presented in his book " Vera Christiana Religio," ii. 423 ; his doctrine of the resurrection, iii. 772.

Synagogues, iii. 337.

Synergistic Controversy, ii. 720.

T.

Tables of the Decalogue, iii. 274.

Talmud,
the doctrine of, concerning Sheol, iii. 734.

Tappan, Chancellor Henry P. (University of Michigan),
" Review of Edwards : " definition of the self-determining power of the will, ii. 294.

Taylor, Isaac, L. L. D. (d. 1865),
what is immaterial can have no relation to space : it can have no " ubi," iii. 713 ; neither can it have any relation to time, or duration measured by succession, iii. 714 ; hence, he infers that the soul has a spiritual (yet a material) body, through which it acts when the outward body dies, iii. 714.

Taylor, Bishop Jeremy (d. 1667),
his " Ductor Dubitantium," on the celibacy of the clergy, iii. 376 ; he says that all the points of difference between the Church of England and the Church of Rome serve the ends of covetousness and ambition, iii. 455 ; the souls of believers are after death happy in paradise as distinguished from heaven, iii. 742.

Taylor, Doctor Nathaniel (d. 1858),
a free agent must have plenary power to do whatever is required, iii. 11; happiness is the chief good, iii. 11 ; self-love, or the desire of happiness, constitutional and, therefore, innocent, is the determining motive in all voluntary action, iii. 12 ; sin consists in seeking our happiness in the creature : holiness in seeking our happiness in God, iii. 12 ; regeneration is a change of purpose, a determination to seek happiness in

the Orthodox all represented in that Council, i. 455 ff. ; sense in which the Council used the words ὑπόστασις, οὐσία, and ὁμοούσιος, i. 454; corresponding difficulty in the Latin Church in determining the meaning of the words, " substantia," " subsistentia," and "persona," i. 454; modification of the Nicene Creed by the Council of Constantinople, A. D. 381, i. 457; the so-called Athanasian Creed, i. 457; points decided by the Council of Nice, against the Sabellians, i. 459; against the Arians and Semi-Arians, i. 459; use made by the Arians of the Septuagint version of Proverbs viii. 22, i. 455; Nicene doctrine as to the mutual relation of the persons of the Trinity, i. 460; doctrine of the Nicene fathers as to the subordination of the Son to the Father, and of the Spirit to the Son, i. 462 ff. ; the eternal generation of the Son as taught by them, i. 468; meaning of John v. 26, i. 470; the eternal sonship of the Second Person of the Trinity, i. 471 ff. ; the relation of the Spirit to the Father and the Son, i. 477; difference between the Greek and Latin churches on that point, i. 477; philosophical statements of the doctrine of the Trinity, i. 478 ff.

Trommius,
on the word βαπτίζω, iii. 529.

Trullo, Council in (A. D. 692),
permitted the marriage of priests and deacons : which is still allowed in the Greek Church, iii. 376.

Trust,
the primary element of faith, iii. 42 ; Protestants assert and Romanists deny that trust enters into the nature of saving faith, iii. 91 ff.

Truth,
according to Scripture is that which is trustworthy : it is that which is what it appears or is declared to be, i. 436 ; the truth of God as a divine attribute, is that perfection of his nature which renders Him in every aspect worthy of entire confidence, i. 437 ; it is therefore the foundation not only of all religion but also of all knowledge, i. 437 ; theological distinctions on the subject, i. 437 ; modern philosophical theologians resolve the truth of God into the uniformity of law, i. 438 ; revealed truth gradually communicated, iii. 288 ; sacredness of truth between man and man, iii. 437 ; are there any cases in which the obligation to speak the truth ceases ? iii. 442 ff.

Truths, Necessary,
(see *Intuitions, Primary Beliefs*), the denial of such truths the most fatal form of scepticism, i. 192, 198, 340.

Turrettin, Francis (d. 1687),
on the nature of the divine attributes and their relation to the divine essence, i. 370 ; the eternal generation of the Son relates to his person and not to his essence : " sic Filius est Deus a seipso, licet non sit a seipso Filius," i. 468 ; on the doctrine of concursus : " causa secunda non potest movere, nisi moveatur," i. 598; how this doctrine can be reconciled with the responsibility of men for their sins, i. 603 ; on the nature of the penalty for Adam's sin which comes upon his posterity, ii. 211 ; the distinction between the covenant of redemption and the cove-

nant of grace, ii. 359 ; the sense in which the Virgin Mary may be called the Mother of God, ii. 393; the acts of Christ belong to each of his three offices : his death was the sacrifice of a priest, the teaching of a prophet, and the triumph of a king, ii. 461 ; the sense in which Christ bore the penalty of the law, ii. 473 ; on Bellarmin's view of efficacious grace, ii. 678 ; the sense in which the Spirit's influence may be called physical, ii. 685 ; the distinction between regeneration and conversion, iii. 3, 4 ; distinction between knowledge and faith, iii. 61 ; the sinner, he says, is not required to believe that his sins are remitted, but that they will be remitted to him as penitent and believing, iii. 100 ; the sense in which the righteousness of Christ is imputed to the believer, iii. 145 ; he quotes from Bellarmin a clear admission of the Protestant doctrine on that subject, iii. 146; the world is to be renewed, and not annihilated at the last day, iii. 853.

Turrianus,
a Jesuit who defended the genuineness of the decretals of Isidore ; effectually answered by Blondell (A. D. 1628), iii. 451.

Twesten, Professor Augustus D. Chr. (Berlin),
successor of Schleiermacher in the University of Berlin : as a theologian, shows greater deference to the teachings of Scripture than his predecessor, i. 9 ; he endeavours to combine the two theories, that the glory of God and that the production of the highest amount of happiness is the end of creation, i. 436.

Tyler, Professor Samuel (Washington, D. C.),
his " Progress of Philosophy : " his view of Hamilton's doctrine that God is an object of faith, but not of knowledge, i. 350 ; he himself teaches that, as our intelligence of God is by analogy, it matters little whether the conviction be called knowledge or faith, i. 360.

Tyndall, Professor John (London), the physics of the brain throw no light on the facts of consciousness : that a definite thought and a definite molecular action of the brain occur simultaneously teaches us nothing of the relation of the one to the other, i. 251 ; the evolution of life and especially of mind from lifeless matter pronounced an absurdity too monstrous to be entertained, provided matter be what it is generally taken to be, ii. 8, 9 ; but if spirit and matter are only two opposite faces of the " same great mystery," the case is different, ii. 9 ; the evolution hypothesis does not solve the mystery of the universe, it only transposes the conception of the origin of life to the indefinitely distant past, ii. 10 ; everything is to be referred to the operation of physical causes ; no evidence of spontaneous action, *i. e.*, of will, ever having occurred in nature, iii. 696 ; prayer for rain is as absurd as praying that the St. Lawrence should roll up the Falls of Niagara, iii. 696.

Tyso,
his " Defence of the Personal Reign of Christ" : says that the Gospel is not designed for the conversion of the world : it has never converted a single village, iii. 864.

U.

Ubiquity,
of the human nature of Christ, according to Lutherans, is a consequence of the hypostatical union, ii. 408 ff.; the relation of the ubiquity of Christ's body to the Lutheran doctrine concerning the Lord's supper, ii. 414 f., iii. 670 ff.

Ullmann, Professor,
his "Reformers before the Reformation," his classification of the mediæval mystics, i. 76; the pantheistical tendency of their system, i. 77; its corrupting influence among the people, i. 77; the central point of Christianity is the oneness of Deity and humanity effected by the incarnation of God and the deification of man, i. 174; the life of Christ is Christianity, i. 174; the oneness of God and man the fundamental idea of Schleiermacher's theology as of Christianity itself, ii. 428, iii. 20.

Ultramontanism,
the Italian or (Jesuit) theory of Papacy as distinguished from the Gallican, iii. 452.

Understanding,
as distinguished from knowing, i. 50.

"Unigenitus," Bull,
issued by Clement XI. against the Jansenists, ii. 680; propositions condemned in that bull, ii. 680.

Union,
nature of the union of the soul and body, ii. 45, 378; the hypostatical union of the divine and human nature in Christ, ii. 387 ff.; union of the believer with Christ, ii. 581, iii. 227, 104, 127.

United States, the,
a Christian and Protestant nation, iii. 343.

Unity of the Human Race,
as to origin and species, ii. 77 ff.;

Universalism, Hypothetical,
theory of, ii. 726.

Universal Salvation, iii. 870 ff.

Universe,
Scriptural account of its origin, i. 553; the nebular hypothesis, i. 551; hylozoistic theory, i. 552; evolution theory, ii. 4 ff., 11 ff., 22 ff.

'Υπόστασις, i. 453.

Ursinus, Zachary (d. 1583),
one of the principal authors of the Heidelberg Catechism: his view of the nature of the union between the body of Christ and the bread in the Lord's Supper, iii. 642.

Utility,
not the ground of the right of property, iii. 422.

V.

Valence, Council of (A. D. 529),
decided in favour of the Augustinian doctrine, ii. 168.

Validity,
of the sacraments: on what validity depends, iii. 523; how far does it depend upon the administrator, answer of Romanists to that question, iii. 524; the answer given in the standards of the Lutheran and Reformed Churches, iii. 524 f.; validity of lay-baptism, iii. 514 f., 525.

Values, Fictitious,
the sinfulness of taking advantage of the necessities of our fellow men to demand an exorbitant price for what they need, iii. 436.

Venema, Hermann,
one of the Reformed theologians who adopted the theory of mediate imputation, ii. 207.

Vermittelungstheologie, ii. 452; a failure, ii. 453.

Veronica Giuliani (canonized 1839), the miracles of which she was the subject, iii. 456.

" **Vestiges of Creation,**"
advocates the hypothesis that living plants and animals are developed from a simple cell, by physical laws, ii. 11 f.

Vicarious,
the meaning of the word, ii. 475 ; the sense in which the sacrifices of the Old Testament were vicarious, ii. 499 ; the sense in which the sufferings of Christ were vicarious, ii. 476.

Victorinus (d. 303),
on the intermediate state, iii. 739.

Vincent of Lerins (d. 450),
one of the heads of the semi-Pelagian party : his work " Commonitorium " of great authority among Romanists, and of high repute among Protestants : he was the author of the formula concerning the rule of faith, " Quod ubique, quod semper, quod ab omnibus creditum est," ii. 165 ; his testimony to the general prevalence of Arianism, i. 145.

Vindicatory Justice,
an instinctive feeling and judgment common to the nature of all moral beings, i. 238, 420 ; involved in the conviction of sin, i. 421 ; taught in Scripture, i. 423, ii. 489 ff. ; difference between vindicatory and vindictive, ii. 489. See *Justice.*

Virgin Mary,
the Immaculate conception of, a disputed point among Romanists, ii. 176, iii. 289 ; the sense in which she is called the Mother of God, ii. 393, 401 f. ; idolatrous worship paid to her in the Church of Rome, iii. 285 ff. ; psalter of, iii. 286.

Virtue,
the theory that it consists in benevolence, or the desire or purpose to promote happiness, the foundation of *Optimism*, which see : the doctrine contrary to our moral nature, i. 420, 433, ii. 145 ff. ;

this theory of the nature of virtue the formative principle of many systems of theology ancient and modern, i. 433, iii. 8 ff.

Visible Church. See *Church.*

Vital Force,
specifically different from any mere physical force, i. 291 ; never developed out of dead matter, i. 266 ; Huxley's arguments against that proposition, i. 268 ff. ; his arguments in support of it, ii. 6 ff. ; relation of God's efficiency to vital processes, i. 610.

" **Vitium,**"
the distinction sometimes made between " vitium " and " peccatum," ii. 230.

Vitringa, Campegius (d. 1722),
his definition of sin, ii. 180 ; objections to his distinction between " vitium " and " peccatum," ii. 230 ; on the forensic sense of the word " to justify," iii. 146 ; in his " Observationes Sacræ " he teaches that the Jewish Sabbath was simply a day of relaxation, iii. 337 ; on the baptism of heathen children committed to the care of Christian missionaries, iii. 562.

Vitringa, Campegius the Younger (d. 1723),
adopted the theory of mediate imputation, ii. 207.

Vocation,
Scriptural usage of the word, ii. 639 ; New Testament usage of the words καλέω, κλῆσις, and κλητός, ii. 639 f. ; the external call, what it includes, ii. 641 ; to whom addressed, ii. 642 ff. ; the reason why it is addressed indiscriminately to all men, ii. 649 ; the external call always attended by more or less of the influence of the Spirit (common grace), ii. 654 ; different views on this subject, ii. 656 ff. ; this influence of the Spirit distinct from the mere

moral power of the truth, ii. 660 ; this influence of the Spirit to be distinguished from the providential efficiency of God, ii. 665 ; proof of the universality of this influence of the Spirit, ii. 668 ff. ; its effects, ii. 670 ff. ; effectual calling, ii. 675 ; the different answers to the question, Why is it efficacious? ii. 675 ff. ; the Augustinian answer is that the influence of the Spirit in effectual calling is almighty, ii. 680 ff. ; inferences which flow from the assumed correctness of that answer, ii. 683 ff. ; proof that the Augustinian doctrine as above stated is correct and Scriptural, ii. 689 ff. ; argument from Ephesians i. 17–19, ii. 695 ff. ; argument from regeneration, the effect produced, ii. 700 ; argument from related doctrines, ii. 704 f. ; argument from experience, ii. 706 ; objections to the doctrine considered, ii. 709 ; history of the doctrine of grace : the early patristic period, ii. 710 ; the Pelagian doctrine, ii. 711 ; Semi-Pelagianism, ii. 712 ; scholastic period, ii. 714 ; the Tridentine doctrine, ii. 717 ; the Synergistic controversy, ii. 720 ; difference of opinion in the Reformed Church, ii. 724 ; supernaturalism and rationalism, ii. 728.

Vogelsang, ii. 211.

Voluntary Acts,
the sense in which Pelagians use the word voluntary, when they say that men are responsible for voluntary acts alone, ii. 153, 156, 251.

Vows,
their nature, iii. 315 ; conditions under which they are lawful, iii. 315 f. ; the danger attending their frequent use, iii. 318 ; the grounds on which the Re-

formers declared that monastic vows were not binding, iii. 319.

Vulgate,
declared authoritative by the Council of Trent, i. 107.

W.

Wahl,
βάπτομαι, iii. 529.

Wallace, Alfred Russel,
" Contributions to the Theory of Natural Selection "; he advocates the Darwinian theory as to the origin of species, ii. 17, 18 ; nevertheless he denies that the theory is applicable to man, ii. 33 ; he comes to the conclusion, however, that "matter is nothing," it is only force, and force is mind, so that " the whole universe *is* the will of one Supreme intelligence," i. 297.

War,
when lawful, iii. 365.

Warren, Dr. W. F.,
a Wesleyan : his " Systematische Theologie "; the ability of the natural man to coöperate with the grace of God, he says, is Semi-Pelagianism, ii. 329 ; and the doctrine that men have by nature the power perfectly to keep the commandments of God, he pronounces pure Pelagianism, ii. 329 ; he teaches, however, that every human being has a measure of grace (unless he has cast it away), and that those who faithfully use this gracious gift, will be accepted of God in the day of judgment, whether Jew or Greek, Christian or Heathen, ii. 329.

Washing of Regeneration,
Titus iii. 5, iii. 595.

Waterland,
on baptismal regeneration, iii. 597.

Watson, Richard (d. 1833),
" Theological Institutes " : a high

712 ; according to Augustine the principal penalty which has come on all men, is spiritual death, ii. 163.

Wilful Desertion,
a legitimate ground of divorce, iii. 393.

Will, the,
different meanings of the word, i. 402, ii. 288 ; when the freedom of the will is spoken of, the word "will" is to be understood of the faculty of self-determination, ii. 288 ; different forms of the doctrine of necessity, ii. 280 ff. ; different forms of the doctrine of contingency, ii. 282 ff. ; the doctrine of certainty ; the meaning of the term, ii. 284 ; different ways in which this doctrine of the will has been stated, ii. 284 ff. ; different senses of the word motive, ii. 289 ; different senses of the word cause, and the sense in which a motive can be said to be the cause of a volition, ii. 289 f. ; difference between liberty of an agent and liberty of his will, ii. 290 ; difference between liberty and ability, ii. 291 ; difference between self-determination and self-determination of the will, ii. 294 ; proof that a free act may be perfectly certain as to its occurrence, ii. 295 ff. ; argument from Scripture, ii. 299 ; argument from consciousness, ii. 303 ; from the moral character of volitions, ii. 304 ; from their rational character, ii. 304 ; from the principle that every effect must have a sufficient cause, ii. 306.

Will of God,
what is meant by the word in this connection, i. 402 ; the sense in which the divine will is free, i. 403 ; distinction between the decretive and preceptive will of God, i. 403 ; antecedent and consequent, absolute and conditional, i. 404 ; in what sense the will of God is the ground of moral obligation, i. 405.

"Will,"
as a verb : its different meanings, iii. 872.

Wilson, Professor Horace Hayman (d. 1860),
" Lectures on the Religion of the Hindus" : the effect of the pantheism of the Hindus on their religion, i. 313 ; on the cycles through which in countless ages the universe, according to the Hindus, is constantly passing, iii. 786 ; no analogy between their doctrine and the Scriptural doctrine of the resurrection, iii. 787.

Winer, Professor George Benedict (d. 1858),
" Comparative Darstellung " comparison of the Protestant and Romish theories of the Church, i. 136 ; he represents Romanists as teaching that original sin consists simply in the loss of original righteousness, ii. 177 ; his " Biblische Realwörterbuch," on the worship of the golden calf set up by Jeroboam, iii. 293 ; on our Lord's command " Swear not at all," iii. 310.

Wisdom of God,
distinction between wisdom and knowledge, i. 401 ; this distinction denied by modern speculative theologians, i. 401 f.

Wiseman, Cardinal Nicholas (d. 1865),
the Catholic principle of faith, he says, is that the Church teaches the truth, iii. 751 ; his argument for purgatory from our Lord's declaration that blasphemy against the Holy Ghost shall not be forgiven in the world to come, iii. 752 ; on the Romish doctrine of satisfac-

tion, iii. 753; on the power
of the Church to remit sin, iii.
758, 759; the Cardinal's admission that this assumed
power has been greatly abused,
iii. 761.

Witsius, Hermann (d. 1708),
on the distinction between the
covenant of redemption and the
covenant of grace, ii. 359.

Wolf, Professor Christian (1679–
1754),
adopted the philosophy of Leibnitz and applied it to the defence and explication of Christian doctrine, i. 5, 45; his
influence tended to substitute
human reason in the place of
divine authority as the ground
of our convictions of religious
truth, i. 46; taught that an
atheist, if consistent in obeying the law of nature, would
act as a Christian acts, iii. 261.

Wonders, Lying, i. 630, iii. 452.

Woolsey, Dr. Theodore D. (New
Haven),
"Essay on Divorce": he does
not understand First Corinthians vii. 15, to teach that
desertion justifies divorce, iii.
397; the old Catholic theory
of marriage, which prohibits
divorce for any cause, productive of great evil, iii. 401; the
new marriage law of England
a great improvement on the
old one, iii. 402; the laws of
the several States of this Union
relating to divorce, iii. 403 ff.

Word, the,
the sense in which the Bible is
the Word of God, iii. 466; the
knowledge of its doctrines is for
adults indispensable to their
salvation, iii. 466, i. 25 ff., ii.
646; it is a divinely appointed
means of grace, iii. 466; its
power not due, as Rationalists
teach, merely to the moral
power of its truths, iii. 470;
nor to an inherent, supernatural, permanent power, accord-

ing to the Lutheran doctrine,
iii. 479 ff.; but to the attending influence of the Holy Spirit,
iii. 472 ff.

Wordsworth, Bishop Christopher
(Lincoln),
wilful desertion a legitimate
ground of divorce, iii. 395 f.

Works,
men are to be judged according
to their works, i. 27; by this
rule of judgment all men are
under condemnation, i. 29; the
gospel proposes a method of
salvation not founded on the
merit of the sinner's own work,
i. 30; the covenant of works,
ii. 117; the works excluded
from the ground of justification, not merely ceremonial
works, as Rationalists say, iii.
134; not merely the perfect
works required by the Adamic
covenant, as the Arminians
say, iii. 136; not merely works
done before regeneration, as
Romanists 'teach, iii. 135; but
works of our own of any and
every kind, iii. 137; good
works, iii. 231; works of supererogation, iii. 234; relation of
the believer's works to his reward: Romish doctrine, iii.
241; Protestant doctrine, iii.
244.

World, the,
the universe: is not eternal, but
an effect produced in time, i.
208 ff.; the end of the world,
iii. 792, 851; not to be annihilated, iii. 852; what the Bible
teaches of the destruction of
the world, to be understood of
our earth, iii. 853.

Worship,
meaning of the Hebrew and
Greek words so translated, iii.
281; the meaning of the English word, iii. 281; different
kinds or degrees of worship,
iii. 281; wherein divine worship consists, iii. 281; Christ

INDEX

OF

TEXTS COMMENTED UPON.

SYSTEMATIC THEOLOGY

INTRODUCTION.

CHAPTER I.

ON METHOD.

§ 1. *Theology a Science.*

In every science there are two factors : facts and ideas ; or, facts and the mind. Science is more than knowledge. Knowledge is the persuasion of what is true on adequate evidence. But the facts of astronomy, chemistry, or history do not constitute the science of those departments of knowledge. Nor does the mere orderly arrangement of facts amount to science. Historical facts arranged in chronological order, are mere annals. The philosophy of history supposes those facts to be understood in their causal relations. In every department the man of science is assumed to understand the laws by which the facts of experience are determined; so that he not only knows the past, but can predict the future. The astronomer can foretell the relative position of the heavenly bodies for centuries to come. The chemist can tell with certainty what will be the effect of certain chemical combinations. If, therefore, theology be a science, it must include something more than a mere knowledge of facts. It must embrace an exhibition of the internal relation of those facts, one to another, and each to all. It must be able to show that if one be admitted, others cannot be denied.

The Bible is no more a system of theology, than nature is a system of chemistry or of mechanics. We find in nature the facts which the chemist or the mechanical philosopher has to examine, and from them to ascertain the laws by which they are determined. So the Bible contains the truths which the theologian has to collect, authenticate, arrange, and exhibit in their internal relation to each other. This constitutes the difference between biblical and systematic theology. The office of the former is to ascertain and state the facts of Scripture. The office of the latter is to take those facts, determine their relation to each other and to other cognate truths, as well as to vindicate them and show their harmony and consistency. This is not an easy task, or one of slight importance.

Necessity for System in Theology.

It may naturally be asked, why not take the truths as God has seen fit to reveal them, and thus save ourselves the trouble of showing their relation and harmony?

The answer to this question is, in the first place, that it cannot be done. Such is the constitution of the human mind that it cannot help endeavoring to systematize and reconcile the facts which it admits to be true. In no department of knowledge have men been satisfied with the possession of a mass of undigested facts. And the students of the Bible can as little be expected to be thus satisfied. There is a necessity, therefore, for the construction of systems of theology. Of this the history of the Church affords abundant proof. In all ages and among all denominations, such systems have been produced.

Second, A much higher kind of knowledge is thus obtained, than by the mere accumulation of isolated facts. It is one thing, for example, to know that oceans, continents, islands, mountains, and rivers exist on the face of the earth; and a much higher thing to know the causes which have determined the distribution of land and water on the surface of our globe; the configuration of the earth; the effects of that configuration on climate, on the races of plants and animals, on commerce, civilization, and the destiny of nations. It is by determining these causes that geography has been raised from a collection of facts to a highly important and elevated science. In like manner, without the knowledge of the laws of attraction and motion, astronomy would be a confused and unintelligible collection of facts. What is true of other sciences is true of theology. We cannot know what God has revealed in his Word unless we understand, at least in some good measure, the relation in which the separate truths therein contained stand to each other. It cost the Church centuries of study and controversy to solve the problem concerning the person of Christ; that is, to adjust and bring into harmonious arrangement all the facts which the Bible teaches on that subject.

Third, We have no choice in this matter. If we would discharge our duty as teachers and defenders of the truth, we must endeavor to bring all the facts of revelation into systematic order and mutual relation. It is only thus that we can satisfactorily exhibit their truth, vindicate them from objections, or bring them to bear in their full force on the minds of men.

Fourth, Such is evidently the will of God. He does not teach men astronomy or chemistry, but He gives them the facts out of which those sciences are constructed. Neither does He teach us systematic theology, but He gives us in the Bible the truths which, properly understood and arranged, constitute the science of theology. As the facts of nature are all related and determined by physical laws, so the facts of the Bible are all related and determined by the nature of God and of his creatures. And as He wills that men should study his works and discover their wonderful organic relation and harmonious combination, so it is his will that we should study his Word, and learn that, like the stars, its truths are not isolated points, but systems, cycles, and epicycles, in unending harmony and grandeur. Besides all this, although the Scriptures do not contain a system of theology as a whole, we have in the Epistles of the New Testament, portions of that system wrought out to our hands. These are our authority and guide.

§ 2. *Theological Method.*

Every science has its own method, determined by its peculiar nature. This is a matter of so much importance that it has been erected into a distinct department. Modern literature abounds in works on Methodology, *i. e.*, on the science of method. They are designed to determine the principles which should control scientific investigations. If a man adopts a false method, he is like one who takes a wrong road which will never lead him to his destination. The two great comprehensive methods are the *à priori* and the *à posteriori*. The one argues from cause to effect, the other from effect to cause. The former was for ages applied even to the investigation of nature. Men sought to determine what the facts of nature must be from the laws of mind or assumed necessary laws. Even in our own day we have had Rational Cosmogonies, which undertake to construct a theory of the universe from the nature of absolute being and its necessary modes of development. Every one knows how much it cost to establish the method of induction on a firm basis, and to secure a general recognition of its authority. According to this method, we begin with collecting well-established facts, and from them infer the general laws which determine their occurrence. From the fact that bodies fall toward the centre of the earth, has been inferred the general law of gravitation, which we are authorized to apply far beyond the limits of actual experience. This inductive method is founded upon two principles : First, That there are laws of nature (forces) which are the proximate causes of natural phenomena. Secondly, That those laws are uniform ; so that we are certain that the same causes, under the same circumstances, will produce the same effects. There may be diversity of opinion as to the nature of these laws. They may be assumed to be forces inherent in matter ; or, they may be regarded as uniform modes of divine operation ; but in any event there must be some cause for the phenomena which we perceive around us, and that cause must be uniform and permanent. On these principles all the inductive sciences are founded ; and by them the investigations of natural philosophers are guided.

The same principle applies to metaphysics as to physics ; to psychology as well as to natural science. Mind has its laws as well as matter, and those laws, although of a different kind, are as permanent as those of the external world.

The methods which have been applied to the study of theology are too numerous to be separately considered. They may, perhaps, be reduced to three general classes : First, The Speculative ; Second, The Mystical ; Third, The Inductive. These terms are, indeed, far from being precise. They are used for the want of better to designate the three general methods of theological investigation which have prevailed in the Church.

§ 3. *The Speculative Method.*

Speculation assumes, in an *à priori* manner, certain principles, and from them undertakes to determine what is and what must be. It decides on all truth, or determines on what is true from the laws of the mind, or from axioms involved in the constitution of the thinking principle within us. To this head must be referred all those systems which are founded on any *à priori* philosophical assumptions. There are three general forms in which this speculative method has been applied to theology.

Deistic and Rationalistic Form.

1. The first is that which rejects any other source of knowledge of divine things than what is found in nature and the constitution of the human mind. It assumes certain metaphysical and moral axioms, and from them evolves all the truths which it is willing to admit. To this class belong the Deistical and strictly Rationalistic writers of the past and present generations.

Dogmatic Form.

2. The second is the method adopted by those who admit a supernatural divine revelation, and concede that such a revelation is contained in the Christian Scriptures, but who reduce all the doctrines thus revealed to the forms of some philosophical system. This was done by many of the fathers who endeavored to exalt πίστις into γνῶσις, i. e., the faith of the common people into philosophy for the learned. This was also to a greater or less degree the method of the schoolmen, and finds an illustration even in the " Cur Deus Homo " of Anselm, the father of scholastic theology. In later times Wolf applied the philosophy of Leibnitz to the explanation and demonstration of the doctrines of revelation. He says, " Scripture serves as an aid to natural theology. It furnishes natural theology with propositions which ought to be demonstrated ; consequently the philosopher is bound not to invent but to demonstrate."[1] This method is still in vogue. Men lay down certain principles, called axioms, or first truths of reason, and from them deduce the doctrines of religion by a course of argument as rigid and remorseless as that of Euclid. This is sometimes done to the entire overthrow of the doctrines of the Bible, and of the most intimate moral convictions not only of Christians but of the mass of mankind. Conscience is not allowed to mutter in the presence of the lordly understanding. It is in the spirit of the same method that the old scholastic doctrine of realism is made the basis of the Scriptural doctrines of original sin and redemption. To this method the somewhat ambiguous term Dogmatism has been applied, because it attempts to reconcile the doctrines of Scripture with reason, and to rest their authority on rational evidence. The result of this method has always been to transmute, as far as it succeeded, faith into knowledge, and to attain this end the teachings of the Bible have been indefinitely modified. Men are expected to believe, not on the authority of God, but on that of reason.

Transcendentalists.

3. Thirdly, and preëminently, the modern Transcendentalists are addicted to the speculative method. In the wide sense of the word they are Rationalists, as they admit of no higher source of truth than Reason. But as they make reason to be something very different from what it is regarded as being by ordinary Rationalists, the two classes are practically very far apart. The Transcendentalists

Theol. Nat., Prolegg. § 22 ; Frankf. and Leipz. 1736, vol. 1. p. 22.

also differ essentially from the Dogmatists. The latter admit an external, supernatural, and authoritative revelation. They acknowledge that truths not discoverable by human reason are thereby made known. But they maintain that those doctrines when known may be shown to be true on the principles of reason. They undertake to give a demonstration independent of Scripture of the doctrines of the Trinity, the Incarnation, Redemption, as well as of the immortality of the soul and a future state of retribution. Transcendentalists admit of no authoritative revelation other than that which is found in man and in the historical development of the race. All truth is to be discovered and established by a process of thought. If it be conceded that the Bible contains truth, it is only so far as it coincides with the teachings of philosophy. The same concession is freely made concerning the writings of the heathen sages. The theology of Daub, for example, is nothing more than the philosophy of Schelling. That is, it teaches just what that philosophy teaches concerning God, man, sin, redemption, and the future state. Marheinecke and Strauss find Hegelianism in the Bible, and they therefore admit that so far the Bible teaches truth. Rosenkranz, a philosopher of the same school, says Christianity is the absolute religion, because its fundamental principle, namely, the oneness of God and man, is the fundamental principle of his philosophy. In his " Encyklopädie " (p. 3) he says : " The only religion which conforms to reason is Christianity, because it regards man as the form in which God has revealed himself. Its theology is therefore anthropology, and its anthropology is theology. The idea of (Gottmenschheit) the godhead of man, is the key of Christianity, in which as Lessing says, lies its rationality."

These are the principal forms of the speculative method in its application to theology. These topics will present themselves for fuller consideration in a subsequent chapter.

§ 4. *The Mystical Method.*

Few words have been used with greater latitude of meaning than mysticism. It is here to be taken in a sense antithetical to speculation. Speculation is a process of thought ; mysticism is matter of feeling. The one assumes that the thinking faculty is that by which we attain the knowledge of truth. The other, distrusting reason, teaches that the feelings alone are to be relied upon, at least in the sphere of religion. Although this method has been unduly pressed, and systems of theology have been constructed under its guidance, which are either entirely independent of the Scriptures, or in which the doctrines of the Bible have been modified and perverted, it is not to be denied that great authority is due to our moral nature in matters of religion.   It has ever been a great evil in the Church that men have allowed the logical understanding, or what they call their reason, to lead them to conclusions which are not only contrary to Scripture, but which do violence to our moral nature.   It is conceded that nothing contrary to reason can be true. But it is no less important to remember that nothing contrary to our moral nature can be true.   It is also to be admitted that conscience is much less liable to err than reason ; and when they come into conflict, real or apparent, our moral nature is the stronger, and will assert its authority in spite of all we can do.   It is rightfully supreme in the soul, although, with the reason and the will, it is in absolute subjection to God, who is infinite reason and infinite moral excellence.

Mysticism as applied to Theology.

Mysticism, in its application to theology, has assumed two principal forms, the supernatural and the natural.   According to the former, God, or the Spirit of God, holds direct communion with the soul ; and by the excitement of its religious feelings gives it intuitions of truth, and enables it to attain a kind, a degree, and an extent of knowledge, unattainable in any other way.   This has been the common theory of Christian mystics in ancient and modern times.   If by this were meant merely that the Spirit of God, by his illuminating influence, gives believers a knowledge of the truths objectively revealed in the Scriptures, which is peculiar, certain, and saving, it would be admitted by all evangelical Christians. And it is because such Christians do hold to this inward teaching of the Spirit, that they are often called Mystics by their opponents. This, however, is not what is here meant.   The mystical method, in its supernatural form, assumes that God by his immediate intercourse with the soul, reveals through the feelings and by means, or in the way of intuitions, divine truth independently of the outward teaching of his Word ; and that it is this inward light, and not the Scriptures, which we are to follow.

According to the other, or natural form of the mystical method, it is not God, but the natural religious consciousness of men, as excited and influenced by the circumstances of the individual, which becomes the source of religious knowledge.   The deeper and purer the religious feelings, the clearer the insight into truth.   This illumination or spiritual intuition is a matter of degree.   But as all men have a religious nature, they all have more or less clearly the apprehension of religious truth. The religious consciousness of men in different ages and nations, has been historically developed under diverse influences, and hence we have diverse forms of religion, — the Pagan, the Mohammedan, and the Christian. These do not stand related as true and false, but as more or less pure. The appearance of Christ, his life, his work, his words, his death, had a wonderful effect on the minds of men. Their religious feelings were more deeply stirred, were more purified and elevated than ever before. Hence the men of his generation, who gave themselves up to his influence, had intuitions of religious truth of a far higher order than mankind had before attained. This influence continues to the present time. All Christians are its subjects. All, therefore, in proportion to the purity and elevation of their religious feelings, have intuitions of divine things, such as the Apostles and other Christians enjoyed. Perfect holiness would secure perfect knowledge.

Consequences of the Mystical Method.

It follows from this theory, — (1.) That there are no such things as revelation and inspiration, in the established theological meaning of those terms. Revelation is the supernatural objective presentation or communication of truth to the mind, by the Spirit of God. But according to this theory there is, and can be, no such communication of truth. The religious feelings are providentially excited, and by reason of that excitement the mind perceives truth more or less clearly, or more or less imperfectly. Inspiration, in the Scriptural sense, is the supernatural guidance of the Spirit, which renders its subjects infallible in the communicating truth to others. But according to this theory, no man is infallible as a teacher. Revelation and inspiration are in different degrees common to all men. And there is no reason why they should not be as perfect in some believers now as in the days of the Apostles. (2.) The Bible has no infallible authority in matters of doctrine. The doctrinal propositions therein contained are not revelations by the Spirit. They are only the forms under which men of Jewish culture gave expression to their feelings and intuitions. Men of different culture, and under other circumstances, would have used other forms or adopted other doctrinal statements. (3.) Christianity, therefore, neither consists in a system of doctrines, nor does it contain any such system. It is a life, an influence, a subjective state ; or by whatever term it may be expressed or explained, it is a power within each individual Christian determining his feelings

and his views of divine things.   (4.) Consequently the duty of a
theologian is not to interpret Scripture, but to interpret his own
Christian consciousness; to ascertain and exhibit what truths concerning God are implied in his feelings toward God; what truths
concerning Christ are involved in his feelings toward Christ; what
the feelings teach concerning sin, redemption, eternal life, etc., etc.

This method found its most distinguished and influential advocate
in Schleiermacher, whose "Glaubenslehre" is constructed on this
principle.   By Twesten — his successor in the chair of Theology in
the University of Berlin — it is held in greater subjection to the normal authority of Scripture.   By others, again, of the same school,
it has been carried out to its utmost extreme.   We are at present,
however, concerned only with its principle, and neither with the
details of its application, nor with its refutation.

§ 5. *The Inductive Method.*

It is so called because it agrees in everything essential with the
inductive method as applied to the natural sciences.

First, The man of science comes to the study of nature with certain assumptions.   (1.) He assumes the trustworthiness of his sense
perceptions.   Unless he can rely upon the well-authenticated testimony of his senses, he is deprived of all means of prosecuting his
investigations.   The facts of nature reveal themselves to our faculties of sense, and can be known in no other way.   (2.) He must
also assume the trustworthiness of his mental operations.   He must
take for granted that he can perceive, compare, combine, remember,
and infer; and that he can safely rely upon these mental faculties in
their legitimate exercise.   (3.) He must also rely on the certainty
of those truths which are not learned from experience, but which
are given in the constitution of our nature.   That every effect must
have a cause; that the same cause under like circumstances, will
produce like effects; that a cause is not a mere uniform antecedent,
but that which contains within itself the reason why the effect
occurs.

Second, The student of nature having this ground on which to
stand, and these tools wherewith to work, proceeds to perceive,
gather, and combine his facts.   These he does not pretend to manufacture, nor presume to modify.   He must take them as they are.
He is only careful to be sure that they are real, and that he has
them all, or, at least all that are necessary to justify any inference
which he may draw from them, or any theory which he may build
upon them.

Third, From facts thus ascertained and classified, he deduces the laws by which they are determined. That a heavy body falls to the ground is a familiar fact. Observation shows that it is not an isolated fact; but that all matter tends toward all other matter; that this tendency or attraction is in proportion to the quantity of matter; and its intensity decreases in proportion to the square of the distance of the attracting bodies. As all this is found to be universally and constantly the case within the field of observation, the mind is forced to conclude that there is some reason for it; in other words, that it is a law of nature which may be relied upon beyond the limits of actual observation. As this law has always operated in the past, the man of science is sure that it will operate in the future. It is in this way the vast body of modern science has been built up, and the laws which determine the motions of the heavenly bodies; the chemical changes constantly going on around us; the structure, growth, and propagation of plants and animals, have, to a greater or less extent, been ascertained and established. It is to be observed that these laws or general principles are not derived from the mind, and attributed to external objects, but derived or deduced from the objects and impressed upon the mind.

A. *The Inductive Method as applied to Theology.*

The Bible is to the theologian what nature is to the man of science. It is his store-house of facts; and his method of ascertaining what the Bible teaches, is the same as that which the natural philosopher adopts to ascertain what nature teaches. In the first place, he comes to his task with all the assumptions above mentioned. He must assume the validity of those laws of belief which God has impressed upon our nature. In these laws are included some which have no direct application to the natural sciences. Such, for example, as the essential distinction between right and wrong; that nothing contrary to virtue can be enjoined by God; that it cannot be right to do evil that good may come; that sin deserves punishment, and other similar first truths, which God has implanted in the constitution of all moral beings, and which no objective revelation can possibly contradict. These first principles, however, are not to be arbitrarily assumed. No man has a right to lay down his own opinions, however firmly held, and call them "first truths of reason," and make them the source or test of Christian doctrines. Nothing can rightfully be included under the category of first truths, or laws of belief, which cannot stand the tests of universality and necessity, to which many add self-evidence. But self-evidence is included in universality and necessity, in so far, that nothing which is not self-evident can be universally believed, and what is self-evident forces itself on the mind of every intelligent creature.

Facts to be collected.

In the second place, the duty of the Christian theologian is to ascertain, collect, and combine all the facts which God has revealed concerning himself and our relation to Him. These facts are all in the Bible. This is true, because everything revealed in nature, and in the constitution of man concerning God and our relation to Him, is contained and authenticated in Scripture. It is in this sense that " the Bible, and the Bible alone, is the religion of Protestants." It may be admitted that the truths which the theologian has to reduce to a science, or, to speak more humbly, which he has to arrange and harmonize, are revealed partly in the external works of God, partly in the constitution of our nature, and partly in the religious experience of believers; yet lest we should err in our inferences from the works of God, we have a clearer revelation of all that nature reveals, in his word; and lest we should misinterpret our own consciousness and the laws of our nature, everything that can be legitimately learned from that source will be found recognized and authenticated in the Scriptures; and lest we should attribute to the teaching of the Spirit the operations of our own natural affections, we find in the Bible the norm and standard of all genuine religious experience. The Scriptures teach not only the truth, but what are the effects of the truth on the heart and conscience, when applied with saving power by the Holy Ghost.

The Theologian to be guided by the same rules as the Man of Science.

In the third place, the theologian must be guided by the same rules in the collection of facts, as govern the man of science.

1. This collection must be made with diligence and care. It is not an easy work. There is in every department of investigation great liability to error. Almost all false theories in science and false doctrines in theology are due in a great degree to mistakes as to matters of fact. A distinguished naturalist said he repeated an experiment a thousand times before he felt authorized to announce the result to the scientific world as an established fact.

2. This collection of facts must not only be carefully conducted, but also comprehensive, and if possible, exhaustive. An imperfect

induction of facts led men for ages to believe that the sun moved
round the earth, and that the earth was an extended plain. In
theology a partial induction of particulars has led to like serious
errors. It is a fact that the Scriptures attribute omniscience to
Christ. From this it was inferred that He could not have had a
finite intelligence, but that the Logos was clothed in Him with a
human body with its animal life. But it is also a Scriptural fact
that ignorance and intellectual progress, as well as omniscience, are
ascribed to our Lord. Both facts, therefore, must be included in
our doctrine of his person. We must admit that He had a human,
as well as a divine intelligence. It is a fact that everything that
can be predicated of a sinless man, is in the Bible, predicated of
Christ; and it is also a fact that everything that is predicated of
God is predicated of our Lord; hence it has been inferred that
there were two Christs, — two persons, — the one human, the other
divine, and that they dwelt together very much as the Spirit dwells
in the believer; or, as evil spirits dwelt in demoniacs. But this
theory overlooked the numerous facts which prove the individual
personality of Christ. It was the same person who said, "I thirst;"
who said, "Before Abraham was I am." The Scriptures teach
that Christ's death was designed to reveal the love of God, and to
secure the reformation of men. Hence Socinus denied that his
death was an expiation for sin, or satisfaction of justice. The
latter fact, however, is as clearly revealed as the former; and therefore both must be taken into account in our statement of the doctrine concerning the design of Christ's death.

Necessity of a complete Induction.

Illustrations without end might be given of the necessity of a
comprehensive induction of facts to justify our doctrinal conclusions. These facts must not be willfully denied or carelessly overlooked, or unfairly appreciated. We must be honest here, as the
true student of nature is honest in his induction. Even scientific
men are sometimes led to suppress or to pervert facts which mili-
tate against their favorite theories; but the temptation to this form
of dishonesty is far less in their case, than in that of the theologian.
The truths of religion are far more important than those of natural
science. They come home to the heart and conscience. They
may alarm the fears or threaten the hopes of men, so that they are
under strong temptation to overlook or pervert them. If, however, we really desire to know what God has revealed we must be
conscientiously diligent and faithful in collecting the facts which He

has made known, and in giving them their due weight. If a geol-
ogist should find in a deposit of early date implements of human
workmanship, he is not allowed to say they are natural productions.
He must either revise his conclusion as to the age of the deposit,
or carry back to an earlier period the existence of man. There is
no help for it. Science cannot make facts; it must take them as
they are. In like manner, if the Bible asserts that Christ's death
was a satisfaction to justice, the theologian is not allowed to merge
justice into benevolence in order to suit his theory of the atonement. If the Scriptures teach that men are born in sin, we cannot
change the nature of sin, and make it a tendency to evil and not
really sin, in order to get rid of difficulty. If it be a Scriptural
fact that the soul exists in a state of conscious activity between
death and the resurrection, we must not deny this fact or reduce
this conscious activity to zero, because our anthropology teaches
that the soul has no individuality and no activity without a body.
We must take the facts of the Bible as they are, and construct our
system so as to embrace them all in their integrity.

Principles to be deduced from facts.

In the fourth place, in theology as in natural science, principles
are derived from facts, and not impressed upon them. The properties of matter, the laws of motion, of magnetism, of light, etc.,
are not framed by the mind. They are not laws of thought. They
are deductions from facts. The investigator sees, or ascertains by
observation, what are the laws which determine material phenomena; he does not invent those laws. His speculations on matters
of science unless sustained by facts, are worthless. It is no less
unscientific for the theologian to assume a theory as to the nature
of virtue, of sin, of liberty, of moral obligation, and then explain the
facts of Scripture in accordance with his theories. His only proper
course is to derive his theory of virtue, of sin, of liberty, of obligation, from the facts of the Bible. He should remember that his
business is not to set forth his system of truth (that is of no account), but to ascertain and exhibit what is God's system, which
is a matter of the greatest moment. If he cannot believe what the
facts of the Bible assume to be true, let him say so. Let the
sacred writers have their doctrine, while he has his own. To this
ground a large class of modern exegetes and theologians, after a
long struggle, have actually come. They give what they regard
as the doctrines of the Old Testament; then those of the Evangelists; then those of the Apostles; and then their own. This is

fair. So long, however, as the binding authority of Scripture is acknowledged, the temptation is very strong to press the facts of the Bible into accordance with our preconceived theories. If a man be persuaded that certainty in acting is inconsistent with liberty of action ; that a free agent can always act contrary to any amount of influence (not destructive of his liberty) brought to bear upon him, he will inevitably deny that the Scriptures teach the contrary, and thus be forced to explain away all facts which prove the absolute control of God over the will and volitions of men. If he hold that sinfulness can be predicated only of intelligent, voluntary action in contravention of law, he must deny that men are born in sin, let the Bible teach what it may. If he believes that ability limits obligation, he must believe independently of the Scriptures, or in opposition to them, it matters not which, that men are able to repent, believe, love God perfectly, to live without sin, at any, and all times, without the least assistance from the Spirit of God. If he deny that the innocent may justly suffer penal evil for the guilty, he must deny that Christ bore our sins. If he deny that the merit of one man can be the judicial ground of the pardon and salvation of other men, he must reject the Scriptural doctrine of justification. It is plain that complete havoc must be made of the whole system of revealed truth, unless we consent to derive our philosophy from the Bible, instead of explaining the Bible by our philosophy. If the Scriptures teach that sin is hereditary, we must adopt a theory of sin suited to that fact. If they teach that men cannot repent, believe, or do anything spiritually good, without the supernatural aid of the Holy Spirit, we must make our theory of moral obligation accord with that fact. If the Bible teaches that we bear the guilt of Adam's first sin, that Christ bore our guilt, and endured the penalty of the law in our stead, these are facts with which we must make our principles agree. It would be easy to show that in every department of theology, — in regard to the nature of God, his relation to the world, the plan of salvation, the person and work of Christ, the nature of sin, the operations of divine grace, men, instead of taking the facts of the Bible, and seeing what principles they imply, what philosophy underlies them, have adopted their philosophy independently of the Bible, to which the facts of the Bible are made to bend. This is utterly unphilosophical. It is the fundamental principle of all sciences, and of theology among the rest, that theory is to be determined by facts, and not facts by theory. As natural science was a chaos until the principle of induction was admitted and faithfully carried out, so theology is a jumble of human speculations, not worth a straw, when men refuse to apply the same principle to the study of the Word of God.

§ 6. *The Scriptures contain all the Facts of Theology.*

This is perfectly consistent, on the one hand, with the admission of intuitive truths, both intellectual and moral, due to our constitution as rational and moral beings ; and, on the other hand, with the controlling power over our beliefs exercised by the inward teachings of the Spirit, or, in other words, by our religious experience. And that for two reasons : First, All truth must be consistent. God cannot contradict himself. He cannot force us by the constitution of the nature which He has given us to believe one thing, and in his Word command us to believe the opposite. And, second, All the truths taught by the constitution of our nature or by religious experience, are recognized and authenticated in the Scriptures. This is a safeguard and a limit. We cannot assume this or that principle to be intuitively true, or this or that conclusion to be demonstrably certain, and make them a standard to which the Bible must conform. What is self-evidently true, must be proved to be so, and is always recognized in the Bible as true. Whole systems of theologies are founded upon intuitions, so called, and if every man is at liberty to exalt his own intuitions, as men are accustomed to call their strong convictions, we should have as many theologies in the world as there are thinkers. The same remark is applicable to religious experience. There is no form of conviction more intimate and irresistible than that which arises from the inward teaching of the Spirit. All saving faith rests on his testimony or demonstrations (1 Cor. ii. 4). Believers have an unction from the Holy One, and they know the truth, and that no lie (or false doctrine) is of the truth. This inward teaching produces a conviction which no sophistries can obscure, and no arguments can shake. It is founded on consciousness, and you might as well argue a man out of a belief of his existence, as out of confidence that what he is thus taught of God is true. Two things, however, are to be borne in mind. First, That this inward teaching or demonstration of the Spirit is confined to truths objectively revealed in the Scriptures. It is given, says the Apostle, in order that we may know things gratuitously given, *i. e.*, revealed to us by God in his Word (1 Cor. ii. 10–16). It is not, therefore, a revelation of new truths, but an illumination of the mind, so that it apprehends the truth, excellence, and glory of things already revealed. And second,

This experience is depicted in the Word of God. The Bible gives us not only the facts concerning God, and Christ, ourselves, and our relations to our Maker and Redeemer, but also records the legitimate effects of those truths on the minds of believers. So that we cannot appeal to our own feelings or inward experience, as a ground or guide, unless we can show that it agrees with the experience of holy men as recorded in the Scriptures.

The Teaching of the Spirit.

Although the inward teaching of the Spirit, or religious experience, is no substitute for an external revelation, and is no part of the rule of faith, it is, nevertheless, an invaluable guide in determining what the rule of faith teaches. The distinguishing feature of Augustinianism as taught by Augustin himself, and by the purer theologians of the Latin Church throughout the Middle Ages, which was set forth by the Reformers, and especially by Calvin and the Geneva divines, is that the inward teaching of the Spirit is allowed its proper place in determining our theology. The question is not first and mainly, What is true to the understanding, but what is true to the renewed heart? The effort is not to make the assertions of the Bible harmonize with the speculative reason, but to subject our feeble reason to the mind of God as revealed in his Word, and by his Spirit in our inner life. It might be easy to lead men to the conclusion that they are responsible only for their voluntary acts, if the appeal is made solely to the understanding. But if the appeal be made to every man's, and especially to every Christian's inward experience, the opposite conclusion is reached. We are convinced of the sinfulness of states of mind as well as of voluntary acts, even when those states are not the effect of our own agency, and are not subject to the power of the will. We are conscious of being sold under sin ; of being its slaves ; of being possessed by it as a power or law, immanent, innate, and beyond our control. Such is the doctrine of the Bible, and such is the teaching of our religious consciousness when under the influence of the Spirit of God. The true method in theology requires that the facts of religious experience should be accepted as facts, and when duly authenticated by Scripture, be allowed to interpret the doctrinal statements of the Word of God. So legitimate and powerful is this inward teaching of the Spirit, that it is no uncommon thing to find men having two theologies, — one of the intellect, and another of the heart. The one may find expression in creeds and systems of divinity, the other in their prayers and hymns. It would be safe for a man to resolve to admit into his theology nothing which is not sustained by the devotional writings of true Christians of every denomination.   It would be easy to construct from such writings, received and sanctioned by Romanists, Lutherans, Reformed, and Remonstrants, a system of Pauline or Augustinian theology, such as would satisfy any intelligent and devout Calvinist in the world.

The true method of theology is, therefore, the inductive, which assumes that the Bible contains all the facts or truths which form the contents of theology, just as the facts of nature are the contents of the natural sciences.   It is also assumed that the relation of these Biblical facts to each other, the principles involved in them, the laws which determine them, are in the facts themselves, and are to be deduced from them, just as the laws of nature are deduced from the facts of nature.   In neither case are the principles derived from the mind and imposed upon the facts, but equally in both departments, the principles or laws are deduced from the facts and recognized by the mind

CHAPTER II.

THEOLOGY.

§ 1. *Its Nature.*

IF the views presented in the preceding chapter be correct, the question, What is Theology ? is already answered. If natural science be concerned with the facts and laws of nature, theology is concerned with the facts and the principles of the Bible. If the object of the one be to arrange and systematize the facts of the external world, and to ascertain the laws by which they are determined ; the object of the other is to systematize the facts of the Bible, and ascertain the principles or general truths which those facts involve. And as the order in which the facts of nature are arranged cannot be determined arbitrarily, but by the nature of the facts themselves, so it is with the facts of the Bible. The parts of any organic whole have a natural relation which cannot with impunity be ignored or changed. The parts of a watch, or of any other piece of mechanism, must be normally arranged, or it will be in confusion and worthless. All the parts of a plant or animal are disposed to answer a given end, and are mutually dependent. We cannot put the roots of a tree in the place of the branches, or the teeth of an animal in the place of its feet. So the facts of science arrange themselves. They are not arranged by the naturalist. His business is simply to ascertain what the arrangement given in the nature of the facts is. If he mistake, his system is false, and to a greater or less degree valueless. The same is obviously true with regard to the facts or truths of the Bible. They cannot be held in isolation, nor will they admit of any and every arrangement the theologian may choose to assign them. They bear a natural relation to each other, which cannot be overlooked or perverted without the facts themselves being perverted. If the facts of Scripture are what Augustinians believe them to be, then the Augustinian system is the only possible system of theology. If those facts be what Romanists or Remonstrants take them to be, then their system is the only true one. It is important that the theologian should know his place. He is not master of the situation. He can no more construct a system of theology to suit his fancy, than the astronomer can adjust the mechanism of the heavens according to his own good pleasure. As the facts of astronomy arrange themselves in a certain order, and will admit of no other, so it is with the facts of theology. Theology, therefore, is the exhibition of the facts of Scripture in their proper order and relation, with the principles or general truths involved in the facts themselves, and which pervade and harmonize the whole.

It follows, also, from this view of the subject, that as the Bible contains one class of facts or truths which are not elsewhere revealed, and another class which, although more clearly made known in the Scriptures than anywhere else, are, nevertheless, so far revealed in nature as to be deducible therefrom, theology is properly distinguished as natural and revealed. The former is concerned with the facts of nature so far as they reveal God and our relation to him, and the latter with the facts of Scripture. This distinction, which, in one view is important, in another, is of little consequence, inasmuch as all that nature teaches concerning God and our duties, is more fully and more authoritatively revealed in his Word.

Definitions of Theology.

Other definitions of Theology are often given.

1. Sometimes the word is restricted to its etymological meaning, " a discourse concerning God." Orpheus and Homer were called theologians among the Greeks, because their poems treated of the nature of the gods. Aristotle classed the sciences under the heads of physics, mathematics, and theology, i. e., those which concern nature, number and quantity, and that which concerns God. The fathers spoke of the Apostle John as the theologian, because in his gospel and epistles the divinity of Christ is rendered so prominent. The word is still used in this restricted sense when opposed to anthropology, soteriology, ecclesiology, as departments of theology in its wider sense.

2. Theology is sometimes said to be the science of the supernatural. But what is the supernatural? The answer to that question depends on the meaning assigned to the word nature. If by nature is meant the external world as governed by fixed laws, then the souls of men and other spiritual beings are not included under the term. In this use of the word nature, the supernatural is synonymous with the spiritual, and theology, as the science of the supernatural, is synonymous with pneumatology. If this view be adopted, psychology becomes a branch of theology, and the theologian must, as such, teach mental philosophy.

The word nature is, however, often taken in a wider sense, so as to include man. Then we have a natural and a spiritual world. And the supernatural is that which transcends nature in this sense, so that what is supernatural is of necessity also superhuman. But it is not necessarily super-angelic. Again, nature may mean everything out of God ; then the supernatural is the divine, and God is the only legitimate subject of theology. In no sense of the word, therefore, is theology the science of the supernatural. Hooker [1] says, " Theology is the science of divine things." If by divine things, or " the things of God," he meant the things which concern God, then theology is restricted to a " discourse concerning God ; " if he meant the things revealed by God, according to the analogy of the expression " things of the Spirit," as used by the Apostle in 1 Cor. ii. 14, then the definition amounts to the more definite one given above.

3. A much more common definition of Theology, especially in our day, is that it is the science of religion. The word religion, however, is ambiguous. Its etymology is doubtful. Cicero [2] refers it to *relegere*, to go over again, to consider. " Religio " is then consideration, devout observance, especially of what pertains to the worship and service of God. " Religens " is devout, conscientious. " Religiosus," in a good sense, is the same as our word religious ; in a bad sense, it means scrupulous, superstitious. " Religentem esse oportet, religiosum nefas." [3] Augustin and Lactantius derive the word from *religare*, to bind back. Augustin [4] says : " Ipse Deus enim fons nostræ beatudinis, ipse omnis appetitionis est finis. Hunc eligentes vel potius religentes amiseramus enim negligentes: hunc ergo religentes, unde et religio dicta perhibetur, ad eum dilectione tendimus ut perveniendo quiescamus." And Lactantius, " Vinculo pietatis obstricti, Deo religati sumus, unde ipsa religio nomen accepit, non, ut Cicero interpretatus est, a religendo." [5] According to this *religio* is the ground of obligation. It is that which binds us to God. Subjectively, it is the inward necessity of union with God. Commonly the word religion, in its objective sense, means " Modus Deum colendi," as when we speak of the Pagan, the Mohammedan, or the Christian religion. Subjectively, it expresses a state of mind. What that state characteristically is, is very variously stated. Most simply it is said to be the state of mind induced by faith in God, and a due sense of our relation to him. Or as Wegscheider expresses it, " Æqualis et con-

[1] *Eccles. Pol.* iii. 8.   [2] *Nat. Deor.* ii. 28.   [3] *Poet. ap. Gell.* iv. 9.
[4] *De Civitate Dei*, x. 3. Edit. of Benedictines, Paris, 1838.   [5] *Instt. Div.* iv. 28.

stans animi affectio, qua homo, necessitudinem suam eandemque æternam, quæ ei cum summo omnium rerum auctore ac moderatore sanctissimo intercedit, intimo sensu complexus, cogitationes, voluntates et actiones suas ad eum referre studet." Or, as more concisely expressed by Bretschneider, " Faith in the reality of God, with a state of mind and mode of life in accordance with that faith." Or, more vaguely, " Recognition of the mutual relation between God and the world " (Fischer), or, " The recognition of a superhuman causality in the human soul and life " (Theile). " Faith founded on feeling in the reality of the ideal " (Jacobi). " The feeling of absolute dependence " (Schleiermacher). " The observance of the moral law as a divine institution " (Kant). " Faith in the moral order of the universe " (Fichte). " The union of the finite with the infinite or God's coming to self-consciousness in the world " (Schelling). [1]

This diversity of views as to what religion is, is enough to prove how utterly vague and unsatisfactory must be the definition of theology as " the science of religion." Besides, this definition makes theology entirely independent of the Bible. For, as moral philosophy is the analysis of our moral nature, and the conclusions to which that analysis leads, so theology becomes the analysis of our religious consciousness, together with the truths which that analysis evolves. And even Christian theology is only the analysis of the religious consciousness of the Christian; and the Christian consciousness is not the natural religious consciousness of men as modified and determined by the truths of the Christian Scriptures, but it is something different. Some say it is to be referred to a new life transmitted from Christ. Others refer everything distinctive in the religious state of Christians to the Church, and really merge theology into ecclesiology.

We have, therefore, to restrict theology to its true sphere, as the science of the facts of divine revelation so far as those facts concern the nature of God and our relation to him, as his creatures, as sinners, and as the subjects of redemption. All these facts, as just remarked, are in the Bible. But as some of them are revealed by the works of God, and by the nature of man, there is so far a distinction between natural theology, and theology considered distinctively as a Christian science.

With regard to natural theology, there are two extreme opinions. The one is that the works of nature make no trustworthy revelation of the being and perfections of God; the other, that

[1] See Hase's *Hutterus Redivivus*, I. § 2.

such revelation is so clear and comprehensive as to preclude the
necessity of any supernatural revelation.

§ 2. *The Facts of Nature Reveal God.*

Those who deny that natural theology teaches anything reliable
concerning God, commonly understand by nature the external,
material universe. They pronounce the ontological and teleological arguments derived from the existence of the world, and from
the evidences of design which it contains, to be unsatisfactory. The
fact that the world is, is a proof that it always has been, in the absence of all evidence to the contrary. And the argument from
design, it is said, overlooks the difference between dead mechanism
and a living organism, between manufacture and growth. That a
locomotive cannot make itself, is no proof that a tree cannot grow.
The one is formed *ab extra* by putting its dead parts together ; the
other is developed by a living principle within. The one necessitates the assumption of a maker external and anterior to itself, the
other excludes, as is said, such assumption. Besides, it is urged
that religious truths do not admit of proof. They belong to the
same category with æsthetic and moral truths. They are the objects of intuition. To be perceived at all, they must be perceived
in their own light. You cannot prove a thing to be beautiful or
good to the man who does not perceive its beauty or excellence.
Hence, it is further urged, that proof of religious truth is unnecessary. The good do not need proof ; the evil cannot appreciate it.
All that can be done is to affirm the truth, and let it awaken, if
possible, the dormant power of perception.

A. *Answer to the above Arguments.*

All this is sophistical. For the arguments in support of the
truths of natural religion are not drawn exclusively from the external works of God. Those which are the most obvious and the
most effective are derived from the constitution of our own nature.
Man was made in the image of God, and he reveals his parentage
as unmistakably as any class of inferior animals reveal the source
from which they sprung. If a horse is born of a horse, the immortal spirit of man, instinct with its moral and religious convictions
and aspirations, must be the offspring of the Father of Spirits.
This is the argument which Paul on Mars' Hill addressed to the
cavilling philosophers of Athens. That the sphere of natural theology is not merely the facts of the material universe is plain from
the meaning of the word nature, which, as we have seen, has many

legitimate senses. It is not only used to designate the external world, but also for the forces active in the material universe, as when we speak of the operations and laws of nature, sometimes for all that falls into the chain of cause and effect as distinguished from the acts of free agents; and, as *natura* is derived from *nascor*, nature means whatever is produced, and therefore includes everything out of God, so that God and nature include all that is.

2. The second objection to natural theology is that its arguments are inconclusive. This is a point which no man can decide for other men. Every one must judge for himself. An argument which is conclusive for one mind may be powerless for other minds. That the material universe began to be ; that it has not the cause of its existence within itself, and therefore must have had an extramundane cause ; and that the infinitely numerous manifestations of design which it exhibits show that that cause must be intelligent, are arguments for the being of God, which have satisfied the minds of the great body of intelligent men in all ages of the world. They should not, therefore, be dismissed as unsatisfactory, because all men do not feel their force. Besides, as just remarked, these arguments are only confirmatory of others more direct and powerful derived from our moral and religious nature.

3. As to the objection that religious truths are the objects of intuition, and that intuitive truths neither need nor admit of proof, it may be answered that in one sense it is true. But self-evident truths may be illustrated ; and it may be shown that their denial involves contradictions and absurdities. All geometry is an illustration of the axioms of Euclid ; and if any man denies any of those axioms, it may be shown that he must believe impossibilities. In like manner, it may be admitted that the existence of a being on whom we are dependent, and to whom we are responsible, is a matter of intuition ; and it may be acknowledged that it is self-evident that we can be responsible only to a person, and yet the existence of a personal God may be shown to be a necessary hypothesis to account for the facts of observation and consciousness, and that the denial of his existence leaves the problem of the universe unsolved and unsolvable. In other words, it may be shown that atheism, polytheism, and pantheism involve absolute impossibilities. This is a valid mode of proving that God is, although it be admitted that his existence after all is a self-evident truth. Theism is not the only self-evident truth that men are wont to deny.

B. *Scriptural Argument for Natural Theology.*

The Scriptures clearly recognize the fact that the works of God reveal his being and attributes.   This they do not only by frequent reference to the works of nature as manifestations of the perfections of God, but by direct assertions.   " The heavens declare the glory of God ; and the firmament sheweth his handy-work.   Day unto day uttereth speech, and night unto night sheweth knowledge. There is no speech nor language, where their voice is not heard. Their line is gone out through all the earth, and their words to the end of the world."   (Ps. xix. 1–4.)   " The idea of perpetual testimony," says Dr. Addison Alexander,[1] " is conveyed by the figure of one day and night following another as witnesses in un-broken succession.   . . . .   The absence of articulate language, far from weakening the testimony, makes it stronger.   Even with-out speech or words, the heavens testify of God to all men."

The sacred writers in contending with the heathen appeal to the evidence which the works of God bear to his perfections :   " Un-derstand, ye brutish among the people : and ye fools, when will ye be wise ?   He that planted the ear, shall he not hear ?   He that formed the eye, shall he not see ?   He that chastiseth the heathen, shall not he correct ?   He that teacheth man knowledge, shall not he know ? "   (Ps. xciv. 8–10.)   Paul said to the men of Lystra, " Sirs, why do ye these things ?   We also are men of like passions with you, and preach unto you that ye should turn from these vanities unto the living God, which made heaven and earth, and the sea, and all things that are therein :   Who in times past suf-fered all nations to walk in their own ways.   Nevertheless he left not himself without witness, in that he did good, and gave us rain from heaven, and fruitful seasons, filling our hearts with food and gladness."   (Acts xiv. 15–17.)   To the men of Athens he said : " God that made the world and all things therein, seeing that he is Lord of heaven and earth, dwelleth not in temples made with hands; neither is worshipped with men's hands, as though he needed anything, seeing he giveth to all life and breath, and all things ; and hath made of one blood all nations of men for to dwell on all the face of the earth, and hath determined the times before appointed, and the bounds of their habitation ; that they should seek the Lord, if haply they might feel after him, and find him, though he be not far from every one of us : for in him we live, and move, and have our being ; as certain also of your own poets

---

[1] *Comm. on Psalms,* in loc.

have said, ' For we are also his offspring.' Forasmuch then as
we are the offspring of God, we ought not to think that the Godhead is like unto gold, or silver, or stone, graven by art and man's
device." (Acts xvii. 24–29.)

Not only the fact of this revelation, but its clearness is distinctly
asserted by the Apostle : " That which may be known of God is
manifest in them ; for God hath shewed it unto them. For the invisible things of him from the creation of the world are clearly
seen, being understood by the things that are made, even his eternal power and Godhead ; so that they are without excuse: because
that when they knew God, they glorified him not as God, neither
were thankful." (Rom. i. 19–21.)

It cannot, therefore, be reasonably doubted that not only the
being of God, but also his eternal power and Godhead, are so revealed in his works, as to lay a stable foundation for natural theology. To the illustration of this subject many important works
have been devoted, a few of which are the following : " Wolf de
Theologia Naturali," " The Bridgewater Treatises," Butler's
" Analogy," Paley's " Natural Theology."

§ 3. *Insufficiency of Natural Theology.*

The second extreme opinion respecting Natural Theology is, that
it precludes the necessity of a supernatural revelation. The question whether the knowledge of God derived from his works, be sufficient to lead fallen men to salvation, is answered affirmatively by
Rationalists, but negatively by every historical branch of the Christian Church. On this point the Greek, the Latin, the Lutheran,
and the Reformed Churches are unanimous. The two former are
more exclusive than the two latter. The Greeks and Latins, in
making the sacraments the only channels of saving grace, deny the
possibility of the salvation of the unbaptized, whether in heathen or
Christian lands. This principle is so essential to the Romish system as to be included in the very definition of the Church, as given
by the authoritative writers of the Papal Church. That definition
is so framed as to exclude from the hope of salvation not only all
unbaptized infants and adults, but all, no matter however enlightened in the knowledge of the Scriptures, and however holy in
heart and life, who do not acknowledge the supremacy of the
bishop of Rome.

The question as to the sufficiency of natural theology, or of the
truths of reason, is to be answered on the authority of the Scriptures. No man can tell *à priori* what is necessary to salvation.

Indeed, it is only by supernatural revelation that we know that any sinner can be saved. It is from the same source alone, we can know what are the conditions of salvation, or who are to be its subjects.

A. *What the Scriptures teach as to the Salvation of Men.*
Salvation of Infants.

What the Scriptures teach on this subject, according to the common doctrine of evangelical Protestants is first : —

1. All who die in infancy are saved. This is inferred from what the Bible teaches of the analogy between Adam and Christ. " As by the offence of one judgment came upon all men to condemnation; even so by the righteousness of one the free gift came upon all men unto justification of life. For as by one man's disobedience many (οἱ πολλοί = πάντες) were made sinners, so by the obedience of one shall many (οἱ πολλοί = πάντες) be made righteous." (Rom. v. 18, 19.) We have no right to put any limit on these general terms, except what the Bible itself places upon them. The Scriptures nowhere exclude any class of infants, baptized or unbaptized, born in Christian or in heathen lands, of believing or unbelieving parents, from the benefits of the redemption of Christ. All the descendants of Adam, except Christ, are under condemnation ; all the descendants of Adam, except those of whom it is expressly revealed that they cannot inherit the kingdom of God, are saved. This appears to be the clear meaning of the Apostle, and therefore he does not hesitate to say that where sin abounded, grace has much more abounded, that the benefits of redemption far exceed the evils of the fall ; that the number of the saved far exceeds the number of the lost.

This is not inconsistent with the declaration of our Lord, in Matthew vii. 14, that only a few enter the gate which leadeth unto life. This is to be understood of adults. What the Bible says is intended for those in all ages, to whom it is addressed. But it is addressed to those who can either read or hear. It tells them what they are to believe and do. It would be an entire perversion of its meaning to make it apply to those to whom and of whom it does not speak. When it is said, " He that believeth not the Son shall not see life ; but the wrath of God abideth on him " (John iii. 36), no one understands this to preclude the possibility of the salvation of infants.

Not only, however, does the comparison, which the Apostle makes between Adam and Christ, lead to the conclusion that as all

are condemned for the sin of the one, so all are saved by the righteousness of the other, those only excepted whom the Scriptures
except ; but the principle assumed throughout the whole discussion
teaches the same doctrine.   That principle is that it is more congenial with the nature of God to bless than to curse, to save than
to destroy.   If the race fell in Adam, much more shall it be restored in Christ.   If death reigned by one, much more shall grace
reign by one.   This " much more " is repeated over and over.
The Bible everywhere teaches that God delighteth not in the
death of the wicked ; that judgment is his strange work.   It is,
therefore, contrary not only to the argument of the Apostle, but
to the whole spirit of the passage (Romans v. 12–21), to exclude
infants from " the all " who are made alive in Christ.

The conduct and language of our Lord in reference to children
are not to be regarded as matters of sentiment, or simply expressive
of kindly feeling.   He evidently looked upon them as the lambs
of the flock for which, as the good Shepherd, He laid down his life,
and of whom He said they shall never perish, and no man could
pluck them out of his hands.   Of such He tells us is the kingdom
of heaven, as though heaven was, in great measure, composed of
the souls of redeemed infants.   It is, therefore, the general belief
of Protestants, contrary to the doctrine of Romanists and Romanizers, that all who die in infancy are saved.

B. *Rule of Judgment for Adults.*

2. Another general fact clearly revealed in Scripture is, that
men are to be judged according to their works, and according to
the light which they have severally enjoyed.   God " will render
to every man according to his deeds : to them who, by patient continuance in well doing, seek for glory, and honour, and immortality,
eternal life ; but unto them that are contentious, and do not obey
the truth but obey unrighteousness, indignation, and wrath, tribu-
lation and anguish, upon every soul of man that doeth evil ; of the
Jew first, and also of the Gentile ; but glory, honour, and peace to
every man that worketh good ; to the Jew first, and also to the
Gentile, for there is no respect of persons with God.   For as many
as have sinned without law shall also perish without law, and as
many as have sinned in the law shall be judged by the law."
(Rom. ii. 6–12.)   Our Lord teaches that those who sinned with a
knowledge of God's will, shall be beaten with many stripes ; and
that those who sinned without such knowledge shall be beaten with
few stripes ; and that it will be more tolerable in the day of judg-

ment for the heathen, even for Sodom and Gomorrah, than for
those who perish under the light of the gospel. (Matt. x. 15 ;
xi. 20–24.) The Judge of all the earth will do right. No human
being will suffer more than he deserves, or more than his own conscience shall recognize as just.

C. *All Men under Condemnation.*

3. But the Bible tells us, that judged according to their works
and according to the light which they have severally enjoyed, all
men will be condemned. There is none righteous ; no, not one.
The whole world is guilty before God. This verdict is confirmed
by every man's conscience. The consciousness of guilt and of
moral pollution is absolutely universal.

Here it is that natural theology utterly fails. It cannot answer
the question, How can man be just with God ? or, How can God
be just and yet justify the ungodly? Mankind have anxiously
pondered this question for ages, and have gained no satisfaction.
The ear has been placed on the bosom of humanity, to catch the
still, small voice of conscience, and got no answer. It has been
directed heavenward, and received no response. Reason, conscience, tradition, history, unite in saying that sin is death ; and,
therefore, that so far as human wisdom and resources are concerned,
the salvation of sinners is as impossible as raising the dead. Every
conceivable method of expiation and purification has been tried
without success.

4. The Scriptures, therefore, teach that the heathen are " without Christ, being aliens from the commonwealth of Israel, and
strangers from the covenants of promise, having no hope, and without God." (Eph. ii. 12.) They are declared to be without excuse, " Because, that when they knew God, they glorified Him not
as God, neither were thankful ; but became vain in their imaginations, and their foolish heart was darkened. Professing themselves
to be wise, they became fools, and changed the glory of the uncorruptible God, into an image made like unto corruptible man, and
to birds, and four-footed beasts, and creeping things. Wherefore
God also gave them up to uncleanness, through the lusts of their
own hearts, to dishonour their own bodies between themselves :
who changed the truth of God into a lie, and worshipped and
served the creature more than the Creator, who is blessed for ever.
Amen." (Rom. i. 21–25.) The Apostle says of the Gentiles that
they " walk in the vanity of their mind, having the understanding
darkened, being alienated from the life of God through the igno-

rance that is in them because of the blindness of their heart:
who being past feeling have given themselves over unto lasciv-
iousness, to work all uncleanness with greediness." (Eph. iv.
17–19.)

5. All men being sinners, justly chargeable with inexcusable
impiety and immorality, they cannot be saved by any effort or
resource of their own.   For we are told that " the unrighteous
shall not inherit the kingdom of God.   Be not deceived ; neither for-
nicators, nor idolaters, nor adulterers, nor effeminate, nor abusers
of themselves with mankind, nor thieves, nor covetous, nor drunk-
ards, nor revilers, nor extortioners, shall inherit the kingdom of
God." (1 Cor. vi. 9.) " For this ye know, that no whoremon-
ger, nor unclean person, nor covetous man, who is an idolater,
hath any inheritance in the kingdom of Christ and of God."
(Eph. v. 5.) More than this, the Bible teaches us that a man
may be outwardly righteous in the sight of men, and yet be a
whitened sepulchre, his heart being the seat of pride, envy, or
malice.   In other words, he may be moral in his conduct, and by
reason of inward evil passions, be in the sight of God the chief of
sinners, as was the case with Paul himself.   And more even than
this, although a man were free from outward sins, and, were it
possible, from the sins of the heart, this negative goodness would
not suffice.   Without holiness " no man shall see the Lord."
(Heb. xii. 14.) " Except a man be born again, he cannot see the
kingdom of God." (John iii. 3.) " He that loveth not, knoweth
not God." (1 John iv. 8.) " If any man love the world, the love
of the Father is not in him." (1 John ii. 15.) " He that loveth
father or mother more than me, is not worthy of me." (1 John,
iv. 8.) Who then can be saved ? If the Bible excludes from the
kingdom of heaven all the immoral; all whose hearts are corrupted by pride, envy, malice, or covetousness; all who love the
world; all who are not holy; all in whom the love of God is not
the supreme and controlling principle of action, it is evident that,
so far as adults are concerned, salvation must be confined to very
narrow limits.   It is also evident that mere natural religion, the
mere objective power of general religious truth, must be as efficacious in preparing men for the presence of God, as the waters of
Syria to heal the leprosy.

D.   *The necessary Conditions of Salvation.*

6. Seeing then that the world by wisdom knows not God ; seeing that men when left to themselves inevitably die in their sins ; it

has "pleased God by the foolishness of preaching to save them that believe." (1 Cor. i. 21.) God has sent his Son into the world to save sinners. Had any other method of salvation been possible, Christ is dead in vain. (Gal. ii. 21; iii. 21.) There is, therefore, no other name whereby men can be saved. (Acts iv. 12.) The knowledge of Christ and faith in Him are declared to be essential to salvation. This is proved: (1.) Because men are declared to be guilty before God. (2.) Because no man can expiate his own guilt and restore himself to the image of God. (3.) Because it is expressly declared that Christ is the only Saviour of men. (4.) Because Christ gave his Church the commission to preach the gospel to every creature under heaven, as the appointed means of salvation. (5.) Because the Apostles in the execution of this commission went everywhere preaching the Word, testifying to all men, Jews and Gentiles, to the wise and the unwise, that they must believe in Christ as the Son of God in order to be saved. Our Lord himself teaching through his forerunner said, "He that believeth on the Son hath everlasting life: and he that believeth not the Son shall not see life; but the wrath of God abideth on him." (John iii. 36.) (6.) Because faith without knowledge is declared to be impossible. "Whosoever shall call upon the name of the Lord shall be saved. How then shall they call on him in whom they have not believed? and how shall they believe in him of whom they have not heard? and how shall they hear without a preacher? and how shall they preach, except they be sent?" (Rom. x. 13–15.)

It is, therefore, as before stated, the common faith of the Christian world, that, so far as adults are concerned, there is no salvation without the knowledge of Christ and faith in Him. This has ever been regarded as the ground of the obligation which rests upon the Church to preach the gospel to every creature.

E. *Objections.*

To the objection that this doctrine is inconsistent with the goodness and justice of God, it may be answered: (1.) That the doctrine only assumes what the objector, if a Theist, must admit, namely, that God will deal with men according to their character and conduct, and that He will judge them according to the light which they have severally enjoyed. It is because the judge of all the earth must do right that all sinners receive the wages of sin, by an inexorable law, unless saved by the miracle of redemption. In teaching, therefore, that there is no salvation for those ignorant of the gospel, the Bible only teaches that a just God will punish sin. (2.) The doctrine of the Church on this subject does not go beyond the facts of the case. It only teaches that God will do what we see He actually does. He leaves mankind, in a large measure, to themselves. He allows them to make themselves sinful and miserable. It is no more difficult to reconcile the doctrine than the undeniable fact with the goodness of our God. (3.) In the gift of his Son, the revelation of his Word, the mission of the Spirit, and the institution of the Church, God has made abundant provision for the salvation of the world. That the Church has been so remiss in making known the gospel is her guilt. We must not charge the ignorance and consequent perdition of the heathen upon God. The guilt rests on us. We have kept to ourselves the bread of life, and allowed the nations to perish.

Some of the older Lutheran divines were disposed to meet the objection in question by saying that the plan of salvation was revealed to all mankind at three distinct epochs. First, immediately after the fall, to Adam ; second, in the days of Noah ; and third, during the age of the Apostles. If that knowledge has been lost it has been by the culpable ignorance of the heathen themselves. This is carrying the doctrine of imputation to its utmost length. It is making the present generation responsible for the apostasy of their ancestors. It leaves the difficulty just where it was.

The Wesleyan Arminians and the Friends, admitting the insufficiency of the light of nature, hold that God gives sufficient grace, or an inward supernatural light, which, if properly cherished and followed, will lead men to salvation. But this is merely an amiable hypothesis. For such universal and sufficient grace there is no promise in the Scripture, and no evidence in experience. Besides, if admitted it does not help the matter. If this sufficient grace does not actually save, if it does not deliver the heathen from those sins upon which the judgment of God is denounced, it only aggravates their condemnation. All we can do is to adhere closely to the teachings of the Bible, assured that the Judge of all the earth will do right ; that although clouds and darkness are round about Him, and his ways past finding out, justice and judgment are the habitation of his throne.

§ 4. *Christian Theology.*

As science, concerned with the facts of nature, has its several departments, as Mathematics, Chemistry, Astronomy, etc., so Theology having the facts of Scripture for its subject, has its distinct and natural departments.   First —

Theology Proper,

Which includes all the Bible teaches of the being and attributes of God; of the threefold personality of the Godhead, or, that the Father, Son, and Spirit are distinct persons, the same in substance and equal in power and glory; the relation of God to the world, or, his decrees and his works of Creation and Providence.   Second, —

Anthropology,

Which includes the origin and nature of man; his original state and probation; his fall; the nature of sin; the effect of Adam's first sin upon himself and upon his posterity.   Third, —

Soteriology,

Including the purpose or plan of God in reference to the salvation of man; the person and work of the Redeemer; the application of the redemption of Christ to the people of God, in their regeneration, justification, and sanctification; and the means of grace. Fourth, —

Eschatology,

That is, the doctrines which concern the state of the soul after death; the resurrection; the second advent of Christ; the general judgment and end of the world; heaven and hell.   And fifth, —

Ecclesiology,

The idea, or nature of the Church; its attributes; its prerogatives; its organization.

It is the suggestive remark of Kliefoth in his "Dogmengeschichte," that to the Greek mind and to the Greek Church, was assigned the task of elaborating the doctrine of the Bible concerning God, i. e., the doctrines of the Trinity and Person of Christ; to the Latin Church the doctrines concerning man; that is, of sin and grace; to the German Church, Soteriology, or the doctrine of justification. Ecclesiology, he says, is reserved for the future, as the doctrine concerning the Church has not been settled by œcumenical authority as have been the doctrines of Theology and Anthropology, and that of justification at least for the Protestant world.

The above classification, although convenient and generally received, is far from being exhaustive. It leaves out of view the law (or at least subordinates it unduly), or rule of moral duty. This is a department in itself, and under the title of Moral Theology, is sometimes, as in the Latin Church, regarded as the most important. Among Protestants it is often regarded as a mere department of Philosophy.

It has been assumed that Theology has to do with the facts or truths of the Bible; in other words, that the Scriptures of the Old and New Testaments are the only infallible rule of faith and practice. This, however, is not a conceded point. Some claim for Reason a paramount, or, at least a coördinate authority in matters of religion. Others assume an internal supernatural light to which they attribute paramount, or coördinate authority. Others rely on the authority of an infallible church. With Protestants, the Bible is the only infallible source of knowledge of divine things. It is necessary, therefore, before entering on our work, briefly to examine these several systems, namely, Rationalism, Mysticism, and Romanism.

CHAPTER III.

§ 1. *Meaning and Usage of the Word.*

By Rationalism is meant the system or theory which assigns undue authority to reason in matters of religion. By reason is not to be understood the Logos as revealed in man, as held by some of the Fathers, and by Cousin and other modern philosophers, nor the intuitional faculty as distinguished from the understanding or the discursive faculty. The word is taken in its ordinary sense for the cognitive faculty, that which perceives, compares, judges, and infers.

Rationalism has appeared under different forms. (1.) The Deistical, which denies either the possibility or the fact of any supernatural revelation, and maintains that reason is both the source and ground of all religious knowledge and conviction. (2.) That which while it admits the possibility and the fact of a supernatural revelation, and that such a revelation is contained in the Christian Scriptures, nevertheless maintains that the truths revealed are the truths of reason ; that is, truths which reason can comprehend and demonstrate. (3.) The third form of Rationalism has received the name of Dogmatism, which admits that many of the truths of revelation are undiscoverable by human reason, and that they are to be received upon authority. Nevertheless, it maintains that those truths when revealed admit of being philosophically explained and established, and raised from the sphere of faith into that of knowledge.

Rationalism in all its forms proceeds on the ground of Theism, that is, the belief of an extramundane personal God. When, therefore, Monism, which denies all dualism and affirms the identity of God and the world, took possession of the German mind, Rationalism, in its old form, disappeared. There was no longer any room for the distinction between reason and God, between the natural and the supernatural. No class of men, therefore, are more contemptuous in their opposition to the Rationalists, than the advocates of the modern, or, as it perhaps may be more properly designated, the modern pantheistic philosophy of Germany.

Although in a measure banished from its recent home, it continues to prevail in all its forms, variously modified, both in Europe and America. Mansel, in his "Limits of Religious Thought," [1] includes under the head of Rationalism every system which makes the final test of truth to be "the direct assent of the human consciousness, whether in the form of logical deduction, or moral judgment, or religious intuition, by whatever previous process these faculties may have been raised to their assumed dignity as arbitrators." This, however, would include systems radically different in their nature.

§ 2. *Deistical Rationalism.*

A. *Possibility of a Supernatural Revelation.*

The first point to be determined in the controversy with the Deistical Rationalists, concerns the possibility of a supernatural revelation. This they commonly deny, either on philosophical or moral grounds. It is said to be inconsistent with the nature of God, and with his relation to the world, to suppose that He interferes by his direct agency in the course of events. The true theory of the universe, according to their doctrine, is that God having created the world and endowed his creatures with their attributes and properties, He has done all that is consistent with his nature. He does not interfere by his immediate agency in the production of effects. These belong to the efficiency of second causes. Or if the metaphysical possibility of such intervention be admitted, it is nevertheless morally impossible, because it would imply imperfection in God. If his work needs his constant interference it must be imperfect, and if imperfect, it must be that God is deficient either in wisdom or power.

That this is a wrong theory of God's relation to the world is manifest. (1.) Because it contradicts the testimony of our moral nature. The relation in which we stand to God, as that relation reveals itself in our consciousness, implies that we are constantly in the presence of a God who takes cognizance of our acts, orders our circumstances, and interferes constantly for our correction or protection. He is not to us a God afar off, with whom we have no immediate concern; but a God who is not far from any one of us, in whom we live, move, and have our being, who numbers the hairs of our head, and without whose notice a sparrow does not fall

[1] Page 47, edit. Boston, 1859.

to the ground.   (2.) Reason itself teaches that the conception of God as a ruler of the world, having his creatures in his hands, able to control them at pleasure, and to hold communion with them, is a far higher conception and more consistent with the idea of infinite perfection, than that on which this system of Rationalism is founded.   (3.) The common consciousness of men is opposed to this doctrine, as is plain from the fact that all nations, the most cultivated and the most barbarous, have been forced to conceive of God as a Being able to take cognizance of human affairs, and to reveal himself to his creatures.   (4.) The argument from Scripture, although not admitted by Rationalists, is for Christians conclusive.   The Bible reveals a God who is constantly and everywhere present with his works, and who acts upon them, not only mediately, but immediately, when, where, and how He sees fit.

B. *Necessity of a Supernatural Revelation.*

Admitting, however, the metaphysical possibility of a supernatural revelation, the next question is whether such a revelation is necessary.   This question must be answered in the affirmative. (1.) Because every man feels that he needs it.   He knows that there are questions concerning the origin, nature, and destiny of man ; concerning sin, and the method in which it can be pardoned and conquered, which he cannot answer.   They are questions, however, which must be answered.   So long as these problems are unsolved, no man can be either good or happy.   (2.) He is equally certain that no man answers these questions for his fellow-men. Every one sees intuitively that they relate to matters beyond the reach of human reason.   What can reason decide as to the fate of the soul after death ?   Can he who has been unable to make himself holy or happy here, secure his own well-being in the eternal future ?   Every man, without a supernatural revelation, no matter how much of a philosopher, knows that death is the entrance on the unknown.   It is the gate into darkness.   Men must enter that gate conscious that they have within them an imperishable life combined with all the elements of perdition.   Is it not self-evident then that immortal sinners need some one to answer with authority the question, What must I do to be saved ?   To convince a man that there is no sin, and that sin does not involve misery, is as impossible as to convince a wretch that he is not unhappy.   The necessity of a divine revelation, therefore, is a simple matter of fact, of which every man is in his heart convinced.   (3.) Admitting that philosophers could solve these great problems to their own satisfaction, What is to become of the mass of mankind? Are they to be left in darkness and despair? (4.) The experience of ages proves that the world by wisdom knows not God. The heathen nations, ancient and modern, civilized and savage, have without exception, failed by the light of nature to solve any of the great problems of humanity. This is the testimony of history as well as of Scripture. (5.) Even where the light of revelation is enjoyed, it is found that those who reject its guidance, are led not only to the most contradictory conclusions, but to the adoption of principles, in most cases, destructive of domestic virtue, social order, and individual worth and happiness. The reason of man has led the great body of those who know no other guide, into what has been well called, " The Hell of Pantheism."

C. *The Scriptures contain such a Revelation.*

Admitting the possibility and even the necessity of a supernatural revelation, Has such a revelation been actually made? This the Deistical Rationalist denies, and the Christian affirms. He confidently refers to the Bible as containing such a revelation, and maintains that its claims are authenticated by an amount of evidence which renders unbelief unreasonable and criminal.

1. In the first place, its authors claim to be the messengers of God, to speak by his authority and in his name, so that what they teach is to be received not on the authority of the writers themselves, nor on the ground of the inherent evidence in the nature of the truths communicated, but upon the authority of God. It is He who affirms what the sacred writers teach. This claim must be admitted, or the sacred writers must be regarded as fanatics or impostors. It is absolutely certain that they were neither. It would be no more irrational to pronounce Homer and Newton idiots, than to set down Isaiah and Paul as either impostors or fanatics. It is as certain as any self-evident truth, that they were wise, good, sober-minded men. That such men should falsely assume to be the authoritative messengers of God, and to be endowed with supernatural powers in confirmation of their mission, is a contradiction. It is to affirm that wise and good men are foolish and wicked.

2. The Bible contains nothing inconsistent with the claim of its authors to divine authority as teachers. It contains nothing impossible, nothing absurd, nothing immoral, nothing inconsistent with any well-authenticated truth. This itself is well-nigh miraculous, considering the circumstances under which the different portions of the Scriptures were written.

3. More than this, the Bible reveals truths of the highest order, not elsewhere made known. Truths which meet the most urgent necessities of our nature ; which solve the problems which reason has never been able to solve. It recognizes and authenticates all the facts of consciousness, all the truths which our moral and religious nature involve, and which we recognize as true as soon as they are presented. It has the same adaptation to the soul that the atmosphere has to the lungs, or the solar influences to the earth on which we live. And what the earth would be without those influences, is, in point of fact, what the soul is without knowledge of the truths which we derive solely from the Bible.

4. The several books of which the Scriptures are composed were written by some fifty different authors living in the course of fifteen hundred years ; and yet they are found to be an organic whole, the product of one mind. They are as clearly a development as the oak from the acorn. The gospels and epistles are but the expansion, fulfilment, the culmination of the protevangelium, " The seed of the woman shall bruise the serpent's head," as uttered to our first parents (Gen. iii. 15). All that intervenes is to the New Testament what the roots, stem, branches, and foliage of the tree are to the fruit. No one book of Scripture can be understood by itself, any more than any one part of a tree or member of the body can be understood without reference to the whole of which it is a part. Those who from want of attention do not perceive this organic relation of the different parts of the Bible, cannot appreciate the argument thence derived in favor of its divine origin. They who do perceive it, cannot resist it.

Argument from Prophecy.

5. God bears witness to the divine authority of the Scriptures by signs and wonders, and divers miracles, and gifts of the Holy Ghost. The leading events recorded in the New Testament were predicted in the Old. Of this any man may satisfy himself by a comparison of the two. The coincidence between the prophecies and the fulfilment admits of no rational solution, except that the Bible is the work of God ; or, that holy men of old spake as they were moved by the Holy Ghost. The miracles recorded in the Scriptures are historical events, which are not only entitled to be received on the same testimony which authenticates other facts of history, but they are so implicated with the whole structure of the New Testament, that they cannot be denied without rejecting the whole gospel, which rejection involves the denial of the best authenticated facts in the history of the world.

Argument from the Effects of the Gospel.

Besides this external supernatural testimony, the Bible is everywhere attended by " the demonstration of the Spirit," which gives to its doctrines the clearness of self-evident truths, and the authority of the voice of God ; analogous to the authority of the moral law for the natural conscience.

6. The Bible ever has been and still is, a power in the world. It has determined the course of history. It has overthrown false religion wherever it is known. It is the parent of modern civilization. It is the only guarantee of social order, of virtue, and of human rights and liberty. Its effects cannot be rationally accounted for upon any other hypothesis than that it is what it claims to be, " The Word of God."

7. It makes known the person, work, the acts, and words of Christ, who is the clearest revelation of God ever made to man. He is the manifested God. His words were the words of God. His acts were the acts of God. His voice is the voice of God, and He said, " The Scripture cannot be broken " (John x. 35). If any man refuse to recognize him as the Son of God, as the infallible teacher, and only Saviour of men, nothing can be said save what the Apostle says, " If our gospel be hid, it is hid to them that are lost : in whom the God of this world hath blinded the minds of them which believe not, lest the light of the glorious gospel of Christ, who is the image of God, should shine unto them. For God, who commanded the light to shine out of darkness, hath shined in our hearts, to give the light of the knowledge of the glory of God in the face of Jesus Christ." (2 Cor. iv. 3, 4, 6.)

Deistical Rationalism is in Germany sometimes called Naturalism, as distinguished from Supernaturalism; as the former denies, and the latter affirms, an agency or operation above nature in the conduct of events in this world. More commonly, however, by Naturalism is meant the theory which denies the existence of any higher power than nature, and therefore is only another name for atheism. It is, consequently, not a proper designation of a system which assumes the existence of a personal God.

§ 3. *The Second Form of Rationalism.*

A. *Its Nature.*

The more common form of Rationalism admits that the Scriptures contain a supernatural revelation. It teaches, however, that the object of that revelation is to make more generally known, and to authenticate for the masses, the truths of reason, or doctrines of natural religion. These doctrines are received by cultivated minds not on the ground of authority, but of rational evidence. The fundamental principle of this class of Rationalists is, that nothing can be rationally believed which is not understood. "Nil credi posse, quod a ratione capi et intelligi nequeat." If asked, Why he believes in the immortality of the soul? the Rationalist answers, Because the doctrine is reasonable. To his mind, the arguments in its favor outweigh those against it. If asked, Why he does not believe the doctrine of the Trinity? he answers, Because it is unreasonable. The philosophical arguments against it outweigh the arguments from reason, in its favor. That the sacred writers teach the doctrine is not decisive. The Rationalist does not feel bound to believe all that the sacred writers teach. The Bible, he admits, contains a Divine revelation. But this revelation was made to fallible men, men under no supernatural guidance in communicating the truths revealed. They were men whose mode of thinking, and manner of arguing, and of presenting truth, were modified by their culture, and by the modes of thought prevailing during the age in which they lived. The Scriptures, therefore, abound with misapprehensions, with inconclusive arguments, and accommodations to Jewish errors, superstitions, and popular beliefs. It is the office of reason to sift these incongruous materials, and separate the wheat from the chaff. That is wheat which reason apprehends in its own light to be true; that is to be rejected as chaff which reason cannot understand, and cannot prove to be true. That is, nothing is true to us which we do not see for ourselves to be true.

B. *Refutation.*

It is sufficient to remark on this form of Rationalism, —

1. That it is founded upon a false principle. It is not necessary to the rational exercise of faith that we should understand the truth believed. The unknown and the impossible cannot be believed; but every man does, and must believe the incomprehensible. Assent to truth is founded on evidence. That evidence may be external or intrinsic. Some things we believe on the testimony of our senses; other things we believe on the testimony of men. Why, then, may we not believe on the testimony of God? A man may believe that paper thrown upon fire will burn, although he does not understand the process of combustion. All men believe that plants grow, and that like begets like; but no man understands

the mystery of reproduction. Even the Positivist who would reduce all belief to zero, is obliged to admit the incomprehensible to be true. And those who will believe neither in God nor spirit because they are invisible and intangible, say that all we know is the unknowable, — we know only force, — but of force we know nothing but that it is, and that it persists. If, therefore, the incomprehensible must be believed in every other department of knowledge, no rational ground can be given why it should be banished from religion.

2. Rationalism assumes that the human intelligence is the measure of all truth. This is an insane presumption on the part of such a creature as man. If a child believes with implicit confidence what it cannot understand, on the testimony of a parent, surely man may believe what he cannot understand, on the testimony of God.

3. Rationalism destroys the distinction between faith and knowledge, which all men and all ages admit. Faith is assent to truth founded on testimony, " credo quod non video." Knowledge is assent founded on the direct or indirect, the intuitive or discursive, apprehension of its object. If there can be no rational faith, if we are to receive as true only what we know and understand, the whole world is beggared. It loses all that sustains, beautifies, and ennobles life.

4. The poor cannot be Rationalists. If we must understand what we believe, even on the principles of the Rationalists, only philosophers can be religious. They alone can comprehend the rational grounds on which the great truths of even natural religion are to be received. Widespread, therefore, as has been the influence of a Rationalistic spirit, it has never taken hold of the people ; it has never controlled the creed of any church ; because all religion is founded on the incomprehensible and the infinite.

5. The protest, therefore, which our religious nature makes against the narrow, cold, and barren system of Rationalism, is a sufficient proof that it cannot be true, because it cannot meet our most urgent necessities. The object of worship must be infinite, and of necessity incomprehensible.

6. Faith implies knowledge. And if we must understand in order to know, faith and knowledge become alike impossible. The principle, therefore, on which Rationalism is founded, leads to Nihilism, or universal negation. Even the latest form of philosophy, taking the lowest possible ground as to religious faith, admits that we are surrounded on every side by the incomprehensible.

Herbert Spencer, in his " First Principles of a New Philosophy,"
asserts, p. 45, " the omnipresence of something which passes comprehension." He declares that the ultimate truth in which all
forms of religion agree, and in which religion and science are in
harmony, is, " That the Power which the universe manifests to us
is utterly inscrutable." [1] The inscrutable, the incomprehensible,
what we cannot understand, must therefore of necessity be rationally the object of faith. And consequently reason, rational demonstration, or philosophical proof is not the ground of faith. We
may rationally believe what we cannot understand. We may be
assured of truths which are encompassed with objections which we
cannot satisfactorily answer.

C. *History.*

The modern form of Deistic Rationalism had its rise in England
during the latter part of the seventeenth, and the first half of the
eighteenth centuries. Lord Herbert, who died as early as 1648,
in his work, " De Veritate, prout distinguitur a Revelatione," etc.,
taught that all religion consists in the acknowledgment of the following truths : 1. The existence of God. 2. The dependence of
man on God, and his obligation to reverence him. 3. Piety consists in the harmony of the human faculties. 4. The essential difference between good and evil. 5. A future state of rewards and
punishment. These he held to be intuitive truths, needing no
proof, and virtually believed by all men. This may be considered
as the confession of Faith of all Deists, and even of those Rationalists who admit a supernatural revelation ; for such revelation, they
maintain, can only authenticate what reason itself teaches. Other
writers quickly followed in the course opened by Lord Herbert ;
as, Toland in his " Christianity without Mystery," 1696, a work
which excited great attention, and drew out numerous refutations.
Toland ended by avowing himself a Pantheist. Hobbes was a
Materialist. Lord Shaftesbury, who died 1773, in his " Characteristics," " Miscellaneous Treatises," and " Moralist," made ridicule the test of truth. He declared revelation and inspiration to
be fanaticism. Collins (died 1729) was a more serious writer.
His principal works were, " An Essay on Free-thinking," and
" The Grounds and Reasons of Christianity." Lord Bolingbroke,
Secretary of State under Queen Anne, " Letters on the Study and
Utility of History." Matthew Tindal, " Christianity as Old as the
Creation." Tindal, instead of attacking Christianity in detail, at-

1 *First Principles of a New Philosophy*, p. 46.

tempted to construct a regular system of Deism. He maintained that God could not intend that men should ever be without a religion adequate to all their necessities, and therefore that a revelation can only make known what every man has in his own reason. This internal and universal revelation contains the two truths : 1. The existence of God. 2. That God created man not for his own sake, but for man's. By far the most able and influential of the writers of this class was David Hume. His " Essays " in four volumes contain his theological views. The most important of these are those on the Natural History of Religion, and on Miracles. His " Dialogues on Natural Religion " is regarded as the ablest work ever written in support of the Deistical, or rather, Atheistical system.

From England the spirit of infidelity extended into France. Voltaire, Rousseau, La Mettrie, Holbach, D'Alembert, Diderot, and others, succeeded for a time in overthrowing all religious faith in the governing classes of society.

Rationalism in Germany.

In Germany the Rationalistic defection began with such men as Baumgarten, Ernesti, and John David Michaelis, who did not deny the divine authority of the Scriptures, but explained away their doctrines. These were followed by such men as Semler, Morus, and Eichhorn, who were thoroughly neological. During the latter part of the last, and first part of the present century, most of the leading church historians, exegetes, and theologians of Germany, were Rationalists. The first serious blow given to their system was by Kant. The Rationalists assumed that they were able to demonstrate the truths of natural religion on the principles of reason. Kant, in his " Critic of Pure Reason," undertook to show that reason is incompetent to prove any religious truth. The only foundation for religion he maintained was our moral consciousness. That consciousness involved or implied the three great doctrines of God, liberty, and immortality. His successors, Fichte and Schelling, carried out the principles which Kant adopted to prove that the outward world is an unknown something, to show that there was no such world ; that there was no real distinction between the ego and non-ego, the subjective and objective ; that both are modes of the manifestation of the absolute. Thus all things were merged into one. This idealistic Pantheism having displaced Rationalism, has already yielded the philosophic throne to a subtle form of Materialism.

Bretschneider's "Entwickelung aller in der Dogmatik vorkommenden Begriffe," gives a list of fifty-two works on the rationalistic controversy in Germany. The English books written against the Rationalists or Deists of Great Britain, and on the proper office of reason in matters of religion, are scarcely less numerous. Some of the more important of these works are the following: "Boyle on Things above Reason," Butler's "Analogy of Religion and Nature," Conybeare's "Defence of Religion," "Hulsean Lectures," Jackson's "Examination," "Jew's Letters to Voltaire," Lardner's "Credibility of the Gospel History," Leland's "Advantage and Necessity of Revelation," Leslie's "Short and Easy Method with Deists." Warburton's "View of Bolingbroke's Philosophy," and his "Divine Legation of Moses," John Wilson's "Dissertation on Christianity," etc., etc. See Stäudlin's "Geschichte des Rationalismus," and a concise and instructive history of theology during the eighteenth century, by Dr. Tholuck in "Biblical Repertory and Princeton Review" for 1828. Leibnitz's "Discours de la Conformité de la Foi avec la Raison," in the Preface to his "Théodicée," and Mansel's "Limits of Religious Thought," deserve the careful perusal of the theological student. The most recent works on this general subject are Lecky's "History of Rationalism in Europe," and "History of Rationalism, embracing a survey of the present state of Protestant Theology," by Rev. John F. Hurst, A. M. The latter is the most instructive publication in the English language on modern skepticism.

§ 4. *Dogmatism, or the Third Form of Rationalism.*

A. *Meaning of the Term.*

It was a common objection made in the early age of the Church against Christianity, by the philosophical Greeks, that its doctrines were received upon authority, and not upon rational evidence. Many of the Fathers, specially those of the Alexandrian school, answered that this was true only of the common people. They could not be expected to understand philosophy. They could receive the high spiritual truths of religion only on the ground of authority. But the educated classes were able and were bound to search after the philosophical or rational evidence of the doctrines taught in the Bible, and to receive those doctrines on the ground of that evidence. They made a distinction, therefore, between πίστις and γνῶσις, faith and knowledge. The former was for the common people, the latter for the cultivated. The objects of faith

were the doctrinal statements of the Bible in the form in which
they are there presented.   The ground of faith is simply the testimony of the Scriptures as the Word of God.   The objects of
knowledge were the speculative or philosophical ideas which underlie the doctrines of the Bible, and the ground on which those ideas
or truths are received and incorporated in our system of knowledge, is their own inherent evidence.   They are seen to be true
by the light of reason.   Faith is thus elevated into knowledge,
and Christianity exalted into a philosophy.   This method was carried out by the Platonizing fathers, and continued to prevail to a
great extent among the schoolmen.   During the Middle Ages the
authority of the Church was paramount, and the freest thinkers
did not venture openly to impugn the doctrines which the Church
had sanctioned.   For the most part they contented themselves
with philosophizing about those doctrines, and endeavoring to show
that they admitted of a philosophical explanation and proof.

Wolfianism.

As remarked in the preceding chapter, this method was revived
and extensively propagated by Wolf (1679–1754, Professor at
Halle and Marburg).   His principal works were "Theologia Naturalis," 1736, "Philos. Practicalis Universalis," 1738, "Philos.
Moralis s. Ethica," 1750, "Vernünftige Gedanken von Gott, der
Welt und der Seele des Menschen, auch allen Dingen überhaupt,"
1720.   Wolf unduly exalted the importance of natural religion.
Although he admitted that the Scriptures revealed doctrines undiscoverable by the unassisted reason of man, he yet insisted that all
doctrines, in order to be rationally received as true, should be
capable of demonstration on the principles of reason.   "He maintained," says Mr. Rose (in his "State of Protestantism in Germany," p. 39), "that philosophy was indispensable to religion, and
that, together with Biblical proofs, a mathematical or strictly demonstrative dogmatical system, according to the principles of reason,
was absolutely necessary.   His own works carried this theory into
practice, and after the first clamors had subsided, his opinions
gained more attention, and it was not long before he had a school
of vehement admirers, who far outstripped him in the use of his
own principles.   We find some of them not content with applying demonstration to the truth of the system, but endeavoring to
establish each separate dogma, the Trinity, the nature of the Redeemer, the Incarnation, the eternity of punishment, on philosophical, and strange as it may appear, some of these truths on mathe-

matical grounds." The language of Wolf himself on this subject has already been quoted on page 5. He expressly states that the office of revelation is to supplement natural religion, and to present propositions which the philosopher is bound to demonstrate. By demonstration is not meant the adduction of proof that the proposition is sustained by the Scriptures, but that the doctrine must be admitted as true on the principles of reason. It is philosophical demonstration that is intended. "Theological Dogmatism," says Mansel,[1] "is an application of reason to the support and defense of preëxisting statements of Scripture. . . . . Its end is to produce a coincidence between what we believe and what we think ; to remove the boundary which separates the comprehensible from the incomprehensible."[2] It attempts, for example, to demonstrate the doctrine of the Trinity from the nature of an infinite being ; the doctrine of the Incarnation from the nature of man and his relation to God, etc. Its grand design is to transmute faith into knowledge, to elevate Christianity as a system of revealed truth into a system of Philosophy.

B. *Refutation.*

The objections to Dogmatism, as thus understood, are, —

1. That it is essentially Rationalistic. The Rationalist demands philosophical proof of the doctrines which he receives. He is not willing to believe on the simple authority of Scripture. He requires his reason to be satisfied by a demonstration of the truth independent of the Bible. This demand the Dogmatist admits to be reasonable, and he undertakes to furnish the required proof. In this essential point, therefore, in making the reception of Christian doctrine to rest on reason and not on authority, the Dogmatist and the Rationalist are on common ground. For although the former admits a supernatural revelation, and acknowledges that for the common people faith must rest on authority, yet he maintains that the mysteries of religion admit of rational or philosophical demonstration, and that such demonstration cultivated minds have a right to demand.

2. In thus shifting faith from the foundation of divine testimony, and making it rest on rational demonstration, it is removed from the Rock of Ages to a quicksand. There is all the difference between a conviction founded on the well-authenticated testimony of God, and that founded on so-called philosophical demonstration, that there is between God and man, the divine and human. Let

[1] *Limits of Religious Thought*, p. 47.   [2] *Ibid.* p. 50.

any man read the pretended philosophical demonstrations of the Trinity, the Incarnation, the resurrection of the body, or any other of the great truths of the Bible, and he will feel at liberty to receive or to reject it at pleasure. It has no authority or certainty. It is the product of a mind like his own, and therefore can have no more power than belongs to the fallible human intellect.

3. Dogmatism is, therefore, in its practical effect, destructive of faith. In transmuting Christianity into a philosophy, its whole nature is changed and its power is lost. It takes its place as one of the numberless phases of human speculation, which in the history of human thought succeed each other as the waves of the sea, — no one ever abides.

4. It proceeds on an essentially false principle. It assumes the competency of reason to judge of things entirely beyond its sphere. God has so constituted our nature, that we are authorized and necessitated to confide in the well-authenticated testimony of our senses, within their appropriate sphere. And in like manner, we are constrained to confide in the operation of our minds and in the conclusions to which they lead, within the sphere which God has assigned to human reason. But the senses cannot sit in judgment on rational truths. We cannot study logic with the microscope or scalpel. It is no less irrational to depend upon reason, or demand rational or philosophical demonstration for truths which become the objects of knowledge only as they are revealed. From the nature of the case the truths concerning the creation, the probation, and apostasy of man, the purpose and plan of redemption the person of Christ, the state of the soul in the future world, the relation of God to his creatures, etc., not depending on general principles of reason, but in great measure on the purposes of an intelligent, personal Being, can be known only so far as He chooses to reveal them, and must be received simply on his authority.

The Testimony of the Scriptures against Dogmatism.

5. The testimony of the Scriptures is decisive on this subject. From the beginning to the end of the Bible the sacred writers present themselves in the character of witnesses. They demand faith in their teachings and obedience to their commands not on the ground of their own superiority in wisdom or excellence ; not on the ground of rational demonstration of the truth of what they taught, but simply as the organs of God, as men appointed by Him to reveal his will. Their first and last, and sufficient reason for faith is, " Thus saith the Lord." The New Testament writers, es-

pecially, repudiate all claim to the character of philosophers. They taught that the Gospel was not a system of truth derived from reason or sustained by its authority, but by the testimony of God. They expressly assert that its doctrines were matters of revelation, to be received on divine testimony. " Eye hath not seen, nor ear heard, neither have entered into the heart of man the things which God hath prepared for them that love him. But God hath revealed them unto us by his Spirit : for the Spirit searcheth all things, yea, the deep things of God. For what man knoweth the things of a man, save the spirit of man which is in him?" (1 Cor. ii. 9–11.) Such being the nature of the Gospel, if received at all it must be received on authority. It was to be believed or taken on trust, not demonstrated as a philosophical system. Nay, the Bible goes still further. It teaches that a man must become a fool in order to be wise ; he must renounce dependence upon his own reason or wisdom, in order to receive the wisdom of God. Our Lord told his disciples that unless they were converted and became as little children, they could not enter into the kingdom of God. And the Apostle Paul, in his Epistle to the Corinthians, and in those addressed to the Ephesians and Colossians, that is, when writing to those imbued with the Greek and with the oriental philosophy, made it the indispensable condition of their becoming Christians, that they should renounce philosophy as a guide in matters of religion, and receive the Gospel on the testimony of God. Nothing, therefore, can be more opposed to the whole teaching and spirit of the Bible, than this disposition to insist on philosophical proof of the articles of our faith. Our duty, privilege, and security are in believing, not in knowing ; in trusting God, and not our own understanding. They are to be pitied who have no more trustworthy teacher than themselves.

6. The instructions of the Bible on this subject are abundantly confirmed by the lessons of experience. From the time of the Gnostics, and of the Platonizing fathers, the attempt has been made in every age to exalt faith into knowledge, to transmute Christianity into philosophy, by demonstrating its doctrines on the principles of reason. These attempts have always failed. They have all proved ephemeral and worthless, — each successive theorizer viewing with more or less contempt the speculations of his predecessors, yet each imagining that he has the gifts for comprehending the Almighty.

These attempts are not only abortive, they are always evil in their effects upon their authors and upon all who are influenced by them. So far as they succeed to the satisfaction of those who make them, they change the relation of the soul to the truth, and, of course, to God. The reception of the truth is not an act of faith, or of trust in God; but of confidence in our own speculations. Self is substituted for God as the ground of confidence. The man's whole inward state is thereby changed. History, moreover, proves that Dogmatism is the predecessor of Rationalism. The natural tendency and the actual consequences of the indulgence of a disposition to demand philosophical demonstration for articles of faith, is a state of mind which revolts at authority, and refuses to admit as true what it cannot comprehend and prove. And this state of mind, as it is incompatible with faith, is the parent of unbelief and of all its consequences. There is no safety for us, therefore, but to remain within the limits which God has assigned us. Let us rely on our senses, within the sphere of our sense perceptions ; on our reason within the sphere of rational truths ; and on God, and God alone, in all that relates to the things of God. He only truly knows, who consents with the docility of a child to be taught of God.

§ 5. *Proper Office of Reason in Matters of Religion.*

A. *Reason Necessary for the Reception of a Revelation.*

Christians, in repudiating Rationalism in all its forms, do not reject the service of reason in matters of religion. They acknowledge its high prerogatives, and the responsibility involved in their exercise.

In the first place, reason is necessarily presupposed in every revelation. Revelation is the communication of truth to the mind. But the communication of truth supposes the capacity to receive it. Revelations cannot be made to brutes or to idiots. Truths, to be received as objects of faith, must be intellectually apprehended. A proposition, to which we attach no meaning, however important the truth it may contain, cannot be an object of faith. If it be affirmed that the soul is immortal, or God is a spirit, unless we know the meaning of the words nothing is communicated to the mind, and the mind can affirm or deny nothing on the subject. In other words, knowledge is essential to faith. In believing we affirm the truth of the proposition believed. But we can affirm nothing of that of which we know nothing. The first and indispensable office of reason, therefore, in matters of faith, is the cognition, or intelligent apprehension of the truths proposed for our reception. This is what theologians are accustomed to call the *usus organicus, seu, instrumentalis, rationis.* About this there can be no dispute.

Difference between Knowing and Understanding.

It is important, however, to bear in mind the difference between knowing and understanding, or comprehending. A child knows what the words "God is a spirit" mean. No created being can comprehend the Almighty unto perfection. We must know the plan of salvation; but no one can comprehend its mysteries. This distinction is recognized in every department. Men know unspeakably more than they understand. We know that plants grow; that the will controls our voluntary muscles; that Jesus Christ is God and man in two distinct natures, and one person forever; but here as everywhere we are surrounded by the incomprehensible. We can rationally believe that a thing is, without knowing how or why it is. It is enough for the true dignity of man as a rational creature, that he is not called upon by his Creator to believe without knowledge, to receive as true propositions which convey no meaning to the mind. This would be not only irrational, but impossible.

B. *Reason must judge of the Credibility of a Revelation.*

In the second place, it is the prerogative of reason to judge of the credibility of a revelation. The word "credible" is sometimes popularly used to mean, easy of belief, *i. e.*, probable. In its proper sense, it is antithetical to incredible. The incredible is that which cannot be believed. The credible is that which can be believed. Nothing is incredible but the impossible. What may be, may be rationally (*i. e.*, on adequate grounds) believed.

A thing may be strange, unaccountable, unintelligible, and yet perfectly credible. What is strange or unaccountable to one mind, may be perfectly familiar and plain to another. For the most limited intellect or experience to make itself the standard of the possible and true, would be as absurd as a man's making his visible horizon the limit of space. Unless a man is willing to believe the incomprehensible, he can believe nothing, and must dwell forever in outer darkness. The most sceptical form of modern philosophy, which reduces faith and knowledge to a minimum, teaches that the incomprehensible is all we know, namely, that force is, and that it is persistent. It is most unreasonable, therefore, to urge as an objection to Christianity that it demands faith in the incomprehensible.

The Impossible cannot be believed.

While this is true and plain, it is no less true that the impossible is incredible, and therefore cannot be an object of faith. Christians concede to reason the *judicium contradictionis*, that is, the prerogative of deciding whether a thing is possible or impossible. If it is seen to be impossible, no authority, and no amount or kind of evidence can impose the obligation to receive it as true. Whether, however, a thing be possible or not, is not to be arbitrarily determined. Men are prone to pronounce everything impossible which contradicts their settled convictions, their preconceptions or prejudices, or which is repugnant to their feelings. Men in former times did not hesitate to say that it is impossible that the earth should turn round on its axis and move through space with incredible rapidity, and yet we not perceive it. It was pronounced absolutely impossible that information should be transmitted thousands of miles in the fraction of a second. Of course it would be folly to reject all evidence of such facts as these on the ground of their being impossible. It is no less unreasonable for men to reject the truths of revelation on the assumption that they involve the impossible, when they contradict our previous convictions, or when we cannot see how they can be. Men say that it is impossible that the same person can be both God and man; and yet they admit that man is at once material and immaterial, mortal and immortal, angel and animal. The impossible cannot be true; but reason in pronouncing a thing impossible must act rationally and not capriciously. Its judgments must be guided by principles which commend themselves to the common consciousness of men. Such principles are the following: —

What is Impossible.

(1.) That is impossible which involves a contradiction; as, that a thing is and is not; that right is wrong, and wrong right. (2.) It is impossible that God should do, approve, or command what is morally wrong. (3.) It is impossible that He should require us to believe what contradicts any of the laws of belief which He has impressed upon our nature. (4.) It is impossible that one truth should contradict another. It is impossible, therefore, that God should reveal anything as true which contradicts any well authenticated truth, whether of intuition, experience, or previous revelation.

Men may abuse this prerogative of reason, as they abuse their free agency. But the prerogative itself is not to be denied. We have a right to reject as untrue whatever it is impossible that God should require us to believe. He can no more require us to believe what is absurd than to do what is wrong.

Proof of this Prerogative of Reason.

1. That reason has the prerogative of the *judicium contradictionis*, is plain, in the first place, from the very nature of the case. Faith includes an affirmation of the mind that a thing is true. But it is a contradiction to say that the mind can affirm that to be true which it sees cannot by possibility be true. This would be to affirm and deny, to believe and disbelieve, at the same time. From the very constitution of our nature, therefore, we are forbidden to believe the impossible. We are, consequently, not only authorized, but required to pronounce anathema an apostle or angel from heaven, who should call upon us to receive as a revelation from God anything absurd, or wicked, or inconsistent with the intellectual or moral nature with which He has endowed us. The subjection of the human intelligence to God is indeed absolute; but it is a subjection to infinite wisdom and goodness. As it is impossible that God should contradict himself, so it is impossible that He should, by an external revelation, declare that to be true which by the laws of our nature He has rendered it impossible we should believe.

2. This prerogative of reason is constantly recognized in Scripture. The prophets called upon the people to reject the doctrines of the heathen, because they could not be true. They could not be true because they involved contradictions and absurdities; because they were in contradiction to our moral nature, and inconsistent with known truths. Moses taught that nothing was to be believed, no matter what amount of external evidence should be adduced in its support, which contradicted a previous, duly authenticated revelation from God. Paul does the same thing when he calls upon us to pronounce even an angel accursed, who should teach another gospel. He recognized the paramount authority of the intuitive judgments of the mind. He says that the damnation of any man is just who calls upon us to believe that right is wrong, or that men should do evil that good may come.

3. The ultimate ground of faith and knowledge is confidence in God. We can neither believe nor know anything unless we confide in those laws of belief which God has implanted in our nature. If we can be required to believe what contradicts those laws, then

the foundations are broken up. All distinction between truth and falsehood, between right and wrong, would disappear. All our ideas of God and virtue would be confounded, and we should become the victims of every adroit deceiver, or minister of Satan, who, by lying wonders, should call upon us to believe a lie. We are to try the spirits. But how can we try them without a standard? and what other standard can there be, except the laws of our nature and the authenticated revelations of God.

C. *Reason must judge of the Evidences of a Revelation.*

In the third place, reason must judge of the evidence by which a revelation is supported.

On this point it may be remarked, —

1. That as faith involves assent, and assent is conviction produced by evidence, it follows that faith without evidence is either irrational or impossible.

2. This evidence must be appropriate to the nature of the truth believed. Historical truth requires historical evidence; empirical truths the testimony of experience; mathematical truth, mathematical evidence; moral truth, moral evidence; and "the things of the Spirit," the demonstration of the Spirit. In many cases different kinds of evidence concur in the support of the same truth. That Jesus is the Christ, the Son of the living God, for example, is sustained by evidence, historical, moral, and spiritual, so abundant that our Lord says of those who reject it, that the wrath of God abideth on them.

3. Evidence must be not only appropriate, but adequate. That is, such as to command assent in every well-constituted mind to which it is presented.

As we cannot believe without evidence, and as that evidence must be appropriate and adequate, it is clearly a prerogative of reason to judge of these several points. This is plain.

1. From the nature of faith, which is not a blind, irrational assent, but an intelligent reception of the truth on adequate grounds.

2. The Scriptures never demand faith except on the ground of adequate evidence. "If I had not done among them," says our Lord, "the works which none other man did, they had not had sin" (John xv. 24); clearly recognizing the principle that faith cannot be required without evidence. The Apostle Paul proves that the heathen are justly liable to condemnation for their idolatry and immorality, because such a revelation of the true God and of the moral law had been made to them, as to leave them without excuse.

3. The Bible regards unbelief as a sin, and the great sin for which men will be condemned at the bar of God.   This presumes that unbelief cannot arise from the want of appropriate and adequate evidence, but is to be referred to the wicked rejection of the truth notwithstanding the proof by which it is attended.   The popular misconception that men are not responsible for their faith, arises from a confusion of ideas.   It is true that men are not blameworthy for not believing in speculative truths, when the cause of their unbelief is ignorance of the fact or of its evidence.   It is no sin not to believe that the earth moves round the sun, if one be ignorant of the fact or of the evidence of its truth.   But wherever unbelief arises from an evil heart, then it involves all the guilt which belongs to the cause whence it springs.   If the wicked hate the good and believe them to be as wicked as themselves, this is only a proof of their wickedness.   If a man does not believe in the moral law; if he holds that might is right, that the strong may rob, murder, or oppress the weak, as some philosophers teach, or if he disbelieve in the existence of God, then it is evident to men and angels that he has been given up to a reprobate mind.   There is an evidence of beauty to which nothing but want of taste can render one insensible ; there is evidence of moral excellence to which nothing but an evil heart can render us blind. Why did the Jews reject Christ, notwithstanding all the evidence presented in his character, in his words, and in his works, that he was the Son of God ?   " He that believeth on him is not condemned : but he that believeth not is condemned already, because he hath not believed in the name of the only begotten Son of God." (John iii. 18.)   The fact, however, that unbelief is a great sin, and the special ground of the condemnation of men, of necessity supposes that it is inexcusable, that it does not arise from ignorance or want of evidence.   " How shall they believe," asks the Apostle, " in him of whom they have not heard." (Rom. x. 14.)   And our Lord says, " This is the condemnation, that light is come into the world, and men loved darkness rather than light, because their deeds were evil."   (John iii. 19.)

4. Another evidence that the Scriptures recognize the necessity of evidence in order to faith, and the right of those to whom a revelation is addressed to judge of that evidence, is found in the frequent command to consider, to examine, to try the spirits, i. e., those who claim to be the organs of the Spirit of God.   The duty of judging is enjoined, and the standard of judgment is given. And then men are held responsible for their decision.

Christians, therefore, concede to reason all the prerogatives it can rightfully claim. God requires nothing irrational of his rational creatures. He does not require faith without knowledge, or faith in the impossible, or faith without evidence. Christianity is equally opposed to superstition and Rationalism. The one is faith without appropriate evidence, the other refuses to believe what it does not understand, in despite of evidence which should command belief. The Christian, conscious of his imbecility as a creature, and his ignorance and blindness as a sinner, places himself before God, in the posture of a child, and receives as true everything which a God of infinite intelligence and goodness declares to be worthy of confidence. And in thus submitting to be taught, he acts on the highest principles of reason.

§ 6. *Relation of Philosophy and Revelation.*

Cicero [1] defines philosophy as " Rerum divinarum et humanarum, causarumque quibus hæ res continentur, scientia." Peemans [2] says, " Philosophia est scientia rerum per causas primas, recto rationis usu comparata." Or, as Ferrier [3] more concisely expresses it, " Philosophy is the attainment of truth by the way of reason." These and other definitions are to be found in Fleming's " Vocabulary of Philosophy."

There is, however, a *philosophia prima*, or first philosophy, which is concerned not so much with what is to be known, as with the faculty of knowledge, which examines the cognitive faculty, determines its laws and its limits. It is the philosophy of philosophy.

Whether we take the word to mean the knowledge of God and nature attained by reason, or the principles which should guide all efforts for the attainment of knowledge, the word is intended to cover the whole domain of human intelligence. Popularly, we distinguish between philosophy and science ; the former having for its sphere the spiritual, the latter, the material. Commonly, philosophy is understood as comprising both departments. Hence we speak of natural philosophy as well as of the philosophy of mind. Such being the compass of the domain which philosophers claim as their own, the proper relation between philosophy and theology becomes a question of vital importance. This is, indeed, the great question at issue in the Rationalistic controversy ; and therefore, at the conclusion of this chapter, all that remains to be done is to give a concise statement of familiar principles.

[1] *De Officiis*, lib. ii, c. 2.   [2] *Introd. ad Philosophiam*, sect. 107.
[3] *Inst. of Metaphys.* p. 2.

Philosophy and Theology occupy Common Ground.

1. Philosophy and Theology occupy common ground. Both assume to teach what is true concerning God, man, the world, and the relation in which God stands to his creatures.

2. While their objects are so far identical, both striving to attain a knowledge of the same truths, their methods are essentially different. Philosophy seeks to attain knowledge by speculation and induction, or by the exercise of our own intellectual faculties. Theology relies upon authority, receiving as truth whatever God in his Word has revealed.

3. Both these methods are legitimate. Christians do not deny that our senses and reason are reliable informants; that they enable us to arrive at certainty as to what lies within their sphere.

4. God is the author of our nature and the maker of heaven and earth, therefore nothing which the laws of our nature or the facts of the external world prove to be true, can contradict the teaching of God's Word. Neither can the Scriptures contradict the truths of philosophy or science.

Philosophers and Theologians should Strive after Unity.

5. As these two great sources of knowledge must be consistent in their valid teachings, it is the duty of all parties to endeavor to exhibit that consistency. Philosophers should not ignore the teachings of the Bible, and theologians should not ignore the teachings of science. Much less should either class needlessly come into collision with the other. It is unreasonable and irreligious for philosophers to adopt and promulgate theories inconsistent with the facts of the Bible, when those theories are sustained by only plausible evidence, which does not command the assent even of the body of scientific men themselves. On the other hand, it is unwise for theologians to insist on an interpretation of Scripture which brings it into collision with the facts of science. Both of these mistakes are often made. The Bible, for example, clearly teaches the unity of the existing races of men, both as to origin and species. Many Naturalists, however, insist that they are diverse, some say, both in origin and kind, and others, in origin if not in species. This is done not only on merely plausible evidence, being one of several possible ways of accounting for acknowledged diversities, but in opposition to the most decisive proof to the contrary. This proof, so far as it is historical and philological, does not fall within the sphere of natural science, and therefore the mere Naturalist disre-

gards it. Comparative philologists hold up their hands at the obtuseness of men of science, who maintain that races have had different origins, whose languages render it clear to demonstration that they have been derived from a common stock. Considering the overwhelming weight of evidence of the divine authority of the Scriptures, and the unspeakable importance of that authority being maintained over the minds and hearts of men, it evinces fearful recklessness on the part of those who wantonly impugn its teachings. On the other hand, it is unwise in theologians to array themselves needlessly against the teachings of science. Romanists and Protestants vainly resisted the adoption of the Copernican theory of our solar system. They interpreted the Bible in a sense contradictory to that theory. So far as in them lay, they staked the authority of the Bible on the correctness of their interpretation. The theory proved to be true, and the received interpretation had to be given up. The Bible, however, has received no injury, although theologians have been taught an important lesson; that is, to let science take its course, assured that the Scriptures will accommodate themselves to all well-authenticated scientific facts in time to come, as they have in time past.

The Authority of Facts.

6. The relation between Revelation and Philosophy (taking the word in its restricted sense) is different from that between Revelation and Science. Or, to express the same idea in different words, the relation between revelation and facts is one thing; and the relation between revelation and theories another thing. Facts do not admit of denial. They are determined by the wisdom and will of God. To deny facts, is to deny what God affirms to be true. This the Bible cannot do. It cannot contradict God. The theologian, therefore, acknowledges that the Scriptures must be interpreted in accordance with established facts. He has a right, however, to demand that those facts should be verified beyond the possibility of doubt. Scientific men in one age or country affirm the truth of facts, which others deny or disprove. It would be a lamentable spectacle to see the Church changing its doctrines, or its interpretation of Scripture, to suit the constantly changing representations of scientific men as to matters of fact.

While acknowledging their obligation to admit undeniable facts, theologians are at liberty to receive or reject the theories deduced from those facts. Such theories are human speculations, and can have no higher authority than their own inherent probability.

The facts of light, electricity, magnetism, are permanent. The theories concerning them are constantly changing. The facts of geology are to be admitted ; the theories of geologists have no coercive authority. The facts of physiology and comparative anatomy may be received ; but no man is bound to receive any of the various conflicting theories of development. Obvious as this distinction between facts and theories is, it is nevertheless often disregarded. Scientific men are disposed to demand for their theories, the authority due only to established facts. And theologians, because at liberty to reject theories, are sometimes led to assert their independence of facts.

The Authority of the Bible higher than that of Philosophy.

7. Philosophy, in its widest sense, being the conclusions of the human intelligence as to what is true, and the Bible being the declaration of God, as to what is true, it is plain that where the two contradict each other, philosophy must yield to revelation ; man must yield to God. It has been admitted that revelation cannot contradict facts ; that the Bible must be interpreted in accordance with what God has clearly made known in the constitution of our nature and in the outward world. But the great body of what passes for philosophy or science, is merely human speculation. What is the philosophy of the Orientals, of Brahmins and Buddhists, of the early Gnostics, of the Platonists, of the Scotists in the Middle Ages; of Leibnitz with his monads and preëstablished harmony ; of Des Cartes and his vortices ; of Kant and his categories ; of Fichte, Schelling, and Hegel, with their different theories of idealistic pantheism ? The answer to that question is, that these systems of philosophy are so many forms of human speculation ; and consequently that so far as these speculations agree with the Bible they are true ; and so far as they differ from it, they are false and worthless. This is the ground which every believer, learned or unlearned, is authorized and bound to take. If the Bible teaches that God is a person, the philosophy that teaches that an infinite being cannot be a person, is false. If the Bible teaches that God creates, controls, regenerates, the philosophy that forbids the assumption that He acts in time, is to be rejected. If the Bible teaches that the soul exists after the dissolution of the body, the philosophy which teaches that man is only the ephemeral manifestation of a generic life in connection with a given corporeal organization, is to be dismissed without further examination. In short, the Bible teaches certain doctrines concerning the nature of God

and his relation to the world; concerning the origin, nature, and destiny of man; concerning the nature of virtue, the ground of moral obligation, human liberty and responsibility; what is the rule of duty, what is right and what is wrong in all our relations to God and to our fellow creatures. These are subjects on which philosophy undertakes to speculate and dogmatize ; if in any case these speculations come into conflict with what is taught or necessarily implied in the Bible, they are thereby refuted, as by a *reductio ad absurdum.* And the disposition which refuses to give up these speculations in obedience to the teaching of the Bible, is inconsistent with Christianity. It is the indispensable condition of salvation through the gospel, that we receive as true whatever God has revealed in his Word. We must make our choice between the wisdom of men and the wisdom of God. The wisdom of men is foolishness with God ; and the wisdom of God is foolishness to the wise of this world.

The relation, therefore, between philosophy and revelation, as determined by the Scriptures themselves, is what every right-minded man must approve. Everything is conceded to philosophy and science, which they can rightfully demand. It is admitted that they have a large and important sphere of investigation. It is admitted that within that sphere they are entitled to the greatest deference. It is cheerfully conceded that they have accomplished much, not only as means of mental discipline, but in the enlargement of the sphere of human knowledge, and in promoting the refinement and well-being of men. It is admitted that theologians are not infallible, in the interpretation of Scripture. It may, therefore, happen in the future, as it has in the past, that interpretations of the Bible, long confidently received, must be modified or abandoned, to bring revelation into harmony with what God teaches in his works. This change of view as to the true meaning of the Bible may be a painful trial to the Church, but it does not in the least impair the authority of the Scriptures. They remain infallible ; we are merely convicted of having mistaken their meaning.

§ 7. *Office of the Senses in Matters of Faith.*

The question, What authority is due to the senses in matters of faith? arose out of the controversy between Romanists and Protestants. The doctrine of transubstantiation, as taught by the Romish Church, contradicts the testimony of our senses of sight, taste, and touch. It was natural for Protestants to appeal to this contradiction as decisive evidence against the doctrine. Romanists reply by denying the competency of the senses to bear testimony in such cases.

Protestants maintain the validity of that testimony on the following grounds : (1.) Confidence in the well-authenticated testimony of our senses, is one of those laws of belief which God has impressed upon our nature ; from the authority of those laws it is impossible that we should emancipate ourselves. (2.) Confidence in our senses is, therefore, one form of confidence in God. It supposes him to have placed us under the necessity of error, to assume that we cannot safely trust the guides in which, by a law of our nature, he constrains us to confide. (3.) All ground of certainty in matters either of faith or knowledge, is destroyed, if confidence in the laws of our nature be abandoned. Nothing is then possible but absolute skepticism. We, in that case, cannot know that we ourselves exist, or that the world exists, or that there is a God, or a moral law, or any responsibility for character or conduct. (4.) All external supernatural revelation is addressed to the senses. Those who heard Christ had to trust to their sense of hearing ; those who read the Bible have to trust to their sense of sight ; those who receive the testimony of the Church, receive it through their senses. It is suicidal, therefore, in the Romanists to say that the senses are not to be trusted in matters of faith.

All the arguments derived from the false judgments of men when misled by the senses, are answered by the simple statement of the proposition, that the senses are to be trusted only within their legitimate sphere. The eye may indeed deceive us when the conditions of correct vision are not present ; but this does not prove that it is not to be trusted within its appropriate limits.

CHAPTER IV.

MYSTICISM.

§ 1. *Meaning of the Words Enthusiasm and Mysticism.*

IN the popular sense of the word, enthusiasm means a high state of mental excitement. In that state all the powers are exalted, the thoughts become more comprehensive and vivid, the feelings more fervid, and the will more determined. It is in these periods of excitement that the greatest works of genius, whether by poets, painters, or warriors, have been accomplished. The ancients referred this exaltation of the inner man to a divine influence. They regarded persons thus excited as possessed, or having a God within them. Hence they were called *enthusiasts* (ἔνθεος). In theology, therefore, those who ignore or reject the guidance of the Scriptures, and assume to be led by an inward divine influence into the knowledge and obedience of the truth, are properly called Enthusiasts. This term, however, has been in a great measure superseded by the word Mystics.

Few words indeed have been used in such a vague, indefinite sense as Mysticism. Its etymology does not determine its meaning. A μύστης was one initiated into the knowledge of the Greek mysteries, one to whom secret things had been revealed. Hence in the wide sense of the word, a Mystic is one who claims to see or know what is hidden from other men, whether this knowledge be attained by immediate intuition, or by inward revelation. In most cases these methods were assumed to be identical, as intuition was held to be the immediate vision of God and of divine things. Hence, in the wide sense of the word, Mystics are those who claim to be under the immediate guidance of God or of his Spirit.

A. *The Philosophical Use of the Word.*

Hence Mysticism, in this sense, includes all those systems of philosophy, which teach either the identity of God and the soul, or the immediate intuition of the infinite. The pantheism of the Brahmins and Buddhists, the theosophy of the Sufis, the Egyptian, and many forms of the Greek philosophy, in this acceptation of the

term, are all Mystical.   As the same system has been reproduced
in modern times, the same designation is applied to the philosophy
of Spinoza, and its various modifications.   According to Cousin,
" Mysticism in philosophy is the belief that God may be known
face to face, without anything intermediate.   It is a yielding to the
sentiment awakened by the idea of the infinite, and a running up
of all knowledge and all duty to the contemplation and love of
Him." [1]

For the same reason the whole Alexandrian school of theology
in the early Church has been called Mystical.   They characteristically depreciated the outward authority of the Scriptures, and
exalted that of the inward light.   It is true they called that light
reason, but they regarded it as divine.   According to the new
Platonic doctrine, the Λόγος, or impersonal reason of God, is Reason
in man; or as Clemens Alexandrinus said, The Logos was a light
common to all men.   That, therefore, to which supreme authority
was ascribed in the pursuit of truth, was " God within us."   This
is the doctrine of modern Eclecticism as presented by Cousin.
That philosopher says, " Reason is impersonal in its nature.   It is
not we who make it.   It is so far from being individual, that its
peculiar characteristics are the opposite of individuality, namely,
universality and necessity, since it is to Reason we owe the
knowledge of universal and necessary truths, of principles which
we all obey, and cannot but obey. . . . .   It descends from
God, and approaches man.   It makes its appearance in the consciousness as a guest, who brings intelligence of an unknown
world, of which it at once presents the idea and awakens the want.
If reason were personal, it would have no value, no authority beyond the limits of the individual subject. . . . .   Reason is a
revelation, a necessary and universal revelation which is wanting
to no man, and which enlightens every man on his coming into the
world.   Reason is the necessary mediator between God and man,
the Λόγος of Pythagoras and Plato, the Word made Flesh, which
serves as the interpreter of God, and teacher of man, divine and
human at the same time.   It is not indeed the absolute God in his
majestic individuality, but his manifestation in spirit and in truth.
It is not the Being of beings, but it is the revealed God of the
human race." [2]

Reason, according to this system, is not a faculty of the human

[1] *Cours de l'Hist. de la Phil. Mod., Prem. Sér.*, Paris, 1846, vol. ii., leç. 9, 10, pp. 95,120.
[2] *Specimens of Foreign Standard Literature,* edited by George Ripley.   Vol. i.   *Philo-sophical Miscellanies from Cousin, et al.*, pp. 125, 149.

soul, but God in man.   As electricity and magnetism are (or used
to be) regarded as forces diffused through the material world, so
the Λόγος, the divine impersonal reason, .is diffused through the
world of mind, and reveals itself more or less potentially in the
souls of all men.   This theory, in one aspect, is a form of Rationalism, as it refers all our higher, and especially our religious knowledge, to a subjective source, which it designates Reason.   It has,
however, more points of analogy with Mysticism, because, (1.) It
assumes that the informing principle, the source of knowledge and
guide in duty, is divine, something which does not belong to our
nature, but appears as a guest in our consciousness.   (2.) The
office of this inward principle, or light, is the same in both systems.   It is to reveal truth and duty, to elevate and purify the
soul.   (3.) Its authority is the same ; that is, it is paramount if
not exclusive.   (4.) Its very designations are the same.   It is
called by philosophers, God, the Λόγος, the Word ; by Christians,
Christ within us, or, the Spirit.   Thus systems apparently the
most diverse (Cousin and George Fox !) run into each other, and
reveal themselves as reproductions of heathen philosophy, or of
the heresies of the early Church.

Although the Alexandrian theologians had these points of agreement with the Mystics, yet as they were speculative in their whole
tendency, and strove to transmute Christianity into a philosophy,
they are not properly to be regarded as Mystics in the generally
received theological meaning of the term.

B.   *The Sense in which Evangelical Christians are called
Mystics.*

As all Evangelical Christians admit a supernatural influence of
the Spirit of God upon the soul, and recognize a higher form of
knowledge, holiness, and fellowship with God, as the effects of that
influence, they are stigmatized as Mystics, by those who discard
everything supernatural from Christianity.   The definitions of
Mysticism given by Rationalists are designedly so framed as to include what all evangelical Christians hold to be true concerning the
illumination, teaching, and guidance of the Holy Spirit.   Thus
Wegscheider [1] says, " Mysticismus est persuasio de singulari animæ
facultate ad immediatum ipsoque sensu percipiendum cum numine
aut naturis coelestibus commercium jam in hac vita perveniendi,
quo mens immediate cognitione rerum divinarum ac beatitate per-
fruatur."   And Bretschneider [2] defines Mysticism as a " Belief in

---

[1] *Inst.* § 5.   [2] *Systematische Entwickelung*, fourth edit. p. 19.

a continuous operation of God on the soul, secured by special religious exercise, producing illumination, holiness, and beatitude."
Evangelical theologians so far acquiesce in this view, that they say,
as Lange,[1] and Nitsch,[2] " that every true believer is a Mystic." The
latter writer adds, " That the Christian ideas of illumination, revelation, incarnation, regeneration, the sacraments and the resurrection, are essentially Mystical elements. As often as the religious
and church-life recovers itself from formalism and scholastic bar-
renness, and is truly revived, it always appears as Mystical, and
gives rise to the outcry that Mysticism is gaining the ascendency."
Some writers, indeed, make a distinction between Mystik and Mysticismus. " Die innerliche Lebendigkeit der Religion ist allezeit
Mystik" (The inward vitality of religion is ever Mystik), says
Nitsch, but " Mysticismus ist eine einseitige Herrschaft und eine
Ausartung der mystischen Richtung." That is, Mysticism is an
undue and perverted development of the mystical element which
belongs to true religion. This distinction, between Mystik and
Mysticismus, is not generally recognized, and cannot be well expressed in English. Lange, instead of using different words, speaks
of a true and false Mysticism. But different things should be designated by different words. There has been a religious theory, which
has more or less extensively prevailed in the Church, which is distinguished from the Scriptural doctrine by unmistakable characteristics, and which is known in church history as Mysticism, and the
word should be restricted to that theory. It is the theory, variously
modified, that the knowledge, purity, and blessedness to be derived
from communion with God, are not to be attained from the Scriptures and the use of the ordinary means of grace, but by a supernatural and immediate divine influence, which influence (or communication of God to the soul) is to be secured by passivity, a
simple yielding the soul without thought or effort to the divine
influx.

C. *The System which makes the Feelings the Source of
Knowledge.*

A still wider use of the word Mysticism has to some extent been
adopted. Any system, whether in philosophy or religion, which assigns more importance to the feelings than to the intellect, is called
Mystical. Cousin, and after him, Morell, arrange the systems of
philosophy under the heads of Sensationalism, Idealism, Skepticism,

1 In Herzog's *Encyklopädie,* art. " Mystik."
2 *System der Christlichen Lehre,* fifth edit. p. 35.

and Mysticism. The first makes the senses the exclusive or predominant source of our knowledge ; the second, the self, in its
constitution and laws, as understood and apprehended by the intellect ; and Mysticism, the feelings. The Mystic assumes that the
senses and reason are alike untrustworthy and inadequate, as
sources of knowledge ; that nothing can be received with confidence as truth, at least in the higher departments of knowledge, in
all that relates to our own nature, to God, and our relation to Him,
except what is revealed either naturally or supernaturally in the
feelings. There are two forms of Mysticism, therefore.: the one
which assumes the feelings themselves to be the sources of this
knowledge ; the other that it is through the feelings that God makes
the truth known to the soul.[1] " Reason is no longer viewed as the
great organ of truth ; its decisions are enstamped as uncertain,
faulty, and well-nigh valueless, while the inward impulses of our
sensibility, developing themselves in the form of faith or of inspiration, are held up as the true and infallible source of human knowledge. The fundamental process, therefore, of all Mysticism, is to
reverse the true order of nature, and give the precedence to the
emotional instead of the intellectual element of the human mind." [2]
This is declared to be " the common ground of all Mysticism."

Schleiermacher's Theory.

If this be a correct view of the nature of Mysticism ; if it consists in giving predominant authority to the feelings in matters of
religion ; and if their impulses, developing themselves in the form
of faith, are the true and infallible source of knowledge, then
Schleiermacher's system, adopted and expounded by Morell himself in his " Philosophy of Religion," is the most elaborate system
of theology ever presented to the Church. It is the fundamental
principle of Schleiermacher's theory, that religion resides not in the
intelligence, or the will or active powers, but in the sensibility. It
is a form of feeling, a sense of absolute dependence. Instead of
being, as we seem to be, individual, separate free agents, originating our own acts, we recognize ourselves as a part of a great
whole, determined in all things by the great whole, of which we
are a part. We find ourselves as finite creatures over against an
infinite Being, in relation to whom we are as nothing. The Infinite is everything; and everything is only a manifestation of the

[1] See Cousin's *Cours de l'Histoire de la Philosophie*, and Morell's *History of Modern Philosophy*, p. 556 ff.
[2] Morell, p. 560.

Infinite. " Although man," says even Morell, " while in the midst
of finite objects, always feels himself to a certain extent free and
independent ; yet in the presence of that which is self-existent, infinite, and eternal, he may feel the sense of freedom utterly pass
away, and become absorbed in the sense of absolute dependence." [1]
This is said to be the essential principle of religion in all its forms
from Fetichism up to Christianity.   It depends mainly on the degree of culture of the individual or community, in what way this
sense of dependence shall reveal itself: because the more enlightened and pure the individual is, the more he will be able to apprehend aright what is involved in this sense of dependence
upon God.   Revelation is not the communication of new truth to
the understanding, but the providential influences by which the religious life is awakened in the soul.   Inspiration is not the divine
influence which controls the mental operations and utterances of
its subject, so as to render him infallible in the communication of
the truth revealed, but simply the intuition of eternal verities due
to the excited state of the religious feelings.   Christianity, subjectively considered, is the intuitions of good men, as occasioned and
determined by the appearance of Christ.   Objectively considered,
or, in other words, Christian theology, it is the logical analysis, and
scientific arrangement and elucidation of the truths involved in
those intuitions.   The Scriptures, as a rule of faith, have no authority.   They are of value only as means of awakening in us the
religious life experienced by the Apostles, and thus enabling us to
attain like intuitions of divine things.   The source of our religious
life, according to this system, is the feelings, and if this be the characteristic feature of Mysticism, the Schleiermacher doctrine is purely
Mystical.

D. *Mysticism as known in Church History.*

This, however, is not what is meant by Mysticism, as it has appeared in the Christian Church.   The Mystics, as already stated,
are those who claim an immediate communication of divine knowledge and of divine life from God to the soul, independently of the
Scriptures and the use of the ordinary means of grace.   " It de-
spairs," says Fleming, " of the regular process of science ; it believes that we may attain directly, without the aid of the senses or
reason, and by an immediate intuition, the real and absolute principle of all truth, — God." [2]

Mystics are of two classes ; the Theosophists, whose object is

[1] *Philosophy of Religion*, p. 75.   [2] Word "Mysticism."

knowledge, and with whom the organ of communication with God, is the reason ; and the Mystics proper, whose object is, life, purity, and beatitude ; and with whom the organ of communication, or receptivity, is the feelings.   They agree, first, in relying on the immediate revelation or communication of God to the soul ; and secondly, that these communications are to be attained, in the neglect of outward means, by quiet or passive contemplation. " The Theosophist is one who gives a theory of God, or of the works of God, which has not reason, but an inspiration of his own for its basis." [1] " The Theosophists, neither contented with the natural light of reason, nor with the simple doctrines of Scripture understood in their literal sense, have recourse to an internal supernatural light superior to all other illuminations, from which they profess to derive a mysterious and divine philosophy manifested only to the chosen favorites of heaven." [2]

Mysticism not identical with the Doctrine of Spiritual Illumination.

Mysticism, then, is not to be confounded with the doctrine of spiritual illumination as held by all evangelical Christians.   The Scriptures clearly teach that the mere outward presentation of the truth in the Word, does not suffice to the conversion or sanctification of men ; that the natural, or unrenewed man, does not receive the things of the Spirit of God, for they are foolishness unto him ; neither can he know them; that in order to any saving knowledge of the truth, *i. e.*, of such knowledge as produces holy affections and secures a holy life, there is need of an inward supernatural teaching of the Spirit, producing what the Scriptures call " spiritual discernment."   This supernatural teaching our Lord promised to his disciples when He said that He would send them the Spirit of truth to dwell in them, and to guide them into the knowledge of the truth.   For this teaching the sacred writers pray that it may be granted not to themselves only, but to all who heard their words or read their writings.   On this they depended exclusively for their success in preaching or teaching.   Hence believers were designated as πνευματικοί, *a Spiritu Dei illuminati, qui reguntur a Spiritu.*   And men of the world, unrenewed men, are described as those who have not the Spirit.   God, therefore, does hold immediate intercourse with the souls of men.   He reveals himself unto his people, as He does not unto the world.   He gives them the Spirit of revelation in the knowledge of himself. (Eph. i. 17.)   He un-

---

[1] Vaughan, *Hours with the Mystics,* vol. i. p. 45.
[2] Taylor, *Elements of Thought.*   See Fleming, word " Theosophism."

folds to them his glory, and fills them with a joy which passes understanding. All this is admitted; but this is very different from Mysticism. The two things, namely, spiritual illumination and Mysticism, differ, firstly, as to their object. The object of the inward teaching of the Spirit is to enable us to discern the truth and excellence of what is already objectively revealed in the Bible. The illumination claimed by the Mystic communicates truth independently of its objective revelation. It is not intended to enable us to appreciate what we already know, but to communicate new knowledge. It would be one thing to enable a man to discern and appreciate the beauty of a work of art placed before his eyes, and quite another thing to give him the intuition of all possible forms of truth and beauty, independent of everything external. So there is a great difference between that influence which enables the soul to discern the things " freely given to us of God " (1 Cor. ii. 12) in his Word, and the immediate revelation to the mind of all the contents of that word, or of their equivalents.

The doctrines of spiritual illumination and of Mysticism differ not only in the object, but secondly, in the manner in which that object is to be attained. The inward teaching of the Spirit is to be sought by prayer, and the diligent use of the appointed means ; the intuitions of the Mystic are sought in the neglect of all means, in the suppression of all activity inward and outward, and in a passive waiting for the influx of God into the soul. They differ, thirdly, in their effects. The effect of spiritual illumination is, that the Word dwells in us " in all wisdom and spiritual understanding " (Col. i. 9). What dwells in the mind of the Mystic are his own imaginings, the character of which depends on his own subjective state ; and whatever they are, they are of man and not of God.

It differs from the Doctrine of the "Leading of the Spirit."

Neither is Mysticism to be confounded with the doctrine of spiritual guidance. Evangelical Christians admit that the children of God are led by the Spirit of God; that their convictions as to truth and duty, their inward character and outward conduct, are moulded by his influence. They are children unable to guide themselves, who are led by an ever-present Father of infinite wisdom and love. This guidance is partly providential, ordering their external circumstances ; partly through the Word, which is a lamp to their feet ; and partly by the inward influence of the Spirit on the mind. This last, however, is also through the Word, making it intelligible and effectual; bringing it suitably to remembrance.

God leads his people by the cords of a man, *i. e.*, in accordance with the laws of his nature. This is very different from the doctrine that the soul, by yielding itself passively to God, is filled with all truth and goodness ; or, that in special emergencies it is controlled by blind, irrational impulses.

It differs from the Doctrine of " Common Grace."

Finally, Mysticism differs from the doctrine of common grace as held by all Augustinians, and that of sufficient grace as held by Arminians. All Christians believe that as God is everywhere present in the material world, guiding the operation of second causes so that they secure the results which He designs ; so his Spirit is everywhere present with the minds of men, exciting to good and restraining from evil, effectually controlling human character and conduct, consistently with the laws of rational beings. According to the Arminian theory this " common grace " is sufficient, if properly cultured and obeyed, to lead men to salvation, whether Pagans, Mohammedans, or Christians. There is little analogy, however, between this doctrine of common, or sufficient grace, and Mysticism as it has revealed itself in the history of the Church. The one assumes an influence of the Spirit on all men analogous to the providential efficiency of God in nature, the other an influence analogous to that granted to prophets and apostles, involving both revelation and inspiration.

§ 2. *Mysticism in the Early Church.*
A. *Montanism.*

The Montanists who arose toward the close of the second century had, in one aspect, some affinity to Mysticism. Montanus taught that as the ancient prophets predicted the coming of the Messiah through whom new revelations were to be made ; so Christ predicted the coming of the Paraclete through whom further communications of the mind of God were to be made to his people. Tertullian, by whom this system was reduced to order and commended to the higher class of minds, did indeed maintain that the rule of faith was fixed and immutable ; but nevertheless that there was need of a continued supernatural revelation of truth, at least as to matters of duty and discipline. This supernatural revelation was made through the Paraclete ; whether, as was perhaps the general idea among the Montanists, by communications granted, from time to time, to special individuals, who thereby became Christian proph-

ets ; or by an influence common to all believers, which however some
more than others experienced and improved.   The following passage from Tertullian[1] gives clearly the fundamental principle of the
system, so far as this point is concerned: "Regula quidem fidei una
omnino est, sola immobilis et irreformabilis. . . . . Hac lege
fidei manente, cetera jam disciplinæ et conversationis admittunt
novitatem correctionis ; operante scilicet et proficiente usque in
finem gratia Dei. . . . . Propterea Paracletum misit Dominus,
ut, quoniam humana mediocritas omnia semel capere non poterat,
paulatim dirigeretur et ordinaretur et ad perfectum perduceretur
disciplina ab illo vicario Domini Spiritu Sancto.   Quæ est ergo
Paracleti administratio nisi hæc, quod disciplina dirigitur, quod
Scripturæ revelantur, quod intellectus reformatur, quod ad meliora
proficitur ? . . . . Justitia primo fuit in rudimentis, natura
Deum metuens ; dehinc per legem et prophetas promovit in infan-
tiam ; dehinc per evangelium efferbuit in juventutem ; nunc per
Paracletum componitur in maturitatem."

The points of analogy between Montanism and Mysticism are
that both assume the insufficiency of the Scriptures and the ordinances of the Church for the full development of the Christian life ;
and both assert the necessity of a continued, supernatural, revelation from the Spirit of God.   In other respects the two tendencies
were divergent.   Mysticism was directed to the inner life ; Montanism to the outward.   It concerned itself with the reformation
of manners and strictness of discipline.   It enjoined fasts, and
other ascetic practices.   As it depended on the supernatural and
continued guidance of the Spirit, it was on the one hand opposed
to speculation, or the attempt to develop Christianity by philosophy ; and on the other to the dominant authority of the bishops.
Its denunciatory and exclusive spirit led to its condemnation as
heretical.   As the Montanists excommunicated the Church, the
Church excommunicated them.[2]

B. *The so-called Dionysius, the Areopagite.*

Mysticism, in the common acceptation of the term, is antagonistic to speculation.   And yet they are often united.   There have
been speculative or philosophical Mystics.   The father indeed of
Mysticism in the Christian Church, was a philosopher.   About the

---

[1] *De Virgg. Veland.* c. 1. — Edit. Basle, 1562, p. 490.
[2] See Neander's *Dogmengeschichte*, vol. i.   Schwegler, F. C. (disciple of Baur) *Der Mon-
tanismus und die Christliche Kirche des Zweiten Jahrhunderts*, Tub. 1841-48.   A concise
and clear account of Montanism is given in Mosheim's *Commentaries on the Affairs of
Christians before the Time of Constantine*, vol. i. § 66, pp. 497 ff. of Murdock's edition.

year A. D. 523, during the Monothelite controversy certain writings were quoted as of authority as being the productions of Dionysius the Areopagite. The total silence respecting them during the preceding centuries; the philosophical views which they express; the allusions to the state of the Church with which they abound, have produced the conviction, universally entertained, that they were the work of some author who lived in the latter part of the fifth century. The most learned investigators, however, confess their inability to fix with certainty or even with probability on any writer to whom they can be referred. Though their authorship is unknown, their influence has been confessedly great. The works which bear the pseudonym of Dionysius are, "The Celestial Hierarchy," "The Terrestrial Hierarchy," "Mystical Theology," and "Twelve Epistles." Their contents show that their author belonged to the school of the New Platonists, and that his object was to propagate the peculiar views of that school in the Christian Church. The writer attempts to show that the real, esoteric doctrines of Christianity are identical with those of his own school of philosophy. In other words, he taught New Platonism, in the terminology of the Church. Christian ideas were entirely excluded, while the language of the Bible was retained. Thus in our day we have had the philosophy of Schelling and Hegel set forth in the formulas of Christian theology.

New Platonism.

The New Platonists taught that the original ground and source of all things was simple being, without life or consciousness; of which absolutely nothing could be known, beyond that it is. They assumed an unknown quantity, of which nothing can be predicated. The pseudo-Dionysius called this original ground of all things God, and taught that God was mere being without attributes of any kind, not only unknowable by man, but of whom there was nothing to be known, as absolute being is in the language of the modern philosophy, — Nothing; nothing in itself, yet nevertheless the δύναμις τῶν πάντων.

The universe proceeds from primal being, not by any exercise of conscious power or will, but by a process or emanation. The familiar illustration is derived from the flow of light from the sun. With this difference, however. That the sun emits light, is a proof that it is itself luminous; but the fact that intelligent beings emanate from the "ground-being," is not admitted as proof that it is intelligent. The fact that the air produces cheerfulness, say these philosophers, does not prove that the atmosphere experiences joy. We can infer nothing as to the nature of the cause from the nature of the effects.

These emanations are of different orders; decreasing in dignity and excellence as they are distant from the primal source. The first of these emanations is mind, νοῦς, intelligence individualized in different ranks of spiritual beings. The next, proceeding from the first, is soul, which becomes individualized by organic or vital connection with matter. There is, therefore, an intelligence of intelligences, and also a soul of souls ; hence their generic unity. Evil arises from the connection of the spiritual with the corporeal, and yet this connection so far as souls are concerned, is necessary to their individuality. Every soul, therefore, is an emanation from the soul of the world, as that is from God, through the Intelligence.

As there is no individual soul without a body, and as evil is the necessary consequence of union with a body, evil is not only necessary or unavoidable, it is a good.

The end of philosophy is the immediate vision of God, which gives the soul supreme blessedness and rest. This union with God is attained by sinking into ourselves; by passivity. As we are a form, or mode of God's existence, we find God in ourselves, and are consciously one with him, when this is really apprehended ; or, when we suffer God, as it were, to absorb our individuality.

The primary emanations from the ground of all being, which the heathen called gods (as they had gods many and lords many) ; the New Platonists, spirits or intelligences ; and the Gnostics, æons ; the pseudo-Dionysius called angels. These he divided into three triads : (1.) thrones, cherubim, and seraphim ; (2.) powers, lordships, authorities ; (3.) angels, archangels, principalities. He classified the ordinances and officers and members of the Church into corresponding triads : (1.) The sacraments, — baptism, communion, anointing, — these were the means of initiation or consecration ; (2.) The initiators,— bishops, priests, deacons; (3.) The initiated, — monks, the baptized, catechumens.

The terms God, sin, redemption, are retained in this system, but the meaning attached to them was entirely inconsistent with the sense they bear in the Bible and in the Christian Church. The pseudo-Dionysius was a heathen philosopher in the vestments of a Christian minister. The philosophy which he taught he claimed to be the true sense of the doctrines of the Church, as that sense had been handed down by a secret tradition. Notwithstanding its heathen origin and character, its influence in the Church was great and long continued. The writings of its author were translated, annotated and paraphrased, centuries after his death. As there is no effect without an adequate cause, there must have been power in this system and an adaptation to the cravings of a large class of minds.

Causes of the Influence of the Writings of the pseudo-Dionysius.

To account for its extensive influence it may be remarked: (1.) That it did not openly shock the faith or prejudices of the Church. It did not denounce any received doctrine or repudiate any established institution or ordinance. It pretended to be Christian. It undertook to give a deeper and more correct insight into the mysteries of religion. (2.) It subordinated the outward to the inward. Some men are satisfied with rites, ceremonies, symbols, which may mean anything or nothing; others, with knowledge or clear views of truth. To others, the inner life of the soul, intercourse with God, is the great thing. To these this system addressed itself. It proposed to satisfy this craving after God, not indeed in a legitimate way, or by means of God's appointment. Nevertheless it was the high end of union with him that it proposed, and which it professed to secure. (3.) This system was only one form of the doctrine which has such a fascination for the human mind, and which underlies so many forms of religion in every age of the world; the doctrine, namely, that the universe is an efflux of the life of God, — all things flowing from him, and back again to him from everlasting to everlasting. This doctrine quiets the conscience, as it precludes the idea of sin ; it gives the peace which flows from fatalism ; and it promises the absolute rest of unconsciousness when the individual is absorbed in the bosom of the Infinite.[1]

§ 3. *Mysticism during the Middle Ages.*

A. *General Characteristics of this Period.*

The Middle Ages embrace the period from the close of the sixth century to the Reformation. This period is distinguished by three marked characteristics. First, the great development of the Latin Church in its hierarchy, its worship, and its formulated doctrines, as well as in its superstitions, corruptions, and power. Secondly, the extraordinary intellectual activity awakened in the region of speculation, as manifested in the multiplication of seats of learning,

---

[1] See Rixner's *Geschichte der Philosophie,* vol. i. §§ 168–172. Ritter's *Geschichte der Christlichen Philosophie,* vol. ii. pp. 115-135. Herzog's *Encyklopädie.*

in the number and celebrity of their teachers, and in the great
multitude of students by which they were attended, and in the
interest taken by all classes in the subjects of learned discussion.
Thirdly, by a widespread and variously manifested movement of,
so to speak, the inner life of the Church, protesting against the formalism, the corruption, and the tyranny of the external Church.
This protest was made partly openly by those whom Protestants
are wont to call " Witnesses for the Truth ; " and partly within
the Church itself.   The opposition within the Church manifested
itself partly among the people, in the formation of fellowships or
societies for benevolent effort and spiritual culture, such as the
Beguines, the Beghards, the Lollards, and afterwards, " The Brethren of the Common Lot ; " and partly in the schools, or by the
teachings of theologians.

It was the avowed aim of the theologians of this period to justify
the doctrines of the Church at the bar of reason ; to prove that
what was received on authority as a matter of faith, was true as a
matter of philosophy.   It was held to be the duty of the theologian
to exalt faith into knowledge.   Or, as Anselm[1] expresses it : " ra-
tionabili necessitate intelligere, esse oportere omnia illa, quæ nobis
fides catholica de Christo credere præcipit."   Richard à St. Victore
still more strongly asserts that we are bound, " quod tenemus ex
fide, ratione apprehendere et demonstrativæ certitudinis attestatione
firmare."

The First Class of Mediæval Theologians.

Of these theologians, however, there were three classes.   First,
those who avowedly exalted reason above authority, and refused
to receive anything on authority which they could not for themselves, on rational grounds, prove to be true.   John Scotus Erigena
(*Eringeborne*, Irish-born) may be taken as a representative of this
class.   He not only held, that reason and revelation, philosophy
and religion, are perfectly consistent, but that religion and philosophy are identical.   " Conficitur," he says, " inde veram philosophiam esse veram religionem conversimque veram religionem esse
veram philosophiam."[2]   And on the crucial question, Whether faith
precedes science, or science faith, he decided for the latter.   Reason, with him, was paramount to authority, the latter having no
force except when sustained by the former.   " Auctoritas siqui-
dem ex vera ratione processit, ratio vero nequaquam ex auctoritate.
Omnis autem auctoritas, quæ vera ratione non approbatur, infirma
videtur esse.   Vera autem ratio, quum virtutibus suis rata atque

[1] *Cur Deus Homo,* lib. i. cap. 25.   [2] *De Prædest.,* cap. i. 1, Migne, *Patr.,* vol. cxxii. p. 358, a.

immutabilis munitur, nullius auctoritatis adstipulatione roborari indiget." [1] His philosophy as developed in his work, " De Divisione Naturæ," is purely pantheistic. There is with him but one being, and everything real is thought. His system, therefore, is nearly identical with the idealistic pantheism of Hegel; yet he had his trinitarianism, his soteriology, and his eschatology, as a theologian.

The Second Class.

The second and more numerous class of the mediæval theologians took the ground that faith in matters of religion precedes science; that truths are revealed to us supernaturally by the Spirit of God, which truths are to be received on the authority of the Scriptures and the testimony of the Church. But being believed, then we should endeavor to comprehend and to prove them; so that our conviction of their truth should rest on rational grounds. It is very evident that everything depends on the spirit with which this principle is applied, and on the extent to which it is carried. In the hands of many of the schoolmen, as of the Fathers, it was merely a form of rationalism. Many taught that while Christianity was to be received by the people on authority as a matter of faith, it was to be received by the cultivated as a matter of knowledge. The human was substituted for the divine, the authority of reason for the testimony of God. With the better class of the schoolmen the principle in question was held with many limitations. Anselm, for example, taught: (1.) That holiness of heart is the essential condition of true knowledge. It is only so far as the truths of religion enter into our personal experience, that we are able properly to apprehend them. Faith, therefore, as including spiritual discernment, must precede all true knowledge. " Qui secundum carnem vivit, carnalis sive animalis est, de quo dicitur: animalis homo non percipit ea, quæ sunt Spiritus Dei. . . . . Qui non crediderit, non intelliget, nam qui non crediderit, non experietur, et qui expertus non fuerit, non intelliget." [2] " Neque enim quæro intelligere, ut credam, sed credo, ut intelligam. Nam et hoc credo, quia, nisi credidero, non intelligam." [3] (2.) He held that rational proof was not needed as a help to faith. It was as absurd, he said, for us to presume to add authority to the testimony of God by our reasoning, as for a man to prop up Olympus. (3.) He taught that there are doctrines of revelation which transcend our reason, which we cannot rationally pretend to compre-

---

[1] *De Div. Nat.* i. 69 f. Migne, *ut supra*, p. 513, b.

[2] *De Fide Trinitatis*, 2; *Opera*, Paris, 1721, p. 42, B, b, c.

[3] *Proslogium* i · Ibid. p. 30, B, a.

hend or prove, and which are to be received on the simple testimony of God. " Nam Christianus per fidem debet ad intellectum proficere, non per intellectum ad fidem accedere, aut si intelligere non valet, a fide recedere. Sed cum ad intellectum valet pertingere, delectatur, cum vero nequit, quod capere non potest, veneratur." [1]

A third class of the schoolmen, while professing to adhere to the doctrines of the Church, consciously or unconsciously, explained them away.

B. Mediæval Mystics.

Mystics were to be found in all these classes, and therefore they have been divided, as by Dr. Shedd,[2] into the heretical, the orthodox, and an intermediate class, which he designates as latitudinarian. Much to the same effect, Neudecker,[3] classifies them as Theosophist, Evangelical, and Separatist. Ullmann [4] makes a somewhat different classification. The characteristic common to these classes, which differed so much from each other, was not that in all there was a protest of the heart against the head, of the feelings against the intellect, a reaction against the subtleties of the scholastic theologians, for some of the leading Mystics were among the most subtle dialecticians. Nor was it a common adherence to the Platonic as opposed to the Aristotelian philosophy, or to realism as opposed to nominalism. But it was the belief, that oneness with God was the great end to be desired and pursued, and that that union was to be sought, not so much through the truth, or the Church, or ordinances, or Christian fellowship; but by introspection, meditation, intuition. As very different views were entertained of the nature of the " oneness with God," which was to be sought, so the Mystics differed greatly from each other. Some were extreme pantheists; others were devout theists and Christians. From its essential nature, however, the tendency of Mysticism was to pantheism. And accordingly undisguised pantheism was not only taught by some of the most prominent Mystics, but prevailed extensively among the people.

Pantheistic tendency of Mysticism.

It has already been remarked, that the system of the pseudo-Dionysius, as presented in his " Mystical Theology " and other writings, was essentially pantheistic. Those writings were translated

---

[1] Epistolae, lib. ii. epis. 41; Opera, Paris, 1721, p. 357, B, a.
[2] History of Christian Doctrine, vol. i. p. 79.
[3] Lexicon, art. " Mystik."   [4] Reformers before the Reformation.

by Scotus Erigena, himself the most pronounced pantheist of the Middle Ages. Through the joint influence of these two men, a strong tendency to pantheism was developed to a greater or less degree among the mediæval Mystics. Even the associations among the people, such as the Beghards and Lollards, although at first exemplary and useful, by adopting a system of mystic pantheism became entirely corrupt.[1] Believing themselves to be modes of the divine existence, all they did God did, and all they felt inclined to do was an impulse from God, and therefore nothing could be wrong. In our own day the same principles have led to the same consequences in one wing of the German school of philosophy.

It was not only among the people and in these secret fellowships that this system was adopted. Men of the highest rank in the schools, and personally exemplary in their deportment, became the advocates of the theory which lay at the foundation of these practical evils. Of these scholastic pantheistical Mystics, the most distinguished and influential was Henry Eckart, whom some modern writers regard " as the deepest thinker of his age, if not of any age." Neither the time nor the place of his birth is known. He first appears in Paris as a Dominican monk and teacher. In 1304 he was Provincial of the Dominicans in Saxony. Soon after he was active in Strasburg as a preacher. His doctrines were condemned as heretical, although he denied that he had in any respect departed from the doctrines of the Church. From the decision of his archbishop and his provincial council, Eckart appealed to the Pope, by whom the sentence of condemnation was confirmed. This decision, however, was not published until 1329, when Eckart was already dead. It is not necessary here to give the details of his system. Suffice it to say, that he held that God is the only being; that the universe is the self-manifestation of God; that the highest destiny of man is to come to the consciousness of his identity with God; that that end is to be accomplished partly by philosophical abstraction and partly by ascetic self renunciation.

" Although union with God is effected mainly by thinking and consciousness, still it also requires a corresponding act of the will, something practical, such as self-denial and privation, by which man rises above all that is finite. Not only must he lay aside all created things, the world and earthly good, and mortify desire, but more than all he must resign his ' I,' reduce himself to nothing, and become what he was before he issued forth into this temporal state. Nay, man must rise above the chief good, above virtue,

1 Ullmann, vol. ii. ch. 2.

piety, blessedness, and God himself, as things external and superior to his spirit, and it is only when he has thus annihilated self, and all that is not God within him, that nothing remains except the pure and simple divine essence, in which all division is brought into absolute unity." [1]

Another distinguished and influential writer of the same class was John Ruysbroek, born 1293, in a village of that name not far from Brussels. Having entered the service of the Church he devoted himself to the duties of a secular priest until his sixtieth year. when he became prior of a newly-instituted monastery. He was active and faithful, gentle and devout. Whether he was a theist or a pantheist is a matter of dispute. His speculative views were formed more or less under the influence of the writings of the pseudo-Dionysius and of Eckart. Gerson, himself a Mystic, objected to his doctrines as pantheistic; and every one acknowledges that there are not only forms of expression but also principles to be found in his writings which imply the pantheistic theory. He speaks of God as the super-essential being including all beings. All creatures, he taught, were in God, as thoughts before their creation. " God saw and recognized them in himself, as somehow, but not wholly, different from himself, for what is in God, is God." " In the act of self-depletion, the spirit loses itself in the enjoyment of love, and imbibes directly the brightness of God, yea, becomes the very brightness which it imbibes. All who are raised to the sublimity of this contemplative life are one with deifying (deifica) brightness, and become one and the same light as that which they behold. To such a height is the spirit elevated above itself, and made one with God, in respect that in the oneness of that living original in which, according to its uncreated being, it possesses itself, it enjoys and contemplates boundless treasures in the same manner as God himself." Ullmann, who quotes these and similar passages, still maintains that Ruysbroek was a theist, because, as he says, Ruysbroek " distinctly recognizes not only the immanence of God, but what no pantheist can do, his transcendence." Moreover, he " too frequently and too solicitously avers that, in the oneness of the contemplative man with God, he still recognizes a difference between the two, to permit us to ascribe to him the doctrine of an absolute solution of the individual into the Divine substance." [2] A man may aver a difference between the waves and the ocean, between the leaves and the tree, and yet in both cases assert a substantial unity. It is true that no one can intelligently

affirm the transcendence of God, and still hold the extreme form
of pantheism which makes the world the existence-form of God,
his whole intelligence, power, and life. But he may be a Monist.
He may believe that there is but one Being in the universe, that
everything is a form of God, and all life the life of God. Pantheism is Protean. Some moderns speak of a Christian Pantheism.
But any system which hinders our saying " Thou," to God, is fatal
to religion.

Evangelical Mystics.

Bernard of Clairvaux, Hugo and Richard of St. Victor, Gerson,
Thomas à Kempis and others, are commonly referred to the class of
evangelical Mystics.   These eminent and influential men differed
much from each other, but they all held union with God, not in
the Scriptural, but in the mystical sense of that term, as the great
object of desire. It was not that they held that " the beatific
vision of God," the intuition of his glory, which belongs to heaven,
is attainable in this world and attainable by abstraction, ecstatic
apprehension, or passive reception, but that the soul becomes one
with God, if not in substance, yet in life.   These men, however,
were great blessings to the Church.   Their influence was directed
to the preservation of the inward life of religion in opposition to
the formality and ritualism which then prevailed in the Church ;
and thus to free the conscience from subjection to human authority.
The writings of Bernard are still held in high esteem, and " The
Imitation of Christ," by Thomas à Kempis, has diffused itself like
incense through all the aisles and alcoves of the Universal Church.[1]

§ 4. Mysticism at, and after the Reformation.

A. Effect of the Reformation on the Popular Mind.

Such a great and general movement of the public mind as occurred during the sixteenth century, when the old foundations of
doctrine and order in the Church, were overturned, could hardly
fail to be attended by irregularities and extravagancies in the
inward and outward life of the people.   There are two principles
advanced, both Scriptural and both of the last importance, which
are specially liable to abuse in times of popular excitement.

---

[1] See Tholuck, *Sufismus seu Theosophia Persarum Pantheistica.*   C. Schmidt, *Essai sur
les Mystiques du 14me Siècle.*   This writer is the author of most of the excellent articles in
Herzog's *Encyklopädie* on the Mediæval Mystics.   Ullmann's *Reformers before the Reformation.*   Poiret, *Bibliotheca Mysticorum.*   Vaughan's *Hours with the Mystics.*   Helfferich's
Christliche Mystik.   Dorner, *Geschichte der Protestantischen Theologie*, 48–59.

The first is, the right of private judgment.   This, as understood by the Reformers, is the right of every man to decide what a revelation made by God to him, requires him to believe.   It was a protest against the authority assumed by the Church (*i. e.* the Bishops), of deciding for the people what they were to believe.   It was very natural that the fanatical, in rejecting the authority of the Church, should reject all external authority in matters of religion.   They understood by the right of private judgment, the right of every man to determine what he should believe from the operations of his own mind and from his own inward experience, independently of the Scriptures.   But as it is palpably absurd to expect, on such a subject as religion, a certainty either satisfactory to ourselves or authoritative for others, from our own reason or feelings, it was inevitable that these subjective convictions should be referred to a supernatural source.   Private revelations, an inward light, the testimony of the Spirit, came to be exalted over the authority of the Bible.

Secondly, the Reformers taught that religion is a matter of the heart, that a man's acceptance with God does not depend on his membership in any external society, on obedience to its officers, and on sedulous observance of its rites and ordinances; but on the regeneration of his heart, and his personal faith in the Son of God, manifesting itself in a holy life.   This was a protest against the fundamental principle of Romanism, that all within the external organization which Romanists call the Church, are saved, and all out of it are lost.   It is not a matter of surprise that evil men should wrest this principle, as they do all other truths, to their own destruction.   Because religion does not consist in externals, many rushed to the conclusion that externals, — the Church, its ordinances, its officers, its worship, — were of no account.   These principles were soon applied beyond the sphere of religion.   Those who regarded themselves as the organs of God, emancipated from the authority of the Bible and exalted above the Church, came to claim exemption from the authority of the State.   To this outbreak the grievous and long-continued oppression of the peasantry greatly contributed, so that this spirit of fanaticism and revolt rapidly spread over all Germany, and into Switzerland and Holland.

The Popular Disorders not the Effects of the Reformation.

The extent to which these disorders spread, and the rapidity with which they diffused themselves, show that they were not the mere outgrowth of the Reformation.   The principles avowed by the

Reformers, and the relaxation of papal authority occasioned by the Reformation, served but to inflame the elements which had for years been slumbering in the minds of the people. The numerous associations and fellowships, of which mention was made in the preceding section, had leavened the public mind with the principles of pantheistic Mysticism, which were the prolific source of evil. Men who imagined themselves to be forms in which God existed and acted, were not likely to be subject to any authority human or divine, nor were they apt to regard anything as sinful which they felt inclined to do.

These men also had been brought up under the Papacy. According to the papal theory, especially as it prevailed during the Middle Ages, the Church was a theocracy, whose representatives were the subjects of a constant inspiration rendering them infallible as teachers and absolute as rulers. All who opposed the Church were rebels against God, whom to destroy was a duty both to God and man. These ideas Münzer and his followers applied to themselves. They were the true Church. They were inspired. They were entitled to determine what is true in matters of doctrine. They were entitled to rule with absolute authority in church and state. All who opposed them, opposed God, and ought to be exterminated. Münzer died upon the scaffold; thus was fulfilled anew our Lord's declaration, "Those who take the sword, shall perish by the sword."

B. *Mystics among the Reformers.*

Few of the theologians contemporary with Luther took any part in this fanatical movement. To a certain extent this however was done by Carlstadt (Bodenstein), archdeacon and afterwards professor of theology at Wittenberg. At first he coöperated zealously with the great Reformer, but when Storch and Stübener claiming to be prophets, came to Wittenberg during Luther's confinement at Wartburg, and denounced learning and Church institutions, and taught that all reliance was to be placed on the inward light, or supernatural guidance of the Spirit, Carlstadt gave them his support and exhorted the students to abandon their studies and to betake themselves to manual labor. Great disorder following these movements, Luther left his place of seclusion, appeared upon the scene, and succeeded in allaying the tumult. Carlstadt then withdrew from Wittenberg, and ultimately united himself with Schwenkfeld, a more influential opponent of Luther, and who was equally imbued with the spirit of Mysticism.

Schwenkfeld.

Schwenkfeld, a nobleman born 1490, in the principality of Lignitz, in Lower Silesia, was a man of great energy and force of character, exemplary in his conduct, of extensive learning and indefatigable diligence. He at first took an active part in promoting the Reformation, and was on friendly terms with Luther, Melancthon, and the other leading Reformers. Being a man not only of an independent way of thinking, but confident and zealous in maintaining his peculiar opinions, he soon separated himself from other Protestants and passed his whole life in controversy; condemned by synods and proscribed by the civil authorities, he was driven from city to city, until his death, which occurred in 1561.

That Schwenkfeld differed not only from the Romanists, but from Lutherans and Reformed on all the great doctrines then in controversy, is to be referred to the fact that he held, in common with the great body of the Mystics of the Middle Ages, that union or oneness with God, not in nature or character only, but also in being or substance, was the one great desideratum and essential condition of holiness and felicity. To avoid the pantheistic doctrines into which the majority of the Mystics were led, he held to a form of dualism. Creatures exist out of God, and are due to the exercise of his power. In them there is nothing of the substance of God, and therefore nothing really good. With regard to men, they are made good and blessed by communicating to them the substance of God. This communication is made through Christ. Christ is not, even as to his human nature, a creature. His body and soul were formed out of the substance of God. While on earth, in his state of humiliation, this substantial unity of his humanity with God, was undeveloped and unrevealed. Since his exaltation it is completely deified, or lost in the divine essence. It followed from these principles, First, That the external church, with its ordinances and means of grace, was of little importance. Especially that the Scriptures are not, even instrumentally, the source of the divine life. Faith does not come by hearing, but from the Christ within; i. e. from the living substance of God communicated to the soul. This communication is to be sought by abnegation, renunciation of the creature, by contemplation and prayer. Secondly, as to the sacrament of the supper, which then was the great subject of controversy, Schwenkfeld stood by himself. Not admitting that Christ had any material body or blood, he could not admit that the bread and wine were transubstantiated into his body and blood, as Romanists teach; nor that his body and blood were locally present in the sacrament, in, with, and under the bread and wine, as Luther held; nor could he admit the dynamic presence of Christ's body, as taught by Calvin; nor that the Lord's Supper was merely a significant and commemorative ordinance, as Zwingle taught. He held his own doctrine. He transposed the words of Christ. Instead of "This (bread) is my body," he said, the true meaning and intent of Christ was, "My body is bread;" that is, as bread is the staff and source of life to the body, so my body, formed of the essence of God, is the life of the soul.

A third inference from Schwenkfeld's fundamental principle was that the redemption of the soul is purely subjective; something wrought in the soul itself. He denied justification by faith as Luther taught that doctrine, and which Luther regarded as the life of the Church. He said that we are justified not by what Christ has done for us, but by what He does within us. All we need is the communication of the life or substance of Christ to the soul. With him, as with Mystics generally, the ideas of guilt and expiation were ignored.

Later Mystics.

The succession of mystical writers was kept up by such men as Paracelsus, Weigel, Jacob Boehme, and others. The first named was a physician and chemist, who combined natural philosophy and alchemy with his theosophy. He was born in 1493 and died in 1541. Weigel, a pastor, was born in Saxony in 1533, and died in 1588. His views were formed under the influence of Tauler, Schwenkfeld, and Paracelsus. He taught, as his predecessors had done, that the inner word, and not the Scriptures, was the source of true knowledge, that all that God creates is God himself, and that all that is good in man is of the substance of God. The most remarkable writer of this class was Jacob Boehme, who was born near Gorlitz in Silesia, in 1575. His parents were peasants, and he himself a shoemaker. That such a man should write books which have proved a mine of thoughts to Schelling, Hegel, and Coleridge, as well as to a whole class of theologians, is decisive evidence of his extraordinary gifts. In character he was mild, gentle, and devout; and although denounced as a heretic, he constantly professed his allegiance to the faith of the Church. He regarded himself as having received in answer to prayer, on three different occasions, communications of divine light and knowledge which he was impelled to reveal to others. He did not represent the primordial being as without attributes or qualities of which nothing could be predicated, but as the seat of all kinds of forces seeking development. What the Bible teaches of the Trinity, he understood as an account of the development of the universe out of God and its relation to him. He was a theosophist in one sense, in which Vaughan[1] defines the term, " One who gives you a theory of God or of the works of God, which has not reason, but an inspiration of his own for its basis." " The theosophists," says Fleming,[2] "are a school of philosophers who mix enthusiasm with observation, alchemy with theology, metaphysics with medicine, and clothe the whole with a form of mystery and inspiration." [3]

§ 5. *Quietism.*

A. *Its general character.*

Tholuck[4] says " There is a law of seasons in the spiritual, as well as in the physical world, in virtue of which when the time has come, without apparent connection, similar phenomena reveal themselves in different places. As towards the end of the fifteenth century an ecclesiastical-doctrinal reformatory movement passed over the greater part of Europe, in part without apparent connection ; so at the end of the seventeenth a mystical and spiritual tendency was almost as extensively manifested. In Germany, it took the form of Mysticism and Pietism ; in England, of Quakerism ; in France, of Jansenism and Mysticism ; and in Spain and Italy, of Quietism." This movement was in fact what in our day would be called a revival of religion. Not indeed in a form free from grievous errors, but nevertheless it was a return to the religion of the heart, as opposed to the religion of forms. The Mystics of this period, although they constantly appealed to the mediæval Mystics, even to the Areopagite, and although they often used the same forms of expression, yet they adhered much more faithfully to Scriptural doctrines and to the faith of the Church. They did not fall into Pantheism, or believe in the absorption of the soul into the substance of God. They held, however, that the end to be attained was union with God. By this was not meant what Christians generally understand by that term ; congeniality with God, delight in his perfections, assurance of his love, submission to his will, perfect satisfaction in the enjoyment of his favour. It was

[1] *Hours with Mystics,* vol. i. p. 45.   [2] *Vocabulary of Philosophy.*

[3] See Baur's *Christliche Gnosis ;* Dorner's *History of the Doctrine of the Person of Christ,* and his *History of Protestant Theology ;* Hamberger, *Die Lehre des Deutschen Philosophen J. Boehme,* 1844.

[4] Herzog's *Encyklopädie,* art. " Molinos."

something more than all this, something mystical and therefore inexplicable; a matter of feeling, not something to be understood or explained; a state in which all thought, all activity was suspended; a state of perfect quietude in which the soul is lost in God, — an " écoulement et liquefaction de l'âme en Dieu," as it is expressed by St. Francis de Sales. This state is reached by few. It is to be attained not by the use of the means of grace or ordinances of the Church. The soul should be raised above the need of all such aids. It rises even above Christ, insomuch that it is not He whom the soul seeks, nor God in him; but God as God; the absolute, infinite God. The importance of the Scriptures, of prayer, of the sacraments, and of the truth concerning Christ, was not denied; but all these were regarded as belonging to the lower stages of the divine life. Nor was this rest and union with God to be attained by meditation; for meditation is discursive. It implies an effort to bring truth before the mind, and fixing the attention upon it. All conscious self-activity must be suspended in order to this perfect rest in God. It is a state in which the soul is out of itself; a state of ecstasy, according to the etymological meaning of the word.

This state is to be reached in the way prescribed by the older Mystics; first, by negation or abstraction; that is, the abstraction of the soul from everything out of God, from the creature, from all interest, concern, or impression from sensible objects. Hence the connection between Mysticism, in this form, and asceticism. Not only must the soul become thus abstracted from the creature, but it must be dead to self. All regard to self must be lost. There can be no prayer, for prayer is asking something for self; no thanksgiving, for thanksgiving implies gratitude for good done to self. Self must be lost. There must be no preference for heaven over hell. One of the points most strenuously insisted upon was a willingness to be damned, if such were the will of God. In the controversy between Fénélon and Bossuet, the main question concerned disinterested love, whether in loving God the soul must be raised above all regard to its own holiness and happiness. This pure or disinterested love justifies, or renders righteous in the sight of God. Although the Mystics of this period were eminently pure as well as devout, they nevertheless sometimes laid down principles, or at least used expressions, which gave their enemies a pretext for charging them with Antinomianism. It was said, that a soul filled with this love, or reduced to this entire negation of self, cannot sin; " sin is not in, but outside of him; " which was made to mean, that nothing was sin to the perfect. It is an instructive psychological fact that when men attempt or pretend to rise above the law of God, they sink below it; that Perfectionism has so generally led to Antinomianism.

B. *Leaders of this Movement.*

The principal persons engaged in promoting this remarkable religious movement were Molinos, Madame Guyon, and Archbishop Fénélon. Michael Molinos, born 1640, was a Spanish priest. About 1670 he became a resident of Rome, where he gained a great reputation for piety and mildness, and great influence from his position as confessor to many families of distinction. He enjoyed the friendship of the highest authorities in the Church, including several of the cardinals, and the Pope, Innocent XI., himself. In 1675 he published his "Spiritual Guide," in which the principles above stated were presented. Molinos did not claim originality, but professed to rely on the Mystics of the Middle Ages, several of whom had already been canonized by the Church. This, however, did not save him from persecution. His first trial indeed before the Inquisition resulted in his acquittal. But subsequently, through the influence of the Jesuits and of the court of Louis XIV., he was, after a year's imprisonment, condemned. Agreeably to his principle of entire subjection to the Church, he retracted his errors, but failed to secure the confidence of his judges. He died in 1697. His principal work, "Manuductio Spiritualis," or Spiritual Guide, was translated into different languages, and won for him many adherents in every part of the Catholic world. When he was imprisoned, it is said, that twenty thousand letters from all quarters, and many of them from persons of distinction, were found among his papers, assuring him of the sympathy of their authors with him in his spirit and views. This is proof that there were at that time thousands in the Romish Church who had not bowed the knee to the Baal of formalism.

Madame Guyon.

The most prominent and influential of the Quietists, as they were called, was Madame Guyon, born 1648 and died 1717. She belonged to a rich and noble family; was educated in a cloister, married at sixteen to a man of rank and wealth and of three times her age; faithful and devoted, but unhappy in her domestic relations; adhering zealously to her Church, she passed a life of incessant labour, and that, too, embittered by persecution. When still in the cloister she came under the influence of the writings of St. Francis de Sales, which determined her subsequent course. Enthusiastic in temperament, endowed with extraordinary gifts, she soon came to regard herself as the recipient of visions, revelations, and inspirations by which she was impelled to write, and, in the first instance, to devote herself to the conversion of Protestants. Failing in this, she considered it her vocation to become the mother of spiritual children, by bringing them to adopt her views of the inner life. To this object she devoted herself with untiring energy and great success, her adherents, secret and avowed, being numbered by thousands, or, as she supposed, by millions. She thus drew upon herself, although devoted to the Church, the displeasure of the authorities, and was imprisoned for seven years in the Bastile and other prisons in France. The latter years of her life she spent in retirement in the house of her daughter, burdened with physical infirmities, hearing mass every day in her private chapel and communicating every other day. Her principal works were, "La Bible avec des Explications et Réflexions, qui regardent la Vie Intérieure," "Moyen court et très-facile de faire Oraison." This little work excited great attention and great opposition. She was obliged to defend it in an "Apologie du Moyen Court," in 1690, and "Justifications" in 1694, and in 1695 she was forced to retract thirty-five propositions selected therefrom. She published an allegorical poem under the title "Les Torrens." Her minor poetic pieces called "Poésies Spirituelles," in four volumes, are greatly admired for the genius which they display.

Archbishop Fénélon, one of the greatest lights of the Gallican Church, espoused the cause of Madame Guyon, and published, 1697, "Explication des Maximes des Saints sur la Vie Intérieure." As the title intimates, the principles of this book are derived from the earlier Mystics, and specially from the latest of the saints, St. Francis de Sales, who was canonized in 1665, only thirty-three years after his death. Although Fénélon carefully avoided the extravagances of the Mystics of his own day, and although he taught nothing which men venerated in the Church had not taught before him, his book forfeited for him the favour of the court, and was finally condemned by the authorities at Rome. To this condemnation he submitted with the greatest docility. He not only made no defence, but read the brief of condemnation in his own pulpit, and forbade his book being read within his diocese. To this his conscience constrained him, although he probably did not change his views. As the Pope decided against him he was willing to admit that what he said was wrong, and yet what he intended to say he still held to be right.

§ 6. *The Quakers or Friends.*

This widely extended and highly respected body of professing Christians constitute the most permanent and best organized representatives of the principles of Mysticism which have appeared in the Church. They have existed as an organized society nearly two centuries and a half, and number in Europe and America several hundred thousands.

A. *Their Origin and Early History.*

They took their origin and name from George Fox, who was born at Drayton, Leicestershire, England, in 1624. He received only the rudiments of an English education, and was by trade a shoemaker. From boyhood he was remarkable for his quiet, secluded habits. He devoted his leisure to the reading of the Scriptures and meditation. The age in which he lived was one of corruption in the Church and agitation in the State. He was so impressed by the evils which he saw around him that he lost confidence in the teachers of religion and in the ordinances of the church. At last he felt himself called of God, by direct revelation and inspiration, to denounce the existing Church, its organization and officers, and to proclaim a new and spiritual dispensation. This dispensation was to be new only relatively to what had long existed. It was designed as a restoration of the apostolic age, when the church was guided and extended by the Spirit, without the intervention of the written Word, or, as Fox and his followers maintained, of a special order of ministers, but every man and every woman spake as the Spirit gave them utterance.[1]

They were called Quakers either because they themselves trembled when under the influence of the Spirit, or because they were in the habit of calling on those whom they addressed to quake in fear of the judgment of God. The designation has long ceased to be appropriate, as they are characteristically quiet in their worship, and gentle toward those who are without. They call themselves Friends because opposed to violence, contention, and especially to war. At first, however, they were chargeable with many irregularities, which, in connection with their refusing to pay tithes, to take oaths, and to perform military service, gave pretext to frequent and long continued persecutions.

[1] One of the most important works of William Penn bears the title, *Primitive Christianity revived in the Faith and Practice of the People called Quakers.*

The Quakers were at first, as a class, illiterate, but men from the educated classes soon joined them, and by their influence the irregularities connected with the movement were corrected, and the society reduced to a regularly organized form. The most prominent of these men were George Keith, Samuel Fisher, and William Penn. The last named, the son of a British admiral, proved his sincerity by the sacrifices and sufferings to which his adherence to a sect, then despised and persecuted, subjected him. From the influence which he possessed, as the friend and favorite of James II., he was able to do much for his brethren, and having received a grant from the crown, of what is now Pennsylvania, he transported a colony of them to this country and founded one of the most important States of the American Union. The man, however, who did most to reduce the principles of George Fox to order, and to commend them to the religious and literary public, was Robert Barclay. Barclay was a member of a prominent Scottish family, and received the benefit of an extended and varied education. He was born in 1648, and died in 1690. His principal work, " Theologiæ Christianæ Apologia," is an exposition of fifteen theses which he had previously written and printed under the title, " Theses Theologicæ omnibus Clericis et præsertim universis Doctoribus, Professoribus et Studiosis Theologiæ in Academiis Europæ versantibus sive Pontificis sive Protestantibus oblatæ."

B. *Their Doctrines.*

It is impossible to give a satisfactory view of the doctrines of the Quakers. They have no authoritative creed or exposition of doctrine which all who call themselves Quakers acknowledge. Their most prominent writers differ in their views on many important points. The opinions of no one, nor of several authors, can be fairly taken as representing the views of the Society. There are in fact three classes of Quakers.

First. Those who call themselves orthodox, and who differ very little from the great body of evangelical Christians. To this belongs the great majority of the Society both in this country and in Great Britain. This appears from the testimonies repeatedly issued by the " Yearly Meetings," the representative bodies of the Society. This is a much more satisfactory witness of the general faith of the body than the declarations of individual writers, however eminent, for which the Society is not responsible. A very clear and comprehensive summary of the doctrine of Friends is to be found in the " History of Religious Denominations in the United

States," compiled by I. Daniel Rupp. The articles in this work were written by eminent men belonging to the several denominations whose views are represented. That which relates to the Quakers was written by the late Thomas Evans, a prominent minister of the Society, and a truly representative man. Without referring to the peculiar doctrines of the Society, the following extracts show how near the orthodox Quakers (*i. e.*, the Society itself, as represented in its yearly meetings) come to the common faith of Protestant churches.

Doctrines of the Orthodox Friends.

1. As to God, it is said, Quakers "Believe in one only wise, omnipotent, and everlasting God, the creator and upholder of all things visible and invisible; and in one Lord Jesus Christ, by whom are all things, the mediator between God and man; and in the Holy Spirit which proceedeth from the Father and the Son; one God blessed forever. In expressing their views relative to the awful and mysterious doctrine of "the Three that bear record in heaven," they have carefully avoided the use of unscriptural terms, invented to define Him who is undefinable, and have scrupulously adhered to the safe and simple language of Holy Scripture, as contained in Matt. xxviii. 18, 19."

2. As to the person and work of Christ, "They own and believe in Jesus Christ, the beloved and only begotten Son of God, who was conceived of the Holy Ghost, and born of the Virgin Mary. . . . . They believe that He alone is the Redeemer and Saviour of man, the captain of salvation, who saves from sin as well as from hell and the wrath to come, and destroys the works of the devil. He is the seed of the woman that bruises the serpent's head; even Christ Jesus, the Alpha and Omega, the first and last. He is, as the Scriptures of truth say of him, our wisdom, righteousness, sanctification, and redemption, neither is there salvation in any other, for there is no other name under heaven given among men whereby we may be saved."

"The Society of Friends have uniformly declared their belief in the divinity and manhood of the Lord Jesus: that He was both true God and perfect man, and that his sacrifice of himself upon the cross was a propitiation and atonement for the sins of the whole world, and that the remission of sins which any partake of, is only in, and by virtue of, that most satisfactory sacrifice."

3. As to the Holy Ghost, "Friends believe in the Holy Spirit, or Comforter, the promise of the Father, whom Christ declared he

would send in his name, to lead and guide his followers into all truth, to teach them all things, and to bring all things to their remembrance. . . . . They believe that the saving knowledge of God and Christ cannot be attained in any other way than by the revelation of this Spirit ; — for the Apostle says, 'What man knoweth the things of a man, save the spirit of man which is in him ? Even so the things of God knoweth no man, but the Spirit of God. Now we have received not the spirit of the world, but the Spirit which is of God, that we might know the things which are freely given to us of God.' If, therefore, the things which properly appertain to man cannot be discerned by any lower principle than the spirit of man ; those things which properly relate to God and Christ, cannot be known by any power inferior to that of the Holy Spirit."

4. As to man, " They believe that man was created in the image of God, capable of understanding the divine law, and of holding communion with his Maker. Through transgression he fell from this blessed state, and lost the heavenly image. His posterity come into the world in the image of the earthly man ; and, until renewed by the quickening and regenerating power of the heavenly man, Christ Jesus, manifested in the soul, they are fallen, degenerated, and dead to the divine life in which Adam originally stood, and are subject to the power, nature, and seed of the serpent ; and not only their words and deeds, but their imaginations, are evil perpetually in the sight of God. Man, therefore, in this state can know nothing aright concerning God ; his thoughts and conceptions of spiritual things, until he is disjoined from this evil seed and united to the divine light, Christ Jesus, are unprofitable to himself and to others."

5. As to the future state, " The Society of Friends believe that there will be a resurrection both of the righteous and the wicked ; the one to eternal life and blessedness, and the other to everlasting misery and torment, agreeably to Matt. xxv. 31–46 ; John v. 25–30 ; 1 Cor. xv. 12–58. That God will judge the world by that man whom He hath ordained, even Christ Jesus the Lord, who will render unto every man according to his works."

6. As to the Scriptures, " The religious Society of Friends has always believed that the Holy Scriptures were written by divine inspiration, and contain a declaration of all the fundamental doctrines and principles relating to eternal life and salvation, and that whatsoever doctrine or practice is contrary to them, is to be rejected as false and erroneous ; that they are a declaration of the mind and

will of God, in and to the several ages in which they were written, and are obligatory on us, and are to be read, believed, and fulfilled by the assistance of divine grace. . . . . It looks upon them as the only fit outward judge and test of controversies among Christians, and is very willing that all its doctrines and practices should be tried by them, freely admitting that whatsoever any do, pretending to the Spirit, which is contrary to the Scriptures, be condemned as a delusion of the devil."

It thus appears that the orthodox Friends are in sympathy, on all fundamental doctrines, with the great body of their fellow Christians.

Heterodox Friends.

Secondly. There is a class calling themselves Friends, and retaining the organization of the Society, and its usages as to dress, language, and mode of worship, who are really Deists. They admit of no higher authority, in matters of religion, than the natural reason and conscience of man, and hold little if anything as true beyond the truths of natural religion. This class has been disowned by the Society in its representative capacity.

Thirdly. There is a third class which does not constitute an organized or separate body, but includes men of very different views. As has been already remarked, great diversity of opinion existed among the Quakers, especially during the early period of their history. This diversity related to the common doctrines of Christianity, to the nature of the inward guiding light in which all professed to believe, and to the authority due to the sacred Scriptures. Some explicitly denied the doctrine of the Trinity and the satisfaction of Christ ; some seemed to ignore the historical Christ altogether, and to refer everything to the Christ within. Others, while admitting the historical verity of the life of Christ, and of his work on earth, regarded his redemption as altogether subjective. He saves us not by what He has done for us, but exclusively by what He does in us. This, as we have seen, is the characteristic tendency of Mysticism in all its modifications.

C. *The Doctrine of Friends as to the Inward Light given to all Men.*

Still greater diversity of views prevailed as to the nature of the inward light which constitutes the distinguishing doctrine of the Society. The orthodox Quakers on this subject, in the first place, carefully distinguish this " light " from the natural reason and conscience of men ; and also from spiritual discernment, or that inward work of the Spirit, which all Christians acknowledge, by which the soul is enabled to know " the things of the Spirit " as they are revealed in the Scriptures, and without which there can be no saving faith, and no holiness of heart or life. This spiritual illumination is peculiar to the true people of God; the inward light, in which the Quakers believe, is common to all men. The design and effect of the " inward light " are the communication of new truth, or of truth not objectively revealed, as well as the spiritual discernment of the truths of Scripture. The design and effect of spiritual illumination are the proper apprehension of truth already speculatively known.

Secondly. By the inner light the orthodox Quakers understand the supernatural influence of the Holy Spirit, concerning which they teach,— (1.) That it is given to all men. (2.) That it not only convinces of sin, and enables the soul to apprehend aright the truths of Scripture, but also communicates a knowledge of " the mysteries of salvation." " A manifestation of this Spirit they believe is given to every man to profit withal; that it convicts of sin, and, as attended to, gives power to the soul to overcome and forsake it; it opens the mind to the mysteries of salvation, enables it savingly to understand the truths recorded in the Holy Scriptures, and gives it the living, practical, and heartfelt experience of those things which pertain to its everlasting welfare." " He hath communicated a measure of the light of his own Son, a measure of the grace of the Holy Spirit — by which he invites, calls, exhorts, and strives with every man, in order to save him; which light or grace, as it is received and not resisted, works the salvation of all, even of those who are ignorant of Adam's fall, and of the death and sufferings of Christ; both by bringing them to a sense of their own misery, and to be sharers of the sufferings of Christ, inwardly; and by making them partakers of his resurrection, in becoming holy, pure, and righteous, and recovered out of their sins." [1]

Thirdly. The orthodox Friends teach concerning this inward light, as has been already shown, that it is subordinate to the Holy Scriptures, inasmuch as the Scriptures are the infallible rule of faith and practice, and everything contrary thereto is to be rejected as false and destructive.

Barclay's Views.

While such are the views of the orthodox Friends, it must be admitted that many hold a different doctrine. This is true not

[1] Evans.

only of those whom the Society has disowned, but of many men
most prominent in their history. This difference relates both to
what this light is, and to its authority. As to the former of these
points the language employed is so diverse, and so figurative, that it
is difficult to determine its real meaning. Some of the early Quakers
spoke as though they adopted the doctrine of the earlier Mystics,
that this inward principle was God himself, the divine substance.
Others speak of it as Christ, or even the body of Christ, or his life.
Others as "a seed," which is declared to be no part of the nature
of man; no remains of the image of God in which Adam was created; neither is it the substance of God. Nevertheless, it is declared to be "a spiritual substance," in which the Father, Son, and
Holy Ghost are present. This seed comes from Christ, and is
communicated to every man. In some it lies as a seed upon a
rock, which never shows any sign of life. But when the soul receives a visitation of the Spirit, if his influence be not resisted, that
seed is vivified, and develops into holiness of heart and life; by
which the soul is purified and justified. We are not justified by
our works. Everything is due to Christ. He is both "the giver
and the gift." Nevertheless our justification consists in this subjective change.[1]   A distinction is made between a twofold redemption; the one "performed and accomplished by Christ for us
in his crucified body without us; the other is the redemption
wrought by Christ in us." "The first is that whereby a man, as
he stands in the fall, is put in a capacity of salvation, and hath conveyed unto him a measure of that power, virtue, spirit, life, and
grace that was in Christ Jesus, which, as the free gift of God, is
able to counterbalance, overcome, and root out the evil seed, wherewith we are naturally, as in the fall, leavened. The second is that
whereby we witness and know this pure and perfect redemption in
ourselves, purifying, cleansing, and redeeming us from the power of
corruption, and bringing us into unity, favour, and friendship with
God."[2]
With regard to the authority of this inward light, while the
orthodox make it subordinate to the Scriptures, many of the early
Friends made the written, subordinate to the inner, word; and
others, as Barclay himself, make the two coördinate. Although
in this matter he is hardly consistent with himself. He expressly denies that the Scriptures are to us "the fountain" of
truth; that they are "the principal ground of all truth and
knowledge, or yet the adequate primary rule of faith and man-

---

[1] See Barclay's *Apology*, Philadelphia edition, pp. 152, 153.   [2] *Ibid.*, p. 218.

ners." They are, however, "to be esteemed a secondary rule subordinate to the Spirit." Nevertheless, he teaches with equal plainness that what " cannot be proved by Scripture, is no necessary article of faith." [1] Again, he says: We are " willing to admit it as a positive and certain maxim, that whatsoever any do, pretending to the Spirit, which is contrary to the Scriptures, be accounted and reckoned a delusion of the devil." [2] He " freely subscribes to that saying, Let him that preacheth any other gospel than that which hath already been preached by the Apostles, and according to the Scriptures, be accursed." [3] We look on the Scriptures, he says, " as the only fit outward judge of controversies among Christians, and that whatsoever doctrine is contrary unto their testimony, may therefore justly be rejected as false." [4] His whole book, therefore, is an effort to prove from Scripture all the peculiar doctrines of Quakerism.

His theory is, (1.) That all men since the fall are in a state of spiritual death from which they are utterly unable to deliver themselves. He is severe in his denunciation of all Pelagian and semi-Pelagian doctrine. (2.) That God determined, through his Son our Lord Jesus Christ, to make provision for the salvation of all men. (3.) The work of Christ secures the opportunity and means of salvation for every man. (4.) Through him and for his sake " a seed " is given to every man which, under the influence of the Spirit, may be developed into righteousness and holiness, restoring ┼he soul to the image and fellowship of God. (5.) To every man is granted " a day of visitation " in which the Spirit comes to him and exerts an influence which, if not resisted, vivifies this divine seed, and thus gives the opportunity of being saved. (6.) The measure of this divine influence is not the same in all cases. In some it is irresistible, in others, not. In some it is as abundant as in the prophets and Apostles, rendering its subjects as authoritative as teachers as the original Apostles. (7.) The office of the Spirit is to teach and to guide. It is not merely intended to enlighten the mind in the knowledge of truths contained in the Scriptures. It presents truth objectively to the mind. It does not reveal new doctrines, much less doctrines opposed to those revealed in the Scriptures ; but it makes a new and independent revelation of old doctrines. On this point Barclay is very explicit.[5] His discussion of his second and third propositions, — the one concerning " immediate revelation," and the other, " the Scriptures," — sets forth this

---

[1] Barclay's *Apology*, p. 106.　　[2] *Ibid.*, p. 100.　　[3] *Ibid.*, p. 105.
[4] *Ibid.*. p. 100.　　　　　　　　　　　　　　　　　　　[5] See pp. 62–64, 105.

doctrine at length. "We distinguish," he says, "between a revelation of a new gospel and new doctrines, and a new revelation of
the good old gospel and doctrines ; the last we plead for, but the
first we utterly deny." Natural reason reveals certain doctrines,
but this is not inconsistent with a new revelation of the same doctrines in the Scriptures. So the fact that the gospel is revealed in
the Scriptures is not inconsistent with its immediate objective revelation to the soul by the Spirit.

Besides the great doctrines of salvation, there are many things
the Christian needs to know which are not contained in the Scriptures. In these matters he is not left to his own guidance. The
Spirit "guides into all truth." "Therefore," says Barclay, "the
Spirit of God leadeth, instructeth, and teacheth every true Christian whatsoever is needful for him to know." For example,
whether he is to preach ; and, if called to preach, when, where,
and what he shall preach ; where he is to go, and in any emergency what he ought to do. So the Spirit teaches us when and
where we are to pray, and what we are to pray for. As the
Spirit's guidance extends to everything, it should be sought and
obeyed in all things.

Quakerism ignores the distinction between inspired and uninspired men, except as to the measure of the Spirit's influence. He
dwells in all believers, and performs the same office in all. As the
saints of old, before the giving of the law, were under his instruction and guidance, so they continued to enjoy his teaching after
the law was given. All through the Old Testament dispensation
the people of God received immediate revelations and directions.
When Christ came there was a more copious communication of
this influence. These communications were not confined to either
sex, or to any class in the Church. They were not peculiar to the
Apostles, or to ministers, but to every one was given a manifestation of the Spirit to profit withal. The state of the Church, as set
forth in the New Testament as to this matter, continues to the
present time, except that the gifts bestowed are not of the same
miraculous character now that they were then. But as to his revealing, enlightening, teaching, guiding operations, He is as much
present with believers now as during the apostolic age. Then
all spake as the Spirit gave them utterance. When Christians
assembled together every one had his gift: one a psalm, one a
doctrine, another a revelation, another an interpretation. Every
one could speak; but it was to be done decently and in order. If
anything were revealed to one sitting by, he was to hold his peace

until his time came; for God is not the author of confusion. In 1 Cor. xiv. we have the Quaker ideal or model of a Christian assembly. And as the Apostles went hither and thither, not according to their own judgment, but supernaturally guided by the Spirit, so the Spirit guides all believers in the ordinary affairs of life, if they wait for the intimations of his will.

As this doctrine of the Spirit's guidance is the fundamental principle of Quakerism, it is the source of all the peculiarities by which the Society of Friends has ever been distinguished. If every man has within himself an infallible guide as to truth and duty, he does not need external teaching. If it be the office of the Spirit to reveal truth objectively to the mind, and to indicate on all occasions the path of duty; and if his revealing and guiding influence be universal, and immediate, self-evidencing itself as divine, it must of necessity supersede all others; just as the Scriptures supersede reason in matters of religion. The Quakers, therefore, although, as has been shown, acknowledging the divine authority of the Scriptures, make far less of them than other denominations of evangelical Christians. They make very little of the Church and its ordinances; of the Sabbath; of a stated ministry; and nothing of the sacraments as external ordinances and means of grace. In all these respects their influence has been hurtful to the cause of Christ, while it is cheerfully admitted that some of the best Christians of our age belong to the Society of Friends.

§ 7. *Objections to the Mystical Theory.*

The idea on which Mysticism is founded is Scriptural and true. It is true that God has access to the human soul. It is true that He can, consistently with his own nature and with the laws of our being, supernaturally and immediately reveal truth objectively to the mind, and attend that revelation with evidence which produces an infallible assurance of its truth and of its divine origin. It is also true that such revelations have often been made to the children of men. But these cases of immediate supernatural revelation belong to the category of miracles. They are rare and are to be duly authenticated.

The common doctrine of the Christian Church is, that God has at sundry times and in divers manners spoken to the children of men; that what eye hath not seen, or ear heard, what never could have entered into the heart of man, God has revealed by his Spirit to those whom He selected to be his spokesmen to their fellow-men; that these revelations were authenticated as divine, by their char-

acter, their effects, and by signs and wonders, and divers miracles
and gifts of the Holy Ghost; that these holy men of old who
spake as they were moved by the Holy Ghost, communicated the
revelations which they had received not only orally, but in writing,
employing not the words which man's wisdom teacheth, but which
the Holy Ghost teacheth; so that we have in the sacred Scriptures
the things of the Spirit recorded in the words of the Spirit; which
Scriptures, therefore, are the Word of God, — i. e., what God says
to man ; what He declares to be true and obligatory, — and constitute for his Church the only infallible rule of faith and practice.

Romanists, while admitting the infallibility of the written Word,
still contend that it is not sufficient; and hold that God continues in
a supernatural manner to guide the Church by rendering its bishops infallible teachers in all matters pertaining to truth and duty.

Mystics, making the same admission as to the infallibility of
Scripture, claim that the Spirit is given to every man as an inward
teacher and guide, whose instructions and influence are the highest
rule of faith, and sufficient, even without the Scriptures, to secure
the salvation of the soul.

Mysticism has no Foundation in the Scriptures.

The objections to the Romish and Mystical theory are substantially the same.

1. There is no foundation for either in Scriptures. As the Scriptures contain no promise of infallible guidance to bishops, so they
contain no promise of the Spirit as the immediate revealer of truth
to every man. Under the Old Testament dispensation the Spirit
did indeed reveal the mind and purposes of God ; but it was to
selected persons chosen to be prophets, authenticated as divine
messengers, whose instructions the people were bound to receive
as coming from God. In like manner, under the new dispensation,
our Lord selected twelve men, endowed them with plenary knowledge of the Gospel, rendered them infallible as teachers, and required all men to receive their instructions as the words of God.
It is true that during the apostolic age there were occasional communications made to a class of persons called prophets. But this
" gift of prophecy," that is, the gift of speaking under the inspiration of the Spirit, was analogous to the gift of miracles. The one
has as obviously ceased as the other.

It is true, also, that our Lord promised to send the Spirit, who
was to abide with the Church, to dwell in his people, to be their
teacher, and to guide them into the knowledge of all truth. But

what truth ?   Not historical or scientific truth, but plainly revealed
truth; truth which He himself had taught, or made known by his
authorized messengers.   The Spirit is indeed a teacher ; and without his instructions there is no saving knowledge of divine things,
for the Apostle tells us, " The natural man receiveth not the things
of the Spirit of God, for they are foolishness unto him ; neither can
he know them, because they are spiritually discerned."   (1 Cor. ii.
14.)   Spiritual discernment, therefore, is the design and effect of
the Spirit's teaching.   And the things discerned are " the things
freely given to us of God," *i. e.*, as the context shows, the things
revealed to the Apostles and clearly made known in the Scriptures.

The Apostle John tells his readers, " Ye have an unction from
the Holy One, and ye know all things " (1 John ii. 20), and again,
ver. 27, " The anointing which ye have received of Him abideth in
you, and ye need not that any man teach you; but as the same
anointing teacheth you of all things, and is truth, and is no lie, and
even as it hath taught you, ye shall abide in Him."   These passages
teach what all evangelical Christians admit.   First, that true knowledge, or spiritual discernment of divine things, is due to the inward
teaching of the Holy Spirit; and secondly, that true faith, or the
infallible assurance of the truths revealed, is due in like manner to
the " demonstration of the Spirit."   (1 Cor. ii. 4.)   The Apostle
John also says : " He that believeth on the Son of God, hath the
witness in himself."   (1 John v. 10.)   Saving faith does not rest
on the testimony of the Church, nor on the outward evidence of
miracles and prophecy, but on the inward testimony of the Spirit
with and by the truth in our hearts.   He who has this inward testimony needs no other.   He does not need to be told by other men
what is truth; this same anointing teaches him what is truth, and
that no lie is of the truth.   Christians were not to believe every
spirit.   They were to try the spirits whether they were of God.
And the test or criterion of trial was the external, authenticated
revelation of God, as spiritually discerned and demonstrated by
the inward operations of the Spirit.   So now when errorists come
and tell the people there is no God, no sin, no retribution, no need
of a Saviour, or of expiation, or of faith ; that Jesus of Nazareth is
not the Son of God, God manifest in the flesh, the true Christian
has no need to be told that these are what the Apostle calls lies.
He has an inward witness to the truth of the record which God
has given of his Son.

If the Bible gives no support to the Mystical doctrine of the

inward, supernatural, objective revelation of truth made by the
Spirit to every man, that doctrine is destitute of all foundation,
for it is only by the testimony of God that any such doctrine can
be established.

Mysticism is contrary to the Scriptures.

2. The doctrine in question is not only destitute of support from
Scripture, but it contradicts the Scriptures. It is not only opposed
to isolated declarations of the Word of God, but to the whole revealed plan of God's dealing with his people. Everywhere, and
under all dispensations, the rule of faith and duty has been the
teaching of authenticated messengers of God. The appeal has
always been "to the law and testimony." The prophets came
saying, "Thus saith the Lord." Men were required to believe
and obey what was communicated to them, and not what the
Spirit revealed to each individual. It was the outward and not the
inward word to which they were to attend. And under the gospel the command of Christ to his disciples, was, " Go ye into all the
world and preach the gospel to every creature. He that believeth
and is baptized shall be saved" (Mar. xvi. 15, 16), — believeth,
of course, the gospel which they preached. Faith cometh by
hearing. "How," asks the Apostle, " shall they believe in him
of whom they have not heard? and how shall they hear without a
preacher?" (Rom. x. 14.) God, he tells us, hath determined to
save men by the foolishness of preaching. (1 Cor. i. 21.) It is
the preaching of the cross he declares to be the power of God.
(Verse 18.) It is the gospel, the external revelation of the plan
of salvation through Jesus Christ, he says in Rom. i. 16, which "is
the power of God unto salvation to every one that believeth, to the
Jew first, and also to the Greek ; for therein is the righteousness
of God revealed from faith to faith." This idea runs through the
whole New Testament. Christ commissioned his disciples to
preach the gospel. He declared that to be the way in which men
were to be saved. They accordingly went forth preaching everywhere. This preaching was to continue to the end of the world.
Therefore, provision was made for continuing the ministry. Men
called and qualified by the Spirit, were to be selected and set apart
to this work by divine command. And it is in this way, so far,
the world has been converted. In no case do we find the Apostles
calling upon the people, whether Jews or Gentiles, to look within
themselves, to listen to the inner Word. They were to listen to
the outward Word ; to believe what they heard, and were to pray

for the Holy Spirit to enable them to understand, receive, and obey what was thus externally made known to them.

Contrary to the Facts of Experience.

3. The doctrine in question is no less contrary to fact than it is to Scripture. The doctrine teaches that by the inward revelation of the Spirit saving knowledge of truth and duty is given to every man. But all experience shows that without the written Word, men everywhere and in all ages, are ignorant of divine things, — without God, without Christ, and without hope in the world. The sun is not more obviously the source of light, than the Bible is the source of divine knowledge. The absence of the one is as clearly indicated as the absence of the other. It is incredible that an inward revelation of saving truth is made to every man by the Holy Spirit, if the appropriate effects of that revelation are nowhere manifested. It is to be remembered that without the knowledge of God, there can be no religion. Without right apprehensions of the Supreme Being, there can be no right affections towards him. Without the knowledge of Christ, there can be no faith in him. Without truth there can be no holiness, any more than there can be vision without light. As right apprehensions of God, and holiness of heart and life, are nowhere found where the Scriptures are unknown, it is plain that the Scriptures, and not an inward light common to all men, are, by the ordinance of God, the only source to us of saving and sanctifying knowledge.

There is a sense in which, as all evangelical Christians believe, the Spirit is given to every man. He is present with every human mind exciting to good and restraining from evil. To this the order, and what there is of morality in the world, are due. Without this "common grace," or general influence of the Spirit, there would be no difference between our world and hell; for hell is a place or state in which men are finally given up of God. In like manner, there is a general providential efficiency of God by which He coöperates with second causes, in the productions of the wonderful phenomena of the external world. Without that coöperation — the continued guidance of mind — the cosmos would become chaos. But the fact that this providential efficiency of God is universal, is no proof that He everywhere works miracles, that He constantly operates without the intervention of second causes. So, also, the fact that the Spirit is present with every human mind, and constantly enforces the truth present to that mind, is no proof that He makes immediate, supernatural revelations to every human

being. The fact is, we cannot see without light. We have the
sun to give us light. It is vain to say that every man has an
inward light sufficient to guide him without the sun. Facts are
against the theory.

No Criterion by which to judge of the Source of Inward Suggestions.

4. A fourth objection to the Mystical doctrine is that there is no
criterion by which a man can test these inward impulses or revelations, and determine which are from the Spirit of God, and which
are from his own heart or from Satan, who often appears and acts
as an angel of light. This objection, Barclay says, "Bespeaketh
much ignorance in the opposers. . . . . For it is one thing to
affirm that the true and undoubted revelation of God's Spirit is
certain and infallible ; and another thing to affirm that this or that
particular person or people is led infallibly by this revelation in
what they speak or write, because they affirm themselves to be so
led by the inward and immediate revelation of the Spirit." [1] It is
admitted that there is an inward and infallible testimony of the
Spirit in the hearts of believers to the truths objectively revealed in
the Scriptures. It is admitted, also, that there have been immediate
revelations of truth to the mind, as in the case of the prophets and
Apostles, and that these revelations authenticate themselves, or are
attended with an infallible assurance that they come from God.
But these admissions do not invalidate the objection as above stated.
Granted that a man who receives a true revelation knows that it is
from God; how is the man who receives a false revelation to know
that it is not from God ? Many men honestly believe themselves to
be inspired, who are under the influence of some evil spirit, — their
own it may be. The assurance or certainty of conviction may be
as strong in one case as in the other. In the one it is well founded,
in the other it is a delusion. Irresistible conviction is not enough.
It may satisfy the subject of it himself. But it cannot either
satisfy others, or be a criterion of truth. Thousands have been,
and still are, fully convinced that the false is true, and that what is
wrong is right. To tell men, therefore, to look within for an
authoritative guide, and to trust to their irresistible convictions, is
to give them a guide which will lead them to destruction. When
God really makes revelations to the soul, He not only gives an infallible assurance that the revelation is divine, but accompanies it
with evidence satisfactory to others as well as to the recipient that

[1] Barclay's *Apology*, p. 67.

it is from God. All his revelations have had the seal both of internal and external evidence. And when the believer is assured, by the testimony of the Spirit, of the truths of Scripture, he has only a new kind of evidence of what is already authenticated beyond all rational contradiction. Our blessed Lord himself said to the Jews, "If I do not the works of my Father, believe me not. But if I do, though ye believe not me, believe the works." (John x.. 37, 38.) He even goes so far as to say, "If I had not done among them the works which none other man did, they had not had sin." (John xv. 24.) The inward teaching and testimony of the Spirit are Scriptural truths, and truths of inestimable value. But it is ruinous to put them in the place of the divinely authenticated written Word.

The Doctrine productive of Evil.

5. Our Lord says of men, "By their fruits ye shall know them." The same rule of judgment applies to doctrines. Mysticism has always been productive of evil. It has led to the neglect or under-valuing of divine institutions, — of the Church, of the ministry, of the sacraments, of the Sabbath, and of the Scriptures. History shows that it has also led to the greatest excesses and social evils. The Society of Friends has in a good degree escaped these evils: but it has been by a happy inconsistency. They have not carried out their principle. For, while they teach that the inward revelations of the Spirit present the " formal object " of faith; that they are clear and certain, forcing " the well-disposed understanding to assent, irresistibly moving it thereto; " that they are the primary, immediate, and principal source of divine knowledge; that they are not " to be subjected to the examination either of the outward testimony of the Scriptures, or of the natural reason of man, as to a more noble or certain rule or touchstone; " [1] yet they also teach that nothing not contained in the Scriptures can be an article of faith; that we are bound to believe all the Bible teaches; that everything contrary to its teaching is to be rejected as " a delusion of the devil," no matter from what source it may come ; and that the Scriptures are the judge of controversies among Christians; and thus they, as a society, have been preserved from the excesses into which Mystics have generally run. Nevertheless, the Mystical principle of immediate, objective revelation of truth to every man, as his principal and primary rule of faith and practice, has wrought with Friends its legitimate fruit, inasmuch as it has led to comparative neglect of the Scriptures and of the ordinances of the Church.

[1] Barclay's *Second Proposition.*

CHAPTER V.

ROMAN CATHOLIC DOCTRINE CONCERNING THE RULE OF FAITH.

§ 1. *Statement of the Doctrine.*

1. ROMANISTS reject the doctrine of the Rationalists who make human reason either the source or standard of religious truth. It is one of their principles, that faith is merely human when either its object or ground is human. Faith to be divine must have truth supernaturally revealed as its object, and the evidence on which it rests must be the supernatural testimony of God.

2. They reject the Mystical doctrine that divine truth is revealed to every man by the Spirit. They admit an objective, supernatural revelation.

3. They maintain, however, that this revelation is partly written and partly unwritten; that is, the rule of faith includes both Scripture and tradition. Moreover, as the people cannot certainly know what books are of divine origin, and, therefore, entitled to a place in the canon; and as they are incompetent to decide on the meaning of Scripture, or which among the multitude of traditionary doctrines and usages are divine, and which are human, God has made the Church an infallible teacher by which all these points are determined, whose testimony is the proximate and sufficient ground of faith to the people.

So far as the Romish doctrine concerning the Rule of Faith differs from that of Protestants, it presents the following points for consideration: First, The doctrine of Romanists concerning the Scriptures. Second, Their doctrine concerning tradition. Third, Their doctrine concerning the office and authority of the Church as a teacher.

§ 2. *Roman Catholic Doctrine concerning the Scriptures.*

On this subject Romanists agree with Protestants, (1.) In teaching the plenary inspiration and consequent infallible authority of the sacred writings. Of these writings the Council of Trent says that God is their author, and that they were written by the dictation of the Holy Spirit (" Spiritu sancto dictante ").

(2.) They agree with us in receiving into the sacred canon all the books which we regard as of divine authority.

Romanists differ from Protestants in regard to the Scriptures, —

1. In receiving into the canon certain books which Protestants do not admit to be inspired, namely : Tobit, Judith, Sirach, parts of Esther, the Wisdom of Solomon, First, Second, and Third Books of the Maccabees (the Third Book of Maccabees, however, is not included in the Vulgate), Baruch, the Hymn of the Three Children, Susanna, and Bel and the Dragon. These books are not all included by name in the list given by the Council of Trent. Several of them are parts of the books there enumerated. Thus, the Hymn of the Three Children, Susanna, and Bel and the Dragon, appear as parts of the book of Daniel. Some modern theologians of the Romish Church refer all the apocryphal books to what they call " The Second Canon," and admit that they are not of equal authority with those belonging to the First Canon.[1] The Council of Trent, however, makes no such distinction.

Incompleteness of the Scriptures.

2. A second point of difference is that Romanists deny, and Protestants affirm, the completeness of the sacred Scriptures. That is, Protestants maintain that all the extant supernatural revelations of God, which constitute the rule of faith to his Church, are contained in his written word. Romanists, on the other hand, hold that some doctrines which all Christians are bound to believe, are only imperfectly revealed in the Scriptures; that others are only obscurely intimated; and that others are not therein contained at all. The Preface to the Romish Catechism (Quest. 12) says, " Omnis doctrinæ ratio, quæ fidelibus tradenda sit, verbo Dei continetur, quod in scripturam traditionesque distributum est." Bellarmin[2] says expressly, " Nos asserimus, in Scripturis non contineri expressè totam doctrinam necessariam, sive de fide sive de moribus ; et proinde praeter verbum Dei scriptum requiri etiam verbum Dei non-scriptum, *i. e.*, divinas et apostolicas traditiones." On this point the Romish theologians are of one mind ; but what the doctrines are, which are thus imperfectly revealed in the Scriptures, or merely implied, or entirely omitted, has never been authoritatively decided by the Church of Rome. The theologians of that Church, with more or less unanimity, refer to one or the

---

[1] See B. Lamy, *Apparatus Bibl.* lib. ii. c. 5. Jahn's *Einleitung*, Th. i. § 29 ; 2nd edit. Vienna, 1802, p. 132. Moehler's *Symbolik*.

[2] *De Verbo Dei*, iv. 3, tom. i. p. 163, e. edit. Paris, 1608.

other of these classes the following doctrines : (1.) The canon of Scripture. (2.) The inspiration of the sacred writers. (3.) The full doctrine of the Trinity. (4.) The personality and divinity of the Holy Spirit. (5.) Infant baptism. (6.) The observance of Sunday as the Christian Sabbath. (7.) The threefold orders of the ministry. (8.) The government of the Church by bishops. (9.) The perpetuity of the apostleship. (10.) The grace of orders. (11.) The sacrificial nature of the Eucharist. (12.) The seven sacraments. (13.) Purgatory. It lies in the interests of the advocates of tradition to depreciate the Scriptures, and to show how much the Church would lose if she had no other source of knowledge of divine truth but the written word. On this subject the author of No. 85 of the Oxford Tracts, when speaking even of essential doctrines, says,[1] "It is a near thing that they are in the Scriptures at all. The wonder is that they are all there. Humanly judging they would not be there but for God's interposition ; and, therefore, since they are there by a sort of accident, it is not strange they shall be but latent there, and only indirectly producible thence." "The gospel doctrine," says the same writer, "is but indirectly and covertly recorded in Scripture under the surface." [1]

Tradition is always represented by Romanists as not only the interpreter, but the complement of the Scriptures. The Bible, therefore, is, according to the Church of Rome, incomplete. It does not contain all the Church is bound to believe ; nor are the doctrines which it does contain, therein fully or clearly made known.

Obscurity of the Scriptures.

3. The third point of difference between Romanists and Protestants relates to the perspicuity of Scripture, and the right of private judgment. Protestants hold that the Bible, being addressed to the people, is sufficiently perspicuous to be understood by them, under the guidance of the Holy Spirit ; and that they are entitled and bound to search the Scripture, and to judge for themselves what is its true meaning. Romanists, on the other hand, teach that the Scriptures are so obscure that they need a visible, present, and infallible interpreter ; and that the people, being incompetent to understand them, are bound to believe whatever doctrines the Church, through its official organs, declares to be true and divine. On this subject the Council of Trent (Sess. 4), says : " Ad coërcenda petulantia ingenia decernit (Synodus), ut nemo, suæ prudentiæ innixus,

[1] Pages 34 and 35.

in rebus fidei et morum ad ædificationem doctrinæ Christianæ
pertinentium, Sacram Scripturam ad suas sensus contorquens contra eum sensum, quem tenuit et tenet sancta mater Ecclesia, cujus
est judicare de vero sensu et interpretatione Scripturarum Sancta-
rum, aut etiam contra unanimem consensum patrum ipsam scripturam sacram interpretari audeat, etiamsi hujus modi interpre-
tationes nullo unquam tempore in lucem edendæ forent. Qui
contravenerint, per ordinarios declarentur et pœnis a jure statutis
puniantur." Bellarmin[1] says: " Non ignorabat Deus multas in
Ecclesia exorituras difficultates circa fidem, debuit igitur judicem
aliquem Ecclesiæ providere. At iste judex non potest esse Scriptura, neque Spiritus revelans privatus, neque princeps secularis,
igitur princeps ecclesiasticus vel solus vel certe cum consilio et consensu coepiscoporum."

From this view of the obscurity of Scripture it follows that the
use of the sacred volume by the people, is discountenanced by the
Church of Rome, although its use has never been prohibited by
any General Council. Such prohibitions, however, have repeatedly been issued by the Popes; as by Gregory VII., Innocent III.,
Clemens XI., and Pius IV., who made the liberty to read any ver-
nacular version of the Scriptures, dependent on the permission of
the priest. There have been, however, many Romish prelates and
theologians who encouraged the general reading of the Bible. The
spirit of the Latin Church and the effects of its teaching, are pain-
fully manifested by the fact that the Scriptures are practically in-
accessible to the mass of the people in strictly Roman Catholic
countries.

The Latin Vulgate.

4. The fourth point of difference concerns the authority due to
the Latin Vulgate. On this subject the Council of Trent (Sess.
4), says: "Synodus considerans non parum utilitatis accedere
posse Ecclesiæ Dei, si ex omnibus Latinis editionibus quæ circum-
ferentur, sacrorum librorum, quænam pro authentica habenda sit,
innotescat: statuit et declarat, ut hæc ipsa vetus et vulgata editio,
quæ longo tot seculorum usu in ipsa Ecclesia probata est, in pub-
licis lectionibus, disputationibus, prædicationibus et expositionibus
pro authentica habeatur et nemo illam rejicere quovis prætextu audeat vel præsumat." The meaning of this decree is a matter of
dispute among Romanists themselves. Some of the more modern
and liberal of their theologians say that the Council simply intended to determine which among several Latin versions was to be

---

[1] *De Verbo Dei*, iii. 9, tom. i. p. 151, d. *ut sup.*

used in the service of the Church.   They contend that it was not meant to forbid appeal to the original Scriptures, or to place the Vulgate on a par with them in authority.   The earlier and stricter Romanists take the ground that the Synod did intend to forbid an appeal to the Hebrew and Greek Scriptures, and to make the Vulgate the ultimate authority.   The language of the Council seems to favor this interpretation.   The Vulgate was to be used not only for the ordinary purposes of public instruction, but in all theological discussions, and in all works of exegesis.

§ 3. *Tradition.*

The word tradition (παράδοσις) means, (1.) The art of delivering over from one to another.   (2.) The thing delivered or communicated.   In the New Testament it is used (*a.*) For instructions delivered from some to others, without reference to the mode of delivery, whether it be orally or by writing; as in 2 Thess. ii. 15, " Hold the traditions which ye have been taught, whether by word, or our epistle ; " and iii. 6, " Withdraw yourself from every brother that walketh disorderly, and not after the tradition which he received of us."   (*b.*) For the oral instructions of the fathers handed down from generation to generation, but not contained in the Scriptures, and yet regarded as authoritative.   In this sense our Lord so frequently speaks of " the traditions of the Pharisees." (*c.*) In Gal. i. 14, where Paul speaks of his zeal for the traditions of his fathers, it may include both the written and unwritten instructions which he had received.   What he was so zealous about, was the whole system of Judaism as he had been taught it.

In the early Church the word was used in this wide sense.   Appeal was constantly made to " the traditions," *i. e.*, the instructions which the churches had received.   It was only certain churches at first which had any of the written instructions of the Apostles.   And it was not until the end of the first century that the writings of the Evangelists and Apostles were collected, and formed into a canon, or rule of faith.   And when the books of the New Testament had been collected, the fathers spoke of them as containing the traditions, *i. e.*, the instructions derived from Christ and his Apostles.   They called the Gospels " the evangelical traditions," and the Epistles " the apostolical traditions."   In that age of the Church the distinction between the written and unwritten word had not yet been distinctly made.   But as controversies arose, and disputants on both sides of all questions appealed to " tradition," *i. e.*, to what they had been taught ; and when it was found that these traditions differed, one church saying their teachers had always taught them one thing, and another that theirs had taught them the opposite, it was felt that there should be some common and authoritative standard. Hence the wisest and best of the fathers insisted on abiding by the written word, and receiving nothing as of divine authority not contained therein. In this, however, it must be confessed they were not always consistent. Whenever prescription, usage, or conviction founded on unwritten evidence, was available against an adversary, they did not hesitate to make the most of it. During all the early centuries, therefore, the distinction between Scripture and tradition was not so sharply drawn as it has been since the controversies between Romanists and Protestants, and especially since the decisions of the Council of Trent.

Tridentine Doctrine.

That Council, and the Latin Church as a body, teach on this subject, — (1.) That Christ and his Apostles taught many things which were not committed to writing, i. e., not recorded in the Sacred Scriptures. (2.) That these instructions have been faithfully transmitted, and preserved in the Church. (3.) That they constitute a part of the rule of faith for all believers.

These particulars are included in the following extracts from the acts of the Council: " Synodus — perspiciens hanc veritatem et disciplinam contineri in libris scriptis et sine scripto traditionibus, quæ ex ipsius Christi ore ab apostolis acceptae, aut ab ipsis apostolis, Spiritu Sancto dictante, quasi per manus traditæ, ad nos usque pervenerunt ; orthodoxorum patrum exempla secuta, omnes libros tam Veteris quam Novi Testamenti, cum utriusque unus Deus sit auctor, nec non traditiones ipsas, tum ad fidem tum ad mores pertinentes, tanquam vel ore tenus a Christo, vel a Spiritu Sancto dictatas, et continua successione in Ecclesia Catholica conservatas, pari pietatis affectu et reverentia suscipit et veneratur." [1]

Bellarmin [2] divides traditions into three classes: divine, apostolical, and ecclesiastical. " Divinæ dicuntur quæ acceptæ sunt ab ipso Christo apostolos docente, et nusquam in divinis literis inveniuntur. . . . . Apostolicæ traditiones proprie dicuntur illæ, quæ ab apostolis institutæ sunt, non tamen sine assistentia Spiritus Sancti et nihilominus non extant scriptæ in eorum epistolis. . . . . Ecclesiasticæ traditiones proprie dicuntur consuetudines quædam antiquæ vel a prælatis vel a populis inchoatæ, quæ paulatim tacito consensu populorum vim legis obtinuerunt.

[1] Trent. Sess. iv.   [2] De Verbo Dei, iv. 1.

Et quidem traditiones divinæ eandem vim habent, quam divina præcepta sive divina doctrina scripta in Evangeliis. Et similiter apostolicæ traditiones non scriptæ eandem vim habent, quam apostolicæ traditiones scriptæ. . . . . Ecclesiasticæ autem traditiones eandem vim habent, quam decreta et constitutiones ecclesiasticæ scriptæ."

Petrus à Soto, quoted by Chemnitz[1] says, "Infallibilis est regula et catholica. Quacunque credit, tenet, et servat Romana Ecclesia, et in Scripturis non habentur, illa ab apostolis esse tradita; item quarum observationum initium, author et origo ignoretur, vel inveniri non potest, illas extra omnem dubitationem ab apostolis tradita esse."

From this it appears, 1. That these traditions are called unwritten because not contained in the Scriptures. They are, for the most part, now to be found written in the works of the Fathers, decisions of councils, ecclesiastical constitutions, and rescripts of the Popes.

2. The office of tradition is to convey a knowledge of doctrines, precepts, and institutions not contained in Scripture; and also to serve as a guide to the proper understanding of what is therein written. Tradition, therefore, in the Church of Rome, is both the supplement and interpretation of the written word.

3. The authority due to tradition is the same as that which belongs to the Scriptures. Both are to be received " pari pietatis affectu et reverentia." Both are derived from the same source; both are received through the same channel; and both are authenticated by the same witness. This authority, however, belongs properly only to traditions regarded as divine or apostolical. Those termed ecclesiastical are of less importance, relating to rites and usages. Still for them is claimed an authority virtually divine, as they are enjoined by a church which claims to have been endowed by Christ with full power to ordain rites and ceremonies.

4. The criteria by which to distinguish between true and false traditions, are either antiquity and catholicity, or the testimony of the extant Church. Sometimes the one, and sometimes the other is urged. The Council of Trent gives the former; so does Bellarmin, and so do the majority of Romish theologians. This is the famous rule established by Vincent of Lerins in the fifth century, " quod semper, quod ubique, quod ab omnibus." On all occasions, however, the ultimate appeal is to the decision of the Church. Whatever the Church declares to be a part of the revelation committed to her, is to be received as of divine authority, at the peril of salvation.

[1] *Examen Concilii Tridentini*, p. 85, edit. Frankfort, 1574.

§ 4. *The Office of the Church as Teacher.*

1. Romanists define the Church to be the company of men professing the same faith, united in the communion of the same sacraments, subject to lawful pastors, and specially to the Pope. By the first clause they exclude from the Church all infidels and heretics ; by the second, all the unbaptized ; by the third, all who are not subject to bishops having canonical succession ; and by the fourth, all who do not acknowledge the Bishop of Rome to be the head of the Church on earth. It is this external, visible society thus constituted, that God has made an authoritative and infallible teacher.

2. The Church is qualified for this office : first, by the communication of all the revelations of God, written and unwritten ; and secondly, by the constant presence and guidance of the Holy Spirit preserving it from all error in its instructions. On this point the " Roman Catechism," [1] says : " Quemadmodum hæc una Ecclesia errare non potest in fidei ac morum disciplina tradenda, cum a Spiritu Sancto gubernetur ; ita ceteras omnes, quæ sibi ecclesiæ nomen arrogant, ut quæ Diaboli spiritu ducantur, in doctrinæ et morum perniciosissimis erroribus versari necesse est." And Bellarmin,[2] " Nostra sententia est Ecclesiam absolute non posse errare nec in rebus absolute necessariis nec in aliis, quæ credenda vel facienda nobis proponit, sive habeantur expresse in Scripturis, sive non."

3. The Church, according to these statements, is infallible only as to matters of faith and morals. Its infallibility does not extend over the domains of history, philosophy, or science. Some theologians would even limit the infallibility of the Church, to essential doctrines. But the Church of Rome does not make the distinction, recognized by all Protestants, between essential and non-essential doctrines. With Romanists, that is essential, or necessary, which the Church pronounces to be a part of the revelation of God. Bellarmin — than whom there is no greater authority among Romish theologians — says that the Church can err " nec in rebus absolute necessariis nec in aliis," *i. e.*, neither in things in their own nature necessary, nor in those which become necessary when determined and enjoined. It has been disputed among Romanists, whether the Church is infallible in matters of fact as well as in matters of doctrine. By facts, in this discussion, are not meant facts of history or science, but facts involved in doctrinal decisions. When the Pope condemned certain propositions taken from the works of

---

[1] Part I. cap. x. quest. 15.　　　[2] *De Ecclesia Militante*, c. 14.

Jansenius, his disciples had to admit that those propositions were erroneous; but they denied that they were contained, in the sense condemned, in the writings of their master. To this the Jesuits replied, that the infallibility of the Church extended in such cases as much to the fact as to the doctrine. This the Jansenists denied.

The Organs of the Church's Infallibility.

4. As to the organs of the Church in its infallible teaching, there are two theories, the Episcopal and Papal, or, as they are designated from their principal advocates, the Gallican and the Transmontane. According to the former, the bishops, in their collective capacity, as the official successors of the Apostles, are infallible as teachers. Individual bishops may err, the body or college of bishops cannot err. Whatever the bishops of any age of the Church unite in teaching, is, for that age, the rule of faith. This concurrence of judgment need not amount to entire unanimity. The greater part, the common judgment of the episcopate, is all that is required. To their decision all dissentients are bound to submit. This general judgment may be pronounced in a council, representing the whole Church, or in any other way in which agreement may be satisfactorily indicated. Acquiescence in the decisions of even a provincial council, or of the Pope, or the several bishops, each in his own diocese, teaching the same doctrine, is sufficient proof of consent.

The Transmontane Theory.

According to the Papal, or Transmontane theory, the Pope is the organ through which the infallible judgment of the Church is pronounced. He is the vicar of Christ. He is not subject to a general council. He is not required to consult other bishops before he gives his decision. This infallibility is not personal, but official. As a man the Pope may be immoral, heretical, or infidel; as Pope, when speaking *ex cathedra*, he is the organ of the Holy Ghost. The High-Priest among the Jews might be erroneous in faith, or immoral in conduct, but when consulting God in his official capacity, he was the mere organ of divine communication. Such, in few words, is the doctrine of Romanists concerning the Rule of Faith.

In the recent Ecumenical Council, held in the Vatican, after a protracted struggle, the Transmontane doctrine was sanctioned. It is, therefore, now obligatory on all Romanists to believe that the Pope, when speaking *ex cathedra*, is infallible.

§ 5. *Examination of the Romish Doctrine.*

Hundreds of volumes have been written in the discussion of the various points included in the theory above stated. Only a most cursory view of the controversy can be given in such a work as this. So far as Romanists differ from us on the canon of Scripture, the examination of their views belongs to the department of Biblical literature. What concerns their doctrine of the incompleteness and obscurity of the written word, and the consequent necessity of an infallible, visible interpreter, can better be said under the head of the Protestant doctrine of the Rule of Faith. The two points to be now considered are Tradition, and the office of the Church as a teacher. These subjects are so related that it is difficult to keep them distinct. Tradition is the teaching of the Church, and the teaching of the Church is tradition. These subjects are not only thus intimately related, but they are generally included under the same head in the Catholic Symbols. Nevertheless, they are distinct, and involve very different principles. They should, therefore, be considered separately.

§ 6. *Examination of the Doctrine of the Church of Rome on Tradition.*

A. *Difference between Tradition and the Analogy of Faith.*

1. The Romish doctrine of tradition differs essentially from the Protestant doctrine of the analogy of faith. Protestants admit that there is a kind of tradition within the limits of the sacred Scriptures themselves. One generation of sacred writers received the whole body of truth taught by those who preceded them. There was a tradition of doctrine, a traditionary *usus loquendi*, traditionary figures, types, and symbols. The revelation of God in his Word begins in a fountain, and flows in a continuous stream ever increasing in volume. We are governed by this tradition of truth running through the whole sacred volume. All is consistent. One part cannot contradict another. Each part must be interpreted so as to bring it into harmony with the whole. This is only saying that Scripture must explain Scripture.

2. Again, Protestants admit that as there has been an uninterrupted tradition of truth from the protevangelium to the close of the Apocalypse, so there has been a stream of traditionary teaching flowing through the Christian Church from the day of Pentecost to the present time. This tradition is so far a rule of faith

that nothing contrary to it can be true. Christians do not stand isolated, each holding his own creed. They constitute one body, having one common creed. Rejecting that creed, or any of its parts, is the rejection of the fellowship of Christians, incompatible with the communion of saints, or membership in the body of Christ. In other words, Protestants admit that there is a common faith of the Church, which no man is at liberty to reject, and which no man can reject and be a Christian. They acknowledge the authority of this common faith for two reasons. First, because what all the competent readers of a plain book take to be its meaning, must be its meaning. Secondly, because the Holy Spirit is promised to guide the people of God into the knowledge of the truth, and therefore that which they, under the teachings of the Spirit, agree in believing must be true. There are certain fixed doctrines among Christians, as there are among Jews and Mohammedans, which are no longer open questions. The doctrines of the Trinity; of the divinity and incarnation of the eternal Son of God; of the personality and divinity of the Holy Spirit; of the apostasy and sinfulness of the human race; the doctrines of the expiation of sin through the death of Christ and of salvation through his merits; of regeneration and sanctification by the Holy Ghost; of the forgiveness of sins, the resurrection of the body, and of the life everlasting, have always entered into the faith of every recognized, historical church on the face of the earth, and cannot now be legitimately called into question by any pretending to be Christians.

Some of the more philosophical of the Romish theologians would have us believe that this is all they mean by tradition. They insist, they say, only on the authority of common consent. Thus Moehler, Professor of Theology at Munich, in his " Symbolik, oder Darstellung der Dogmatischen Gegensätze," says, " Tradition, in the subjective sense of the word, is the common faith, or consciousness of the Church." [1] " The ever-living word in the hearts of believers." [2] It is, he says, what Eusebius means by the ἐκκλησιαστικὸν φρόνημα; and what Vincent of Lerins intends by the *ecclesiastica intelligentia*, and the Council of Trent by the *universus ecclesiæ sensus*. " In the objective sense of the word," Moehler says that " Tradition is the common faith of the Church as presented in external, historical witnesses through all centuries." " In this latter sense," he tells us, " tradition is commonly viewed when spoken of as a guide to the interpretation of the rule of faith." [3] He admits that in this sense " Tradition contains nothing

[1] Page 356.   [2] Page 357.   [3] Page 358.

beyond what is taught in Scripture; the two as to their contents are one and the same." [1]   Nevertheless, he acknowledges that in the Church of Rome many things were handed down from the Apostles which are not contained in the Scriptures.   This fact he does not deny.   He admits that such additional revelations, or such revelations in addition to those contained in the written word, are of the highest importance.   But he soon dismisses the subject, and devotes his strength to the first-mentioned view of the nature and office of tradition, and holds that up as the peculiar doctrine of Romanism as opposed to the Protestant doctrine.   Protestants, however, admit the fact and the authority of a common consciousness, and a common faith, or common sense of the Church, while they reject the real and peculiar doctrine of Rome on this subject.

B. *Points of Difference between the Romish Doctrine and that of Protestants on Common Consent.*

The points of difference between the Protestant doctrine concerning the common faith of the Church and the Roman Catholic doctrine of tradition are : —

First.   When Protestants speak of common consent of Christians, they understand by Christians the true people of God.   Romanists, on the other hand, mean the company of those who profess the true faith, and who are subject to the Pope of Rome.   There is the greatest possible difference between the authority due to the common faith of truly regenerated, holy men, the temples of the Holy Ghost, and that due to what a society of nominal Christians profess to believe, the great majority of whom may be worldly, immoral, and irreligious.

Secondly.   The common consent for which Protestants plead concerns only essential doctrines; that is, doctrines which enter into the very nature of Christianity as a religion, and which are necessary to its subjective existence in the heart, or which if they do not enter essentially into the religious experience of believers, are so connected with vital doctrines as not to admit of separation from them.   Romanists, on the contrary, plead the authority of tradition for all kinds of doctrines and precepts, for rites and ceremonies, and ecclesiastical institutions, which have nothing to do with the life of the Church, and are entirely outside of the sphere of the promised guidance of the Spirit.   Our Lord, in promising the Spirit to guide his people into the knowledge of truths necessary to their salvation, did not promise to preserve them from error

[1] Page 373

in subordinate matters, or to give them supernatural knowledge of
the organization of the Church, the number of the sacraments, or
the power of bishops. The two theories, therefore, differ not only
as to the class of persons who are guided by the Spirit, but also as to
the class of subjects in relation to which that guidance is promised.

Thirdly. A still more important difference is, that the common
faith of the Church for which Protestants contend, is faith in doctrines plainly revealed in Scripture. It does not extend beyond
those doctrines. It owes its whole authority to the fact that it is a
common understanding of the written word, attained and preserved
under that teaching of the Spirit, which secures to believers a competent knowledge of the plan of salvation therein revealed. On
the other hand, tradition is with the Romanists entirely independent of the Scriptures. They plead for a common consent in doctrines not contained in the Word of God, or which cannot be
proved therefrom.

Fourthly. Protestants do not regard " common consent " either
as an informant or as a ground of faith. With them the written
word is the only source of knowledge of what God has revealed for
our salvation, and his testimony therein is the only ground of our
faith. Whereas, with Romanists, tradition is not only an informant of what is to be believed, but the witness on whose testimony
faith is to be yielded. It is one thing to say that the fact that all
the true people of God, under the guidance of the Spirit, believe
that certain doctrines are taught in Scripture, is an unanswerable
argument that they are really taught therein, and quite another
thing to say that because an external society, composed of all sorts
of men, to whom no promise of divine guidance has been given,
agree in holding certain doctrines, therefore we are bound to receive those doctrines as part of the revelation of God.

C. *Tradition and Development.*

The Romish doctrine of tradition is not to be confounded with
the modern doctrine of development. All Protestants admit that
there has been, in one sense, an uninterrupted development of theology in the Church, from the apostolic age to the present time.
All the facts, truths, doctrines, and principles, which enter into
Christian theology, are in the Bible. They are there as fully and
as clearly at one time as at another; at the beginning as they are
now. No addition has been made to their number, and no new
explanation has been afforded of their nature or relations. The
same is true of the facts of nature. They are now what they

have been from the beginning. They are, however, far better known, and more clearly understood now than they were a thousand years ago. The mechanism of the heavens was the same in the days of Pythagoras as it was in those of La Place ; and yet the astronomy of the latter was immeasurably in advance of that of the former. The change was effected by a continual and gradual progress. The same progress has taken place in theological knowledge. Every believer is conscious of such progress in his own experience. When he was a child, he thought as a child. As he grew in years, he grew in knowledge of the Bible. He increased not only in the compass, but in the clearness, order, and harmony of his knowledge. This is just as true of the Church collectively as of the individual Christian. It is, in the first place, natural, if not inevitable, that it should be so. The Bible, although so clear and simple in its teaching, that he who runs may read and learn enough to secure his salvation, is still full of the treasures of the wisdom and knowledge of God ; full of τὰ βάθη τοῦ θεοῦ, the profoundest truths concerning all the great problems which have taxed the intellect of man from the beginning. These truths are not systematically stated, but scattered, so to speak, promiscuously over the sacred pages, just as the facts of science are scattered over the face of nature, or hidden in its depths. Every man knows that there is unspeakably more in the Bible than he has yet learned, as every man of science knows that there is unspeakably more in nature than he has yet discovered, or understands. It stands to reason that such a book, being the subject of devout and laborious study, century after century, by able and faithful men, should come to be better and better understood. And as in matters of science, although one false theory after another, founded on wrong principles or on an imperfect induction of facts, has passed away, yet real progress is made, and the ground once gained is never lost, so we should naturally expect it to be with the study of the Bible. False views, false inferences, misapprehensions, ignoring of some facts, and misinterpretations, might be expected to come and go, in endless succession, but nevertheless a steady progress in the knowledge of what the Bible teaches be accomplished. And we might also expect that here, too, the ground once surely gained would not again be lost.

But, in the second place, what is thus natural and reasonable in itself is a patent historical fact. The Church has thus advanced in theological knowledge. The difference between the confused and discordant representations of the early fathers on all subjects con-

nected with the doctrines of the Trinity and of the person of
Christ, and the clearness, precision, and consistency of the views
presented after ages of discussion, and the statement of these doctrines by the Councils of Chalcedon and Constantinople, is as great
almost as between chaos and cosmos. And this ground has never
been lost. The same is true with regard to the doctrines of sin
and grace. Before the long-continued discussion of these subjects
in the Augustinian period, the greatest confusion and contradiction
prevailed in the teachings of the leaders of the Church ; during
those discussions the views of the Church became clear and settled. There is scarcely a principle or doctrine concerning the fall
of man, the nature of sin and guilt, inability, the necessity of the
Spirit's influence, etc., etc., which now enters into the faith of
evangelical Christians, which was not then clearly stated and authoritatively sanctioned by the Church. In like manner, before
the Reformation, similar confusion existed with regard to the great
doctrine of justification. No clear line of discrimination was
drawn between it and sanctification. Indeed, during the Middle
Ages, and among the most devout of the schoolmen, the idea of
guilt was merged in the general idea of sin, and sin regarded as
merely moral defilement. The great object was to secure holiness. Then pardon would come of course. The apostolic, Pauline,
deeply Scriptural doctrine, that there can be no holiness until sin
be expiated, that pardon, justification, and reconciliation, must precede sanctification, was never clearly apprehended. This was the
grand lesson which the Church learned at the Reformation, and
which it has never since forgot. It is true then, as an historical
fact, that the Church has advanced. It understands the great doctrines of theology, anthropology, and soteriology, far better now,
than they were understood in the early post-apostolic age of the
Church.

Modern Theory of Development.

Very distinct from the view above presented is the modern theory of the organic development of the Church. This modern
theory is avowedly founded on the pantheistic principles of Schelling and Hegel. With them the universe is the self-manifestation
and evolution of the absolute Spirit. Dr. Schaff[1] says, that this
theory " has left an impression on German science that can never
be effaced ; and has contributed more than any other influence to
diffuse a clear conception of the interior organism of history." In
his work on the " Principles of Protestantism," [2] Dr. Schaff says

[1] *What is Church History?* p. 75.   [2] Page 150.

that Schelling and Hegel taught the world to recognize in history " the ever opening sense of eternal thoughts, an always advancing rational development of the idea of humanity, and its relations to God." This theory of historical development was adopted, and partially Christianized by Schleiermacher, from whom it has passed over to Dr. Schaff, as set forth in his work above quoted, as well as to many other equally devout and excellent men. The basis of this modified theory is realism. Humanity is a generic life, an intelligent substance. That life became guilty and polluted in Adam. From him it passed over by a process of natural, organic development (the same numerical life and substance) to all his posterity, who therefore are guilty and polluted. This generic life the Son of God assumed into union with his divine nature, and thus healed it and raised it to a higher power or order. He becomes a new starting-point. The origin of this new form of life in Him is supernatural. The constitution of his person was a miracle. But from Him this life is communicated by a natural process of development to the Church. Its members are partakers of this new generic life. It is, however, a germ. Whatever lives grows. " Whatever is done is dead." This new life is Christianity. Christianity is not a form of doctrine objectively revealed in the Scriptures. Christian theology is not the knowledge, or systematic exhibition of what the Bible teaches. It is the interpretation of this inner life. The intellectual life of a child expresses itself in one way, of a boy in another way, and of a man in another and higher way. In each stage of his progress the man has views, feelings, and modes of thinking, appropriate to that stage. It would not do for a man to have the same views and thoughts as the child. Yet the latter are just as true, as right, and as proper, for the child, as those of the man for the man. It is thus with the Church. It passes through these stages of childhood, youth, and manhood, by a regular process. During the first centuries the Church had the indistinctness, vagueness, and exaggeration of views and doctrines, belonging to a period of infancy. In the Middle Ages it had a higher form. At the Reformation it advanced to the entrance on another stage. The form assumed by Christianity during the mediæval period, was for that period the true and proper, but not the permanent form. We have not reached that form as to doctrine yet. That will be reached in the Church of the future.

Development as held by some Romanists.

There is still another and very different form of the doctrine of development. It does not assume the Mystical doctrine of the indwelling of the substance of Christ, in the soul, the development of which works out its illumination in the knowledge of the truth, and finally its complete redemption. It admits that Christianity is, or includes a system of doctrine, and that those doctrines are in the Scriptures; but holds that many of them are there only in their rudiments. Under the constant guidance and tuition of the Spirit, the Church comes to understand all that these rudiments contain, and to expand them in their fulness. Thus the Lord's Supper has been expanded into the doctrine of transubstantiation and the sacrifice of the mass; anointing the sick, into the sacrament of extreme unction; rules of discipline into the sacrament of penance, of satisfactions, of indulgences, of purgatory, and masses and prayers for the dead; the prominence of Peter, into the supremacy of the Pope. The Old Testament contains the germ of all the doctrines unfolded in the New; and so the New Testament contains the germs of all the doctrines unfolded, under the guidance of the Spirit, in the theology of the mediæval Church.

Although attempts have been made by some Romanists and Anglicans to resolve the doctrine of tradition into one or other of these theories of development, they are essentially different. The only point of analogy between them is, that in both cases, little becomes much. Tradition has made contributions to the faith and institutions of the Christian Church; and development (in the two latter forms of the doctrine above mentioned) provides for a similar expansion.

The Real Question.

The real *status quæstionis*, on this subject, as between Romanists and Protestants, is not (1) Whether the Spirit of God leads true believers into the knowledge of the truth; nor (2) whether true Christians agree in all essential matters as to truth and duty; nor (3) whether any man can safely or innocently dissent from this common faith of the people of God; but (4) whether apart from the revelation contained in the Bible, there is another supplementary and explanatory revelation, which has been handed down outside of the Scriptures, by tradition. In other words, whether there are doctrines, institutions, and ordinances, having no warrant in the Scriptures, which we as Christians are bound to receive and obey on the authority of what is called common consent. This Romanists affirm and Protestants deny.

D. *Arguments against the Doctrine of Tradition.*

The heads of argument against the Romish doctrine on this subject are the following: —

1. It involves a natural impossibility. It is of course conceded that Christ and his Apostles said and did much that is not recorded in the Scriptures; and it is further admitted that if we had any certain knowledge of such unrecorded instructions, they would be of equal authority with what is written in the Scriptures. But Protestants maintain that they were not intended to constitute a part of the permanent rule of faith to the Church. They were designed for the men of that generation. The showers which fell a thousand years ago, watered the earth and rendered it fruitful for men then living. They cannot now be gathered up and made available for us. They did not constitute a reservoir for the supply of future generations. In like manner the unrecorded teachings of Christ and his Apostles did their work. They were not designed for our instruction. It is as impossible to learn what they were, as it is to gather up the leaves which adorned and enriched the earth when Christ walked in the garden of Gethsemane. This impossibility arises out of the limitations of our nature, as well as its corruption consequent on the fall. Man has not the clearness of perception, the retentiveness of memory, or the power of presentation, to enable him (without supernatural aid) to give a trustworthy account of a discourse once heard, a few years or even months after its delivery. And that this should be done over and over from month to month for thousands of years, is an impossibility. If to this be added the difficulty in the way of this oral transmission, arising from the blindness of men to the things of the Spirit, which prevents their understanding what they hear, and from the disposition to pervert and misrepresent the truth to suit their own prejudices and purposes, it must be acknowledged that tradition cannot be a reliable source of knowledge of religious truth. This is universally acknowledged and acted upon, except by Romanists. No one pretends to determine what Luther and Calvin, Latimer and Cranmer, taught, except from contemporaneous written records. Much less will any sane man pretend to know what Moses and the prophets taught except from their own writings.

Romanists admit the force of this objection. They admit that tradition would not be a trustworthy informant of what Christ and the Apostles taught, without the supernatural intervention of God.

Tradition is to be trusted not because it comes down through the hands of fallible men, but because it comes through an infallibly guided Church. This, however, is giving up the question. It is merging the authority of tradition into the authority of the Church. There is no need of the former, if the latter be admitted. Romanists, however, keep these two things distinct. They say that if the Gospels had never been written, they would know by historical tradition the facts of Christ's life; and that if his discourses and the epistles of the Apostles had never been gathered up and recorded, they would by the same means know the truths which they contain. They admit, however, that this could not be without a special divine intervention.

No Promise of Divine Intervention.

2. The second objection of Protestants to this theory is, that it is unphilosophical and irreligious to assume a supernatural intervention on the part of God, without promise and without proof, merely to suit a purpose, — Deus ex machina.

Our Lord promised to preserve his Church from fatal apostasy; He promised to send his Spirit to abide with his people, to teach them; He promised that He would be with them to the end of the world. But these promises were not made to any external, visible organization of professing Christians, whether Greek or Latin; nor did they imply that any such Church should be preserved from all error in faith or practice; much less do they imply that instructions not recorded by the dictation of the Spirit, should be preserved and transmitted from generation to generation. There is no such promise in the Word of God, and as such preservation and transmission without divine, supernatural interposition, would be impossible, tradition cannot be a trustworthy informant of what Christ taught.

No Criterion.

3. Romanists again admit that many false traditions have prevailed in different ages and in different parts of the Church. Those who receive them are confident of their genuineness, and zealous in their support. How shall the line be drawn between the true and false? By what criterion can the one be distinguished from the other? Protestants say there is no such criterion, and therefore, if the authority of tradition be admitted, the Church is exposed to a flood of superstition and error. This is their third argument against the Romish doctrine on this subject. Romanists, however, say they have a sure criterion in antiquity and universality. They

have formulated their rule of judgment in the famous dictum of Vincent of Lerins: "Quod semper, quod ubique, quod ab omnibus."

Common Consent not a Criterion.

To this Protestants reply, — First, That they admit the authority of common consent among true Christians as to what is taught in the Scriptures. So far as all the true people of God agree in their interpretation of the Bible, we acknowledge ourselves bound to submit. But this consent is of authority only, (*a*) So far as it is the consent of true believers; (*b*) So far as it concerns the meaning of the written word; and, (*c*) So far as it relates to the practical, experimental, or essential doctrines of Christianity. Such consent as to matters outside of the Bible, or even supposed to be in the Bible, if they do not concern the foundation of our faith, is of no decisive weight. The whole Christian world, without one dissenting voice, believed for ages that the Bible taught that the sun moves round the earth. No man now believes it.

Secondly, Common consent as to Christian doctrine cannot be pleaded except within narrow limits. It is only on the gratuitous and monstrous assumption that Romanists are the only Christians, that the least plausibility can be given to the claim of common consent. The argument is really this: The Church of Rome receives certain doctrines on the authority of tradition. The Church of Rome includes all true Christians. Therefore, the common consent of all Christians may be claimed in favour of those doctrines.

But, thirdly, admitting that the Church of Rome is the whole Church, and admitting that Church to be unanimous in holding certain doctrines, that is no proof that that Church has always held them. The rule requires that a doctrine must be held not only *ab omnibus*, but *semper*. It is, however, a historical fact that all the peculiar doctrines of Romanism were not received in the early Church as matters of faith. Such doctrines as the supremacy of the Bishop of Rome; the perpetuity of the apostleship; the grace of orders; transubstantiation; the propitiatory sacrifice of the Mass; the power of the priests to forgive sins; the seven sacraments; purgatory; the immaculate conception of the Virgin Mary, etc., etc., can all be historically traced in their origin, gradual development, and final adoption. As it would be unjust to determine the theology of Calvin and Beza from the Socinianism of modern Geneva; or that of Luther from the theology of the Germans of our day; so it is utterly unreasonable to infer that because the Latin Church believes all that the Council of Trent pronounced to be true, that such was its faith in the first centuries of its history. It is not to be denied that for the first hundred years after the Reformation the Church of England was Calvinistic; then under Archbishop Laud and the Stuarts it became almost thoroughly Romanized; then it became to a large extent Rationalistic, so that Bishop Burnet said of the men of his day, that Christianity seemed to be regarded as a fable "among all persons of discernment." To this succeeded a general revival of evangelical doctrine and piety; and that has been followed by a like revival of Romanism and Ritualism. Mr. Newman[1] says of the present time: "In the Church of England, we shall hardly find ten or twenty neighboring clergymen who agree together; and that, not in non-essentials of religion, but as to what are its elementary and necessary doctrines; or as to the fact whether there are any necessary doctrines at all, any distinct and definite faith required for salvation." Such is the testimony of history. In no external, visible Church, has there been a consent to any form of faith, *semper et ab omnibus.*

The Latin Church is no exception to this remark. It is an undeniable fact of history that Arianism prevailed for years both in the East and West; that it received the sanction of the vast majority of the bishops, of provincial and ecumenical councils, and of the Bishop of Rome. It is no less certain that in the Latin Church, Augustinianism, including all the characteristic doctrines of what is now called Calvinism, was declared to be the true faith by council after council, provincial and general, and by bishops and popes. Soon, however, Augustinianism lost its ascendency. For seven or eight centuries no one form of doctrine concerning sin, grace, and predestination prevailed in the Latin Church. Augustinianism, Semi-Pelagianism, and Mysticism (equally irreconcilable with both), were in constant conflict; and that, too, on questions on which the Church had already pronounced its judgment. It was not until the beginning of the sixteenth century that the Council of Trent, after long conflict within itself, gave its sanction to a modified form of Semi-Pelagianism.

The claim, therefore, for common consent, as understood by Romanists, is contrary to history. It is inconsistent with undeniable facts. This is virtually admitted by Romanists themselves. For with them it is common to say, We believe because the fifth century believed. But this is a virtual admission that their peculiar faith is not historically traceable beyond the fifth century. This

---

[1] *Lectures on Prophet. Office of the Church,* Lond. 1837, pp. 394, 395.

admission of a want of all historical evidence of "common consent" is also involved, as before remarked, in their constant appeal to the authority of the Church. What the Church says is a matter of faith, we, the traditionists affirm, are bound to believe, has always been a matter of faith. The passage from "Petrus á Soto," quoted above, puts the case very concisely : "Quæcunque credit, tenet et servat Romana ecclesia, et in Scripturis non habentur illa ab Apostolis esse tradita." The argument amounts to this. The Church believes on the ground of common consent. The proof that a thing is a matter of common consent, and always has been, is that the Church now believes it.

Inadequacy of the Evidences of Consent.

The second objection to the argument of Romanists from common consent in support of their traditions, is, that the evidence which they adduce of such consent is altogether inadequate. They appeal to the ancient creeds. But there was no creed generally adopted before the fourth century. No creed adopted before the eighth century contains any of the doctrines peculiar to the Church of Rome. Protestants all receive the doctrinal statements contained in what is called the Apostles' creed, and in those of Chalcedon, and of Constantinople, adopted A. D. 681.

They appeal also to the decisions of councils. To this the same reply is made. There were no general councils before the fourth century. The first six ecumenical councils gave no doctrinal decisions from which Protestants dissent. They, therefore, present no evidence of consent in those doctrines which are now peculiar to the Church of Rome.

They appeal again to the writings of the fathers. But to this Protestants object, —

First. That the writings of the apostolic fathers are too few to be taken as trustworthy representatives of the state of opinion in the Church for the first three hundred years. Ten or twenty writers scattered over such a period cannot reasonably be assumed to speak the mind of the whole Church.

Secondly. The consent of these fathers, or of the half of them, cannot be adduced in favour of any doctrine in controversy between Protestants and Romanists.

Thirdly. Almost unanimous consent can be quoted in support of doctrines which Romanists and Protestants unite in rejecting. The Jewish doctrine of the millennium passed over in its grossest form to the early Christian Church. But that doctrine the Church of Rome is specially zealous in denouncing.

Fourthly. The consent of the fathers cannot be proved in support of doctrines which Protestants and Romanists agree in accepting. Not that these doctrines did not then enter into the faith of the Church, but simply that they were not presented.

Fifthly. Such is the diversity of opinion among the fathers themselves, such the vagueness of their doctrinal statements, and such the unsettled *usus loquendi* as to important words, that the authority of the fathers may be quoted on either side of any disputed doctrine. There is no view, for example, of the nature of the Lord's supper, which has ever been held in the Church, for which the authority of some early father cannot be adduced. And often the same father presents one view at one time, and another at a different time.

Sixthly. The writings of the fathers have been notoriously corrupted. It was a matter of great complaint in the early Church that spurious works were circulated; and that genuine works were recklessly interpolated. Some of the most important works of the Greek fathers are extant only in a Latin translation. This is the case with the greater part of the works of Irenæus, translated by Rufinus, whom Jerome charges with the most shameless adulteration.

Another objection to the argument from consent is, that it is a Procrustean bed which may be extended or shortened at pleasure. In every *Catena Patrum* prepared to prove this consent in certain doctrines, it will be found that two or more writers in a century are cited as evincing the unanimous opinion of that century, while double or fourfold the number, of equally important writers, belonging to the same period, on the other side, are passed over in silence. There is no rule to guide in the application of this test, and no uniformity in the manner of its use.

While, therefore, it is admitted that there has been a stream of doctrine flowing down uninterruptedly from the days of the Apostles, it is denied, as a matter of fact, that there has been any uninterrupted or general consent in any doctrine not clearly revealed in the Sacred Scriptures; and not even in reference to such clearly revealed doctrines, beyond the narrow limits of essential truths. And it is, moreover, denied that in any external, visible, organized Church, can the rule, *quod semper, quod ab omnibus,* be applied even to essential doctrines. The argument, therefore, of Romanists in favor of their peculiar doctrines, derived from general consent, is utterly untenable and fallacious. This is virtually admitted by the most zealous advocates of tradition. "Not only," says Professor Newman,[1] "is the Church Catholic bound to teach the truth, but she is divinely guided to teach it; her witness of the Christian faith is a matter of promise as well as of duty; her discernment of it is secured by a heavenly, as well as by a human rule. She is indefectible in it; and therefore has not only authority to enforce it, but is of authority in declaring it. The Church not only transmits the faith by human means, but has a supernatural gift for that purpose; that doctrine which is true, considered as an historical fact, is true also because she teaches it." The author of the Oxford Tract, No. 85, after saying, "We believe mainly because the Church of the fourth and fifth centuries unanimously believed," [2] adds, "Why should not the Church be divine? The burden of proof surely is on the other side. I will accept her doctrines, and her rites, and her Bible — not one, and not the other, but all, — till I have clear proof that she is mistaken. It is I feel God's will that I should do so; and besides, I love these her possessions — I love her Bible, her doctrines, and her rites; and therefore, I believe." [3] The Romanist then believes because the Church believes. This is the ultimate reason. The Church believes, not because she can historically prove that her doctrines have been received from the Apostles, but because she is supernaturally guided to know the truth. "Common consent," therefore, is practically abandoned, and tradition resolves itself into the present faith of the Church.

Tradition not available by the People.

4. Protestants object to tradition as part of the rule of faith, because it is not adapted to that purpose. A rule of faith to the people must be something which they can apply; a standard by which they can judge. But this unwritten revelation is not contained in any one volume accessible to the people, and intelligible by them. It is scattered through the ecclesiastical records of eighteen centuries. It is absolutely impossible for the people to learn what it teaches. How can they tell whether the Church in all ages has taught the doctrine of transubstantiation, the sacrifice of the Mass, or any other popish doctrine. They must take all such doctrines upon trust, *i. e.*, on the faith of the extant Church. But this is to deny that to them tradition is a rule of faith. They are required to believe, on the peril of their souls, doctrines, the pretended evidence of which it is impossible for them to ascertain or appreciate.

[1] *Lectures, ut supra*, pp. 225, 226.   [2] *Oxford Tracts*, No. 85, p. 102.
[3] *Ibid.* p. 115.

5. Romanists argue that such is the obscurity of the Scriptures, that not only the people, but the Church itself needs the aid of tradition in order to their being properly understood. But if the Bible, a comparatively plain book, in one portable volume, needs to be thus explained, What is to explain the hundreds of folios in which these traditions are recorded? Surely a guide to the interpretation of the latter must be far more needed than one for the Scriptures.

Tradition destroys the Authority of the Scriptures.

6. Making tradition a part of the rule of faith subverts the authority of the Scriptures. This follows as a natural and unavoidable consequence. If there be two standards of doctrine of equal authority, the one the explanatory, and infallible interpreter of the other, it is of necessity the interpretation which determines the faith of the people. Instead, therefore, of our faith resting on the testimony of God as recorded in his Word, it rests on what poor, fallible, often fanciful, prejudiced, benighted men, tell us is the meaning of that word. Man and his authority take the place of God. As this is the logical consequence of making tradition a rule of faith, so it is an historical fact that the Scriptures have been made of no account wherever the authority of tradition has been admitted. Our Lord said, that the Scribes and Pharisees made the word of God of no effect by their traditions; that they taught for doctrines the commandments of men. This is no less historically true of the Church of Rome. A great mass of doctrines, rites, ordinances, and institutions, of which the Scriptures know nothing, has been imposed on the reason, conscience, and life of the people. The Roman Catholic religion of our day, with its hierarchy, ritual, image and saint worship; with its absolutions, indulgences, and its despotic power over the conscience and the life of the individual, is as little like the religion of the New Testament, as the present religion of the Hindus with its myriad of deities, its cruelties, and abominations, is like the simple religion of their ancient Vedas. In both cases similar causes have produced similar effects. In both there has been a provision for giving divine authority to the rapidly accumulating errors and corruptions of succeeding ages.

7. Tradition teaches error, and therefore cannot be divinely controlled so as to be a rule of faith. The issue is between Scripture and tradition. Both cannot be true. The one contradicts the other. One or the other must be given up. Of this at least no true Protestant has any doubt. All the doctrines

peculiar to Romanism, and for which Romanists plead the authority
of Scripture, Protestants believe to be anti-scriptural; and therefore they need no other evidence to prove that tradition is not to
be trusted either in matters of faith or practice.

The Scriptures not received on the Authority of Tradition.

8. Romanists argue that Protestants concede the authority of
tradition, because it is on that authority they receive the New
Testament as the word of God. This is not correct. We do not
believe the New Testament to be divine on the ground of the
testimony of the Church. We receive the books included in the
canonical Scriptures on the twofold ground of internal and external evidence. It can be historically proved that those books
were written by the men whose names they bear; and it can also
be proved that those men were the duly authenticated organs of
the Holy Ghost. The historical evidence which determines the
authorship of the New Testament is not exclusively that of the
Christian fathers. The testimony of heathen writers is, in some
respects, of greater weight than that of the fathers themselves.
We may believe on the testimony of English history, ecclesiastical
and secular, that the Thirty-Nine Articles were framed by the
English Reformers, without being traditionists. In like manner
we may believe that the books of the New Testament were written
by the men whose names they bear without admitting tradition to
be a part of the rule of faith.

Besides, external evidence of any kind is a very subordinate
part of the ground of a Protestant's faith in the Scripture. That
ground is principally the nature of the doctrines therein revealed,
and the witness of the Spirit, with and by the truth, to the heart
and conscience. We believe the Scriptures for much the same
reason that we believe the Decalogue.

The Church is bound to stand fast in the liberty wherewith
Christ has made it free, and not to be again entangled with the
yoke of bondage, — a bondage not only to human doctrines and
institutions, but to soul-destroying errors and superstitions.

§ 7. *Office of the Church as a Teacher.*

A. *The Romish Doctrine on this subject.*

Romanists teach that the Church, as an external, visible society,
consisting of those who profess the Christian religion, united in
communion of the same sacraments and subjection to lawful pastors,

and especially to the Pope of Rome, is divinely appointed to be the infallible teacher of men in all things pertaining to faith and practice. It is qualified for this office by the plenary revelation of the truth in the written and unwritten word of God, and by the supernatural guidance of the Holy Spirit vouchsafed to the bishops as official successors of the Apostles, or, to the Pope as the successor of Peter in his supremacy over the whole Church, and as vicar of Christ on earth.

There is something simple and grand in this theory. It is wonderfully adapted to the tastes and wants of men. It relieves them of personal responsibility. Everything is decided for them. Their salvation is secured by merely submitting to be saved by an infallible, sin-pardoning, and grace-imparting Church. Many may be inclined to think that it would have been a great blessing had Christ left on earth a visible representative of himself clothed with his authority to teach and govern, and an order of men dispersed through the world endowed with the gifts of the original Apostles, — men everywhere accessible, to whom we could resort in all times of difficulty and doubt, and whose decisions could be safely received as the decisions of Christ himself. God's thoughts, however, are not as our thoughts. We know that when Christ was on earth, men did not believe or obey Him. We know that when the Apostles were still living, and their authority was still confirmed by signs, and wonders, and divers miracles and gifts of the Holy Ghost, the Church was nevertheless distracted by heresies and schisms. If any in their sluggishness are disposed to think that a perpetual body of infallible teachers would be a blessing, all must admit that the assumption of infallibility by the ignorant, the erring, and the wicked, must be an evil inconceivably great. The Romish theory if true might be a blessing; if false it must be an awful curse. That it is false may be demonstrated to the satisfaction of all who do not wish it to be true, and who, unlike the Oxford Tractarian, are not determined to believe it because they love it.

B. *The Romish definition of the Church is derived from what the Church of Rome now is.*

Before presenting a brief outline of the argument against this theory, it may be well to remark that the Romish definition of the Church is purely empirical. It is not derived from the signification or usage of the word ἐκκλησία in the New Testament; nor from what is there taught concerning the Church. It is merely a statement of what the Church of Rome now is. It is a body professing the same faith, united in the communion of the same sacraments, subject to pastors (*i. e.*, bishops) assumed to be lawful, and to the Pope as the vicar of Christ. Now in this definition it is gratuitously assumed, —

1. That the Church to which the promise of divine guidance is given, is an external, visible organization ; and not the people of God as such in their personal and individual relation to Christ. In other words, it is assumed that the Church is a visible society, and not a collective term for the people of God; as when it is said of Paul that he persecuted the Church ; and of Christ that He loved the Church and gave himself for it. Christ certainly did not die for any external, visible, organized Society.

2. The Romish theory assumes, not only that the Church is an external organization, but that it must be organized in one definite, prescribed form. But this assumption is not only unreasonable, it is unscriptural, because no one form is prescribed in Scripture as essential to the being of the Church; and because it is contrary to the whole spirit and character of the gospel, that forms of government should be necessary to the spiritual life and salvation of men. Moreover, this assumption is inconsistent with historical facts. The Church in all its parts has never been organized according to one plan.

3. But conceding that the Church is an external society, and that it must be organized according to one plan, it is a gratuitous and untenable presumption, that that plan must be the episcopal. It is a notorious fact that diocesan episcopacy did not exist during the apostolic age. It is equally notorious that that plan of government was gradually introduced. And it is no less notorious that a large part of the Church in which Christ dwells by his presence, and which He in every way acknowledges and honours, has no bishops until the present day. The government of the Church by bishops, Romanists admit is one of the institutions which rest not on Scripture, but on tradition for their authority.

4. But should everything else be conceded, the assumption that subjection to the Pope, as the vicar of Christ, is necessary to the existence of the Church, is utterly unreasonable. This is the climax. There is not the slightest evidence in the New Testament or in the apostolic age, that Peter had any such primacy among the Apostles as Romanists claim. There is not only the absence of all evidence that he exercised any jurisdiction over them, but there is abundant evidence to the contrary. This is clear from

Peter, James, and John, being mentioned together as those who appeared to be pillars (Gal. ii. 9), and this distinction was due not to office, but to character. It is moreover clear from the full equality in gifts and authority which Paul asserted for himself, and proved to the satisfaction of the whole Church that he possessed. It is clear from the subordinate position occupied by Peter in the Council of Jerusalem (Acts xv.), and from the severe reproof he received from Paul at Antioch (Gal. ii. 11-21). It is a plain historical fact, that Paul and John were the master-spirits of the Apostolic Church. But admitting the primacy of Peter in the college of Apostles, there is no evidence that such primacy was intended to be perpetual. There is no command to elect a successor to him in that office ; no rules given as to the mode of such election, or the persons by whom the choice was to be made ; and no record of such election having actually been made. Everything is made out of the air. But admitting that Peter was constituted the head of the whole Church on earth, and that such headship was intended to be continued, what evidence is there that the Bishop of Rome was to all time entitled to that office ? It is very doubtful whether Peter ever was in Rome. The sphere of his labors was in Palestine and the East. It is certain he never was Bishop of the Church in that city. And even if he were, he was Primate, not as Bishop of Rome, but by appointment of Christ. According to the theory, he was Primate before he went to Rome, and not because he went there. The simple historical fact is, that as Rome was the seat of the Roman empire, the Bishop of Rome aspired to be the head of the Church, which claim after a long struggle came to be acknowledged, at least in the West.

It is on the four gratuitous and unreasonable assumptions above mentioned, namely, that the Church to which the promise of the Spirit was made is an external, visible organization ; that a particular mode of organization is essential to its existence ; that that mode is the episcopal ; and that it must be papal, *i. e.*, the whole episcopacy be subject to the Bishop of Rome ; — it is on these untenable assumptions that the whole stupendous system of Romanism rests. If any one of them fail, the whole falls to the ground These assumptions are so entirely destitute of any adequate historical proof, that no reasonable man can accept them on their own evidence. It is only those who have been taught or induced to believe the extant Church to be infallible, who can believe them. And they believe not because these points can be proved, but on the assertion of the Church. The Romish Church says

that Christ constituted the Church on the papal system, and therefore, it is to be believed. The thing to be proved is taken for
granted. It is a *petitio principii* from beginning to end.

C. *The Romish Doctrine of Infallibility founded on a Wrong
Theory of the Church.*

The first great argument of Protestants against Romanism concerns the theory of the Church.

God entered into a covenant with Abraham. In that covenant
there were certain promises which concerned his natural descendants through Isaac, which promises were suspended on the national
obedience of the people. That covenant, however, contained the
promise of redemption through Christ. He was the seed in whom
all the nations of the earth were to be blessed. The Jews came
to believe that this promise of redemption, *i. e.*, of the blessings of
the Messiah's reign, was made to them as a nation ; and that it was
conditioned on membership in that nation. All who were Jews
either by descent or proselytism, and who were circumcised, and
adhered to the Law, were saved. All others would certainly perish forever. This is the doctrine which our Lord so pointedly condemned, and against which St. Paul so strenuously argued. When
the Jews claimed that they were the children of God, because they
were the children of Abraham, Christ told them that they might
be the children of Abraham, and yet the children of the devil
(John viii. 33–44) ; as John, his forerunner, had before said, say
not "We have Abraham to our father; for I say unto you, that
God is able of these stones to raise up children unto Abraham."
(Matt. iii. 9.) It is against this doctrine the epistles to the Romans and Galatians are principally directed. The Apostle shows,
(1.) That the promise of salvation was not confined to the Jews,
or to the members of any external organization. (2.) And therefore that it was not conditioned on descent from Abraham, nor on
circumcision, nor on adherence to the Old Testament theocracy.
(3.) That all believers (οἱ ἐκ πίστεως) are the sons, and, therefore,
the heirs of Abraham. (Gal. iii. 7.) (4.) That a man might be a
Jew, a Hebrew of the Hebrews, circumcised on the eighth day,
and touching the righteousness which is of the law blameless, and
yet it avail him nothing. (Phil. iii. 4–6.) (5.) Because he is
not a Jew who is one outwardly; and circumcision is of the heart.
(Romans ii. 28–29.) (6.) And consequently that God could
cast off the Jews as a nation, without acting inconsistently with his
covenant with Abraham, because the promise was not made to the
Israel κατὰ σάρκα, but to the Israel κατὰ πνεῦμα. (Rom. ix. 6–8.)

Romanists have transferred the whole Jewish theory to the Christian Church; while Protestants adhere to the doctrine of Christ and his Apostles. Romanists teach, (1.) That the Church is essentially an external, organized community, as the commonwealth of Israel. (2.) That to this external society, all the attributes, prerogatives, and promises of the true Church belong. (3.) That membership in that society is the indispensable condition of salvation; as it is only by union with the Church that men are united to Christ, and, through its ministrations, become partakers of his redemption. (4.) That all who die in communion with this external society, although they may, if not perfect at death, suffer for a longer or shorter period in purgatory, shall ultimately be saved. (5.) All outside of this external organization perish eternally. There is, therefore, not a single element of the Jewish theory which is not reproduced in the Romish.

Protestant Doctrine of the Nature of the Church.

Protestants, on the other hand, teach on this subject, in exact accordance with the doctrine of Christ and the Apostles : (1.) That the Church as such, or in its essential nature, is not an external organization. (2.) All true believers, in whom the Spirit of God dwells, are members of that Church which is the body of Christ, no matter with what ecclesiastical organization they may be connected, and even although they have no such connection. The thief on the cross was saved, though he was not a member of any external Church. (3.) Therefore, that the attributes, prerogatives, and promises of the Church do not belong to any external society as such, but to the true people of God collectively considered ; and to external societies only so far as they consist of true believers, and are controlled by them. This is only saying what every man admits to be true, that the attributes, prerogatives, and promises pertaining to Christians belong exclusively to true Christians, and not to wicked or worldly men who call themselves Christians. (4.) That the condition of membership in the true Church is not union with any organized society, but faith in Jesus Christ. They are the children of God by faith ; they are the sons of Abraham, heirs of the promise of redemption made to him by faith ; whether they be Jews or Gentiles, bond or free ; whether Protestants or Romanists, Presbyterians or Episcopalians ; or whether they be so widely scattered, that no two or three of them are able to meet together for worship.

Protestants do not deny that there is a visible Church Catholic

on earth, consisting of all those who profess the true religion, together with their children.   But they are not all included in any
one external society.   They also admit that it is the duty of Christians to unite for the purpose of worship and mutual watch and
care.   They admit that to such associations and societies certain
prerogatives and promises belong; that they have, or ought to
have the officers whose qualifications and duties are prescribed in
the Scriptures; that there always have been, and probably always
will be, such Christian organizations, or visible churches.   But they
deny that any one of these societies, or all of them collectively,
constitute the Church for which Christ died; in which He dwells by
his Spirit; to which He has promised perpetuity, catholicity, unity,
and divine guidance into the knowledge of the truth.   Any one
of them, or all of them, one after another, may apostatize from the
faith, and all the promises of God to his Church be fulfilled.   The
Church did not fail, when God reserved to himself only seven thousand in all Israel who had not bowed the knee unto Baal.

Almost all the points of difference between Protestants and Romanists depend on the decision of the question, "What is the
Church?"   If their theory be correct; if the Church is the external society of professing Christians, subject to apostle-bishops (*i. e.*,
to bishops who are apostles), and to the Pope as Christ's vicar on
earth; then we are bound to submit to it; and then too beyond the
pale of that communion there is no salvation.   But if every true
believer is, in virtue of his faith, a member of that Church to which
Christ promises guidance and salvation, then Romanism falls to the
ground.

The Opposing Theories of the Church.

That the two opposing theories of the Church, the Romish and
Protestant, are what has been stated above is so generally known
and so unquestioned, that it is unnecessary to cite authorities on
either side.   It is enough, so far as the doctrine of Romanists is concerned, to quote the language of Bellarmin,[1] that the marks of the
Church are three: "Professio veræ fidei, sacramentorum commu-
nio, et subjectio ad legitimum pastorem, Romanum Pontificem. —
Atque hoc interest inter sententiam nostram et alias omnes, quod
omnes aliæ requirunt internas virtutes ad constituendum aliquem
in Ecclesia, et propterea Ecclesiam veram invisibilem faciunt; nos
autem credimus in Ecclesia inveniri omnes virtutes, — tamen ut
aliquis aliquo modo dici possit pars veræ Ecclesiæ, — non putamus
requiri ullam internam virtutem, sed tantum externam professionem

---

[1] *De Ecclesia Militante*, II. Disputationes, edit. Paris, 1608, vol. ii. p. 108, d.

fidei, et sacramentorum communionem, quæ sensu ipso percipitur. Ecclesia enim est cœtus hominum ita visibiliş et palpabilis, ut est cœtus Populi Romani, vel regnum Galliæ aut respublica Venetorum." The Lutheran Symbols define the Church as, " Congregatio sanctorum." [1] " Congregatio sanctorum et vere credentium." [2] " Societas fidei et Spiritus Sancti in cordibus." [3] " Congregatio sanctorum, qui habent inter se societatem ejusdem evangelii seu doctrinæ, et ejusdem Spiritus Sancti, qui corda eorum renovat, sanctificat et gubernat ; " and [4] " Populus spiritualis, non civilibus ritibus distinctus a gentibus, sed verus populus Dei renatus per Spiritum Sanctum." [5]

The Symbols of the Reformed Churches present the same doctrine.[6] The Confessio Helvetica says, " Oportet semper fuisse, nunc esse et ad finem usque seculi futuram esse Ecclesiam, *i. e.*, e mundo evocatum vel collectum cœtum fidelium, sanctorum inquam omnium communionem, eorum videlicet, qui Deum verum in Christo servatore per verbum et Spiritum Sanctum vere cognoscunt et rite colunt, denique omnibus bonis per Christum gratuito oblatis fide participant." [7] Confessio Gallicana : " Affirmamus ex Dei verbo, Ecclesiam esse fidelium cœtum, qui in verbo Dei sequendo et pura religione colenda consentiunt, in qua etiam quotidie proficiunt." [8] Confessio Belgica : " Credimus et confitemur unicam Ecclesiam catholicam seu universalem, quæ est sancta congregatio seu cœtus omnium fidelium Christianorum, qui totam suam salutem ab uno Jesu Christo exspectant, abluti ipsius sanguine et per Spiritum ejus sanctificati atque obsignati. Hæc Ecclesia sancta nullo est aut certo loco sita et circumscripta, aut ullis certis personis astricta aut alligata : sed per omnem orbem terrarum sparsa atque diffusa est." [9] The same doctrine is found in the answer to the fifty-fourth question in the Heidelberg Catechism. In the Geneva Catechism to the question, " Quid est Ecclesia ? " the answer is, " Corpus ac societas fidelium, quos Deus ad vitam æternam prædestinavit." [10]

Winer in his " Comparative Darstellung," [11] thus briefly states the two theories concerning the Church. Romanists, he says, " define the Church on earth, as the community of those baptized in the name of Christ, united under his Vicar, the Pope, its visible head. Protestants, on the other hand, as the communion

---

1 *Augsburg Confession*, art. 7.
3 *Apol. A. C.*, art. 4, pp. 144, 145, Hase.
5 See Hase, *Libri Symbolici*.
7 II. cap. 17, p. 499, Niem.
9 Art. 27, p. 379, *ibid.*
11 Page 165.

2 *Ibid.* art. 8.
4 *Ibid.* p. 146.
6 See Niemeyer, *Coll. Confess.*
8 Art. 27, p. 336, *ibid.*
10 Page 135, *ibid.*

of saints, that is, of those who truly believe on Christ, in which the gospel is purely preached and the sacraments properly administered."

Proof of the Protestant Doctrine of the Church.

This is not the place to enter upon a formal vindication of the Protestant doctrine of the nature of the Church. That belongs to the department of ecclesiology. What follows may suffice for the present purpose.

The question is not whether the word Church is not properly used, and in accordance with the Scriptures, for visible, organized bodies of professing Christians, or for all such Christians collectively considered. Nor is it the question, whether we are to regard as Christians those who, being free from scandal, profess their faith in Christ, or societies of such professors organized for the worship of Christ and the administration of his discipline, as being true churches. But the question is, whether the Church to which the attributes, prerogatives, and promises pertaining to the body of Christ belong, is in its nature a visible, organized community; and specially, whether it is a community organized in some one exclusive form, and most specially on the papal form; or, whether it is a spiritual body consisting of true believers. Whether when the Bible addresses a body of men as " the called of Jesus Christ," " beloved of God," " partakers of the heavenly calling; " as " the children of God, joint heirs with Christ of a heavenly inheritance; " as " elect according to the foreknowledge of God the Father, through sanctification and sprinkling of the blood of Christ; " as " partakers of the like precious faith with the Apostles; " as " those who are washed, and sanctified, and justified in the name of the Lord Jesus and by the Spirit of our God; " as those who being dead in sin, had been " quickened and raised up and made to sit together in heavenly places with Christ Jesus; " it means the members of an external society as such, and because such, or, the true people of God? The question is, whether when to the men thus designated and described, Christ promised to be with them to the end of the world, to give them his Spirit, to guide them unto the knowledge of the truth, to keep them through the power of the Spirit, so that the gates of hell should not prevail against them — he means his sincere or his nominal disciples, — believers or unbelievers? These questions admit of but one answer. The attributes ascribed to the Church in Scripture belong to true believers alone. The promises made to the Church are fulfilled only to believers. The relation in which the Church stands to God and

Christ is sustained alone by true believers. They only are the children and heirs of God; they only are the body of Christ in which He dwells by his Spirit; they only are the temple of God, the bride of Christ, the partakers of his glory. The doctrine that a man becomes a child of God and an heir of eternal life by membership in any external society, overturns the very foundations of the gospel, and introduces a new method of salvation. Yet this is the doctrine on which the whole system of Romanism rests. As, therefore, the Apostle shows that the promises made to Israel under the Old Testament, the promise of perpetuity, of extension over the whole earth, of the favour and fellowship of God, and all the blessings of the Messiah's reign, were not made to the external Israel as such, but to the true people of God; so Protestants contend that the promises made to the Church as the body and bride of Christ are not made to the external body of professed Christians, but to those who truly believe on him and obey his gospel.

The absurdities which flow from the substitution of the visible Church for the invisible, from transferring the attributes, prerogatives, and promises which belong to true believers, to an organized body of nominal or professed believers, are so great that Romanists cannot be consistent. They cannot adhere to their own theory. They are forced to admit that the wicked are not really members of the Church. They are " in it " but not " of it." Their connection with it is merely external, as that of the chaff with the wheat. This, however, is the Protestant doctrine. The Romish doctrine is precisely the reverse. Romanists teach that the chaff is the wheat; that the chaff becomes wheat by external connection with the precious grain. Just so certain, therefore, as that chaff is not wheat; that nominal Christians, as such, are not true Christians; just so certain is it that no external society consisting of good and bad, is that Church to which the promise of Christ's presence and salvation is made. It is as Turrettin says,[1] " πρῶτον ψεῦδος pontificiorum in tota controversia est, ecclesiam metiri velle ex societatis civilis modulo, ut ejus essentia in externis tantum et in sensus incurrentibus consistat, et sola professio fidei sufficiat ad membrum ecclesiæ constituendum, nec ipsa fides et pietas interna ad id necessario requirantur."

D. *The Doctrine of Infallibility founded on the False Assumption of the Perpetuity of the Apostleship.*

As the first argument against the doctrine of Romanists as to the

1 Locus XVIII. ii. 12.

infallibility of the Church is, that it makes the Church of Rome to be the body to which the attributes, prerogatives, and promises of Christ to true believers belong; the second is that it limits the promise of the teaching of the Spirit, to the bishops as successors of the Apostles. In other words, Romanists falsely assume the perpetuity of the Apostleship. If it be true that the prelates of the Church of Rome, or of any other church, are apostles, invested with the same authority to teach and to rule as the original messengers of Christ, then we must be bound to yield the same faith to their teaching, and the same obedience to their commands, as are due to the inspired writings of the New Testament. And such is the doctrine of the Church of Rome.

Modern Prelates are not Apostles.

To determine whether modern bishops are apostles, it is necessary in the first place to determine the nature of the Apostleship, and ascertain whether modern prelates have the gifts, qualifications, and credentials of the office. Who then were the Apostles? They were a definite number of men selected by Christ to be his witnesses, to testify to his doctrines, to the facts of his life, to his death, and specially to his resurrection. To qualify them for this office of authoritative witnesses, it was necessary, (1.) That they should have independent and plenary knowledge of the gospel. (2.) That they should have seen Christ after his resurrection. (3.) That they should be inspired, *i. e.*, that they should be individually and severally so guided by the Spirit as to be infallible in all their instructions. (4.) That they should be authenticated as the messengers of Christ, by adherence to the true gospel, by success in preaching (Paul said to the Corinthians that they were the seal of his apostleship, 1 Cor. ix. 2); and by signs and wonders and divers miracles and gifts of the Holy Ghost. Such were the gifts and qualifications and credentials of the original Apostles; and those who claimed the office without possessing these gifts and credentials, were pronounced false apostles and messengers of Satan.

When Paul claimed to be an apostle, he felt it necessary to prove, (1.) That he had been appointed not by man nor through men, but immediately by Jesus Christ. (Gal. i. 1.) (2.) That he had not been taught the gospel by others, but received his knowledge by immediate revelation. (Gal. i. 12.) (3.) That he had seen Christ after his resurrection. (1 Cor. ix. 1 and xv. 8.) (4.) That he was inspired, or infallible as a teacher, so that men were bound to recognize his teachings as the teaching of Christ.

(1 Cor. xiv. 37.) (5.) That the Lord had authenticated his apostolic mission as fully as he had done that of Peter. (Gal. ii. 8.) (6.) "The signs of an apostle," he tells the Corinthians, "were wrought among you in all patience, in signs, and wonders, and mighty deeds." (2 Cor. xii. 12.)

Modern prelates do not claim to possess any one of these gifts. Nor do they pretend to the credentials which authenticated the mission of the Apostles of Christ. They claim no immediate commission ; no independent knowledge derived from immediate revelation ; no personal infallibility ; no vision of Christ ; and no gift of miracles. That is, they claim the authority of the office, but not its reality. It is very plain, therefore, that they are not apostles. They cannot have the authority of the office without having the gifts on which that authority was founded, and from which it emanated. If a man cannot be a prophet without the gift of prophecy ; or a miracle-worker without the gift of miracles ; or have the gift of tongues without the ability to speak other languages than his own ; no man can rightfully claim to be an apostle without possessing the gifts which made the original Apostles what they were. The deaf and dumb might as reasonably claim to have the gift of tongues. The world has never seen or suffered a greater imposture than that weak, ignorant, and often immoral men, should claim the same authority to teach and rule that belonged to men to whom the truth was supernaturally revealed, who were confessedly infallible in its communication, and to whose divine mission God himself bore witness in signs and wonders, and divers miracles and gifts of the Holy Ghost. The office of the Apostles as described in the New Testament, was, therefore, from its nature incapable of being transmitted, and has not in fact been perpetuated.

There is no command given in the New Testament to keep up the succession of the Apostles. When Judas had apostatized, Peter said his place must be filled, but the selection was to be confined to those, as he said, " which have companied with us all the time that the Lord Jesus went in and out among us, beginning from the baptism of John unto that same day that He was taken up from us." (Acts i. 21, 22.) The reason assigned for this appointment was not that the Apostleship might be continued, but that the man selected might be " a witness with us of his resurrection." " And they gave forth their lots ; and the lot fell upon Matthias ; and he was numbered with the eleven Apostles." And that was the end. We never hear of Matthias afterward. It is very doubtful whether this appointment of Matthias had any validity. What is here recorded (Acts, i. 15-26), took place before the Apostles had been endued with power from on high (Acts i. 8), and, therefore, before they had any authority to act in the premises. Christ in his own time and way completed the number of his witnesses by calling Paul to be an Apostle. But, however this may be, here if ever *exceptio probat regulam.* It proves that the ranks of the Apostles could be filled, and the succession continued only from the number of those who could bear independent witness of the resurrection and doctrines of Christ.

Besides the fact that there is no command to appoint apostles, there is clear evidence that the office was not designed to be perpetuated. With regard to all the permanent officers of the Church, there is, (1.) Not only a promise to continue the gifts which pertained to the office, and the command to appoint suitable persons to fill it, but also a specification of the qualifications to be sought and demanded; and (2.) a record of the actual appointment of incumbents; and (3.) historical evidence of their continuance in the Church from that day to this. With regard to the Apostleship, all this is wanting. As we have seen, the gifts of the office have not been continued, there is no command to perpetuate the office, no directions to guide the Church in the selection of proper persons to be apostles, no record of their appointment, and no historical evidence of their continuance; on the contrary, they disappear entirely after the death of the original twelve. It might as well be asserted that the Pharaohs of Egypt, or the twelve Cæsars of Rome have been continued, as that the race of apostles has been perpetuated.

It is true that there are a few passages in which persons other than the original twelve seem to be designated as apostles. But from the beginning of the Church until of late, no one has ventured on that account to regard Barnabas, Silas, Timothy, and Titus, as apostles, in the official sense of the word. All the designations given to the officers of the Church in the New Testament, are used in different senses. Thus, " presbyter " or " elder," means, an old man, a Jewish officer, an officer of the Church. The word " deacon," means, a domestic, sometimes a secular officer, sometimes any minister of the Church; sometimes the lowest order of church officers. Because Paul and Peter call themselves " deacons," it does not prove that their office was to serve tables. In like manner the word " apostle " is sometimes used in its etymological sense " a messenger," sometimes in a religious sense, as we use the word " missionary; " and sometimes in its strict official sense, in which it is confined to the immediate messengers of Christ. Nothing can be plainer from the New Testament than that neither Silas nor Timothy, nor any other person, is ever spoken of as the official equal of the twelve Apostles. These constitute a class by themselves. They stand out in the New Testament as they do in all Church history, as the authoritative founders of the Christian Church, without peers or colleagues.

If, then, the Apostleship, from its nature and design, was incapable of transmission ; if there be this decisive evidence from Scripture and history, that it has not been perpetuated, then the whole theory of the Romanists concerning the Church falls to the ground. That theory is founded on the assumption that prelates are apostles, invested with the same authority to teach and rule, as the original messengers of Christ. If this assumption is unfounded, then all claim to the infallibility of the Church must be given up; for it is not pretended that the mass of the people is infallible nor the priesthood, but simply the episcopate. And bishops are infallible only on the assumption that they are apostles, in the official sense of the term. This they certainly are not. The Church may make priests, and bishops, and even popes; but Christ alone can make an Apostle. For an Apostle was a man endowed with supernatural knowledge, and with supernatural power.

E. *Infallibility founded on a False Interpretation of the Promise of Christ.*

The third decisive argument against the infallibility of the Church is, that Christ never promised to preserve it from all error. What is here meant is that Christ never promised the true Church, that is, " the company of true believers," that they should not err in doctrine. He did promise that they should not fatally apostatize from the truth. He did promise that He would grant his true disciples such a measure of divine guidance by his Spirit, that they should know enough to be saved. He, moreover, promised that He would call men into the ministry, and give them the qualifications of faithful teachers, such as were the presbyters whom the Apostles ordained in every city. But there is no promise of infallibility either to the Church as a whole, or to any class of men in the Church. Christ promised to sanctify his people; but this was not a promise to make them perfectly holy in this life. He promised to give them joy and peace in believing ; but this is not a promise to make them perfectly happy in this life, — that they should have no trials or sorrows. Then, why should the promise to teach be a promise to render infallible. As the Church has gone through the world bathed in tears and blood, so has she gone soiled with sin and error. It is just as manifest that she has never been infallible, as that she has never been perfectly holy. Christ no more promised the one than the other.

F. *The Doctrine contradicted by Facts.*

The fourth argument is that the Romish doctrine of the infallibility of the Church is contradicted by undeniable historical facts. It therefore cannot be true. The Church has often erred, and therefore it is not infallible.

Protestants believe that the Church, under all dispensations, has been the same. It has always had the same God ; the same Redeemer ; the same rule of faith and practice (the written Word of God, at least from the time of Moses), the same promise of the presence and guidance of the Spirit, the same pledge of perpetuity and triumph. To them, therefore, the fact that the whole visible Church repeatedly apostatized during the old economy — and that, not the people only, but all the representatives of the Church, the priests, the Levites, and the elders — is a decisive proof that the external, visible Church may fatally err in matters of faith. No less decisive is the fact that the whole Jewish Church and people, as a church and nation, rejected Christ. He came to his own, and his own received him not. The vast majority of the people, the chief priests, the scribes and the elders, refused to recognize him as the Messiah. The Sanhedrim, the great representative body of the Church at that time, pronounced him worthy of death, and demanded his crucifixion. This, to Protestants, is overwhelming proof that the Church may err.

Romanists, however, make such a difference between the Church before and after the advent of Christ, that they do not admit the force of this argument. That the Jewish Church erred, they say, is no proof that the Christian Church can err. It will be necessary, therefore, to show that according to the principles and admissions of Romanists themselves, the Church has erred. It taught at one time what it condemned at another, and what the Church of Rome now condemns. To prove this, it will suffice to refer to two undeniable examples.

It is to be borne in mind that by the Church, in this connection, Romanists do not mean the true people of God ; nor the body of professing Christians ; nor the majority of priests, or doctors of divinity, but the episcopate. What the body of bishops of any age teach, all Christians are bound to believe, because these bishops are so guided by the Spirit as to be infallible in their teaching.

The Arian Apostasy.

The first great historical fact inconsistent with this theory is, that the great majority of the bishops, both of the Eastern and Western Church, including the Pope of Rome, taught Arianism, whic the whole Church, both before and afterwards, condemned. The decision of three hundred and eighty bishops at the Council of Nice, ratified by the assent of the great majority of those who did not attend that Council, is fairly taken as proof that the visible Church at that time taught, as Rome now teaches, that the Son is consubstantial with the Father. The fact that some dissented at the time, or that more soon joined in that dissent; or, that in a few years, in the East, the dissentients were in the majority, is not considered as invalidating the decision of that Council as the decision of the Church; because a majority of the bishops, as a body, were still in favor of the Nicene doctrine. Then, by parity of reasoning, the decisions of the two contemporary councils, one at Seleucia in the East, the other at Ariminum in the West, including nearly eight hundred bishops, ratified as those decisions were by the great majority of the bishops of the whole Church (including Liberius, the bishop of Rome), must be accepted as the teaching of the visible Church of that age. But those decisions, according to the previous and subsequent judgment of the Church, were heretical. It has been urged that the language adopted by the Council of Ariminum admits of an orthodox interpretation. In answer to this, it is enough to say, (1.) That it was drawn up, proposed, and urged by the avowed opponents of the Nicene Creed. (2.) That it was strenuously resisted by the advocates of that creed, and renounced as soon as they gained the ascendency. (3.) That Mr. Palmer himself admits that the Council repudiated the word " consubstantial " as expressing the relation of the Son to the Father. But this was the precise point in dispute between the Orthodox and semi Arians.

Ancients and moderns unite in testifying to the general prevalence of Arianism at that time. Gregory Nazianzen says,[1] " Nam si perpaucos exceperis, ... omnes (pastores) tempori obsecuti sunt : hoc tantum inter eos discriminis fuit, quod alii citius, alii seriùs in eam fraudem inciderunt, atque, alii impietatis duces antistitesque se præbuerunt." Jerome says : " Ingemuit totus

[1] *Orat.* **xxi.** t. i. p. 387, edition Paris, 1609.

orbis terrarum, et Arianum se esse miratus est." [1]   He also says: [2]
" Ecclesia non parietibus consistit, sed in dogmatum veritate, Ecclesia ibi est ubi fides vera est.   Ceterum ante annos quindecim
aut viginti parietes omnes hic ecclesiarum hæretici (Ariani) pos-
sidebant, Ecclesia autem vera illic erat, ubi vera fides erat." It
is here asserted that the whole world had become Arian ; and that
all the churches were in the possession of heretics.   These statements must be taken with due allowance.   They nevertheless
prove that the great majority of the bishops had adopted the Arian,
or semi-Arian Creed.   To the same effect Athanasius says:
" Quæ nunc ecclesia libere Christum adorat? Si quidem ea, si
pia est, periculo subjacet ? . . . .   Nam si alicubi pii et
Christi studiosi (sunt autem ubique tales permulti) illi itidem, ut
Prophetæ et magnus ille Elias, absconduntur, ... et in
speluncas et cavernas terræ sese abstrudunt, aut in solitudine
aberrantes commorantur." [3]   Vincent of Lerins [4] says: " Ariano-
rum venenum non jam portiunculam quamdam, sed pene orbem
totum contaminaverat, adeo ut prope cunctis Latini sermonis epis-
copis partim vi partim fraude deceptis caligo quædam mentibus ef-
funderetur."   To these ancient testimonies any number of authorities from modern theologians might be added.   We give only the
testimony of Dr. Jackson, one of the most distinguished theologians of the Church of England : " After this defection of the
Romish Church in the bishop Liberius, the whole Roman empire
was overspread with Arianism." [5]

Whatever doubt may exist as to details, the general fact of this
apostasy cannot be doubted.   Through defection from the truth,
through the arts of the dominant party, through the influence of
the emperor, the great majority of the bishops did join in condemnation of Athanasius, and in subscribing a formula of doctrine
drawn up in opposition to the Nicene Creed ; a formula afterwards
renounced and condemned ; a formula which the Bishop of Rome
was banished for two years for refusing to sign, and restored to his
see when he consented to subscribe.   If, then, we apply to this
case the same rules which are applied to the decisions of the Nicene Council, it must be admitted that the external Church apostatized as truly under Constantius, as it professed the true faith under
Constantine.   If many signed the Eusebian or Arian formula in-

[1] *Dialogus contra Luciferanos*, 19, vol. ii. p. 172 c., edit. Migne, Paris, 1845.
[2] Comment. on Ps. cxxxiii., vol. vii. p. 1223 a, edit. Migne.
[3] " Ad Solitariam Vitam Agentes Epist.," *Works*, p. 846, edit. Paris, 1627.
[4] *Comm.* I. iv. p. 642, vol. l. Migne, *Patrol.*, Paris, 1846.
[5] *On the Church*, p. 160. Edited by W. Goode. Philadelphia, 1844.

sincerely, so did many hypocritically assent to the decrees of Nice. If many were overborne by authority and fear in the one case, so they were in the other. If many revoked their assent to Arianism, quite as many withdrew their consent to the Athanasian doctrine.

The Romish Evasion of this Argument.

In dealing with this undeniable fact, Romanists and Romanizers are forced to abandon their principle. Their doctrine is that the external Church cannot err, that the majority of the bishops living at any one time cannot fail to teach the truth. But under the reign of the Emperor Constantius, it is undeniable that the vast majority, including the Bishop of Rome, did renounce the truth. But, says Bellarmin,[1] the Church continued and was conspicuous in Athanasius, Hilary, Eusebius, and others. And Mr. Palmer, of Oxford says,[2] " The truth was preserved under even Arian bishops." But the question is not, whether the truth shall be preserved and confessed by the true children of God, but whether any external, organized body, and specially the Church of Rome, can err in its teaching. Romanists cannot be allowed, merely to meet an emergency, to avail themselves of the Protestant doctrine that the Church may consist of scattered believers. It is true as Jerome teaches in the passage above quoted, " Ubi fides vera est, ibi Ecclesia est." But that is our doctrine, and not the doctrine of Rome. Protestants say with full confidence, " Ecclesia manet et manebit." But whether in conspicuous glory as in the time of David, or in scattered believers as in the days of Elias, is not essential.

The Church of Rome rejects the Doctrines of Augustine.

A second case in which the external church (and specially the Church of Rome) has departed from what it had itself declared to be true, is in the rejection of the doctrines known in history as Augustinian. That the peculiar doctrines of Augustine, including the doctrine of sinful corruption of nature derived from Adam, which is spiritual death, and involves entire inability on the part of the sinner to convert himself or to coöperate in his own regeneration; the necessity of the certainly efficacious operation of divine grace; the sovereignty of God in election and reprobation, and the certain perseverance of the saints; were sanctioned by the whole Church, and specially by the Church of Rome, cannot be disputed. The eighteenth chapter of Wiggers' " Augustinianism and Pelagianism," is headed, " The final adoption of the Augustinian system

---

[1] *De Ecclesia*, lib. iii. c. 16.   [2] *On the Church*, vol. ii. p. 187.

for all Christendom by the third ecumenical council of Ephesus, A. D. 431." It is not denied that many of the eastern bishops, perhaps the majority of them, were secretly opposed to that system in its essential features. All that is insisted upon is that the whole Church, through what Romanists recognize as its official organs, gave its sanction to Augustine's peculiar doctrines; and that so far as the Latin Church is concerned this assent was not only for the time general but cordial. It is no less certain that the Council of Trent, while it condemned Pelagianism, and even the peculiar doctrine of semi-Pelagians, who said that man began the work of conversion, thus denying the necessity of preventing grace (*gratia preveniens*), nevertheless repudiated the distinguishing doctrines of Augustine and anathematized all who held them.

G.   *The Church of Rome now teaches Error.*

A fifth argument against the infallibility of the Church of Rome, is that, that Church now teaches error. Of this there can be no reasonable doubt, if the Scriptures be admitted as the standard of judgment.

1. It is a monstrous error, contrary to the Bible, to its letter and spirit, and shocking to the common sense of mankind, that the salvation of men should be suspended on their acknowledging the Pope to be the head of the Church in the world, or the vicar of Christ. This makes salvation independent of faith and character. A man may be sincere and intelligent in his faith in God and Christ, and perfectly exemplary in his Christian life, yet if he does not acknowledge the Pope, he must perish forever.

2. It is a grievous error, contrary to the express teachings of the Bible, that the sacraments are the only channels of communicating to men the benefits of redemption. In consequence of this false assumption, Romanists teach that all who die unbaptized, even infants, are lost.

3. It is a great error to teach as the Church of Rome does teach, that the ministers of the gospel are priests; that the people have no access to God or Christ, and cannot obtain the remission of sins or other saving blessings, except through their intervention and by their ministrations; that the priests have the power not only of declarative, but of judicial and effective absolution, so that those and those only whom they absolve stand acquitted at the bar of God. This was the grand reason for the Reformation, which was a rebellion against this priestly domination; a demand on the part of the people for the liberty wherewith Christ had made them free, —

the liberty to go immediately to him with their sins and sorrows, and find relief without the intervention or permission of any man who has no better right of access than themselves.

4. The doctrine of the merit of good works as taught by Romanists is another most prolific error. They hold that works done after regeneration have real merit (*meritum condigni*), and that they are the ground of the sinner's justification before God. They hold that a man may do more than the law requires of him, and perform works of supererogation, and thus obtain more merit than is necessary for his own salvation and beatification. That this superfluous merit goes into the treasury of the Church, and may be dispensed for the benefit of others. On this ground indulgences are granted or sold, to take effect not only in this life but in the life to come.

5. With this is connected the further error concerning Purgatory. The Church of Rome teaches that those dying in the communion of the Church, who have not in this life made full satisfaction for their sins, or acquired sufficient merit to entitle them to admission into heaven, do at death pass into a state of suffering, there to remain until due satisfaction is made and proper purification is effected. There is no necessary termination to this state of purgatory but the day of judgment or the end of the world. It may last for a thousand or many thousands of years. But Purgatory is under the power of the keys. The sufferings of souls in that state may be alleviated or shortened by the authorized ministers of the Church. There is no limit to the power of men who are believed to hold the keys of heaven in their hand, to shut and no man opens, and open and no man shuts. Of all incredibilities the most incredible is that God would commit such power as this, to weak, ignorant, and often wicked men.

6. The Romish Church teaches grievous error concerning the Lord's Supper. It teaches, (1.) That when consecrated by the priest the whole substance of the bread and the whole substance of the wine are transmuted into the substance of the body and blood of Christ. (2.) That as his body is inseparable from his soul and divinity, where the one is there the other must be. The whole Christ, therefore, body, soul, and divinity, is present in the consecrated wafer, which is to be worshipped as Christ himself is worshipped. This is the reason why the Church of England in her Homilies pronounces the service of the Mass in the Romish Church idolatrous. (3.) That Church further teaches that the body and blood of Christ thus locally and substantially present in the Eu-

charist are offered as a true propitiatory sacrifice for the forgiveness of sin, the application of which is determined by the intention of the officiating priests.

7. Idolatry consists not only in the worship of false gods, but in the worship of the true God by images. The second Commandment of the Decalogue expressly forbids the bowing down to, or serving the likeness of anything in heaven above or in the earth beneath. In the Hebrew the words used are, הִשְׁתַּחֲוָה and עָבַד. In the Septuagint the words are, οὐ προσκυνήσεις αὐτοῖς, οὐδὲ μὴ λατρεύσεις αὐτοῖς. In the Vulgate it reads, "Non adorabis ea neque coles." The precise thing, therefore, that is forbidden is that which the Church of Rome permits and enjoins, namely, the use of images in religious worship, prostration before them, and doing them reverence.

8. Another great error of the Church of Rome is the worship of saints and angels, and especially of the Virgin Mary. It is not merely that they are regarded as objects of reverence, but that the service rendered them involves the ascription of divine attributes. They are assumed to be everywhere present, able to hear and answer prayer, to help and to save. They become the ground of confidence to the people, and the objects of their religious affections. They are to them precisely what the gods of the heathen were to the Greeks and Romans.

Such are some of the errors taught by the Church of Rome, and they prove that that Church instead of being infallible, is so corrupt that it is the duty of the people of God to come out of it and to renounce its fellowship.

H. *The Recognition of an Infallible Church incompatible with either Religious or Civil Liberty.*

A church which claims to be infallible, *ipso facto*, claims to be the mistress of the world ; and those who admit its infallibility, thereby admit their entire subjection to its authority. It avails nothing to say that this infallibility is limited to matters of faith and morals, for under those heads is included the whole life of man, religious, moral, domestic, social, and political.

A church which claims the right to decide what is true in doctrine and obligatory in morals, and asserts the power to enforce submission to its decisions on the pain of eternal perdition, leaves no room for any other authority upon earth. In the presence of the authority of God, every other disappears.

With the claim to infallibility is inseparably connected the claim to pardon sin.   The Church does not assume merely the right to declare the conditions on which sin will be forgiven at the bar of God, but it asserts that it has the prerogative to grant, or to withhold that forgiveness.   "Ego te absolvo," is the formula the Church puts into the mouth of its priesthood.   Those who receive that absolution are saved ; those whom the Church refuses to absolve must bear the penalty of their offences.

An infallible church is thus the only institute of salvation. All within its pale are saved; all without it perish.   Those only are in the Church who believe what it teaches, who do what it commands, and are subject to its officers, and especially its head, the Roman pontiff.   Any man, therefore, whom the Church excommunicates is thereby shut out of the kingdom of heaven ; any nation placed under its ban is not only deprived of the consolations of religious services, but of the necessary means of salvation.

If the Church be infallible, its authority is no less absolute in the sphere of social and political life.   It is immoral to contract or to continue an unlawful marriage, to keep an unlawful oath, to enact unjust laws, to obey a sovereign hostile to the Church.   The Church, therefore, has the right to dissolve marriages, to free men from the obligations of their oaths, and citizens from their allegiance, to abrogate civil laws, and to depose sovereigns.   These prerogatives have not only been claimed, but time and again exercised by the Church of Rome.   They all of right belong to that Church, if it be infallible.   As these claims are enforced by penalties involving the loss of the soul, they cannot be resisted by those who admit the Church to be infallible.   It is obvious, therefore, that where this doctrine is held there can be no liberty of opinion, no freedom of conscience, no civil or political freedom.   As the recent ecumenical Council of the Vatican has decided that this infallibility is vested in the Pope, it is henceforth a matter of faith with Romanists, that the Roman pontiff is the absolute sovereign of the world.   All men are bound, on the penalty of eternal death, to believe what he declares to be true, and to do whatever he decides is obligatory.

CHAPTER VI.

THE PROTESTANT RULE OF FAITH.

§ 1. *Statement of the Doctrine."*

ALL Protestants agree in teaching that "the word of God, as contained in the Scriptures of the Old and New Testaments, is the only infallible rule of faith and practice."

In the Smalcald Articles,[1] the Lutheran Church says: "Ex patrum — verbis et factis non sunt exstruendi articuli fidei — Regulam autem aliam habemus, ut videlicet verbum Dei condat articulos fidei et præterea nemo, ne angelus quidem." In the "Form of Concord,"[2] it is said: "Credimus, confitemur et docemus, unicam regulam et normam secundum quam omnia dogmata omnesque doctores æstimari et judicari oporteat, nullam omnino aliam esse, quam prophetica et apostolica scripta cum V. tum N. Testamenti."

The symbols of the Reformed churches teach the same doctrine. Confessio Helvetica, II.[3] says: "In scriptura sancta habet universalis Christi Ecclesia plenissime exposita, quæcunque pertinent cum ad salvificam fidem, tum ad vitam Deo placentem.[4] Non alium in causa fidei judicem, quam ipsum Deum per Scripturas sacras pronuntiantem, quid verum sit, quid falsum, quid sequendum sit quidne fugiendum. Confessio Gallicana:[5] Quum hæc (SS.) sit omnis veritatis summa, complectens quidquid ad cultum Dei et salutem nostram requiritur, neque hominibus neque ipsis etiam angelis fas esse dicimus quicquam ei verbo adjicere vel detrahere vel quicquam prorsus in eo immutare." In the Thirty-Nine Articles of the Church of England,[6] it is said: "Holy Scripture containeth all things necessary to salvation: so that whatsoever is not read therein, nor may be proved thereby, is not to be required of any man, that it should be believed as an article of faith, or be thought requisite or necessary to salvation." The Westminster Confession[7] teaches: "Under the name of Holy Scripture, or the Word of God written, are now contained all the books of the Old and New Testament, which are these: etc. . . . . All

---

[1] Part ii. 2, 15; Hase *Lib. Sym.* p. 308.   [2] Page 570, *ibid.*
[3] C. i. p. 467, *ibid.*   [4] C. ii. p. 479, *ibid.*
[5] Art. v. p. 330, *ibid.*   [6] Art. 6.   [7] Ch. i. § 2.

which are given by inspiration of God, to be the rule of faith and life.[1] The whole counsel of God concerning all things necessary for his own glory, man's salvation, faith, and life, is either expressly set down in Scripture, or by good and necessary consequence may be deduced from Scripture; unto which nothing at any time is to be added whether by new revelations of the Spirit or traditions of men.[2] All things in Scripture are not alike plain in themselves, nor alike clear unto all; yet those things which are necessary to be known, believed, and observed, for salvation, are so clearly propounded and opened in some place of Scripture or other, that not only the learned, but the unlearned, in a due use of the ordinary means, may attain unto a sufficient understanding of them."

From these statements it appears that Protestants hold, (1.) That the Scriptures of the Old and New Testaments are the Word of God, written under the inspiration of the Holy Spirit, and are therefore infallible, and of divine authority in all things pertaining to faith and practice, and consequently free from all error whether of doctrine, fact, or precept. (2.) That they contain all the extant supernatural revelations of God designed to be a rule of faith and practice to his Church. (3.) That they are sufficiently perspicuous to be understood by the people, in the use of ordinary means and by the aid of the Holy Spirit, in all things necessary to faith or practice, without the need of any infallible interpreter.

The Canon.

Before entering on the consideration of these points, it is necessary to answer the question, What books are entitled to a place in the canon, or rule of faith and practice? Romanists answer this question by saying, that all those which the Church has decided to be divine in their origin, and none others, are to be thus received. Protestants answer it by saying, so far as the Old Testament is concerned, that those books, and those only, which Christ and his Apostles recognized as the written Word of God, are entitled to be regarded as canonical. This recognition was afforded in a twofold manner: First, many of the books of the Old Testament are quoted as the Word of God, as being given by the Spirit; or the Spirit is said to have uttered what is therein recorded. Secondly, Christ and his Apostles refer to the sacred writings of the Jews — the volume which they regarded as divine — as being what it claimed to be, the Word of God. When we refer to the Bible as

[2] *Ibid.* § 6.   [2] *Ibid.* § 7.

of divine authority, we refer to it as a volume and recognize all the writings which it contains as given by the inspiration of the Spirit. In like manner when Christ or his Apostles quote the " Scriptures," or the " law and the prophets," and speak of the volume then so called, they give their sanction to the divine authority of all the books which that volume contained. All, therefore, that is necessary to determine for Christians the canon of the Old Testament, is to ascertain what books were included in the " Scriptures " recognized by the Jews of that period. This is a point about which there is no reasonable doubt. The Jewish canon of the Old Testament included all the books and no others, which Protestants now recognize as constituting the Old Testament Scriptures. On this ground Protestants reject the so-called apocryphal books. They were not written in Hebrew and were not included in the canon of the Jews. They were, therefore, not recognized by Christ as the Word of God. This reason is of itself sufficient. It is however confirmed by considerations drawn from the character of the books themselves. They abound in errors, and in statements contrary to those found in the undoubtedly canonical books.

The principle on which the canon of the New Testament is determined is equally simple. Those books, and those only which can be proved to have been written by the Apostles, or to have received their sanction, are to be recognized as of divine authority. The reason of this rule is obvious. The Apostles were the duly authenticated messengers of Christ, of whom He said, " He that heareth you, heareth me."

§ 2. *The Scriptures are Infallible, i. e., given by Inspiration of God.*

The infallibility and divine authority of the Scriptures are due to the fact that they are the word of God ; and they are the word of God because they were given by the inspiration of the Holy Ghost.

A. *The Nature of Inspiration.   Definition.*

The nature of inspiration is to be learnt from the Scriptures ; from their didactic statements, and from their phenomena. There are certain general facts or principles which underlie the Bible, which are assumed in all its teachings, and which therefore must be assumed in its interpretation. We must, for example, assume, (1.) That God is not the unconscious ground of all things ; nor an unintelligent force ; nor a name for the moral order of the universe ; nor mere causality ; but a Spirit, — a self-conscious, intelligent, voluntary agent, possessing all the attributes of our spirits without limitation, and to an infinite degree. (2.) That He is the creator of the world, and extra-mundane, existing before, and independently of it; not its soul, life, or animating principle; but its maker, preserver, and ruler. (3.) That as a spirit He is everywhere present, and everywhere active, preserving and governing all his creatures and all their actions. (4.) That while both in the external world and in the world of mind He generally acts according to fixed laws and through secondary causes, He is free to act, and often does act immediately, or without the intervention of such causes, as in creation, regeneration, and miracles. (5.) That the Bible contains a divine, or supernatural revelation. The present question is not, Whether the Bible is what it claims to be; but, What does it teach as to the nature and effects of the influence under which it was written?

On this subject the common doctrine of the Church is, and ever has been, that inspiration was an influence of the Holy Spirit on the minds of certain select men, which rendered them the organs of God for the infallible communication of his mind and will. They were in such a sense the organs of God, that what they said God said.

B. *Inspiration Supernatural.*

This definition includes several distinct points. First. Inspiration is a supernatural influence. It is thus distinguished, on the one hand, from the providential agency of God, which is everywhere and always in operation; and on the other hand, from the gracious operations of the Spirit on the hearts of his people. According to the Scriptures, and the common views of men, a marked distinction is to be made between those effects which are due to the efficiency of God operating regularly through second causes, and those which are produced by his immediate efficiency without the intervention of such causes. The one class of effects is natural; the other, supernatural. Inspiration belongs to the latter class. It is not a natural effect due to the inward state of its subject, or to the influence of external circumstances.

No less obvious is the distinction which the Bible makes between the gracious operations of the Spirit and those by which extraordinary gifts are bestowed upon particular persons. Inspiration, therefore, is not to be confounded with spiritual illumination. They differ, first, as to their subjects. The subjects of inspiration are a few selected persons; the subjects of spiritual illumination are all true believers. And, secondly, they differ as to their design. The design of the former is to render certain men infallible as teachers ; the design of the latter is to render men holy ; and of course they differ as to their effects. Inspiration in itself has no sanctifying influence. Balaam was inspired. Saul was among the prophets. Caiaphas uttered a prediction which " he spake not of himself." (John xi. 51.) In the last day many will be able to say to Christ, "Lord, Lord, have we not prophesied in thy name? and in thy name have cast out devils? and in thy name done many wonderful works?" To whom he will say : " I never knew you ; depart from me, ye that work iniquity." (Matt. vii. 22, 23.)

C. *Distinction between Revelation and Inspiration.*

Second. The above definition assumes a difference between revelation and inspiration. They differ, first, as to their object. The object of revelation is the communication of knowledge. The object or design of inspiration is to secure infallibility in teaching. Consequently they differ, secondly, in their effects. The effect of revelation was to render its recipient wiser. The effect of inspiration was to preserve him from error in teaching. These two gifts were often enjoyed by the same person at the same time. That is, the Spirit often imparted knowledge, and controlled in its communication orally or in writing to others. This was no doubt the case with the Psalmists, and often with the Prophets and Apostles. Often, however, the revelations were made at one time, and were subsequently, under the guidance of the Spirit, committed to writing. Thus the Apostle Paul tells us that he received his knowledge of the gospel not from man, but by revelation from Jesus Christ ; and this knowledge he communicated from time to time in his discourses and epistles. In many cases these gifts were separated. Many of the sacred writers, although inspired, received no revelations. This was probably the fact with the authors of the historical books of the Old Testament. The evangelist Luke does not refer his knowledge of the events which he records to revelation, but says he derived it from those " which from the beginning were eyewitnesses, and ministers of the Word." (Luke i. 2.) It is immaterial to us where Moses obtained his knowledge of the events recorded in the book of Genesis ; whether from early documents, from tradition, or from direct revelation. No more causes are to be assumed for any effect than are necessary. If the sacred writers had sufficient sources of knowledge in themselves, or in those about them, there is no need to assume any direct revelation. It is enough for us that they were rendered infallible as teachers.

This distinction between revelation and inspiration is commonly
made by systematic writers. Thus Quenstedt (1685) [1] says: "Dis-
tingue inter revelationem et inspirationem. Revelatio vi vocis est
manifestatio rerum ignotarum et occultarum, et potest fieri multis
et diversis modis. . . . . Inspiratio . . . . est interna conceptum
suggestio, seu infusio, sive res conceptæ jam ante scriptori fuerint
cognitæ, sive occultæ. Illa potuit tempore antecedere scriptionem,
hæc cum scriptione semper fuit conjuncta et in ipsam scriptionem
influebat." Often, however, the distinction in question is overlooked. In popular language, inspiration is made to include both
the supernatural communication of truth to the mind, and a supernatural control in making known that truth to others. The two
gifts, however, differ in their nature, and should therefore be distinguished. Confounding them has sometimes led to serious error.
When no revelation was necessary, no inspiration is admitted.
Thus Grotius says: " Vere dixi non omnes libros qui sunt in He-
bræo Canone dictatos a Spiritu Sancto. Scriptos esse cum pio
animi motu, non nego; et hoc est quod judicavit Synagoga Magna,
cujus judicio in hac re stant Hebræi. Sed a Spiritu Sancto dictari
historias nihil fuit opus: satis fuit scriptorem memoria valere circa
res spectatas, aut diligentia in describendis veterum commentariis." [2]
It is an illogical conclusion, however, to infer that because a historian did not need to have the facts dictated to him, that therefore
he needed no control to preserve him from error.

D. *Inspired Men the Organs of God.*

A third point included in the Church doctrine of inspiration is,
that the sacred writers were the organs of God, so that what they
taught, God taught. It is to be remembered, however, that when
God uses any of his creatures as his instruments, He uses them
according to their nature. He uses angels as angels, men as
men, the elements as elements. Men are intelligent voluntary
agents; and as such were made the organs of God. The sacred
writers were not made unconscious or irrational. The spirits of the
prophets were subject to the prophets. (1 Cor. xiv. 32.) They
were not like calculating machines which grind out logarithms with
infallible correctness. The ancients, indeed, were accustomed to
say, as some theologians have also said, that the sacred writers were
as pens in the hand of the Spirit; or as harps, from which He drew
what sounds He pleased. These representations were, however,

---

[1] *Theologia,* i. iv. ii. quæst. iii. ἔχθεσις, 3; edit. Wittenberg, 1685, p. 68, a.
[2] " Votum pro Pace Ecclesiastica." *Opera,* Londini, 1679, t. iii. p. 672.

intended simply to illustrate one point, namely, that the words uttered or recorded by inspired men were the words of God. The Church has never held what has been stigmatized as the mechanical theory of inspiration. The sacred writers were not machines. Their self-consciousness was not suspended; nor were their intellectual powers superseded. Holy men spake as they were moved by the Holy Ghost. It was men, not machines; not unconscious instruments, but living, thinking, willing minds, whom the Spirit used as his organs. Moreover, as inspiration did not involve the suspension or suppression of the human faculties, so neither did it interfere with the free exercise of the distinctive mental characteristics of the individual. If a Hebrew was inspired, he spake Hebrew; if a Greek, he spake Greek; if an educated man, he spoke as a man of culture; if uneducated, he spoke as such a man is wont to speak. If his mind was logical, he reasoned, as Paul did; if emotional and contemplative, he wrote as John wrote. All this is involved in the fact that God uses his instruments according to their nature. The sacred writers impressed their peculiarities on their several productions as plainly as though they were the subjects of no extraordinary influence. This is one of the phenomena of the Bible patent to the most cursory reader. It lies in the very nature of inspiration that God spake in the language of men ; that He uses men as his organs, each according to his peculiar gifts and endowments. When He ordains praise out of the mouth of babes, they must speak as babes, or the whole power and beauty of the tribute will be lost. There is no reason to believe that the operation of the Spirit in inspiration revealed itself any more in the consciousness of the sacred writers, than his operations in sanctification reveal themselves in the consciousness of the Christian. As the believer seems to himself to act, and in fact does act out of his own nature ; so the inspired penmen wrote out of the fulness of their own thoughts and feelings, and employed the language and modes of expression which to them were the most natural and appropriate. Nevertheless, and none the less, they spoke as they were moved by the Holy Ghost, and their words were his words.

E. *Proof of the Doctrine.*

That this is the Scriptural view of inspiration; that inspired men were the organs of God in such a sense that their words are to be received not as the words of men, but as they are in truth, as the words of God (1 Thess. ii. 13), is proved, —

1. From the signification and usage of the word. It is, of

course, admitted that words are to be understood in their historical sense.   If it can be shown what idea the men living in the
apostolic age attached to the word θεόπνευστος and its equivalents,
that is the idea which the Apostles intended to express by them.
All nations have entertained the belief not only that God has access
to the human mind and can control its operations, but that He at
times did take such possession of particular persons as to make them
the organs of his communications.   Such persons were called by
the Greeks θεοφόροι (those who bore a God within them) ; or,
ἔνθεος (those in whom a God dwelt).   In the Septuagint the word
πνευματοφόρος is used in the same sense.   In Josephus,[1] the idea is
expressed by the phrase " τῷ θείῳ πνεύματι κεκινήμενος ; " to which the
words of Peter (2 Peter i. 21) exactly answer, ὑπὸ πνεύματος φερόμ
ενοι; and what is written by men under this influence of the Spirit
is called γραφὴ θεόπνευστος.   (2 Tim. iii. 16.)   Gregory of Nyssa,[2]
having quoted the words of our Lord in Matt. xxii. 43, " How then
doth David in Spirit call him Lord," adds, οὐκοῦν τῇ δυνάμει τοῦ Πνεύ
ματος οἱ θεοφορούμενοι τῶν ἁγίων ἐμπνέονται, καὶ διὰ τοῦτο πᾶσα γραφὴ θεόπνευστος λέγεται, διὰ τὸ τῆς θείας ἐμπνεύσεως εἶναι διδασκαλίαν, that is,
" Hence those of the saints who by the power of the Spirit are full
of God are inspired, and therefore all Scripture is called θεόπνευστος,
because the instruction is by divine inspiration."   The idea of inspiration is therefore fixed.   It is not to be arbitrarily determined.
We must not interpret the word or the fact, according to our theories of the relation of God to the world, but according to the
usage of antiquity, sacred and profane, and according to the doctrine which the sacred writers and the men of their generation are
known to have entertained on the subject.   According to all antiquity, an inspired man was one who was the organ of God in what
he said, so that his words were the words of the god of which he
was the organ.   When, therefore, the sacred writers use the same
words and forms of expression which the ancients used to convey
that idea, they must in all honesty be assumed to mean the same
thing.

Argument from the Meaning of the Word Prophet.

2. That this is the Scriptural idea of inspiration is further proved
from the meaning of the word prophet.   The sacred writers divide
the Scriptures into the " law and the prophets."   As the law was
written by Moses, and as Moses was the greatest of the prophets,
it follows that all the Old Testament was written by prophets.   If,
therefore, we can determine the Scriptural idea of a prophet, we

---

[1] *Antiquities*, iv. 6, 5.   [2] *Contra Eunomium Orat.* vi. t. ii. p. 187; Paris, 1615.

shall thereby determine the character of their writings and the authority due to them. A prophet, then, in the Scriptural sense of the term, is a spokesman, one who speaks for another, in his name, and by his authority; so that it is not the spokesman but the person for whom he acts, who is responsible for the truth of what is said. In Exodus vii. 1, it is said, "See, I have made thee a god to Pharaoh; and Aaron thy brother shall be thy prophet," *i. e.*, thy spokesman. This is explained by what is said in Exodus iv. 14–16, "Is not Aaron the Levite thy brother? I know that he can speak well. . . . . Thou shalt speak unto him, and put words into his mouth; and I will be with thy mouth, and with his mouth, and will teach you what ye shall do. And he shall be thy spokesman unto the people; and he shall be, even he shall be, to thee instead of a mouth, and thou shalt be to him instead of God." (See Jeremiah xxxvi. 17, 18.) This determines definitely, what a prophet is. He is the mouth of God; one through whom God speaks to the people; so that what the prophet says God says. So when a prophet was consecrated, it was said, "Behold, I have put my words in thy mouth." (Jer. i. 9; Is. li. 16.) That this is the Scriptural idea of a prophet is moreover evident from the formulas, constantly recurring, which relate to his duties and mission. He was the messenger of God; he spoke in the name of God; the words, "Thus saith the Lord," were continually in his mouth. "The word of the Lord" is said to have come to this prophet and on that; "the Spirit came upon," "the power," or "hand" of God was upon him; all implying that the prophet was the organ of God, that what he said, he said in God's name and by his authority. It is true, therefore, as Philo [1] says, προφήτης γάρ ἴδιον οὐδὲν ἀποφθέγγεται ἀλλότρια δὲ πάντα ὑπηχοῦντος ἑτέρου.

This is precisely what the Apostle Peter teaches when he says (2 Peter i. 20, 21), "No prophecy of the Scripture is of any private interpretation. For the prophecy came not in old time by the will of man: but holy men spake as they were moved (φερόμενοι, *borne along* as a ship by the wind) by the Holy Ghost." Prophecy, *i. e.*, what a prophet said, was not human, but divine. It was not the prophet's own interpretation of the mind and will of God. He spoke as the organ of the Holy Ghost.

What the Prophets said God said.

3. It is another decisive proof that the sacred writers were the organs of God in the sense above stated, that whatever they said

---

[1] *Opera*, t. iv. p. 116, ed. Pfeiff.

the Spirit is declared to have said. Christ himself said that David
by the Spirit called the Messiah Lord. (Matt. xxii. 43.) David
in the 95th Psalm said, " To-day if ye will hear his voice, harden
not your heart; " but the Apostle (Heb. iii. 7), says that these
were the words of the Holy Ghost. Again, in ch. x. 15, the same
Apostle says, " Whereof the Holy Ghost also is a witness to us:
for after that he had said before, This is the covenant that I will
make with them after those days, saith the Lord." Thus quoting
the language of Jeremiah xxxi. 33, as the language of the Holy
Ghost. In Acts iv. 25, the assembled Apostles said, " with one
accord," " Lord thou art God. . . . . Who by the mouth of
thy servant David hast said, Why did the heathen rage ? " In
Acts xxviii. 25, Paul said to the Jews, " Well spake the Holy
Ghost by Esaias the prophet unto our fathers." It is in this way
that Christ and his Apostles constantly refer to the Scriptures,
showing beyond doubt that they believed and taught, that what the
sacred writers said the Holy Ghost said.

Inspiration of the New Testament Writers.

This proof bears specially, it is true, only on the writings of the
Old Testament. But no Christian puts the inspiration of the Old
Testament above that of the New. The tendency, and we may
even say the evidence, is directly the other way. If the Scriptures
of the old economy were given by inspiration of God, much more
were those writings which were penned under the dispensation of
the Spirit. Besides, the inspiration of the Apostles is proved,
(1.) From the fact that Christ promised them the Holy Spirit,
who should bring all things to their remembrance, and render
them infallible in teaching. It is not you, He said, that speak,
but the Spirit of my Father speaketh in you. He that heareth
you heareth me. He forbade them to enter upon their office
as teachers until they were endued with power from on high.
(2.) This promise was fulfilled on the day of Pentecost, when the
Spirit descended upon the Apostles as a mighty rushing wind, and
they were filled with the Holy Ghost, and began to speak as
the Spirit gave them utterance (*dabat eloqui*, as the Vulgate more
literally renders the words). From this moment they were new
men, with new views, with new spirit, and with new power and
authority. The change was sudden. It was not a development.
It was something altogether supernatural; as when God said, Let
there be light, and there was light. Nothing can be more unreasonable than to ascribe this sudden transformation of the Apostles

from narrow-minded, bigoted Jews, into enlightened, large-minded, catholic Christians, to mere natural causes. Their Jewish prejudices had resisted all the instructions and influence of Christ for three years, but gave way in a moment when the Spirit came upon them from on high. (3.) After the day of Pentecost the Apostles claimed to be the infallible organs of God in all their teachings. They required men to receive what they taught not as the word of man but as the word of God (1 Thess. ii. 13); they declared, as Paul does (1 Cor. xiv. 37), that the things which they wrote were the commandments of the Lord. They made the salvation of men to depend on faith in the doctrines which they taught. Paul pronounces anathema even an angel from heaven who should preach any other gospel than that which he had taught. (Gal. i. 8.) John says that whoever did not receive the testimony which he bore concerning Christ, made God a liar, because John's testimony was God's testimony. (1 John v. 10.) "He that knoweth God, heareth us; he that is not of God, heareth not us." (iv. 6.) This assertion of infallibility, this claim for the divine authority of their teaching, is characteristic of the whole Bible. The sacred writers all, and everywhere, disclaim personal authority; they never rest the obligation to faith in their teachings, on their own knowledge or wisdom; they never rest it on the truth of what they taught as manifest to reason or as capable of being proved by argument. They speak as messengers, as witnesses, as organs. They declare that what they said God said, and, therefore, on his authority it was to be received and obeyed.

The Testimony of Paul.

The Corinthians objected to Paul's preaching that he did not attempt any rational or philosophical proof of the doctrines which he propounded; that his language and whole manner of discourse were not in accordance with rhetorical rules. He answers these objections, — first, by saying that the doctrines which he taught were not the truths of reason, were not derived from the wisdom of men, but were matters of divine revelation; that he simply taught what God declared to be true; and secondly, that as to the manner of presenting these truths, he was the mere organ of the Spirit of God. In 1 Cor. ii. 7–13, he sets forth this whole subject in the clearest and most concise manner. The things which he taught, which he calls "the wisdom of God," "the things of the Spirit," i. e., the gospel, the system of doctrine taught in the Bible, he says, had never entered into the mind of man. God had re-

vealed those truths by his Spirit; for the Spirit is the only competent source of such knowledge. "For what man knoweth the
things of a man, save the spirit of man which is in him? even so,
the things of God knoweth no man, but the Spirit of God." So
much for the source of knowledge, and the ground on which the
doctrines he taught were to be received. As to the second objection, which concerned his language and mode of presentation, he
says, These things of the Spirit, thus revealed, we teach "not in
the words which man's wisdom teacheth; but which the Holy
Ghost teacheth," πνευματικοῖς πνευματικὰ συγκρίνοντες, combining spiritual with spiritual, i. e., clothing the truths of the Spirit in the
words of the Spirit. There is neither in the Bible nor in the writings of men, a simpler or clearer statement of the doctrines of
revelation and inspiration. Revelation is the act of communicating divine knowledge by the Spirit to the mind. Inspiration is the
act of the same Spirit, controlling those who make the truth known
to others. The thoughts, the truths made known, and the words in
which they are recorded, are declared to be equally from the Spirit.
This, from first to last, has been the doctrine of the Church, notwithstanding the endless diversity of speculations in which theologians have indulged on the subject. This then is the ground
on which the sacred writers rested their claims. They were the
mere organs of God. They were his messengers. Those who
heard them, heard God; and those who refused to hear them,
refused to hear God. (Matt. x. 40; John xiii. 20.)

4. This claim to infallibility on the part of the Apostles was duly
authenticated, not only by the nature of the truths which they communicated, and by the power which those truths have ever exerted
over the minds and hearts of men, but also by the inward witness
of the Spirit of which St. John speaks, when he says, "He that
believeth on the Son of God hath the witness in himself" (1 John
v. 10); "an unction from the Holy One." (1 John ii. 20.) It
was confirmed also by miraculous gifts. As soon as the Apostles
were endued with power from on high, they spake in "other
tongues;" they healed the sick, restored the lame and the blind.
"God also," as the Apostle says (Heb. ii. 4), "bearing them witness, both with signs, and wonders, and with divers miracles, and
gifts of the Holy Ghost, according to his own will." And Paul
tells the Corinthians that the signs of an Apostle had been wrought
among them "in all patience, in signs, and wonders, and mighty
deeds." (2 Cor. xii. 12.) The mere working of miracles was not
an evidence of a divine commission as a teacher. But when a

man claims to be the organ of God, when he says that God speaks through him, then his working of miracles is the testimony of God to the validity of his claims. And such testimony God gave to the infallibility of the Apostles.

The above considerations are sufficient to show, that according to the Scriptures, inspired men were the organs, or mouth of God, in the sense that what they said and taught has the sanction and authority of God.

F. *Inspiration extends equally to all Parts of Scripture.*

This is the fourth element of the Church doctrine on this subject. It means, first, that all the books of Scripture are equally inspired. All alike are infallible in what they teach. And secondly, that inspiration extends to all the contents of these several books. It is not confined to moral and religious truths, but extends to the statements of facts, whether scientific, historical, or geographical. It is not confined to those facts the importance of which is obvious, or which are involved in matters of doctrine. It extends to everything which any sacred writer asserts to be true.

This is proved, (1) Because it is involved in, or follows as a necessary consequence from, the proposition that the sacred writers were the organs of God. If what they assert, God asserts, which, as has been shown, is the Scriptural idea of inspiration, their assertions must be free from error. (2.) Because our Lord expressly says, " The Scripture cannot be broken " (John x. 35), *i. e.,* it cannot err. (3.) Because Christ and his Apostles refer to all parts of the Scriptures, or to the whole volume, as the word of God. They make no distinction as to the authority of the Law, the Prophets, or the Hagiographa. They quote the Pentateuch, the historical books, the Psalms, and the Prophets, as all and equally the word of God. (4.) Because Christ and the writers of the New Testament refer to all classes of facts recorded in the Old Testament as infallibly true. Not only doctrinal facts, such as those of the creation and probation of man ; his apostasy ; the covenant with Abraham ; the giving the law upon Mount Sinai ; not only great historical facts, as the deluge, the deliverance of the people out of Egypt, the passage of the Red Sea, and the like ; but incidental circumstances, or facts of apparently minor importance, as *e. g.* that Satan tempted our first parents in the form of a serpent ; that Moses lifted up a serpent in the wilderness ; that Elijah healed Naaman, the Syrian, and was sent to the widow in Sarepta ; that David ate the shew-bread in the temple ; and even that great stumbling-block, that Jonah was three days in the whale's belly, are all referred to by our Lord and his Apostles with the sublime simplicity and confidence with which they are received by little children. (5.) It lies in the very idea of the Bible, that God chose some men to write history; some to indite psalms; some to unfold the future; some to teach doctrines. All were equally his organs, and each was infallible in his own sphere. As the principle of vegetable life pervades the whole plant, the root, stem, and flower; as the life of the body belongs as much to the feet as to the head, so the Spirit of God pervades the whole Scripture, and is not more in one part than in another. Some members of the body are more important than others; and some books of the Bible could be far better spared than others. There may be as great a difference between St. John's Gospel and the Book of Chronicles as between a man's brain and his hair; nevertheless the life of the body is as truly in the hair as in the brain.

G. *The Inspiration of the Scriptures extends to the Words.*

1. This again is included in the infallibility which our Lord ascribes to the Scriptures. A mere human report or record of a divine revelation must of necessity be not only fallible, but more or less erroneous.

2. The thoughts are in the words. The two are inseparable. If the words, priest, sacrifice, ransom, expiation, propitiation, purification by blood, and the like, have no divine authority, then the doctrine which they embody has no such authority.

3. Christ and his Apostles argue from the very words of Scripture. Our Lord says that David by the Spirit called the Messiah Lord, *i. e.*, David used that word. It was in the use of a particular word, that Christ said (John x. 35), that the Scriptures cannot be broken. "If he call them gods unto whom the word of God came, and the Scripture cannot be broken," etc. The use of that word, therefore, according to Christ's view of the Scripture, was determined by the Spirit of God. Paul, in Gal. iii. 16, lays stress on the fact, that in the promise made to Abraham, a word used is singular and not plural, "seed," "as of one," and not "seeds as of many." Constantly it is the very words of Scripture which are quoted as of divine authority.

4. The very form in which the doctrine of inspiration is taught in the Bible, assumes that the organs of God in the communication of his will were controlled by Him in the words which they used. "I have put my words in thy mouth." (Jer. i. 9.) "It is not ye

that speak, but the Spirit of your Father which speaketh in you."
(Matt. x. 20.)   They spake " as the Spirit gave them utterance."
(Acts ii. 4.)   " Holy men of God spake as they were moved by
the Holy Ghost."   (2 Pet. i. 21.)   All these, and similar modes
of expression with which the Scriptures abound, imply that the
words uttered were the words of God.   This, moreover, is the
very idea of inspiration as understood by the ancient world.   The
words of the oracle were assumed to be the words of the divinity,
and not those selected by the organ of communication.   And this,
too, as has been shown, was the idea attached to the gift of prophecy.   The words of the prophet were the words of God, or he
could not be God's spokesman and mouth.   It has also been shown
that in the most formally didactic passage in the whole Bible on
this subject (1 Cor. ii. 10–13), the Apostle expressly asserts that the
truths revealed by the Spirit, he communicated in words taught by
the Spirit.

Plenary Inspiration.

The view presented above is known as the doctrine of plenary
inspiration.   Plenary is opposed to partial.   The Church doctrine
denies that inspiration is confined to parts of the Bible ; and affirms that it applies to all the books of the sacred canon.   It denies
that the sacred writers were merely partially inspired ; it asserts
that they were fully inspired as to all that they teach, whether of
doctrine or fact.   This of course does not imply that the sacred
writers were infallible except for the special purpose for which
they were employed.   They were not imbued with plenary knowledge.   As to all matters of science, philosophy, and history, they
stood on the same level with their contemporaries.   They were infallible only as teachers, and when acting as the spokesmen of God.
Their inspiration no more made them astronomers than it made
them agriculturists.   Isaiah was infallible in his predictions, although
he shared with his countrymen the views then prevalent as to the
mechanism of the universe.   Paul could not err in anything he
taught, although he could not recollect how many persons he had
baptized in Corinth.   The sacred writers also, doubtless, differed
as to insight into the truths which they taught.   The Apostle Peter
intimates that the prophets searched diligently into the meaning of
their own predictions.   When David said God had put " all things "
under the feet of man, he probably little thought that " all things "
meant the whole universe.   (Heb. ii. 8.)   And Moses, when he
recorded the promise that childless Abraham was to be the father
" of many nations," little thought that it meant the whole world.

(Rom. iv. 13). Nor does the Scriptural doctrine on this subject imply that the sacred writers were free from errors in conduct. Their infallibility did not arise from their holiness, nor did inspiration render them holy. Balaam was inspired, and Saul was among the prophets. David committed many crimes, although inspired to write psalms. Peter erred in conduct at Antioch; but this does not prove that he erred in teaching. The influence which preserved him from mistakes in teaching was not designed to preserve him from mistakes in conduct.

H.   *General Considerations in Support of the Doctrine.*

On this point little need be said. If the questions, What is the Scriptural doctrine concerning inspiration? and, What is the true doctrine? be considered different, then after showing what the Scriptures teach on the subject, it would be necessary to prove that what they teach is true. This, however, is not the position of the Christian theologian. It is his business to set forth what the Bible teaches. If the sacred writers assert that they are the organs of God; that what they taught He taught through them; that they spoke as they were moved by the Holy Ghost, so that what they said the Holy Spirit said, then, if we believe their divine mission, we must believe what they teach as to the nature of the influence under which they spoke and wrote. This is the reason why in the earlier period of the Church there was no separate discussion of the doctrine of inspiration. That was regarded as involved in the divine origin of the Scriptures. If they are a revelation from God, they must be received and obeyed; but they cannot be thus received without attributing to them divine authority, and they cannot have such authority without being infallible in all they teach.

The organic unity of the Scriptures proves them to be the product of one mind. They are not only so united that we cannot believe one part without believing the whole; we cannot believe the New Testament without believing the Old; we cannot believe the Prophets without believing the Law; we cannot believe Christ without believing his Apostles; but besides all this they present the regular development, carried on through centuries and millenniums, of the great original promise, " The seed of the woman shall bruise the serpent's head." This development was conducted by some forty independent writers, many of whom understood very little of the plan they were unfolding, but each contributed his part to the progress and completion of the whole.

If the Bible be the work of one mind, that mind must be the

mind of God. He only knows the end from the beginning. He only could know what the Bible reveals. No one, says the Apostle, knows the things of God but the Spirit of God. He only could reveal the nature, the thoughts, and purposes of God. He only could tell whether sin can be pardoned. No one knows the Son but the Father. The revelation of the person and work of Christ is as clearly the work of God as are the heavens in all their majesty and glory.

Besides, we have the witness in ourselves. We find that the truths revealed in the Bible have the same adaptation to our souls that the atmosphere has to our bodies. The body cannot live without air, which it receives and appropriates instinctively, with full confidence in its adaptation to the end designed. In like manner the soul receives and appropriates the truths of Scripture as the atmosphere in which alone it can breathe and live. Thus in receiving the Bible as true, we necessarily receive it as divine. In believing it as a supernatural revelation, we believe its plenary inspiration.

This doctrine involves nothing out of analogy with the ordinary operations of God. We believe that He is everywhere present in the material world, and controls the operations of natural causes. We know that He causes the grass to grow, and gives rain and fruitful seasons. We believe that He exercises a like control over the minds of men, turning them as the rivers of water are turned. All religion, natural and revealed, is founded on the assumption of this providential government of God. Besides this, we believe in the gracious operations of his Spirit, by which He works in the hearts of his people to will and to do ; we believe that faith, repentance, and holy living are due to the ever-present influence of the Holy Spirit. If, then, this wonder-working God everywhere operates in nature and in grace, why should it be deemed incredible that holy men should speak as they were moved by the Holy Ghost, so that they should say just what He would have them say, so that their words should be his words.

After all Christ is the great object of the Christian's faith. We believe him and we believe everything else on his authority. He hands us the Old Testament and tells us that it is the Word of God ; that its authors spoke by the Spirit ; that the Scriptures cannot be broken. And we believe on his testimony. His testimony to his Apostles is no less explicit, although given in a different way. He promised to give them a mouth and a wisdom which their adversaries could not gainsay or resist. He told them to take no thought what they should say, " For the Holy Ghost shall

teach you in the same hour what ye ought to say." (Luke xii.
12.) " It is not ye that speak but the Spirit of your Father which
speaketh in you." He said to them " he that receiveth you receiveth me "; and He prayed for those who should believe on Him
through their word. We believe the Scriptures, therefore, because
Christ declares them to be the Word of God. Heaven and earth
may pass away, but his word cannot pass away.

I. *Objections.*

A large class of the objections to the doctrine of inspiration,
which for many minds are the most effective, arise from the rejection of one or other of the presumptions specified on a preceding
page. If a man denies the existence of a personal, extramundane
God, he must deny the doctrine of inspiration, but it is not necessary in order to prove that doctrine that we should first prove the
being of God. If he denies that God exerts any direct efficiency
in the government of the world, and holds that everything is the
product of fixed laws, he cannot believe what the Scriptures teach
of inspiration. If the supernatural be impossible, inspiration is
impossible. It will be found that most of the objections, especially
those of recent date, are founded on unscriptural views of the relation of God to the world, or on the peculiar philosophical views
of the objectors as to the nature of man or of his free agency.

A still larger class of objections is founded on misconceptions of
the doctrine. Such objections are answered by the correct statement of what the Church believes on the subject. Even a man so
distinguished for knowledge and ability as Coleridge, speaks with
contempt of what he regards as the common theory of inspiration,
when he utterly misunderstands the real doctrine which he opposes.
He says : " All the miracles which the legends of monk or rabbi
contain, can scarcely be put in competition, on the score of complication, inexplicableness, the absence of all intelligible use or purpose, and of circuitous self-frustration, with those that must be
assumed by the maintainers of this doctrine, in order to give effect
to the series of miracles by which all the nominal composers of the
Hebrew nation before the time of Ezra, of whom there are any remains, were successively transformed into *automaton* compositors,"[1]
etc. But if the Church doctrine of inspiration no more assumes
that the sacred writers " were transformed into automaton compositors," than that every believer is thus transformed in whom God
" works to will and to do," then all such objections amount to

[1] " Confessions of an Inquiring Spirit," *Works*, Harpers, N. Y., 1853, vol. v. p. 612.

nothing. If God, without interfering with a man's free agency, can make it infallibly certain that he will repent and believe, He can render it certain that he will not err in teaching. It is in vain to profess to hold the common doctrine of Theism, and yet assert that God cannot control rational creatures without turning them into machines.

Discrepancies and Errors.

But although the theologian may rightfully dismiss all objections founded on the denial of the common principles of natural and revealed religion, there are others which cannot be thus summarily disposed of. The most obvious of these is, that the sacred writers contradict each other, and that they teach error. It is, of course, useless to contend that the sacred writers were infallible, if in point of fact they err. Our views of inspiration must be determined by the phenomena of the Bible as well as from its didactic statements. If in fact the sacred writers retain each his own style and mode of thought, then we must renounce any theory which assumes that inspiration obliterates or suppresses all individual peculiarities. If the Scriptures abound in contradictions and errors, then it is vain to contend that they were written under an influence which precludes all error. The question, therefore, is a question of fact. Do the sacred writers contradict each other? Do the Scriptures teach what from any source can be proved not to be true? The question is not whether the views of the sacred writers were incorrect, but whether they taught error? For example, it is not the question Whether they thought that the earth is the centre of our system? but, Did they teach that it is?

The objection under consideration, namely, that the Bible contains errors, divides itself into two. The first, that the sacred writers contradict themselves, or one the other. The second, that the Bible teaches what is inconsistent with the facts of history or science.

As to the former of these objections, it would require, not a volume, but volumes to discuss all the cases of alleged discrepancies. All that can be expected here is a few general remarks : (1.) These apparent discrepancies, although numerous, are for the most part trivial ; relating in most cases to numbers or dates. (2.) The great majority of them are only apparent, and yield to careful examination. (3.) Many of them may fairly be ascribed to errors of transcribers. (4.) The marvel and the miracle is that there are so few of any real importance. Considering that the different books of the Bible were written not only by different authors, but by men of all degrees of culture, living in the course of fifteen hundred or two thousand years, it is altogether unaccountable that they should agree perfectly, on any other hypothesis than that the writers were under the guidance of the Spirit of God. In this respect, as in all others, the Bible stands alone. It is enough to impress any mind with awe, when it contemplates the Sacred Scriptures filled with the highest truths, speaking with authority in the name of God, and so miraculously free from the soiling touch of human fingers. The errors in matters of fact which skeptics search out bear no proportion to the whole. No sane man would deny that the Parthenon was built of marble, even if here and there a speck of sandstone should be detected in its structure. Not less unreasonable is it to deny the inspiration of such a book as the Bible, because one sacred writer says that on a given occasion twenty-four thousand, and another says that twenty-three thousand, men were slain. Surely a Christian may be allowed to tread such objections under his feet.

Admitting that the Scriptures do contain, in a few instances, discrepancies which with our present means of knowledge, we are unable satisfactorily to explain, they furnish no rational ground for denying their infallibility. " The Scripture cannot be broken." (John x. 35.) This is the whole doctrine of plenary inspiration, taught by the lips of Christ himself. The universe teems with evidences of design, so manifold, so diverse, so wonderful, as to overwhelm the mind with the conviction that it has had an intelligent author. Yet here and there isolated cases of monstrosity appear. It is irrational, because we cannot account for such cases, to deny that the universe is the product of intelligence. So the Christian need not renounce his faith in the plenary inspiration of the Bible, although there may be some things about it in its present state which he cannot account for.

Historical and Scientific Objections.

The second great objection to the plenary inspiration of the Scripture is that it teaches what is inconsistent with historical and scientific truth.

Here again it is to be remarked, (1.) That we must distinguish between what the sacred writers themselves thought or believed, and what they teach. They may have believed that the sun moves round the earth, but they do not so teach. (2.) The language of the Bible is the language of common life; and the language of common life is founded on apparent, and not upon scientific truth.

It would be ridiculous to refuse to speak of the sun rising and
setting, because we know that it is not a satellite of our planet.
(3.) There is a great distinction between theories and facts. Theories are of men. Facts are of God. The Bible often contradicts
the former, never the latter. (4.) There is also a distinction to be
made between the Bible and our interpretation. The latter may
come into competition with settled facts ; and then it must yield.
Science has in many things taught the Church how to understand
the Scriptures. The Bible was for ages understood and explained
according to the Ptolemaic system of the universe; it is now explained without doing the least violence to its language, according
to the Copernican system. Christians have commonly believed
that the earth has existed only a few thousands of years. If geologists finally prove that it has existed for myriads of ages, it will be
found that the first chapter of Genesis is in full accord with the facts,
and that the last results of science are embodied on the first page
of the Bible. It may cost the Church a severe struggle to give up
one interpretation and adopt another, as it did in the seventeenth
century, but no real evil need be apprehended. The Bible has
stood, and still stands in the presence of the whole scientific world
with its claims unshaken. Men hostile or indifferent to its truths
may, on insufficient grounds, or because of their personal opinions,
reject its authority; but, even in the judgment of the greatest
authorities in science, its teachings cannot fairly be impeached.

It is impossible duly to estimate the importance of this subject.
If the Bible be the word of God, all the great questions which
for ages have agitated the minds of men are settled with infallible
certainty. Human reason has never been able to answer to its own
satisfaction, or to the assurance of others, the vital questions, What
is God ? What is man ? What lies beyond the grave ? If there
be a future state of being, what is it? and How may future blessedness be secured? Without the Bible, we are, on all these subjects, in utter darkness. How endless and unsatisfying have been
the answers to the greatest of all questions, What is God? The
whole Eastern world answers by saying, " That He is the unconscious ground of being." The Greeks gave the same answer for
philosophers, and made all nature God for the people. The moderns have reached no higher doctrine. Fichte says the subjective
Ego is God. According to Schelling, God is the eternal movement of the universe, subject becoming object, object becoming
subject, the infinite becoming finite, and the finite infinite. Hegel
says, Thought is God. Cousin combines all the German answers

to form his own.   Coleridge refers us to Schelling for an answer
to the question, What is God?   Carlyle makes force God.   A
Christian child says : " God is a Spirit, infinite, eternal, and unchangeable in his being, wisdom, power, holiness, justice, goodness, and truth."   Men and angels veil their faces in the presence
of that answer.   It is the highest, greatest, and most fruitful truth
ever embodied in human language.   Without the Bible, we are
without God and without hope.   The present is a burden, and the
future a dread.

§ 3.   *Adverse Theories.*

Although substantial unanimity as to the doctrine of inspiration
has prevailed among the great historical Churches of Christendom,
yet there has been no little diversity of opinion among theologians
and philosophical writers.   The theories are too numerous to be
examined in detail.   They may, perhaps, be advantageously referred to the following classes.

A.   *Naturalistic Doctrine.*

There is a large class of writers who deny any supernatural
agency in the affairs of men.   This general class includes writers
who differ essentially in their views.

First.   There are those who, although Theists, hold the mechanical theory of the universe.   That is, they hold that God having
created the world, including all that it contains, organic and inorganic, rational and irrational, and having endowed matter with its
properties and minds with their attributes, leaves it to itself.   Just
as a ship, when launched and equipped, is left to the winds and to
its crew.   This theory precludes the possibility not only of all
miracles, prophecy, and supernatural revelation, but even of all
providential government, whether general or special.   Those who
adopt this view of the relation of God to the world, must regard
the Bible from beginning to end as a purely human production.
They may rank it as the highest, or as among the lowest of the
literary works of men ; there is no possibility of its being inspired
in any authorized sense of that word.

Secondly.   There are those who do not so entirely banish God
from his works.   They admit that He is everywhere present, and
everywhere active ; that his providential efficiency and control are
exercised in the occurrence of all events.   But they maintain that
He always acts according to fixed laws ; and always in connection
and coöperation with second causes.   According to this theory,
also, all miracles and all prophecy, properly speaking, are excluded.

A revelation is admitted, or at least, is possible. But it is merely providential. It consists in such an ordering of circumstances, and such a combination of influences as to secure the elevation of certain men to a higher level of religious knowledge than that attained by others. They may also, in a sense, be said to be inspired in so far as that inward, subjective state is purer, and more devout, as well as more intelligent than that of ordinary men. There is no specific difference, however, according to this theory, between inspired and uninspired men. It is only a matter of degrees. One is more and another less purified and enlightened. This theory also makes the Bible a purely human production. It confines revelation to the sphere of human knowledge. No possible degree of culture or development can get anything more than human out of man. According to the Scriptures, and to the faith of the Church, the Bible is a revelation of the things of God ; of his thoughts and purposes. But who knoweth the things of God, asks the Apostle, but the Spirit of God? The things which the Bible purports to make known, are precisely those things which lie beyond the ken of the human mind. This theory, therefore, for bread gives us a stone ; for the thoughts of God, the thoughts of man.

Schleiermacher's Theory.

Thirdly. There is a theory far more pretentious and philosophical, and which of late years has widely prevailed, which in reality differs very little from the preceding. It agrees with it in the main point in that it denies anything supernatural in the origin or composition of the Bible. Schleiermacher, the author of this theory, was addicted to a philosophy which precluded all intervention of the immediate efficiency of God in the world. He admits, however, of two exceptions : the creation of man, and the constitution of the person of Christ. There was a supernatural intervention in the origin of our race, and in the manifestation of Christ. All else in the history of the world is natural. Of course there is nothing supernatural in the Bible ; nothing in the Old Testament which the Adamic nature was not adequate to produce ; and nothing in the New Testament, which Christianity, the life of the Church, a life common to all believers, is not sufficient to account for.

Religion consists in feeling, and specifically in a feeling of absolute dependence (or an absolute feeling of dependence) *i. e.*, the consciousness that the finite is nothing in the presence of the Infinite, — the individual in the presence of the universal. This consciousness involves the unity of the one and all, of God and man.

"This system," says Dr. Ullmann, one of its more moderate and effective advocates, "is not absolutely new. We find it in another form in ancient Mysticism, especially in the German Mystics of the Middle Ages. With them, too, the ground and central point of Christianity is the oneness of Deity and humanity effected through the incarnation of God, and deification of man." [1]

Christianity, therefore, is not a system of doctrine; it is not, subjectively considered, a form of knowledge. It is a life. It is the life of Christ. Ullmann again says explicitly: "The life of Christ *is* Christianity." [2] God in becoming man did not take upon himself, "a true body and *a* reasonable soul," but generic humanity; *i. e.*, humanity as a generic life. The effect of the incarnation was to unite the human and divine as one life. And this life passes over to the Church precisely as the life of Adam passed over to his descendants, by a process of natural development. And this life is Christianity. Participation of this divine-human life makes a man a Christian.

The Christian revelation consists in the providential dispensations connected with the appearance of Christ on the earth. The effect of these dispensations and events was the elevation of the religious consciousness of the men of that generation, and specially of those who came most directly under the influence of Christ. This subjective state, this excitement and elevation of their religious life, gave them intuitions of religious truths, "eternal verities." These intuitions were by the logical understanding clothed in the form of doctrines. This, however, was a gradual process as it was effected only by the Church-life, *i. e.*, by the working of the new divine-human life in the body of believers.[3] Mr. Morell in expounding this theory, says: [4] "The essential germ of the religious life is concentrated in the absolute feeling of dependence, — a feeling which implies nothing abject, but, on the contrary, a high and hallowed sense of our being inseparably related to Deity." On the preceding page he had said, "Let the subject become as nothing — not, indeed, from its intrinsic insignificance or incapacity of moral action, but by virtue of the infinity of the object to which it stands

[1] *Studien und Kritiken*, 1845, p. 59.
[2] *Studien und Kritiken*, January 1845; translated in *The Mystical Presence*, by Dr. J. W. Nevin.
[3] The English reader may find this theory set forth, in Morell's *Philosophy of Religion*; in Archdeacon Wilberforce's work on the Incarnation; in Maurice's *Theological Essays*; in the *Mystical Presence*, by Dr. John W. Nevin, and in the pages of the Mercersburg *Quarterly Review*, a journal specially devoted to the defence of Schleiermacher's doctrines and of those of the same general character.
[4] *Philosophy of Religion*, p. 77.

consciously opposed ; and the feeling of dependence must become *absolute ;* for all finite power is as nothing in relation to the Infinite."

Christianity, as just stated, is the life of Christ, his human life, which is also divine, and is communicated to us as the life of Adam was communicated to his descendants. Morell, rather more in accordance with English modes of thought, says,[1] " Christianity, like every other religion, consists essentially in a state of man's inner consciousness, which develops itself into a system of thought and activity only in a community of awakened minds ; and it was inevitable, therefore, that such a state of consciousness should require time, and intercourse, and mutual sympathy, before it could become moulded into a decided and distinctive form." He represents the Apostles as often meeting together and deliberating on essential points, correcting each other's views ; and, after years of such fellowship, Christianity was at last brought into form.

Revelation is declared to be a communication of truth to our intuitional consciousness. The outward world is a revelation to our sense-intuitions ; beauty is a revelation to our esthetic intuitions ; and " eternal verities," when intuitively perceived, are said to be revealed ; and this intuition is brought about by whatever purifies and exalts our religious feelings. " Revelation," says Morell, " is a process of the intuitional consciousness, gazing upon eternal verities ; while theology is the reflection of the understanding upon those vital intuitions, so as to reduce them to a logical and scientific expression." [2]

Inspiration is the inward state of mind which enables us to apprehend the truth. " Revelation and inspiration," says Morell, " indicate one united process, the result of which upon the human mind is, to produce a state of spiritual intuition, whose phenomena are so extraordinary, that we at once separate the agency by which they are produced from any of the ordinary principles of human development. And yet this agency is applied in perfect consistency with the laws and natural operations of our spiritual nature. Inspiration does not imply anything generically new in the actual processes of the human mind ; it does not involve any form of intelligence essentially different from what we already possess ; it indicates rather the elevation of the religious consciousness, and with it, of course, the power of spiritual vision, to a degree of intensity peculiar to the individuals thus highly favoured of God." [3] The only difference, therefore, between the Apostles and ordinary Christians is as to their relative holiness.

---

[1] *Philosophy of Religion*, page 104.   [2] Page 141   [3] Page 151.

According to this theory there is no specific difference between genius and inspiration. The difference is simply in the objects apprehended and the causes of the inward excitement to which the apprehension is due. " Genius," says Morell, " consists in the possession of a remarkable power of intuition with reference to some particular object, a power which arises from the inward nature of a man being brought into unusual harmony with that object in its reality and its operations." [1] This is precisely his account of inspiration. " Let," he says, " there be a due purification of the moral nature, — a perfect harmony of the spiritual being with the mind of God, — a removal of all inward disturbances from the heart, and what is to prevent or disturb this immediate intuition of divine things." [2]

This theory of inspiration, while retaining its essential elements, is variously modified. With those who believe with Schleiermacher, that man " is the form in which God comes to conscious existence on our earth," it has one form. With Realists who define man to be " the manifestation of generic humanity in connection with a given corporeal organization;" and who believe that it was generic humanity which Christ took and united in one life with his divine nature, which life is communicated to the Church as his body, and thereby to all its members; it takes a somewhat different form. With those again who do not adopt either of these anthropological theories, but take the common view as to the constitution of man ; it takes still a different, and in some respects, a lower, form. In all, however, inspiration is the intuition of divine truths due to the excitement of the religious nature, whatever that nature may be.

Objections to Schleiermacher's Theory.

To this theory in all its forms it may be objected, —

1. That it proceeds upon a wrong view of religion in general and of Christianity in particular. It assumes that religion is a feeling, a life. It denies that it is a form of knowledge, or involves the reception of any particular system of doctrine. In the subjective sense of the word, all religions (i. e., all religious doctrines) are true, as Twesten says,[3] but all are not equally pure, or equally adequate expressions of the inward religious principle. According to the Scriptures, however, and the common conviction of Christians,

---

[1] *Philosophy of Religion,* page 184.   [2] Page 186.
[3] *Dogmatik,* vol. i. p. 2. " Das Verhältniss des Erkennen zur Religion." Hase's *Dogmatik,* " Jede Religion als Ergebniss einer Volksbildung ist angemesen oder subj. wahr; wahr an sich ist die, welche der vollendeten Ausbildung der Menschheit entspricht." See also his *Hutterus Redivivus.*

religion (subjectively considered) is the reception of certain doctrines as true, and a state of heart and course of action in accordance with those doctrines. The Apostles propounded a certain system of doctrines; they pronounced those to be Christians who received those doctrines so as to determine their character and life. They pronounced those who rejected those doctrines, who refused to receive their testimony, as antichristian; as having no part or lot with the people of God. Christ's command was to teach; to convert the world by teaching. On this principle the Apostles acted and the Church has ever acted from that day to this. Those who deny Theism as a doctrine, are atheists. Those who reject Christianity as a system of doctrine, are unbelievers. They are not Christians. The Bible everywhere assumes that without truth there can be no holiness; that all conscious exercises of spiritual life are in view of truth objectively revealed in the Scriptures. And hence the importance everywhere attributed to knowledge, to truth, to sound doctrine, in the Word of God.

2. This theory is inconsistent with the Scriptural doctrine of revelation. According to the Bible, God presents truth objectively to the mind, whether by audible words, by visions, or by the immediate operations of his Spirit. According to this theory, revelation is merely the providential ordering of circumstances which awaken and exalt the religious feelings, and which thus enable the mind intuitively to apprehend the things of God.

3. It avowedly confines these intuitions, and of course revealed truth, to what are called "eternal verities." But the great body of truths revealed in Scripture are not "eternal verities." The fall of man; that all men are sinners; that the Redeemer from sin was to be of the seed of Abraham, and of the house of David; that He was to be born of a virgin, to be a man of sorrows; that He was crucified and buried; that He rose again the third day; that He ascended to heaven; that He is to come again without sin to salvation, although truths on which our salvation depends, are not intuitive truths; they are not truths which any exaltation of the religious consciousness would enable any man to discover of himself.

4. According to this theory the Bible has no normal authority as a rule of faith. It contains no doctrines revealed by God, and to be received as true on his testimony. It contains only the thoughts of holy men; the forms in which their understandings, without supernatural aid, clothed the "intuitions" due to their religious feelings. "The Bible," says Morell,[1] "cannot in strict

---

[1] *Philosophy of Religion*, ch. 8, p. 143, London ed. 1849.

accuracy of language be termed a revelation, since a revelation
always implies an actual process of intelligence in a living mind;
but it contains the records in which those minds who enjoyed the
preliminary training or the first brighter revelation of Christianity,
have described the scenes which awakened their own religious
nature to new life, and the high ideas and aspirations to which that
new life gave origin." The Old Testament is the product of "the
religious consciousness" of men who lived under a rude state of
culture; and is of no authority for us. The New Testament is
the product of "the religious consciousness" of men who had experienced the sanctifying influence of Christ's presence among
them. But those men were Jews, they had Jewish modes of thinking. They were familiar with the services of the old dispensation;
were accustomed to think of God as approachable only through a
priesthood; as demanding expiation for sin, and regeneration of
heart; and promising certain rewards and forms of blessedness in
a future state of existence. It was natural for them, therefore, to
clothe their "intuitions" in these Jewish modes of thought. We,
in this nineteenth century, may clothe ours in very different forms,
i. e., in very different doctrines, and yet "the eternal verities" be
the same.

Different men carry this theory to very different lengths. Some
have such an inward experience that they can find no form for expressing what they feel, so suitable as that given in the Bible, and
therefore they believe all its great doctrines. But the ground of
their faith is purely subjective. It is not the testimony of God
given in his Word, but their own experience. They take what
suits that, and reject the rest. Others with less Christian experience, or with no experience distinctively Christian, reject all the
distinctive doctrines of Christianity, and adopt a form of religious
philosophy which they are willing to call Christianity.

5. That this theory is antiscriptural has already been said. The
Bible makes revelation as therein contained to be the communication of doctrines to the understanding by the Spirit of God. It
makes those truths or doctrines the immediate source of all right
feeling. The feelings come from spiritual apprehension of the
truth, and not the knowledge of truth from the feelings. Knowledge is necessary to all conscious holy exercises. Hence the Bible
makes truth of the greatest importance. It pronounces those
blessed who receive the doctrines which it teaches, and those
accursed who reject them. It makes the salvation of men to depend upon their faith. This theory makes the creed of a man or
of a people of comparatively little consequence.

In the Church, therefore, Christianity has always been regarded as a system of doctrine. Those who believe these doctrines are Christians; those who reject them, are, in the judgment of the Church, infidels or heretics. If our faith be formal or speculative, so is our Christianity; if it be spiritual and living, so is our religion. But no mistake can be greater than to divorce religion from truth, and make Christianity a spirit or life distinct from the doctrines which the Scriptures present as the objects of faith.

B. *Gracious Inspiration.*

This theory belongs to the category of natural or supernatural, according to the meaning assigned to those terms. By natural effects are commonly understood those brought about by natural causes under the providential control of God. Then the effects produced by the gracious operations of the Spirit, such as repentance, faith, love, and all other fruits of the Spirit, are supernatural. And consequently the theory which refers inspiration to the gracious influence of the Spirit, belongs to the class of the supernatural. But this word is often used in a more limited sense, to designate events which are produced by the immediate agency or volition of God without the intervention of any second cause. In this limited sense, creation, miracles, immediate revelation, regeneration (in the limited sense of that word), are supernatural. As the sanctification of men is carried on by the Spirit by the use of the means of grace, it is not a supernatural work, in the restricted sense of the term.

There are many theologians who do not adopt either of the philosophical theories of the nature of man and of his relation to God, above mentioned; and who receive the Scriptural doctrine as held by the Church universal, that the Holy Spirit renews, sanctifies, illuminates, guides, and teaches all the people of God; and yet who regard inspiration to be one of the ordinary fruits of the Spirit. Inspired and uninspired men are not distinguished by any specific difference. The sacred writers were merely holy men under the guidance of the ordinary influence of the Spirit. Some of those who adopt this theory extend it to revelation as well as to inspiration. Others admit a strictly supernatural revelation, but deny that the sacred writers in communicating the truths revealed were under any influence not common to ordinary believers. And as to those parts of the Bible (as the Hagiographa and Gospels), which contain no special revelations, they are to be regarded as the devotional writings or historical narratives of devout but fallible men.   Thus Coleridge, who refers inspiration to that "grace and communion with the Spirit which the Church, under all circumstances, and every regenerate member of the Church, is permitted to hope and instructed to pray for;" makes an exception in favour of "the law and the prophets, no jot or tittle of which can pass unfulfilled." [1] The remainder of the Bible, he holds, was written under the impulse and guidance of the gracious influence of the Spirit given to all Christian men.   And his friends and followers, Dr. Arnold, Archdeacon Hare, and specially Maurice, ignore this distinction and refer the whole Bible "to an inspiration the same as what every believer enjoys." [2]   Thus Maurice says,[3] "We must forego the demand which we make on the conscience of young men, when we compel them to declare that they regard the inspiration of the Bible as generically unlike that which God bestows on His children in this day."

Objections to the Doctrine that Inspiration is common to all Believers.

That this theory is anti-scriptural is obvious. 1. Because the Bible makes a marked distinction between those whom God chose to be his messengers, his prophets, his spokesmen, and other men. This theory ignores that distinction, so far as the people of God is concerned.

2. It is inconsistent with the authority claimed by these special messengers of God.   They spoke in his name.   God spoke through them.   They said, "Thus saith the Lord," in a sense and way in which no ordinary believer dare use those words.   It is inconsistent with the authority not only claimed by the sacred writers, but attributed to them by our Lord himself.   He declared that the Scripture could not be broken ; that it was infallible in all its teachings.   The Apostles declare those anathema who did not receive their doctrines.   This claim to divine authority in teaching was confirmed by God himself in signs, and wonders, and divers miracles, and gifts of the Holy Ghost.

3. It is inconsistent with the whole nature of the Bible, which is and professes to be a revelation of truths not only undiscoverable by human reason, but which no amount of holiness could enable the mind of man to perceive.   This is true not only of the strictly prophetic revelations relating to the future, but also of all things

---

[1] "Confessions of an Inquiring Spirit," Letter 7, *Works*, N. Y., 1853, vol. v. p. 619.
[2] See Bannerman, *Inspiration of the Scriptures*, Edinburgh, 1865, pp. 145, 232.
[3] *Theological Essays*, p. 339, Cambridge, 1853.

concerning the mind and will of God. The doctrines of the Bible are called μυστήρια, *things concealed*, unknown and unknowable, except as revealed to the holy Apostles and prophets by the Spirit. (Eph. iii. 5.)

4. It is inconsistent with the faith of the Church universal, which has always made the broadest distinction between the writings of the inspired men and those of ordinary believers. Even Romanists, with all their reverence for the fathers, never presumed to place their writings on a level with the Scriptures. They do not attribute to them any authority but as witnesses of what the Apostles taught. If the Bible has no more authority than is due to the writings of pious men, then our faith is vain and we are yet in our sins. We have no sure foundation for our hopes of salvation.

C. *Partial Inspiration.*

Under this head are included several different doctrines.

1. Many hold that only some parts of Scripture are inspired, *i. e.*, that the writers of some books were supernaturally guided by the Spirit, and the writers of others were not. This, as mentioned above, was the doctrine of Coleridge, who admitted the inspiration of the Law and the Prophets, but denied that of the rest of the Bible. Others admit the New Testament to be inspired to an extent to which the Old was not. Others again hold the discourses of Christ to be infallible, but no other part of the sacred volume.

2. Others limit the inspiration of the sacred writers to their doctrinal teaching. The great object of their commission was to give a faithful record of the revealed will and purpose of God, to be a rule of faith and practice to the Church. In this they were under an influence which rendered them infallible as religious and moral teachers. But beyond these limits they were as liable to error as other men. That there should be scientific, historical, geographical mistakes; errors in the citation of passages, or in other unessential matters; or discrepancies as to matters of fact between the sacred writers, leaves their inspiration as religious teachers untouched.

3. Another form of the doctrine of partial, as opposed to plenary inspiration, limits it to the thoughts, as distinguished from the words of Scripture. Verbal inspiration is denied. It is assumed that the sacred writers selected the words they used without any guidance of the Spirit, to prevent their adopting improper or inadequate terms in which to express their thoughts.

4. A fourth form of the doctrine of partial inspiration was early

introduced and has been widely adopted. Maimonides, the greatest
of the Jewish doctors since the time of Christ, taught as early as
the twelfth century that the sacred writers of the Old Testament
enjoyed different degrees of divine guidance. He placed the inspiration of the Law much above that of the Prophets ; and that
of the Prophets higher than that of the Hagiographa. This idea
of different degrees of inspiration was adopted by many theologians,
and in England for a long time it was the common mode of representation. The idea was that the writers of Kings and Chronicles
needed less, and that they received less of the divine assistance
than Isaiah or St. John.[1]

In attempting to prove the doctrine of plenary inspiration the
arguments which bear against all these forms of partial inspiration
were given or suggested. The question is not an open one. It is
not what theory is in itself most reasonable or plausible, but simply,
What does the Bible teach on the subject? If our Lord and his
Apostles declare the Old Testament to be the Word of God ; that
its authors spake as they were moved by the Holy Ghost ; that
what they said, the Spirit said ; if they refer to the facts and to the
very words of Scripture as of divine authority ; and if the same
infallible divine guidance was promised to the writers of the New
Testament, and claimed by themselves ; and if their claim was
authenticated by God himself ; then there is no room for, as there
is no need of, these theories of partial inspiration. The whole Bible
was written under such an influence as preserved its human authors
from all error, and makes it for the Church the infallible rule of
faith and practice.

§ 4. *The Completeness of the Scriptures.*

By the completeness of the Scriptures is meant that they contain all the extant revelations of God designed to be a rule of faith
and practice to the Church. It is not denied that God reveals himself, even his eternal power and Godhead, by his works, and has
done so from the beginning of the world. But all the truths thus
revealed are clearly made known in his written Word. Nor is it
denied that there may have been, and probably were, books written by inspired men, which are no longer in existence. Much less
is it denied that Christ and his Apostles delivered many discourses

---

[1] This view of different degrees of inspiration was adopted by Lowth: *Vindication of the
Divine Authority and Inspiration of the Old and New Testaments.* Whitby, in the Preface to
his *Commentary.* Doddridge, *Dissertation on the Inspiration of the New Testament.* Hill,
Lectures on Divinity. Dick, *Essay on the Inspiration of the Holy Scriptures.* Wilson.
Evidences of Christianity. Henderson, *Divine Inspiration.*

which were not recorded, and which, could they now be known and authenticated, would be of equal authority with the books now regarded as canonical. All that Protestants insist upon is, that the Bible contains all the extant revelations of God, which He designed to be the rule of faith and practice for his Church ; so that nothing can rightfully be imposed on the consciences of men as truth or duty which is not taught directly or by necessary implication in the Holy Scriptures. This excludes all unwritten traditions, not only ; but also all decrees of the visible Church ; all resolutions of conventions, or other public bodies, declaring this or that to be right or wrong, true or false. The people of God are bound by nothing but the Word of God. On this subject little need be said. The completeness of Scripture, as a rule of faith, is a corollary of the Protestant doctrine concerning tradition. If that be true, the former must also be true. This Romanists do not deny. They make the Rule of Faith to consist of the written and unwritten word of God, *i. e.*, of Scripture and tradition. If it be proved that tradition is untrustworthy, human, and fallible, then the Scriptures by common consent stand alone in their authority. As the authority of tradition has already been discussed, further discussion of the completeness of the Scriptures becomes unnecessary.

It is well, however, to bear in mind the importance of this doctrine. It is not by Romanists only that it is denied, practically at least, if not theoretically. Nothing is more common among Protestants, especially in our day, than the attempt to coerce the conscience of men by public opinion ; to make the opinions of men on questions of morals a rule of duty for the people, and even for the Church. If we would stand fast in the liberty wherewith Christ has made us free, we must adhere to the principle that in matters of religion and morals the Scriptures alone have authority to bind the conscience.

§ 5. *Perspicuity of the Scriptures. The Right of Private Judgment.*

The Bible is a plain book. It is intelligible by the people. And they have the right, and are bound to read and interpret it for themselves ; so that their faith may rest on the testimony of the Scriptures, and not on that of the Church. Such is the doctrine of Protestants on this subject.

It is not denied that the Scriptures contain many things hard to be understood ; that they require diligent study ; that all men need the guidance of the Holy Spirit in order to right knowledge and true faith.   But it is maintained that in all things necessary to salvation they are sufficiently plain to be understood even by the unlearned.

It is not denied that the people, learned and unlearned, in order to the proper understanding of the Scriptures, should not only compare Scripture with Scripture, and avail themselves of all the means in their power to aid them in their search after the truth, but they should also pay the greatest deference to the faith of the Church.   If the Scriptures be a plain book, and the Spirit performs the functions of a teacher to all the children of God, it follows inevitably that they must agree in all essential matters in their interpretation of the Bible.   And from that fact it follows that for an individual Christian to dissent from the faith of the universal Church (*i. e.*, the body of true believers), is tantamount to dissenting from the Scriptures themselves.

What Protestants deny on this subject is, that Christ has appointed any officer, or class of officers, in his Church to whose interpretation of the Scriptures the people are bound to submit as of final authority.   What they affirm is that He has made it obligatory upon every man to search the Scriptures for himself, and determine on his own discretion what they require him to believe and to do.

The arguments in support of the former of these positions have already been presented in the discussion concerning the infallibility of the Church.   The most obvious reasons in support of the right of private judgment are, —

1. That the obligations to faith and obedience are personal. Every man is responsible for his religious faith and his moral conduct.   He cannot transfer that responsibility to others ; nor can others assume it in his stead.   He must answer for himself ; and if he must answer for himself, he must judge for himself.   It will not avail him in the day of judgment to say that his parents or his Church taught him wrong.   He should have listened to God, and obeyed Him rather than men.

2. The Scriptures are everywhere addressed to the people, and not to the officers of the Church either exclusively, or specially. The prophets were sent to the people, and constantly said, " Hear, O Israel," " Hearken, O ye people." Thus, also, the discourses of Christ were addressed to the people, and the people heard him gladly.   All the Epistles of the New Testament are addressed to the congregation, to the " called of Jesus Christ ; " " to the beloved of God ; " to those " called to be saints ; " " to the sanctified in Christ Jesus ; " " to all who call on the name of Jesus Christ our

Lord ; " " to the saints which are in (Ephesus), and to the faithful in Jesus Christ ; " or " to the saints and faithful brethren which
are in (Colosse) ; " and so in every instance. It is the people who
are addressed. To them are directed these profound discussions of
Christian doctrine, and these comprehensive expositions of Christian duty. They are everywhere assumed to be competent to understand what is written, and are everywhere required to believe
and obey what thus came from the inspired messengers of Christ.
They were not referred to any other authority from which they
were to learn the true import of these inspired instructions. It is,
therefore, not only to deprive the people of a divine right, to forbid
the people to read and interpret the Scriptures for themselves ; but
it is also to interpose between them and God, and to prevent their
hearing his voice, that they may listen to the words of men.

The People commanded to search the Scriptures.

3. The Scriptures are not only addressed to the people, but the
people were called upon to study them, and to teach them unto their
children. It was one of the most frequently recurring injunctions
to parents under the old dispensation, to teach the Law unto their
children, that they again might teach it unto theirs. The "holy oracles " were committed to the people, to be taught by the people ;
and taught immediately out of the Scriptures, that the truth might
be retained in its purity. Thus our Lord commanded the people
to search the Scriptures, saying, " They are they which testify of
me." (John v. 39.) He assumed that they were able to understand what the Old Testament said of the Messiah, although its
teachings had been misunderstood by the scribes and elders, and by
the whole Sanhedrim. Paul rejoiced that Timothy had from his
youth known the Holy Scriptures, which were able to make him
wise unto salvation. He said to the Galatians (i. 8, 9), " Though
we, or an angel from heaven, — if any *man* preach any other gospel unto you than that ye have received, let him be accursed."
This implies two things, — first, that the Galatian Christians, the
people, had a right to sit in judgment on the teaching of an Apostle,
or of an angel from heaven ; and secondly, that they had an infallible
rule by which that judgment was to be determined, namely, a previous authenticated revelation of God. If, then, the Bible recognizes the right of the people to judge of the teaching of Apostles
and angels, they are not to be denied the right of judging of the
doctrines of bishops and priests. The principle laid down by the
Apostle is precisely that long before given by Moses (Deut. xiii.

1–3), who tells the people that if a prophet should arise, although he worked wonders, they were not to believe or obey him, if he taught them anything contrary to the Word of God. This again assumes that the people had the ability and the right to judge, and that they had an infallible rule of judgment. It implies, moreover, that their salvation depended upon their judging rightly. For if they allowed these false teachers, robed in sacred vestments, and surrounded by the insignia of authority, to lead them from the truth, they would inevitably perish.

4. It need hardly be remarked that this right of private judgment is the great safeguard of civil and religious liberty. If the Bible be admitted to be the infallible rule of faith and practice in accordance with which men are bound on the peril of their souls, to frame their creed and conduct; and if there be a set of men who have the exclusive right of interpreting the Scripture, and who are authorized to impose their interpretations on the people as of divine authority, then they may impose on them what conditions of salvation they see fit. And the men who have the salvation of the people in their hands are their absolute masters. Both reason and experience fully sustain the dictum of Chillingworth,[1] when he says, " He that would usurp an absolute lordship and tyranny over any people, need not put himself to the trouble and difficulty of abrogating and disannulling the laws, made to maintain the common liberty ; for he may frustrate their intent, and compass his own design as well, if he can get the power and authority to interpret them as he pleases, and add to them what he pleases, and to have his interpretations and additions stand for laws ; if he can rule his people by his laws, and his laws by his lawyers." This is precisely what the Church of Rome has done, and thereby established a tyranny for which there is no parallel in the history of the world. What renders this tyranny the more intolerable, is, that, so far as the mass of the people is concerned, it resolves itself into the authority of the parish priest. He is the arbiter of the faith and morals of his people. No man can believe unless the ground of faith is present to his mind. If the people are to believe that the Scriptures teach certain doctrines, then they must have the evidence that such doctrines are really taught in the Bible. If that evidence be that the Church so interprets the sacred writings, then the people must know what is the Church, *i. e.*, which of the bodies claiming to be the Church, is entitled to be so regarded. How are the people, the uneducated masses, to determine that question ? The

1 *Works*, p. 105.

priest tells them. If they receive his testimony on that point, then how can they tell how the Church interprets the Scriptures? Here again they must take the word of the priest. Thus the authority of the Church as an interpreter, which appears so imposing, resolves itself into the testimony of the priest, who is often wicked, and still oftener ignorant. This cannot be the foundation of the faith of God's elect. That foundation is the testimony of God himself speaking his word, and authenticated as divine by the testimony of the Spirit with and by the truth in the heart of the believer.

§ 6. *Rules of Interpretation.*

If every man has the right, and is bound to read the Scriptures, and to judge for himself what they teach, he must have certain rules to guide him in the exercise of this privilege and duty. These rules are not arbitrary. They are not imposed by human authority. They have no binding force which does not flow from their own intrinsic truth and propriety. They are few and simple.

1. The words of Scripture are to be taken in their plain historical sense. That is, they must be taken in the sense attached to them in the age and by the people to whom they were addressed. This only assumes that the sacred writers were honest, and meant to be understood.

2. If the Scriptures be what they claim to be, the word of God, they are the work of one mind, and that mind divine. From this it follows that Scripture cannot contradict Scripture. God cannot teach in one place anything which is inconsistent with what He teaches in another. Hence Scripture must explain Scripture. If a passage admits of different interpretations, that only can be the true one which agrees with what the Bible teaches elsewhere on the same subject. If the Scriptures teach that the Son is the same in substance and equal in power and glory with the Father, then when the Son says, " The Father is greater than I," the superiority must be understood in a manner consistent with this equality. It must refer either to subordination as to the mode of subsistence and operation, or it must be official. A king's son may say, " My father is greater than I," although personally his father's equal. This rule of interpretation is sometimes called the analogy of Scripture, and sometimes the analogy of faith. There is no material difference in the meaning of the two expressions.

3. The Scriptures are to be interpreted under the guidance of the Holy Spirit, which guidance is to be humbly and earnestly sought. The ground of this rule is twofold: First, the Spirit is

promised as a guide and teacher. He was to come to lead the people of God into the knowledge of the truth. And secondly, the Scriptures teach, that "the natural man receiveth not the things of the Spirit of God : for they are foolishness unto him ; neither can he know them, because they are spiritually discerned." (1 Cor. ii. 14.) The unrenewed mind is naturally blind to spiritual truth. His heart is in opposition to the things of God. Congeniality of mind is necessary to the proper apprehension of divine things. As only those who have a moral nature can discern moral truth, so those only who are spiritually minded can truly receive the things of the Spirit.

The fact that all the true people of God in every age and in every part of the Church, in the exercise of their private judgment, in accordance with the simple rules above stated, agree as to the meaning of Scripture in all things necessary either in faith or practice, is a decisive proof of the perspicuity of the Bible, and of the safety of allowing the people the enjoyment of the divine right of private judgment.

SYSTEMATIC THEOLOGY

PART I.

THEOLOGY PROPER

CHAPTER I.

ALL men have some knowledge of God. That is, they have the conviction that there is a Being on whom they are dependent, and to whom they are responsible. What is the source of this conviction? In other words, what is the origin of the idea of God? To this question three answers have been given. First, that it is innate. Second, that is a deduction of reason; a conclusion arrived at by a process of generalization. Third, that it is to be referred to a supernatural revelation, preserved by tradition.

§ 1. *The Knowledge of God is Innate.*

A. *What is meant by Innate Knowledge.*

By innate knowledge is meant that which is due to our constitution, as sentient, rational, and moral beings. It is opposed to knowledge founded on experience; to that obtained by *ab extra* instruction; and to that acquired by a process of research and reasoning.

It cannot be doubted that there is such knowledge, *i. e.*, that the soul is so constituted that it sees certain things to be true immediately in their own light. They need no proof. Men need not be told or taught that the things thus perceived are true. These immediate perceptions are called intuitions, primary truths, laws of belief, innate knowledge, or ideas. Provided we understand what is meant, the designation is of minor importance. The doctrine of innate knowledge, or intuitive truths, does not imply that the child is born with knowledge in conscious exercise in the mind. As knowledge is a form or state of the intelligence, and as that is a state of consciousness, knowledge, in the sense of the act of knowing, must be a matter of consciousness; and, therefore, it is said, cannot be innate. The new-born child has no conscious conviction of the existence of God. But the word knowledge is sometimes used in a passive sense. A man knows what lies dormant in his mind. Most of our knowledge is in that state. All the facts

of history stored in the memory, are out of the domain of consciousness, until the mind is turned to them.   It is not inconceivable,
therefore, that the soul as it comes into the world may be stored
with these primary truths which lie dormant in the mind, until
roused by the due occasion.   This, however, is not what is meant by
innate knowledge.   The word innate simply indicates the source
of the knowledge.   That source is our nature; that which is born
with us.   Nor does the doctrine of innate knowledge imply that the
mind is born with ideas, in the sense of "patterns, phantasms, or
notions," as Locke calls them; nor that it is furnished by nature
with a set of abstract principles, or general truths.   All that is
meant is, that the mind is so constituted that it perceives certain
things to be true without proof and without instruction.

These intuitive truths belong to the several departments of the
senses, the understanding, and our moral nature.   In the first place,
all our sense perceptions are intuitions.   We apprehend their objects immediately, and have an irresistible conviction of their
reality and truth.   We may draw erroneous conclusions from our
sensations; but our sensations, as far as they go, tell us the truth.
When a man feels pain, he may refer it to the wrong place, or to
a wrong cause; but he knows that it is pain.   If he sees an object,
he may be mistaken as to its nature; but he knows that he sees,
and that what he sees is the cause of the sensation which he experiences.   These are intuitions, because they are immediate perceptions of what is true.   The conviction which attends our sensations is due not to instruction but to the constitution of our
nature.

In the second place, there are intuitions of the intellect.   That
is, there are certain truths which the mind perceives to be true
immediately, without proof or testimony.   Such are the axioms of
geometry.   No man needs to have it proved to him that the part
of a thing is less than the whole; or that a straight line is the
shortest distance between two given points.   It is an intuitive truth
that "nothing" cannot be a cause; that every effect must have a
cause.   This conviction is not founded on experience, because
experience is of necessity limited.   And the conviction is not merely
that every effect which we or other men have observed has had
a cause; but that in the nature of things there can be no effect
without an adequate cause.   This conviction is said to be an innate
truth, not because the child is born with it so that it is included in
its infant consciousness, nor because the abstract principle is laid
up in the mind, but simply because such is the nature of the mind,

that it cannot but see these things to be true. As we are born with the sense of touch and sight, and take cognizance of their appropriate objects as soon as they are presented ; so we are born with the intellectual faculty of perceiving these primary truths as soon as they are presented.

In the third place, there are moral truths which the mind intuitively recognizes as true. The essential distinction between right and wrong ; the obligation of virtue ; responsibility for character and conduct ; that sin deserves punishment ; are examples of this class of truths. No man needs to be taught them. No one seeks for further evidence of their being truths than that which is found in their nature.

There is another remark to be made in reference to the intuitions of the mind. The power of intuitional perception is capable of being increased. It is in fact greater in one man than in other men. The senses of some persons are far more acute than those of others. The senses of hearing and touch are greatly exalted in the case of the blind. It is the same with the intellect. What is self-evident to one man, has to be proved to another. It is said that all the propositions of the First Book of Euclid were as plain at first sight to Newton as the axioms. The same is true in our moral and religious nature. The more that nature is purified and exalted, the clearer is its vision, and the wider the scope of its intuitions. It is not easy to see, therefore, why Sir William Hamilton should make simplicity a characteristic of intuitive truths. If a proposition be capable of resolution into simpler factors, it may still to a powerful intellect be seen as self-evidently true. What is seen immediately, without the intervention of proof, to be true, is, according to the common mode of expression, said to be seen intuitively.

It is, however, only of the lower exercises of this power that we can avail ourselves in our arguments with our fellow men. Because a truth may be self-evident to one mind, it does not follow that it must be so to all other minds. But there is a class of truths so plain that they never fail to reveal themselves to the human mind, and to which the mind cannot refuse its assent. Hence the criteria of those truths which are accepted as axioms, and which are assumed in all reasoning, and the denial of which renders all faith and all knowledge impossible, are universality and necessity What all believe, and what all men must believe, is to be assumed as undeniably true. These criteria indeed include each other. If a truth be universally admitted, it must be because no man can rationally call it to question. And if it be a matter of necessary belief, it must be accepted by all who possess the nature out of the constitution of which the necessity arises.

B. *Proof that the Knowledge of God is Innate.*

The question now is, Whether the existence of God is an intuitive truth? Is it given in the very constitution of our nature? Is it one of those truths which reveal themselves to every human mind, and to which the mind is forced to assent? In other words, has it the characteristics of universality and necessity? It should be remarked that when universality is made a criterion of intuitive truths, it is intended to apply to those truths only which have their foundation or evidence in the constitution of our nature. As to the external world, if ignorance be universal, error may be universal. All men, for example, for ages believed that the sun moves round the earth; but the universality of that belief was no evidence of its truth.

When it is asked, Whether the existence of God is an intuitive truth, the question is equivalent to asking, Whether the belief in his existence is universal and necessary? If it be true that all men do believe there is a God, and that no man can possibly disbelieve his existence, then his existence is an intuitive truth. It is one of those given in the constitution of our nature; or which, our nature being what it is, no man can fail to know and to acknowledge.

Such has been the common opinion in all ages. Cicero[1] says: " Esse Deos, quoniam insitas eorum, vel potius innatas cognitiones habemus." Tertullian[2] says of the heathen of his day, that the common people had a more correct idea of God than the philosophers. Calvin[3] says: " Hoc quidem recte judicantibus semper constabit, insculptum mentibus humanis esse divinitatis sensum, qui deleri nunquam potest." The whole tendency in our day is to make the existence of God so purely a matter of intuition as to lead to the disparagement of all argument in proof of it. This extreme, however, does not justify the denial of a truth so important as that God has not left any human being without a knowledge of his existence and authority.

The word God, however, is used in a very wide sense. In the Christian sense of the word, " God is a spirit, infinite, eternal, and unchangeable, in his being, wisdom, power, holiness, justice, goodness, and truth." This sublime idea of God no human mind ever

[1] *De Natura Deorum*, i. 17.   [2] *Testimonium Animæ*.   [3] *Institutio*, i. iii. 3.

attained either intuitively or discursively, except under the light of a supernatural revelation. On the other hand, some philosophers dignify motion, force, or the vague idea of the infinite, with the name of God. In neither of these senses of the word is the knowledge of God said to be innate, or a matter of intuition. It is in the general sense of a Being on whom we are dependent, and to whom we are responsible, that the idea is asserted to exist universally, and of necessity, in every human mind. It is true that if this idea is analyzed, it will be found to embrace the conviction that God is a person, and that He possesses moral attributes, and acts as a moral governor. Nothing is asserted as to how far this analysis is made by uneducated and uncivilized men. All that is maintained is that this sense of dependence and accountability to a being higher than themselves exists in the minds of all men.

The Knowledge of God is Universal.

In proof of this doctrine, reference may be made —

1. To the testimony of Scripture. The Bible asserts that the knowledge of God is thus universal. This it does both directly and by necessary implication. The Apostle directly asserts in regard to the heathen as such without limitation, that they have the knowledge of God, and such knowledge as to render their impiety and immorality inexcusable. " Because that when they knew God," he says, " they glorified him not as God, neither were thankful." (Rom. i. 19–21.) He says of the most depraved of men, that they know the righteous judgment of God, that those who commit sin are worthy of death. (Rom. i. 32.) The Scripture everywhere addresses men as sinners; it calls upon them to repent; it threatens them with punishment in case of disobedience; or promises pardon to those who turn from their sins. All this is done without any preliminary demonstration of the being of God. It assumes that men know that there is a God, and that they are subject to his moral government. It is true that the Bible at times speaks of the heathen as not knowing God, and says that they are without God. But this, as explained by the context in which such declarations appear, and by the general teaching of the Scriptures, only means that the heathen are without correct, or saving knowledge of God; that they are without his favour, do not belong to the number of his people, and of course are not partakers of the blessedness of those whose God is the Lord. In teaching the universal sinfulness and condemnation of men; their inexcusableness for idolatry and immorality; and

in asserting that even the most degraded are conscious of guilt and just exposure to the divine judgment, the Bible takes for granted that the knowledge of God is universal, that it is written on the heart of every man.

This is still more apparent from what the Bible teaches of the law as written on the heart. The Apostle tells us that those who have a written revelation, shall be judged by that revelation; that those who have no externally revealed law, shall be judged by the law written on the heart. That the heathen have such a law, he proves first, from the fact that "they do by nature the things contained in the law," i. e., they do under the control of their nature the things which the law prescribes; and secondly, from the operations of conscience. When it condemns, it pronounces something done, to be contrary to the moral law; and when it approves, it pronounces something to be conformed to that law. (Rom. ii. 12–16.) The recognition of God, therefore, that is, of a being to whom we are responsible, is involved in the very idea of accountability. Hence every man carries in the very constitution of his being as a moral agent, the evidence of the existence of God. And as this sense of sin and responsibility is absolutely universal, so must also, according to the Bible, be the knowledge of God.

2. The second argument in favor of the universality of this knowledge, is the historical one. History shows that the religious element of our nature is just as universal as the rational or social one. Wherever men exist, in all ages and in all parts of the world, they have some form of religion. The idea of God is impressed on every human language. And as language is the product and revelation of human consciousness, if all languages have some name for God, it proves that the idea of God, in some form, belongs to every human being.

Objections to the Assumption that the Knowledge of God is Universal.

There are two objections often urged against the doctrine that the knowledge of God results from the very constitution of our nature, and is therefore universal. The one is, that travellers and missionaries report the existence of some tribes so degraded that they could discover in them no traces of this knowledge. Even if the fact be admitted that such tribes have no idea of God, it would not be conclusive. Should a tribe of idiots be discovered, it would not prove that reason is not an attribute of our nature. If any community should come to light in which infanticide was universal, it would not prove that parental love was not one of the instincts of humanity.   But the probability is that the fact is not as reported. It is very difficult for foreigners to get acquainted with the interior life of those who differ from themselves so much in their intellectual and moral condition.   And besides, Christians attach such an exalted meaning to the word God, that when they see no evidence of the presence of that exalted conception in the minds of the heathen, they are apt to conclude that all knowledge of God is wanting.   Unless such people show that they have no sense of right and wrong, no consciousness of responsibility for character and conduct, there is no evidence that they have no knowledge of such a being as God.

The other objection is drawn from the case of the deaf and dumb, who sometimes say that previous to instruction, the idea of God never entered their minds.   To this the same answer may be given.   The knowledge obtained by Christian instruction so much surpasses that given by intuition, that the latter seems as nothing. It is hardly conceivable that a human soul should exist in any state of development, without a sense of responsibility, and this involves the idea of God.   For the responsibility is felt to be not to self, nor to men, but to an invisible Being, higher than self, and higher than man.

The Belief in God Necessary.

But if it be admitted that the knowledge of God is universal among men, is it also a necessary belief?   Is it impossible for the mind to dispossess itself of the conviction that there is a God? Necessity, as remarked above, may be considered as involved in universality, at least in such a case as this.   There is no satisfactory way of accounting for the universal belief in the existence of God, except that such belief is founded on the very constitution of our nature.   Nevertheless, these two criteria of intuitive truths are generally distinguished, and are in some aspects distinct.

The question then is, Is it possible for a sane man to disbelieve in the existence of God?   This question is commonly answered in the negative.   It is objected, however, that facts prove the contrary.   No man has ever been found, who denies that two and two make four, whereas atheists abound in every age and in every part of the world.

There, are, however, different kinds of necessary truths.

1. Those the opposite of which is absolutely unthinkable.   That every effect must have a cause, that a part of a given thing is less than the whole, are propositions the opposites of which cannot have

any meaning. When a man says that something is nothing, he expresses no thought. He denies what he affirms, and therefore says nothing.

2. There are truths concerning external or material things, which have a power to constrain belief different from that power which pertains to truths concerning the mind. A man cannot deny that he has a body ; and he cannot rationally deny that he has a will. The impossibility in both cases may be equal, but they are of different kinds, and affect the mind differently.

3. Again, there are truths which cannot be denied without doing violence to the laws of our nature. In such cases the denial is forced, and can only be temporary. The laws of our nature are sure sooner or later to assert themselves, and constrain an opposite belief. A pendulum when at rest hangs perpendicularly to the horizon. It may by extraneous force be made to hang at any degree of inclination. But as soon as such force is removed, it is sure to swing back to its normal position. Under the control of a metaphysical theory, a man may deny the existence of the external world, or the obligation of the moral law ; and his disbelief may be sincere, and for a time persistent ; but the moment the speculative reasons for his disbelief are absent from his mind, it of necessity reverts to its original and natural convictions. It is also possible that a man's hand may be so hardened or cauterized as to lose the sense of touch. But that would not prove that the hand in man is not normally the great organ of touch. So it is possible that the moral nature of a man may be so disorganized by vice or by a false philosophy as to have its testimony for the existence of God effectually silenced. This, however, would prove nothing as to what that testimony really is. Besides this, insensibility and the consequent unbelief cannot last. Whatever rouses the moral nature, whether it be danger, or suffering, or the approach of death, banishes unbelief in a moment. Men pass from skepticism to faith, in many cases, instantaneously ; not of course by a process of argument, but by the existence of a state of consciousness with which skepticism is irreconcilable, and in the presence of which it cannot exist. This fact is illustrated continually, not only in the case of the uneducated and superstitious, but even in the case of men of the highest culture. The simple fact of Scripture and experience is, that the moral law as written upon the heart is indelible ; and the moral law in its nature implies a lawgiver, one from whom that law emanates, and by whom it will be enforced. And, therefore, so long as men are moral creatures, they will and must believe

in the existence of a Being on whom they are dependent, and to whom they are responsible for their character and their conduct. To this extent, and in this sense, therefore, it is to be admitted that the knowledge of God is innate and intuitive ; that men no more need to be taught that there is a God, than they need to be taught there is such a thing as sin. But as men are ignorant of the nature and extent of sin, while aware of its existence, until instructed by the Word of God, and enlightened by his Spirit; so they greatly need the same sources of instruction to give them any adequate knowledge of the nature of God, and of their relations to Him.

§ 2. *The Knowledge of God is not due to a Process of Reasoning.*

Those who are unwilling to admit that the idea of God is innate as given in the very constitution of man, generally hold that it is a necessary, or, at least, a natural deduction of reason. Sometimes it is represented as the last and highest generalization of science. As the law of gravitation is assumed to account for a large class of the phenomena of the universe, and as it not only does account for them, but must be assumed in order to understand them ; so the existence of an intelligent first cause is assumed to account for the existence of the universe itself, and for all its phenomena. But as such generalizations are possible only for cultivated minds, this theory of the origin of the idea of God, cannot account for belief in his existence in the minds of all men, even the least educated.

Others, therefore, while regarding this knowledge to be the result of a course of reasoning, make the process far more simple. There are many things which children and illiterate persons learn, and can hardly avoid learning, which need not be referred to the constitution of their nature. Thus the existence of God is so obviously manifested, by everything within and around us, the belief in that existence is so natural, so suited to what we see and what we need, that it comes to be generally adopted. We are surrounded by facts which indicate design ; by effects which demand a cause. We have a sense of the infinite which is vague and void, until filled with God. We have a knowledge of ourselves as spiritual beings, which suggests the idea of God, who is a spirit. We have the consciousness of moral qualities, of the distinction between good and evil, and this makes us think of God as a being of moral perfections. All this may be very true, but it is not an adequate account of the facts of the case. It does not give a satisfactory reason for the universality and strength of the conviction of the existence of God. Our own consciousness teaches us that this is

not the ground of our own faith. We do not thus reason ourselves into the belief that there is a God; and it is very obvious
that it is not by such a process of ratiocination, simple as it is, that
the mass of the people are brought to this conclusion.

Moreover, the process above described does not account for the
origin of our belief in God, but only gives the method by which
that belief is confirmed and developed. Very little is given by intuition in any case, at least to ordinary minds. What is thus discovered needs to be expanded, and its real contents unfolded. If
this be true with the intuitions of sense and of the understanding,
why should it not be so of our religious nature?

The truth is, that all the faculties and feelings of our minds and
bodies have their appropriate objects; and the possession of the
faculties supposes the existence of those objects. The senses suppose the existence and reality of the objects of sense. The eye, in
its very structure, supposes that there is such an element as light;
the sense of hearing would be unaccountable and inconceivable
without sound; and the sense of touch would be inconceivable
were there no tangible objects. The same is true of our social
affections; they necessitate the assumption that there are relations
suited to their exercises. Our moral nature supposes that the dis
tinction between right and wrong is not chimerical or imaginary.
In like manner, our religious feelings, our sense of dependence, our
consciousness of responsibility, our aspirations after fellowship with
some Being higher than ourselves, and higher than anything which
the world or nature contains, necessitates the belief in the existence
of God. It is indeed said that if this belief is intuitive and necessary, there is no virtue in it. This objection overlooks the fact
that the moral character of our feelings depends on their nature
and not on their origin. They may spring from the constitution
of our nature, and yet be good or evil as the case may be. A
mother's love for her child is instinctive; the absence of the ma-
ternal affection in a mother is something unnatural and monstrous,
the object of universal condemnation. The sense of pity, of justice, the feelings of benevolence, are instinctive, but none the less
virtuous. The same is true of our religious feelings, and of the
belief which they involve. We cannot help feeling that we are responsible, and it is right that we should feel so. The man who has
brought himself to a state of insensibility to all moral obligation, is
what the Scriptures call a "reprobate." Adam believed in God
the moment he was created, for the same reason that he believed
in the external world. His religious nature, unclouded and unde-

filed, apprehended the one with the same confidence that his senses apprehended the other. It is of great importance that men should know and feel that they are by their very nature bound to believe in God ; that they cannot emancipate themselves from that belief, without derationalizing and demoralizing their whole being.

§ 3. *Knowledge of God not due exclusively to Tradition.*

There are some theologians who are unable to believe that the knowledge of God can be referred either to the constitution of our nature, or to any process of reasoning. Not only the exalted view of the Divine Being presented in the Bible, but the simple and perverted apprehensions of his nature prevailing among the heathen, they say must be referred to an original supernatural revelation. Such a revelation was made to our first parents, and from them passed over to their descendants. When the knowledge thus communicated began to die out among men, God again revealed himself to Abraham, and made him and his posterity the depositaries of the truth. Either, therefore, from the remains of the primitive revelation, or by radiation from the chosen people, all the knowledge of God existing in the world has been derived. The attempt is made to show that the more remote any people were from the Jews, the less did they know of God ; and the more any nation enjoyed of intercourse with the people to whom God had committed his oracles, the more correct and extended was their knowledge.

This view, although arising from reverence for the Word of God, is evidently extreme. It is true that the further we go back in the history of the world, the nearer we approach the primal revelation, the purer is the knowledge concerning Him. It may also be true, as a general rule, that the more any people were brought under the influence of the truth as held by the chosen people of God, the more enlightened they became. It may further be conceded that those who with the Bible in their hands reject its teachings, and give themselves up to their own speculations, turn, as the Apostle expresses it, " the truth of God into a lie," losing all knowledge of the living and true God. All this, however, does not prove that the knowledge of God is not written on the heart. Our intuitive perceptions need to be cherished, developed, and interpreted. We know from Scripture that the law is written in characters which cannot be obliterated, upon the souls of all men, and yet it has been perverted, misinterpreted, or disregarded by men in every age and in every part of the world.

§ 4. *Can the Existence of God be proved?*

A large class of theologians and philosophers deny that the existence of God is susceptible of proof. This is done on different grounds.

First. It is said that the knowledge of God being intuitive, it is not a proper subject of proof. This is the position taken by that class of theologians who resolve all religion into feeling, and by the modern school of speculative philosophers, who make such a wide distinction between the reason and the understanding; the former being the intuitional, and the latter the discursive faculty. Eternal and necessary truths belong to the province of the reason; subordinate truths to the sphere of the understanding. It is the understanding that argues and concludes. The reason apprehends by immediate vision. What relates to God, as the eternal, infinite, necessary Being, belongs to the province of reason, and not to that of the understanding. Even such theistic writers as Twesten [1] say that the good need no proof that God is, and that the wicked .are not susceptible of conviction. You cannot prove that a thing is beautiful, or that it is good. So neither can you prove that there is a God. The fallacy of this statement is obvious. Beauty and goodness are qualities which must be discerned by the mind, just as the objects of sight are discerned by the eye. As it is true that you cannot prove to a blind man that an object is red, so you cannot prove to a peasant that the " Paradise Lost " is sublime. But the existence of God is an objective fact. It may be shown that it is a fact which cannot be rationally denied. Although all men have feelings and convictions which necessitate the assumption that there is a God; it is, nevertheless, perfectly legitimate to show that there are other facts which necessarily lead to the same conclusion.

Besides, it is to be remembered that theistical arguments are designed to prove not only that there is a necessity for the assumption of an extra-mundane and eternal Being, but mainly, to show what that Being is; that He is a personal Being, self-conscious, intelligent, moral. All this may lie inclosed in the primary intuition, but it needs to be brought out and established.

Secondly. Another class of objections against all theistical arguments, relates to the arguments themselves. They are pronounced fallacious, as involving a *petitio principii;* or declared to be invalid as derived from false premises; or leading to conclusions other than that intended to be established. Of this every man must judge for

[1] *Vorlesungen.*

himself. They have been regarded as sound and conclusive by the wisest men, from Socrates to the present day. Of course the argument on the principle of causation must be invalid to those who deny that there is any such thing as an efficient cause; and the argument from design can have no force for those who deny the possibility of final causes.

Most of the objections to the conclusiveness of the arguments in question arises from a misapprehension of what they are intended to prove. It is often assumed that each argument must prove the whole doctrine of Theism ; whereas one argument may prove one element of that doctrine ; and other arguments different elements. The cosmological argument may prove the existence of a necessary and eternal Being; the teleological argument, that that Being is intelligent ; the moral argument that He is a person possessing moral attributes. The arguments are not designed so much to prove the existence of an unknown being, as to demonstrate that the Being who reveals himself to man in the very constitution of his nature must be all that Theism declares him to be. Such writers as Hume, Kant, Coleridge, and the whole school of transcendental philosophers, have more or less expressly denied the validity of the ordinary arguments for the existence of a personal God.

CHAPTER II.

THEISM.

THEISM is the doctrine of an extra-mundane, personal God, the creator, preserver, and governor of the world. The design of all arguments on this subject is to show that the facts around us, and the facts of consciousness, necessitate the assumption of the existence of such a Being. The arguments usually urged on this subject are the Ontological, the Cosmological, the Teleological, and the Moral.

§ 1. *The Ontological Argument.*

This is a metaphysical *à priori* argument. It is designed to show that the real objective existence of God is involved in the very idea of such a Being. It is commonly made to include all arguments which are not *à posteriori;* that is, which do not proceed from effect to cause. It has, therefore, been presented in different forms. The principal of which are the following : —

1. That in which it is presented by Anselm in his " Monologium," and more fully and definitely in his " Proslogium." The argument is substantially this. That which exists *in re* is greater than that which exists only in the mind. We have an idea of an infinitely perfect Being ; but actual existence is included, in infinite perfection. Because, if actual existence be a perfection, and if God is not actually existent, then we can conceive of a Being greater than God. His words [1] are, " Et certe id, quo majus cogitari nequit, non potest esse in intellectu solo. Si enim vel in solo intellectu est, potest cogitari esse et in re, quod majus est. . . . . Existit ergo procul dubio aliquid, quo majus cogitari non valet, et in intellectu et in re." This argument assumes that existence is of the nature of a perfection. It adds, however, nothing to the idea. The idea in itself may be complete, although there be no objective existence to answer to it. Anselm regarded the negation of the existence of God as impossible ; for God is the highest truth, the highest being, the highest good, of whom all other truth and good are the manifestations. Necessity of existence is included, according to this doctrine, in the idea of absolute perfection. In

---

[1] *Proslogium* ii., *Opera*, Paris, 1721, p. 30, b.

other words, it is included in the idea of God.   And as every man
has the idea of God, he must admit his actual existence ; for what
is necessary is of course actual.   It does not follow from our idea
of a man, that he actually exists, because man is not necessarily
existent.   But it is absurd to say that a necessarily existing Being,
does not exist.   If this argument has any validity, it is unimpor-
tant.   It is only saying that what must be actually is.   If the idea
of God as it exists in every man's mind includes that of actual
existence, then so far as the idea goes, he who has the one has the
other.   But the argument does not show how the ideal implies the
real.[1]

Des Cartes' Argument.

2. Des Cartes' argument was in this form.   We have the idea
of an infinitely perfect Being.   As we are finite, that idea could
not have originated with us.   As we are conversant only with the
finite, it could not have originated from anything around us.   It
must, therefore, have come from God, whose existence is thus a
necessary assumption.   " Habemus ideam Dei, hujusque ideæ real-
itas objectiva nec formaliter nec eminenter in nobis continetur, nec
in ullo alio præterquam in ipso Deo potest contineri ; ergo hæc idea
Dei, quæ in nobis est, requirit Deum pro causa ; Deusque proinde
existit." [2]   It is true we have many ideas or conceptions to which
there is no answering existence.   But in such cases the ideas are
arbitrary, or voluntary creations of our own minds.   But the idea
of God is necessary ; we cannot help having it.   And having it,
there must be a Being who answers to it.   Des Cartes illustrates
his argument by saying, that as it is included in our idea of a triangle, that its angles are equal to two right angles, it is so in fact.
The cases, however, are not parallel.   It is only saying that a triangle is what it is, namely, a three-sided figure, whose angles are
equal to two right angles.   But the existence of God as a fact is
not included in the definition of Him.   Kant expresses this in philosophical language, saying that if the predicate be removed, the
subject is removed ; because an analytic judgment is a mere analysis, or full statement of what is in the subject.   The judgment
that the angles of a triangle are equal to two right angles, is only
an analysis of the subject.   It is a simple statement of what a triangle is ; and therefore, if you take away the equality of the
angles, you take away the triangle.   But in a synthetic judgment,

---

[1] On this argument see Ritter's *Geschichte der Christlichen Philosophie*, vol. iii. pp. 334
340.   Shedd's *History of Doctrine*, i. pp. 229–237.   Baur's *Dreieinigkeitslehre*, ii. 374.
[2] *Meditationes de Prima Philosophia*, prop. ii. p. 89, edit. Amsterdam, 1685.

there is a synthesis, a putting together. Something is added in the judgment which is not in the subject. In this case that something is actual existence. We may infer from the idea of a perfect being, that he is wise and good; but not that he actually is; because reality is something added to the mere idea.

The only difference between the argument of Des Cartes and that of Anselm, appears to be merely formal. The one infers the existence of God, in order to account for the idea; the other argues that actual existence is included in the idea. The same illustration, therefore, is employed by the advocates of both. The argument of Anselm is the same as that derived from the definition of a triangle. You cannot think of a triangle without thinking of it as having three angles; so you cannot think of God without thinking of Him as actually existent; because actual existence enters as essentially into the idea of God, as " triangularity " enters into that of a triangle. There are, doubtless, minds which are affected by this kind of reasoning; but it has no power over the generality of men.

Dr. Samuel Clarke's Argument.

3. Dr. Samuel Clarke, equally distinguished as a mathematician, as a linguist, and as a metaphysician, published in 1705, his celebrated " Demonstration of the Being and Attributes of God." So far as the Being of God is concerned his argument is à priori. Nothing, he says, is necessarily existent, the non-existence of which is conceivable. We can conceive of the non-existence of the world; therefore the world is not necessarily existing and eternal. We cannot, however, conceive of the non-existence of space and duration; therefore space and duration are necessary and infinite. Space and duration, however, are not substances; therefore, there must be an eternal and necessary substance (i. e., God), of which they are the accidents. This argument at best gives us only the idea of a necessary and infinite something; which no class of antitheists are disposed to deny. To determine what this eternal substance is, what attributes belong to it, reference must be made to the phenomenal world, and the argument becomes à posteriori. It has been objected to Dr. Clarke's argument that it is not properly à priori. It infers from the existence of time and space the existence of a substantial Being.

Cousin's Argument.

4. Cousin, in his "Elements of Psychology," repeats continually the same argument in a somewhat different form. The idea of the infinite, he says, is given in that of the finite. We cannot have the one without having the other. "These two ideas are logical correlatives; and in the order of their acquisition, that of the finite and imperfect precedes the other; but it scarcely precedes it. It is not possible for the reason, as soon as consciousness furnishes the mind with the idea of the finite and imperfect, not to conceive the idea of the infinite and perfect. Now, the infinite and perfect is God."[1] Here again the argument is, that that is real of which we have an idea. This is not indeed assumed as a general proposition. We can imagine, says Cousin, a gorgon, or centaur, and we can imagine them not to exist; but it is not in our power, when the finite and imperfect are given, not to conceive of the infinite and perfect. This is not a chimera, he says, it is the necessary product of reason; and, therefore, it is a legitimate product. The idea of the finite and imperfect is a primitive idea, given in the consciousness; and therefore, the correlative idea of the infinite and perfect given by necessity and by the reason, must also be primitive.[2] At other times he presents this subject in a different light. He teaches that, as the mind in perception takes cognizance of the object as a real existence, distinct from itself, so the reason has an apprehension, or immediate cognition of the Infinite, with a necessary conviction of its reality as distinguished (in one sense) from itself. Self, nature, and God are alike and equally involved in the intuitive apprehension of the mind; and they are inseparable. This is very different from the common doctrine of the knowledge of God as innate, or intuitive. The latter doctrine only assumes that such is the nature of the human soul that it is intuitively convinced of its dependence on, and responsibility to a Being other than, and higher than itself. The former assumes, with the German philosophers, especially Schelling, the immediate cognition of the Infinite by the reason.

Admitting with Cousin that the ideas of the finite and infinite are correlative; that we cannot have the one without having the other; and that the mind by a rational necessity is convinced that if there be a finite, there must be an infinite; it remains to be asked, What that Infinite is? With Cousin, the Infinite is the All. Theism therefore gains nothing from these metaphysical arguments.

[1] *Elements of Psychology*, p. 375.   Translated by Prof. Henry, New York, 1856.
[2] Page 376.

§ 2. *The Cosmological Argument.*

This is founded on the principle of a sufficient cause. Syllogisti-
cally stated, the argument stands thus : Every effect must have an
adequate cause. The world is an effect. Therefore the world
must have had a cause outside of itself and adequate to account for
its existence.

A. *Causation.*

The validity and the meaning of this argument, depend on the
sense given to the words effect and cause. If an effect be correctly
defined to be an event, or product, not due to anything in itself,
but produced by something out of itself; and if by cause be understood, an antecedent to whose efficiency the effect is due ; then the
conclusion is inevitable, that the existence of the world supposes
the existence of a cause adequate to its production, provided it can
be proved that the world is an effect, *i. e.*, that it is not self-caused
or eternal.

It is well known, however, that since Hume propounded his
theory, all efficient causes have been discarded by a large class of
philosophers. The senses take cognizance of nothing but the sequence of events. One follows another. That which uniformly
precedes, we call cause ; that which uniformly follows, we call the
effect. As sequence is all the senses detect, that is all we have
any right to assume. The idea that there is anything in the
antecedent which determines the effect to be as it is and no otherwise, is altogether arbitrary. A cause, therefore, is nothing but an
invariable antecedent, and an effect an invariable consequent.

Mr. Stuart Mill[1] modified Hume's definition of cause as Dr.
Brown of Edinburgh had done before him. The former says, " It
is necessary to our using the word cause, that we should believe
not only that the antecedent always has been followed by the consequent, but that, as long as the present constitution of things en-
dures, it always will be so." So Dr. Brown[2] says, " A cause in
the fullest definition which it philosophically admits of, may be said
to be that which immediately precedes any change, and which,
existing at any time in similar circumstances, has been always, and
will be always immediately followed by a similar change." It is
obvious that this definition is not only arbitrary, but that it is inconsistent with the fundamental principles of Hume's philosophy,
and that of his followers, namely, that all our knowledge is founded
on experience. Experience relates to the past. It cannot guar-

---

[1] *Logic*, p. 203. New York, 1855.   [2] *Inquiry*, p. 17. Edinburgh, 1818.

antee the future.   If we believe that a given consequent always will follow a given antecedent, there must be some other ground for that conviction than that it always has done so.   Unless there be something in the nature of the antecedent to secure the sequence of the effect, there is no rational ground for the belief that the future must be like the past.

The Common Doctrine on the Subject.

The common doctrine on this subject includes the following points.   (1.) A cause is something.   It has a real existence.   It is not merely a name for a certain relation.   It is a real entity, a substance.   This is plain because a nonentity cannot act.   If that which does not exist can be a cause, then nothing can produce something, which is a contradiction.   (2.) A cause must not only be something real, but it must have power or efficiency.   There must be something in its nature to account for the effects which it produces.   (3.) This efficiency must be adequate ; that is, sufficient and appropriate to the effect.   That this is a true view of the nature of a cause is plain.   (1.) From our own consciousness. We are causes.   We can produce effects.   And all three of the particulars above mentioned are included in our consciousness of ourselves as cause.   We are real existences ; we have power ; we have power adequate to the effects which we produce.   (2.) We can appeal to the universal consciousness of men.   All men attach this meaning to the word cause in their ordinary language.   All men assume that every effect has an antecedent to whose efficiency it is due.   They never regard mere antecedence, however uniform in the past, or however certain in the future, as constituting a causal relation.   The succession of the seasons has been uniform in the past, and we are confident that it will continue uniform in the future ; yet no man says that winter is the cause of summer.   Every one is conscious that cause expresses an entirely different relation from that of mere antecedence.   (3.) This view of the nature of causation is included in the universal and necessary belief, that every effect must have a cause.   That belief is not that one thing must always go before another thing ; but that nothing can occur, that no change can be produced, without the exercise of power or efficiency somewhere ; otherwise something could come out of nothing.

This subject is discussed by all the metaphysicians from Aristotle downwards, and especially since the promulgation of the new doctrine adopted by Hume.[1]   It is one of the great services rendered

---

[1] See Reid's *Intellectual Powers*; Stewart's *Philosophical Essays*; Brown's *Inquiry*, and

by Dr. McCosh to the cause of truth, that he has defended the authority of those primary beliefs which lie at the foundation of all knowledge.

Intuitive Conviction of the Necessity of a Cause.

But admitting a cause to be not merely an invariable antecedent, but that to whose power the effect is due, " Ens quod in se continet rationem, cur aliud existat,"[1] as it is defined by Wolf, it remains to be asked, What is the foundation of the universal belief that every effect must have a cause? Hume says it is founded on experience, and therefore is limited by it. We see that every effect within the sphere of our observation is preceded by a cause, and we may reasonably expect that the same is true beyond the sphere of our observation. But of this we know nothing. It would be presumptuous to determine from what takes place on our little globe, what must be the law of the universe. The fact that, as far as we see, every effect has a cause, gives us no right to assume that the universe must have had a cause. Kant says that the law of cause and effect is only in our minds. Men view things in that relation; but they have no assurance that that relation holds in the world outside of themselves.

The common doctrine of the schools is, that it is an intuitive truth, a first, or self-evident principle. That is, that it is something which all men do believe, and which all men must believe. There are no self-evident, intuitive truths, if the fact that they have been denied by one or more speculative philosophers be considered proof that they are not matters of universal and necessary belief. Personal identity, the real existence of the external world, the essential distinction between right and wrong, have all been denied. Nevertheless, all men do, and all men must believe these truths. The denial of them is forced and temporary. Whenever the mind reverts to its normal state, the belief returns. So the principle of causation has been denied; yet every man is forced by the constitution of his nature to admit it, and constantly to act upon it. A man may believe that the universe is eternal; but that it began to be without a cause — that it sprang out of nothing — it is impossible to believe.

We are reduced, therefore, to this alternative. The universe is. It therefore either has been from all eternity, or it owes its existence to a cause out of itself, adequate to account for its being what it is. The theistical argument is, that the world is an effect; that

---

Essay on Cause and Effect; Sir William Hamilton's *Works;* Dr. McCosh's *Intuitions of the Mind.*　　　　　[1] See his *Ontologia,* II. iii. 2, § 881.

it has not the cause of existence in itself, that it is not eternal, and therefore we are necessitated to assume the existence of a great First Cause to whose efficiency the existence of the universe is to be referred.

B. *The World is an Effect.*

1. The first argument to prove that the world as a whole is not self-existent and eternal, is, that all its parts, everything that enters into its composition, is dependent and mutable. A whole cannot be essentially different from its constituent parts. An infinite number of effects cannot be self-existent. If a chain of three links cannot support itself, much less can a chain of a million of links. Nothing multiplied by infinity is nothing still. If we do not find the cause of our existence in ourselves, nor our parents in themselves, nor their progenitors in themselves, going back *ad infinitum* is only adding nothing to nothing. What the mind demands is a sufficient cause, and no approach to it is made by going back indefinitely from one effect to another. We are forced, therefore, by the laws of our rational nature, to assume the existence of a self-existent cause, *i. e.*, a Being endued with power adequate to produce this ever-changing phenomenal world. In all ages thinking men have been forced to this conclusion. Plato and Aristotle argued from the existence of motion, that there must be an ἀεικίνη-τον ἑαυτὸ κινοῦν, *an eternal self-moving power*, or *primum movens*, as it was called by the Schoolmen. The validity of this argument is acknowledged by almost all classes of philosophers, at least so far as to admit that we are forced to assume the existence of an eternal and necessary Being. The theistical argument is, that if everything in the world be contingent, this eternal and necessary Being must be an extramundane First Cause.

Historical Argument.

2. The second argument is the historical one. That is, we have historical evidence that the race of man, for example, has existed only a few thousand years. That mankind has existed from eternity is absolutely incredible. Even if we adopt the development theory, it affords no relief. It only substitutes millions for thousands of years. Both are equally insignificant when compared to eternity. Darwin's germ-cell as necessarily demands a self-existing cause out of itself, as a fully developed man, or the whole race of man, or the universe itself. We are shut up to the conclusion that the universe sprang out of nothing, or that there is a self-existing, eternal, extramundane Being.

Geological Argument.

3. The geological argument is to the same effect. Geologists as a class agree as to the following facts : (1.) That the extant *genera* of plants and animals inhabiting our earth, began to be within a comparatively short period in the history of our globe. (2.) That neither experience nor science, neither fact nor reason, justify the assumption of spontaneous generation. That is, there is no evidence that any living organism is ever produced by mere physical causes. Every such organism is either immediately created, or is derived from some other organism having life, already existing. (3.) Genera and species are permanent. One never passes into another. A fish never becomes a bird, nor a bird a quadruped. Modern theorists have indeed questioned these facts ; but they still are admitted by the great body of scientific men, and the evidence in their favour is overwhelming to the ordinary mind. If these principles be conceded, it follows that all the extant plants and animals on the earth began to be. And if they began to be, they were created, and therefore there must be a Creator. These considerations are merely collateral. The main argument is the one first mentioned, namely, the absolute impossibility of conceiving either of an infinite succession of contingent events, or of the origin of the universe out of nothing.

C. Objections.   Hume's Doctrine.

There are only two objections to this cosmological argument which need be noticed. The one is directed to the principle on which it is founded, and the other to the conclusion drawn from it. Hume begins his " Treatise on Human Nature," by laying down the principle that the perceptions of the human mind resolve themselves into impressions and ideas. By impressions he means " all our sensations, passions, and emotions, as they make their first appearance in the soul." By ideas is meant " the faint images of these in thinking and reasoning." [1] There can, therefore, be no idea which is not derived from some previous impression. This is the fundamental principle of his whole system. From this it follows that all our knowledge is founded on experience. We have certain impressions made by external things, and certain passions and emotions ; these are the only sources of our ideas, and therefore of our knowledge. When [2] he comes to apply this principle

---

[1] *Treatise of Human Nature*, Part i. § 1; *Works*, vol. i. Edinburgh, 1826.
[2] In Part iii. § 14.

to the nature and origin of our idea of causation, he says, all we can know on the subject is that one object or event is contiguous and antecedent to another. This is all we perceive ; all of which we can have an "impression." We have no impression of power, efficacy, energy, force, or whatever equivalent term we may choose to use. Therefore, there is no such thing. There is no such thing as efficacy or power either in mind or matter. When we use such words we have, he says, " really no distinct meaning." [1] When we see events or changes in uniform sequence, we get the habit, or, as he says, " we feel the determination," [2] to expect the consequent when we see its accustomed antecedent. Necessity, force, power, efficacy, therefore, are nothing but " a determination to carry our thoughts from one object to another." [3] " The necessity of power, which unites causes and effects, lies in the determination of the mind to pass from the one to the other. The efficacy or energy of causes is neither placed in the causes themselves, nor in the Deity, nor in the concurrence of these two principles ; but belongs entirely to the soul, which considers the union of two or more objects in all past instances." [4] Hume was fully aware of the paradoxical character of his view of causation and of its far-reaching consequences, although he insisted that his argument in its support was unanswerable. In immediate connection with the preceding quotation, he says : " I am sensible, that of all the paradoxes which I have had, or shall hereafter have, occasion to advance in the course of this treatise, the present one is the most violent, and that 'tis merely by dint of solid proof and reasoning I can ever hope it will have admission, and overcome the inveterate prejudices of mankind." [5] What he calls inveterate prejudices, are really laws of belief which God has impressed on our nature, and which all the sophistry of philosophers can never subvert.

The conclusions which Hume draws from his doctrine show his appreciation of its importance. (1.) It follows, he says, from his principle that there is no difference between causes as efficient, formal, material, exemplary, or final ; nor between cause and occasion. (2.) " That the common distinction betwixt moral and physical necessity is without any foundation in nature." " The distinction which we often make betwixt power and the exercise of it, is equally without foundation." (3.) " That the necessity of a cause to every beginning of existence is not founded on any arguments either demonstrative or intuitive." (4.) " We can never

---

[1] *Treatise of Human Nature*, vol. i. p. 216.   [2] Page 219.   [3] Page 219.
[4] Page 220.   [5] Page 220.

have reason to believe that any object exists, of which we cannot form an idea." [1] By this fourth corollary, he has reference to such things as substance, from which we receive no impression, and consequently of which we can have no idea, and therefore cannot rationally believe to exist. The same may be said of God.

In the beginning of the following section,[2] Hume with a boldness almost unparalleled says: "According to the precedent doctrine, there are no objects which, by the mere survey, without consulting experience, we can determine to be the causes of any other; and no objects which we can certainly determine in the same manner not to be causes. Anything may produce anything. Creation, annihilation, motion, reason, volition, all these may arise from one another, or from any other object we can imagine. Nor will this appear strange if we compare two principles explained above, that the constant conjunction of objects determines their causation; and that, properly speaking, no objects are contrary to each other but existence and non-existence. Where objects are not contrary, nothing hinders them from having that constant conjunction on which the relation of cause and effect totally depends."

If there be any such argument as the *reductio ad absurdum*, surely this theory of Hume refutes itself. (1.) He admits the trustworthiness of consciousness so far as "impressions" are concerned; then how can he reject the intuitions of sense, reason, and conscience? (2.) If we have no knowledge which is not derived from impressions, and no right to believe in the existence of anything of which we have not an idea derived from an impression, then we cannot believe in substance, soul, or God. (3.) For the same reason we cannot believe that there is any such thing as power or efficiency, or any difference between efficient and final causes, *i. e.*, between the expansive force of steam and the intention of the mechanist who makes a steam-engine. (4.) In like manner, we must believe that something can come out of nothing, that there is no reason that what begins to be should have a cause, even an antecedent; and, therefore, that "anything can produce anything," *e. g.*, a human volition, the universe. (5.) He cannot even state his theory without contradicting himself. He speaks of one thing "producing" another. But according to his doctrine there is no such thing as production, because he denies that there is any such thing as power or efficiency.

It is universally admitted that we have no foundation for knowledge or faith, but the veracity of consciousness. This principle

---

[1] *Treatise of Human Nature*, vol. i. pp. 226–228.   [2] § 15.

must be kept constantly in view, and must be often reiterated. Any doctrine, therefore, which contradicts the facts of consciousness, or the laws of belief which God has impressed on our nature, must be false. If, therefore, it can be shown that there are certain truths which men are constrained by the constitution of their nature to believe, those truths are to be retained in despite of all the arts of sophistry. If, therefore, it be a fact of consciousness that we ourselves are something, an *ens*, a substance, and that we have power, that we can produce effects, then it is certain that there is such a thing as power, and efficient cause. If, moreover, it be an intuitive and necessary truth that every effect must have a cause, that *ex nihilo nihil fit*, then it is absolutely certain that if the world began to be, it had an adequate cause of its existence out of itself. And, therefore, if the arguments to prove that the world is not self-existing and eternal be sound, the cosmological argument is valid and conclusive.

The Second Objection.

The other form of objection is directed not against the premises on which the cosmological argument is founded, but against the conclusion which Theists draw from them. It is admitted that something now exists; that nonentity cannot be the cause of real existence; therefore, something must have existed from eternity. It is also admitted that a *regressus ad infinitum*, or an eternal series of effects, is impossible. There must, therefore, be an eternal, self-existing Being. This is all the cosmological argument fairly proves. It does not prove that this necessary Being is extramundane, much less that it is a personal God. It may be an eternal substance of which things mutable are the phenomena.[1]

The cosmological argument is not intended to prove all that Theists hold to be true concerning God. It is enough that it proves that we must admit the existence of an eternal and necessary Being. Other arguments prove that that Being is self-conscious and intelligent. The argument, moreover, fairly proves that this Being is extramundane; for the principle of causation is that everything contingent must have the cause of its existence out of itself.

§ 3. The Teleological Argument.

A. Its Nature.

This argument also admits of being stated in a syllogistic form. Design supposes a designer. The world everywhere exhibits marks

[1] See Strauss's *Dogmatik*, vol. i. p. 382.

of design.   Therefore the world owes its existence to an intelligent author.

By design is intended, — (1.) The selection of an end to be attained. (2.) The choice of suitable means for its attainment. (3.) The actual application of those means for the accomplishment of the proposed end.

Such being the nature of design, it is a self-evident truth, or, even an identical proposition, that design is indicative of intelligence, will, and power.   It is simply saying that intelligence in the effect implies intelligence in the cause.

It is moreover true that the intelligence indicated by design is not in the thing designed.   It must be in an external agent.   The mind indicated in a book is not in the book itself, but in the author and printer.   The intelligence revealed by a calculating machine, or any similar work of art, is not in the material employed, but in the inventor and artist.   Neither is the mind indicated in the structure of the bodies of plants and animals, in them, but in Him who made them.   And in like manner the mind indicated in the world at large must be in an extramundane Being.   There is, indeed, this obvious difference between the works of God and the works of man.   In every product of human art dead materials are fashioned and united to accomplish a given end ; but the organized works of nature are animated by a living principle.   They are fashioned as it were from within outward.   In other words, they grow ; they are not constructed.   In this respect there is a great difference between a house and a tree or the human body.   But, nevertheless, in both cases, the mind is external to the thing produced ; because the end, the thought, is prior to the product.   As the thought or idea of a machine must be in the mind of the mechanist, before the machine is made ; so the idea or thought of the eye must be anterior to its formation.   "It is a simple and pregnant conclusion," says Trendelenburg,[1] "that so far as design is realized in the world, thought as its ground has preceded it."   And this thought, he goes on to say, is not dead, as a figure or model, it is connected with will and power.   It is, therefore, in the mind of a person who has the ability and purpose to carry it out.   He further says, " tiefsinnige Zweckmässigkeit bewustlos und blind," cannot be imagined, i. e., a blind and unconscious adaptation of means to an end is inconceivable.

As the conviction that design implies an intelligent agent is intuitive and necessary, it is not limited to the narrow sphere of our

---

[1] *Log. Untersuchungen*, 2nd edit. Leipzig, 1862, vol. ii. p. 28.

experience. The argument is not, Every house, ship, telescope, or
other instrument or machine, we ever saw had an intelligent maker,
therefore we may take it for granted that any similar work of art
was not formed by chance or by the operation of blind, unconscious
forces. The argument rather is, Such is the nature of design, that
it of necessity implies an intelligent agent ; and, therefore, whereever, or whenever we see evidence of design we are convinced
that it is to be referred to the operation of mind. On this ground
we are not only authorized, but compelled to apply the argument
from design far beyond the limits of experience, and to say : It is
just as evident that the world had an intelligent creator, as that a
book had an author. If a man can believe that a book was written
by chance, or by blind, unconscious force, then, and not otherwise,
can he rationally deny the validity of the argument from design in
proof of the existence of a personal God.

B. Evidences of Design in the World.

This is a boundless subject. One of the most important and
valuable of the " Bridgewater Treatises," the volume by Dr.
Charles Bell, is devoted to " The Hand, its mechanism and vital
endowments as evincing design." Hundreds of volumes would not
be sufficient to exhibit the evidence of the intelligent adaptation of
means to an end, which the world everywhere affords. In the few
pages now at command all that can be attempted, is an indication
of the nature of this evidence.[1]

Design in Single Organs.

1. No work of human art can compare with the nicety and completeness of the separate organs of organized bodies for the purpose for which they are designed. In the eye, for example, there

[1] It may be well to give the titles of the valuable series of the Bridgewater Treatises devoted to this subject, besides the work of Dr. Bell mentioned in the text. The volumes are,
The Adaptation of External Nature to the Moral and Intellectual Constitution of Man, by Dr.
Thomas Chalmers; *On the Adaptation of External Nature to the Physical Constitution of Man*,
by John Kidd; *Astronomy and General Physics treated in Reference to Natural Theology*, by
William Whewell; *Animal and Vegetable Physiology considered in Reference to Natural Theology*, by Peter Mark Roget; *Geology and Mineralogy considered in Reference to Natural
Theology*, by William Buckland; *The Power, Wisdom, and Goodness of God as manifested in
the Creation of Animals*, by William Kirby; *Chemistry, Meteorology, and the Function of Di-
gestion considered in Reference to Natural Theology*, by William Prout. *The Ninth Bridge-
water Treatise*, by C. Babbage; *Footprints of the Creator*, by Hugh Miller; *Théologie de la
Nature*, by H. Durkheim (1852, 3 vols. 8vo.); Butler's *Analogy of Religion and Nature;*
Paley's *Natural Theology;* Dr. McCosh's *Typical Forms and Special Ends in Creation;* Dr.
James Buchanan's *Faith in God and Modern Atheism compared*, 2 vols. 8vo. ; and Dr. John
Tulloch's (Principal of St. Mary's College, St. Andrew's) *Theism; The Witness of Reason
and Nature to an All-Wise and Beneficent Creator*, may also be mentioned.

is the most perfect optical instrument constructed in accordance with the hidden laws of light. We find there the only nerve in the body susceptible of the impressions of light and color. That nerve is spread out on the retina. The light is admitted through an orifice in the ball, which opening by the most delicate arrangement of muscles is enlarged or contracted, according to the degree of light which falls on the retina, which enlargement or contraction is not dependent on the will, but on the stimulus of the light itself. Light, however, merely passing through an orifice would make no image of the object from which it was reflected. It is, therefore, made to pass through lenses perfect in form so to refract the rays as to bring them to a proper focus on the retina. If the inner chamber of the eye were white, it would so reflect the rays entering the pupil at every angle as to render vision impossible. That chamber, and that alone, is lined with a black pigment. By a delicate muscular arrangement the eye is enabled to adapt itself to the distance of external objects so that the proper focus may be preserved. These are a small part of the wonders exhibited by this single organ of the body. This organ was fashioned in the darkness of the womb, with a self-evident reference to the nature and properties of light, of which the creature for whose use it was fashioned had neither knowledge or experience. If the eye, therefore, does not indicate the intelligent adaptation of means to an end, no such adaptation can be found in any work of human ingenuity.

The same remarks apply to the ear. In its cavity lies the auditory nerve. A tortuous passage is formed in the bony structure of the skull. The orifice of that passage is covered by a membrane to receive the vibration of the air ; on the centre of that membrane rests the termination of a small bone so connected as to convey those vibrations to the only nerve capable of receiving or interpreting them, or of transmitting them to the brain. It is by this organ, constructed according to the recondite principles of acoustics, that our intercourse with our fellow-men is principally kept up ; through which the marvels of speech, all the charms of music and eloquence become possible for man.

We cannot live without a constant supply of oxygen, which must every moment be brought to act upon the blood, to vitalize it, and by combining with the carbon it contains fit it for renewed use. The infant, therefore, comes into the world with an apparatus prepared for that purpose. In its formative state, it did not breathe. Yet it had lungs. They were given for a foreseen necessity. Nothing can exceed the intricacy, complication, or beauty of the organ or system of organs thus prepared, for the absolutely necessary and continuous purification of the blood, and for its distribution in an uninterrupted flux and reflux to every part of the body. This process goes on without our supervision. It is as regular during sleep as during our waking hours.

Food is as necessary for our support as air. The unborn infant needs no food. It is included in the circulation of its mother. In the state on which it is soon to enter food will be a necessity. Full provision is made beforehand for its reception and use. Teeth are embedded in the jaw for its mastication; salivary glands to furnish the fluid for its chemical preparation for the stomach; an œsophagus to convey it to the stomach, where it meets with a fluid found nowhere else, capable of dissolving and digesting it. It then comes into contact with a set of absorbent vessels which select from it the elements suited for the wants of the body and reject all the rest. The valuable portion is poured into the blood by which it is distributed, each constituent going to its own place and answering its predestined purpose ; carbon to be consumed to keep up the vital heat, lime to the bones, fibrine to the muscles, phosphorus to the brain and nerves.

The child before birth has no need of organs for locomotion or for apprehending external objects. But it was foreseen that it would need them, and therefore they are prepared beforehand. The bones are grooved for the reception of muscles, and have projections for points of support; joints of all kinds, hinge and ball and socket, for the flexure of the limbs ; the instruments for motion, the contractile fibres, arranged and attached, according to the strict laws of mechanics, so as best to secure the two ends of symmetry and power. Thus the body is a perfect marvel of mechanical contrivances. The several organs, therefore, of the animal frame, viewed separately, present the most incontestible evidence of foresight, intelligence, and wisdom. This, however, is only a small part of the evidence of design furnished even by the body.

Design in the Relation of one Organ to Another.

2. Every animal is a complete whole. Each part has a designed and predetermined reference to every other part. The organs of sight, hearing, breathing, nutrition, locomotion, etc., are so arranged and adjusted as to answer a common purpose to the best advantage. Besides, these organs, although common to all animals (at least to all above the lowest), are modified in each genus and species to

meet its peculiar necessities. If the animal is to live on the land all its organs are adapted to that condition. If it is to live in the water or move through the air, all is prepared beforehand for that destination. And more than this, if one organ be designed for some special use, all the rest are modified in accordance with that purpose. If the stomach is suited for the digestion of flesh, then the teeth, the limbs, the claws, are all adapted to secure and prepare the proper aliment. So complete is the adaptation that the anatomist can determine from a single bone the genus or species to which the animal belonged. Birds which wade in the water have long legs and long necks. Those which float on the surface, have web feet, and feathers impenetrable by water; two things which have causal relation, and which are united by a kind of intelligence external to the animal itself. Birds which fly in the air are fitted for their destiny by hollow bones, wide-spread wings, and great accumulation of muscles on the breast. Those which climb trees have feet and tail adapted for that purpose, and, as in the case of the wood-pecker, a sharp bill for boring the tree and a barbed tongue to seize its food. These modifications of animal structure are endless, all showing an external intelligence cognizant of the necessities of every distinct species.

The Adaptation of the Organs to the Instinct of Animals.

3. There is a correspondence between the organs of every animal and the instincts by which it is endowed. Beasts and birds of prey having the instinct to feed on flesh have all the organs requisite to satisfy this inward craving. Those having an instinct for vegetable food, have teeth and stomachs adapted for that purpose. The bee whose body secretes wax, has the instinct to build cells; the spider furnished with the peculiar viscid matter, and apparatus for spinning it, makes a web and watches for its prey. So it is throughout all animated nature. Here then are two very distinct things: instinct and corporeal organs; the instinct cannot account for the organs nor the organs for the instinct; and yet they are never found the one without the other. They of necessity, therefore, imply an intelligence which implants the instinct and furnishes the appropriate organs.

Argument from Prevision.

4. There cannot be a more decisive proof of intelligence than prevision; preparation for an event in the future. The world is full of evidence of such prevision. It is seen not only in the prep-

aration of the organs of sight, hearing, breathing, nutrition, etc. for necessities still future; but still more strikingly in the provision made for the support of young animals as soon as they are born. In the mammalia before the birth of the offspring, the breast or udder begins to swell; it commences the secretion of milk, so that the moment the young animal enters the world he finds prepared the most nutritious and suitable food the world contains. The egg furnishes a still more instructive illustration. It consists of albumen and the yolk. To the yolk is attached a minute germ or cell. When by heat the germ begins to develop, if nourishment were not provided and at hand, it would of necessity perish. But the yolk is there to supply the needed material out of which the future animal is fashioned. If this does not indicate a foreseeing mind and a providing power, then the most skilful productions of human skill and kindness do not prove the intelligence of man. Where then is this intelligence? Not in the parent bird, for it understands nothing about it. Not in mere blind forces of nature. There may possibly be room for question where to place it; but to deny that these provisions indicate an intelligent agency somewhere, is altogether irrational.

Vegetable Organisms.

5. The vegetable kingdom is as full of the indications of benevolent design as the animal. Plants have their organism and their physiology. Their structure, in their organs for growth and reproduction, is quite as marvellous as that of most species of the animal kingdom. They constitute an essential part in the great system of nature, without which there could be no sentient life on our globe. Animals cannot live on inorganic matter. It is the province of the plant to reduce this matter into such a state as to be fit for the support of animal life. If it were not therefore for the functions of the leaf which transmutes the inorganic into the organic, there could be no sentient life on our earth. Is there no design here? Is there no intelligent adaptation of one part of the great system of nature to another?

From the Adaptations of Nature.

6. This leads to another department of the subject. The evidences of design are not confined to the separate organs of the plant or animal; nor to the relations of these organs to each other; nor, in the case of animals, to the instinct which impels to the proper use of those organs; they are to be found just as abundantly

in the adaptation of external nature to the necessities of animal
and vegetable life.   Neither plants nor animals could exist without
light, air, heat, water, and soil, to produce the common food of all
living things.   Who created the light and heat and diffuses them
over the whole earth?   Who made the sun from which they radi-
ate?   Who constituted the atmosphere with its chemical adjust-
ments, precisely what is necessary for the support of life, everywhere and always the same, and poured it round our globe?   How
is it that water at a certain temperature evaporates, rises in mist,
is gathered into clouds, is carried everywhere by the winds, and
falls in rain to fertilize the earth?   The eye supposes light, as the
lungs suppose air; the appetite of hunger supposes food, and the
power of digestion.   Food supposes soil, light, heat, and water.
Surely this is one great system.   There is unity and mutual relation in all its parts.   It must have had one author, and He must
be infinite in intelligence and goodness.

All living Creatures on the Earth have Organic Relations.

7. The design indicated in nature is, however, not confined to
the individual organisms and to their relations to the world around
them, but it has in the progress of science been discovered, that
the whole vegetable and animal world has been constructed on
one comprehensive plan.   As there is a relation of one organ of a
given plant or animal to all others and to the whole, so the whole
race of plants, and the whole race of animals are related.   There
are certain typical forms of which all the infinite variety of plants
are modifications; and certain other types of which the innumerable genera, species, and varieties of animals are only modifications;
and these modifications are precisely of the kind to suit each species for its end, and for the circumstances in which it is to live.
So obviously is this the case that Professor Agassiz's " Essay on
Classification," is, to say the least, as strong an argument for the
being of God as any of the " Bridgewater Treatises."   And it is
so regarded by its illustrious author.   On page 10 of his " Contributions to the Natural History of the United States," he says,
" I know those who hold it to be very unscientific to believe that
thinking is not something inherent in matter, and that there is an
essential difference between inorganic and living and thinking
beings.   I shall not be prevented by any such pretensions of a false
philosophy from expressing my conviction that as long as it cannot
be shown that matter or physical forces do actually reason, I shall
consider any manifestation of thought as evidence of the existence

of a thinking Being as the author of such thought, and shall look upon an intelligent and intelligible connection between the facts of nature as direct proof of the existence of a thinking God, as certainly as man exhibits the power of thinking, when he recognizes their natural relation."

Evidence that the Earth was designed for Man.

8. It is not only, however, the living organisms inhabiting our earth, which exhibit such evidence of an intelligent creator, but also the earth itself. If a father, who when he provides a home for his children, fits it up with all the necessities and all the luxuries which they can possibly need, gives indisputable evidence of intelligence and love, then are those attributes to be ascribed to Him who fitted up this world to be the home of his creatures. This is seen, as already intimated, in the constitution of the atmosphere, in the distribution of light and heat, of electricity and magnetism, in the establishment of those laws which secure the regular succession of the seasons, in the preparation of soil by the disintegration of rocks, the falling of rain, the deposition of dew which falls gently with life-giving power on the thirsty earth; in innumerable other provisions and dispositions of the forces of nature without which neither vegetable nor animal life could be sustained. There are many special provisions of this kind which fill the mind with gratitude and wonder. It is a general law that bodies contract as they become colder. Water, however, when it freezes expands and becomes lighter. If it were not for this benevolent exception to the general law, not only would the inhabitants of all our rivers perish, but the greater part of the temperate zone would be uninhabitable. It is no answer to this argument to say that there are a few other exceptions to this law. We may not know the final cause why bismuth should expand on cooling; but this does not prevent our knowing why ice is made lighter than water. Our not understanding one sentence in a book, does not prove that it has no meaning, nor that we cannot understand another sentence.

The whole configuration of the earth, its position in relation to the sun, and the inclination of its axis, are obviously intended to render it a suitable residence for the creatures by which it is inhabited. Their well-being depends on the distribution of land and water on its surface; on the elevation of its mountain ranges and plateaus, and on the ocean currents which are determined by the configuration of its coasts. If North and South America were not connected by the narrow Isthmus of Darien, Great Britain and the northwestern portions of Europe would be uninhabitable. They owe the moderate temperature which they enjoy to the immense body of warm water, which is prevented by that Isthmus from flowing into the Pacific, being floated in a northeasterly direction across the Atlantic. When we see such benevolent arrangements among men, we refer them instinctively and by a rational necessity to a benevolent and intelligent agent. No rational ground exists for refusing to ascribe like arrangements in nature to a similar source. Is it any more an evidence of prudent or benevolent fore-sight that a man should store away abundant fuel for himself or others, knowing that winter is approaching, than that God has laid up inexhaustible stores of coal in the bowels of the earth, for the use of his children on the earth?

Cosmical Arrangements.

9. The argument for design founded on cosmical arrangements is so vast a subject that it seems absurd even to refer to it, in a single paragraph. The simple facts are, that our globe is one of eight primary planets which revolve round the sun. The most distant of these planets is some three thousand millions of miles from the central luminary. These planets all move in the same direction, in nearly circular orbits, in nearly the same plane, and with so equable a motion that each performs its revolutions in the proper time. The stability of the system depends on these circumstances. To secure these results matter must attract matter according to its quantity and the square of its distance. The central body must be of such mass as to hold the planets in their course. The centrifugal and centripetal forces must be exactly balanced, to prevent the planets from flying off into space, or falling into the sun. Each planet must have been projected with a precise definite velocity to secure its orbit being nearly a circle, rather than any other curve. The central body alone, in accordance with the evident plan, is luminous and heat-producing. All the others are opaque and cold. These are facts, which Sir Isaac Newton says he is "forced to ascribe to the counsel and contrivance of a voluntary agent."[1] Since the time of Newton, indeed, it has been the commonly received theory that the planets were at one time fluid, highly heated, and luminous; and that they have become opaque in the process of cooling. But this only puts the argument one step back. The fact is that a most wonderful and beneficent result has been accomplished. The question How? is of minor im-

[1] Newton's *First Letter to Bentley*, quoted by Tulloch, *Theism*, edit. N. Y. 1855, p. 109

portance. It is the beneficence of the result which indicates mind, and this indication of mind implies a " voluntary agent."

Our solar system itself, therefore, is vast, varied, and well ordered. Our system, however, is one of probably hundreds of millions. At least astronomers assert their knowledge of a hundred million of suns, some of which are incalculably larger than ours. Sirius is calculated to shine with a light equal to two hundred and fifty of our suns ; Alcyone with that of twelve thousand suns. The nearest of these stars is separated from the outer planet of our system twenty-one billions of miles. These millions of stars are not scattered equally through space, but are gathered into groups, the members of which bear an obvious relation to each other.

Besides these systems in which planets are assumed to revolve around suns, there are others in which suns revolve around suns, at distances proportioned to their magnitude. The light emanating from these great luminaries is of different colors, white, red, blue.

Then more distant in space float the unresolved nebulæ. Whether these nebulæ are vast continents of stars too distant to be distinguishable, or cosmical matter in a formative state, is still an open question with astronomers. Two thousand have been counted in the northern hemisphere, and one thousand in the southern. They assume every variety of form ; some are spherical, some fan-shaped, some spiral, some in circular rings. It is estimated that the light of some of the stars has been many thousand years in reaching our earth, although travelling at the rate of more than ten millions of miles a minute.

Throughout this vast universe order reigns. In the midst of endless variety, there is unity. The same laws of gravitation, of light, and of heat everywhere prevail. Confusion and disorder are the uniform result of chance or blindly operating forces. Order is the sure indication of mind. What mind! what wisdom! what power! what beneficence! does this all but infinite universe display!

" The result of our whole experience," said Sir Gilbert Eliot, writing to Hume himself, " seems to amount to this : — There are but two ways in which we have ever observed the different parcels of matter to be thrown together, — either at random, or with design and purpose. By the first, we have never seen produced a regular complicated effect, corresponding to a certain end ; by the second, we uniformly have. If, then, the works of nature and the productions of men resemble each other in this one general characteristic, will not even experience sufficiently warrant us to ascribe to both a similar, though proportionable, cause." [1]

This argument from design is constantly urged in the Old Testament, which appeals to the heavens and the earth as revealing the being and perfections of God. The Apostle Paul says that the living God, who made heaven and earth, and the sea and all that is therein, hath not left himself without a witness. (Acts xiv. 15–17.) He demonstrated to the Athenians the nature of God from his works and from our relation to him as his offspring. (Acts xvii. 23–31.) To the Romans he said that the eternal power and Godhead of the Supreme Being, are clearly seen, being understood by the things that are made. (Rom. i. 20.) The ancient philosophers drew the same conclusion from the same premises. Anaxagoras argued that νοῦς, *mind*, must be admitted as controlling everything in the world, because everything indicates design. Socrates constantly dwells on this as the great proof of the being of God. Cicero [2] says that it is as impossible that an ordered world could be formed by the fortuitous concurrence of atoms, as that a book should be composed by the throwing about letters at random. Trendelenburg,[3] after referring to that passage, says : " It is perhaps more difficult to assume, that by the blind combination of chemical and physical elements and forces, any one even of the organs of the body should be formed, — the eye, for example, so clear, sharp, and all-seeing, — much less the harmonious union of organs which make up the body, than that a book should be made by chance, by throwing types about."

Philo presents the argument in its simplest syllogistic form. " No work of art is self-made. The world is the most perfect work of art. Therefore, the world was made by a good and most perfect Author. Thus we have the knowledge of the existence of God." [4] All the Christian fathers and subsequent theologians have reasoned in the same way. Even Kant, although denying its conclusiveness, says that the teleological argument should always be treated with respect. It is, he says, the oldest, the clearest, and the best adapted to the human mind.

[1] Dr. Buchanan's *Analogy a Guide to Truth and an Aid to Faith*, edit. Edinburgh, 1864, p. 414.
[2] *De Natura Deorum*, ii. 37.   [3] *Logische Untersuchungen*, vol. ii. p. 64
[4] *De Monarchia*, i. § 4, edit. Leipsig, 1828, vol. iv. p. 290.

§ 4. *Objections to the Argument from Design.*

A. *The Denial of Final Causes.*

The doctrine of final causes in nature must stand or fall with the doctrine of a personal God. The one cannot be denied without denying the other. And the admission of the one involves the admission of the other. By final cause is not meant a mere tendency, or the end to which events either actually or apparently tend; but the end contemplated in the use of means adapted to attain it. The contemplation of an end, is a mental act. The selection and use of means adapted to attain such end, are both intelligent and voluntary acts. But an intelligent voluntary agent is a person.[1] In other words, the use of means to accomplish a contemplated end is a function of personality, or at least of intelligent agency.

Such being the nature of final causes, they are of course denied, (1.) By the positivist, who believes nothing but facts of which the senses take cognizance; and who admits of no other causation than regularity of sequence. As efficiency, intention, and mind are not perceived by the senses, they are not, and cannot be philosophically admitted. (2.) By those who, while they admit such a thing as force, and, therefore, in that sense, a cause, allow of no distinction between physical, vital, and mental causes, or forces; and who maintain that the one can be resolved into either of the others. The advocates of this theory make thought a product of the brain; and have as their watch-word, " Ohne Phosphor kein Gedanke." Of course phosphorus must be before thought, and therefore there can be no final cause in the production of phosphorus, or of anything else. (3.) Final causes are denied by those who regard the universe as the development of the infinite Being under the operation of necessary law. Of that Being no intelligence, consciousness, or will can be predicated. Consequently there can be no preconceived design to be accomplished, either by the universe as a whole, or by any of its parts. According to Spinoza, therefore, final causes are " humana figmenta et deliria."

If you should ask a peasant, where a tree or the body of an animal came from, he would probably answer, " Why, it grew." That for him is the final fact. And so it is for all the advocates of the above-named theories. Thus it is that extremes (the peasant's thought and the savant's theory) meet. What more, what

---

[1] This is in accordance with the accepted theological definition of a person as a " suppositum intelligens."

deeper thought is found in the words of Stuart Mill than in the peasant's answer, when the logician says: "Sequences entirely physical and material, as soon as they had become sufficiently familiar to the human mind, came to be thought perfectly natural, and were regarded not only as needing no explanation themselves, but as being capable of affording it to others, and even of serving as the ultimate explanation of things in general." [1]

B. *Objections of Hume and Kant.*

Hume's answer to the argument from design, or final causes, is, that our knowledge is limited by experience. We have often seen houses, ships, engines, and other machines made, and therefore, when we see similar products of human skill we are authorized to infer that they too were constructed by an intelligent author. But the world belongs to an entirely different category; we have never seen a world made; and therefore we have no rational ground for assuming that this world had a maker. "When two species of objects," says Hume,[2] "have always been observed to be conjoined together, I can infer, by custom, the existence of one whenever I see the existence of the other, and this I call an argument from experience. But how this argument can have place, where the objects, as in the present case, are single, individual, without parallel, or specific resemblance, may be difficult to explain. And will any man tell me with a serious countenance, that an orderly universe must arise from some thought and art, like the human, because we have experience of it? To ascertain this reasoning, it were requisite that we had experience of the origin of worlds; and it is not sufficient surely that we have seen ships and cities arise from human art and contrivance." What experience teaches is that design implies intelligence; *i. e.*, that we never see the adaptation of means to an end without having evidence that such adaptation is the work of an intelligent agent. And, therefore, even under the guidance of experience we infer that wherever we see design, whether in nature or in art, there must be an intelligent agent. But experience is not the ground or limit of this conviction. It is an intuitive truth, self-evident from its nature, that design cannot be accounted for on the ground of chance or necessity. Let any man try to persuade himself that a watch is the product of chance, and he will see how futile is the attempt.

Kant presents substantially the same objection as Hume when

---

1 *Logic*, edit. London, 1851, vol. i. p. 366.
2 "Dialogues on Natural Religion," *Works*, edit. Edinburgh, 1826, vol. ii. p. 449.

he says that the concatenation of cause and effect is confined to the external world, and therefore that it is illogical to apply the principle of causation to account for the existence of the external world itself. He further objects that the evidences of design in nature would prove only a demiurgus, or world-builder, and not an extramundane God. It is further urged against the sufficiency of the teleological argument, that even if it proved the author of the world to be distinct from it, it would not prove him to be infinite, because the world is finite, and we cannot infer an infinite cause from a finite effect.

Answer to the Objections.

In answer to these objections it may be remarked that what the argument from design is intended to prove, and what it does prove, is, (1.) That the Author of the universe is an intelligent and voluntary agent. (2.) That He is extramundane and not merely the life, or soul of the world, for the design is shown not simply or chiefly by the moulding of organized bodies by a principle acting from within outward; but by the adaptation of things external to such organisms, to their various necessities; and by the disposition and orderly arrangement of immense bodies of matter, separated by millions, or even billions of miles. (3.) The immensity of the universe through the whole of which design is manifest, proves that its cause must be adequate to the production of such an effect; and if the effect be, as it is to us, incomprehensibly great, the cause must be so also. And incomprehensibly great and infinitely great, are practically equivalent. But besides, the cosmological argument proves that God is not only maker, but creator. And creation implies the possession of infinite power. Not only because the difference between existence and non-existence is infinite, but because in Scripture creation is always represented as the peculiar work of the infinite God. So far as we know all creature power is limited to self-action, or to the more or less limited control of what already exists.

What has already been said may be a sufficient answer to the objection that while design does indeed prove intelligence, yet that intelligence may be in matter itself, or in nature (a *vis insita*), as in the soul of the world. These points, as they are generally presented, concern more properly the relation of God to the world, than his existence. They involve the admission of the existence of an intelligence somewhere, adequate to account for all the phenomena of the universe. They involve consequently the denial that these phenomena are to be referred either to chance, or the action of mere physical laws. Where that intelligence is placed, is not the question. Wherever placed it must be a person ; and not merely an unintelligent force acting according to necessary law. For the evidence of voluntary action and of benevolence is as clear as that of intelligence. And the considerations already urged prove that this voluntary, intelligent Being must be extramundane; a conclusion which is rendered still more evident from our relation to Him as responsible and dependent.

C. *Miscellaneous Objections.*

1. It is objected that both in the vegetable and animal kingdoms there are malformations, abnormal productions, which are inconsistent with the idea of the control of an infinite intelligence. This is at best merely an argument from our ignorance. Admitting that there are in nature some things which we cannot account for, this does not invalidate the argument drawn from the innumerable cases of benevolent design. If Mr. Babbage's calculating machine should once in many million of times present the wrong number, this would not prove that there was no intelligence manifested in its construction. It is not necessary even to assume that such apparently irregular action is to be referred to the imperfection of the machine. For what we know, its maker may have a reason for such action, which we cannot discover. In every extended piece of music, discords here and there occur, which pain the ear, and which those unskilled in music cannot account for, but which the competently instructed perceive are taken up and resolved into a higher harmony. If a prince should give us a chest containing millions in coin and jewels, we should not question his kind intention, even should we find among them a spurious dime for whose presence we could not account. It would be insane to reject the Bible with all its sublime and saving truths, because there may be in it a few passages which we cannot understand, and which in themselves seem inconsistent with the perfection of its author. No man refuses to believe in the sun and to rejoice in its light because there are dark spots on its surface for which he cannot account. Ignorance is a very healthful condition of our present state of being.

Useless Organs.

2. A second objection of much the same kind is founded on the fact that we find members in organized bodies for which they have no use. For example, men have mammæ; the whale has teeth

which are never developed and which the animal does not need; animals have bones which they never use; birds and crocodiles have their skulls formed of separate bones as well as viviparous animals, although in their case there seems to be no utility in such arrangement. Even Professor Owen urges this objection. In his work on " Limbs," [1] he says, " I think it will be obvious that the principle of final adaptation fails to satisfy all the conditions of the problem. That every segment and almost every bone which is present in the human hand and arm should exist in the fin of the whale," where they are not needed, does not appear consistent with the principle. Again, in another place, he says, [2] " The cranium of the bird, which is composed in the adult of a single bone, is ossified from the same number of points as in the human embryo, without the possibility of a similar purpose being subserved thereby, in the extrication of the chick from the fractured egg-shell . . . . These, and a hundred such facts force upon the contemplative anatomist the inadequacy of the teleological hypothesis."

On this it may be remarked: (1.) That the objection bears only on the individual organism of plants or animals, whereas the evidences of design are scattered over the whole universe. (2.) This objection also is founded on our ignorance. The argument is that because we cannot see the reason for a certain arrangement, no such reason exists. (3.) It takes the lowest view of utility, namely, that which contemplates the immediate wants of the individual organism. Things which are not needed for its necessities may answer a much higher end. In a great building use is not the only end contemplated; there are symmetry and unity, æsthetic ends of as much value as mere comfort or convenience. Scientific men have demonstrated that all animals are in their structure only modifications of four typical forms. These forms are preserved in all the genera and species included under these general classes. The presence, therefore, of these characteristic features of the type, even where not needed for the individual, serve to indicate the unity of the plan on which the whole animal kingdom is constructed. We must remember that what we do not see, cannot disprove the reality of what we do see.

Instinct.

3. A third objection is sometimes derived from the operations of instinct. Instinct, according to Dr. Reid, is " a natural blind impulse to certain actions, without having any end in view, without deliberation, and very often without any conception of what we

[1] Page 39.   [2] *Homologies*, p. 73.

do." [1] Dr. Whately also says: "An instinct is a blind tendency to a mode of action independent of any consideration on the part of the agent, of the end to which the action leads." Paley defines it to be "a propensity prior to experience and independent of instruction." [2] The argument is that as "a blind impulse" contemplating no end, effects all the marvellous contrivances which we see in the works of irrational animals, similar contrivances in nature cannot prove intelligence in the author of nature. The answer to this argument is : —

1. That it is founded on a wrong definition of instinct. It is not a blind impulse. It is that measure of intelligence given to animals which enables them to sustain their lives, to continue their race, and to answer the necessities of their being. Within certain limits this form of intelligence, both in man and in irrational animals, acts blindly. The impulse which leads the young of all animals to seek their nourishment in the appropriate way and in the proper place, is no doubt blind. The same is also probably true of the impulse which leads many animals to make provision in summer for the necessities of winter. Neither can it be supposed that the bee has always and everywhere constructed its cell according to the nicest mathematical principles, under the guidance of an intelligent apprehension of those principles. These operations which are performed without instructions, and always from age to age in the same way, indicate a guidance which may be called blind in so far that those under its influence do not devise the plan on which they act, although they may know the end they have in view. But the intelligence of animals goes far beyond these narrow limits. Not only does the beaver construct his dam according to the nature of the locality and the force of the stream on which he fixes his habitations, but we constantly see it, as well as other animals, varying its mode of operation to suit special emergencies. Instinct, therefore, as designating the principle which controls the action of irrational animals, is not blind, but intelligent. It admits of the contemplation of an end, and of the selection and application of means appropriate for its accomplishment. Even admitting, therefore, that the intelligence manifested in nature is of the same kind as that manifested by animals, yet the difference in degree is infinite.

2. No measure, however, of intellect of the grade or character of instinct is sufficient to account for the phenomena of the uni-

---

[1] *Active Powers*, iii. i. 2, vol. iv. p. 48: edit. Charlestown, 1815.
[2] *Natural Theology*, chap. xviii.

verse. Instinct is concerned with the wants of individual organism. But who adapts the organs of an animal to its instincts? Who adapts external nature, air, light, heat, water, food, etc., etc., to its necessities? What relation has instinct to the stellar universe?

3. Moreover, these instincts themselves are among the phenomena to be accounted for. If they are blind impulses, can they be accounted for, in all their variety and in all their accommodation to the nature and wants of animals, by a blind impulse pervading all things? The fact is that the adaptation of external nature to the instincts of the different classes of animals, and of their instincts to external nature, affords one of the most convincing proofs of an intellect exterior to both, and ordering the one in relation to the other.

4. It is to be remembered, although the topic of a separate argument, that the soul of man with all its wonderful powers and capacities, intellectual, moral, and religious, is one of the facts to be accounted for. To trace the existence of the soul of man to " a blind impulse," is to assume that the effect immeasurably transcends its cause, which is assuming an effect without a cause.

5. All these objections take for granted the eternal existence of matter, and the eternity of physical forces. As these are, they must have existed from eternity, or have begun to be. If they began to be they must have had a cause outside of themselves. That cause cannot be nonentity. It must be a self-existing, eternal substance, having the intelligence, power, will, and benevolence adequate to account for the universe and all that it contains. That is, the cause of the universe must be a personal God.

§ 5. *The Moral, or Anthropological Argument.*

A. *Nature of the Argument.*

As the image of the sun reflected from a mirror, or the smooth surface of a lake, reveals to us that the sun is, and what it is ; so the soul of man, just as clearly, and just as certainly, reveals that God is and what He is. The reflection of the sun does not teach us everything that is true concerning that luminary ; it does not reveal its internal constitution, nor tell us how its light and heat are maintained from age to age. In like manner the soul, as the image of God, does not reveal all that God is. In both cases, and equally in both cases, what is revealed is true, that is, trustworthy. It answers to the objective reality. As we know that the sun really is what its reflection represents him as being, so we know that God is what the nature of the human soul declares Him to be. Doubt in the one case is just as unreasonable, and we may say, just as impossible as in the other.

It has been shown in the preceding chapter that every man has in his own nature the evidence of the existence of God, an evidence which never can be obliterated, and which will force conviction on the most unwilling. It is no less true that every man has in himself the same irresistible evidence that God is an extramundane personal Being; that He is intelligent, voluntary, and moral; that He knows; that He has the right to command; and that He can punish and can save.

It may naturally be asked, If this be so; if every man has in his own nature a witness whose competency he cannot question, and whose testimony he cannot ignore, What is the use of arguing about the matter? For two reasons, first, because even self-evident truths are often denied; and secondly, because men, in their present moral state, are under a strong temptation to deny the existence of a holy and just God; and thirdly, because efforts are constantly made to pervert or contradict the testimony of our nature to the existence and nature of God.

B. *Argument from the Existence of the Mind.*

Every man has in his own consciousness the evidence of the existence of mind. He knows that he is an intelligent, personal being. He knows that his personality does not reside in his body, but in his soul. It is included in the facts of consciousness that the soul and body are distinct, that they are different substances having not only different but incompatible attributes. That such is the general conviction of men is plain from all languages recognizing the distinction; and from the fact that it is never denied except by speculative or theoretical writers. The common consciousness of men as revealed by their forms of speech, and by their avowals, and by the universal belief, in some form, of a state of conscious existence after death, bears witness to the truth that the soul is something different from, and far superior to the body. How is the existence of this immaterial, thinking, immortal substance which we call self, to be accounted for? That it has not always existed is undeniable. If it began to be, it must have the cause of its existence out of itself. That cause cannot be the soul of the parent, for that also is an effect. It began to be. And it is universally admitted that an infinite series of effects is unthinkable. If the soul cannot be accounted for by derivation in unending series of steps from those who preceded us, neither can it be conceived of as a product of the body, or of physical forces and combinations. It would seem to be a self-evident proposition, that the effect cannot contain in it more than is in its cause; that intelligence cannot be the product of what is unintelligent. This also is confirmed by all experience.

We are conversant in our present state, first, with matter, with its properties and laws or forces; secondly, with vegetable life; thirdly, with animal life; and fourthly, with mind, endowed with a life of a much higher order. These different elements, or kinds of existence, although marvellously combined and intermingled, are distinct. As a fact of experience, mere matter with its physical forces never originates vegetable life; vegetable life of itself never originates or passes over into animal life; and animal life never originates, and is never developed into intellectual or spiritual life. There is an impassable gulf between these several departments of being. As soon as the principle of life leaves a plant or animal, the physical forces belonging to matter work its dissolution. These are facts indelibly impressed on the convictions of the mass of mankind. They are conclusions to which universal experience has led the minds of all men. They are indeed denied by certain scientific men; but the theory on which that denial is founded involves the denial of so many intuitive and necessary truths; it does such violence to the laws of belief impressed upon our nature, and on the validity of which all knowledge depends, that it can never be more than a precarious and temporary belief on the part of those who adopt it, and can never have control over the minds of men. This is not the place to enter upon the discussion of the theory of materialism. We have a right to appeal to the general conviction of mankind that mind cannot be the product of matter. If this be so, as our minds are not self-existent and eternal, it must be true, as even the heathen believed, that our spirits owe their existence to Him who is the Father of spirits.

C. *From the Nature of the Soul.*

There are two laws, or general facts, which seem to characterize all the works of nature. By nature is here meant all things out of God. The first of these laws is, that whatever capacities, necessities, or desires exist, or are found in any organism, adequate provision is made to meet and satisfy them all. This is obviously true with regard to the vegetable world. Plants have organs for the selection of the materials necessary for their growth and maturity, from the soil ; organs for the absorption of carbon from the atmosphere ; the capacity of being appropriately affected by light and heat ; organs of propagation designed for the continuance of each after its kind. All these necessities are met. Soil, atmosphere, light, heat, and water, are all provided. The same is no less true with regard to the animal world in all its endless variety of forms. Food, light, heat, air, and water, are suited to their several necessities ; to their organs, and to their instincts. If they have the appetite of hunger, they have organs for the appropriation of their food, and for its digestion ; the instinct for its selection, and food suited to each, is ever at hand. So of all the other necessities of their nature.

The second law, or general fact is, that all these living organisms reach perfection, and fully accomplish the end of their being. That is, they become all they are capable of being. All that belongs to their nature is fully developed. All their capacities are fully exercised, and all their wants fully satisfied.

These two things are true of every living creature within the compass of human knowledge, except Man. So far as his body is concerned, they are true in regard to him also. His physical necessities are all met by the present circumstances of his being. His body becomes all that it is capable of being, in this stage of existence. But these things are not true with regard to his soul. It has capacities which are not fully developed in this world, and never can be. It has desires, aspirations, and necessities for which the world does not furnish the appropriate objects. It is, therefore, as evidently designed and adapted for a higher and spiritual state of existence, as his body is adapted to the present order of things. The soul of man has, in the first place, intellectual powers capable of indefinite expansion, which in this world never reach their utmost limit. With these is connected a desire of knowledge which is never satisfied. In the second place, the soul of man has a capacity for happiness which nothing in the world, nor the whole world could it be attained, can by possibility fill. The animal is satisfied. Its capacity for happiness is here fully provided for. In the third place, the soul has aspirations to which nothing in this life corresponds. It longs for fellowship with what is far above itself ; what is boundless, and eternal. In the fourth place, with all these powers, desires, and aspirations, it is conscious of its weakness, insufficiency, and dependence. It must have an object to worship, to love, to trust ; a Being who can satisfy all its necessities, and under whose guardianship it can be safe from those powers of evil to which it knows that it is on all sides and at all times exposed; a Being whose existence, and whose relation to itself, can explain all the mysteries of its own being, and secure its felicity in the future, on which it knows it must soon enter. Just as certainly as hunger in the animal supposes that there is food adapted to still its cravings, so certainly does this hunger of the soul suppose that there is some Being in the universe to satisfy its necessities. In both cases the craving is natural, universal, and imperative.

It cannot be that man is an exception to the laws above-mentioned; that he alone, of all that lives, has capacities, desires, necessities, for which no provision has been made. God is the correlative of man, in the sense that the existence of such a creature as man necessitates the assumption of such a Being as God.

D. *From the Moral Nature of Man.*

The familiar facts of consciousness on this subject are, —

1. That we have, by the constitution of our nature, a sense of right and wrong; we perceive or judge some things to be right, and others to be wrong. This perception is immediate. As the reason perceives some things to be true, and others false; and as the senses take immediate knowledge of their appropriate objects, so the soul takes immediate cognizance of the moral character of feelings and acts. The reason, the senses, and the conscience are alike infallible within certain limits, and liable to error beyond those limits.

2. Our moral perceptions or judgments are *sui generis*. They have their peculiar, distinctive character, which belongs to no other of our states of consciousness. The right is as distinct from the true, the proper, the agreeable, or the expedient, as these latter are from our sensations. The right is that which we are bound to do and to approve; the wrong is that which we are bound to avoid and to disapprove. Moral obligation, as expressed by the word "ought," is a simple and primary idea. It can be understood only by those who have felt it. And it can be confounded with nothing else.

3. These moral judgments are independent. They are not under the control of the understanding or of the will. No man can will to regard an axiom as false, or think that black is white, or white black. Nor can any sophistry of the understanding lead him to such false judgment. In like manner, no man can will to believe

that to be right which his conscience tells him to be wrong; nor can he argue himself into the conviction that he has done right, when his conscience tells him he has done wrong.

4. Our moral judgments, or, in other words, the conscience, has an authority from which we cannot emancipate ourselves. We can neither deny nor ignore it. It has a lordship. It commands, and it forbids. And we are bound to obey. It has power also to enforce its decisions. It can reward and punish. Its rewards are among the greatest blessings we can enjoy. Its punishments are the most intolerable agony the human soul can endure.

5. Our moral judgments involve the idea of law, i. e., of a rule or standard to which we are bound to be conformed. When we judge a thing to be right, we judge it to be conformed to the moral law; when we judge it to be wrong, we judge that is not conformed to that law.

6. This law has an authority which it does not derive from us. It is essentially different from a sense of propriety, or perception of expediency. It is something imposed upon us, and to which we are required to be conformed by an authority out of ourselves.

7. Our moral nature involves, therefore, a sense of responsibility. We must answer for what we are, and for what we do. This responsibility is not to ourselves, not to society, nor to being in general. It must be to a person; that is, to a Being who knows what we are, what we do, and what we ought to be and do; who approves of the right, and disapproves of the wrong; and who has the power and the purpose to reward and punish us according to our character and conduct. Sin, from its very nature, as it reveals itself in our consciousness, involves not only a sense of pollution, or moral degradation, but also a sense of guilt; i. e., a conviction that we deserve punishment, that we ought to be punished, and, therefore, that punishment is inevitable.

If such be the facts of our moral nature, it is plain that we are under the necessity of assuming the existence of an extramundane, personal God, on whom we are dependent, and to whom we are responsible. This is undoubtedly the ground for the conviction of the being of God, which has universally prevailed among men. Having the idea given in the constitution of their nature, or being under an inward necessity of believing in such a Being, cultivated men have sought and found evidence of his existence in the world without them. But these external proofs have neither been as general nor as operative as those derived from what we ourselves are, and from what we know that we deserve. Such men, there-

fore, as Kant, and Sir William Hamilton, while denying the validity of all other arguments for the existence of God, admit that our
nature forces us to believe that He is, and that He is a person.

Our Moral Feelings not due to Education.

It is indeed objected that these phenomena of our moral nature
are due to education or to superstition. To this it is answered, first,
that moral truths have a self-evidencing light. They can no more
be denied than the intuitions of sense and reason. It may even be
said that our moral judgments have greater certainty than any
other of our convictions. Men believe absurdities. They believe
what contradicts the evidence of their senses. But no man ever
has, or ever can believe that malignity is a virtue. In the second
place, what is universal cannot be accounted for by peculiarities of
culture. All men are moral beings; all have this sense of moral
obligation, and of responsibility ; and no man can free himself from
these convictions. The Apostle, therefore, speaking out of the
common consciousness of men, as well as under the guidance of
the Holy Spirit, speaks of sinners as " knowing the judgment of
God " (Rom. i. 32) ; that is, a sense of sin involves the knowledge
of a righteous God.

We then are placed in the midst of a vast universe, of which
we constitute a part. We are forced not merely by the desire of
knowledge, but from the necessities of our nature, to ask, How did
this universe originate ? How is it sustained? To what does it
tend ? What are we ? Whence did we come ? Whither are we
going ? These questions must be answered. This complicated
problem must be solved. To refer everything to chance, is no solution. It is a frivolous denial that any solution is necessary, that
such questions need any answer. To refer everything to necessity,
is to say that the existence of things as they are is the ultimate
fact. The universe is, and always has been, and always must be.
It is the evolution of necessary being by necessary laws. This is
all we can know, and all that need be known. This, however, is
no solution. It is merely the denial that any solution is possible.
Could this theory be accepted with regard to the outward world, it
leaves all the phenomena of man's nature — intellectual, moral,
and religious — unaccounted for. Theism is a solution. It assumes the existence of an eternal and necessary Being; a Spirit,
and therefore intelligent, voluntary, self-conscious, and endowed
with moral perfections. This hypothesis accounts for the origin of
the universe. " In the beginning God created the heaven and

the earth." This is a satisfactory answer to the first question. It accounts for all the universe is, its immensity, its variety, its order, its numberless organisms, the adaptation of external nature to the wants of all living things. It accounts for the nature of man. It gives what that nature demands, — an infinite object of love, confidence, and adoration. It reveals who it is to whom we are responsible, and on whom we are dependent. We know that this solution is true, because it is a solution. It meets all the facts of the case. And it so meets them that it cannot fail to be accepted as true, either intelligently or blindly. The God whom all men ignorantly worship, the Scriptures reveal, not only in the certainty of his existence, but in the plenitude of his perfections.

CHAPTER III

§ 1. *What is meant by Anti-Theism.*

As Theism is the doctrine of an extramundane, personal God, the creator, preserver, and governor of all things, any doctrine which denies the existence of such a Being is anti-theistic. Not only avowed Atheism, therefore, but Polytheism, Hylozoism, Materialism, and Pantheism, belong to the class of anti-theistic theories.

Atheism.

Atheism does not call for any separate discussion. It is in itself purely negative. It affirms nothing. It simply denies what Theism asserts. The proof of Theism is, therefore, the refutation of Atheism. Atheist is, however, a term of reproach. Few men are willing to call themselves, or to allow others to call them by that name. Hume, we know, resented it. Hence those who are really atheists, according to the etymological and commonly received meaning of the word, repudiate the term. They claim to be believers in God, although they assign to that word a meaning which is entirely unauthorized by usage. Thus Helvetius[1] says, "There is no man of understanding who does not admit an active principle in nature; therefore there is no atheist. He is not an atheist who says that motion is God; because in fact motion is incomprehensible, as we have no clear idea of it, because it only manifests itself by its effects, and by it all things are performed in the universe." Cousin[2] says, "Atheism is impossible, because the existence of God is implied in every affirmation. If a man believes that he exists, he must believe in the power of thought, and that is God." In like manner Herbert Spencer claims to be religious. He does not oppose religion, but dogmas. He acknowledges inscrutable power. He reduces all our knowledge to the two facts, "That force is," and "Force is persistent." Force, however, is perfectly inscrutable and incomprehensible. On this principle he attempts

---

[1] "De l'Homme," *Works*, edit. Paris, 1793, vol. iii. p. 221, note.
[2] *Introduction to the General History of Philosophy*, vol. i. p. 169.

to reconcile religion and science. The ultimate principle of religion, that in which all religions agree, is that there is an inscrutable power which is the cause of all things. This also is the ultimate principle of science. They have therefore a common ground. Nothing can be predicated of this cause ; not consciousness ; not intelligence ; not will ; only that it is a force. This is all the God the new philosophy leaves us.[1]

Language, however, has its rights. The meaning of words cannot be changed at the pleasure of individuals. The word God, and its equivalents in other languages, have a definite meaning, from which no man is at liberty to depart. If any one says he believes in God, he says he believes in the existence of a personal, self-conscious being. He does not believe in God, if he only believes in "motion," in "force," in "thought," in "moral order," in "the incomprehensible," or in any other abstraction.

Theists also have their rights. Theism is a definite form of belief. For the expression of that belief, the word Theism is the established and universally recognized term. We have the right to retain it ; and we have the right to designate as Atheism, all forms of doctrine which involve the denial of what is universally understood by Theism.

Is Atheism possible?

The question has often been discussed, Whether Atheism is possible ? The answer to the question depends on the meaning of the term. If the question be, Whether a man can emancipate himself from the conviction that there is a personal Being to whom he is responsible for his character and conduct, and who will punish him for his sins ? it must be answered in the negative. For that would be to emancipate himself from the moral law, which is impossible. If, however, the question means, Whether a man may, by speculation or otherwise, bring himself into such a state as to lose the consciousness of the belief of God as written in his heart, and free himself, for a time, from its power ? it must be answered affirmatively. A man may, in this sense, deny his individuality or identity ; the real, objective existence of soul or body, mind or matter ; the distinction between right and wrong. But this is unnatural, and cannot last. It is like deflecting a spring by force. The moment the force is removed, the spring returns to its normal position. Men, therefore, often pass in a moment from a state of entire skepticism to a state of unquestioning faith ; not of course by a process of argument, but by a change in their inward state. This transition from unbelief to faith, though thus sudden, and although not produced by an intellectual process, is perfectly rational. The feelings which rise in the mind contain evidence of the truth which the understanding cannot resist. It is also a familiar psychological fact, that skepticism and faith may, in a certain sense, coexist in the mind. An idealist while abiding by his theory, has nevertheless an inward conviction of the reality of the external world. So the speculative atheist lives with the abiding conviction that there is a God to whom he must render an account.

§ 2. *Polytheism.*

As the word implies, Polytheism is the theory which assumes the existence of many gods. Monotheism was the original religion of our race. This is evident not only from the teachings of the Scriptures, but also from the fact that the earliest historical form of religious belief is monotheistic. There are monotheistic hymns in the Vedas, the most ancient writings now extant, unless the Pentateuch be an exception.

The first departure from monotheism seems to have been nature worship. As men lost the knowledge of God as creator, they were led to reverence the physical elements with which they were in contact, whose power they witnessed, and whose beneficent influence they constantly experienced. Hence not only the sun, moon, and stars, the great representatives of nature, but fire, air, and water, became the objects of popular worship. We accordingly find that the Vedas consist largely of hymns addressed to these natural elements.

These powers were personified, and soon it came to be generally believed that a personal being presided over each. And these imaginary beings were the objects of popular worship.

While the mass of the people really believed in beings that were "called gods" (1 Cor. viii. 5), many of the more enlightened were monotheists, and more were pantheists. The early introduction and wide dissemination of pantheism are proved from the fact that it lies at the foundation of Brahminism and Buddhism, the religions of the larger part of the human race for thousands of years.

There can be little doubt that when the Aryan tribes entered India, fifteen hundred or two thousand years before Christ, pantheism was their established belief. The unknown, and "unconditioned" infinite Being, reveals itself according to the Hindu system, as Brahma, Vishnu, and Shiva, — that is, as Creator, Preserver, and Restorer. These were not persons, but modes of manifestation. It was in this form that the idea of an endless process of development of the infinite into the finite, and of the return of the finite into the infinite, was expressed. It was from this pantheistic principle that the endless polytheism of the Hindus naturally developed itself; and this determined the character of their whole religion. As all that is, is only a manifestation of God, everything remarkable, and especially the appearance of any remarkable man, was regarded as an "avatar," or incarnation of God, in one or other of his modes of manifestation, as Brahma, Vishnu, or Shiva. And as evil is as actual as good, the one is as much a manifestation, or, *modus existendi*, of the infinite Being as the other. And hence there are evil gods as well as good. In no part of the world has pantheism had such a field for development as in India, and nowhere has it brought forth its legitimate effects in such a portentous amount of evil. Nowhere has polytheism been carried to such revolting extremes.

Among the Egyptians, Greeks, and Romans polytheism assumed a form determined by the character of the people. The Greeks rendered it bright, beautiful, and sensual; the Romans were more decorous and sedate. Among barbarous nations it has assumed forms much more simple, and in many cases more rational.

In the Bible the gods of the heathen are declared to be "vanity," and "nothing," mere imaginary beings, without power either to hurt or to save. (Jer. ii. 28; Isa. xli. 29; xlii. 17; Ps. cvi. 28.) They are also represented as δαιμόνια (1 Cor. x. 20). This word may express either an imaginary, or a real existence. The objects of heathen worship are called gods, even when declared to be nonentities. So they may be called "demons," without intending to teach that they are "spirits." As the word, however, generally in the New Testament, does mean "evil spirits," it is perhaps better to take it in that sense when it refers to the objects of heathen worship. This is not inconsistent with the doctrine that the gods of the heathen are "vanities and lies." They are not what men take them to be. They have no divine power. Paul says of the heathen before their conversion, "ἐδουλεύσατε τοῖς φύσει μὴ οὖσι θεοῖς" (Gal. iv. 8). The prevalence and persistency of Polytheism show that it must have a strong affinity with fallen human nature. Although, except in pantheism, it has no philosophical basis, it constitutes a formidable obstacle to the progress of true religion in the world.

§ 3. *Hylozoism.*

Hylozoism, from ὕλη, *matter*, and ζωή, *life*, is properly the doctrine that matter is endued with life.   And this is the form in which the doctrine was held by many of its advocates.   All matter, and every particle of matter, besides its physical properties, has a principle of life in itself, which precludes the necessity of assuming any other cause for the phenomena of life exhibited in the world.   In this form Hylozoism does not differ from Materialism.

Most commonly, however, the term is used to designate a system which admits a distinction between mind and matter, but considers them as intimately and inseparably united, as the soul and body in man.   God, according to this view, is the soul of the world; an intelligent power everywhere present, to which are to be referred all the manifestations of design in the external world, and all the activity of the human soul.   The relation, however, of the soul to the body, is a very imperfect illustration of the relation of God to the world according to the hylozoistic system.   The soul is really exterior to the body, and independent of it, at least for its existence and activity.   It is not the life of the body.   It neither fashions nor preserves it.   It is not even conscious of the vital activity by which the body is developed and sustained.   Whereas according to the hylozoistic theory, the soul of the world is its plastic principle, the inward source of all its organizations and of all its activities.

The leading principles of this theory as developed by the Stoics are, (1.) There are two constituent principles of the universe, one active, the other passive.   The passive principle is matter, without form and without properties, *i. e.*, inert.   The active principle is mind, dwelling in matter its organizing formative power, *i. e.*, God.   (2.) The universe is therefore to be viewed under three aspects: (*a.*) As the all-forming power; the *natura naturans*, or, ἡ φύσις τεχνική.   (*b.*) The world as formed by this living, inward principle.   The living κόσμος, or *natura naturata.*   (*c.*) The identity of the two, as they form one whole.   It is only by an act of the mind that the one is distinguished from the other.   Therefore the world, as including both, or as the identity of both, is formed with the greatest wisdom, and by a necessary process, for the laws of nature are the laws of reason.   Cicero,[1] expounding this system, says, " Natura, non artificiosa solum, sed plane artifex ab eodem Zenone dicitur; consultrix, et provida utilitatum opportunitatumque omnium.   Censet [Zeno] enim artis maxime proprium est creare et gignere, quodque in operibus nostrarum artium manus officiet, id multo artificiosius naturam officere."

---

[1] *De Natura Deorum,* ii. 22, p. 1116, edit. Leipzig, 1850.

(3.) The universe, therefore (The All-one), of which God is the soul and Nature the body, is living, immortal, rational, and perfect (ζῶον ἀθάνατον, λογικὸν, τέλειον). God, as the controlling, operative principle in all things, acts according to necessary, although rational laws. (4.) The souls of men are of the same nature with the soul of the world, but as individual existences, passing away when the life of the body ceases. (5.) The highest end of life is virtue; and virtue is living according to reason.[1]

This system in one of its forms is nearly identical with Materialism, and in the other with Pantheism. There is no personal God to whom we are responsible, no freedom of the will; therefore, no sin, and no conscious existence after death.

§ 4. *Materialism.*

Materialism is that system which ignores the distinction between matter and mind, and refers all the phenomena of the world, whether physical, vital, or mental, to the functions of matter.

A. *The Doctrine of Epicurus.*

Epicurus taught, (1.) That as *ex nihilo nihil fit*, the universe has always existed, and must continue to exist forever. (2.) That space, and the number of bodies which it contains, are infinite. (3.) These bodies are of two kinds, simple and compound. The simple bodies are atoms possessing form, magnitude, and weight. They are indivisible, unalterable, and indestructible. This is also the doctrine of modern science. Faraday[2] says, " A particle of oxygen is ever a particle of oxygen, — nothing can in the least wear it. If it enters into combination, and disappears as oxygen; if it pass through a thousand combinations, animal, vegetable, and mineral — if it lie hid for a thousand years, and then be evolved, it is oxygen with its first qualities, neither more nor less. It has all its original force, and only that; the amount of force which it disengaged when hiding itself, has again to be employed in a reverse direction when it is set at liberty." (4.) These atoms have their peculiar forces, distinct from their mere gravity. This, too, is the doctrine of modern science. It is included in what Faraday says in the passage just quoted. " Molecules," say the scientific men of our day, " have been endowed with forces which give rise to various chemical qualities, and these never change either in their nature or

---

[1] See Rixner's *Geschichte der Philosophie*, vol. i. sect. 120.
[2] See Youmans' *Conservation and Correlation of Forces*, p. 372.

in their amount." [1] (5.) Epicurus taught that the quantity of matter, and of course the amount of force in the world, is always the same. Neither can be increased or diminished. (6.) The atoms, of which the number is infinite, move through space with incredible velocity under the guidance of necessary physical laws. (7.) By the combination of these atoms under the influence of gravity and other physical forces, the universe was formed, and became a cosmos. This is very nearly the nebular hypothesis. (8.) The soul is material ; or, in other words, all mental phenomena are due to the properties of matter. This, also, is proclaimed as the last result of modern science. (9.) The soul, of course, ceases to exist when the body dies ; *i. e.*, as death is the cessation of the vital, so it is also of the intellectual functions of the individual. The atoms of which the man is composed, with the forces which belong to them, continue to exist, and may enter into the composition of other men. But the man, as an individual, ceases to exist. This, almost in so many words, is the avowed doctrine of many physicists of the present day. (10.) Sensation is for us the only source of knowledge. By remembering former sensations, we form ideas, and by the combination of ideas we form judgments. Almost the very words of Hume, and the doctrine of the whole school of which he is the representative. (11.) As Epicurus held that nothing is incorporeal except a vacuum, he of necessity includes all the forms of existence under the head of matter. As there is no mind or spirit, there is no God, and no moral law. Virtue is only a prudent regard to happiness. In a certain sense he admitted the existence of Gods, but they were corporeal beings having no concern with the affairs of men.[2]

A recent German writer,[3] in Herzog's " Encyklopädie," under the head of Materialismus, says that notwithstanding the great progress of modern science, the Materialists of our day have not advanced a step upon the system of Epicurus. That system, probably owing to the dominant influence of the higher philosophy of Plato and Aristotle, did not exert much influence on the ancient mind, or on the progress of human thought. It was not until modern times that Materialism gained any great power as a philosophical theory.

---

[1] *Croonian Lectures on Matter and Force.* Given at the Royal College of Physicians, in 1868. By Henry Bruce Jones, A. M., M. D., F. R. S., London, 1868, p. 17.

[2] Rixner's *Geschichte der Philosophie*, i. 303–318. Ritter's *History of Philosophy* translated by A. J. W. Morrison, iii. 399–447.

[3] F. Fabri.

B. *Materialism in England during the Eighteenth Century.*

Hobbes (1588–1679) anticipated the movement towards Materialism which manifested itself in England during the last century. " He made sensation the real basis of every mental operation, the sole originator of our ideas, the sole medium and test of truth.[1] As, therefore, we can perceive through sensation only what is material, he concluded that matter is the only reality, and that whatever exists to us must accordingly be a part of the material universe. The whole process of scientific investigation was thus reduced to the doctrine of bodies, beyond which, he maintained, there can be no knowledge whatever accessible to the human mind. This knowledge, however, does not refer simply to the existence of bodies, but also to their changes, of all which changes the ultimate principle is motion. The doctrine of bodies, therefore, includes the knowledge of all phenomena in relation to their probable causes; and of all possible causes as known from their observed effects. . . . . The mind itself he viewed as wholly material, the phenomena of consciousness being the direct result of our organization. The one great and fundamental fact of mind is sensation, which is nothing more or less than the effect of material objects around us, exerted by means of pressure or impact upon that material organization which we term the mind." [2] Thus it appears that Hobbes anticipated the great result of modern science, that all force may be resolved into motion.

Locke (1632–1704).

The introduction of Materialism into England during the last century is generally attributed to the influence of Locke's philosophy. Locke himself was far from being a Materialist, and the advocates of his system strenuously insist that his principles have no legitimate tendency to obliterate the distinction between matter and mind. Locke, however, in combating the doctrine of " innate ideas," in the sense of abstract truths, seemed to deny that the mind was so constituted as to apprehend truth intuitively, and beyond the range of experience. He compared the mind to a " *tabula rasa.*" This figure suggests that all our knowledge is from without, as the slate contributes nothing to the matter written upon it. He defined ideas to be " anything with which the mind is immediately occupied when we think." The origin of these

---

[1] *Leviathan*, chap. i.
[2] Morell's *History of Modern Philosophy*, New York, 1848, pp. 71, 72.

ideas, he said, was sensation and reflection. If by reflection he meant the observation of the phenomena of the mind, his theory is one thing. If it mean the process of recalling, combining, analyzing, and otherwise ' elaborating the impressions upon us from without, his theory is another. Probably Locke himself, and certainly many of his followers, took it in the latter sense; and thus the two sources of ideas, or of knowledge, are reduced to one, and that one is sensation. But as sensation can give us the knowledge only of what is external and material, the theory in this form seemed to leave no room for the higher ideas of eternal and necessary truths. Locke attempts to account for our ideas, of time, space, infinity, cause, and even of right and wrong, from observation, *i. e.*, from observation of what is without, or from impressions made upon our senses. It is a common criticism upon Locke's great work, that in it he does not distinguish between the occasion and the source of our ideas. Our experience furnishes the occasion, and it may be the necessary condition, of waking the mind to the perception not only of the fact experienced, but also of the intuitive apprehension of the universal and necessary truth which the fact involves. If we did not see effects produced around us, and did not ourselves exercise efficiency, we might never have the idea of causation; but the conviction that every effect must have a cause is an intuitive judgment, which experience can neither produce nor limit. It is not from the observed tendency of some acts to produce happiness, and of others to produce misery, that we get the idea of the essential distinction between right and wrong; but from the constitution of the mind. Although Locke, and many of his disciples, were satisfied with his method of accounting for our ideas of God, of spirit, and of moral and religious truths, yet it is also certain that many of his followers felt justified on his principles to discard them.

Hartley (1705–1757).

Hartley was a physician and a physiologist. Physiology and psychology have intimate relations. It is perhaps natural that those who devote themselves specially to the former, should make little of the latter. It is the marked characteristic of our age, so far as physicists are concerned, that it tries to merge psychology entirely into physiology. Hartley adopted the principles of Locke, and endeavored to show how it is that external things produce sensation and thought. This he did by his theory of vibrations. "The objects of the external world affect in some manner the extreme ends of the nerves, which spread from the brain as centre to every part of the body. This affection produces a vibration, which is continued along the nerve by the agency of an elastic ether, until it reaches the brain, where it constitutes the phenomenon we term sensation. When a sensation has been experienced several times, the vibratory movement from which it arises acquires the tendency to repeat itself spontaneously, even when the external object is not present. These repetitions or relics of sensations are ideas, which in their turn possess the property of recalling each other by virtue of mutual association among themselves." [1] This doctrine of association of ideas is the most important part of his system. He insists principally on the following law : " An idea is sometimes associated with another through the medium of a third ; but in process of time this intermediate idea may be disregarded, and yet the connection between the first and third may, notwithstanding, remain. Thus the idea of pleasure, which is so indissolubly connected with money, arises from the conveniences which it is able to procure, while in the mind of the miser the conveniences are lost sight of, and the very possession of the money itself is regarded as containing the whole enjoyment. In this way Hartley accounts for almost all the emotions and passions of the human mind. The domestic affections, for instance, arise from the transference of the pleasure derived from parental kindness to the parent itself ; the social and patriotic affections from transferring the pleasures of society to the country which affords them ; in like manner, also, the moral and religious affections, the love of virtue and the love of God, arise from the pleasures connected with virtuous and pious conduct, being transferred to the law of action, or to the supreme Lawgiver, from whom these pleasures have emanated." [2] The connection of this theory with Materialism is obvious. If vibrations of the brain constitute sensation, and if the relics, or spontaneous repetitions of these vibrations constitute thought and feeling, then all mental and moral acts are mere affections of our material organism. It is also obvious that, according to this theory, there is no more freedom in volition than in sensation. The former is a mode, or relic of the latter. Although this tendency of his system was undeniable, and although his successors drew these conclusions from his principles, Hartley himself was not a Materialist. He was a very religious man. It is not at all uncommon for a man to hold a speculative theory inconsistent with his faith.

Morell [3] quotes the following criticism of Hartley's doctrine from

---

[1] *Observations on Man*, chap. i. sect. 2, and Morell, p. 98.   [2] Morell. p. 99.
[3] Page 97.

the " Edinburgh Review " : " There may be," says the reviewer, " little shakings in the brain, for anything we know, and there may even be shakings of a different kind accompanying every act of thought or perception ; — but that the shakings themselves are the thought or perception, we are so far from admitting, that we find it absolutely impossible to comprehend what is meant by the assertion. The shakings are certain throbbings, vibrations, or stirrings, in a whitish, half-fluid substance like custard, which we might see perhaps, or feel, if we had eyes and fingers sufficiently small or fine for the office. But what should we see or feel, upon the supposition that we could detect by our senses, everything that actually took place in the brain ? We should see the particles of this substance change their place a little, move a little up or down, to the right or the left, round about or zigzag, or in some other course or direction. This is all that we could see, if Dr. Hartley's conjecture were proved by actual observation ; because this is all that exists in motion, according to our conception of it, and all that we mean when we say that there is motion in any substance. Is it intelligible, then, to say, that this motion, the whole of which we see and comprehend, is thought and feeling, and that thought and feeling will exist, wherever we can excite a similar motion in a similar substance ? — In our humble apprehension the proposition is not so much false, as utterly unmeaning and incomprehensible." [1]

If history repeats itself, so does philosophy. What the " Edinburgh Review " said of Hartley nearly seventy years ago, Professor Tyndall says of the Materialists of our day. " The passage from the physics of the brain to the corresponding facts of consciousness is unthinkable. Granted that a definite thought and a definite molecular action in the brain occur simultaneously ; we do not possess the intellectual organ, nor apparently any rudiment of the organ, which would enable us to pass, by a process of reasoning, from the one phenomenon to the other. They appear together, but we do not know why. Were our minds and senses so expanded, strengthened, and illuminated, as to enable us to see and feel the very molecules of the brain ; were we capable of following all their motions, all their grouping, all their electric discharges, if such there be ; and were we intimately acquainted with the corresponding states of thought and feeling, we should probably be as far as ever from the solution of the problem, How are these physical processes connected with the facts of consciousness ? The

[1] *Edinburgh Review*, Oct. 1806, p. 157.

chasm between the two classes of phenomena would still remain intellectually impassable.   Let the consciousness of love, for example, be associated with a right-handed spiral motion of the molecules of the brain, and the consciousness of hate with a left-handed spiral motion.   We should then know when we love that the motion is in one direction, and when we hate that the motion is in the other, but the ' Why ?' would still remain unanswered.   In affirming that the growth of the body is mechanical, and that thought, as exercised by us, has its correlative in the physics of the brain, I think the position of the ' Materialist' is stated as far as that position is a tenable one.   I think the Materialist will be able finally to maintain this position against all attacks; but I do not think, as the human mind is at present constituted, that he can pass beyond it.   I do not think he is entitled to say that his molecular grouping and his molecular motions explain everything.   In reality they explain nothing." [1]

Priestley (1733–1804).

Priestley owes his permanent reputation to his important discoveries in the department of physical science.   He was, however, prominent during his life for the part he took in philosophical and theological controversies.   Devoted to science, the senses were for him the great sources of knowledge ; all others, except supernatural revelation which he admitted, he distrusted.   He adopted with enthusiasm the theory of Hartley which resolved thought and feeling into vibrations of the brain.   Hartley, he said, had done more for the doctrine of mind than Newton accomplished for the theory of the material universe.   He did not hesitate to avow himself a Materialist.   "Priestley," says Morell,[2] "rested the truth of Materialism upon two deductions.   The first was, that thought and sensation are essentially the same thing — that the whole variety of our ideas, however abstract and refined they may become, are, nevertheless, but modifications of the sensational faculty. . . . . The second deduction was, that all sensation, and, consequently, all thought, arises from the affections of our material organization, and therefore consists entirely in the motion of the material particles of which the nerves and brain are composed."   He was a necessitarian, and in morals a utilitarian.   Believing, however, in God and in divine revelation, he admitted a future state of existence.   As the Bible teaches the doctrine of the resurrection of the

---

[1] "Address before British Association," *Athenæum*, for August 29, 1868. Quoted in Perowne's *Hulsean Lectures*, for 1868 ; Appendix, Note A

[2] Page 102.

body, Priestley believed that man would be restored to conscious existence when that event occurred. His principal works bearing on this subject are : " Examination of Reid, Beattie, and Oswald," " Doctrine of Philosophical Necessity Explained," " Disquisitions relating to Matter and Spirit," and " Hartley's Theory of the Human Mind, with Essays relating to the subject of it."

Hume is regarded as their master by the most advanced physicists of the modern scientific school, so far as their general principles and method of philosophizing are concerned. He was neither a Materialist nor an Idealist, but rather a Nihilist, as his great object was to show that no certainty could be attained in any department of knowledge. He affirmed nothing and denied everything. Such knowledge as we have comes from sensation, therefore, he maintained that as we have no sensation of efficiency, we can have no idea of it, and no evidence of its reality. A cause is not that which produces an effect, but simply that which uniformly precedes it. Consequently, anything can be the cause of anything. Again, as we have no perception by the senses of substance, there can be no such thing. This applies to mind as well as matter. Nothing exists to us but our thoughts and feelings. We are " nothing but a bundle or collection of different perceptions, which succeed each other with an inconceivable rapidity, and are in perpetual flux and movement."

C. *Materialism in France during the Eighteenth Century.*

The sensational philosophy, as it is called, found a much more congenial soil in France than in England. Locke's " Essay " was translated into the language of that country and made the subject of comments and lectures. His leading principles were adopted without the limitations and qualifications with which he had presented them, and conclusions drawn from them which Locke would have been the first to repudiate.

Condillac, one of the first and most influential of the disciples of Locke, in his first work, ' Essai sur l'Origine des Connaissances Humaines," differed comparatively little from the English philosopher. But in his " Traité des Sensations," he virtually discarded " reflection " as a source of our ideas, and regarded all thoughts, feelings, and volitions as " transformed sensations." " While he answered the question concerning the relation between the soul and body, by assuming their identity, he took theistic ground in accounting for the origin of the world. This middle ground was occupied also, at least ostensibly, by Diderot and D'Alembert in the French

" Encyclopédie," who, notwithstanding their sensational theory as to
the source of our knowledge, and their making happiness the ground
of morals and end of life, not only maintained theistic principles,
but insisted on the necessity of a divine revelation. This, however,
was probably more a matter of prudence than of conviction." [1]

These, however, were only the first steps. The extreme of
materialistic atheism was soon reached and avowed. La Mettrie
published his " L'Histoire Naturelle de l'Ame " in 1745, his
" L'Homme Machine," the same year, and his " L'Homme Planté "
in 1749. Helvetius published his work " De l'Esprit " in 1758.
His book entitled " De l'Homme " was published after his death.
The climax was reached by Baron d'Holbach in his " Système de
la Nature," in which Materialism, fatalism, and atheism were
openly avowed. According to this system matter and motion are
eternal ; thought is an agitation of the nerves ; the soul the result
of our corporeal organization ; the will the strongest sensation ; the
ground of morals a regard to our own happiness. There is no
freedom, no morality, no future existence, no God. When these
principles got hold of the popular mind, then came the end.

D. *Positivism.*

Comte, the author of the " Positive Philosophy," was born in
1798, and died in 1859. The greater part of his life was passed
in poverty and neglect. His only occupation was teaching. Ten
years were devoted to the preparation of a course of lectures on
philosophy which secured him wealth and fame. He called his
system " Philosophie Positive," because it purported " to assume
nothing beyond the content of observed facts."

The fundamental principle of the " Positive Philosophy " is the
one so often referred to, namely, that the senses are the only source
of our knowledge, hence nothing exists but matter. There is no
mind distinct from matter ; no such thing as efficiency ; no causes,
whether first or final ; no God ; no future state of existence for
man. Theology and psychology are, therefore, banished from the
domain of science. Science is solely occupied in the observation
of facts, and in deducing from them the laws by which they are
determined. These laws, however, are not forces operating in a
uniform manner, but simply statements of the actual order in the
sequence of events. This sequence is not only uniform but necessary. Our business is simply to ascertain what it is. The only
method by which this can be done is observation. This task is

---

[1] F. Fabri in Herzog's *Real-Encyclopädie*, art. " Materialismus."

much easier in some departments than in others ; for in some the facts to be observed are less numerous and less complicated. In mathematics and astronomy the facts are all of one kind ; whereas in physiology and sociology they are of very different kinds, and vastly more complicated. The same rule, however, applies to all departments. In all, the sequence of events is uniform and neces- sary ; and if we can only, by a sufficient induction of facts, ascer- tain what the law of sequence is, we shall be able to predict the future as certainly in one department as in another. The astrono- omer can tell what will be the position of the stars and planets a century hence. The Positivist will be able to foretell with equal certainty how a man will act in any given circumstances, and what will be the progress and state of society in time to come.

It follows, therefore, according to the Positive Philosophy, — (1.) That all our knowledge is confined to physical phenomena. (2.) That all we can know of such phenomena is, that they are, and the relations in which they stand to each other. (3.) That these relations are all included under the heads of sequence and resemblance. (4.) These relations constitute the laws of nature, and are invariable. (5.) As everything that exists is material, these laws, or " invariable relations of succession and resemblance," control all the phenomena of mind, as we call it, and of social life and of history, as well as those of nature, in the common sense of that word. (6.) As everything is included in the department of physics, everything is controlled by physical laws, and there is no more freedom in human acts than in the motions of the stars ; and, therefore, the one can be predicted with the same certainty as the other.

The following quotations from the " Philosophie Positive," " freely translated and condensed by Harriet Martineau," [1] include all the points above mentioned.

" The first characteristic of the Positive Philosophy is that it regards all phenomena as subjected to invariable natural laws. Our business is, — seeing how vain is any research into what are called causes, whether first or final, — to pursue an accurate dis- covery of these laws, with a view to reducing them to the smallest possible number." [2] " Our positive method of connecting phenom- ena is by one or other of two relations, — that of similitude or that of succession, — the mere fact of such resemblance or succession being all that we can pretend to know ; and all that we need to know ; for this perception comprehends all knowledge which consists in elucidating something by something else, — in now explaining, and now foreseeing certain phenomena, by means of the resemblance or sequence of other phenomena." [1] " If we regard these functions [of the mind] under their statical aspect, — that is, if we consider the conditions under which they exist, — we must determine the organic circumstances of the case, which inquiry involves it with anatomy and physiology. If we look at the dynamic aspect, we have to study simply the exercise and results of the intellectual powers of the human race, which is neither more nor less than the general object of the Positive Philosophy." [2]

Comte is obliged to use the word " power," and to speak of its exercise, yet all his philosophy denies the existence of any such thing as efficiency. The laws which determine events are nothing more than facts of uniform sequence. According to the passage just quoted, one department of psychology (the statical) belongs to anatomy and physiology ; the other (the dynamic) to the observed sequence of certain facts called intellectual. The sequence is invariable. The intervention of will is necessarily excluded, because philosophy, at least Positivism, is nothing unless it secures the power of prevision. But free acts cannot be foreseen by man. Hence Comte says, " The arbitrary can never be excluded while political phenomena are referred to will, divine or human, instead of being connected with invariable natural laws." [3]   " If social events were always exposed to disturbance by the accidental intervention of the legislator, human or divine, no scientific prevision of them would be possible." [4]

Intellectual exercises being regarded as a function of the brain, Comte says, " The positive theory of the intellectual and affective functions is therefore henceforth unchangeably regarded as consisting in the study, both rational and experimental, of the various phenomena of internal sensibility, which are proper to the cerebral ganglia, apart from their external apparatus. It is, therefore, simply a prolongation of animal physiology, properly so called, when this is extended so as to include the fundamental and ultimate attributes." [5]

Comte, being an ardent phrenologist, founded one of the arguments for his system on the organization of the brain ; but his great dependence was upon the law of human development. He admitted no essential difference between man and irrational animals. The superiority of man is only in the degree of his intelli-

[1] *Philosophie Positive*, vol. ii. p. 515.   [2] Vol. i. p. 11.   [3] Vol. ii. p. 47.
[4] *Ibid.* p. 73.   [5] See Prof. Porter's *Human Intellect*, p. 54.

gence, which is due to his better physical organization. According to Comte, the whole human race, and every individual man, passes through three distinct stages, which he calls the theological, the metaphysical, and the positive. During the first stage all events are referred to supernatural causes. In the first part of this stage of their progress, men were fetich-worshippers; then they gradually became polytheists, and monotheists. This he endeavors to prove historically in regard to the Greeks, the Romans, and the inhabitants of western Europe. As men outgrew the fetich age, so they outgrew the polytheistic and monotheistic forms of belief. That is, they ceased to refer phenomena to the agency of supernatural beings.

During the metaphysical stage, phenomena are referred to unseen causes, to occult powers, or forces, that is, to something which the senses cannot detect. This also has passed away, and men have come to recognize the great fact that there are no spiritual agencies in the universe, no efficient causes, nothing but events to be arranged according to the laws of sequence and resemblance. The order of events is invariable and necessary. What it has been in the past, it will be in the future. As this is the law of the development of the race collectively, so it is of the individual man. Every one, in his progress from infancy to manhood, passes through these several stages, the theological, the metaphysical, and the positive. We first believe in supernatural agencies (witches, ghosts, souls, angels, etc.); then in occult causes; then only in facts discerned by the senses. The history of the race and the experience of the individual man are thus made the broad and sure foundation of the Positive Philosophy.

Remarks.

1. Considering that the advocates of this philosophy are a mere handful; considering that nine hundred and ninety-nine millions of the thousand millions of our race still believe in God, it is a rather violent assumption that mankind have reached the stage of Positivism. It may be readily admitted that the progress of science and of Christianity has banished alchemy, astrology, witchcraft, and necromancy from enlightened portions of our race, but it has had a scarcely discernible effect in banishing belief in mind as distinct from matter, or in efficient causes, or in God. Admitting, therefore, the principle of the argument to be correct, the conclusion arrived at is contradicted by facts.

2. The principle itself, however, is a groundless assumption.

There has been no such development of the race, and there is no such development of the individual man, as the argument supposes. Much less is it true, as Comte maintains, that these several methods of dealing with phenomena are antagonistic and mutually exclusive; that if we believe in spiritual agents, we cannot believe in unseen, metaphysical causes; and that if we believe in the latter we cannot believe in the former. The fact is, the great mass of mankind, educated and uneducated, believe in both. They believe in God and mind, as well as in occult causes, such as electricity, magnetism, and other physical forces; which, in Comte's sense of the word, are metaphysical.

With regard to this assumed law of progress, Prof. Huxley, who is as completely emancipated from the trammels of authority as any man of science now living, says, in the first place, that Comte contradicts himself as to this fundamental principle. In proof he quotes a long passage from the "Philosophie Positive," in which Comte teaches, — "(a.) As a matter of fact, the human intellect has *not* been invariably subjected to the law of the three states, and, therefore, the necessity of the law *cannot* be demonstrable *à priori.* (b.) Much of our knowledge of all kinds has *not* passed through the three states, and more particularly, as M. Comte is careful to point out, not through the first. (c.) The positive state has more or less coexisted with the theological, from the dawn of human intelligence. And, by way of completing the series of contradictions, the assertion that the three states are 'essentially different and even radically opposed,' is met a little lower on the same page by the declaration that 'the metaphysical state is, at bottom, nothing but a simple general modification of the first.'" "Men of science," he adds, "are not in the habit of paying much attention to 'laws' stated in this fashion." [1]

After showing that the individual man does not pass through these several states, Prof. Huxley says, "What is true of the individual is, *mutatis mutandis,* true of the intellectual development of the species. It is absurd to say of men in a state of primitive savagery, that all their conceptions are in a theological state. Nine tenths of them are eminently realistic, and as 'positive' as ignorance and narrowness can make them." [2]

Besides, it is not true that the race of men now existing on the earth, were in their primitive state fetich-worshippers, or that they

[1] *Lay Sermons,* pp. 174, 175.
[2] Huxley's *Lay Sermons, Addresses,* etc., London, 1870, No. VIII. " The Scientific Aspects of Positivism," p. 178.

gradually rose to polytheism and monotheism. The reverse is true. Not only revelation, but all history and tradition, go to show that the primitive state of our race was its highest state, at least so far as religion is concerned. Monotheism was the earliest form of religion among men. To that succeeded nature-worship and pantheism, and to that polytheism. It is a historical fact that monotheism was not reached by a process of development. Monotheism was first; it gradually perished from among men, except as miraculously preserved among the Hebrews, and from them diffused through the medium of, or rather, in the form of, Christianity. It extends nowhere beyond the influence, direct or indirect, of the supernatural revelation contained in the Bible. This is a fact which scientific men should not overlook in their deductions.

3. Comte was guilty of the unfairness of confining his survey to a small portion of the nations of the earth; and that the portion too which had been brought under the influence of Christianity. If the law which he sought to establish be universal and necessary, it must have operated from the beginning in India and China as well as in Europe. The millions of those regions have not reached the monotheistic, much less the metaphysical, and still less the positive stage of development. India especially furnishes a striking refutation of this theory. The Hindus are a highly intellectual race. Their language and literature are on a par with those of Greece and Rome. Their philosophers, nearly three thousand years ago, anticipated the highest results reached by the Schellings and Hegels of our day. Yet of all the nations of the earth the Hindus are the least materialistic, or positive, in their views of nature. With them the supernatural or spiritual is alone real. The Hindus, therefore, cannot be subject to that universal and necessary law of development which is assumed as the foundation of the Positive Philosophy.

4. It is of course presumptuous and idle to attempt to reason men out of their senses, or to convince them that what their very nature teaches them is true, is utterly false and untrustworthy. This, however, Comte not only attempts, but his whole system is founded on the assumption that our nature is a delusion and a lie. That is, it is founded on the assumption that intuitive truths are false. It is intuitively true that we are free agents. This Comte denies. It is intuitively true that there is a specific and essential difference between right and wrong. This is denied. It is intuitively true that every effect has an efficient cause. This too is denied. It is intuitively true that there is a God to whom men

are responsible for their character and conduct. This also is denied. Had all the intellect and all the knowledge ever possessed by men and angels been concentrated in the person of Comte, it had still been folly in him to attempt to found a system involving the denial of such truths as these. The Christian is not afraid to say one thing more. It is intuitively true, to all who have eyes to see, that Jesus Christ is the Son of God, and that his gospel is the wisdom of God and the power of God unto salvation, and that it is absolutely impossible that any theory which is opposed to these divine intuitions can be true.

Another illustration of the presumptuous character of this philosophy is found in what it teaches concerning Sociology. Scientific men of all countries have long been laboriously engaged in making meteorological observations, and yet such are the number and complexity of the causes which determine the state of the weather, that no man is able to predict how the wind will blow forty-eight hours, much less, a year, in advance. The causes which determine human action in the individual and in society, are far more complex and inscrutable than those which determine the state of the weather. Yet Comte assumes to have reduced Sociology to a science, vying with mathematics in certainty. " I will venture to say," is his confident assertion, " that Sociological science, though only established by this book, already rivals mathematical science itself, not in precision and fecundity, but in positivity and rationality." [1]

Practical Applications of Positivism.

The practical applications of this philosophy are very serious. Positivism claims the right of absolute and universal control over all human affairs; over education, politics, social organization, and religion. As the progress of science has banished all liberty of opinion or of action from the departments of mathematics and astronomy, so it must banish it from every other department of human thought and activity. Speaking of liberty of conscience, Comte says: " Negative as we now see this dogma to be, signifying release from old authority, while waiting for the necessity of positive science, the absolute character supposed to reside in it gave it energy to fulfil its revolutionary destination. . . . . This dogma can never be an organic principle; and, moreover, it constitutes an obstacle to reorganization, now that its activity is no longer absorbed by the demolition of the old political order. . . . . Can it be supposed," he asks, " that the most important and the most deli-

1 *Philosophie Positive*, vol. ii. p. 516.

cate conceptions, and those which by their complexity are accessible to only a small number of highly prepared understandings, are
to be abandoned to the arbitrary and variable decisions of the least
competent minds." [1] This argument is conclusive. If social life,
the acts of men, are as much and as certainly determined by physical laws as material changes, those who have ascertained these
laws are entitled to control all other men. As it would be prepos-
terous to allow men to build our houses or navigate our ships who
would not obey the laws of nature, so it would be absurd, on this
hypothesis, to allow those ignorant of social laws to govern society.
Comte avows his admiration, not of popish doctrine, but of the
papal organization, which in the new order of things he proposes
to continue. " Papal infallibility," he says,[2] " was a great intellectual and social advance." Prof. Huxley pithily characterizes Positivism, in this regard, as " Catholicism *minus* Christianity."

Religion is not excepted from this absolute subjection. The
Positive Philosophy, as it denies the existence of the soul and the
being of God, would seem to leave no place for religion. Comte
placed on the title-page of his " Discours sur l'Ensemble du Posi-
tivisme," the announcement that his design was to reorganize society "sans Dieu ni Roi." Nevertheless, as men must have, as they
always have had, some religion, a philosophy which aspired to absolute dominion over all the departments of human life, must make
some provision for this universal, although imaginary, necessity of
our nature. Comte, therefore, published a catechism of religious
belief, and a ritual of religious worship. The object of worship
was to be the aggregate of humanity formed by the absorption of
the successive generations of men. Every great man has two forms
of existence. one conscious before death ; the other after death,
unconscious, in the hearts and intellects of other men. The God
of the Positive Philosophy is, therefore, the aggregate of the mem-
ories of great men. " Undoubtedly," says Huxley, " ' Dieu ' disappeared, but the ' Noveau Grand-Être Suprême,' a gigantic fetich,
turned out bran-new by M. Comte's own hands, reigned in his
stead. ' Roi ' also was not heard of; but in his place I found a
minutely-defined social organization, which, if it ever came into
practice, would exert a despotic authority such as no sultan has
rivalled, and no Puritan presbytery in its palmiest days could hope
to excel. While, as for the ' culte systématique de l'humanité,' I,
in my blindness, could not distinguish it from sheer Popery, with

---

[1] *Philosophie Positive*, vol. ii. pp. 14, 15.　　　　[2] *Ibid.* vol. ii. p. 268.

M. Comte in the chair of St. Peter, and the names of most of the saints changed." [1]

There are, however, to be two forms of worship, the one private, the other public. The special object of the former is woman, because she is the most perfect representative of humanity. As "Mother, she excites veneration ; as wife, affection ; and as daughter, kindness." To excite these sentiments, ideal woman is to be worshipped. Humanity, or the memory of great men, is the object for public worship, regarding which minute details are given. The new religion is to have ten sacraments, a peculiar architecture, and an extended hierarchy, under the control of one absolute High Priest. Such is the system which Comte was allowed to believe would supersede the gospel of Jesus Christ. It has already almost passed away. Among the advanced men of science in England there is scarcely one so poor as to do it reverence.[2]

E. *Scientific Materialism.*

Leading Principles.

The leading principles of the modern scientific form of Materialism are embraced, by some at least, who do not consider themselves Materialists. They, however, adopt the language of the system, and avow principles which, in their generally accepted meaning, constitute what in the history of human thought is known as Materialism.

The most important of these principles are the following, many of which, however, are not peculiar to the system.

1. Matter and force are inseparable. Wherever there is matter there is force, and wherever there is force there is matter. This proposition, at least in the first instance, is to be understood only of physical force.

---

[1] *Lay Sermons*, etc., p. 164.

[2] Professor Huxley says: "For these sixteen years, it has been a periodical source of irritation to me to find M. Comte put forward as a representative of scientific thought; and to observe that writers whose philosophy had its legitimate parent in Hume, or in themselves, were labelled 'Comtists,' or 'Positivists,' by public writers, even in spite of vehement protests to the contrary. It has cost Mr. Mill hard rubbings to get that label off; and I watch Mr. Spencer, as one regards a good man struggling with adversity, still engaged in eluding its adhesiveness, and ready to tear away skin and all, rather than let it stick. My own turn might come next; and, therefore, when an eminent prelate the other day gave currency and authority to the popular confusion, I took an opportunity of incidentally re-vindicating Hume's property in the so-called 'New Philosophy,' and at the same time of repudiating Comtism on my own behalf." — *Ut supra*, p. 165. The mistake complained of is a very natural one, as Comte and Hume have so much in common. Professor Huxley's quotation from Faust is in point here: —

"Ungefähr sagt das der Pfarrer auch
Nur mit ein bischen andern Worten."

2. All physical forces, such as light, heat, chemical affinities, electricity, magnetism, etc., etc., are convertible. Light may be converted into heat, and heat into light ; either into electricity, and electricity into either ; and so through the whole range. This is what is called the correlation of forces. Count Rumford, in a communication to the Royal Society of London, in 1798, satisfied that the heat generated in boring cannon could not be otherwise accounted for, advanced the doctrine that heat is a peculiar mode of motion. Since then the doctrine has been generalized, and it is now the commonly received opinion that all the physical forces are resolvable into motion. This generalization, however, is not accepted by all scientific men. They find it impossible to conceive how gravitation, which acts instantaneously at all distances, can be motion. It is simply a force which tends to produce motion.

3. This motion, however, is not of a fluid, or ether, or any other imponderable substance peculiar to each particular kind of force. As sound consists in, or rather, is produced by the vibrations of the atmosphere, it was natural to assume that light was the undulation of one medium, heat of another, electricity of another. This theory is discarded. The motion intended is motion in the molecules of the matter affected. When iron is heated, nothing is added to it. There is no imponderable substance called caloric. All that occurs is, that the molecules of the iron are agitated in a particular way. If the iron be magnetized, it is only a different kind of motion imparted to its constituent atoms. So of all other kinds of force. When, however, light or heat is radiated from a distant object, the motion which constitutes these forces must be transmitted through some medium. For where there is motion, there must be something that moves. And, therefore, if heat be motion in the molecules of the sun, that heat could not reach us unless there was some material medium between us and the sun.

4. The physical forces are not only convertible one into any of the others, but they are quantitively equivalent ; that is, a given amount of heat will produce an amount of light or of electricity, or of any other force, which, if it could be utilized, would reproduce precisely that amount of heat. A cannon-ball, when it impinges on a target, produces heat enough to give it the velocity which it had at the moment of contact. A certain amount of light and heat derived from the sun is expended in the formation of a certain amount of wood or coal ; that amount of wood or coal will furnish precisely the amount of light and heat which was expended in its production. Count Rumford experimented to determine the quan-

titive relation between motion and heat, and arrived at very nearly the same conclusion as that reached by Dr. Joule of Manchester, England, who found that one pound of matter, falling seven hundred and seventy-two feet, will produce heat enough to raise the temperature of a pound of water one degree of Fahrenheit. This is now received as the unit of force.

5. Force is indestructible. It is never increased or diminished. What is lost in one form is taken up in another. Forces are, therefore, indestructible, convertible, and imponderable agents. This correlation and conservation of forces is declared by Dr. Carpenter, the eminent physiologist, to be " now amongst the best established generalizations of physical science," and the greatest scientific triumph of the age; " thanks," as he says, " to the labors of Faraday, Grove, Joule, Thomson, and Tyndall, to say nothing of those of Helmholtz and other distinguished continental savans." [1]

Correlation of the Physical and Vital Forces.

So long as this doctrine of the correlation of forces is confined to the department of physics, it is a purely scientific question, in which the theologian has no special interest. Unhappily it has not been thus confined. Dr. Carpenter, in the paper just quoted, says, " Every thoughtful physiologist must desire to see the same course of inquiry thoroughly pursued in regard to the phenomena of living bodies." [2] The first step in that direction, he adds, was taken by Dr. Mayer of Germany, in his remarkable treatise on " Organic Movement in its Relation to Material Changes."

There appear to be three forms of opinion among scientific men, of the " advanced " school, as to the relation between vital and physical forces. First, there are some, of whom Dr. Carpenter is one, who hold that the forces by which vital processes are carried on, are light, heat, electricity, and so forth, but that these are directed or controlled by a force of a different kind, called " a directing agency."

Dr. Carpenter's Theory.

Dr. Carpenter denies that there is any such thing as vitality, or vital force, or *nisus formativus*, or Bildungstrieb. Two germs may be selected between which neither the microscope nor chemical analysis can detect the slightest difference ; yet one develops

[1] See *Correlation and Conservation of Forces.* A collection of papers by distinguished scientific men. By Edward L. Youmans, M. D. New York, 1865, p. 405.
[2] *Ibid.* p. 405.

into a fish, another into a bird. Why is this? Dr. Carpenter answers because of a " directing agency " residing in the germ. His language is: " The prevalent opinion has until lately been, that this power is inherent in the germ; which has been supposed to derive from its parent not merely its material substance, but a *nisus formativus*, Bildungstrieb, or germ-force, in virtue of which it builds itself up into the likeness of its parent, and maintains itself in that likeness until the force is exhausted, and at the same time imparting a fraction of it to each of its progeny." [1] This opinion he rejects; but adds, " When we look carefully into the question, we find that what the germ really supplies, is not the force, but the directive agency; thus rather resembling the control exercised by the superintendent builder, who is charged with working out the design of the architect, than the bodily force of the workmen who labor under his guidance in the construction of the fabric." [2] The conclusion at which he arrives is " that the correlation between heat and the organizing force of plants is not less intimate than that which exists between heat and motion. The special attribute of the vegetable germ is its power of utilizing, after its own peculiar fashion, the heat which it receives, and of applying a constructive power to the building up of its fabric after its characteristic type." [3]

On this doctrine of Carpenter it may be remarked, (1.) That it seems to be self-contradictory. He denies to the germ a *nisus formativus*, or, Bildungstrieb, and attributes to it " a constructive power." What is the difference? The English phrase is a literal translation of the German word. (2.) He says that " heat and the organizing force of plants " are correlated, *i. e.*, they are convertible one into the other and are quantitively equivalent; and yet the relation between them is analogous to that between a superintending builder and the strength of the workmen. According to this, the physical strength of the hod-man is convertible into the intellect of the builder and is its quantitive equivalent. We do not see how this contradiction is to be avoided, unless he uses the phrases " constructive force," ".organizing force," sometimes for the " directing agency " in the germ, and sometimes, for the physical forces which that agency controls. But if he distinguishes between the " directing agency " and " the organizing force," then there is no correlation between the physical force and " the vital activity of the germ."

---

[1] See *Correlation and Conservation of Forces*, p. 411.   [2] *Ibid.* p. 412.
[3] *Ibid.* p. 119. Also, *New Quarterly Journal of Science* for 1864.

3. According not only to the common, but to the latest, opinion of physiologists, the germ supplies something more than "a directing agency" (which must itself be a force).   It not only directs, but it effects, or produces changes.   It is an operative force, acting not by, but against physical forces or chemical affinities; counteracting them as long as it continues.   As soon as the germ or plant or tissue dies, the physical forces obtain ascendency and disintegration takes place.   This Dr. Carpenter himself admits.   The most marked characteristic, he says, which distinguishes "vital from every kind of physical activity," is, "the fact that a germ endowed with life, develops itself into an organism of a type resembling that of its parent; that this organism is the subject of incessant changes, which all tend, in the first place, to the evolution of its typical form; and subsequently to its maintenance in that form, *notwithstanding the antagonism of chemical and physical agencies*, which are continually tending to produce its disintegration; but that, as its term of existence is prolonged, its conservative power declines so as to become less and less able to resist these disintegrating forces, to which it finally succumbs, leaving the organism to be resolved by their agency into the components from which its materials were originally drawn." [1]   This does not mean that chemical agencies have no part to act in the growth and development of plants and animals, but it certainly does mean that the vital force or life is an agency or power different from any kind of physical force.   Life and physical force, therefore, are not identical.   They are not correlated.   The former is not a mere form of the latter.

One of the most eminent of living physiologists is Dr. John Marshall, and he, although far from belonging to the old school, distinctly takes the ground that there is a vital force which cannot be resolved into any of the physical forces operative in the external, inorganic world.   He says: [2] "All the strictly physical processes within the body, whether chemical, mechanical, thermic, electric, or photic, are performed by modifications of the common force which produces similar phenomena in the inorganic world around us.   There exists, however, in the living animal, as in the living vegetable organism, a special formative or organizing energy, evolving the perfect animal or plant from the primitive ovum or ovule, developing its various tissues and organs, and conserving them from the commencement to the termination of its individual

[1] Youmans, p. 407.
[2] *Outlines of Physiology*, Smith's Philadelphia edition, 1868, p. 932.

existence. The influence of this force, moreover, extends from the parent to the offspring, generation after generation." This is the commonly received doctrine, that physical phenomena are to be referred to physical forces; vital phenomena to vital force; and mental phenomena to mind. The new doctrine, however, is that all phenomena are to be referred to physical forces, no other forces being either known or knowable.

The more advanced Opinions.

The second view adopted in reference to the relation of physical to vital force, is, that if there be any difference it cannot be known. Physical forces are known. They can be measured. They can not only be converted one into another, but can be proved to be quantitively equivalent. If any other kind of force be assumed to account for vital phenomena, the assumption is gratuitous. It is taking for granted that something exists of which we know, and can know nothing. It must, therefore, lie beyond the sphere of science and is of no importance. Even Dr. Carpenter uses such language as this: " Another class of reasoners have cut the knot which they could not untie, by attributing all the actions of living bodies for which physics and chemistry cannot account, to a hypothetical ' vital principle ; ' a shadowy agency that does everything in its own way, but refuses to be made the subject of scientific examination; like the ' od-force,' or the 'spiritual power' to which the lovers of the marvellous are so fond of attributing the mysterious movements of turning and tilting tables." [1] " If a man asks me," says Prof. Huxley, " what the politics of the inhabitants of the moon are, and I reply, that I do not know; that neither I, nor any one else, have any means of knowing; and that, under these circumstances, I decline to trouble myself about the subject at all, I do not think he has any right to call me a skeptic." [2] It is thus he banishes vitality from the sphere of science, because everything, except matter and its functions, belongs to the region of the unknown and the unknowable. Prof. Tyndall and Herbert Spencer take, at times, the same ground.

But, although such writers as Dr. Carpenter, in apparent contradiction to their own admissions, acknowledge the existence of " a directing agency " in the living germ, the majority of the writers of this school refuse to recognize any such agency or force as a scientific truth. The only difference between the second and

---

[1] Youmans, p. 402.
[2] " Physical Basis of Life " in his *Lay Sermons*, p. 158.

third views on this general subject, above referred to, is, that according to the one, the assumption of vital as distinct from physical force, is regarded as gratuitous and unnecessary ; according to the other, any such assumption is declared to be unphilosophical, and to be utterly discarded. The same writer sometimes takes one, and sometimes the other of these grounds.

The Argument for the Correlation of Physical and Vital Forces.

Thus Prof. Huxley, although a few years since a firm advocate of vital, as distinct from physical force, in his discourse on the " Physical Basis of Life," takes the opposite ground. The argument is this: the elements furnished by the mineral kingdom are taken up by the plant, and, under the influence of light and heat, transformed into organized matter. The products of vegetation, starch, sugar, fibrine, etc., are purely material. This is true even of protoplasm, or living matter, or the physical basis of life, as it is called, which is elaborated by the plant out of the lifeless materials furnished by the soil and the atmosphere. There is indeed a great difference between the products of vegetation and the lifeless elements out of which they are formed. But so there is between the elements of water and water itself. If an electric spark be passed through a volume of oxygen and hydrogen gas, it becomes water, which weighs precisely as much as the volume of the two gases of which it is composed. It is oxygen and hydrogen in combination, and nothing more. Yet the properties of the water are entirely different from those of the oxygen and hydrogen. In like manner there is a great difference between the properties of the carbonic acid, the water, and the ammonia, of which the plant is composed, and the living plant itself. But as it would be unphilosophical to assume the existence of an unknown something called aquosity to account for the difference between water and its elements, it is no less unphilosophical to assume the existence of an unknown something called vitality to account for the difference between it and the lifeless materials of which living matter is composed.

Animal Life.

In like manner all the phenomena of animal life are referred to the physical forces inseparable from the matter which composes the animal structure. It is true the functions of matter in the animal tissues are higher than in those of the plant. But the advocates of the theory under consideration, endeavor to reduce the difference between animal and vegetable life to a minimum. It is only the upper surface of the leaf which is susceptible of the peculiar effects of light. So it is only the optic nerve that is affected in a way which is necessary to vision. The sensitive plant contracts when touched ; and so does the animal muscle when the proper stimulus, nervous or electric, is applied. In short, as all the operations of vegetable life are due to physical forces, so all the phenomena of animal life are due to the same causes.

On this subject Prof. Huxley says : " The matter of life is composed of ordinary matter, differing from it only in the manner in which its atoms are aggregated. It is built up of ordinary matter, and again resolved into ordinary matter when its work is done." [1] By protoplasm, or matter of life, he sometimes means matter which exhibits the phenomena of life ; and sometimes, matter which having been elaborated by the plant or animal, is capable of supporting life. Hence he calls boiled mutton protoplasm.

The only difference between inorganic, lifeless matter, and living plants or animals, is in the manner in which their atoms are aggregated. " Carbon, hydrogen, oxygen, and nitrogen, are all lifeless bodies. Of these, carbon and oxygen unite, in certain proportions, and under certain conditions, to give rise to carbonic acid ; hydrogen and oxygen produce water ; nitrogen and hydrogen give rise to ammonia. These new compounds, like the elementary bodies of which they are composed, are lifeless. But when they are brought together, under certain conditions they give rise to the still more complex body, protoplasm, and this protoplasm exhibits the phenomena of life. I see no break in this series of steps in molecular complication, and I am unable to understand why the language which is applicable to any one term of the series may not be used to any of the others. . . . . When hydrogen and oxygen are mixed in a certain proportion, and an electric spark is passed through them, they disappear, and a quantity of water, equal in weight to the sum of their weights, appears in their place. There is not the slightest parity between the passive and active powers of the water and those of the oxygen and hydrogen which have given rise to it." [2] " What justification is there, then, for the assumption of the existence in the living matter of a something which has no representative, or correlative, in the not living matter which gave rise to it ? What better philosophical status has ' vitality ' than ' aquosity ? ' And why should ' vitality ' hope for a better fate than the other ' itys ' which have disappeared since Martinus Scriblerus accounted for the operation of the meat-jack

[1] *Lay Sermons*, p. 144.   [2] *Ibid.* p. 149.

by its inherent ' meat-roasting quality,' and scorned the materialism of those who explained the turning of the spit by a certain mechanism worked by the draught of the chimney ? . . . . If the properties of water may be properly said to result from the nature and
disposition of its component molecules, I can find no intelligible
ground for refusing to say that the properties of protoplasm result
from the nature and disposition of its molecules." [1]

The doctrine, therefore, is, that carbonic acid, water, and ammonia, lifeless bodies, under certain conditions, become living matter, not in virtue of any new force or principle communicated to
them, but solely in virtue of a different arrangement of their molecules.   Of this living matter all plants and animals are composed,
and to the properties or physical forces inherent in the matter of
which they are composed, all the phenomena of vegetable and animal life are to be referred.   " Protoplasm," says Prof. Huxley, " is
the clay of the potter : which, bake it and paint it as he will, remains clay, separated by artifice and not by nature, from the com-
monest brick or sun-dried clod." [2]   As the brick, no matter what
its shape or color, can have no properties not inherent in the clay,
so vegetable or animal organisms can have no properties which do
not belong to protoplasm, which, in the last analysis, is nothing but
carbonic acid, water, and ammonia.

Professor Huxley is not only a distinguished naturalist, but a
popular lecturer and preacher of " Lay Sermons," and thus has
become a representative man among the advocates of this new form
of Materialism.   He is, however, very far from standing alone.
" Some of the most distinguished living physicists, chemists, and
naturalists," says Dr. Beale, " have accepted this physical theory
of life.   They have taught that life is but a mode of ordinary force,
and that the living thing differs from the non-living thing, not in
quality, or essence, or kind, but merely in degree." [3]   "So long,"
says the same writer, " as the advocates of the physical doctrine
of life contented themselves with ridiculing ' vitality ' as a fiction
and a myth, because it could not be made evident to the senses,
measured or weighed, or proved scientifically to exist, their position was not easily assailed ; but now when they assert dogmati-
cally that vital force is only a form or mode of ordinary motion,
they are bound to show that the assertion rests upon evidence, or
it will be regarded by thoughtful men as one of a large number
of fanciful hypotheses, advocated only by those who desire to swell

---

[1] Lay Sermons, p. 151.   [2] Ibid. p. 142.
[3] Protoplasm; or Life, Matter, and Mind, by Lionel S. Beale, M. B., F. R. S.   Second
Edition, London, 1870, p. 3.

the ranks of the teachers and expounders of dogmatic science, which, although pretentious and authoritative, must ever be intolerant and unprogressive." [1]

Mental Phenomena.

Not only are the operations of vegetable and animal life, according to the new doctrine, due to physical forces, but the same is true of all mental operations. If the argument from analogy is valid in the one case, it is valid in the other. If we must believe that the properties of protoplasm, or living matter, are to be referred to the mode in which its molecules are aggregated, because the properties of water are due to the peculiar aggregation of the atoms of which its elements, hydrogen and oxygen, are composed ; then we must believe that all thought and feeling are due to the molecular composition and movements of the brain atoms. Accordingly, Professor Huxley, after saying that "vitality" has no better philosophical standing than "aquosity," warns his readers that they cannot stop with that admission. "I bid you beware," he says, "that in accepting these conclusions, you are placing your feet on the first rung of a ladder, which in most people's estimation is the reverse of Jacob's, and leads to the antipodes of heaven. It may seem a small thing to admit that the dull vital actions of a fungus or a foraminifer are the properties of their protoplasm, and are the direct results of the nature of the matter of which they are composed. But if, as I have endeavored to prove to you, their protoplasm is essentially identical with, and most readily converted into, that of any animal, I can discover no logical halting-place, between the admission that such is the case, and the further concession that all vital action may with equal propriety be said to be the result of the molecular forces of the protoplasm which displays it. And if so, it must be true, in the same sense and to the same extent, that the thoughts to which I am now giving utterance, and your thoughts regarding them, are the expression of molecular changes in that matter of life which is the source of our other vital phenomena." [2] "Further," he says, "I take it to be demonstrable that it is utterly impossible to prove that anything whatever may not be the effect of a material and necessary cause, and that human logic is equally incompetent to prove that any act is really spontaneous. A really spontaneous act is one which, by the assumption, has no cause [*i. e.* no material cause, for he admits no other] ; and the attempt to prove such a negative as this is, on the

---

[1] *Protoplasm*, p. 4.   [2] *Lay Sermons*, pp. 151, 152.

face of the matter, absurd. And while it is thus a philosophical impossibility to demonstrate that any given phenomenon is not the effect of a material cause, any one who is acquainted with the history of science will admit that its progress has in all ages meant, and now more than ever means, the extension of the province of what we call matter and causation, and the concomitant gradual banishment from all regions of human thought of what we call spirit and spontaneity." [1] " After all, what do we know of this terrible ' matter,' except as a name for the unknown and hypothetical cause of states of our own consciousness ? And what do we know of that ' spirit' over whose threatened extinction by matter a great lamentation is arising, ... except that it is also a name for an unknown and hypothetical cause or condition of states of consciousness ? In other words, matter and spirit are but names for the imaginary substrata of groups of natural phenomena." [2] " As surely as every future grows out of past and present, so will the physiology of the future gradually extend the realm of matter and law until it is co-extensive with knowledge, with feeling, and with action.[3] He cites the often-quoted exhortation of Hume, and enforces " the most wise advice " which it contains. "If we take in our hand," says Hume, " any volume of divinity or school-metaphysics, for instance ; let us ask, does it contain any abstract reasoning concerning quantity or number ? No. Does it contain any experimental reasoning concerning matter of fact or existence ? No. Commit it, then, to the flames ; for it can contain nothing but sophistry and illusion." [4]

The history of human speculation does not furnish a more explicit avowal of Materialism than that contained in the above quotations. All known effects are ascribed to material causes. Spirit is declared to have only an imaginary existence. Spontaneity is pronounced an absurdity. Necessity is affirmed to be inexorable and universal. Yet Huxley says he is no Materialist. This in a sense is true. He is not a Materialist, because he believes in neither matter nor spirit. He avows himself a disciple of Hume, who taught that we know nothing but impressions and ideas. Substance, whether material or spiritual, efficiency, and God, are banished from the sphere of knowledge to that of " sophistry and illusion." He avows his fellowship with Herbert Spencer, the fundamental principle of whose " New Philosophy " is, that all we know, or can know, is, that force is and that it is persistent, while

---

[1] *Lay Sermons*, pp. 155, 156.   [2] *Ibid.* p. 157.   [3] *Ibid.* p. 156.
[4] Hume, *Works*, edit. Edinburgh, 1826, iv. p. 193.

force itself is absolutely inscrutable. This blots the soul and God out of existence, except as those words indicate an unknown force. But as he also holds that all forces are convertible, the distinction between material and mental forces, whether human or divine, is obliterated. He avails himself of the common assumption that his theory does not degrade spirit, but exalts matter. It is the verdict of history, however, as Julius Müller truly says, " That every attempt to spiritualize matter ends in materializing spirit." On this subject Spencer says : " Men who have not risen above that vulgar conception which unites with matter the contemptuous epithets ' gross' and ' brute,' may naturally feel dismay at the proposal to reduce the phenomena of life, of mind, and of society, to a level with those which they think so degraded. . . . . The course proposed does not imply a degradation of the so-called higher, but an elevation of the so-called lower." [1] This at least is an avowal that the phenomena of life, mind, and society are to be referred to material or physical causes. This, indeed, he repeatedly asserts. After insisting on the transformation of physical forces into chemical, and these into vital, he adds, " Many will be alarmed by the assertion that the forces which we distinguish as mental, come within the same generalization. Yet there is no alternative but to make this concession.[2] . . . . Any hesitation to admit that between the physical forces and the sensations there exists a correlation like that between the physical forces themselves, must disappear on remembering how the one correlation like the other, is not qualitive only, but quantitive." [3] " Various classes of facts unite to prove that the law of metamorphosis, which holds among the physical forces, holds equally between them and the mental forces. . . . . How this metamorphosis takes place — how a force existing as motion, light, or heat, can become a mode of consciousness," is mysterious ; but he adds, it is not a greater mystery " than the transformations of physical forces into each other." [4]

Dr. Maudsley, a distinguished writer of the same school,[5] says, " Few, if any, will now be found to deny that with each display of mental power there are correlative changes in the material substratum ; that every phenomenon of mind is the result, as manifest energy, of some change, molecular, chemical, or vital, in the nervous elements of the brain." Again, he says,[6] " With regard to the manifold phenomena of mind ; by observation of them, and abstraction from the particular, we get the general conception, or

[1] *First Principles*, New York, 1869, p. 556.   [2] *Ibid.* p. 211.   [3] *Ibid.* p. 212.
[4] *Ibid.* p. 217.   [5] *Physiology and Pathology of Mind*, Lond. 1868, p. 42.   [6] *Ibid.* p. 43.

the essential idea of mind, an idea which has no more existence out of the mind, than any other abstract idea or general term. In virtue, however, of that powerful tendency in the human mind to make the reality conformable to the idea, a tendency which has been at the bottom of so much confusion in philosophy, this general conception has been converted into an objective entity, and allowed to tyrannize over the understanding. A metaphysical abstraction has been made into a spiritual entity and a complete barrier thereby interposed in the way of positive investigation."

The passages quoted above are a fair specimen of the kind of reasoning in which scientific men frequently indulge. In the first quotation, there are two clauses presented as equivalent, which are in fact essentially different; and substituting the one for the other is just a silent and subtle begging of the question. The first says that every mental act is attended by a molecular change in the brain. The other in effect says, the molecular change is the mental act. These two propositions are as different as day and night. The theory is that a certain kind of molecular motion in iron *is* heat; and a certain kind of molecular motion in the brain *is* thought. And all the proof, as far as the latter is concerned, is that the one attends the other. But the formation of an image on the retina attends sight, and yet does not prove that the image is our consciousness when we see.

Again, in the second passage, Dr. Maudsley says that "mind is an abstract idea," which has no existence outside " of the mind," *i. e.*, outside of itself. An abstract idea has an abstract idea, which it makes into an objective entity. Men who deny the objective existence of mind, can no more think, speak, or write without recognizing its existence, than an idealist can act without recognizing the existence of the external world. Any theory which involves a denial of the laws of our nature is of necessity absurd.

The German Physicists.

As might be expected, the scientific men of the continent are more outspoken in their Materialism than those of England. A late German writer, Th. Otto Berger, Oberlehrer für Mathematik und Physik,[1] says: Materialism is the philosophy of the five senses, it admits nothing but on the testimony of sensation, and therefore denies the existence of the soul, of God, and of everything supersensuous. In its modern form, it teaches that as the material is alone true and real, it is uncreated and eternal. It

---

[1] *Evangelischer Glaube, römischer Irrglaube, und weltlicher Unglaube*, Gotha, 1870.

always has been and always will be. It is indestructible, and, in
its elements, unchangeable. Force is inseparable from matter.
According to the theory no matter is without force, and no force is
without matter. No force exists of itself; and, therefore, there is
none to which the creation of matter is to be referred. The universe as it now is, is due to the gradual evolution of the two elements, matter and force; which evolution proceeds under the operation of fixed laws. The lower organisms are first formed; then the
higher, until man appears. All life, whether animal, vegetable, or
spiritual, is due to the working of physical and chemical forces in
matter. As no power exists but in matter, there can be no divine
Being with creative power nor any created human soul. Berger
quotes Virchow as saying, " The scientific naturalist knows only
bodies and the properties of bodies." All that is beyond them he
pronounces " transcendental, and the transcendental is the chimerical." He also quotes B. C. Vogt, as saying, " We admit of no
creator, either in the beginning, or in the course of the world's
history; and regard the idea of a self-conscious, extramundane
creator as ridiculous." Man, according to these writers, consists
only of a material body; all mental acts and states are of the brain.
When the body dies, the man ceases to exist. " The only immortality," says Moleschott, " is, that when the body is disintegrated,
its ammonia, carbonic acid, and lime, serve to enrich the earth,
and to nourish plants, which feed other generations of men." [1]

F. *Refutation.*

As Materialism, in its modern form, in all that is essential to the
theory, is the same that it was a thousand years ago, the old arguments against it are as available now as they ever were. Its fundamental affirmation is, that all the phenomena of the universe,
physical, vital, and mental, are to be referred to unintelligent physical forces; and its fundamental negation is, that there is no such
objective entity as mind or spirit. If, therefore, it can be shown
that unintelligent force cannot account for all the phenomena of the
universe; and that there is such an objective entity or substance,
as mind, the theory is refuted. There are two methods of combating any given theory. The one is the scientific, which calls in
question the accuracy or the completeness of the data on which it
is founded, or the validity of the inferences deduced from them.
The other is the shorter and easier method of the *reductio ad
absurdum.* The latter is just as legitimate and valid as the

[1] See Berger, I. iii. 5; part i. pp. 264 to 271.

former. It is to be remembered that every theory includes two factors; facts and principles; or, facts and inferences drawn from them. The facts may be admitted, when the principles or inferences may be denied. Thus the facts on which Materialists insist may, for the most part at least, be acknowledged; while the sweeping inferences which they draw from them, in the eye of reason may not be worth a straw. All such inferences must be rejected whenever they conflict with any well-established truth, whether of intuition, experience, or of divine revelation.

Three general theories have been proposed to solve the great problem of the universe: the Materialistic, the Pantheistic, and the Theistic. According to the first all the phenomena of the universe are due to matter and its forces; according to the second, in its most rational form, all power, activity, and life, are the power, activity, and life of the one universal mind. The third, or Theistic theory, assumes the existence of an infinite, extramundane God, who created matter, endowed with forces, and finite minds gifted with intelligence and will; and that all the ordinary phenomena of the universe are proximately due to these physical and mental forces as constantly upheld and controlled by the omnipresent wisdom and power of God. It may be doubted whether any amount of argument can deepen the conviction that the Theistic solution of this great problem is the true one. It is seen to be true, because it is seen to be a solution. It satisfactorily accounts for all the facts of consciousness and observation. It satisfies the reason, the heart, and the conscience. It is in fact self-evidently true, in the sense that no man to whom it has been once proposed, can ever permanently shake off the conviction of its truth. The other theories are not solutions. They may account for some classes of facts, but not for others. Our present concern, however, is with Materialism.

Materialism contradicts the Facts of Consciousness.

1. The primary principle of all knowledge is the knowledge of self. This must be assumed. Unless we *are* we cannot *know*. This knowledge of self is a knowledge that we are something; a real existence; not merely a state or mode of something else; but that the self is a substance, a real, objective entity. It is, moreover, a knowledge not only that we are a substance, but also that we are an individual subsistence, which thinks, feels, and wills. Here, then, is mind, *i. e.*, an individual, intelligent, voluntary agent, necessarily included in the first, and the most essential of all truths. If this be denied, then Hume is right, and we can

know nothing. It is, moreover, included in this knowledge of the Self, that the body is not the Ego. Although the body is intimately, and even vitally united to the substance in which our personality resides, it is nevertheless objective to it. It is the organ which the Self uses, and by which it holds communion with the external world. That these are really facts of consciousness, and not merely *dicta*, or arbitrary assumptions, is clear because they are universally and of necessity recognized. They are imbedded in all human languages ; they are involved in all expressions of human thought; they are of necessity assumed by those who theoretically deny them. The Materialist cannot think, or speak, or write, without assuming the existence of mind as distinct from matter, any more than the Idealist can live and act without assuming the existence of the external world.

Our knowledge of mind, therefore, as a thinking substance, is the first, and most certain, and the most indestructible of all forms of knowledge ; because it is involved in self-knowledge, or self-consciousness, which is the indispensable condition of all knowledge. That which knows is, in the order of nature, before that which is known. It is impossible, therefore, that the Materialist can have any higher evidence of the existence of matter, or of force, than that which every man has, in his own consciousness, of the existence of mind. To deny the one is as unreasonable as to deny the other. Neither can be denied, except theoretically. As a matter of fact, every man believes in matter, and every man believes in mind. What are our sensations which are relied upon so confidently to give us knowledge of physical phenomena, but states of consciousness ? If consciousness is to be trusted in reporting the testimony of the senses, why is it not to be trusted when it reports the facts of our interior life ? If it is believed when it says there is something visible and tangible without us, why should it not be believed when it says there is something which thinks and wills within us? If unreliable in the one case, it is unreliable in the other ; and if unreliable in either, the whole foundation of knowledge and of all faith is swept away. Confidence in the veracity of consciousness is our only security from the wildest, the most irrational, and the most degrading skepticism.

It may be said, however, that the Materialist does not deny that there is something within us that thinks and wills. He only says that that something is the brain. This, however, is to ignore one half of the testimony which consciousness really bears. It testifies not only that there are such sensations as those of sight and touch, but that there is a real objective substance which is tangible and visible. That is to say, we believe in virtue of the constitution of our nature, and therefore of necessity, when we see or touch, that the objects of our sense-perceptions have a real, objective existence. This every man believes, and cannot help believing. And in like manner, when he thinks, feels, or wills, he believes, in virtue of the constitution of his nature, and therefore by a like necessity, that he himself is an intelligent, feeling, and voluntary substance. That is, he believes that the Self is mind, or spirit, to which the body is objective, and therefore different from the Self. The belief in mind, therefore, is involved in the belief of self-existence. Consciousness gives us the assurance that the Self is an intelligent, voluntary agent, or spirit.

2. Another fact of consciousness which Materialism denies, either avowedly or by necessary implication, is the fact of free agency. This, indeed, is involved in what has already been said. Nevertheless there are those who admit the existence of mind who deny that man is a free agent. It needs no proof that consciousness attests that men have the power of self-determination. Every man knows this to be true with regard to himself. Every man recognizes the fact with regard to his fellow-men. This again is a conviction which no obduracy of the conscience, and no sophistry of argument can permanently obliterate from the human mind. This, however, Materialism denies. Physical forces act necessarily and uniformly. In referring all mental action to physical forces, Materialism cannot but exclude all freedom of action. There is no spontaneity in chemical affinity, in light, heat, or electricity ; yet to these forces all vital and mental phenomena are referred. If thought be a certain kind of molecular motion of the brain, it is no more free than that other kind of molecular motion called heat. And this is the more obviously true, if they are correlative, the one being changed into the other. Accordingly Materialists, as a general thing, are avowed necessitarians. This is not only true of the Positivists, but the doctrine that human action is determined by necessary laws, is the foundation of their whole system of Social Science. And Professor Huxley, as we have seen, pronounces a spontaneous act, from the nature of the case, an absurdity. It is for him a causeless effect. Every man, therefore, who knows that he is a free agent, knows that Materialism cannot be true.

3. Materialism contradicts the facts of our moral and religious consciousness. Our moral perceptions are the clearest, the most

certain, and the most authoritative of all of our cognitions. If a man is shut up to deny either the testimony of his senses or the truths of reason, on the one hand, or the testimony of his moral nature on the other, all experience shows that he will give up sense and reason, and bow to the authority of conscience. He cannot help it. No man can free himself from the sense of sin, or of accountability. These moral convictions involve in them, or, at least, necessitate the belief in a God to whom we must give an account. But Materialism, in banishing all mind in man, leaves nothing to be accountable; and in banishing all mind from the universe, leaves no Being to whom an account can be rendered. To substitute for an intelligent, extramundane, personal God, mere "inscrutable force," is a mockery, an insult. Our whole moral and religious nature declares any such theory to be false. It cannot be true unless our whole nature be a lie. And our nature cannot be a lie, unless, as Sir William Hamilton says, the whole universe be "a dream of a dream." To call upon men to worship gravitation, and sing hallelujahs to the whirlwind, is to call upon them to derationalize themselves. The attempt is as idle as it is foolish and wicked.

This argument from the facts of consciousness against Materialism, is met by the assertion that consciousness is not to be trusted. Dr. Maudsley devotes the greater part of the first chapter of his book on the "Physiology of the Mind," to the establishment of this point. He argues that self-consciousness is unreliable in the information which it does give, and incompetent to give any account of a large part of our mental activity. It gives no account of the mental phenomena of the infant, of the uncultivated adult, and of the insane; no account of the bodily conditions which underlie every mental manifestation; no account of the large field of unconscious mental action exhibited, not only in the unconscious assimilation of impressions, but in the registrations of ideas and of their associations, in their latent existence and influence when not active, and their recall into activity; and no account of the influence organically exerted on the brain by other organs of the body. That is, consciousness does not tell us all things, and sometimes tells us wrong. Cannot the same be said of the senses? Can they inform us of everything which goes on in the body? Do they not often deceive us? Are not the sensations of the delirious and the maniac altogether untrustworthy? Does it follow from this that our senses are never to be relied upon? What then becomes of the physical sciences, which are founded on the trustworthiness of

the senses.   The fact is that if the testimony of consciousness is
not to be received as to our mental operations, it cannot be received as to our sensations.   If we have no trustworthy evidence
of the existence of mind, we have no valid evidence of the existence of matter; and there is no universe, no God.   All is nothing.

Happily men cannot emancipate themselves from the laws of
their nature.   They cannot help believing the well-attested testimony of their senses, and they cannot help believing the testimony
of consciousness as to their personal identity, and as to the real,
objective existence of the soul as the subject of their thoughts, feelings, and volitions.   As no man can refuse to believe that he has
a body, so no man can refuse to believe that he has a soul, and that
the two are distinct as the Self and the Not-Self.

Materialism contradicts the Truths of Reason.

1.   It is intuitively true that every effect must have a cause.
This does not mean merely that every effect must have an antecedent; or, as Hume says, that anything may be the cause of anything.   Nor does it mean merely that every effect must have an
efficient cause.   But it means that the antecedent or cause of every
effect must have that kind and degree of efficiency which will
rationally account for the effect.

There are two general classes of effects with which we are familiar, and which are specifically different, and therefore must have
specifically different causes.   The one class consists of effects
which do not, the other of those which do indicate design.   In the
latter we see evidence of a purpose, of foresight, of provision for
the future, of adaptation, of choice, of spontaneity, as well as of
power.   In the former all these indications are absent.   We see
around us innumerable effects belonging to each of these classes.
We see water constantly flowing from a higher to a lower level;
vapor constantly ascending from the sea; heat producing expansion, cold contraction, water extinguishing fire, alkalies correcting
acidity, etc., etc.   On the other hand, the world is crowded with
works of human intelligence ; with statues, pictures, houses, ships,
complicated machines for different purposes, with books, libraries,
hospitals prepared for the wants of the sick, with institutions of
learning, etc., etc.   No man can help believing that these classes
of effects are specifically different, nor can he help believing that
they are due to causes specifically different.   In other words, it is
self-evident that an unintelligent cause cannot produce an intelli-

gent effect; it cannot purpose, foresee, organize, or choose. Professor Joule may determine through what space a weight must fall to produce a given amount of heat; but can he tell how far it must fall to write a poem, or produce a Madonna? Such a cause has no tendency to produce such an effect. And to suppose it to operate from eternity, is only to multiply eternally, nothing by nothing, it is nothing still.

If every man recognizes the absurdity of referring all the works of human ingenuity and intellect to unintelligent, physical force, how much greater is the absurdity of referring to blind force the immeasurably more stupendous, complicated, and ordered works of God, everywhere indicative of purpose, foresight, and choice. Of this absurdity Materialism is guilty. It teaches, in its modern form, that to carbonic acid, water, and ammonia, with the molecular forces they contain, is the causal efficiency to which all organisms from the fungus to man, and all vital and mental phenomena, are to be referred. This is the doctrine elaborately proposed and defended in Professor Huxley's paper on the "Physical Basis of Life." That paper is devoted to establishing two propositions. The first is, "That all animal and vegetable organisms are essentially alike in power, in form, and in substance; and the second, That all vital and intellectual functions are the properties of the molecular dispositions and changes of the material basis (protoplasm) of which the various animals and vegetables consist." [1] He even intimates, after referring to a clock which marks the time, and the phases of the moon, as an illustration of the vital and intellectual phenomena of the universe, as produced by molecular motions and combinations, "that the existing world lay potentially in the cosmic vapor; and that a sufficient intelligence could, from a knowledge of the properties of the molecules of that vapor, have predicted, say the state of the Fauna of Britain in 1869, with as much certainty as one can say what will happen to the vapor of the breath in a cold winter's day." [2] On this it is obvious to remark, in the first place, that it is not one whit in advance of the theory of Epicurus propounded more than two thousand years ago. As the whole mass of thinking men have turned their backs on that theory from that day to this, it is not probable that the reassertion of it, however confidently made, will have much effect upon

[1] *As regards Protoplasm in relation to Professor Huxley's Essay on the Physical Basis of Life*, by James Hutchison Stirling, F. R. C. S., LL. D. Edit. New Haven, p. 15.
[2] See *Life, Matter, and Mind*, by Lionel S. Beale, M. B., F. R. S., London, 1870, p. 17 Dr. Beale quotes from a paper by Professor Huxley in the first number of the *Academy*, p. 13.

men who have either heads or hearts. In the second place, it gives no rational account of the origin of the universe, and of the wonders which it contains. It violates the fundamental intuitive truth that every effect must have an adequate cause, inasmuch as it refers intelligent effects to unintelligent causes; all the libraries in the world, for example, to " the properties of the molecules," of carbonic acid, water, and ammonia.

2. A second truth of Reason which Materialism contradicts is that an infinite succession of effects is as unthinkable as a self-supporting chain of an infinite number of links. The modern doctrine is that lifeless matter never becomes living except when brought into contact with previous living matter. It is the office of the living plant to take up the dead elements of the inorganic world and imbue them with life. The plant, therefore, must either precede protoplasm, which is impossible, as it is composed of protoplasm; or the protoplasm must precede the plant, which is equally impossible, because the plant alone, in the first instance, can make protoplasm; or there must be an infinite succession. That is, an infinite number of causeless effects, which is no less impossible. The doctrine of spontaneous generation, or of life originating out of dead matter, is repudiated by the most advanced advocates of the modern form of Materialism. Professor Huxley has done the cause of truth good service by his able refutation of that doctrine.[1] Whatever may be the ultimate decision of the question as to the origin of life, it is enough for the present that the modern advocates of Materialism admit that living matter can only come from matter already alive. This admission, it is now urged, is fatal to their theory, as it necessitates the assumption of an eternal effect. If dead matter can only be made alive by previous living matter, there must be a source of life outside of matter, or life never could have begun.

Materialism inconsistent with the Facts of Experience.

It is generally admitted that in nature, i. e., in the external world, there are four distinct spheres, or, as they are sometimes called, planes of existence. First, the common chemical compounds, which constitute the mineral kingdom; second, the vegetable kingdom; third, the irrational animal world; and fourth, Man. It is admitted that all the resources of science are incompe-

---

[1] See his Address as President of the British Association, reported in the *London Athenæum*, September 17th, 1870. The little that is necessary to say on the subject of spontaneous generation in such a work as this, is reserved until the question concerning the origin of man comes up for consideration.

tent to raise matter from one of these planes to another. The plant contains ingredients derived from the mineral kingdom, with something specifically different. The animal contains all that is in the plant, with something specifically different. Man contains all that enters into the constitution of the plant and animal, with something specifically different. The lifeless elements of the mineral kingdom, under " the influence of preëxistent living matter," and not otherwise, become living and life-supporting matter in the plant. The products of vegetable life, in like manner, become the matter of animal tissues and organs, but only under the influence of preëxisting living animal tissues. So, also, the products of the vegetable and animal kingdoms are received into the human system, and become connected with the functions and phenomena of the intellectual and moral life of man, but never otherwise than in the person of a man. This outstanding fact, vouched for by the whole history of our globe, proves that there is something in the plant which is not in lifeless matter; something in the animal which is not in the plant, and something in man which is not in the animal. To assume, with the Materialist, that the organizing life of the plant comes out of lifeless matter; that the sensitive and voluntary life of the animal comes out of the insensible and involuntary life of the plant; or that the rational, moral, and spiritual life of Man comes out of the constituents of the animal, is to assume as a fact something which all experience contradicts. We are not forgetful of the theories which refer these different grades or orders of existence to some process of natural development. We here, however, refer only to the outstanding fact of history, that, in the sphere of human experience, lifeless matter does not become organizing and living, in virtue of its own physical forces; nor the plant an animal; nor the animal a man from anything in the plant or animal, but only in virtue of an *ab extra* vital influence. It is indeed said that as the same chemical elements combined in one way, have certain properties ; and when combined in another way, have other properties; so the same elements combined in one way in lifeless matter and in other ways, in plants, animals, and man, may account for all their distinctive characteristics. But it is to be remembered that the properties of chemical compounds, however varied, are chemical, and nothing more ; whereas, in vital organisms the properties or phenomena are specifically different from mere chemical effects. They have no relation to each other, any more than gravity to beauty; and, therefore, the one cannot account for the other.

Materialism is Atheistic.

Atheism is the denial of an extramundane personal God. In saying that Materialism is Atheism, it is not meant that all Materialists are atheists. Some, as for example, Dr. Priestley, confine the application of their principles to the existing order of things. They admit the being of God to whom they refer the creation of the world. The number, however, of such illogical Materialists is small. Leaving out of view these exceptional cases, the philosophers of this school may be divided into three classes, —

(1.) Avowed atheists. To this class belong the Epicureans; the French skeptics of the last century; the Positivists; and a large part of the physicists of the present generation, especially in Europe. (2.) Those who repudiate the charge of atheism, because they admit the necessary existence of an inscrutable force. But inscrutable force is not God. In rejecting the doctrine of an extramundane Spirit, self-conscious, intelligent, and voluntary, the First Cause of all things, they reject Theism; and the denial of Theism is Atheism. (3.) Those whose principles involve the denial of an extramundane God. To this class belong all those who deny the distinction between matter and mind; who deny the " supersensual," and "supernatural," who affirm that physical force is the only kind of force of which we have any knowledge; and who maintain that thought is in such a sense a product of the brain, that where there is no brain there can be no thought. Büchner, who although an avowed atheist, is, as to this point, a fair representative of the whole school, says that the fundamental principle (der oberste Grundsatz) of our philosophy is, " No matter without force; and no force without matter." " A spirit without a body," he adds, " is as unthinkable as electricity or magnetism without the matter of which they are affections." [1] This he makes the ground of his argument to prove the impossibility of the existence of the soul after death. The principle, if admitted, is equally conclusive against the existence of God. As Materialism leaves us no God to reverence and trust, no Being to whom we are responsible; and as it denies any conscious existence after death, it can be adopted only on the sacrifice of the higher attributes of our nature; and its whole tendency must be to demoralize and degrade.

The Correlation of Physical and Vital and Mental Forces.

Besides the considerations urged above against Materialism as a general theory, it may be proper to say a few words in reference

[1] *Kraft und Stoff*, Zehnte Auflage, Leipzig, 1869. p. 200

to its modern scientific form.   It is admitted that it is the province
of scientific men to discuss scientific questions ; and that much injury to the cause of truth has followed the attempts of men not
devoted to such pursuits, undertaking to adjudicate in such cases.
Physicists are wont to take high ground on this subject, and to
warn off as intruders all metaphysicians and theologians, all who
are devoted to the study of the supersensuous and the supernatural.
They are not allowed to be heard on questions of science.   The
rule must work both ways.   If metaphysicians and theologians
must be silent on matters of science, then scientific men devoted to
the study of the sensuous, are not entitled to be dictatorial in what
regards the supersensuous.   A man may be so habituated to deal
with quantity and number, as to become incapable of appreciating
beauty or moral truth.   In like manner a man may be so devoted
to the examination of what his senses reveal, as to come to believe
that the sensible alone is true and real.   The senses have their
rights, and so have reason and conscience; and the votaries of
sense are not entitled to claim the whole domain of knowledge as
exclusively their own.

While, therefore, it is conceded that it belongs specially to scientific men to deal with scientific subjects, yet other classes have
some rights which are not to be denied.   They have the right to
judge for themselves on the validity of the arguments of scientific
men ; and they have the right to appeal from one scientific man to
another, and from the few to the many.   So far as the correlation
of physical and vital forces is concerned, it is not only a new doctrine, but as yet is adopted only by " advanced thinkers," as they
are called, and call themselves.   Dr. H. B. Jones, F. R. S., one
of the more modest advocates of the doctrine,[1] says, " We are only
just entering upon the inquiry how far our ideas of conservation
and correlation of energy can be extended to the biological sciences."   And certain it is that the leading men of science, both in
Europe and America, are firm believers in vital and mental forces,
as distinct in kind, from all physical forces operative in the inorganic world.

The Arguments for such Correlation are Invalid.
The Argument from Analogy.

It has already been stated on the authority of the advocates of
the theory, that their first and most important argument in its
support is from analogy.   The physical forces are all correlated ;

---

[1] *Croonian Lectures*, p. 66.

one is convertible into either of the others; all may be resolved
into motion.   This creates, as it is said, a strong presumption, that
all force, whatever its phenomena, is essentially the same thing.
If one kind of motion is heat, another electricity, another light, it
is fair to infer that vitality is only another kind of motion, and
thought and feeling another.   As there is no reason for assuming
a specific force for light, and another for heat, therefore it is unnecessary, and unphilosophical, to assume a specific kind of force
to account for vital or mental phenomena.   Prof. Barker of Yale
College, says,[1] "To-day, as truly as seventy-five years ago when
Humboldt wrote, the mysterious and awful phenomena of life,
are commonly attributed to some controlling agent residing in
the organism — to some independent presiding deity, holding it in
absolute subjection."   This presiding agent is called " vital fluid,"
" *materia vitæ diffusa*," " vital force."   " All these names," he
adds, " assume the existence of a material or immaterial something,
more or less separable from the material body, and more or less
identical with the mind or soul, which is the cause of the phenomena of living beings.   But as science moved irresistibly onward,
and it became evident that the forces of inorganic nature were
neither deities nor imponderable fluids, separable from matter, but
were simple affections of it, *analogy demanded a like concession in
behalf of vital force.*   From the notion that the effects of heat were
due to an imponderable fluid called caloric, discovery passed to the
conviction that heat was but a motion of material particles, and
hence inseparable from matter; to a like assumption concerning
vitality [namely, that it also is but a motion of material particles], it
was now but a step.   The more advanced thinkers in science of
to-day, therefore, look upon the life of the living form as inseparable from its substance, and believe that the former is purely phenomenal, and only a manifestation of the latter.   Denying the
existence of a special vital force as such, they retain the term only
to express the sum of the phenomena of living beings."

The argument from analogy is presented, as we have seen, in
another form, by Huxley and others.   The properties of water are
very different from those of the hydrogen and oxygen of which it
is composed.   Yet no one supposes that those properties are due to
anything else than the material composition of the water itself.   So
also the phenomena of living matter, and of the human brain, are
very different from those of the elements which enter into their
constitution; but this affords no presumption that there is any

[1] *Correlation of Vital and Physical Forces*, p. 5.

" vital force " or " mind " to account for this difference, any more than the peculiar properties of water justify the assumption of the existence of anything distinct from its material element.   Vitality and mind, we are told, have no better philosophical status than aquosity.

Dr. Stirling [1] states the case thus : " If it is by its mere chemical and physical structure that water exhibits certain properties called aqueous, it is also by its mere chemical and physical structure that protoplasm exhibits certain properties called vital.   All that is necessary in either case is, ' under certain conditions,' to bring the chemical constituents together.   If water is a molecular complication, protoplasm is equally a molecular complication, and for the description of the one or the other, there is no change of language required.   A new substance with new qualities results in precisely the same way here, as a new substance with new qualities there ; and the derivative qualities are not more different from the primitive qualities in the one instance, than the derivative qualities are different from the primitive qualities in the other.   Lastly, the *modus operandi* of preëxistent protoplasm is not more unintelligible than that of the electric spark.   The conclusion is irresistible, then, that all protoplasm being reciprocally convertible, and consequently identical, the properties it displays, vitality and intellect included, are as much the result of molecular constitution, as those of water itself."   This analogy is two-fold ; having reference to chemical composition on the one hand, and to the antecedent stimulus which determines it on the other.   " As regards chemical composition, we are asked, by virtue of the analogy obtaining, to identify, as equally simple instances of it, protoplasm here and water there ; and, as it regards the stimulus in question, we are asked to admit the action of the electric spark in the one case to be quite analogous to the action of preëxisting protoplasm in the other."

In answer to this argument Dr. Stirling goes on to show that the analogy holds only as to chemical and physical properties. " One step farther and we see not only that protoplasm has, like water, a chemical and physical structure ; but that, unlike water, it has also an organized or organic structure.   Now this, on the part of protoplasm, is a possession in excess ; and with relation to that excess there can be no grounds for analogy."   " Living pro-

---

[1] *As Regards Protoplasm in Relation to Professor Huxley's Essay on the Physical Basis of Life,* by James Hutchison Stirling, F. R. C. S., LL. D.   Edinburgh, Blackwood & Sons. Republished as one of the Yale University series, p. 39.   This is considered to be the best refutation of the theory of the correlation of physical and vital force.

toplasm, namely, is identical with dead protoplasm," says Dr. Stirling, " only so far as its chemistry is concerned (if even so much as that) ; and it is quite evident, consequently, that difference between the two cannot depend on that in which they are identical—cannot depend on the chemistry.   Life, then, is no affair of chemical and physical structure, and must find its explanation in something else.   It is thus that, lifted high enough, the light of the analogy between water and protoplasm is seen to go out." [1]   Water and its elements, hydrogen and oxygen, are as to the *kind* of power which they exhibit on a level.   " But not so protoplasm, where, with preservation of the chemical and physical likeness there is the addition of the unlikeness of life, of organization, and of ideas.   But the addition is a new world — a new and higher world, the world of a self-realizing thought, the world of an *entelechy*." [2]   " There are certainly different states of water, as ice and steam ; but the relation of the solid to the liquid, or of either to the vapor, surely offers no analogy to the relation of protoplasm dead to protoplasm alive.   That relation is not an analogy but an antithesis, the antithesis of antitheses.   In it, in fact, we are in the presence of the one incommunicable gulf — the gulf of all gulfs — that gulf which Mr. Huxley's protoplasm is as powerless to efface as any other material expedient that has ever been suggested since the eyes of men first looked into it — the mighty gulf between death and life." [3]

" The differences alluded to (they are, in order, organization and life, the objective idea — design, and the subjective idea — thought), it may be remarked, are admitted by those very Germans to whom protoplasm, name and thing, is due.   They, the most advanced and innovating of them, directly avow that there is present in the cell ' an architectonic principle that has not yet been detected.'   In pronouncing protoplasm capable of active or vital movements, they do by that refer, they admit also, to an immaterial force, and they ascribe the processes exhibited by protoplasm — in so many words — not to the molecules, but to organization and life." [4]

" Was it molecular powers that invented a respiration — that perforated the posterior ear to give a balance of air ; that compensated the *fenestra ovalis* by a *fenestra rotunda ;* that placed in the auricular sacs those otolithes, those express stones for hearing ?   Such machinery !   The *chordæ tendineæ* are, to the valves of the heart, exactly adjusted check-strings ; and the contractile *columnæ*

1 *As Regards Protoplasm*, etc., pp. 41, 42.   2 *Ibid.* p. 42.   3 *Ibid.* p. 42.   4 *Ibid.* p. 43.

carneæ are set in, under contraction and expansion, to equalize their length to their office. . . . . Are we to conceive such machinery, such apparatus, such contrivances, merely molecular ? Are molecules adequate to such things — molecules in their blind passivity, and dead, dull, insensibility ? . . . . Surely in the presence of these manifest ideas, it is impossible to attribute the single peculiar feature of protoplasm — its vitality, namely — to mere molecular chemistry. Protoplasm, it is true, breaks up into carbon, hydrogen, oxygen, and nitrogen, as water does into hydrogen and oxygen ; but the watch breaks similarly up into mere brass, and steel, and glass. The loose materials of the watch — even its chemical material if you will — replace its weight, quite as accurately as the constituents, carbon, etc., replace the weight of the protoplasm. But neither these nor those replace the vanished idea, which was alone the important element."[1] There is, therefore, something in protoplasm which cannot be weighed or otherwise measured, and to which the vital phenomena are to be referred.

If then the argument from analogy fails in its application to vital phenomena, there can be no pretence that it is valid in its application to the phenomena of mind. If we refuse to take the first step, even Professor Huxley cannot require us to take those which follow.

Further Arguments of the Materialists.

Besides the analogical argument, Materialists insist that there is direct evidence of the correlation of physical, with vital, and mental force. Let it be remembered what this means. Correlated forces are such as may be converted, the one into the other, and which are consequently in their nature identical. The thing, therefore, in this case, to be proved is that light, heat, etc., can be changed into life and thought, and that the latter are identical with the former, both classes being resolvable into motion of the molecules of matter.

The proof is substantially this. The animal body generates heat by the combustion of the carbon of the food which it receives, precisely as heat is produced by the combustion of carbon out of the body. And it has been experimentally proved that the quantity of heat produced in the body, is precisely the same, due allowances being made, as the same amount of carbon would produce if burnt out of the body. Vital heat, therefore, is identical with physical heat.

[1] *As regards Protoplasm*, etc., pp. 47. 48.

Again, muscular force is produced precisely in the same way as physical force. The potential energy of the fuel moves the steam-engine. Its work or power is measured and determined by the amount of power stored in the wood or coal consumed in its production. The source and measure of muscular power, are in like manner to be found in the food we eat. Its potential energy, derived from the sun as is the case with the potential energy of wood and coal, when liberated, produces its due amount, so much and no more, of muscular power. Muscular power, therefore, is as purely physical, produced in the same way, and measured by the same standard, as the power of the steam-engine.

In like manner, " nervous energy, or that form of force, which, on the one hand, stimulates a muscle to contract, and on the other, appears in forms called mental," is merely physical. It comes from the food we eat. It moves. The rate of its motion is determined to be ninety-seven feet in a second. Its effects are analogous to those of electricity. It is, therefore, for these and similar reasons, inferred that " nerve-force is a transmuted potential energy." This is no less true of nerve-force when manifested in the form of thought and feeling. Every external manifestation of thought-force, argues Professor Huxley, is a muscular one, and therefore analogous to other forces producing similar effects. Besides, it has been proved that every exercise of thought or feeling is attended by an evolution of heat, which shows that thought is resolved into heat. " Can we longer doubt, then, that the brain, too, is a machine for the conversion of energy? Can we longer refuse to believe that even thought is, in some mysterious way, correlated to the other natural forces? and this, even in face of the fact that it has never yet been measured ? " [1]

To unscientific men of ordinary intelligence, to men not devoted to the study of the sensuous, it is a matter of astonishment that such arguments should be regarded as valid. Admitting all the above *facts*, what do they prove ? Admitting that animal heat is the same in source and nature with heat outside the body; admitting that muscular power is physical in its nature and mode of production; admitting that nerve-force is also physical; what then ? Do these facts give any solution of the mysteries of life, of organization, alimentation, or reproduction? Do they in any measure account for the formation of the eye or ear; for the mutual relations and interdependence of the organs of the body ?

[1] See Professor Barker's *Lecture*, above referred to, for a summary of these arguments, page 24.

Admitting these forces to be physical; who or what uses them? What guides their operation so as to answer a preconceived design? Admitting muscular power to be physical, what calls it into exercise at one time and not at another; beginning, continuing, or suspending it, at pleasure? It is plain that the facts adduced, are no solution either of vital or of voluntary phenomena. And when we come to thought, admitting that mental action is attended by a development of heat, does that prove that thought and heat are identical? When ashamed we blush, when afraid we become pale; do these facts prove that shame and fear and their bodily effects are one and the same thing? Does concomitancy prove identity? In proving the former, do you establish the latter? Do the facts adduced prove that shame is heat and heat shame, and that the one may be converted into the other? All the world knows that sorrow produces tears; but no one infers from this coincidence that sorrow and salt water are identical. Even Professor Tyndall, one of "the advanced thinkers," tells the Materialists, that when they have proved everything they claim to prove, they have proved nothing. They leave the connection between mind and body precisely where it was before.[1]

Direct Arguments against the Theory of the Correlation of Physical, and Vital, and Mental Forces.

1. They are heterogeneous. All physical forces are alike. They all tend to produce motion. They all tend to equilibrium. They are all measurable, by weight, or velocity, or by their sensible effects. They are all unintelligent. They act by necessity, without choice, without reference to an end. In all these respects mental forces are directly the reverse. They do not produce motion, they only guide and control it. They resist a state of equilibrium. They counteract physical force. As soon as vitality is gone, the chemical forces come into play and the plant or animal decays. They cannot be measured. Forces which do not admit of measurement, do not admit of correlation, for correlation involves sameness in quantity. "Thought," says President Barnard, "cannot be a physical force, because thought admits of no measure. I think it will be conceded without controversy that there is no form of material substance, and no known force of a physical nature (and there are no other forces), of which we cannot in some form definitely express the quantity, by reference to

[1] *Athenæum* for August 29, 1868, quoted in *Hulsean Lectures for* 1868: Appendix, Note A.

some conventional measuring unit. . . . . No such means of measuring mental action has been suggested. No such means can be conceived. . . . . Now, I maintain that a thing which is unsusceptible of measure cannot be a quantity; and that a thing that is not even a quantity, cannot be a force." [1]

Again, vital and mental force act with intelligence, with forethought, with freedom, and with design. Wherever the intelligence may reside, it is perfectly evident that all vital operations are carried on in execution of a purpose. Heat and electricity can no more fashion an eye than brass and steel can make a watch, or pen and paper write a book. Intelligent force, therefore, differs in kind from unintelligent force. They are not only different, but contradictory; the affirmation of the one is the negation of the other.

Professor Joseph Henry.

Prof. Joseph Henry, of the Smithsonian Institute, is admitted to be one of the most eminent naturalists of the age; distinguished not only for the thoroughness of his researches, but for soundness of judgment, and for the rare gift of being able to appreciate different kinds of evidence. He admits the correlation of physical forces, but protests against the obliteration of the distinction between them and vitality and mind. "The body," he says, "has been called ' the house we live in,' but it may be more truly denominated the machine we employ, which, furnished with power, and all the appliances for its use, enables us to execute the intentions of our intelligence, to gratify our moral natures, and to commune with our fellow beings. This view of the nature of the body is the furthest removed possible from Materialism; it requires a separate thinking principle. To illustrate this, let us suppose a locomotive engine equipped with steam, water, fuel, — in short, with the potential energy necessary to the exhibition of immense mechanical power; the whole remains in a state of dynamic equilibrium, without motion, or signs of life or intelligence. Let the engineer now open a valve which is so poised as to move with the slightest touch, and almost with a volition, to let on the power to the piston; the machine now awakes, as it were, into life. It rushes forward with tremendous power; it stops instantly, it returns again, it may be, at the command of the master of the train; in short, it exhibits signs of life and intelligence. Its power is now

[1] *The Recent Progress of Science, with an Examination of the asserted identity of the Mental Powers with Physical Forces.* An Address before the American Association for the Advancement of Science. August, 1868. By Frederick A. P. Barnard, S. T. D., LL. D.. pp. 41, 42.

controlled by mind, — it has, as it were, a soul within it." [1] This illustration holds just so far as it was intended to hold. The intellect which controls the engine is not in it, nor is it affected by its changes. Nevertheless, in the body, as well as in the engine, the controlling intellect is equally distinct from the physical force, which both so wonderfully exhibit.

In more direct reference to vitality, Professor Henry says : " Vitality gives startling evidence of the immediate presence of a direct, divine, and spiritual essence, operating with the ordinary forces of nature, but being in itself entirely distinct from them. This view of the subject is absolutely necessary in carrying out the mechanical theory of the equivalency of heat and the correlation of the ordinary physical forces. Among the latter vitality has no place, and knows no subjection to the laws by which they are governed." [2]

Dr. Beale.

Dr. Beale [3] is equally explicit. He constantly insists that what acts voluntarily, with choice to accomplish an end, cannot be physical ; and that in vital and mental operations there is unquestionable evidence of such voluntary action. He says, " I regard ' vitality ' as a power of a peculiar kind, exhibiting no analogy whatever to any known forces. It cannot be a property of matter, because it is in all respects essentially different in its actions from all acknowledged properties of matter. The vital property belongs to a different category altogether." [4] He argues also to prove that organization cannot be referred to physical force. " It cannot be maintained that the atoms arrange themselves, and devise what positions each is to take up, — and it would be yet more extravagant to attribute to ordinary force or energy, atomic rule and directive agency. We might as well try to make ourselves believe that the laboratory fire made and. lighted itself, that the chemical compounds put themselves into the crucible, and the solutions betook themselves to the beakers in the proper order, and in the exact proportions required to form certain definite compounds. But while all will agree that it is absurd to ignore the chemist in the laboratory, many insist upon ignoring the presence of anything representing the chemist in the living matter which they call the ' cell-laboratory.' In the one case the chemist works and guides, but in

---

[1] Paper in the *Agricultural Report*, 1854–1855, p. 448.   [2] Page 441.
[3] *Protoplasm ; or Life, Matter, and Mind.* By Lionel S. Beale, M. B., F. R. S. Second Edition. London, J. Churchill & Sons, 1870. Dr. Beale is an authority in the department of Physiology. His book, *How to work with the Microscope*, has reached a fourth edition.
[4] Page 103.

the other, it is maintained, the lifeless molecules of matter are
themselves the active agents in developing vital phenomena. . . .
No one has proved, and no one can prove, that mind and life are
in any way related to chemistry and mechanics. . . . . Neither
can it be said that life works *with* physical and chemical forces, for
there is no evidence that this is so.   On the other hand it is quite
certain that life overcomes, in some very remarkable and unknown
manner, the influence of physical forces and chemical affinities." [1]
On a former page he had said, " In order to convince people that
the actions of living beings are not due to any mysterious vitality
or vital force or power, but are in fact physical and chemical in
their nature, Professor Huxley gives to matter which is alive, to
matter which is dead, and to matter which is completely changed
by roasting or boiling, the very same name.   The matter of sheep
and mutton and man and lobster and egg is the same, and, according to Huxley, one may be transubstantiated into the other.   But
how ?   By ' subtle influences,' and ' under sundry circumstances,'
answers this authority.   And all these things alive, or dead, or
roasted, he tells us are made of protoplasm, and this protoplasm is
the physical basis of life, or the basis of physical life.   But can this
discoverer of ' subtle influences ' afford to sneer at the fiction of
vitality ?   By calling things which differ from one another in many
qualities by the same name, Huxley seems to think he can annihilate distinctions, enforce identity, and sweep away the difficulties
which have impeded the progress of previous philosophers in their
search after unity.   Plants, and worms, and men are all protoplasm, and protoplasm is albuminous matter, and albuminous matter consists of four elements, and these four elements possess certain properties, by which properties all differences between plants,
and worms, and men, are to be accounted for.   Although Huxley
would probably admit that a worm was not a man, he would tell
us that by ' subtle influences ' the one thing might be easily converted into the other, and not by such nonsensical fictions as ' vitality,' which can neither be weighed, measured, nor conceived." [2]

   In the latter portion of his book Dr. Beale shows that the brain
is not a gland to secrete thought as the liver does bile ; nor is
thought a function of the brain, nor the result of mechanical or
chemical action ; nor is the brain a voltaic battery giving shocks
of thought, as Stuart Mill conjectures ; but it is the organ of the
mind, not for generating, but for expressing thought.

---

[1] *Protoplasm*, etc., pp. 116, 117   [2] *Ibid.* p. 16.

Mr. Wallace.

To quote only one more authority, we refer to the eminent naturalist Wallace, the friend and associate of Darwin, and the zealous defender of his theory. "If," says he, "a material element, or a combination of a thousand material elements in a molecule, are alike unconscious, it is impossible for us to believe, that the mere addition of one, two, or a thousand other material elements to form a more complex molecule, could in any way tend to produce a self-conscious existence. To say that mind is a product or function of protoplasm, or of its molecular changes, is to use words to which we can attach no clear conception. You cannot have, in the whole, what does not exist in any of the parts; . . . . either all matter is conscious, or consciousness is something distinct from matter; and in the latter case, its presence in material forms is a proof of the existence of conscious beings, outside of, and independent of, what we term matter." [1]

Vital and Physical Forces not Convertible.

2. A second argument against the doctrine of the correlation of vital and physical forces is that in fact they are not convertible. Motion and heat are said to be correlated, because one can be changed into the other, measure for measure. But no one has ever changed death into life, dead matter into living matter. This Professor Huxley admits. If the simplest living cell once dies, all the science in the world cannot make it alive. What is dead can be made alive only by being taken up and assimilated by that which is still living. The life, therefore, is not due to the chemical properties of that which is dead. So far as chemistry is concerned, there is no known difference between protoplasm dead and protoplasm alive; and yet there is all the difference between them of life and death. That difference, therefore, is not chemical. Until scientific men can actually change heat and electricity into life, and go about raising the dead, men will be slow to believe that heat and life are identical; and until they can transmute physical force into intelligence and will, they cannot convert "thinkers" into Materialists.

3. Another argument against this theory is the inadequacy of the cause to the assumed effect. The doctrine is that the relation

---

[1] *Contributions to the Theory of Natural Selection.* A series of Essays. By Alfred Russel Wallace, author of *The Malay Archipelago,* etc., etc. McMillan & Co., London, 1870. p. 365.

between correlated forces is quantitive ; so much of the one will produce so much of the other.   But we know that great mental agitation may be produced by the mere sight of certain objects, and that these mental states may call into action violent muscular force. According to the hypothesis, the impression on the nerves of sight or hearing is first transformed into mental force, and that again into muscular and molar energy.   This, President Barnard, who presents this argument, pronounces to be absurd, " since it makes a small force equivalent to a large one." [1]

President Barnard further argues against this theory from the fact that the mental states produced by impressions on the senses are, at least in many cases, obviously due not to the physical impression, but to the idea therewith connected.   If you insult a Frenchman in English, it produces no effect ; if the insult be expressed in his own language, it rouses him to fury.   The meaning of the words is not a physical force, and yet it is to the meaning the effect is due.   Dr. Barnard says, " when it is demanded of us to pronounce as physicists that spiritual existence is an absurdity and religion a dream, it seems to me that no choice is left us but to proclaim our dissent, or to be understood by our silence to accept the doctrine as our own.   When such is the alternative, for one I feel bound to speak, and to declare my conviction that as physicists we have nothing to do with mental philosophy ; and that in endeavouring to reduce the phenomena of mind under the laws of matter, we wander beyond our depth, we establish nothing certain, we bring ridicule upon the name of positive science, and achieve but a single undeniable result, that of unsettling in the minds of multitudes convictions which form the basis of their chief happiness." [2]

4. Physicists cannot carry out their own theory.   Even those least susceptible of the force of the supersensuous, are compelled to admit that there is more in mental and vital action than blind physical force can account for.   Dr. Carpenter, as we have seen, assumes the presence of " a directive agency ; " the Germans of an " architectonic principle " unknown, and uncorrelated, in living matter, to explain undeniable facts for which physical force furnishes no solution.   Others, whose spiritual nature is not so entirely subjected to the sensible, break down entirely.   Thus Professor Barker, of Yale College, after devoting his whole lecture to prove that vital force and even thought " are correlated to other natural forces " (*i. e.*, identical with them), comes at the end to

[1] Barnard's *Address*, p. 45.   [2] *Ibid.* p. 49.

ask : " Is it only this ? Is there not behind this material substance,
a higher than molecular power in the thoughts which are immor-
talized in the poetry of a Milton or a Shakespeare, the art creations of a Michael Angelo or a Titian, the harmonies of a Mozart
or a Beethoven ? Is there really no immortal portion separable
from this brain-tissue, though yet mysteriously united to it ? In a
word, does this curiously fashioned body inclose a soul, God-given,
and to God returning ? Here science veils her face, and bows in
reverence before the Almighty. We have passed the boundaries
by which physical science is inclosed. No crucible, no subtle mag-
netic needle can answer now our questions. No word but His who
formed us can break the awful silence. In the presence of such a
revelation science is dumb, and faith comes in joyfully to accept
that higher truth which can never be the object of physical demonstration." [1]

It thus appears, after all, that there is in man a soul ; that the
soul is not the body, nor a function of it ; that it is the subject and
agent of our thoughts, feelings, and volitions. But this is precisely the thing which the lecture is devoted to disproving. Thus
Professor Barker's science gives up the ghost at the feet of his religion. It quenches its torch in the fountain of an order of truths
higher than those which admit of " physical demonstration." The
πρῶτον ψεῦδος of the whole theory is, that nothing is true which cannot be physically demonstrated ; that is, which cannot be felt,
weighed, or otherwise measured.

Wallace, the Naturalist.

A still more striking illustration of the insufficiency of materialistic principles is furnished by the distinguished naturalist, Alfred
Russel Wallace, above quoted. After devoting his whole book to
the defence of the doctrine of natural selection, which refers the origin of all species and genera of plants and animals to the blind operation of physical forces, he comes to the conclusion that there are
no such forces ; that all is " Mind." Matter has no existence. Matter is force, and force is mind ; so that " the whole universe is not
merely dependent on, but actually *is* the WILL of higher intelligences, or one Supreme Intelligence." [2] He holds that instead of
admitting the existence of an unknown something called matter,
and that mind is " another thing, either a product of this matter
and its supposed inherent forces, or distinct from, and co-existent

---

[1] Barker's *Lecture*, pp. 26, 27.
[2] *Contributions to the Theory of Natural Selection*, p. 368.

with it ; " . . . . it is a " far simpler and more consistent belief, that matter, as an entity distinct from force, does not exist; and that force is a product of MIND. Philosophy," he adds, " had long demonstrated our incapacity to prove the existence of matter, as usually conceived, while it admitted the demonstration to each of us of our own self-conscious, ideal existence. Science has now worked its way up to the same result, and this agreement between them should give us some confidence in their combined teaching." [1] Thus, by one step, the gulf between Materialism and idealistic pantheism is passed. This, at least, is a concession that physical forces cannot account for the phenomena of life and mind ; and that is conceding that Materialism as a theory is false.

The great mistake of Materialists is that they begin at the wrong end. They begin with blind, lifeless matter ; and endeavor to deduce from it and its molecular changes, all the infinite marvels of organization, life, and intelligence which the universe exhibits. This is an attempt to make everything out of nothing. The human mind, in its normal state, always begins with God ; who, as the Bible teaches us, is an Infinite Spirit, and therefore self-conscious, intelligent, and voluntary ; the creator of all things ; of matter with its properties, and of finite minds with their powers ; and who controls all things by his ever present wisdom and might; so that all the intelligence indicated in unintelligent forces is only one form of the infinite intelligence of God. This is the solution of the problem of the universe given in the Scriptures ; a solution which satisfies our whole nature, rational, moral, and religious.

All works on Psychology, and on the history of Philosophy, contain discussions on the principles of Materialism. Chapter iv. of Dr. Buchanan's able work, " Faith in God and Modern Atheism Compared," is devoted to the history and examination of that theory. See also chapter ii. of the Introduction to Professor Porter's elaborate work, " The Human Intellect." Professor Porter gives, on page 40, a copious account of the literature of the subject. In Herzog's "Real-Encyklopädie," article Materialismus, an account is given of the principal recent German works against the modern form of the doctrine.

Among the most important works on this subject, besides the writings of Comte and his English disciples, J. Stuart Mill, and H. G. Lewes, are Herbert Spencer's " First Principles of a New System of Philosophy," and his " Biology " in two volumes ; Maudsley's " Physiology and Pathology of Mind ; " Laycock (Professor

---

[1] *Contributions to the Theory of Natural Selection*, p. 369.

in the University of Edinburgh), " Mind and Brain ; " Huxley's
" Discourse on the Physical Basis of Life ; " his " Evidence of
Man's Place in Nature ; " and " Introduction to the Classification
of Animals ; " and his " Lay Sermons and Essays ; " Professor
Tyndall's " Essay on Heat ; " " The Correlation and Conservation
of Forces : A Series of Expositions, by Professor Grove, Professor
Helmholtz, Dr. Mayer, Dr. Faraday, Professor Liebig, and Dr.
Carpenter ; with an Introduction by Edward L. Youmans, M. D. ; "
Alexander Bain (Professor of Logic in the University of Aber-
deen), " The Senses and the Intellect ; " " The Emotions and the
Will ; " " Mental and Moral Science ; " " Kraft und Stoff, von
Ludwig Büchner, Zehnte Auflage. Leipzig, 1869." By the same
author, " Die Stellung des Menschen in der Natur in Vergangen-
heit, Gegenwart und Zukunft. Oder Woher kommen wir ? Wer
sind wir ? Wohin gehen wir ? Leipzig, 1869." Also, " Sechs
Vorlesungen uber die Darwin'sche Theorie von der Verwandlung
der Arten und die erste Entstehung der Organismenwelt. Leipzig,
1868."

§ 5. *Pantheism.*

A. *What Pantheism is.*

If the etymology of the word Pantheism be allowed to determine
its meaning, the answer to the question, What is Pantheism ? is
easy. The universe is God, and God is the universe. Τὸ πᾶν Θεὸς
ἐστι. This is not only the signification of the word and the popular
idea usually attached to it, but it is the formal definition often given
of the term. Thus Wegscheider says, " Pantheismus [est] ea sententia, qua mundum non secretum a numine ac disparatum, sed
ad ipsam Dei essentiam pertinere quidam opinati sunt."[1] This,
however, is pronounced by the advocates of the doctrine to be
a gross misrepresentation. The idea that the universe, as the
aggregate of individual things, is God, is, they say, a form of
thought, which the earliest philosophy of the East had surmounted.
It might as well be said that the contents of a man's consciousness,
at any one time, were the man himself ; or that the waves of the
ocean were the ocean itself. It is because so many Pantheists
take the word in the sense above indicated, that they deny that
they are Pantheists, and affirm their belief in the being of God.
As the system which is properly designated Pantheism, does exclude the popular view of the subject, derived from the etymology
of the word ; and as it has been held in very different forms, it is

[1] *Institutiones Theologiæ,* fifth edit., Halle, 1826, p. 215.

not easy to give a concise and satisfactory answer to the question, What is Pantheism? The three principal forms in which the doctrine has been presented, are, (1.) That which ascribes to the Infinite and Universal Being, the attributes (to a certain extent at least) of both mind and matter, namely, thought and extension. (2.) That which ascribes to it only the attributes of matter, Materialistic Pantheism. (3.) That which ascribes to it only the attributes of spirit, Idealistic Pantheism.

General Principles of the System.

For the purpose of theological instruction it is sufficient to state what these several systems unite in denying, and what they substantially agree in affirming.

1. They deny all dualism in the universe. The essential distinction between matter and mind, between soul and body, between God and the world, between the Infinite and the Finite is repudiated. There is but one substance, but one real Being. Hence the doctrine is called Monism, or, the All-One doctrine. "The idea," says Cousin,[1] " of the finite, of the infinite, and of their necessary connection as cause and effect, meet in every act of intelligence, nor is it possible to separate them from each other; though distinct, they are bound together, and constitute at once a triplicity and unity." " The first term (the infinite), though absolute, exists not absolutely in itself, but as an absolute cause which must pass into action, and manifest itself in the second (the finite). The finite cannot exist without the infinite, and the infinite can only be realized by developing itself in the finite."

All philosophy is founded, he says, on the ideas of "unity and multiplicity," " of substance and phenomenon." " Behold," he says, " all the propositions which we had enumerated reduced to a single one, as vast as reason and the possible, to the opposition of unity and plurality, of substance and phenomenon, of being and appearance, of identity and difference."[2] All men, he says, believe, " as it were, in a combination of phenomena which would cease to be at the moment in which the eternal substance should cease to sustain them; they believe, as it were, in the visible manifestation of a concealed principle which speaks to them under this cover, and which they adore in nature and in consciousness."[3] "As God is made known only in so far as he is absolute cause, on this account,

[1] *Psychology*, by Henry, first edition, p. xviii.
[2] *History of Philosophy*, translated by Wight, N. Y. 1852, p. 78.
[3] *Ibid.* p. 121.

in my opinion, he cannot but produce, so that the creation ceases
to be unintelligible, and God is no more without a world than a
world without God." [1] It is one of the most familiar aphorisms of
the German philosophers, " Ohne Welt kein Gott; und ohne Gott
keine Welt."

Renan in his " Vie de Jésus," understands by Pantheism, materialism, or the denial of a living God. This would exclude all
the forms of the doctrines held by idealistic pantheists in all ages.
Dr. Calderwood pronounces Sir William Hamilton's doctrine of
creation pantheistic, because it denies that the sum of existence can
either be increased or diminished. Sir William Hamilton teaches
that when we say God created the world out of nothing, we can
only mean that " He evolves existence out of Himself." Although
all the forms of Pantheism are monistic, except Hylozoism, which
is properly dualistic, yet the mere doctrine of the unity of substance
does not constitute Pantheism. However objectionable the doctrine may be that everything that exists, even unorganized matter,
is of the substance of God, it has been held by many Christian
Theists. This does not necessarily involve the denial of the essential distinction between matter and mind.

2. However they differ as to the nature of the Infinite as such,
whether it be matter or spirit; or that of which both thought and
extension (potentially) can be predicated; or, whether it be
thought itself, or force, or cause, or nothing, *i. e.*, that of which
nothing can be affirmed or denied; a simple unknown quantity;
they all agree that it has no existence either before or out of the
world. The world is, therefore, not only consubstantial, but coeternal with God.

3. This of course precludes the idea of creation; except as an
eternal and necessary process.

4. They deny that the Infinite and Absolute Being in itself has
either intelligence, consciousness, or will. The Infinite comes into
existence in the Finite. The whole life, consciousness, intelligence,
and knowledge, at any time, of the former, is the life, consciousness, intelligence, and knowledge of the latter, *i. e.*, of the world.
" Omnes (mentes)," says Spinoza, " simul Dei æternum et infinitum intellectum constituunt." [2] " God alone is, and out of Him is
nothing." [3] " Seine Existenz als Wesen ist unser Denken von ihm;
aber seine reale Existenz ist die Natur, zu welcher das einzelne
Denkende als moment gehört." [4]

---

[1] *Psychology*, fourth edition, N. Y. 1856, p. 447.
[2] *Ethices*, v. xl. schol., edit. Jena, 1803, p. 297.
[3] Fichte, *Von seligen Leben*, p. 143, edit. Berlin, 1806.
[4] Strauss, *Dogmatik*, i. p. 517.

5. Pantheism denies the personality of God. Personality as well as consciousness implies a distinction between the Self and the Not Self; and such distinction is a limitation inconsistent with the nature of the Infinite. God, therefore, is not a person who can say I, and who can be addressed as Thou. As He comes into existence, intelligence, and consciousness only in the world, He is a person only so far as He comprehends all personalities, and the consciousness of the sum of finite creatures constitutes the consciousness of God. " The true doctrine of Hegel on this subject," says Michelet,[1] " is not that God is a person as distinguished from other persons; neither is He simply the universal or absolute substance. He is the movement of the Absolute ever making itself subjective ; and in the subjective first comes to objectivity or to true existence." " God," he adds, " according to Hegel, is the only true personal Being." " As God is eternal personality, so He eternally produces his other self, namely, Nature, in order to come to self-consciousness."

It follows of necessity from the doctrine, that God is the substance of which the universe is the phenomenon; that God has no existence but in the world ; that the aggregate consciousness and life of the Finite is, for the time being, the whole consciousness and life of the Infinite ; that the Infinite cannot be a person distinct from the world, to whom we can say, Thou. On this point Cousin says, " Take away my faculties, and the consciousness that attests them to me, and I am not for myself. It is the same with God ; take away nature, and the soul, and every sign of God disappears." [2] What the soul would be without faculties and without consciousness, that is God without the universe. An unconscious God, without life, of whom nothing can be predicated but simple being, is not only not a person, but he is, for us, nothing.

6. Man is not an individual subsistence. He is but a moment in the life of God ; a wave on the surface of the sea ; a leaf which falls and is renewed year after year.

7. When the body, which makes the distinction of persons among men, perishes, personality ceases with it. There is no conscious existence for man after death. Schleiermacher, in his " Discourses," says, the piety in which he was nurtured in his youth, " remained with me when the God and immortality of my childhood disappeared from my doubting sight." [3] On this avowal, Mr. Hunt, curate of St. Ives, Hunts, comments : " The ' God and immortality ' of his

---

1 *Geschichte der letzen Systeme der Philosophie in Deutschland*, vol. ii. p. 647.
2 *Lectures on the True, the Beautiful, and the Good*, trans. Wight, N.Y., 1854, p. 365.
8 Hunt's *Essay on Pantheism*, London. 1866, p. 312.

childhood disappeared. The personal God whom the Moravians worshipped was exchanged for the impersonal Divinity of philosophy. Nor did this theology seem impious. No, it was the very essence of true religion." There is good reason to believe that with regard to the personal existence of the soul after death, Schleiermacher sacrificed his philosophy, as he certainly did in other points, to his religion. This, however, only the more clearly shows how inconsistent the pantheistic view of the nature of God is with the doctrine of conscious existence after death. The absorption of the soul in God, of the Finite into the Infinite, is the highest destiny that Pantheism can acknowledge for man.

8. As man is only a mode of God's existence, his acts are the acts of God, and as the acts of God are necessary, it follows that there can be no freedom of the will in man. Spinoza says,[1] " Hinc sequitur mentem humanam partem esse infiniti intellectus Dei : ac proinde cum dicimus, mentem humanam hoc vel illud percipere, nihil aliud dicimus, quam quod Deus, non quatenus infinitus est, sed quatenus per naturam humanæ mentis explicatur, sive quatenus humanæ mentis essentiam constituit, hanc vel illam habeat ideam." " In mente nulla est absoluta sive libera voluntas. Mens certus et determinatus modus cogitandi est adeoque suarum actionum non potest esse causa libera." [2] " Eodem hoc modo demonstratur, in mente nullam dari facultatem absolutam intelligendi, cupiendi, amandi, etc." [3]

Cousin says, " We are thus arrived then in the analysis of the me, by the way of psychology still, at a new aspect of ontology, at a substantial activity, anterior and superior to all phenomenal activity, which produces all the phenomena of activity, survives them all, and renews them all, immortal and inexhaustible, in the destruction of its temporary manifestations." [4] Thus our activity is only a temporary manifestation of the activity of God. All our acts are his acts.[5]

Mr. Hunt, analyzing Spinoza's system, and using mainly his language on this point, says, " Spinoza ascribed to God a kind of freedom : a free necessity. But to created existences even this kind of freedom is denied. ' There is nothing contingent in the nature of beings ; all things on the contrary are determined by the necessity of the Divine nature, to exist and to act, after a certain fashion.' ' Nature produced ' is determined by ' nature produ-

---

[1] *Ethices*, part ii. prop. xi. coroll., vol. ii. p. 87, edit. Jena, 1803.

[2] *Ibid.* prop. xlviii. *Demon.* vol. ii. p. 121.   [3] *Ibid.* Scholium.

[4] *Elements of Psychology*, translated by Henry, N. Y. 1856, p. 429.

[5] *Princeton Review*, 1856, p. 368.

cing.' It does not act, it is acted upon. The soul of man is a Spiritual automaton. . . . . There can be nothing arbitrary in the necessary developments of the Divine essence." [1]

As Pantheism makes creation an eternal, necessary, and continuous evolution of the Infinite Being, all liberty of second causes is of necessity excluded. A distinction may be made between the necessity by which a stone falls to the ground, and the necessity by which a mind thinks; but the necessity is as absolute in the one case as in the other. Liberty in man is rational self-determination, that is, spontaneity determined by reason. But reason in man is impersonal, according to Pantheism. It is God as explicated in us. All the acts of the human mind are the acts of God as determined by the necessity of his nature. The same doctrine of fatalism is involved in the idea that history is merely the self-evolution of God. One idea, or phase of the Infinite Being, is exhibited by one age or nation, and a different one by another. But the whole is as much a necessary process of evolution as the growth of a plant.

Sir William Hamilton, therefore, says that Cousin destroys liberty by divorcing it from intelligence, and that his doctrine is inconsistent not only with Theism but with morality, which cannot be founded "on a liberty which at best only escapes necessity by taking refuge with chance." [2] And Morell, a eulogist of Cousin, says, that according to Cousin : "God is the ocean, we are but the waves; the ocean may be one individuality, and each wave another; but still they are essentially one and the same. We see not how Cousin's Theism can possibly be consistent with any idea of moral evil ; neither do we see how, starting from such a dogma, he can ever vindicate and uphold his own theory of human liberty. On such Theistic principles, all sin must be simply defect, and all defect must be absolutely fatuitous." [3]

9. Pantheism in making man a mode of God's existence, and in denying all freedom of the will, and in teaching that all " phenomenal activity" is "a transient manifestation " of the activity of God, precludes the possibility of sin. This does not mean that there is in man no sentiment of approbation or disapprobation, no subjective difference between right and wrong. This would be as absurd as to say that there is no difference between pleasure and pain. But if God be at once God, nature, and humanity; if reason in us be God's reason ; his intelligence our intelligence, his activity our activity ; if God be the substance of which the world is the

---

[1] *Essay on Pantheism*, p. 231.   [2] Hamilton's *Discussions*, p. 43.
[3] *History of Modern Philosophy*, N. Y. 1848, p. 660.

phenomenon ; if we are only moments in the life of God, then there can be nothing in us which is not in God.   Evil is only limitation, or undeveloped good.   One tree is larger and finer than another ; one mind is more vigorous than another ; one mode of action more pleasurable than another ; but all alike are modes of God's activity. Water is water, whether in the puddle or in the ocean ; and God is God, in Nero or St. John.   Hegel says that sin is something unspeakably higher than the law-abiding motion of the planets, or the innocence of plants.   That is, it is a higher manifestation of the life of God.

Spinoza teaches that " sin is nothing positive.   It exists for us but not for God.   The same things which appear hateful in men are regarded with admiration in animals. . . . .   It follows then that sin, which only expresses an imperfection, cannot consist in anything which expresses a reality.   We speak improperly, applying human language to what is above human language, when we say that we sin against God, or that men offend God." [1]

It is the necessary consequence of the doctrine that God is the universal Being, that the more of being the more of God, and therefore the more of good.   And consequently the less of being, the less of good.   All limitation, therefore, is evil ; and evil is simply limitation of being.   Spinoza [2] says, " Quo magis unusquisque — suum esse conservare conatur et potest, eo magis virtute præditus est ; contra quatenus unusquisque — suum esse conservare negligit, eatenus est impotens."   In the demonstration of this proposition, he says, " Virtus est ipsa humana potentia," [3] making power and goodness identical.   Professor Baur of Tübingen,[4] says : " Evil is what is finite ; for the finite is negative ; the negation of the infinite."

It is only, as just said, another form of this doctrine that power, or strength, is in man the only good.   This does not mean the strength to submit to injury ; the strength of self-sacrifice ; the strength to be humble and to resist evil passion ; but the power to carry out our own purposes in opposition to the will, interests, or happiness of others.   That is, that might is right.   The victor is always right, the vanquished is always wrong.   This is only one manifestation of God, suppressing or superseding a less perfect manifestation.   Spinoza's doctrine is, " To the pursuit of what is agreeable, and the hatred of the contrary, man is compelled by his nature, for ' every one desires or rejects by necessity, according to the laws of his nature, that which he judges good or bad.'   To

---

[1] Hunt, p. 231.
[3] *Ibid.*

[2] *Ethices*, iv. prop. xx., vol. ii. p. 217, edit. Jena, 1803.
[4] In the Tübingen *Zeitschrift*, 1834, Drittes Heft, p. 233.

follow this impulse is not only a necessity but it is the right and the duty of every man, and every one should be reckoned an enemy who wishes to hinder another in the gratification of the impulses of his nature. The measure of every one's right is his power. The best right is that of the strongest ; and as the wise man has an absolute right to do all which reason dictates, or the right of living according to the laws of reason, so also the ignorant and foolish man has a right to live according to the laws of appetite." [1] A more immoral and demoralizing principle was never expressed in human language. To say that it is the duty of every man to seek his own gratification, to satisfy the impulses of his nature ; that he is an enemy who attempts to hinder that gratification ; that the only limit to such gratification is our power ; that men have the right, if so inclined, to live according to the laws of appetite, is to say that there is no such thing as moral obligation ; no such thing as right or wrong.

Cousin repeats *ad nauseam* the doctrine that might is right ; that the strongest is always the best. " We usually see in success," he says, " only a triumph of force, ... I hope I have shown that, inasmuch as there always must be a vanquished party, and inasmuch as the vanquished party is always that which ought to be vanquished, to accuse the vanquisher and to take part against victory, is to take part against humanity, and to complain of the progress of civilization. It is necessary to go further ; it is necessary to prove that the vanquished party deserves to be vanquished ; that the vanquishing party not only serves the cause of civilization, but that it is better, and more moral than the vanquished party." " Virtue and prosperity, misfortune and vice, are in necessary harmony." " Feebleness is a vice, and, therefore, it is always punished and beaten." " It is time," he says, " that philosophy of history put beneath its feet the declamations of philanthropy." [2] It must, of course, be true, if God is the life of the world, all power his power, every act his act, not only that there can be no sin, but that the most powerful are always morally (if that word has any meaning) the best ; and that might is right. This is the theory on which hero worship is founded, not only among the heathen, but among Christians, so called, of our day.

10. Pantheism is self deification. If God comes to existence only in the world, and if everything that is, is a manifestation of God, it follows that (so far as this earth is concerned, and so far as

---

[1] Hunt, p. 233.

[2] Cousin's *History of Modern Philosophy*, translated by Wight, New York, 1852, vol. i. pp. 186, 187, 189.

pantheists allow or acknowledge) the soul of man is the highest form of the existence of God. As the souls of men differ very much one from another, one being much superior to others, the greater the man the more divine he is, *i. e.*, the more does he represent God; the more of the divine essence does he reveal. The highest step of development is reached only by those who come to the consciousness of their identity with God. This is the precise doctrine of the Hindus, who teach that when a man is able to say, "I am Brahm," the moment of his absorption into the infinite Being has arrived. This is the ground on which the pantheistic philosophers rest their claim of preëminence; and the ground on which they concede the preëminence of Christ. He, more than any other man, saw into the depths of his own nature. He was able to say as no other man could say, "I and the Father are one." But the difference between Christ and other men is only one of degree. The human race is the incarnation of God, which is a process from eternity to eternity. "Mankind," says Strauss, "is the Godman; the key of a true Christology is, that the predicates which the Church gives to Christ, as an individual, belong to an idea, a generic whole."[1]

11. There is only one step further, and that is, the deification of evil. That step Pantheists do not hesitate to take; so far as evil exists it is as truly a manifestation of God as good. The wicked are only one form of the self-manifestation of God; sin is only one form of the activity of God. This dreadful doctrine is explicitly avowed.

Rosenkranz says,[2] "Die dritte Consequenz endlich ist die, dass Gott der Sohn auch als identisch gesetzt ist mit dem Subject, in welchem die religiöse Vorstellung den Ursprung des Bösen anschaut, mit dem Satan, Phosphoros, Lucifer. Diese Verschmelzung begründet sich darin, dass der Sohn innerhalb Gottes das Moment der Unterscheidung ist, in dem Unterschied aber die Möglichkeit der Entgegensetzung und Entzweiung angelegt ist. Der Sohn ist der selbstbewusste Gott." Such a sentence as the foregoing has never been written in English, and, we trust, never will be. The conclusion it avows, however, is unavoidable. If God be everything, and if there be a Satan, God must be Satan. Rosenkranz says, that the mind is horrified at such language, only because it does not recognize the intimate connection between good and evil; that evil is in good, and good in evil. Without evil there can be no good.

---

[1] *Dogmatik*, ii. p. 215.   [2] *Encyklopädie*, p. 51.

It is because of this deification of evil, that a recent German writer[1] said that this system should be called Pandiabolism instead of Pantheism. He, if we mistake not, is the author of the article in Hengstenberg's "Kirchen-Zeitung,"[2] in which it is said, "this is the true positive blasphemy of God — this veiled blasphemy — this diabolism of the deceitful angel of light — this speaking of reckless words, with which the man of sin sets himself in the temple of God, showing himself that he is God. The Atheist cannot blaspheme with such power as this; his blasphemy is merely negative. He merely says : ' There is no God.' It is only out of Pantheism that a blasphemy can proceed, so wild, of such inspired mockery, so devoutly godless, so desperate in its love of the world, — a blasphemy so seductive, and so offensive that it may well call for the destruction of the world."

Pantheism, however, becomes all things to all men. To the pure it gives scope for a sentimental religious feeling which sees God in every thing and every thing in God. To the proud it is the source of intolerable arrogance and self-conceit. To the sensual it gives authority for every form of indulgence. The body being a mode of God's extension, according to Spinoza's theory, as the mind is a mode of the divine intelligence, the body has its divine rights as well as the soul. Even some of the most reputable of the Pantheistic school, do not hesitate to say in reference to the trammels of morality : "It is well that the rights of our sensual nature should, from time to time, be boldly asserted."[3] This system, therefore, as even the moderate Tholuck says, "comes to the same result with the materialism of French encyclopedists, who mourned over mankind for having sacrificed the real pleasures of time for the imaginary pleasures of eternity, and the protracted enjoyments of life, for the momentary happiness of a peaceful death."

Pantheism, therefore, merges everything into God. The universe is the existence-form of God ; that is, the universe is his existence. All reason is his reason ; all activity is his activity ; the consciousness of creatures, is all the consciousness God has of himself ; good and evil, pain and pleasure, are phenomena of God ; modes in which God reveals himself, the way in which He passes from Being into Existence. He is not, therefore, a person whom we can worship and in whom we can trust. He is only the substance of which the universe and all that it contains are the ever

<hr />

[1] Leo, the historian, we believe.   [2] 1836, p. 575.
[3] Bischer, quoted in *Evangelische Kirchen-Zeitung*, 1839, p. 31.

changing manifestation. Pantheism admits of no freedom, no responsibility, no conscious life after death. Cousin sums up the doctrine in this comprehensive paragraph : " The God of consciousness is not an abstract God, a solitary monarch exiled beyond the limits of creation, upon the desert throne of a silent eternity, and of an absolute existence which resembles even the negation of existence. He is a God at once true and real, at once substance and cause, always substance and always cause, being substance only in so far as He is cause, and cause only so far as He is substance, that is to say, being absolute cause, one and many, eternity and time, space and number, essence and life, indivisibility and totality, principle, end, and centre, at the summit of Being and at its lowest degree, infinite and finite together, triple, in a word, that is to say, at the same time God, nature, and humanity. In fact, if God be not everything, He is nothing." [1]

History of Pantheism.

Pantheism has proved itself to be the most persistent as well as the most wide-spread form of human thought relative to the origin and nature of the universe, and its relation to the Infinite Being, whose existence in some form seems to be a universal and necessary assumption. Pantheistic ideas underlie almost all the forms of religion which have existed in the world. Polytheism, which has been almost universal, has its origin in nature worship ; and nature-worship rests on the assumption that Nature is God, or, the manifestation, or existence form of the infinite unknown. Of course it is only the briefest outline of the different forms of this portentous system of error, that can be given in these pages.

B. Brahminical Pantheism.

Ethnographically the Hindus belong to the same race as the Greeks, Romans, and other great European nations. In prehistoric periods one division of the great Aryan family spread itself westward over the territory which now constitutes Europe. Another division extended south and east and entered India, displacing almost entirely the original inhabitants of that large, diversified, and fertile region.

Long before Greece or Rome became cultivated communities, and when Europe was the home only of uncivilized barbarians, India was covered with rich and populous cities ; the arts had

---

[1] *Philosophical Fragments*, Preface to First Edition. See *History of Modern Philosophy*, translated by Wight, N. Y. 1852, vol. i. pp. 112, 113.

reached the highest state of development; a literature and language which, in the judgment of scholars, rival those of Greece and Rome, had been produced, and systems of philosophy as profound, as subtle, and as diversified as the human mind ever elaborated, were already taught in her schools.

The Hindus number nearly two hundred millions of souls. They are now, in the essential principles of their philosophy, their religion, and their social organization, what they were a thousand years before the birth of Christ. Never in the history of the world has a form of religious philosophy been so extensively embraced, so persistently adhered to, or so effective in moulding the character and determining the destiny of a people.

Few questions of the kind, therefore, are of deeper interest than what the true character of the Hindu religion actually is. The decision of that question is not free from difficulty; and it has, therefore, received very different answers. The difficulty in this case arises from various sources.

1. The religious books of the Hindus are not only written in Sanskrit, a language unintelligible, except to a small class of learned men, but they are exceedingly voluminous. The Vedas, the most ancient and authoritative, fill fourteen volumes folio. The Institutes of Menu, the Puranas, and the sacred poems, "Ramayana" and "Mahabhrata," are equally extensive. The former of these poems consists of a hundred thousand verses, and the latter of four hundred thousand, while the Æneid has only twelve thousand, and the Iliad twenty-four thousand. Sir William Jones said that the student of the Hindu literature and religion, found himself in the presence of infinity.

2. It is not only, however, the voluminousness of the authoritative sacred books, but the character of their contents, which creates the difficulty of getting a clear idea of the system which they teach. The Vedas consist mainly of hymns of various ages, interspersed with brief, obscure, philosophical or theological explanations and comments. The Puranas are filled with extravagant legends; which are to be interpreted historically, and which mythically, it is difficult to decide.

3. The spirit of exaggeration is so characteristic of the Hindu mind that statements meant to be understood literally shock the mind by their extravagance. Thus their books make the earth a circular plane one hundred and seventy millions of miles in diameter; they speak of mountains sixty miles high, and of periods of four thousand millions of millions of years.

The Religion of the Hindus not originally Monotheistic.

It is a common opinion that the Hindu religion was originally and for centuries monotheistic; that out of monotheism gradually rose the present complicated and monstrous polytheism, and that contemporaneously among the philosophical class, were developed the different forms of Pantheism. But this is contrary to well established facts, and is altogether unsatisfactory as a solution of the great problem of Hindu life.

It is indeed true, as we know from the Bible, that monotheism was the earliest form of religion among men. And it is also true in all probability that the Vedas, which are collections of ancient hymns, contain some which belong to the monotheistic period. Most of those, however, which appear to assume the existence of one God, are to be understood in a pantheistic and not in a theistic sense. These recognize one divine Being, but that one includes all the other forms of being. The history of religion shows that when monotheism failed among men because " they did not like to retain God in their knowledge," it was replaced by the worship of nature. This nature-worship assumed two forms. The different elements, as fire, air, and water, were personified, endowed with personal attributes and divine powers, giving rise to polytheism. Or nature as a whole was the object of worship, giving rise to Pantheism.

It is evident that among the highly intellectual Aryans who settled in India, between one and two thousand years before Christ, the pantheistic view had obtained the ascendency, not as a philosophical theory merely, but as a religious doctrine. It became, and has continued until this day, the foundation of the religious, civil, and social life of the Hindu. It is this which gives it its paramount importance. It stands alone in history. In no other case, among no other people, has Pantheism become the controlling form of religious belief among the people, so as to determine their institutions and to mould their character. The Hindus, therefore, have an interest for Christians and for the religious philosopher which attaches to no other heathen nation. They show, and were doubtless intended to show, what are the legitimate effects of Pantheism. That doctrine has had dominant control for millenniums, over a highly cultivated and intelligent people, and in their character and state we see its proper fruits.

It was Pantheistic.

That the religion of the Hindus is fundamentally pantheistic, is evident —

1. From what their sacred writings teach of the Supreme Being. It is designated by a word in the neuter gender, Brahm. It is never addressed as a person. It is never worshipped. It has no attributes but such as may be predicated of space. It is said to be eternal, infinite, immutable. It is said to have continued for untold ages in the state of unintelligent, unconscious being. It comes to existence, to consciousness, and life, in the world. It unfolds itself through countless ages in all the forms of finite existence; and then by a like gradual process all things are resolved into unconscious being. The illustrations of the origin of the world commonly employed are sparks issuing from a burning mass; or, better, vapour rising from the ocean, condensing and falling back to the source whence it came. Being as such, or the Infinite, is, therefore, viewed in three aspects: as coming to existence, as developing itself in the world, as receiving everything back into the abyss of simple being. These different aspects are expressed by the words, Brahma, Vishnu, and Shiva, to which our terms, Creator, Preserver, and Destroyer, answer very imperfectly.

We have here the constantly recurring pantheistic formula, Thesis, Analysis, Synthesis; Being, Development, Restoration. The Infinite, the Finite, and their Identity. The principal difference between the Brahminical system and the theories of the later pantheists, is that the latter make the universe co-eternal with God. The Infinite from eternity to eternity develops itself in the Finite. Whereas, according to the former, there was an inconceivably long period of repose antecedent to the process of development, and that process after millions of millions of ages, is to be followed by a like period of unconsciousness and rest.

Relation of Infinite Being to the World.

2. The relation of God to the world, or rather of the Infinite to the Finite, is the same in the Brahminical, as in other pantheistic systems. That relation has been already intimated. It is that of identity. The world is the existence-form of God. God is everything, good and evil; and everything is God. But in very different degrees. There is more of Being (*i. e.*, of God) in a plant than in unorganized matter; more in an animal than in the plant; more in man than in either; more in one man, or race of men, than in another.

Relation of Pantheism to Polytheism.

3. The vast polytheistic system of the Hindus is founded on Pantheism and is its logical consequence. In the first place, as just remarked, Brahma, Vishnu, and Shiva, commonly called the Hindu Trinity, are not persons, but personifications, or different aspects under which Infinite Being is to be regarded. In the second place, as the Infinite Being manifests itself in different degrees in different persons and things, anything extraordinary in nature, any remarkable man, is regarded as a special manifestation or embodiment of God. Hence the frequent *avatars* or incarnations of the Hindu mythology. In this way the gods may be, and have been indefinitely multiplied. Any person or thing, or quality, may be deified as a manifestation of infinite Being. In the third place, this accounts for the facts that the Hindu gods are regarded as destitute of moral excellence, and that even evil, as under the name of *Kali*, the goddess of cruelty and patroness of murderers, may be the special object of reverence. In the fourth place, no god, not even Brahma or Vishnu, is, according to the Hindu system, immortal. All gods and goddesses are at length to be merged in the abyss of infinite, unconscious Being.

Effect of Pantheism on Religion.

4. Pantheism, as it makes being, God, as it recognizes no attribute but power in the objects of worship, divorces morality from religion. It is not in the power of any system, however sincerely embraced, to reverse the laws of our nature. And, therefore, in despite of the prevalence of a doctrine which denies the possibility of either sin or virtue, and makes everything dependent on fate, or the power of arbitrary being, the people in various ways recognize the obligation of the moral law and the excellence of virtue. But this has nothing to do with their religion. The great object of all religious observances was final absorption in God; their proximate object was to propitiate some power by which the worshipper would be raised one or more steps toward the state in which that absorption is possible. On this point Professor Wilson says: [1] " Entire dependence upon Krishna, or any other favorite deity, not only obviates the necessity of virtue, but it sanctifies vice. Conduct is wholly immaterial. It matters not how atrocious a sinner a man may be, if he paints his face, his breast, his arms with certain sec-

[1] *Essays and Lectures chiefly on the Religion of the Hindus*, vol. ii. p. 75; edit. London, 1862.

tarial marks; or, which is better, if he brands his skin permanently with them with a hot iron stamp; if he is constantly chanting hymns in honor of Vishnu, or, what is equally efficacious, if he spends hours in the simple reiteration of his name or names; if he die with the word Hari, or Ráma, or Krishna on his lips, and the thought of him in his mind, he may have lived a monster of iniquity, — he is certain of heaven." "Certain of heaven," is a Christian form of expression, and conveys an idea foreign to the Hindu mind. What such a worshipper hopes and expects is that when next born into this the world it may be in a higher state and so much the nearer his final absorption. As Professor Wilson is not only moderate, but almost apologetic in the account which he gives of the religion of the Hindus, the above quoted statement cannot be suspected of unfairness or exaggeration.

Character of the Hindu Worship.

The two leading characteristics of the Hindu worship are cruelty and indecency. And these are sufficiently accounted for by the Pantheism which underlies the whole system. Pantheism denies the distinction between virtue and vice; it recognizes no attribute but power; it deifies evil; it "sanctifies vice;" passion, sensual or malignant, is as much a mode of divine manifestation as the most heroic virtue. Indeed, there is no room for the idea of moral excellence. Hence the prescriptions of religion have reference almost exclusively to rites and ceremonies. The Brahmin when he rises must bathe in a certain way, stand in a certain posture, extend his fingers in a prescribed manner; he must salute the rising sun, resting on one foot; he must repeat certain words. When he eats, the dish must be placed according to rule; he must make prescribed motions with his hands, and so on through the whole day. Every act is prescribed, everything is religious; everything either defiles or purifies, ceremonially, but of moral defilement or purity there seems to be in their religion no recognition.

The Anthropology of the Hindus.

5. The anthropology of the Hindus proves the pantheistic character of their whole system. Man is only a part of God, a mode of his existence. He is compared to a portion of sea-water inclosed in a bottle and thrown into the ocean. The water in the bottle is the same in nature as that without. As soon as the bottle is broken the water within it is lost in the surrounding ocean. Another illustration of the destiny of the soul is that of a lump of

salt thrown into the ocean, which immediately disappears. Its individuality is lost. This absorption of the soul is the highest beatification which Pantheism offers to its votaries. But this, in the case of the vast majority of men, can be attained only after a long process of transmigrations extending, it may be, through millions of years. If a man be faithful and punctilious in his religious observances, he comes into the world after death in a higher state. Thus, a Soudra may become a Brahmin. But if unfaithful, he will be born in a lower form, it may be, in that of a reptile. It is thus, by these alternations, that the wished for absorption in Brahm is ultimately attained. With regard to the sacred, or Brahminical caste, the process may be shorter. A Brahmin's life is divided, according to the Institutes of Menu, into four periods : childhood; student life ; life as householder ; and finally, the ascetic period. As soon as a Brahmin feels the approach of old age, he is directed to retire from the world ; to live as a hermit; to subsist only on herbs ; to deny himself all business and enjoyment, that by continued self-negation he may not only destroy the power of the body, and free himself from the influence of the things seen and temporal, but also lose the consciousness of his individuality, and be able at last to say, " I am Brahm," and then he is lost in the infinite.

The Hindu life is dominated by this doctrine of absorption in God after a long series of transmigrations, and by the division of the people into castes, which has in like manner its foundation in their theory of the relation of God to the world, or, of the Infinite to the Finite. The Brahminical, or sacred class, is a higher manifestation of God than the military class ; the military, than the mercantile ; the mercantile, than the servile. This is popularly expressed by saying that the first proceeds from the head, the second from the arms, the third from the body, and the fourth from the feet of Brahm. The member of one of the lower castes cannot pass into either of those above him, except that by merit (ritual observances) he may on his next birth into the world be advanced to a higher grade ; and one of a higher caste, by neglect of the prescribed rule of living, may at his next birth find himself degraded into a lower caste, or even into a beast or a reptile. Hence the horror of losing caste, which places a man out of the line of advancement, and consigns him to an almost endless state of degradation.

The Effect of Pantheism on the Social Life of the Hindus.

6. The whole religious and social life of the Hindu is controlled
by the radical principle that all things are God, or modes of his
existence, and all destined to return to Him again. To a Hindu
his individual existence is a burden. It is a fall from God. Hence
to get back, to be lost in the Infinite, is the one great object of
desire and effort. As this end is not to be attained by virtue, but
by asceticism, by propitiation of the gods, their religion is simply
a round of unmeaning ceremonies, or acts of self-denial, or self-
torture. Their religion, therefore, tends to destroy all interest in
the present life, which is regarded as a burden and degradation.
It cuts the nerves of exertion. It presents no incentive to virtue.
It promotes vice. It has all the effects of fatalism. The influence
of the worship of deities without moral excellence, some of them
monsters of iniquity ; the belief that cruelty and obscenity are ac-
ceptable to these deities, and secure their favor, cannot be otherwise than debasing. The world, therefore, sees in India the practical working of Pantheism. The system has been in unrestricted
operation, not as a philosophy, but as a practical religious belief, for
thousands of years, and among a people belonging to the most
favored of the various races of men, and the result is before our
eyes.

" Greece and India," says Max Müller, " are, indeed, the two
opposite poles in the historical development of the Aryan man.
To the Greek, existence is full of life and reality ; to the Hindu it
is a dream, an illusion. . . . . The Hindu enters this world as a
stranger ; all his thoughts are directed to another world ; he takes
no part even where he is driven to act ; and when he sacrifices his
life, it is but to be delivered from it. No wonder that a nation like
the Indian cared so little for history ; no wonder that social and
political virtues were little cultivated, and the ideas of the useful
and the beautiful scarcely known to them. With all this, however, they had what the Greek was as little capable of imagining
as they were of realizing the elements of Grecian life. They shut
their eyes to this world of outward seeming and activity, to open
them full on the world of thought and rest. Their life was a
yearning after eternity ; their activity a struggle to return into that
divine essence from which this life seemed to have severed them.
Believing as they did in a divine and really existing eternal Being

---

[1] *A History of Ancient Sanskrit Literature, so far as it illustrates the Primitive Religion
of the Brahmans,* pp. 18, 19.

($\tau\grave{o}$ ὄντως ὄν), they could not believe in the existence of this passing world.   If the one existed, the other could only seem to exist ; if they lived in the one, they could not live in the other.   Their existence on earth was to them a problem, their eternal life a certainty.   The highest object of their religion was to restore that bond by which their own self (âtman) was linked to the eternal Self (paramâtman) ; to recover that unity which had been clouded and obscured by the magical illusions of reality, by the so-called Mâyâ of creation."

In order to show " How largely this idea of the Âtman, as the Divine Spirit, entered into the early religious and philosophical speculations of the Indians," he quotes from one of the Vedas a Dialogue in which, among other things, one of the speakers says : " Whosoever looks for this world, for the gods, for all beings, for this universe, elsewhere than in the Divine Spirit, should be abandoned by them all.   This Brahmahood, this kshatra-power, this world, these gods, these beings, this universe, all is the Divine Spirit." [1]   The illustrations used by the speaker to show the relation of the phenomenal universe to God, are derived from the sounds issuing from a drum or a lute, smoke rising from a fire, vapour from the sea.   He adds, " It is with us, when we enter into the Divine Spirit, as if a lump of salt was thrown into the sea ; it becomes dissolved into the water (from which it was produced), and is not to be taken out again.   But wherever you take the water and taste it, it is salt.   Thus is this great, endless, and boundless Being but one mass of knowledge.   As the water becomes salt, and the salt becomes water again, thus has the Divine Spirit appeared from out the elements and disappears again into them.   When we have passed away, there is no longer any name." [2]

There can therefore be no reasonable doubt that Pantheism lies at the foundation of all the religion of India.   There is, indeed, the same difference between the present complex and corrupt polytheism of the Hindus and the teachings of the Vedas, that there is between the Roman Catholicism of our day and primitive Christianity.   There is, however, this important distinction between the two cases.   Popery is a perversion of Christianity by the introduction of incongruous elements derived from Jewish and heathen sources, whereas the religion of modern India is the legitimate and logical result of the principles of the earliest and purest of the Hindu sacred writings.

The most accessible sources of information on the literature and

[1] *History of Ancient Sanskrit Literature*, etc., p. 23.   [2] *Ibid.* p. 21.

religion of India, are the writings of Sir William Jones ; the writings of Colebrooke ; the Journal of the Asiatic Society ; the works of Prof. Wilson of Oxford, specially his " Essays and Lectures on the Religion of the Hindus " ; Max Müller's work just quoted. Dr. Duff's " India and Indian Missions," and the histories of India, by Macaulay, Elphinstone, *et al.*

C. *Grecian Pantheism.*

The remark of Max Müller, that " Greece and India are the two opposite poles of the development of the Aryan man," is strikingly correct. The Greek believed in, and lived for the present and the visible ; the Indian believed in, and lived for the invisible and the future. Nevertheless there was a tendency in the higher minds among the Greeks to adopt the same speculative views as to God and the universe, the Infinite and the Finite, as prevailed in India. With the Greek, however, it was a matter of speculation ; with the Hindu, it was a practical religious belief.

Speaking in general terms, the different forms of Grecian philosophy are characterized by the effort to reduce all the forms of existence to unity ; to discover some one substance, principle, or power, to which all modes of manifestation of being could be referred. Sometimes this one substance was assumed to be material ; sometimes spiritual ; sometimes the obvious incompatibility between the phenomena of mind and those of matter, forced the admission of two eternal principles : the one active, the other passive ; the one spiritual, the other material. The fundamental principle or idea, therefore, of the Grecian philosophy was pantheistic, either in its materialistic, spiritualistic, or hylozoistic form.

The Ionic School.

The earliest school among the Greeks was the Ionic, represented by Thales the Milesian, Anaximander and Anaximenes also of Miletus, and Heraclitus of Ephesus. These philosophers flourished from about 600 to 500 b. c. They were all materialistic in their theories. With Thales the one primal universal substance was water ; with Anaximenes it was air ; with Heraclitus it was fire. " It was the endeavour of this oldest of the Ionic philosophies, to deduce the origin of all things from one simple radical cause, a cosmical substance, in itself unchangeable, but entering into the change of phenomena ; and this was why these philosophers had no room in their doctrine for gods, or transmundane beings, fashioning and

ruling things at will; and, in fact, Aristotle also remarked of the
old physiologists, that they had not distinguished the moving cause
from matter." [1] Of Heraclitus, Döllinger, in his able work "The
Gentile and the Jew in the Courts of the Temple of Christ," says
he "meant by his 'fire,' an ethereal substance as primal matter, the
all-pervading and animating soul of the universe; a matter which
he conceived to be not merely actual fire, but caloric, and this
being at the same time the only power at work in the world, all-
creative and destructive in turns, was, to speak generally, the one
real and veritable existence among all things. For everything had
its origin only in the constant modification of this eternal and primal fire: the entire world was a fire dying out and rekindling itself
in a fixed succession, while the other elements are but fire converted by condensation or rarefaction into a variety of forms. Thus
the idea of a permanent being is a delusion; everything is in a
state of perpetual flux, an eternal-going to be (Werden), and in
this stream spirit is hurried along as well as body, swallowed up
and born afresh. . . . . Heraclitus, as any thorough-going
Pantheist would, called the common soul of the world, the all-comprehending primal fire, Zeus; and the flux of perpetual change
and tendency to be, into which it enters, he termed poetically
Zeus playing by himself." [2]

Cousin says, "For the Ionic school in both its stages, there was
no other God than nature. Pantheism is inherent in its system.
What is Pantheism? It is the conception of the universe, τὸ πᾶν,
as alone existing, as self-sufficient, and having its explanation in
itself. All nascent philosophy is a philosophy of nature, and thus
is inclined to Pantheism. The sensationalism of the Ionians of
necessity took that form; and, to speak honestly, Pantheism is
nothing but atheism." [3]

Cousin frames the definition of Pantheism so as to exclude his
own system. With him the material universe alone is not God.
He believes in "God, nature, and humanity." But these three
are one. "If God," he says, "be not everything, He is nothing."
This, however, is as truly Pantheism (although in a more philosophical form), as the Materialism of the Ionians.

The Eleatic School.

The Eleatic or Italian school, of which Xenophanes, Parmenides,
and Zeno, are the principal representatives, was inclined to the

[1] Döllinger, *The Gentile and the Jew*, translated by Darnell, London, 1862, vol. i. p. 250.
[2] *Ibid.* vol. i. p. 252.   [3] *Histoire Generale de la Philosophie*, Paris, 1863, vol. i. p. 107.

other extreme of denying the very existence of matter. Of these philosophers, Cousin says, " They reduced everything to an existence absolute, which approached nearly to Nihilism, or the denial of all existence."[1] Of Xenophanes, born in Colophon 617 B. C., Döllinger[2] says, " With all his assertions of monotheistic sound, he was still a Pantheist, and, indeed, a material Pantheist, and is universally understood to be such by the ancients. Certainly there was present to his mind the idea of a being, one and spiritual, embracing the whole complement of existence and thought within nimself; yet this being was in his view but the general naturepower ; the unity of God was to him identical with the unity of the world, and this again but the manifestation of the invisible being, called God, and therefore also he explained it to be uncreate, everlasting, and imperishable." It is hard to see how this differs from the modern pantheistic doctrine, that God is the substance of which the world is the phenomenon ; or why Xenophanes should be regarded as a materialist more than Schelling or Cousin.

Parmenides of Elea about 500 B. C. was more of an idealist. He attained to the idea of a pure and simple being in opposition to the material principle of the Ionic school. This " being," however, was not a " pure metaphysical idea, for," says Döllinger, " he so expressed himself as to seèm to represent it at one time as corporeal, and extended in space, at another as thinking. ' To think, and the object of which the thought is, are one and the same,' was a saying of his. . . . . There was no bridge for Parmenides that had led from this pure simple ' being ' to the world of phenomena, of the manifold, and of motion ; and therefore he denied the reality of all we see ; the whole world of sense owed its existence only to the illusions of sense and the empty notions of mortal men built thereon."[3] Thus Parmenides anticipated Schelling in teaching the identity of subject and object.

The Stoics.

The Stoics take their origin from Zeno of Cittium, in Cyprus (340–260 B. C). Their doctrine has already been noticed under the head of Hylozoism. Döllinger, indeed, says, " The Stoic system is utter Materialism, built upon Heraclitic doctrine. It adopted corporeal causes only, and is only acquainted with two principles — matter, and an activity resident in matter, from eternity, as power, and giving it form. Everything real is body ; there are no incor-

---

[1] *Histoire Generale de la Philosophie*, Paris, 1867, vol. i. p. 116; edit. 1863, p. 111.
[2] *The Gentile and the Jew*, vol. i. p. 260.   [3] *Ibid.* vol. i. p. 261

poreal things, as our abstractions, space, time, etc., have merely an existence in our thoughts; so all that really exists can only be known through the senses." [1] This judgment, however, is modified by what he says elsewhere. It is very plain that the later Stoics, especially among the Latins, as Seneca and Marcus Aurelius, regarded the general principle which animated matter as having all the attributes of mind. On this point Döllinger says, " The two principles, matter and power, are to the Stoics but one and the same thing viewed in different relations. Matter required for its existence a principle of unity to give it form and keep it together; and this, the active element, is inconceivable without matter, as a subject in and on which it exists and dwells, and in which it works and moves. Thus, the positive element is matter; yet conceived without properties; the active one, running through and quickening all, is God in matter. But in truth, God and matter are identical; in other words, the Stoic doctrine is hylozoic Pantheism."

" God is, therefore, the world-soul, and the world itself no aggregate of independent elements, but an organized, living being, whose complement and life is a single soul, or primal fire, exhibiting divers degrees of expansion and heat. . . . . God, then, in his physical aspect, is the world-fire, or vital heat, all-penetrating, the one only cause of all life and all motion, and, at the same time, the necessity that rules in the world: but, on the other side, as the universal cause can only be a soul full of intelligence and wisdom, he is the world-intelligence, a blest being, and the author of the moral law, who is ever occupied with the government of the world, although he is precisely this world itself." [2] " The one substance is God and nature together, of which all that comes into being, and ceases to be, all generation and dissolution, are mere modifications. Seneca explains Zeus or God's being at once the world and the world's soul by pointing to man, who feels himself to be a single being and yet again as one consisting of two substances, body and soul." [3]

The Stoics adopted the Hindu doctrine of the dissolution of all things, and the redevelopment of God in the world, after long successive periods. " In the great conflagration which takes place after the expiration of a world period or great year," all organized beings will be destroyed, all multiplicity and difference be lost in God's unity; which means, all will become ether again. But forthwith, like the phœnix recovering life from his own ashes, the formation of the world begins afresh; God trans-

[1] *The Gentile and the Jew*, vol. i. p. 349. [2] *Ibid.* pp. 349–350. [3] *Ibid.* p. 350.

forms himself once more by a general renovation into a world, in which the same events, under similar circumstances, are again to be repeated down to the minutest detail.   Many of these great catastrophes have already happened, and the process of burning by fire will follow again upon this regeneration, and so on *ad infinitum.*[1]

This system as well as every other form of Pantheism, excludes all moral freedom; everything is under the law of absolute necessity.   It therefore precludes the idea of sin.   " Acts of vice, Chrysippus said, are movements of universal nature, and in conformity with the divine intelligence.   In the economy of the great world, evil is like chaff falling, — as unavoidable and worthless. Evil also was said by this school to do the service of making the good known, and yet at last all must resolve itself into God." [2]

Thus the Ionic, the Eleatic, and the Stoic forms of Grecian philosophy were in their fundamental principles pantheistic.   The two great philosophic minds of Greece, and of the world, however, were Plato and Aristotle, the one the philosopher of the ideal world, and the other of the natural.   The latter was the disciple of the former, although in most points of doctrine, or at least of method, his antagonist.   It is only with the views of these mind-controlling men, concerning the nature of the supreme Being, and of his relation to the phenomenal world, that the theologian as such has anything to do.   And this, unfortunately, with regard to both, is the point in regard to which their teachings are the most obscure.

Plato.

Plato united in his comprehensive intellect, and endeavoured to harmonize the elements of the different doctrines of his predecessors in the field of speculation.   " The Socratic doctrine of the absolute good and beautiful, and of the Deity revealing himself to man as a kind Providence, formed the basis on which he started. As channels for the Heraclitic doctrine of the perpetual coming into being and flux of all things, together with the Eleatic one of the eternal immutability of the one and only Being, the dogma of Anaxagoras of a world-ruling spirit was serviceable to him, and with it he had the skill to connect the Pythagorean view of the universe, as an animated intelligent whole, in a spiritualized form." [3]   These are sufficiently incongruous materials.   An intelligent Deity exercising a providential control over the world; the Heraclitic doctrine which involved the denial of all reality and re-

[1] *The Gentile and the Jew,* vol. i. p. 351.   [2] *Ibid.* p. 351.   [3] *Ibid.* p. 307.

solved everything into a perpetual flow of phenomena ; the Eleatic doctrine of a one and only Being ; and the Pythagorean idea of the universe as an animated and intelligent whole. It was not possible but that first one, and then another of these elements should be made the more prominent, and consequently that the great philosopher should speak sometimes as a Theist and sometimes as a Pantheist. Neither was it possible that these incongruous elements should be moulded into a consistent system. It is not, therefore, a matter of surprise that Döllinger, one of the greatest admirers of Plato and one of the ablest expounders of his writings, should immediately add to the passage above quoted. " Plato never arrived at a finished system, rounded off and perfect in itself; nevertheless there is unmistakable evidence in his works of a continual progress, an effort after an increasing depth of foundation, and a stronger internal articulation, joined to a wonderful exuberance of ideas, often excessively bold." [1]

Plato was not a Theist, in the ordinary and Christian sense of that word. He did not recognize the existence of an extramundane God, the creator, preserver, and governor of the world, on whom we are dependent and to whom we are responsible. With him God is not a person. As Anselm and the Realists generally admitted the existence of " rationality " as distinct from rational beings ; a general principle which became individual and personal in angels and men ; so Plato admitted the existence of an universal intelligence, or νοῦς, which becomes individualized in the different orders of intelligent beings, gods, demons, and men. God with him was an Idea ; the Idea of the Good ; which comprehended and gave unity to all other ideas.

Ideas.

What then were ideas in Plato's sense of the term ? They were not mere thoughts, but the only real entities, of which the phenomenal and sensible are the representations or shadows. He illustrated their nature by supposing a man in a dark cave entirely ignorant of the external world, with a bright light shining behind him, while between him and the light there continually passes a procession of men, animals, trees, etc. The moving shadows of these things would be projected on the wall of the cavern, and the man would necessarily suppose that the shadows were the realities. These ideas are immutable and eternal, constituting the essence or real being of all phenomenal existence. " Plato teaches that for as

[1] *The Gentile and the Jew*, p. 307.

many general signs of our conceptions as we have, there are so
many really existing things, or Ideas, in the intelligible world corresponding : to man these are the only solid and worthy objects of
thought and knowledge ; for they are eternal and immutable, existing only in themselves, but separate from all things and individual, while their manifold copies, the things perceptible by sense, are
ever fluctuating and transitory.   Independent of time and space,
as well as of our intellect and its conceptions, Ideas belong to a
world of their own, of another sphere, transcending sense.   They
are not the thoughts of God, but the objects of his thought ; and,
according to them, He created the world in matter.   They only and
God are really existing beings ; and therefore earthly things have
but the shadow of an existence, and that only derived from a certain participation in the Ideas, their types." [1]

The Relation of Ideas, in Plato's Philosophy, to God.

What is the relation of these ideas to God ?   This is the decisive question so far as the theology of Plato is concerned.   Unfortunately it is not a question easily answered.   It is a point about
which the commentators differ ; some saying that Plato leaves the
matter undecided, sometimes identifying ideas with God, and at
others representing them as distinct ; others say that he clearly
identifies ideas with God, or includes them in the divine essence ;
while others again understand him as making a marked distinction
between God and the ideas after which the universe was moulded.
It is not easy to reconcile what Döllinger says on this subject.   In
the passage above quoted he says that ideas are not the thoughts
of God, but the objects of his thought.   But on the same page [2] he
says, " These Ideas are not to be conceived as beside and external
to God.   They are founded in God, and God is the all comprehensive Idea, embracing all partial archetypes in an unity."
He had before said, that with Plato Ideas and God are the only
" really existing beings."   If this be so, and if God is "the all-
comprehensive idea, embracing all others in unity," then God is
the only really existing Being ; and we have pure Pantheism.
According to Cousin, Plato not only gave ideas a real and proper
existence, but, " en dernière analyse il les place dans la raison
divine : c'est la qu' elles existent substantiellement." [3]   Döllinger, in
commenting on a passage in the Timæus, in which " God is styled
the Father, who has begotten the world like a son, as an image of

---

[1] *The Gentile and the Jew*, vol. i. pp. 308 and 309.   [2] *Ibid.* p. 309.
[3] *Histoire Générale de la Philosophie*, Paris, 1863, p. 122.

the eternal gods, *i. e.*, ideas ; " says, " Had Plato really intended here to explain the idea of procreation as a communication of essence, he would have been a pure Pantheist." [1]   Plato, however, he says [2] " is no Pantheist ; matter is, with him, entirely distinct from God ; still he has a pantheistical bias in his system ; for all that there is of intelligence in the world, down even to man, belongs, in his view, to the divine substance." Plato, therefore, escapes Pantheism only by admitting the eternity of matter; but this eternal matter is as near nothing as possible.   It is not corporeal.   It is " something not yet entity."

As Plato made ideas eternal and immutable ; as they were all included in the idea of God, *i. e.*, in God ; and as they constitute the only really existing beings, all that is phenomenal or that affects the senses being mere shadows of the real, it can hardly be denied that his system in its essential character is really pantheistical.   It is, however, an ideal Pantheism.   It does not admit that matter or evil is a manifestation of God, or mode of his existence. Only what is good, is God ; but all that really is, is good.

The Cosmogony of Plato.

Plato's cosmogony and anthropology confirm this view of his theology.   Nothing has ever been created.   All that is, is eternal ; not indeed in form, but in substance.   Matter, something material, has always existed.   This in itself is lifeless, but it has " a soul," an unintelligent force by which chaotic or disorderly agitation or motion is produced.   This unintelligent force God endowed with a portion of his own intelligence or νοῦς, and it becomes the world-soul, *i. e.*, the Demiurgus, the formative principle of the world. God is not therefore himself even the framer of the world.   This is the work of the Demiurgus.   This world-soul pervades the visible universe, and constitutes one living, animated whole.   This " world-soul " is individualized in star-gods, demons, and human souls.   Thus Plato's system makes room for polytheism.

The Nature of the Soul.

The soul, according to this theory, consists of intelligence which is of the substance of God, and of elements derived from the world-soul as distinguished from the νοῦς which did not originally belong to it.   All evil arises from the connection of the divine element in man with matter.   The object of life is to counteract this evil influence by contemplation and communion with the ideal

---

[1] *The Gentile and the Jew*, vol. i. p. 329.   [2] *Ibid.* p. 312.

world. Plato taught the preëxistence as well as the immortality
of the soul. ·Its state in the present stage of existence being determined by its course in its previous forms of being. It is, however, according to his common mode of representation, strictly
immortal. " Plato's monotheistic conception of God," says Döllinger,[1] " is one of the most refined to which ante-Christian speculation attained ; yet he contributed nothing whatever to the knowledge of the perfect, living, personality of God, and its absolute and
unconditional liberty." His monotheism, it would seem, consisted
in the acknowledgment of a universal intelligence which manifested
itself as reason in all rational beings.

Aristotle.

Aristotle, although the disciple, was the great opponent of Plato
and his philosophy. He rejected Plato's doctrine of ideas as chimerical, as a hypothesis which was unnecessary and without evidence. In like manner he denied the existence of preëxistent matter out of which the world was fashioned. He believed the world
to be eternal both in matter and form. It is, and there is no reason
to doubt that it always has been and always will be. He admitted
the existence of mind in man ; and, therefore, assumed that there
is an infinite intelligence, of which reason in man is a manifestation. But this infinite intelligence, which he called God, was pure
intelligence, destitute of power and of will ; neither the creator
nor the framer of the world ; unconscious, indeed, that the world
exists ; as it is occupied exclusively in thought of which it is itself
the object. The world and God are coeternal ; and yet, in a certain sense, God is the cause of the world. As a magnet acts on
matter, or as the mere presence of a friend stirs the mind, so God
unconsciously operates on matter, and awakens its dormant powers.
As the universe is a cosmos, an ordered system ; and as innumerable organized beings, vegetable and animal, exist in the world,
Aristotle assumed that there are " forms " inherent in matter, which
determine the nature of all such organizations. This is very much
what in modern language would be called " vital force," " vitality,"
" vis formativa," " Bildungstrieb," or Agassiz's " immaterial principle," which is different in every distinct species, and which constitutes the difference between one species and another. The soul
is the " forma " of the man. " It is the principle that gives form,
motion, and development to the body, the entelecheia of it ; i. e.,
that substance, which only manifests itself in the body which is
formed and penetrated by it, and continues energizing in it as the

1 *The Gentile and the Jew*, p. 329.

principle of life, determining and mastering matter. Thus, the
body is nothing of itself; it is what it is, only through the soul,
the nature and being of which it expresses, to which it stands in
the relation of a medium in which the object, the soul, is realized ;
and so it cannot be imagined without the body, nor the body without it ; one must be produced contemporaneously with the other." [1]
Of course there can be no immortality of the soul. As no plant is
immortal, as the vital principle does not exist separately from the
plant, so the soul has no existence separate from the body. The
two begin and end together. " The really human in the soul, that
which has come into being, must also pass away, the understanding even ; only the divine reason is immortal ; but, as the memory
belongs to the sensitive soul, and individual thought depends on the
understanding or passive *nous* only, all self-consciousness must
cease with death." [2] " Thus, then, Aristotle's doctrine of the soul
shows that his defect, as well as that of Plato, and indeed of all
antiquity, was his imperfect acquaintance with the idea of personality ; and on that head he cannot be acquitted of a pantheistic tendency." [3] " His God is not a really personal one, or is only an
imperfect personality." [4] " The *nous*, or reason, allows souls, with
their bodies, to sink back into nothingness, from which they severally issued. It alone exists on, ever the same and unalterable ;
for it is no other than the divine *nous* in individual existence, the
divine intelligence enlightening the night of human understanding,
and must be conceived just as much the prime mover of human
discursive thought and knowledge, as of his will." [5]

This brief review of the Grecian philosophy in its relation to
theology, shows that in all its forms it was more or less pantheistic.
This remark will not be recognized as correct by those, who with
Cousin, limit the use of the word Pantheism to designate either the
doctrine which makes the material universe God ; or that which
denies the existence of anything but matter and physical force,
which is atheism ; nor by those who take the word strictly as
meaning the theory which admits of only one substance, which is
the substance of God ; and which consequently makes matter as
much a mode of God's existence as mind. Its correctness, however, will be admitted by those who mean by Pantheism the doctrine which makes all the intelligence in the world the intelligence
of God, and all intellectual activity modes of the activity of God,
and which necessarily precludes the possibility of human liberty
and responsibility.

[1] *The Gentile and the Jew*, p. 338.   [2] *Ibid.* p. 339.   [3] *Ibid.* p. 340.
[4] *Ibid.* p. 336.   [5] *Ibid.* p. 339.

The authorities on this subject are, so far as Plato and Aristotle are concerned, of course their own writings ; with regard to those philosophers whose works are not preserved, or of which only fragments are extant, their systems are more or less fully detailed by the ancient writers, as Plutarch and Cicero. The general reader will find the information he needs in one or more of the numerous histories of philosophy ; as those of Brucker, Ritter, Tenneman, and Cousin ; among the latest and best of which is Döllinger's " The Gentile and the Jew in the Courts of the Temple of Christ," London, 1862.

D. *Mediæval Pantheism.*

The Neo-Platonists.

Pantheism, as it appeared in the Middle Ages, took its form and character from Neo-Platonism. This was an eclectic system in which the Eleatic doctrine of the unity of all being was combined with the Platonic doctrine concerning the phenomenal universe. The philosophers recognized as the representatives of this school are Plotinus (A. D. 205–270), Porphyry (born A. D. 233), Jamblichus in the fourth century, and Proclus in the fifth. Neo-Platonism was monism. It admitted of only one universal Being. This Being considered in itself was inconceivable and indescribable. It was revealed, or self-manifested in the world-soul, and world-reason, which constituted a trinity ; one substance in different aspects or modes of manifestation. The world is therefore " the affluence of God," as fire emits heat. The soul of man is a mode of God's existence, a portion of his substance. Its destiny is absorption in the infinite Being. This was not to be attained by thought, or by meditation, but by ecstasy. This constituted the peculiar feature of the Neo-Platonic school. " Union with God " was to be attained by " a mystical self-destruction of the individual person (Ichheit) " in God.[1] Schwegler [2] says : " From the introduction of Christianity monism has been the character and the fundamental tendency of the whole modern philosophy." This remark, coming from an advocate of that theory, must be taken with no small amount of allowance. It is, however, true that almost all the great departures from the simplicity of the truth as revealed in the sacred Scriptures, have assumed more or less distinctly a pantheistic tendency.

---

[1] *History of Philosophy.* Translated from the German by Julius H. Seelye, p. 157.
[2] *Ibid.* p. 158.

John Scotus Erigena.

The most pronounced Pantheist among the schoolmen was John
Scotus Erigena. Little is known of his origin or history. From
his name Scotus and designation Erigena (son of Erin), it has
been generally assumed that he was an Irishman. It is known
that he enjoyed the protection and patronage of Charles the Bald
of France, and that he taught in Paris and perhaps in England.

His principal work is that " De Divisione Naturæ." By nature
he means all being. The fourfold divisions which he makes of
nature, are only so many manifestations or aspects under which
the one Being is revealed or is to be contemplated. Those divisions
are : (1.) That which creates and is not created. (2.) That
which creates and is created. (3.) That which does not create
but is created. (4.) That which neither creates nor is created.
" This division of nature," says Ritter,[1] " is made simply to show
that all is God, since the four natures are only revelations of God."

Scotus agreed with most philosophers in making philosophy and
religion identical, and in admitting no higher source of knowledge
than human reason. " Conficitur," he says, " veram esse philosophiam veram religionem, conversimque veram religionem esse
veram philosophiam." [2]

The leading principles of his philosophy are the following:
(1.) The distinction with him between being and not-being, is
not that between something and nothing, between substantial existence and non-existence, but between affirmation and negation.
Whatever may be affirmed *is ;* whatever is denied *is* not. (2.) All
being consists in thought. Nothing is but as it exists in the mind
and consciousness. (3.) With God, being, thought, and creating
are identical. God's being consists in thinking, and his thoughts
are things. In other words, the thought of God is the real being
of all that is. (4.) Consequently the world is eternal. God and
the world are identical. He is the " *totum omnium.*"

His system is, therefore, a form of idealistic Pantheism. Ritter
devotes the ninth book of his " Geschichte der Christlichen Philosophie," [3] to the exposition of the philosophy of Scotus. The few
following passages from the " De Divisione Naturæ," are sufficient
to show the correctness of the above statement of his principles.

" Intellectus enim omnium in Deo essentia omnium est. Siqui-
dem id ipsum est Deo cognoscere, priusquam fiunt, quæ facit, et

---

[1] *Geschichte der Christlichen Philosophie*, vol. iii. p. 224.
[2] *De Prædest.* cap. i. 1, Migne, *Patr.*, vol. cxxii. p. 358, a.   [3] Vol. iii. pp. 206–296.

facere, quæ cognoscit. Cognoscere ergo et facere Dei unum est." [1]
"Maximus ait: Quodcunque intellectus comprehendere potuerit, id
ipsum fit." [2] "Intellectus enim rerum veraciter ipsæ res sunt, dicente Sancto Dionysio, ' Cognitio eorum, quæ sunt, ea, quæ sunt,
est. ' " [3] "Homo est notio quædam intellectualis in mente divina
æternaliter facta. Verissima et probatissima definitio hominis est
ista : et non solum hominis, verum etiam omnium quæ in divina
sapientia facta sunt." [4] Omnis visibilis et invisibilis creatura Theophania, i. e., divina apparitio potest appelari.[5] "Num negabis cre-
atorem et creaturam unum esse ? " [6] "Creation [with Erigena] is
nothing else than the Lord of creation ; God in some ineffable
manner created in the creation." [7]

Scotus translated the works of the so-called St. Dionysius, the
Areopagite, and in so doing prepared the way for that form of mystical Pantheism which prevailed through the Church down to the
period of the Reformation. The pseudo-Dionysius was a Neo-
Platonist. His object was to give the doctrine of Plotinus a Christian aspect. He adopted the principle of the unity of all being.
All creatures are of the essence of God. But instead of placing
the self-manifestation of God in nature, in the world-soul, he placed
it principally in the hierarchy of rational being, — cherubim, seraphim, thrones, principalities, and powers, and souls of men. The
destiny of all rational creatures, is reunion with God; and this
reunion, as the Neo-Platonists taught, was to be attained by ecstasy
and the negation of Self. It was this system, which, in common
with all other forms of Pantheism, precluded the idea of sin, which
was reproduced by the leading mystics of the Middle Ages, and
which, when it found its way among the people as it did with the
Beghards and Brethren of the Free Spirit, produced, as substantially the same system has done in India, its legitimate fruits of
evil. Of the mystical Pantheism of the Middle Ages, however,
enough has already been said in the Introduction, in the chapter
on Mysticism.

E. *Modern Pantheism.*

Spinoza.

The revival of Pantheism since the Reformation is principally
due to Spinoza ; he was born at Amsterdam in 1634, and died at
Ghent in the forty-fourth year of his age. He was descended from
a wealthy Jewish Portuguese family, and enjoyed the advantage of

---

[1] *De Divisione Naturæ*, II. 20; edit. Westphalia, 1838, p. 118.
[2] *Ibid.* I. 9, p. 9.   [3] *Ibid.* II. 8, p. 95.   [4] *Ibid.* IV. 7, p. 330.
[5] *Ibid.* III. 19, p. 240.   [6] *Ibid.* II 9, p. 88.   [7] Ritter, vol. iii. p. 234.

a highly finished education.   He early devoted himself to the study of philosophy, and was at first a disciple of Des Cartes.   Leibnitz characterizes the system of Spinoza as Cartesianism run wild.   Des Cartes distrusted the testimony of the senses.   His starting-point was the consciousness of existence, " I think."   In that proposition the existence of a thinking substance is necessarily included.   The outward world produces impressions on this thinking substance. But after all, these sensations thus produced, are only states of self-consciousness.   Self, therefore, and its varying states, are all of which we have direct knowledge.   It is not all, however, that Des Cartes believed actually existed.   He was a sincere Catholic, and died in communion with the Church.   He acknowledged not only the existence of mind, but also of God and of matter.   Our knowl- edge, however, of God and of matter as substances distinct from our minds, was arrived at by a process of reasoning.   The validity of that process Spinoza denied.   He admitted the existence of only one substance, and gave such a definition of the word as precluded the possibility of there being more substances than one.   With him substance is that which exists of itself, of necessity, and is abso- lutely independent.   There is, therefore, but one substance possi- ble.   We come, however, everywhere into contact with two classes of phenomena : those of thought and those of extension.   Thought and extension, therefore, are the two attributes of the one infinite substance.   Individual things are the modes under which the in- finite substance is constantly manifested.   In Spinoza's system there are the three radical ideas of substance, attribute, and mode. Of these that of substance alone has any reality.   The other two are mere appearances.   If we look at anything through a glass colored red the object will appear red ; if the glass be blue, the object will appear blue ; but the color is not really an attribute of the object. Thus substance (the one) appears to us under one aspect as thought and under another as extension.   The difference is appar- ent and not real.   The finite has therefore no real existence.   The universe is sunk into the Infinite ; and the Infinite is a substance of which nothing can be affirmed.   Of the Infinite nothing can be denied, and therefore nothing can be affirmed for " omnis deter- minatio est negatio."   The Infinite, therefore, is practically nothing.

A sufficient account of modern Pantheism in its general features, as represented by Fichte, Schelling, and Hegel, and their succes- sors and disciples, has been given already at the commencement of this chapter.   More detailed information may be found in the numerous recent histories of philosophy, as those of Morell, Schwegler, Michelet, and Rosenkranz, and in Hunt's "History of Pantheism."

F. *Conclusion.*

The fact that Pantheism has so extensively prevailed in every age and in every part of the world, is a proof of its fascination and power. Apart from a divine revelation, it seems to have been regarded as the most probable solution of the great problem of the universe. Nevertheless it is so unsatisfactory, and does such violence to the laws of our nature, that it has never to any extent taken hold on the hearts of the people. India may be regarded as furnishing an exception to this remark. But even there, although Pantheism was the ground form of the popular religion, it had to resolve itself into polytheism in order to meet the necessities of the people. Men must have a personal god whom they can worship and to whom they can pray.

The most obvious remark to be made of the whole system is that it is a hypothesis. From its very nature it is incapable of proof. It is a mere theory assumed to account for the phenomena of the universe. If it did satisfactorily account for them, and did not contradict the teachings of the Bible, it might be safely admitted. But it is not only inconsistent with all that the Scriptures reveal concerning the nature of God and his relation to the world, but it contradicts the laws of belief which God has impressed on our nature, subverts the very foundation of religion and morality, and involves even the deification of sin.

Had we no divine revelation on the subject, Theism merely as a theory could not fail to secure the assent of every devout mind in preference to Pantheism. Theism supposes the existence of a personal, extramundane God, the creator and preserver of the universe ; everywhere present in his wisdom and power, directing all events to the accomplishment of his infinitely wise designs. It supposes the material universe to be distinct from God, dependent on his will, upheld by his power, and pregnant with physical forces ever active under his control. It supposes that man is the creature of God, owing his existence to the will of God, created after his image, a free, rational, moral, and accountable agent, capable of knowing, loving, and worshipping God as a Spirit infinite in his being and perfections. Although this theory may have, for the reason, some problems, such as the origin and prevalence of evil, without a satisfactory solution, yet as it meets and satisfies all the demands of our nature, and solves the problem as to the origin and nature of the universe, it commends itself to the reason, the heart, and the conscience with a force which no sophistry of speculation can resist.

Pantheism, on the other hand, does violence to our nature, and contradicts the intuitive convictions of consciousness.

1. We are conscious that we are. free agents. This is a truth which no man can deny with regard to himself, and which every man assumes with regard to others. This truth Pantheism denies. It makes our activity only a form of the activity of God, and assumes that his acts are determined by necessity as much as the development of a plant or animal.

2. It is intuitively certain that there is a real distinction between moral good and evil: that the one is that to which man is bound to be conformed, and the other that which he is bound to hate and to avoid; that the one deserves approbation, and that the other deserves disapprobation, and merits punishment. These are convictions which belong to the rational nature of man; and they cannot be destroyed without destroying his rationality. Pantheism, however, pronounces these convictions delusions; that there is no such thing as sin, in the sense above stated; that what we call sin is mere weakness; imperfect development, as unavoidable as feebleness in an infant. It goes further: it pronounces evil good. It makes the sinful acts and passions of men as much the acts and states of God as holy acts and holy feelings. There is no good but being; and the men of power are the men of being; and, therefore, the strongest are the best; the weak are to be despised; they deserved to be conquered and trodden under foot. Hence where Pantheism has become a religion the deities who represent evil are the most honoured and worshipped.

3. Pantheism not only destroys the foundation of morals, but it renders all rational religion impossible. Religion supposes a personal Being endowed not only with intelligence and power, but with moral excellence; and to be rational, that Being must be infinite in all his perfections. Pantheism, however, denies that an infinite Being can be a person; that it is intelligent, self-conscious, or possessed of moral attributes. It is just as impossible to worship such a Being as it is to worship the atmosphere, or the law of gravitation, or the axioms of Euclid.

4. It is no extravagance to say that Pantheism is the worst form of atheism. For mere atheism is negative. It neither deifies man nor evil. But Pantheism teaches that man, the human soul, is the highest form in which God exists; and that evil is as much a manifestation of God as good; Satan as the ever-blessed and adorable

Redeemer.   Beyond this it is impossible for the insanity of wickedness to go.

5. Man, according to this system, is no more immortal than the leaves of the forest, or the waves of the sea.   We are transient forms of universal Being.

Our nature is indestructible; as it is impossible that we should not believe in our own individual existence, in our free agency, in our moral obligations; in our dependence and responsibility to a Being capable of knowing what we are and what we do, and of rewarding and punishing as He sees fit, so it is impossible that Pantheism should ever be more than a philosophical speculation, where the moral nature of man has once been developed by the knowledge of the living and true God.

CHAPTER IV.

THE KNOWLEDGE OF GOD.

HAVING considered the arguments in favor of the doctrine that God is, and also the various systems opposed to Theism, we come now to consider the question, Can God be known? and if so, How? that is, How does the mind proceed in forming its idea of God, and, How do we know that God really is what we believe Him to be?

§ 1. *God can be known.*

It is the clear doctrine of the Scriptures that God can be known. Our Lord teaches that eternal life consists in the knowledge of God and of Jesus Christ, whom He hath sent. The Psalmist says, "In Judah is God known" (Ps. lxxvi. 1). Isaiah predicts, that "the earth shall be full of the knowledge of the Lord" (Is. xi. 9). Paul says even of the heathen, that they knew God, but did not like to retain that knowledge (Rom. i. 19, 20, 21, 28).

A. *State of the Question.*

It is, however, important distinctly to understand what is meant when it is said, God can be known.

1. This does not mean that we can know all that is true concerning God. There were some among the ancient philosophers who taught that the nature of God can be as fully understood and determined as any other object of knowledge. The modern speculative school teaches the same doctrine. Among the propositions laid down by Spinoza, we find the following: " Cognitio æternæ et infinitæ essentiæ Dei, quam unaquæque idea involvit, est adæquata et perfecta." [1] Hegel says, that God is, only so far as He is known. The sin against the Holy Ghost, according to Hegel, is to deny that He can be known.[2] Cousin holds the same doctrine. " God in fact," he says, " exists to us only in so far as He is known." [3]

According to Schelling, God is known in his own nature by

---

[1] *Ethices*, ii. prop. xlvi. edit. Jena, 1803, vol. ii. p. 119.

[2] See Mansel's *Limits of Religious Thought*, Boston, 1859, p. 301.

[3] Sir William Hamilton's *Discussions*, p. 16. *Princeton Review* on *Cousin's Philosophy*, 1856.

direct intuition of the higher reason.   He assumes that there is in
man a power which transcends the limits of the ordinary consciousness (an Anschauungs Vermögen), which takes immediate cognizance of the Infinite.   Hegel says that " Man knows God only so
far as God knows Himself in man ; this knowledge is God's self-
consciousness, but likewise a knowledge of the same by man, and
this knowledge of God by man is the knowledge of man by God." [1]
Cousin finds this knowledge in the common consciousness of men.
That consciousness includes the knowledge of the Infinite as well
as of the finite.   We know the one just as we know the other, and
we cannot know the one without knowing the other.   These philosophers all admit that we could not thus know God unless we were
ourselves God.   Self-knowledge, with them, is the knowledge of
God.   Reason in man, according to Cousin, does not belong to his
individuality.   It is infinite, impersonal, and divine.   Our knowledge of God, therefore, is only God knowing Himself.   Of course
it is in no such sense as this that the Scriptures and the Church
teach that God can be known.

God Inconceivable.

2. It is not held that God, properly speaking, can be conceived
of ; that is, we cannot form a mental image of God.   " All conception," says Mr. Mansel,[2] "implies imagination."   To have a
valid conception of a horse, he adds, we must be able " to combine " the attributes which form " the definition of the animal "
into " a representative image."   Conception is defined by Taylor
in the same manner, as " the forming or bringing an image or idea
into the mind by an effort of the will."   In this sense of the word
it must be admitted that the Infinite is not an object of knowledge.
We cannot form an image of infinite space, or of infinite duration,
or of an infinite whole.   To form an image is to limit, to circum-
scribe.   But the infinite is that which is incapable of limitation.
It is admitted, therefore, that the infinite God is inconceivable.
We can form no representative image of Him in our minds.   The
word, however, is often, and perhaps commonly, used in a less
restricted sense.   To conceive is to think.   A conception is
therefore a thought, and not necessarily an image.   To say,
therefore, that God is conceivable, in common language, is merely
to say that He is thinkable.   That is, that the thought (or idea)
of God involves no contradiction or impossibility.   We cannot

---

[1] *Werke*, xii. p. 496, edit. Berlin, 1840.
[2] *Prolegomena Logica*, edit. Boston, 1860, p. 34.

think of a round square, or that a part is equal to the whole.
But we can think that God is infinite and eternal.

God Incomprehensible.

3. When it is said that God can be known, it is not meant that
He can be comprehended. To comprehend is to have a complete
and exhaustive knowledge of an object. It is to understand its nature and its relations. We cannot comprehend force, and specially
vital force. We see its effect, but we cannot understand its nature
or the mode in which it acts. It would be strange that we should
know more of God than of ourselves, or of the most familiar objects
of sense. God is past finding out. We cannot understand the
Almighty unto perfection. To comprehend is (1.) To know the
essence as well as the attributes of an object. (2.) It is to know
not some only, but all of its attributes. (3.) To know the relation
in which these attributes stand to each other and to the substance
to which they belong. (4.) To know the relation in which the
object known stands to all other objects. Such knowledge is
clearly impossible in a creature, either of itself or of anything out
of itself. It is, however, substantially thus that the transcendentalists claim to know God.

Our Knowledge of God Partial.

4. It is included in what has been said, that our knowledge of
God is partial and inadequate. There is infinitely more in God
than we have any idea of; and what we do know, we know imperfectly. We know that God knows; but there is much in his
mode of knowing, and in its relation to its objects, which we cannot
understand. We know that He acts; but we do not know how
He acts, or the relation which his activity bears to time, or things
out of Himself. We know that He feels; that He loves, pities, is
merciful, is gracious; that He hates sin. But this emotional element of the divine nature is covered with an obscurity as great,
but no greater, than that which rests over his thoughts or purposes.
Here again our ignorance, or rather, the limitation of our knowledge
concerning God, finds a parallel in our ignorance of ourself. There
are potentialities in our nature of which, in our present state of
existence, we have no idea. And even as to what we are now, we
know but little. We know that we perceive, think, and act; we
do not know how. It is perfectly inscrutable to us how the mind
takes cognizance of matter; how the soul acts on the body, or the
body on the mind. But because our knowledge of ourselves is

thus partial and imperfect, no sane man would assert that we have no self-knowledge.

The common doctrine on this subject is clearly expressed by Des Cartes: [1] "Sciri potest, Deum esse infinitum et omnipotentem, quanquam anima nostra, utpote finita, id nequeat comprehendere sive concipere; eodem nimirum modo, quo montem manibus tangere possumus, sed non ut arborem, aut aliam quampiam rem brachiis nostris non majorem amplecti: comprehendere enim est cogitatione complecti; ad hoc autem, ut sciamus aliquid, sufficit, ut illud cogitatione attingamus."

Even Spinoza [2] says: "Ad quæstionem tuam, an de Deo tam claram, quam de triangulo habeam ideam, respondeo affirmando. Non dico, me Deum omnino cognoscere; sed me quædam ejus attributa, non autem omnia, neque maximam intelligere partem, et certum est, plurimorum ignorantiam, quorundam eorum habere notitiam, non impedire. Quum Euclidis elementa addiscerem, primo tres trianguli angulos duobus rectis æquari intelligebam; hancque trianguli proprietatem clare percipiebam, licet multarum aliarum ignarus essem."

While, therefore, it is admitted not only that the infinite God is incomprehensible, and that our knowledge of Him is both partial and imperfect; that there is much in God which we do not know at all, and that what we do know, we know very imperfectly; nevertheless our knowledge, as far as it goes, is true knowledge. God really is what we believe Him to be, so far as our idea of Him is determined by the revelation which He has made of Himself in his works, in the constitution of our nature, in his word, and in the person of his Son. To know is simply to have such apprehensions of an object as conform to what that object really is. We know what the word Spirit means. We know what the words infinite, eternal, and immutable, mean. And, therefore, the sublime proposition, pregnant with more truth than was ever compressed in any other sentence, "God is a Spirit, infinite, eternal, and immutable," conveys to the mind as distinct an idea, and as true (i. e., trustworthy) knowledge, as the proposition "The human soul is a finite spirit." In this sense God is an object of knowledge. He is not the unknown God, because He is infinite. Knowledge in Him does not cease to be knowledge because it is omniscience; power does not cease to be power because it is omnipotence; any more than space ceases to be space because it is infinite.

---

1 Epistolæ, I., cx., edit. Amsterdam, 1682.
2 Epistola lx. vol. i. p. 659, edit. Jena, 1802.

B. *How do we know God?*

How does the mind proceed in forming its idea of God? The older theologians answered this question by saying that it is by the way of negation, by the way of eminence, and by the way of causality. That is, we deny to God any limitation; we ascribe to Him every excellence in the highest degree; and we refer to Him as the great First Cause every attribute manifested in his works. We are the children of God, and, therefore, we are like Him. We are, therefore, authorized to ascribe to Him all the attributes of our own nature as rational creatures, without limitation, and to an infinite degree. If we are like God, God is like us. This is the fundamental principle of all religion. This is the principle which Paul assumed in his address to the Athenians (Acts xvii. 29): " Forasmuch then as we are the offspring of God, we ought not to think that the Godhead is like unto gold, or silver, or stone, graven by art and man's device." For the same reason we ought not to think that He is simple being, or a mere abstraction, a name for the moral order of the universe, or the unknown and unknowable cause of all things, — mere inscrutable force. If we are his children, He is our Father, whose image we bear, and of whose nature we partake. This, in the proper sense of the word, is Anthropomorphism, a word much abused, and often used in a bad sense to express the idea that God is altogether such a one as ourselves, a being of like limitations and passions. In the sense, however, just explained, it expresses the doctrine of the Church and of the great mass of mankind. Jacobi[1] well says: " We confess, therefore, to an Anthropomorphism inseparable from the conviction that man bears the image of God; and maintain that besides this Anthropomorphism, which has always been called Theism, is nothing but atheism or fetichism."

C. *Proof that this Method is Trustworthy.*

That this method of forming an idea of God is trustworthy, is proved, —

1. Because it is a law of nature. Even in the lowest form of fetichism the life of the worshipper is assumed to belong to the object which he worships. The power dreaded is assumed to possess attributes like our own. In like manner under all the forms of polytheism, the gods of the people have been intelligent personal agents. It is only in the schools of philosophy that we find a differ-

---

[1] " Von den göttlichen Dingen," *Werke,* iii. pp. 422, 423, edit. Leipzig, 1816.

ent method of forming an idea of the Godhead. They have substituted τὸ ὄν for ὁ ὤν, τὸ θεῖον for ὁ Θεός, τὸ ἀγαθόν for ὁ ἀγαθός. It is here as with regard to the knowledge of the external world. The mass of mankind believe that things are what they perceive them to be. This philosophers deny. They affirm that we do not perceive the things themselves, but certain ideas, species, or images of the things; that we have, and can have, no knowledge of what the things themselves really are. So they say we can have no knowledge of what God is ; we only know that we are led to think of Him in a certain way, but we are not only not authorized to believe that our idea corresponds to the reality, but, say they, it is certain that God is not what we take Him to be. As the people are right in the one case, so are they in the other. In other words, our conviction that God is what He has revealed Himself to be, rests on the same foundation as our conviction that the external world is what we take it to be. That foundation is the veracity of consciousness, or the trustworthiness of the laws of belief which God has impressed upon our nature. " Invincibility of belief," according to Sir William Hamilton, " is convertible with the truth of belief," [1] although, unhappily, on this subject, he did not adhere to his own principle, " That what is by nature necessarily believed to be, truly is." [2] No man has more nobly or more earnestly vindicated this doctrine, which is the foundation of all science and of all faith. " Consciousness," he says, " once convicted of falsehood, an unconditioned scepticism, in regard to the character of our intellectual being, is the melancholy but only rational result. Any conclusion may now with impunity be drawn against the hopes and the dignity of human nature. Our personality, our immateriality, our moral liberty, have no longer an argument for their defence. ‘ Man is the dream of a shadow.’ God is the dream of that dream." [3] The only question, therefore, is, Are we invincibly led to think of God as possessing the attributes of our rational nature ? This cannot be denied; for universality proves invincibility of belief. And it is a historical fact that men have universally thus thought of God. Even Mr. Mansel [4] exclaims against the transcendentalists, " Fools, to dream that man can escape from himself, that human reason can draw aught but a human portrait of God." True, he denies the correctness of that portrait ; or, at least, he asserts that we cannot know whether it is correct or not. But this

[1] Philosophy, edit. Wight, New York, 1854, p. 233.   [2] Ibid. p. 226.
[3] Ibid. p. 234.
[4] Limits of Religious Thought, edit. Boston, 1859, pp. 56, 57.

is not now the question. He admits that we are forced by the constitution of our nature thus to think of God. And by the fundamental principle of all true philosophy, what we are forced to believe must be true. It is true, therefore, that God really is what we take Him to be, when we ascribe to Him the perfections of our own nature, without limitation, and to an infinite degree.

Our Moral Nature demands this Idea of God.

2. It has already been shown, when speaking of the moral argument for the existence of God, that all men are conscious of their accountability to a being superior to themselves, who knows what they are and what they do, and who has the will and purpose to reward or punish men according to their works. The God, therefore, who is revealed to us in our nature, is a God who knows, and wills, and acts; who rewards and punishes. That is, He is a person; an intelligent, voluntary agent, endowed with moral attributes. This revelation of God must be true. It must make known to us what God really is, or our nature is a lie. All this Mr. Mansel, who holds that God cannot be known, admits. He admits that a sense of dependence on a superior power is "a fact of the inner consciousness;" that this superior power is "not an inexorable fate, or immutable law, but a Being having at least so far the attributes of personality, that He can show favour or severity to those dependent upon Him, and can be regarded by them with the feelings of hope, and fear, and reverence, and gratitude."[1] No man, however, is, or can be grateful to the sun, or to the atmosphere, or to unintelligent force. Gratitude is a tribute of a person to a person. Again, the same author admits that "the moral reason, or will, or conscience of man, call it by what name we please, can have no authority save as implanted in him by some higher spiritual Being, as a law emanating from a law-giver."[2] "We are thus compelled," he says, "by the consciousness of moral obligation, to assume the existence of a moral [and of course of a personal] Deity, and to regard the absolute standard of right and wrong as constituted by the nature of that Deity."[3] Our argument from these facts is, that if our moral nature compels us to believe that God is a person, He must be a person, and consequently that we arrive at a true knowledge of God by attributing to Him the perfections of our own nature.

---

[1] *Limits of Religious Thought*, etc., p. 120.   [2] *Ibid.* p. 121.
[3] *Ibid.* p. 122.

Our Religious Nature makes the same Demand.

3. The argument from our religious, as distinct from our moral nature, is essentially the same. Morality is not all of religion. The one is as much a law and necessity of our nature as the other. To worship, in the religious sense of the word, is to ascribe infinite perfection to its object. It is to express to that object our acknowledgments for the blessings we enjoy, and to seek their continuance ; it is to confess, and praise, and pray, and to adore. We cannot worship the law of gravity, or unconscious force, or the mere order of the universe. Our religious nature, in demanding an object of supreme reverence, love, and confidence, demands a personal God, a God clothed with the attributes of a nature like our own ; who can hear our confessions, praises, and prayers ; who can love, and be loved ; who can supply our wants, and fill all our capacities for good. Thus again it appears that unless our whole nature is a contradiction and a falsehood, we arrive at a true knowledge of God when we ascribe to Him the perfections of our own nature.

Mr. Mansel admits that our nature does demand a personal and moral Deity ; but, he says, " the very conception of a moral nature is in itself the conception of a limit, for morality is the compliance with a law ; and a law, whether imposed from within or from without, can only be conceived to operate by limiting the range of possible actions." [1] In like manner he says, " The only human conception of personality is that of limitation." Therefore, if God be infinite, he can neither be a person, nor possess moral attributes. This is the argument of Strauss, and of all other pantheists, against the doctrine of a personal God. Mr. Mansel admits the force of the argument, and says we must renounce all hope of knowing what God is, and be content with " regulative knowledge," which teaches not what God really is, but what He wills us to think Him to be. We are thus forbidden to trust to our necessary beliefs. We must not regard as true what God by the constitution of our nature forces us to believe. This is to subvert all philosophy and all religion, and to destroy the difference between the rational and the irrational. Why is this contradiction between reason and conscience, between our rational and moral nature, assumed to exist ? Simply because philosophers choose to give such a definition of morality and personality that neither can be predicated of an infinite Being. It is not true that either

[1] *Limits of Religious Thought*, etc., p. 127.

morality or personality imply any limitation inconsistent with absolute perfection. We do not limit God when we say He cannot be irrational as well as rational, unconscious as well as conscious, finite as well as infinite, evil as well as good. The only limitation admitted is the negation of imperfection. Reason is not limited when we say it cannot be unreason ; or spirit, when we say that it is not matter ; or light, when we say it is not darkness ; or space, when we say it is not time. We do not, therefore, limit the Infinite, when we exalt Him in our conceptions from the unconscious to the conscious, from the unintelligent to the intelligent, from an impersonal something to the absolutely perfect personal Jehovah. All these difficulties arise from confounding the ideas of infinite and all.

4. The fourth argument on this subject is, that if we are not justified in referring to God the attributes of our own nature, then we have no God. The only alternative is anthropomorphism (in this sense) or Atheism. An unknown God, a God of whose nature and of whose relation to us we know nothing, to us is nothing. It is a historical fact that those who reject this method of forming our idea of God, who deny that we are to refer to Him the perfections of our own nature, have become atheists. They take the word " spirit," and strip from it consciousness, intelligence, will, and morality ; and the residue, which is blank nothing, they call God. Hamilton and Mansel take refuge from this dreadful conclusion in faith. They say that reason forbids the ascription of these, or of any other attributes, to the Infinite and Absolute, but that faith protests against this conclusion of the reason. Such protest, however, is of no account, unless it be rational. When Kant proved that there was no rational evidence of the existence of God, and fell back from the speculative to the practical reason (i. e., from reason to faith), his followers universally gave up all faith in a personal God. No man can believe in the impossible. And if reason pronounces that it is impossible that the Infinite should be a person, faith in His personality is an impossibility. This Mr. Mansel does not admit. For while he says that it is a contradiction to affirm the Infinite to be a person, or to possess moral attributes, he nevertheless says that, " Anthropomorphism is the indispensable condition of all human theology ; "[1] and he quotes from Kant[2] this passage : " We may confidently challenge all natural theology to name a single distinctive attribute of the Deity, whether denoting intelligence or will, which, apart from anthropomorphism, is anything

[1] *Limits of Religious Thought*, etc., p. 261.
[2] " Kritik der Praktischen Vernunft." *Works*, edit. Rosenkranz, vol. viii. p. 282.

more than a mere word, to which not the slightest notion can be attached, which can serve to extend our theoretical knowledge." It is greatly to be lamented that men should teach that the only way in which it is possible for us to form an idea of God, leads to no true knowledge. It does not teach us what God is, but what we are forced against reason to think He is.

Argument from the Revelation of God in Nature.

5. A fifth argument is from the fact that the works of God manifest a nature like our own. It is a sound principle that we must refer to a cause the attributes necessary to account for its effects. If the effects manifest intelligence, will, power, and moral excellence, these attributes must belong to the cause. As, therefore, the works of God are a revelation of all these attributes on a most stupendous scale, they must belong to God in an infinite degree. This is only saying that the revelation made of God in the external world agrees with the revelation which He has made of himself in the constitution of our own nature. In other words, it proves that the image of himself which He has enstamped on our nature is a true likeness.

Argument from Scripture.

6. The Scriptures declare God to be just what we are led to think He is, when we ascribe to Him the perfections of our own nature in an infinite degree. We are self-conscious, so is God. We are spirits, so is He. We are voluntary agents, so is God. We have a moral nature, miserably defaced indeed, God has moral excellence in infinite perfection. We are persons, so is God. All this the Scriptures declare to be true. The great primal revelation of God is as the "I am," the personal God. All the names and titles given to Him ; all the attributes ascribed to Him ; all the works attributed to Him, are revelations of what He truly is. He is the Elohim, the Mighty One, the Holy One, the Omnipresent Spirit ; He is the creator, the preserver, the governor of all things. He is our Father. He is the hearer of prayer ; the giver of all good. He feeds the young ravens. He clothes the flowers of the field. He is Love. He so loved the world as to give his only begotten Son, that whosoever believeth on Him might not perish but have everlasting life. He is merciful, long-suffering, abundant in goodness and truth. He is a present help in every time of need ; a refuge, a high tower, an exceeding great reward. The relations in which, according to the Scriptures, we stand to God, are such as we can sustain only to a being who is like ourselves. He

is our ruler, and father, with whom we can commune. His favour is our life, his loving-kindness better than life. This sublime revelation of God in his own nature and in his relation to us is not a delusion. It is not mere regulative truth, or it would be a deceit and mockery. It makes God known to us as He really is. We therefore know God, although no creature can understand the Almighty unto perfection.

Argument from the Manifestation of God in Christ.

7. Finally, God has revealed Himself in the person of his Son. No man knoweth the Father but the Son; and he to whom the Son shall reveal Him. Jesus Christ is the true God. The revelation which He made of Himself was the manifestation of God. He and the Father are one. The words of Christ were the words of God. The works of Christ were the works of God. The love, mercy, tenderness, the forgiving grace, as well as the holiness, the severity and power manifested by Christ, were all manifestations of what God truly is. We see, therefore, as with our own eyes, what God is. We know that although infinite and absolute, He can think, act, and will; that He can love and hate; that He can hear prayer and forgive sin; that we can have fellowship with Him, as one person can commune with another. Philosophy must veil her face in the presence of Jesus Christ, as God manifest in the flesh. She may not presume in that presence to say that God is not, and is not known to be, what Christ himself most clearly was. This doctrine that God is the object of certain and true knowledge lies at the foundation of all religion, and therefore must never be given up.

§ 2.   God cannot be fully known.

The modern German philosophers take the ground that all science, all true philosophy, must be founded on the knowledge of being, and not of phenomena. They reject the authority of the senses and of consciousness, and teach that it is only by the immediate cognition of the Absolute that we arrive at any true or certain knowledge. God, or rather, the Infinite, can be as thoroughly known and comprehended as the simplest object of sense or of consciousness; He is, only so far as He is known.

It would seem impossible that the presumption of men should be so extreme that such a creature as man should pretend to understand the Almighty to perfection, when in fact he cannot understand himself or the simplest objects with which he is in daily contact. The assumption is that being, as such, Infinite and Absolute Being, can be known; that is, that we can determine what it is, and the necessary laws by which it is developed into the phenomenal world. This knowledge is attained *à priori;* not by any induction or deduction from our own nature or the facts of experience, but by an immediate act of cognition, which transcends all consciousness. The great service rendered by Sir William Hamilton and Mr. Mansel to the cause of truth was to demonstrate the utter futility of this pretended philosophy of the Infinite, on the principles of its advocates. To the common mind it needed no refutation, being intuitively seen to be impossible and absurd.

Sir William Hamilton's Argument.

Hamilton shows, in the first place, that the immediate intuition of Schelling, which Hegel ridiculed as a mere imagination, the dialectics of Hegel, which Schelling pronounced a mere play of words, and the impersonal reason of Cousin which enters into our consciousness but not into our personality, utterly fail to give us a knowledge of the Infinite. " Existence," he says, " is revealed to us only under specific modifications, and these are known only under the conditions of our faculties of knowledge. Things in themselves, matter, mind, God, all in short that is not finite, relative, and phenomenal, as bearing no analogy to our faculties, is beyond the verge of our knowledge." [1] In what sense Hamilton places God " beyond the verge of our knowledge " will be seen in the sequel. It is, however, self-evident that our knowledge must be limited by our faculties of knowing. Other animals may have senses which we do not possess. It is utterly impossible that we should have the kind of knowledge due to the exercise of those senses. It is probable that there are faculties dormant in our nature which are not called into activity in our present state of being. It is clear that we cannot now attain the knowledge which those faculties may hereafter enable us to attain. It is just as plain that we cannot cognize the Infinite, in the sense of these philosophers, as that we cannot see a spirit, or guide ourselves in space, as does the carrier-pigeon or the migrating salmon.

Only the Infinite can know the Infinite.

2. In the second place, it is admitted that none but the Infinite can know the Infinite, and to know God in this sense, it is admitted that we must be God. " Schelling claimed for the mind of man, what Kant had demonstrated to be impossible, a faculty of intel-

[1] *Discussions,* p. 23.

lectual intuition which is apart from sense, above consciousness, and released from the laws of the understanding, and which comprehends the absolute by becoming the absolute, and thus knows God by being God." [1] This assumption that man is God, shocks the reason and common sense of men as well as outrages their religious and moral convictions.

3. In the third place, Hamilton and Mansel demonstrate that, assuming the definitions of the Absolute and Infinite given by the transcendentalists, the most contradictory conclusions may logically be deduced from them.   " There are three terms familiar as household words in the vocabulary of philosophy, which must be taken into account in every system of metaphysical theology.   To conceive the Deity as He is, we must conceive him as First Cause, as absolute, and as infinite.   By First Cause, is meant that which produces all things, and is itself produced of none.   By the Absolute, is meant that which exists in and by itself, having no necessary relation to any other being.   By the Infinite, is meant that which is free from all possible limitation ; that than which a greater is inconceivable, and which, consequently, can receive no additional attribute or mode of existence which it had not from all eternity." [2]

According to these definitions, in the sense in which they are intended to be taken, it follows : —

1. That the Infinite and Absolute must include the sum of all being. For " that which is conceived as absolute and infinite must be conceived as containing within itself the sum, not only of all actual, but of all possible modes of being.   For if any actual mode can be denied of it, it is related to that mode and limited by it ; and if any possible mode can be denied of it, it is capable of becoming more than it now is, and such a capability is a limitation." [3]

2. If the Absolute and Infinite be as above defined, it cannot be the object of knowledge. To know is to limit. It is to distinguish the object of knowledge from other objects. We cannot conceive, says Hamilton, of an absolute whole ; i. e., of a whole so great that we cannot conceive of it as a part of a greater whole. We cannot conceive of an infinite line, or of infinite space, or of infinite duration. We may as well think without thought, as to assign any limit beyond which there can be no extension, no space, no duration. " Goad imagination to the utmost, it still sinks paralyzed within the bounds of time." [4] It follows, therefore, from the very nature of knowledge, according to Hamilton, that the Infinite and Absolute cannot be known.

---

[1] *Progress of Philosophy*, by S. Tyler, LL.D., p. 200.   [2] Mansel, p. 75.
[3] Mansel, p. 76.   [4] Hamilton's *Discussions*, p. 35.

The Infinite cannot Know.

3. It also follows from these premises, that the Infinite cannot know. All knowledge is limitation and difference. It supposes a distinction between subject and object, between the knower and what is known, inconsistent with the idea of the Absolute.

4. It follows also that the Absolute cannot be conscious, for consciousness involves a distinction between the self and the not-self. It is knowledge of ourselves as distinct from what is not ourselves. Even if conscious only of itself, there is the same distinction between subject and object ; the self as subject and a mode of the self as the object of consciousness.   " The almost unanimous voice of philosophy," says Mansel, " in pronouncing that the Absolute is both one and simple must be accepted as the voice of reason also, so far as reason has any voice in the matter."   " The conception of an absolute and infinite consciousness contradicts itself." [1]

The Absolute cannot be Cause.

5. It is equally clear that the Absolute and Infinite cannot be cause. Causation implies relation ; the relation of efficiency to the effect. It also implies change ; change from inaction to activity. It moreover implies succession, and succession implies existence in time.   " A thing existing absolutely (*i. e.*, not under relation)," says Hamilton, " and a thing existing absolutely as a cause, are contradictory."   He quotes Schelling [2] as saying, " He would deviate wide as the poles from the idea of the Absolute, who would think of defining its nature by the notion of activity." " But he who would define the Absolute by the notion of a cause," he adds, " would deviate still more widely from its nature, inasmuch as the notion of a cause involves not only the notion of a determination to activity, but of a determination to a particular, nay a dependent, kind of activity." [3]   " The three conceptions, the Cause, the Absolute, the Infinite, all equally indispensable, do they not," asks Mr. Mansel, [4] " imply contradiction to each other, when viewed in conjunction, as attributes of one and the same Being?   A cause cannot, as such, be absolute : the Absolute cannot, as such, be cause."

6. According to the laws of our reason and consciousness, there can be no duration without succession, but succession as implying change cannot be predicated of the Absolute and Infinite, and yet without succession there can be no thought or consciousness ; and,

[1] Mansel, pp. 78, 79.   [2] Bruno, p. 171.   [3] *Discussions*, p. 40.   [4] Mansel, p. 77.

therefore, to say that God is eternal is to deny that He has either thought or consciousness.

7. Again, " Benevolence, holiness, justice, wisdom," says Mansel, " can be conceived by us only as existing in a benevolent and holy and just and wise being, who is not identical with any one of his attributes, but the common subject of them all ; in one word, in a person.   But personality, as we conceive it, is essentially a limitation and a relation. — To speak of an absolute and infinite person, is simply to use language to which, however true it may be in a superhuman sense, no mode of human thought can possibly attach itself." [1]

The Conclusion to which Hamilton's Argument leads.

What then is the result of the whole matter ?   It is, that if the definitions of the Absolute and Infinite adopted by transcendentalists be admitted, the laws of reason lead us into a labyrinth of contradictions.   If their idea of an infinite and absolute Being be correct, then it must include all being actual and possible ; it can neither know nor be the object of knowledge ; it cannot be conscious, or cause, or a person, or the subject of any moral attribute. Hamilton infers from all this, that a philosophy of the Absolute is a sheer impossibility ; that the Absolute, from its nature and from the necessary limits of human thought, is unknowable, and consequently that the stupendous systems of pantheistic atheism which had been erected on the contrary assumption, must fall to the ground.   Those systems have indeed already fallen by their own weight.   Although only a few years ago they claimed the homage of the intellectual world and boasted of immutability, they have at the present time scarcely a living advocate.

Unhappily, however, Hamilton, like Samson, is involved in the ruin which he created.   In overthrowing pantheism he overthrows Theism.   All that he says of the Absolute as unknowable, he affirms to be true of God.   All the contradictions which attend the assumption of an absolute and infinite being as the ground of philosophy, he says attend the assumption of an infinite God.

§ 3. Hamilton's Doctrine.

A. God an Object of Faith, but not of Knowledge.

The sense in which Hamilton and his followers represent God as unknowable, has been a matter of dispute.   When he says that we can know that God is, but not what He is, he says only what

[1] Mansel, pp. 102, 103.

had been said a hundred times before. Plato had said that the search after God was difficult, and that when He is found, it is impossible to declare his nature. Philo still more explicitly teaches that the divine essence is without qualities or attributes, and as we know nothing of any essence but by its distinguishing attributes, God in his own nature is altogether unknowable.[1] This is repeated continually by the Greek and Latin fathers; who, however, in most cases at least, meant nothing more than that God is incomprehensible. Others again, in asserting the incapacity of man to know God, refer to his spiritual blindness occasioned by sin. Therefore, while they deny that God can be known by the unregenerate, they affirm that He is known by those to whom the Son has revealed Him. In like manner although the Apostle asserts that even the heathen know God, he elsewhere speaks of a kind of knowledge due to the saving illumination of the Holy Spirit. It is in the sense that God is past finding out that the devout Pascal says,[2] " We know there is an infinite, but we are ignorant of its nature. . . . . We may well know that there is a God, without knowing what He is." And even John Owen says, " All the rational conceptions of the minds of men are swallowed up and lost, when they would exercise themselves directly on that which is absolute, immense, eternal, and infinite. When we say it is so, we know not what we say, but only that it is not otherwise. What we deny of God we know in some measure — but what we affirm we know not; only we declare what we believe and adore." [3] Professor Tyler adds, that while the philosophy of Hamilton " confines our knowledge to the conditioned [the finite], it leaves faith free about the unconditioned [the infinite]; indeed constrains us to believe in it by the highest law of our intelligence."

Although Hamilton often uses the same language when speaking of God as unknowable, as that employed by others, his meaning is very different. He really teaches an ignorance of God destructive of all rational religion, because inconsistent with the possibility of faith.

Different Kinds of Ignorance.

There are different kinds of ignorance. First, there is the ignorance of the idiot, which is blank vacuity. In him the statement of a proposition awakens no mental action whatever. Secondly, there is the ignorance of a blind man, of colour. He does not know what colour is; but he knows there is something which answers to

---

[1] Strauss, *Dogmatik*, i. p. 527.   [2] *Pensées*, partie II. art. iii. 5.
[3] Tyler's *Progress of Philosophy*, second edit. p. 147.

that word and which produces a certain effect on the eyes of those who see. He may even understand the laws by which the production of colour is determined. A blind man has written a treatise on optics. Thirdly, there is the ignorance under which the mind labors when it can prove contradictory propositions concerning the same object, as that the same figure is both square and round. And fourthly, there is the ignorance of imperfect knowledge. Paul speaks of knowing what passes knowledge.

Our ignorance of God, according to Hamilton, is neither the ignorance of the idiot nor of imperfect knowledge, but it is analogous to the ignorance of a blind man of colours, and more definitely, the ignorance we labor under with regard to any object of which we can prove contradictions.

Proof that Hamilton Denies that we can Know God.

That this view of his doctrine is correct is proved, (1.) Because he asserts in such broad terms that God cannot be known; that He is not only inconceivable, but incogitable. (2.) Because, he says, that we know that God is not, and cannot be, what we think He is. It is not merely that we cannot determine with certainty that our idea of God is correct, but we know that it is not correct. " To think that God is, as we can think Him to be," he says, " is blasphemy. The last and highest consecration of all true religion, must be an altar, 'Αγνώστῳ Θεῷ, ' To the unknown and unknowable God.' "[1] (3.) Because both he and Mansel continually assert that the Infinite cannot be a person; cannot know; cannot be cause; cannot be conscious; cannot be the subject of any moral attributes. To think of God as infinite, and to think of Him as a person is an impossibility. (4.) The illustrations which these writers employ determine clearly their meaning. Our ignorance of God is compared to our incapacity to conceive of two straight lines inclosing a portion of space; or to think " a circular parallelogram." It is not merely that we cannot understand such a figure, but we see that, in the nature of things, any such figure is impossible. So we not only cannot understand how God can be absolute and yet a person, but we see that an absolute person is as much a contradiction as a square circle. (5.) Accordingly Herbert Spencer and others, in carrying out Hamilton's principles, come to the conclusion not only that we cannot know God, but that it is impossible that a personal God should exist. There can be no such being.

[1] *Discussions*, p. 22.

Hamilton's Doctrine of God as an object of Faith.

Hamilton and Mansel, however, are not only Theists, but Christians. They believe in God, and they believe in the Scriptures as a divine revelation. They endeavor to avoid what seem to be the inevitable consequences of their doctrine, by adopting two principles : first, that the unthinkable is possible, and, therefore, may be believed. By the unthinkable is meant that which the laws of reason force us to regard as self-contradictory. On this subject Mansel says : " It is our duty to think of God as personal, and it is our duty to believe that He is infinite. It is true that we cannot reconcile these two representations with each other ; as our conception of personality involves attributes apparently contradictory to the notion of infinity. But it does not follow that this contradiction exists anywhere but in our own minds : it does not follow that it implies any impossibility in the absolute nature of God. . . . . It proves that there are limits to man's power of thought ; and it proves no more." [1] The conclusion is, that as whatever is possible is credible, therefore, as it is possible that God though infinite may be a person, his personality may be rationally believed.

The Unthinkable, or Impossible, cannot be an object of Faith.

On this it may be remarked, —

1. That there is a great difference between the irreconcilable and the self-contradictory. In the one case the difficulty arises, or may arise, out of our ignorance or mental weakness ; in the other, it arises out of the nature of the things themselves. Many things are irreconcilable to a child which are not so to a man. Many things are irreconcilable to one man and not to another ; to men and not to angels. But the self-contradictory is impossible, and is seen to be so by all orders of mind. That two and two should make twenty, or that the same figure should be a square and a circle, is just as irreconcilable to an angel as to a child. What is self-contradictory cannot possibly be true. Now, according to Hamilton and Mansel, infinity and personality are not only irreconcilable, but contradictory. The one affirms what the other denies. According to their doctrine the Infinite cannot be a person, and a person cannot be infinite, any more than the Infinite can be finite, or the finite infinite. The one of necessity excludes the other. If you affirm the one, you deny the other. There is a great difference between not seeing how a thing is, and clearly

[1] *Limits of Religious Thought*, p. 106.

seeing that it cannot be. Hamilton and Mansel constantly assert that an absolute person is a contradiction in terms. And so it is, if their definition of the absolute be correct ; and if a contradiction, it is impossible.

2. If to our reason the personality of an infinite God be a contradiction, then it is impossible rationally to believe that He is a person. It is in vain to say that the contradiction is only in our mind. So is faith in our mind. It is impossible for one and the same mind to see a thing to be false, and believe it to be true. For the reason to see that a thing is a contradiction, is to see it to be false ; and to see it to be false, and to believe it to be true, is a contradiction in terms. Even if to other and higher minds the contradiction does not exist, so long as it exists in the view of any particular mind, for that mind faith in its truth is an impossibility.

It may be said that a man's reason may convince him that the external world does not really exist, while his senses force him to believe in its reality. So reason may pronounce the personality of God a contradiction, and conscience force us to believe that He is a person. This is to confound consecutive with contemporaneous states of mind. It is possible for a man to be an idealist in his study, and a realist out of doors. But he cannot be an idealist and a realist at one and the same time. The mind is a unit. A man's reason is the man himself; so is his conscience, and so are all his other faculties. It is the one substantive self that thinks and believes. To assume, therefore, that by necessity he must think one way and believe another ; that the laws of his reason force him to regard as false what his conscience or senses force him to regard as true, is to destroy his rationality. It is also to impugn the wisdom and goodness of our Creator, for it supposes Him to have put one part of our constitution in conflict with another ; to have placed us under guides who alternately force us to move in opposite directions. It even places this contradiction in God himself. For what reason, in its legitimate exercise, says, God says; and what conscience, in its legitimate exercise, says, God says. If, therefore, reason says that God is not a person, and conscience says that He is, then — with reverence be it spoken — God contradicts Himself.

Knowledge essential to Faith.

It is one of the distinguishing doctrines of Protestants that knowledge is essential to faith. This is clearly the doctrine of Scripture. How can they believe on Him of whom they have not heard ? is the pertinent and instructive query of the Apostle. Faith

includes the affirmation of the mind that a thing is true and trustworthy.   But it is impossible for the mind to affirm anything of
that of which it knows nothing. Romanists indeed say that if a man
believes that the Church teaches the truth, then he believes all the
Church teaches, although ignorant of its doctrines.   It might as
well be said that because a child has confidence in his father, therefore he knows all his father knows.   Truth must be communicated
to the mind, and seen to be possible, before, on any evidence, it
can be believed.   If, therefore, we cannot know God, we cannot
believe in Him.

B. *Regulative Knowledge.*

The second principle which Hamilton and Mansel adopt to save
themselves from scepticism is that of regulative knowledge.   We
are bound to believe that God is what the Scriptures and our moral
nature declare Him to be.   This revelation, however, does not
teach us what God really is, but merely what He wills us to believe
concerning Him.   Our senses, they say, tell us that things around
us are, but not what they are.   We can, however, safely act on
the assumption that they really are what they appear to be.   Our
senses, therefore, give only regulative knowledge ; *i. e.*, knowledge
sufficient to regulate our active life.   So we do not, and cannot,
know what God really is ; but the representations contained in the
Scriptures are sufficient to regulate our moral and religious life.
We can safely act on the assumption that He really is what we are
thus led to think Him to be, although we know that such is not the
fact.

We must be " content," says Mansel,[1] " with those regulative
ideas of the Deity, which are sufficient to guide our practice, but
not to satisfy our intellect, — which tell us not what God is in
Himself, but how He wills that we should think of Him."
" Though this kind of knowledge," says Hampden,[2] " is abundantly
instructive to us in point of sentiment and action ; teaches us, that
is, both how to feel, and how to act towards God ; — for it is the
language that we understand, the language formed by our own experience and practice ; — it is altogether inadequate in point of
science."   Regulative knowledge, therefore, is that which is designed to regulate our character and practice.   It need not be
true.   Nay, it may be, and is demonstrably false ; for Hamilton
says it is blasphemy to think that God really is what we take Him
to be.

[1] *Limits of Religious Thought*, p. 132.
[2] *Bampton Lectures*, 1832, p. 54.

Objections to the Doctrine of Regulative Knowledge.

1. The first remark on this doctrine of regulative knowledge is, that it is self-contradictory. Regulative truth is truth designed to accomplish a given end. Design, however, is the intelligent and voluntary adaptation of means to an end; and the intelligent adaptation of means to an end, is a personal act. Unless, therefore, God be really a person, there can be no such thing as regulative knowledge. Mr. Mansel says, we cannot know what God is in Himself, " but only how He wills that we should think of Him." Here " will " is attributed to God; and the personal pronouns are used, and must be used in the very statement of the doctrine. That is, we must assume that God is really (and not merely in our subjective apprehensions) a person, in order to believe in regulative knowledge, which form of knowledge supposes that He is not, or may not be a person. This is a contradiction.

2. Regulative knowledge is, from the nature of the case, powerless, unless its subjects regard it as well founded. Some parents educate their children in the use of fictions and fairy tales; but belief in the truth of these is essential to their effect. So long as the world believed in ghosts and witches, the belief had power. As soon as men were satisfied that there were no such real existences, their power was gone. Had the philosophers convinced the Greeks that their gods were not real persons, there would have been an end to their mythology. And if Hamilton and his disciples can convince the world that the Infinite cannot be a person, the regulative influence of Theism is gone. Men cannot be influenced by representations which they know are not conformed to the truth.

3. This theory is highly derogatory to God. It supposes Him to propose to influence his creatures by false representations; revealing Himself as Father, Governor, and Judge, when there is no objective truth to answer to these representations. And worse than this, as remarked above, it supposes Him to have so constituted our nature as to force us to believe what is not true. We are constrained by the laws of our rational and moral being to think of God as having a nature like our own, and yet we are told it is blasphemy so to regard Him. The theory supposes a conflict between reason and conscience, — between our rational and moral nature. The latter forcing us to believe that God is a person, and the former declaring personality and deity to be contradictory ideas. We do not forget that Mr. Mansel says that the incogitable may be real.

that the contradiction is in our own minds, and not necessarily in the nature of things. But this amounts to nothing; for he says continually that the Absolute cannot be a person, cannot be a cause, cannot be conscious, cannot either know or be known. He says, " A thing — an object — an attribute — a person — or any other term signifying one out of many possible objects of consciousness, is by that very relation necessarily declared to be finite." [1] That is, if God be a person, He is of necessity finite. Here the personality of God is said not only to be incogitable, or inconceivable, but impossible. And this is the real doctrine of his book. It must be so. It is intuitively true that the whole cannot be a part of itself; and if the Infinite be " the All," then it cannot be one out of many. If men adopt the principles of pantheists, they cannot consistently avoid their conclusions. Hamilton teaches not merely that God may not be what we think Him to be, but that He cannot so be ; that we are ignorant what He is ; that He is to us an unknown God. If God, by the laws of our reason, thus forces us to deny his personality, and by the laws of our moral nature makes it not only a duty, but a necessity to believe in his personality, then our nature is chaotic. Man, in that case, is not the noble creature that was formed in the image of God.

4. This doctrine of regulative knowledge destroys the authority of the Scriptures. If all that the Bible teaches concerning the nature of God and concerning his relation to the world, reveals no objective truth, gives us no knowledge of what God really is, then what it teaches concerning the person, offices, and work of Christ, may all be unreal, and there may be no such person and no such Saviour.

C.   *Objections to the whole Theory.*

1. The first and most obvious fallacy in the theory of Hamilton and Mansel, as it appears to us, lies in their definition of the Absolute and Infinite, or in the language of Hamilton, the Unconditioned. By the Absolute they mean that which exists in and of itself, and out of all relation. The Infinite is that, than which nothing greater can be conceived or is possible ; which includes all actual and all possible modes of being. Mansel subscribes to the dictum of Hegel that the Absolute must include all modes of being, good as well as evil. In like manner the Infinite must be All. For if any other being exists, the Infinite must of necessity be limited, and, therefore, is no longer infinite.

These definitions determine everything. If the Absolute be that

[1] *Limits of Religious Thought,* p. 107.

which is incapable of all relation, then it must be alone ; nothing
but the Absolute can be actual or possible.   Then it can neither
know nor be known.   And if the Infinite be all, then again there
can be no finite.   Then it is just as certain that the Absolute and
Infinite cannot be cause, or conscious, or a person, as that a square
cannot be a circle, or the whole a part of itself.   When a definition leads to contradictions and absurdities, when it leads to conclusions which are inconsistent with the laws of our nature, and
when it subverts all that consciousness, common sense, and the
Bible declare to be true, the only rational inference is that the
definition is wrong.   This inference we have the right to draw in
the present case.   The very fact that the definitions of the Absolute and Infinite which Hamilton and Mansel have adopted from
the transcendentalists, lead to all the fearful conclusions which
they draw from them, is proof enough that they must be wrong.
They are founded upon purely speculative *à priori* grounds.   They
can have no authority.   For if, as these philosophers say, the Absolute and Infinite cannot be known, how can it be defined ?   Neither the etymology nor the usage of the words in question justifies
the above given definitions of them.   Absolute (*ab* and *solvo*) means,
free, unrestrained, independent ; as when we speak of an absolute
monarch or absolute promise ; or, unlimited, as when we speak of
absolute space.   The word is also used in the sense of finished, or
perfect.   An absolute being is one that is free, unlimited, independent, and perfect.   God is absolute, because He is not dependent for his existence, nature, attributes, or acts, on any other being.
He is unlimited, by anything out of Himself or independent of his
will.   But this does not imply that He is the only being ; nor that
in order to be absolute He must be dead, unconscious, or without
thought or will.   Much less does the word infinite, as applied to
God, imply that He must include all forms of being.   Space may
be infinite without being duration, and duration may be infinite
without being space.   An infinite spirit does not include material
forms of existence, any more than an infinite line is an infinite surface or an infinite solid.   When it is said that anything is infinite,
all that is properly meant is that no limit is assignable or possible
to it as such.   An infinite line is that to which no limit can be
assigned as a line ; infinite space is that to which no limit can be
assigned as space ; an infinite spirit is a spirit which is unlimited in
all the attributes of a spirit.   It is a great mistake to assume that
the infinite must be all.   Infinite power is not all power, but
simply power to whose efficiency no limitation can be assigned ;

and infinite knowledge is not all knowledge, but simply knowledge to the extent of which no limit is possible. So too an infinite substance is not all substance, but a substance which is not excluded from any portion of space by other substances, or limited in the manifestation of any of its attributes or functions by anything out of itself. God, therefore, may be a Spirit infinite, eternal, and immutable in his being and perfections, without being matter, and sin, and misery.

It may be said that as infinite space must include all space, so an infinite being must of necessity include all modes of being. This, however, is a mere play on words. Infinite is sometimes inclusive of all, not from the meaning of the word, but from the nature of the subject of which infinitude is predicated. Infinite space must include all space, because space is in its nature one. But an infinite line does not include all lines, because there may be any number of lines; and an infinite being is not all being, because there may be any number of beings.

It must excite the wonder and indignation of ordinary men to see the fundamental truths of religion and morality endangered or subverted out of deference to the assumption that the Absolute must be unrelated.

Wrong Definition of Knowledge.

2. The second fallacy involved in Hamilton's theory concerns his idea of knowledge. When it is said that God is unknowable, everything depends on what is meant by knowledge. With him to know is to understand, to have a distinct conception, or mental image. This is evident from his using interchangeably the words unthinkable, unknowable, and inconceivable. Thus on a single page [1] Mansel uses the phrases that of which " we do not and cannot think," that " which we cannot conceive," and " that which we are unable to comprehend," as meaning one and the same thing. This is also proved from the manner in which other words and phrases are employed; for example, the Infinite, the Absolute, an absolute beginning, an absolute whole, an absolute part, any increase or diminution of the complement of being. The only sense, however, in which these things are unthinkable, is, that we cannot form a mental image of them. A distinguished German professor, when anything was said to which he could not assent, was accustomed to spread out his hands and close his eyes and say, " Ich kann gar keine Anschauung davon machen." *I cannot see it with*

1 Page 110.

my mind's eye, I cannot make an image of it. This seems to be a materialistic way of looking at things. The same may be said of cause, substance, and soul, of none of which can we frame a mental image; yet they are not unthinkable. A thing is unthinkable only when it is seen to be impossible, or when we can attach no meaning to the words, or proposition, in which it is stated. This impossibility of intelligent thought may arise from our weakness. The problems of the higher mathematics are unthinkable to a child. Or, the impossibility may arise from the nature of the thing itself. That a triangle should have four sides, or a circle be a square, is absolutely unthinkable. But in neither of these senses is the Infinite unthinkable. It is not impossible, for Hamilton and Mansel both admit that God is in fact infinite; nor is that proposition unintelligible. It conveys a perfectly clear and distinct idea to the mind. When the mind affirms to itself that space is infinite, *i. e.*, that it cannot be limited, it knows what it means just as well as when it says that two and two are four. Neither is an absolute beginning unthinkable. If, indeed, by absolute beginning is meant uncaused beginning, the coming into existence of something out of nothing, and produced by nothing, then it is impossible and therefore incogitable. But the dictum is applied to a creation *ex nihilo*, which is declared to be unthinkable. This, however, is denied. We will to move a limb, and it moves. God said, Let there be light, and light was. The one event is just as intelligible as the other. In neither case can we comprehend the *nexus* between the antecedent and the consequent, between the volition and the effect; but as facts they are equally thinkable and knowable.

It is not possible to give the evidence scattered through the writings of Hamilton and Mansel, that they use the word "to know" in the sense of comprehending, or, forming a mental image of the object known. Mansel [1] quotes the following sentence from Dr. McCosh's work on the "Method of the Divine Government," namely, "The mind seeks in vain to embrace the infinite in a positive image, but is constrained to believe, when its efforts fail, that there is a something to which no limits can be put." This sentence Mansel says may be accepted "by the most uncompromising adherent" of Sir W. Hamilton's doctrine, that the infinite is unthinkable and unknowable. To know, therefore, according to Hamilton and Mansel, is to form a mental image of; and as we cannot form such an image of God, God cannot be known. Mansel is disposed to think that this reduces the controversy to a

[1] Page 280.

matter of words.   And Dr. Tyler, in his able exposition of Hamilton's philosophy, says,[1] "So it be admitted, as it must, that all our intelligence of God is by analogy, it matters but little, practically, whether the conviction be called knowledge, belief, or faith." It is, however, very far from being a dispute about words.   For Hamilton constantly asserts that God is not, and cannot be, what we think He is.   Then we have no God.   For what is God as infinite, if as Mansel says, " The Infinite, if it is to be conceived at all, must be conceived as potentially everything and actually nothing." [2]

What is meant by Knowledge.

Knowledge is the perception of truth.   Whatever the mind perceives, whether intuitively or discursively, to be true, that it knows. We have immediate knowledge of all the facts of consciousness; and with regard to other matters, some we can demonstrate, some we can prove analogically, some we must admit or involve ourselves in contradictions and absurdities.   Whatever process the mind may institute, if it arrives at a clear perception that a thing is, then that thing is an object of knowledge.   It is thus we know the objects with which heaven and earth are crowded.   It is thus we know our fellow men.   With regard to anything without us, when our ideas, or convictions concerning it, correspond to what the thing really is, then we know it.   How do we know that our nearest friend has a soul, and that that soul has intelligence, moral excellence, and power ?   We cannot see or feel it.   We cannot form a mental image of it.   It is mysterious and incomprehensible.   Yet we know that it is, and what it is, just as certainly as we know that we ourselves are, and what we are.   In the same way we know that God is, and what He is.   We know that He is a spirit, that He has intelligence, moral excellence, and power to an infinite degree.   We know that He can love, pity, and pardon ; that He can hear and answer prayer.   We know God in the same sense and just as certainly as we know our father or mother.   And no man can take this knowledge from us, or persuade us that it is not knowledge, but a mere irrational belief.

Hamilton's Doctrine Leads to Scepticism.

3. The principles on which Hamilton and Mansel deny that God can be known, logically lead to scepticism.   Hamilton has indeed rendered invaluable service to the cause of truth by his

[1] See *Progress of Philosophy*, by Samuel Tyler, LL.D., p. 207.
[2] *Limits of Religious Thought*, p. 94.

defence of what is, perhaps, infelicitously called the "Philosophy of Common Sense." The principles of that philosophy are: (1.) That what is given in consciousness is undoubtedly true. (2.) That whatever the laws of our nature force us to believe, must be accepted as true. (3.) That this principle applies to all the elements of our nature, to the senses, the reason, and the conscience. We cannot rationally or consistently with our allegiance to God, deny what our senses, reason, or conscience pronounce to be true. (4.) Neither the individual man, nor the cause of truth, however, is to be left to the mercy of what any one may choose to say reason or conscience teaches. Nothing is to be accepted as the authoritative judgment of either reason or conscience, which does not bear the criteria of universality and necessity.

Hamilton has drawn from the stores of his erudition, in this department perhaps unexampled, proof that these principles have been recognized by the leading philosophic minds in all ages. He himself sustains them with earnestness as the safeguards of truth. He impressively asserts that if consciousness once be convicted of falsehood, all is lost; we have then no resting place for either science or religion; that absolute scepticism follows, if it be denied that necessity and universality of belief are not decisive proof of the truth of what is thus believed. Even Stuart Mill admits that "whatever is known to us by consciousness, is known beyond possibility of question." [1] Mr. Mansel tells us that it is from consciousness we get our idea of substance, of personality, of cause, of right and wrong, in short of everything which lies at the foundation of knowledge and religion; and therefore if consciousness deceive us we have nothing to depend upon. Mansel thus expounds the famous aphorism of Des Cartes, "Cogito ergo sum," i. e., "I, who see, and hear, and think, and feel, am the one continuous self, whose existence gives unity and connection to the whole. Personality comprises all that we know of that which exists; relation to personality comprises all that we know of that which seems to exist." [2] "Consciousness," he says, "gives us the knowledge of substance. We are a substantive existence." [3] "I exist as I am conscious of existing; and conscious self is itself the *Ding an sich*, the standard by which all representations of personality must be judged, and from which our notion of reality, as distinguished from appearance, is originally derived." [4] Hamilton

[1] *Logic*, Introduction, p. 4, edit. N. Y. 1846.
[2] *Limits of Religious Thought*, p. 105.
[3] *Ibid.* p. 288.   [4] *Ibid.* p. 291.

and Mansel therefore teach that the veracity of consciousness is the foundation of all knowledge, and that the denial of that veracity inevitably leads to absolute scepticism. Nevertheless they teach that our senses deceive us; that reason deceives us; that conscience deceives us; that is, that our sensuous, rational, and moral consciousness are alike deceptive and unreliable.

Our senses give us the knowledge of the external world. They teach us that things are, and what they are. It is admitted that the universal and irresistible belief of men, as that belief is determined by their sense and consciousness, is that things really are what to our senses they appear to be. Philosophers tell us this is a delusion. Kant says that they certainly are not what we take them to be. Mansel says this is going rather too far. We cannot know, indeed, what they are, but it is possible that they are in fact what they appear to be. In either case they are to us an unknown quantity, and the senses deceive us. They assume to teach more than they have a right to teach, and we are bound to believe them.

Kant teaches that our reason, that the necessary laws of thought which govern our mental operations, lead to absolute contradictions. In this Hamilton and Mansel fully agree with him. They tell us that reason teaches that the Absolute must be all things actual and possible; that there cannot be an absolute or infinite person, or cause; that being and not-being are identical; that the infinite is "potentially all things and actually nothing." These and similar contradictions are said to be inevitable results of all attempts to know God as an Absolute and Infinite Being. "The conception of the Absolute and Infinite, from whatever side we view it, appears encompassed with contradictions. There is a contradiction in supposing such an object to exist, whether alone or in conjunction with others; and there is a contradiction in supposing it not to exist. There is a contradiction in conceiving it as one, and there is a contradiction in conceiving it as many. There is a contradiction in conceiving it as personal; and there is a contradiction in conceiving it as impersonal. It cannot without contradiction be represented as active; nor, without equal contradiction, be represented as inactive. It cannot be conceived as the sum of all existence; nor yet can it be conceived of as a part only of that sum." [1] Yet all this we are called upon to believe; for it is our duty, he says, to believe that God is infinite and absolute. That is, we are bound to believe what our rational consciousness pronounces to be contradictory and impossible.

[1] *Limits of Religious Thought*, p. 85.

Conscience, or our moral consciousness, is no less deceptive. Mr. Mansel admits that we are conscious of dependence and of moral obligation ; that this involves what he calls " the consciousness of God," *i. e.*, that we stand in the relation to God of one spirit to another spirit, of one person to another person ; a person so superior to us as to have rightfully supreme authority over us, and who has all the power and all the moral perfections which enter into our idea of God. But all this is a delusion. It is a delusion, because what our moral consciousness thus teaches involves all the contradictions and absurdities above mentioned ; because it is said to teach not what God is, but only what it is desirable that we should think He is ; and because we are told that it is blasphemy to think that He is what we take Him to be.

The theory, therefore, of Hamilton and Mansel as to the knowledge of God is suicidal. It is inconsistent with the veracity of consciousness, which is the fundamental principle of their philosophy. The theory is an incongruous combination of sceptical principles with orthodox faith, the anti-theistic principles of Kant with Theism. One or the other must be given up. We cannot believe in a personal God, if an infinite person be a contradiction and absurdity.

God has not so constituted our nature as to make it of necessity deceptive. The senses, reason, and conscience, within their appropriate spheres, and in their normal exercise, are trustworthy guides. They teach us real, and not merely apparent or regulative truth. Their combined spheres comprehend all the relations in which we, as rational creatures, stand to the external world, to our fellow-men, and to God. Were it not for the disturbing element of sin, we know not that man, in full communion with his Maker, whose favour is light and life, would have needed any other guides. But man is not in his original and normal state. In apostatizing from God, man fell into a state of darkness and confusion. Reason and conscience are no longer adequate guides as to " the things of God." Of fallen men, the Apostle says : " That when they knew God, they glorified him not as God, neither were thankful, but became vain in their imaginations, and their foolish heart was darkened. Professing themselves to be wise, they became fools ; and changed the glory of the uncorruptible God into an image made like to corruptible man, and to birds, and four-footed beasts, and creeping things " (Rom. i. 21–23) ; or, worse yet, into an absolute and infinite being, without consciousness, intelligence, or moral character ; a being which is potentially all things, and actually nothing. It is true, therefore, as the same Apostle tells us, that the world by wisdom knows not God. It is true in a still higher sense, as the Lord himself says, that no man " knoweth the Father, save the Son, and he to whomsoever the Son will reveal Him." (Matt. xi. 27.)

Necessity of a Supernatural Revelation.

We need, therefore, a divine supernatural revelation. Of this revelation, it is to be remarked, first, that it gives us real knowledge. It teaches us what God really is; what sin is; what the law is; what Christ and the plan of salvation through Him are; and what is to be the state of the soul after death. The knowledge thus communicated is real, in the sense that the ideas which we are thus led to form of the things revealed conform to what those things really are. God and Christ, holiness and sin, heaven and hell, really are what the Bible declares them to be. Sir William Hamilton[1] divides the objects of knowledge into two classes: those derived from within, from the intelligence; and those derived from experience. The latter are of two kinds: what we know from our own experience, and what we know from the experience of others, authenticated to us by adequate testimony. In the generally received sense of the word this is true knowledge. No man hesitates to say that he knows that there was such a man as Washington, or such an event as the American Revolution. If the testimony of men can give us clear and certain knowledge of facts beyond our experience, surely the testimony of God is greater. What He reveals is made known. We apprehend it as it truly is. The conviction that what God reveals is made known in its true nature, is the very essence of faith in the divine testimony. We are certain, therefore, that our ideas of God, founded on the testimony of his Word, correspond to what He really is, and constitute true knowledge. It is also to be remembered that while the testimony of men is to the mind, the testimony of God is not only to, but also within the mind. It illuminates and informs; so that the testimony of God is called the demonstration of the Spirit.

The second remark concerning the revelation contained in the Scriptures is, that while it makes known truths far above the reach of sense or reason, it reveals nothing which contradicts either. It harmonizes with our whole nature. It supplements all our other knowledge, and authenticates itself by harmonizing the testimony of enlightened consciousness with the testimony of God in his Word.

[1] *Lectures on Logic.* Lecture 32d.

The conclusion, therefore, of the whole matter is, that we know God in the same sense in which we know ourselves and things out of ourselves. We have the same conviction that God is, and that He is, in Himself, and independently of our thought of Him, what we take Him to be. Our subjective idea corresponds to the objective reality. This knowledge of God is the foundation of all religion ; and therefore to deny that God can be known, is really to deny that rational religion is possible. In other words, it makes religion a mere sentiment, or blind feeling, instead of its being what the Apostle declares it to be, a λογικὴ λατρεία, *a rational service ;* the homage of the reason as well as of the heart and life. " Our knowledge of God," says Hase, " developed and enlightened by the Scriptures, answers to what God really is, for He cannot deceive us as to his own nature." [1]

---

[1] See on this subject, Sir William Hamilton's *Discussions on Philosophy and Literature ,* Hamilton's *Lectures on Metaphysics and Logic,* edited by Rev. Henry L. Mansel and John Veitch, M. A.; *Philosophy of Sir William Hamilton,* arranged and edited by O. W. Wight, translator of Cousin's *History of Modern Philosophy; The Limits of Religious Thought,* eight lectures on the Bampton Foundation, by Henry Longueville Mansel, B. D.; Calderwood's *Philosophy of the Infinite;* Dr. McCosh's works on the *Method of the Divine Government; The Intuitions of the Mind; Defence of Fundamental Truths; Princeton Review,* April, 1862, *Philosophy of the Absolute,* an article by Dr. Charles W. Shields; October, 1861, Review of Dr. Hickok's *Rational Psychology,* by Dr. Stephen Alexander; and *A Philosophical Confession of Faith,* by the same writer, a very able and concise statement of fundamental principles, in the number for July, 1867, of the same journal. See also Mill's *Review of Hamilton's Philosophy,* and the admirable work of Professor Noah Porter, of New Haven, on the *Human Intellect,* part fourth, chap. viii.

CHAPTER V.

NATURE AND ATTRIBUTES OF GOD.

§ 1. *Definitions of God.*

THE question whether God can be defined, depends for its answer on what is meant by definition. Cicero[1] says, "Est definitio, earum rerum, quæ sunt ejus rei propriæ, quam definire volumus, brevis et circumscripta quædam explicatio." In this sense God cannot be defined. No creature, much less man, can know all that is proper to God; and, therefore, no creature can give an exhaustive statement of all that God is.

To define, however, is simply to bound, to separate, or distinguish; so that the thing defined may be discriminated from all other things. This may be done (1.) By stating its characteristics. (2.) By stating its genus and its specific difference. (3.) By analyzing the idea as it lies in our minds. (4.) By an explanation of the term or name by which it is denoted. All these methods amount to much the same thing. When we say we can define God, all that is meant is, that we can analyze the idea of God as it lies in our mind; or, that we can state the class of beings to which He belongs, and the attributes by which He is distinguished from all other beings. Thus, in the simple definition, God is *ens perfectissimum*, the word *ens* designates Him as a being, not an idea, but as that which has real, objective existence; and absolute perfection distinguishes Him from all other beings. The objection to this and most other definitions of God is, that they do not bring out with sufficient fulness the contents of the idea. This objection bears against such definitions as the following: *Ens absolutum*, the self-existent, independent being; and that by Calovius, "Deus est essentia spiritualis infinita;" and Reinhard's[2] "Deus est, Natura necessaria, a mundo diversa, summas complexa perfectiones et ipsius mundi causa;" or Baumgarten's "Spiritus perfectissimus, rationem sui ipsius rerumque contingentium omnium seu mundi continens;" or, that of Morus, "Spiritus perfectissimus, conditor, conservator,

---

[1] *De Oratore*, i. 42, 189, edit. Leipzig, 1850, p. 84.
[2] *Dogmatik*, p. 92.

et gubernator mundi." Probably the best definition of God ever penned by man, is that given in the "Westminster Catechism": "God is a Spirit, infinite, eternal, and unchangeable, in his being, wisdom, power, holiness, justice, goodness, and truth." This is a true definition; for it states the class of beings to which God is to be referred. He is a Spirit; and He is distinguished from all other spirits in that He is infinite, eternal, and unchangeable in his being and perfections. It is also a complete definition, in so far as it is an exhaustive statement of the contents of our idea of God.

In what sense, however, are these terms used? What is meant by the words "being," and "perfections," or "attributes" of God? In what relation do his attributes stand to his essence and to each other? These are questions on which theologians, especially during the scholastic period, expended much time and labor.

Being of God.

By *being* is here meant that which has a real, substantive existence. It is equivalent to substance, or essence. It is opposed to what is merely thought, and to a mere force or power. We get this idea, in the first place, from consciousness. We are conscious of self as the subject of the thoughts, feelings, and volitions, which are its varying states and acts. This consciousness of substance is involved in that of personal identity. In the second place, a law of our reason constrains us to believe that there is something which underlies the phenomena of matter and mind, of which those phenomena are the manifestation. It is impossible for us to think of thought and feeling, unless there be something that thinks and feels. It is no less impossible to think of action, unless there be something that acts; or of motion, unless there be something that moves. To assume, therefore, that mind is only a series of acts and states, and that matter is nothing but force, is to assume that nothing (nonentity) can produce effects.

God, therefore, is in his nature a substance, or essence, which is infinite, eternal, and unchangeable; the common subject of all divine perfections, and the common agent of all divine acts. This is as far as we can go, or need to go. We have no definite idea of substance, whether of matter or mind, as distinct from its attributes. The two are inseparable. In knowing the one we know the other. We cannot know hardness except as we know something hard. We have, therefore, the same knowledge of the essence of God, as we have of the substance of the soul. All we have to do in reference to the divine essence, as a Spirit, is to deny of it, as we do of our own spiritual essence, what belongs to material substances; and to affirm of it, that in itself and its attributes it is infinite, eternal, and unchangeable. When, therefore, we say there is a God, we do not assert merely that there is in our minds the idea of an infinite Spirit; but that, entirely independent of our idea of Him, such a Being really exists. Augustine [1] says, "Deus est quædam substantia; nam quod nulla substantia est, nihil omnino est. Substantia ergo aliquid esse est."

If, therefore, a divine essence, infinite, eternal, and unchangeable, exists, this essence existed before and independent of the world. It follows also that the essence of God is distinct from the world. The Scriptural doctrine of God is consequently opposed to the several forms of error already mentioned; to Hylozoism, which assumes that God, like man, is a composite being, the world being to Him what the body is to us; to Materialism, which denies the existence of any spiritual substance, and affirms that the material alone is real; to extreme Idealism, which denies not only the reality of the internal world, but all real objective existence, and affirms that the subjective alone is real; to Pantheism, which either makes the world the existence form of God, or, denying the reality of the world, makes God the only real existence. That is, it either makes nature God, or, denying nature, makes God everything.

§ 2. *Divine Attributes.*

To the divine essence, which in itself is infinite, eternal, and unchangeable, belong certain perfections revealed to us in the constitution of our nature and in the word of God. These divine perfections are called attributes as essential to the nature of a divine Being, and necessarily involved in our idea of God. The older theologians distinguished the attributes of God, (1.) From predicates which refer to God in the concrete, and indicate his relation to his creatures, as creator, preserver, ruler, etc. (2.) From properties, which are technically the distinguishing characteristics of the several persons of the Trinity. There are certain acts or relations peculiar or proper to the Father, others to the Son, and others to the Spirit. And (3.) From accidents or qualities which may or may not belong to a substance, which may be acquired or lost. Thus holiness was not an attribute of the nature of Adam, but an accident, something which he might lose and still remain a man; whereas intelligence was an attribute, because the loss of intelligence involves the loss of humanity.

---

[1] *Enarratio in Psalmum*, lxviii. i. 5, edit. Benedictines, voi. iv. p. 988 c.

The perfections of God, therefore, are attributes, without which He would cease to be God.

Relation of the Attributes to the Essence of God.

In attempting to explain the relation in which the attributes of God stand to his essence and to each other, there are two extremes to be avoided. First, we must not represent God as a composite being, composed of different elements ; and, secondly, we must not confound the attributes, making them all mean the same thing, which is equivalent to denying them all together. The Realists of the Middle Ages tended to the former of these extremes, and the Nominalists to the other. Realists held that general terms express not merely thoughts, or abstract conceptions in our minds, but real or substantive, objective existence. And hence they were disposed to represent the divine attributes as differing from each other *realiter*, as one *res* or thing differs from another. The Nominalists, on the other hand, said general terms are mere words answering to abstractions formed by the mind. And consequently when we speak of different attributes in God, we only use different words for one and the same thing. Occam, Biel, and other Nominalists, therefore, taught that " Attributa divina nec rei, nec rationis distinctione, inter se aut ab essentia divina distingui ; sed omnem distinctionem esse solum in nominibus." The Lutheran and Reformed theologians tended much more to the latter of these extremes than to the former. They generally taught, in the first place, that the unity and simplicity of the divine essence precludes not only all physical composition of constituent elements, or of matter and form, or of subject and accidents ; but also all metaphysical distinction as of act and power, essence and existence, nature and personality ; and even of logical difference, as genus and specific difference.

In the second place, the theologians were accustomed to say that the attributes of God differ from his essence *non re, sed ratione.* This is explained by saying that things differ *ex natura rei*, when they are essentially different as soul and body ; while a difference *ex ratione* is merely a difference in us, *i. e.*, in our conceptions, *i. e.*, " quod distincte solum concipitur, cum in re ipsa distinctum non sit." Hence the divine attributes are defined as " conceptus essentiæ divinæ inadequatæ, ex parte rei ipsam essentiam involventes, eandemque intrinsice denominantes. Aquinas says, " Deus est unus re et plures ratione, quia intellectus noster ita multipliciter apprehendit Deum, sicuti res multipliciter ipsum representant." The language of the

Lutheran theologian Quenstedt [1] exhibits the usual mode of representing this subject: " Si proprie et accurate loqui velimus, Deus nullas habet proprietates, sed mera et simplicissima est essentia quæ nec realem differentiam nec ullam vel rerum vel modorum admittit compositionem. Quia vero simplicissimam Dei essentiam uno adequato conceptu adequate concipere non possumus, ideo inadequatis et distinctis conceptibus, inadequate essentiam divinam repræsentantibus, eam apprehendimus, quos inadequatos conceptus, qui a parte rei essentiæ divinæ identificantur, et a nobis per modum affectionum apprehenduntur, attributa vocamus." And again, " Attributa divina a parte rei et in se non multa sunt, sed ut ipsa essentia divina, ita et attributa, quæ cum illa identificantur, simplicissima unitas sunt; multa vero dicuntur (1.) συγκαταβατικῶς, ad nostrum concipiendi modum, ... (2.) ἐνεργητικῶς, in ordine ad effecta." [2] The favorite illustration to explain what was meant by this unity of the divine attributes, was drawn from the sun. His ray, by one and the same power (as was then assumed) illuminates, warms, and produces chemical changes, not from any diversity in it, but from diversity in the nature of the objects on which it operates. The force is the same; the effects are different. The meaning of these theologians is further determined by their denying that the relation of attribute and essence in God is analogous to the relation of intelligence and will to the essence of the soul in man; and also by the frequently recurring declaration, borrowed from the schoolmen, that God is *actus purus*. Schleiermacher goes still further in the same direction. With him the divine attributes are mere Beziehungen, or relations of God to us. He commonly resolves them into mere causality. Thus he defines the holiness of God to be that causality in Him which produces conscience in us.

Divine Attributes.

A third and less objectionable way of representing the matter is adopted by those who say with Hollazius : " Attributa divina ab essentia divina et a se invicem, distinguuntur non nominaliter neque realiter sed formaliter, secundum nostrum concipiendi modum, non sine certo distinctionis fundamento." [3] This is very different from saying that they differ *ratione tantum*. Turrettin says the attributes are to be distinguished not *realiter*, but *virtualiter;* that is, there is a real foundation in the divine nature for the several attributes ascribed to Him.

[1] *Theologia*, part I. cap. viii. § 2, edit. Leipzig, 1715, p. 426.
[2] *Ibid.* II. cap. viii. § 2, p. 426.
[3] *Examen Theologicum*, edit. Leipzig, 1763, p. 235.

It is evident that this question of the relation of the divine attributes to the divine essence merges itself into the general question of the relation between attributes and substance. It is also evident that this is a subject about which one man knows just as much as another; because all that can be known about it is given immediately in consciousness.

This subject has already been referred to. We are conscious of ourselves as a thinking substance. That is, we are conscious that that which is ourselves has identity, continuance, and power. We are further conscious that the substance self thinks, wills, and feels. Intelligence, will, and sensibility, are its functions, or attributes, and consequently the attributes of a spirit. These are the ways in which a spirit acts. Anything which does not thus act, which has not these functions or attributes, is not a spirit. If you take from a spirit its intelligence, will, and sensibility, nothing remains; its substance is gone; at least it ceases to be a spirit. Substance and attributes are inseparable. The one is known in the other. A substance without attributes is nothing, *i. e.*, no real existence. What is true of spiritual substances is true of matter. Matter, without the essential properties of matter, is a contradiction.

We know, therefore, from consciousness, as far as it can be known, the relation between substance and its attributes. And all that can be done, or need be done, is to deny or correct the false representations which are so often made on the subject.

The Divine Attributes do not differ merely in our Conceptions.

To say, as the schoolmen, and so many even of Protestant theologians, ancient and modern, were accustomed to say, that the divine attributes differ only in name, or in our conceptions, or in their effects, is to destroy all true knowledge of God. Thus even Augustine confounds knowledge and power, when he says,[1] " Nos ista, quæ fecisti videmus quia sunt : tu autem quia vides ea, sunt." So Scotus Erigena [2] says, " Non aliud est ei videre, aliud facere ; sed visio illius voluntas ejus est, et voluntas operatio." Thomas Aquinas [3] says the same thing : " Deus per intellectum suum causat res, cum suum esse sit suum intelligere." And again, " Scientia (Dei) causat res ; nostra vero causatur rebus et dependat ab eis." Even Mr. Mansel,[4] to aggravate our ignorance of God, speaks of Him as " an intellect whose thought creates its own object." It is

---

[1] *Confessiones*, XIII. xxxviii. 53, edit. Benedictines, vol. i. p. 410 b.
[2] *De Divisione Naturæ*, iii. 29, edit. Westphalia, 1838, p. 264.
[3] *Summa*, I. xiv. 8, edit. Cologne, 1640, p. 30.   [4] *Limits*, p. 195

obvious that, according to this view, God is simply a force of which
we know nothing but its effects. If in God eternity is identical
with knowledge, knowledge with power, power with ubiquity, and
ubiquity with holiness, we are using words without meaning when
we attribute any perfection to God. We must, therefore, either
give up the attempt to determine the divine attributes from our
speculative idea of an infinite essence, or renounce all knowledge
of God, and all faith in the revelation of Himself, which He has
made in the constitution of our nature, in the external world, and
in his Word. Knowledge is no more identical with power in God
than it is in us. Thought in Him is no more creative than is
thought in us. Otherwise creation is eternal, and God creates
everything — all the thoughts, feelings, and volitions of his creatures, good and evil ; and God is the only real agent, and the only
real being in the universe. According to this doctrine, also, there
can be no difference between the actual and the possible, for the
one as well as the other is always present to the divine mind. It
would also follow that the creation must be infinite, or God finite.
For if knowledge is causative, God creates all He knows, and you
must limit his knowledge if you limit creation. It need hardly be
remarked that this doctrine is derogatory to God. It is not only
a much higher idea, but one essential to personality, that there
should be a real distinction between the divine attributes. That
which from its nature and by necessity does all that it can do, is
a force, and not a person. It can have no will. The doctrine in
question, therefore, is essentially pantheistic. " However much,"
says Martensen, " we must guard our idea of God from being degraded by anything that is merely human, from all false Anthropomorphism, yet we can find in Nominalism only the denial of God
as He is revealed in the Scriptures. It is the denial of the very
essence of faith, if it is only in our thoughts that God is holy and
righteous, and not in his own nature; if it is we who so address Him,
and not He who so reveals Himself. We teach, therefore, with
the Realists (of one class), that the attributes of God are objectively true as revealed, and therefore have their ground in the divine essence." There is a kind of Realism, as Martensen admits,
which is as destructive of the true idea of God as the Nominalism
which makes his attributes differ only in name. It grants, indeed,
objective reality to our ideas ; but these ideas, according to it, have
no real subject. " The idea of omnipotence, righteousness, and
holiness," he says, " is a mere blind thought, if there be not an
omnipotent, righteous, and holy One." [1]

1 *Dogmatik.* p. 113.

The Divine Attributes not to be resolved into Causality.

It amounts to much the same doctrine, to resolve all the attributes of God into causality. It was a principle with some of the schoolmen, " Affectus in Deo denotat effectum." This was so applied as to limit our knowledge of God to the fact that God is the cause of certain effects. Thus, when we say God is just, we mean nothing more than that He causes misery to follow sin ; when we say He is holy, it only means that He is the cause of conscience in us. As a tree is not sweet, because its fruit is luscious, so God is not holy, He is only the cause of holiness. Against this application of the principle, Aquinas himself protested, declaring, " Cum igitur dicitur, Deus est bonus ; non est sensus, Deus est causa bonitatis ; vel Deus non est malus. Sed est sensus : Id, quod bonitatem dicimus in creaturis, præexistit in Deo ; et hoc quidem secundum modum altiorem. Unde ex hoc non sequitur, quod Deo competat esse bonum, in quantum causat bonitatem ; sed potius e converso, quia est bonus, bonitatem rebus diffundit." [1] And the Lutheran theologian, Quenstedt, says, " Dicunt nonnulli, ideo Deum dici justum, sanctum, misericordem, veracem, etc., non quod revera sit talis, sed quod duntaxat sanctitatis, justitiæ, misericordiæ, veritatis, etc., causa sit et auctor in aliis. Sed si Deus non est vere misericors, neque vere perfectus, vere sanctus, etc., sed causa tantum misericordiæ et sanctitatis in aliis, ita etiam et nos pariter juberemur esse non vere misericordes, non vere perfecti, etc., sed sanctitatis saltem et misericordiæ in aliis auctores." [2]

The Divine Attributes differ Virtualiter.

Theologians, to avoid the blank ignorance of God which must follow from the extreme view of the simplicity of his essence, which requires us to assume that the divine attributes differ only in our conceptions, or as expressing the diverse effects of the activity of God, made a distinction between the *ratio rationantis* and the *ratio rationatæ*. That is, the reason as determining, and the reason as determined. The attributes, they say, differ not *re*, but *ratione ;* not in our subjective reason only ; but there is in God a reason why we think of Him as possessing these diverse perfections. This idea, as before stated, was often expressed by saying that the divine attributes differ neither *realiter*, nor *nominaliter*, but *virtualiter*. If this be understood to mean that the divine perfections are really what the Bible declares them to be ; that God truly

[1] *Summa*, I. xiii. 2, edit. Cologne. 1640, p. 28. [2] *Theologia*, I. viii. § ii. 2, p. 431.

thinks, feels, and acts ; that He is truly wise, just, and good ; that He is truly omnipotent, and voluntary, acting or not acting, as He sees fit; that He can hear and answer prayer; it may be admitted. But we are not to give up the conviction that God is really in Himself what He reveals Himself to be, to satisfy any metaphysical speculations as to the difference between essence and attribute in an infinite Being.   The attributes of God, therefore, are not merely different conceptions in our minds, but different modes in which God reveals Himself to his creatures (or to Himself) ; just as our several faculties are different modes in which the inscrutable substance self reveals itself in our consciousness and acts.   It is an old saying, " Qualis homo, talis Deus."   And Clemens Alexandrinus [1] says, " If any one knows himself, he will know God." And Leibnitz expresses the same great truth when he says,[2] " The perfections of God are those of our own souls, but He possesses them without limit.   He is an ocean of which we have only received a few drops.   There is in us something of power, something of knowledge, something of goodness ; but these attributes are in entireness in Him."   There is indeed danger in either extreme ; danger of degrading God in our thoughts, by reducing Him to the standard of our nature, and danger of denying Him as He is revealed.   In our day, and among educated men, and especially among students of philosophy, the latter danger is by far the greater of the two.   We should remember that we lose God, when we lose our confidence in saying Thou ! to Him, with the assurance of being heard and helped.

§ 3. *Classification of the Divine Attributes.*

On few subjects have greater thought and labor been expended than on this.   Perhaps, however, the benefit has not been commensurate with the labor.   The object of classification is order, and the object of order is clearness.   So far as this end is secured, it is a good.   But the great diversity of the methods which have been proposed, is evidence that no one method of arrangement has such advantages as to secure for it general recognition.

1. Some, as has been seen, preclude all necessity of a classification of the attributes, by reducing them all to unity, or regarding them as different phases under which we contemplate the Supreme Being as the ground of all things.   With them the whole discussion of the divine attributes is an analysis of the idea of the Infinite and Absolute.

---

1 *Pædagogus*, III. i. edit. Cologne, 1688, p. 214 a.
2 " Théodicée," Preface, *Works*, p. 469, edit. Berlin, 1840.

2. Others arrange the attributes according to the mode in which we arrive at the knowledge of them. We form our idea of God, it is said, (1.) By the way of causation ; that is, by referring to Him as the great first cause every virtue manifested by the effects which He produces. (2.) By the way of negation ; that is, by denying to Him the limitations and imperfections which belong to his creatures. (3.) By the way of eminence, in exalting to an infinite degree or without limit the perfections which belong to an infinite Being. If this is so, the attributes conceived of by one of these methods belong to one class, and those conceived of, or of which we attain the knowledge by another method, belong to another class. This principle of classification is perhaps the one most generally adopted. It gives rise, however, really but to two classes, namely, the positive and negative, *i. e.*, those in which something is affirmed, and those in which something is denied concerning God. To the negative class are commonly referred simplicity, infinity, eternity, immutability ; to the positive class, power, knowledge, holiness, justice, goodness, and truth. Instead of calling the one class ·negative and the other positive, they are often distinguished as absolute and relative. By an absolute attribute is meant one which belongs to God, considered in Himself, and which implies no relation to other beings ; by a relative attribute is meant one which implies relation to an object. They are also distinguished as immanent and transient, as communicable and incommunicable. These terms are used interchangeably. They do not express different modes of classification, but are different modes of designating the same classification. Negative, absolute, immanent, and incommunicable, are designations of one class ; and positive, relative, transitive, and communicable, are designations of the other class.

3. A third principle of classification is derived from the constitution of our own nature. In man there is the substance or essence of the soul, the intellect, and the will. Hence, it is said, we can most naturally arrange the attributes of God under three heads. First, those pertaining to his essence ; second, those referring to his intellect ; and third, those referring to his will, the word "will" being taken in its most comprehensive sense.

4. Others again seek the principle of classification in the nature of the attributes themselves. Some include the idea of moral excellence, and others do not. Hence they are distinguished as natural and moral. The word natural, however, is ambiguous. Taking it in the sense of what constitutes or pertains to the nature, the holiness and justice of God are as much natural as his power

or knowledge. And on the other hand, God is infinite and eternal in his moral perfections, although infinity and eternity are not distinctively moral perfections. In the common and familiar sense of the word natural, the terms natural and moral express a real distinction.

5. Schleiermacher's method is, of course, peculiar. It is based on the characteristic principle of his system, that all religion is founded on a sense of dependence, and all theology consists in what that sense of dependence teaches us. He does not treat of the divine attributes in any one place, but here and there, as they come up according to his plan. Our sense of dependence does not awaken in our consciousness a feeling of opposition to God's eternity, omnipotence, omnipresence, or omniscience. These, therefore, are treated of in one place. But we, as dependent creatures, are conscious of opposition to God's holiness and righteousness. These, therefore, belong to another head. And as this opposition is removed through Christ, we are brought into relation to God's grace or love, and to his wisdom. These form a third class.

That so many different principles of classification have been adopted, and that each of those principles is carried out in so many different ways, shows the uncertainty and difficulty attending the whole subject. It is proposed in what follows to accept the guidance of the answer given in the " Westminster Catechism," to the question, What is God ? It is assumed in that answer that God is a self-existent and necessary Being ; and it is affirmed of Him, I. That He is a Spirit. II. That as such He is infinite, eternal, and immutable. III. That He is infinite, eternal, and immutable, (1.) In his being. (2.) In all that belongs to his intelligence, namely, in his knowledge and wisdom. (3.) In all that belongs to his will, namely, his power, holiness, justice, goodness, and truth. Whatever speculative objections may be made to this plan, it has the advantage of being simple and familiar.

§ 4. *Spirituality of God.*

A. *The Meaning of the Word " Spirit."*

The fundamental principle of interpretation of all writings, sacred or profane, is that words are to be understood in their historical sense ; that is, in the sense in which it can be historically proved that they were used by their authors and intended to be understood by those to whom they were addressed. The object of language is the communication of thought. Unless words are taken in the sense in which those who employ them know they will be understood, they fail of their design. The sacred writings being the words of God to man, we are bound to take them in the sense in which those to whom they were originally addressed must inevitably have taken them. What is the meaning of the word "spirit?" or rather, What is the *usus loquendi* of the Hebrew and Greek words to which our word "spirit" corresponds? In answering this question, we learn what our Lord meant when he said God is a Spirit. Originally the words רוּחַ and πνεῦμα meant the moving air, especially the breath, as in the phrase πνεῦμα βίου; then any invisible power ; then the human soul. In saying, therefore, that God is a Spirit, our Lord authorizes us to believe that whatever is essential to the idea of a spirit, as learned from our own consciousness, is to be referred to God as determining his nature. On this subject consciousness teaches, and has taught all men, —

1. That the soul is a substance ; that our thoughts and feelings have a common ground, of which they are the varying states or acts. Substance is that which has an objective existence, and has permanence and power. Even Kant says: "Wo Handlung, mithin Thätigkeit und Kraft ist, da ist auch Substanz," where operation, and consequently activity and power are, there is substance.[1] This is not only the common conviction of men, but it is admitted by the vast majority of philosophers. As before remarked, that there should be action without something acting, is as unthinkable as that there should be motion without something moving.

2. Consciousness teaches that the soul is an individual subsistence. This is included in the consciousness of the unity, identity, and permanence of the soul. It is not that we are conscious simply of certain states of the soul, from which we infer its substance and subsistence ; but that such are the contents of the knowledge given to us in the consciousness of self. Des Cartes' famous aphorism, *Cogito ergo sum,* is not a syllogism. It does not mean that existence is inferred from the consciousness of thought ; but that the consciousness of thought involves the consciousness of existence. Des Cartes himself so understood the matter, for he says : " Cum advertimus nos esse res cogitantes, prima quædam notio est quæ ex nullo syllogismo concluditur; neque etiam cum quis dicit ' Ego cogito, ergo sum, sive existo,' existentiam ex cogitatione per syllogismum deducit, sed tanquam rem per se notam simplici mentis intuitu agnoscit." [2]   Mansel says : " Whatever may be the va-

---

[1] *Werke,* edit. Leipzig, 1838, vol. ii. p. 173.

[2] *Meditationes de Prima Philosophia, Responsio ad Secundas Objectiones, III.,* edit. Amsterdam, 1685. p. 74

riety of the phenomena of consciousness, sensations by this or that organ, volitions, thoughts, imaginations, of all we are immediately conscious as affections of one and the same self. It is not by any after-effort of reflection that I combine together sight and hearing, thought and volition, into a factitious unity or compounded whole : in each case I am immediately conscious of myself seeing and hearing, willing and thinking. This self-personality, like all other simple and immediate presentations, is indefinable ; but it is so because it is superior to definition." [1] This individual subsistence is thus involved in the consciousness of self, because in self-consciousness we distinguish ourselves from all that is not ourselves.

3. As power of some kind belongs to every substance, the power which belongs to spirit, to the substance self, is that of thought, feeling, and volition. All this is given in the simplest form of consciousness. We are not more certain that we exist, than that we think, feel, and will. We know ourselves only as thus thinking, feeling, and willing, and we therefore are sure that these powers or faculties are the essential attributes of a spirit, and must belong to every spirit.

4. Consciousness also informs us of the unity or simplicity of the soul. It is not compounded of different elements. It is composed of substance and form. It is a simple substance endowed with certain attributes. It is incapable of separation or division.

5. In being conscious of our individual subsistence, we are conscious of personality. Every individual subsistence is not a person. But every individual subsistence which thinks and feels, and has the power of self-determination, is a person ; and, therefore, the consciousness of our subsistence, and of the powers of thought and volition, is the consciousness of personality.

6. We are also conscious of being moral agents, susceptible of moral character, and the subjects of moral obligation.

7. It need not be added that every spirit must possess self-consciousness. This is involved in all that has been said. Without self-consciousness we should be a mere power in nature. This is the very ground of our being, and is necessarily involved in the idea of self as a real existence.

It is impossible, therefore, to overestimate the importance of the truth contained in the simple proposition, God is a Spirit. It is involved in that proposition that God is immaterial. None of the properties of matter can be predicated of Him. He is not extended or divisible, or compounded, or visible, or tangible. He has neither

---

[1] *Prolegomena Logica*, Boston, 1860, p. 123. See also Dr. McCosh's *Intuitions of the Mind*, p. 148.

bulk nor form. The Bible everywhere recognizes as true the intuitive convictions of men. One of those convictions is that spirit is not matter, or matter spirit; that different and incompatible attributes cannot belong to the same substance. In revealing, therefore, to us that God is a Spirit, it reveals to us that no attribute of matter can be predicated of the divine essence. The realistic dualism which lies at the bottom of all human convictions, underlies also all the revelations of the Bible.

B. *Consequences of the Spirituality of God.*

If God be a spirit, it follows of necessity that He is a person,— a self-conscious, intelligent, voluntary agent. As all this is involved in our consciousness of ourselves as spirit, it must all be true of God, or God is of a lower order of being than man.

It follows also that God is a simple Being, not only as not composed of different elements, but also as not admitting of the distinction between substance and accidents. Nothing can either be added to, or taken from God. In this view the simplicity, as well as the other attributes of God, are of a higher order than the corresponding attributes of our spiritual nature. The soul of man is a simple substance; but it is subject to change. It can gain and lose knowledge, holiness, and power. These are in this view accidents in our substance. But in God they are attributes, essential and immutable.

Finally, it follows from God's being a spirit, that He is a moral as well as an intelligent Being. It is involved in the very nature of rational voluntary being, that it should be conformed to the rule of right, which in the case of God is his own infinite reason. These are primary truths, which are not to be sacrificed to any speculative objections. It is vain to tell us that an infinite spirit cannot be a person, because personality implies self-consciousness, and self-consciousness implies the distinction between the self and the not-self, and this is a limitation. It is equally vain to say that God cannot have moral excellence, because moral goodness implies conformity to law, and conformity to law again is inconsistent with the idea of an absolute Being. These are empty speculations; and even if incapable of a satisfactory solution, would afford no rational ground for rejecting the intuitive truths of reason and conscience. There are mysteries enough in our nature, and yet no sane man denies his own personal existence and moral accountability. And he is worse than insane who is beguiled by such sophistries into renouncing his faith in God as a personal spirit and a loving Father.

The Scriptures confirm these Views.

It need hardly be remarked that the Scriptures everywhere represent God as possessing all the above-mentioned attributes of a spirit. On this foundation all religion rests; all intercourse with God, all worship, all prayer, all confidence in God as preserver, benefactor, and redeemer. The God of the Bible is a person. He spoke to Adam. He revealed himself to Noah. He entered into covenant with Abraham. He conversed with Moses, as a friend with friend. He everywhere uses the personal pronouns. He says, "I am," that "is my name." I am the Lord your God. I am merciful and gracious. Call upon me, and I will answer you. Like as a father pitieth his children, so the Lord pitieth them that fear Him. O thou that hearest prayer, to thee shall all flesh come. Our Lord has put into our lips words which reveal that God is a spirit, and all that being a spirit implies, when He teaches us to say: "Our Father who art in heaven. Hallowed be thy name. Thy kingdom come. Thy will be done." Everywhere the God of the Bible is contrasted with the gods of the heathen, as a God who sees, hears, and loves. These are not *regulative*, they are real truths. God does not mock us when He thus presents Himself to us as a personal Being with whom we can have intercourse, and who is everywhere present to help and save. "To human reason," says Mansel, "the personal and the infinite stand out in apparently irreconcilable antagonism; and the recognition of the one in a religious system almost inevitably involves the sacrifice of the other." [1] This cannot be so. According to the Bible, and according to the dictates of our own nature, of reason as well as of conscience, God is a spirit, and being a spirit is of necessity a person; a Being who can say I, and to whom we can say Thou.

§ 5. *Infinity.*

Although God reveals Himself as a personal Being capable of fellowship with man, whom we can worship and love, and to whom we can pray with the assurance of being heard and answered; nevertheless He fills heaven and earth; He is exalted above all we can know or think. He is infinite in his being and perfections. The ideas with which we are most familiar are often those of which we are the least able to give an intelligent account. Space, time, and infinity, are among the most difficult problems of human thought. What is space? is a question which has never been satisfactorily answered. Some say it is nothing; where nothing is,

[1] *Limits.* p. 148.

space is not; it is "negation defined by boundary lines;" others, with Kant and Hamilton, say that it is "a condition of thought," "the subjective condition of sensibility;" others that it is an attribute or accident of God; others that it is that in which real existences can act and move. Notwithstanding these conflicting statements of philosophers, and the real obscurity of the subject, every man knows clearly and definitely what the word "space" means, although no man may be able to define it satisfactorily. It is much the same with the idea of infinity. If men would be content to leave the word in its integrity, as simply expressing what does not admit of limitation, there would be no danger in speculating about its nature. But in all ages wrong views of what the infinite is, have led to fatal errors in philosophy and religion. Without attempting to detail the speculations of philosophers on this subject, we shall simply endeavor to state what is meant when it is said that God is infinite in his being and perfections.

The Idea of Infinity not merely Negative.

Being, in this connection, is that which is or exists. The being of God is his essence or substance, of which his perfections are the essential attributes or modes of manifestation. When it is said that God is infinite as to his being, what is meant is, that no limitation can be assigned to his essence. It is often said that our idea of the infinite is merely negative. There is a sense in which this may be true, but there is a sense in which it is not true. It is true that the form of the proposition is negative when we say that no limit can be assigned to space, or possible duration, or to the being of God. But it implies the affirmation that the object of which infinity is predicated is illimitable. It is as much a positive idea which we express when we say a thing is infinite as when we say that it is finite. We cannot, indeed, form a conception or mental image of an infinite object, but the word nevertheless expresses a positive judgment of the mind. Sir William Hamilton and others, when they say that the infinite is a mere negation, mean that it implies a negation of all thought. That is, we mean nothing when we say that a thing is infinite. As we know nothing of the inhabitants of the other planets of our system, if such there be, or of the mode in which angels and disembodied spirits take cognizance of material objects, our ideas on such subjects are purely negative, or blank ignorance. "The infinite," Mansel says, "is not a positive object of human thought." [1] Every man, however, knows that the propositions "Space is infinite," and "Space is finite," express

[1] *Prolegomena Logica*, Boston, 1860, p. 52.

different and equally definite thoughts. When, therefore, we say that God is infinite, we mean something; we express a great and positive truth.

A. *The Infinite not the All.*

The infinite, although illimitable and incapable of increase, is not necessarily all. An infinite body must include all bodies, infinite space all portions of space, and infinite duration all periods of duration. Hence Mr. Mansel says that an infinite being must of necessity include within itself all actual and all possible forms or modes of being. So said Spinoza, many of the schoolmen, and even many Christian theologians. The sense in which Spinoza and Mansel make this assertion is the fundamental principle of Pantheism. Mr. Mansel, as we have seen, escapes that conclusion by appealing to faith, and teaching that we are constrained to believe what reason pronounces to be impossible, which itself is an impossibility. The sense in which theologians teach that an infinite being must comprehend within it all being, is, that in the infinite is the cause or ground of all that is actual or possible. Thus Howe[1] says, " Necessary being must include all being." But he immediately adds, not in the same way, " It comprehends all being, besides what itself is, as having had, within the compass of its productive power, whatsoever hath actually sprung from it; and having within the compass of the same power, whatsoever is still possible to be produced." This, however, is not the proper meaning of the words, nor is it the sense in which they are generally used. What the words mean, and what they are generally intended to mean by those who use them is, that there is only one being in the universe; that the finite is merely the *modus existendi*, or manifestation of the Infinite. Thus Cousin says, God must be " infinite and finite together, ... at the summit of being and at its humblest degree . . . . ; at once God, nature, and humanity."[2] Even some of the Remonstrants regard this as the necessary consequence of the doctrine of the infinitude of the divine essence. Episcopius[3] says, " Si essentia Dei sic immensa est, tum intelligi non potest quomodo et ubi aliqua creata essentia esse possit. Essentia enim creata non est essentia divina; ergo aut est extra essentiam divinam, aut, si non est extra eam, est ipsa essentia illa, et sic omnia sunt Deus et divina essentia." "God is infinite," says Jacob Böhme, "for God is all." This, says Strauss,[4] is exactly the doctrine of the modern philosophy.

1 " Living Temple," *Works*, London, 1724, vol. i. p. 70.
2 *History of Modern Philosophy*, translated by Wight. New York, 1852, vol. i. p. 113.
3 *Institutiones Theologicæ*, iv. ii. 13, edit. Amsterdam, 1550, vol. i. p. 294.
4 *Dogmatik*. vol. i. p. 556

It has already been remarked in a previous chapter, in reference to this mode of reasoning, that it proceeds on a wrong idea of the infinite. A thing may be infinite in its own nature without precluding the possibility of the existence of things of a different nature. An infinite spirit does not forbid the assumption of the existence of matter. There may even be many infinites of the same kind, as we can imagine any number of infinite lines. The infinite, therefore, is not all. An infinite spirit is a spirit to whose attributes as a spirit no limits can be set. It no more precludes the existence of other spirits than infinite goodness precludes the existence of finite goodness, or infinite power the existence of finite power. God is infinite in being because no limit can be assigned to his perfections, and because He is present in all portions of space. A being is said to be present wherever it perceives and acts. As God perceives and acts everywhere, He is everywhere present. This, however, does not preclude the presence of other beings. A multitude of men even may perceive and act at the same time and place. Besides, we have very little knowledge of the relation which spirit bears to space. We know that bodies occupy portions of space to the exclusion of other bodies; but we do not know that spirits may not coexist in the same portion of space. A legion of demons dwelt in one man.

B. *Infinitude of God in relation to Space.*

The infinitude of God, so far as space is concerned, includes his immensity and his omnipresence. These are not different attributes, but one and the same attribute, viewed under different aspects. His immensity is the infinitude of his being, viewed as belonging to his nature from eternity. He fills immensity with his presence. His omnipresence is the infinitude of his being, viewed in relation to his creatures. He is equally present with all his creatures, at all times, and in all places. He is not far from any one of us. "The Lord is in this place," may be said with equal truth and confidence, everywhere. Theologians are accustomed to distinguish three modes of presence in space. Bodies are in space circumscriptively. They are bounded by it. Spirits are in space definitively. They have an *ubi*. They are not everywhere, but only somewhere. God is in space repletively. He fills all space. In other words, the limitations of space have no reference to Him. He is not absent from any portion of space, nor more present in one portion than in another. This of course is not to be understood of extension or diffusion. Extension is a property of matter, and cannot be predicated of God. If extended, He would be capable of division and separation ; and part of God would be here, and part elsewhere. Nor is this omnipresence to be understood as a mere presence in knowledge and power. It is an omnipresence of the divine essence. Otherwise the essence of God would be limited. The doctrine, therefore, taught by the older Socinians that the essence of God is confined to heaven (wherever that may be), and that He is elsewhere only as to his knowledge and efficiency, is inconsistent with the divine perfections and with the representations of Scripture. As God acts everywhere, He is present everywhere ; for, as the theologians say, a being can no more act where he is not than when he is not.

The older and later theologians agree in this view of the divine immensity and omnipresence. Augustine [1] says God is not to be regarded as everywhere diffused, as the air or the light : " Sed in solo cœlo totus, et in sola terra totus, et in cœlo et in terra totus, et nullo contentus loco, sed in seipso ubique totus." Thomas Aquinas says,[2] Deus " est in omnibus per potentiam, in quantum omnia ejus potestati subduntur ; est per præsentiam in omnibus, in quantum omnia nuda sunt et aperta oculis ejus. Est in omnibus per essentiam in quantum adest omnibus ut causa essendi sicut dictum est." Quenstedt says,[3] "Est Deus ubique illocaliter, impartibiliter, efficaciter ; non definitive ut spiritus, non circumscriptive ut corpora, sed repletivè citra sui multiplicationem, extensionem, divisionem, inclusionem, aut commixtionem more modoque divino incomprehensibili." The Bible teaches the infinitude of God, as involving his immensity and omnipresence, in the clearest terms. He is said to fill all in all, *i. e.*, the universe in all its parts. (Eph. i. 23.) " Am I a God at hand, saith the Lord, and not a God afar off? Can any hide himself in secret places that I shall not see him ? saith the Lord. Do not I fill heaven and earth ? saith the Lord." (Jer. xxiii. 23, 24.) " Whither shall I go from thy Spirit ? or whither shall I flee from thy presence ? If I ascend up into heaven, thou art there : if I make my bed in hell, behold, thou art there. If I take the wings of the morning, and dwell in the uttermost parts of the sea ; even there shall thy hand lead me, and thy right hand shall hold me." (Ps. cxxxix. 7–12.) It is " in Him we (*i. e.*, all creatures) live, and move, and have our being." (Acts xvii. 28.) Everywhere in the Old and in the New Testament, God is repre-

1 *De Præsentia Dei seu Epistola* clxxxvii. iv. 14, edit. Benedictines, vol. ii. p. 1023, d.
2 *Summa*, i. viii. 3, edit. Cologne, 1640, p. 16.
3 *Theologia*, i. viii. § 1, p. 413.

sented as a spiritual Being, without form, invisible, whom no man hath seen or can see; dwelling in the light which no man can approach unto, and full of glory; as not only the creator, and preserver, but as the governor of all things; as everywhere present, and everywhere imparting life, and securing order; present in every blade of grass, yet guiding Arcturus in his course, marshalling the stars as a host, calling them by their names; present also in every human soul, giving it understanding, endowing it with gifts, working in it both to will and to do. The human heart is in his hands; and He turneth it even as the rivers of water are turned. Whereever, throughout the universe, there is evidence of mind in material causes, there, according to the Scriptures, is God, controlling and guiding those causes to the accomplishment of his wise designs. He is in all, and over all things; yet essentially different from all, being over all, independent, and infinitely exalted. This immensity and omnipresence of God, therefore, is the ubiquity of the divine essence, and consequently of the divine power, wisdom, and goodness. As the birds in the air and the fish in the sea, so also are we always surrounded and sustained by God. It is thus that He is infinite in his being, without absorbing all created beings into his own essence, but sustaining all in their individual subsistence, and in the exercise of their own powers.

§ 6. *Eternity.*

A. *Scriptural Doctrine.*

The infinitude of God relatively to space, is his immensity or omnipresence; relatively to duration, it is his eternity. As He is free from all the limitations of space, so He is exalted above all the limitations of time. As He is not more in one place than in another, but is everywhere equally present, so He does not exist during one period of duration more than another. With Him there is no distinction between the present, past, and future; but all things are equally and always present to Him. With Him duration is an eternal now. This is the popular and the Scriptural view of God's eternity. "Before the mountains were brought forth, or ever thou hadst formed the earth and the world, even from everlasting to everlasting thou art God." (Ps. xc. 2.) "Of old hast thou laid the foundation of the earth: and the heavens are he work of thy hands. They shall perish, but thou shalt endure: yea, all of them shall wax old like a garment; as a vesture shalt thou change them, and they shall be changed: but thou art the

same, and thy years shall have no end." (Ps. cii. 25–27.)   He is
" The high and lofty One that inhabiteth eternity." (Is. lvii. 15.)
" I am the first and I am the last; and besides me there is no
God." (Is. xliv. 6.)   " A thousand years in thy sight are but as
yesterday when it is past." (Ps. xc. 4.)   " One day is with the
Lord as a thousand years, and a thousand years as one day."
(2 Pet. iii. 8.)   He is " the same yesterday, and to-day, and forever." (Heb. xiii. 8.)   God is He " which is [ever is], and which
was, and which is to come." (Rev. i. 4.)   Throughout the Bible
He is called the eternal or everlasting God; who only hath immortality.   The primal revelation of Himself to his covenant people
was as the " I am."

What is taught in these and similar passages, is, first, that God
is without beginning of years or end of days.   He is, and always
has been, and always will be; and secondly, that to Him there is
neither past nor future ; that the past and the future are always
and equally present to Him.

B. *Philosophical View.*

These are Scriptural facts, and necessarily follow from the nature
of God as self-existent, infinite, and immutable.   With these representations the teaching of theologians for the most part agrees.
Thus Augustine says: "Fuisse et futurum esse non est in ea [*scil.*
vita divina], sed esse solum, quoniam æterna est : nam fuisse et futurum esse non est æternum." [1]   " Nec tu tempore tempora præcedis, alioquin non omnia tempora præcederes sed præcedis omnia
præterita celsitudine semper præsentis æternitatis ; et superas omnia
futura, quia illa futura sunt et cum venerint præterita erunt ; tu
autem idem ipse es, et anni tui non deficiunt." [2]   Aquinas, to the
same effect says, " Æternitas est tota simul." [3]   Or, as the schoolmen generally were accustomed to say, " In æternitate est unicum
instans semper præsens et persistens ; " or, as they otherwise expressed it, " Eternitas est interminabilis vitæ simul et perfecta
possessio."   The same view of this attribute is given by the later
theologians.   Thus Quenstedt says, " Æternitas Dei est duratio
vel permanentia essentiæ divinæ interminabilis, sine principio et fine
carens, et indivisibilis, omnem omnino successionem excludens." [4]

The only thing open to question in these statements is, the denial of all succession in the divine consciousness.   Our idea of

---

1 *Confessiones*, IX. x. 24, edit. Benedictines, vol. i. p. 283, c.
2 *Ibid.* XI. xiii. 16, p. 338, a.   3 *Summa*, I. x. 4, edit. Cologne, 1640, p. 16.
4 *Theologia*, I. viii. § I. xvii. p. 413.

eternity is arrived at from our idea of time. We are conscious of
existence in space, and we are conscious of protracted or continuous existence. The ideas of space and duration are necessarily
given in the consciousness of continuous existence. We see also that
events succeed each other, that their occurrence is separated by a
longer or shorter period of duration, just as bodies are separated by
a greater or less interval in space. We therefore know, from consciousness or from experience, of no kind of duration which is not
successive. Instead of saying, as is commonly done, that time is duration measured by succession, which supposes that duration is antecedent to that by which it is measured, and independent of it, it is
maintained by some that duration without succession is inconceivable and impossible. As space is defined to be " negation betwixt the
boundary-lines of form," so time is said to be " the negation betwixt
the boundary-points of motion." Or, in other words, time is " the
interval which a body in motion marks in its transit from one point
of space to another." [1] Hence, if there be no bodies having form,
there is no space ; and if there is no motion, there is no time. " If
all things were annihilated, time as well as space must be annihilated ;
for time is dependent on space. If all things were annihilated, there
could be no transition, no succession of one object with respect to
another ; for there would be no object in being, — all would be
perfect emptiness, nothingness, non-being-ness. Under an entire
annihilation, there could be neither space nor time." [2] The same
writer [3] elsewhere says, " Were the earth, as well as the other
globes of space, annihilated, much more would time be annihilated
therewith." [4] All this, however, is to be understood, it is said,
of "objective time, that is, of time as dependent upon created
material conditions." [5] As objective timelessness follows from the
annihilation of material existences, so timelessness as regards
thinking personalities is conceivable only on the destruction of
thought. " We have seen that there can be a state of timelessness for material creation, only by destroying its operation, that is,
its attribute of motion : precisely in analogy therewith, there can
be a state of timelessness for intellectual creation, only by destroying the laws of intellect, that is, its operation of thinking." [6] If,
therefore, God be a person, or a thinking Being, He cannot be

[1] Jamieson, p. 199.   [2] *Ibid.* p. 163.
[3] Rev. George Jamieson, M. A., one of the ministers of the parish of Old Machar, Aber-
deen. *The Essentials of Philosophy, wherein its constituent Principles are traced throughout
the various Departments of Science with analytical Strictures on the Views of some of our
leading Philosophers.*
[4] *Ibid.* p. 200.   [5] *Ibid.*   [6] *Ibid*

timeless ; there must be succession ; one thought or state must follow another.   To deny this, it is said, is to deny the personality of
God.   The dictum, therefore, of the schoolmen, and of the theologians, that eternity precludes succession — that it is a persistent,
unmoving Now — is according to this repudiated.

There are, however, two senses in which succession is denied to
God.   The first has reference to external events.   They are ever
present to the mind of God.   He views them in all their relations,
whether causal or chronological.   He sees how they succeed each
other in time, as we see a passing pageant, all of which we may
take in in one view.   In this there is perhaps nothing which absolutely transcends our comprehension.   The second aspect of the
subject concerns the relation of succession to the thoughts and acts
of God.   When we are ignorant, it is wise to be silent.   We
have no right to affirm or deny, when we cannot know what our
affirmation or denial may involve or imply.   We know that God
is constantly producing new effects, effects which succeed each
other in time ; but we do not know that these effects are due to
successive exercises of the divine efficiency.   It is, indeed, incomprehensible to us how it should be otherwise.   The miracles of
Christ were due to the immediate exercise of the divine efficiency.
We utter words to which we can attach no meaning, when we say
that these effects were due, not to a contemporaneous act or volition of the divine mind, but to an eternal act, if such a phrase be
not a solecism.   In like manner we are confounded when we are
told that our prayers are not heard and answered in time — that
God is timeless — that what He does in hearing and answering
prayer, and in his daily providence, He does from eternity.   It is
certain that God is subject to all the limitations of personality, if
there be any.   But as such limitations are the conditions of his
being a person and not a mere involuntary force, they are the conditions of his infinite perfection.   As constant thought and activity are involved in the very nature of a spirit, these must belong
to God; and so far as thinking and acting involve succession,
succession must belong to God.   There are mysteries connected
with chronological succession, in our nature, which we cannot
explain.   We know that in dreams months may be compressed
into moments, and moments extended to months, so far as our consciousness is concerned.   We know that it often happens to those
near death, that all the past becomes instantly present.   Had God
so constituted us that memory was as vivid as present consciousness, there would to us be no past, so far as our personal exist-

ence is concerned. It is not impossible that, hereafter, memory may become a consciousness of the past; that all we ever thought, felt, or did, may be ever present to the mind; that everything written on that tablet is indelible. Persons who, by long residence in foreign countries, have entirely lost all knowledge of their native language, have been known to speak it fluently, and understand it perfectly, when they came to die. Still more wonderful is the fact, that uneducated persons, hearing passages read in an unknown language (Greek or Hebrew, for example), have, years after, when in an abnormal, nervous state, repeated those passages correctly, without understanding their meaning. If unable to comprehend ourselves, we should not pretend to be able to comprehend God. Whether we can understand how there can be succession in the thoughts of Him who inhabits eternity or not, we are not to deny that God is an intelligent Being, that He actually thinks and feels, in order to get over the difficulty. God is a person, and all that personality implies must be true of Him.

Modern Philosophical Views.

The modern philosophy teaches that " Die Ewigkeit ist die Einheit in dem Unterschiede der Zeitmomente — Ewigkeit und Zeit verhalten sich wie die Substanz und deren Accidentien." [1] That is, Eternity is the unity underlying the successive moments of time, as substance is the unity underlying the accidents which are its manifestations. Schleiermacher's illustration is borrowed from our consciousness. We are conscious of an abiding, unchanging self, which is the subject of our ever changing thoughts and feelings. By the eternity of God, therefore, is meant nothing more than that He is the ground-being of which the universe is the ever changing phenomenon. The eternity of God is only one phase of his universal causality. " Unter der Ewigkeit Gottes verstehen wir die mit allem Zeitlichen auch die Zeit selbst bedingende schlechthin zeitlose Ursächlichkeit Gottes." [2] To attain this philosophical view of eternity, we must accept the philosophical view of the nature of God upon which it is founded, namely, that God is merely the designation of that unknown and unknowable something of which all other things are the manifestations. To give up the living, personal God of the Bible and of the heart, is an awful sacrifice to specious, logical consistency. We believe what we cannot understand. We believe what the Bible teaches as

---

[1] Strauss, *Dogmatik*, i. p. 561.
[2] *Christliche Glaube*, I. § 52, *Werke*, edit. Berlin, 1842, vol. iii p. 268.

facts; that God always is, was, and ever will be, immutably the same; that all things are ever present to his view; that with Him there is neither past nor future; but nevertheless that He is not a stagnant ocean, but ever living, ever thinking, ever acting, and ever suiting his action to the exigencies of his creatures, and to the accomplishment of his infinitely wise designs. Whether we can harmonize these facts or not, is a matter of minor importance. We are constantly called upon to believe that things are, without being able to tell how they are, or even how they can be.

§ 7. *Immutability.*

The immutability of God is intimately connected with his immensity and eternity, and is frequently included with them in the Scriptural statements concerning his nature. Thus, when it is said, He is the First and the Last; the Alpha and Omega, the same yesterday, to-day, and forever; or when in contrast with the ever changing and perishing world, it is said: " They shall be changed, but thou art the same; " it is not his eternity more than his immutability that is brought into view. As an infinite and absolute Being, self-existent and absolutely independent, God is exalted above all the causes of and even above the possibility of change. Infinite space and infinite duration cannot change. They must ever be what they are. So God is absolutely immutable in his essence and attributes. He can neither increase nor decrease. He is subject to no process of development, or of self-evolution. His knowledge and power can never be greater or less. He can never be wiser or holier, or more righteous or more merciful than He ever has been and ever must be. He is no less immutable in his plans and purposes. Infinite in wisdom, there can be no error in their conception; infinite in power, there can be no failure in their accomplishment. He is " the Father of lights, with whom is no variableness, neither shadow of turning." (James i. 17.) " God is not a man that He should lie; neither the son of man that He should repent; hath He said and shall He not do it? or hath He spoken, and shall He not make it good? " (Num. xxiii. 19.) " I am the Lord, I change not." (Mal. iii. 6.) " The counsel of the Lord standeth forever; the thoughts of his heart to all generations." (Ps. xxxiii. 11.) " There are many devices in a man's heart; nevertheless, the counsel of the Lord, that shall stand." (Prov. xix. 21.) " The Lord of Hosts hath sworn, saying, Surely as I have thought, so shall it come to pass; and as I have purposed, so shall it stand." (Is. xiv. 24.) " I am God, and there is none like me, declaring the end from the beginning, and from ancient times the things that are not yet done, saying, My counsel shall stand, and I will do all my pleasure." (Is. xlvi. 9, 10.) Those passages of Scripture in which God is said to repent, are to be interpreted on the same principle as those in which He is said to ride upon the wings of the wind, or to walk through the earth. These create no difficulty.

Philosophical Statement.

Theologians, in their attempts to state, in philosophical language, the doctrine of the Bible on the unchangeableness of God, are apt to confound immutability with immobility. In denying that God can change, they seem to deny that He can act. Augustine says, on this subject: "Non invenies in Deo aliquid mutabilitatis; non aliquid, quod aliter nunc sit, aliter paulo ante fuerit. Nam ubi invenis aliter et aliter, facta est ibi quædam mors: mors enim est, non esse quod fuit." [1] Quenstedt uses language still more open to objection, when he says that the immutability of God is "Perpetua essentiæ divinæ et omnium ejus perfectionum identitas, negans omnem omnino motum cum physicum, tum ethicum." [2] Turrettin is more cautious, and yet perhaps goes too far. He says: "Potestas variandi actus suos, non est principium mutabilitatis in se, sed tantum in objectis suis; nisi intelligatur *de variatione internorum suorum actuum*, quos voluntas perfecta non variat, sed imperfecta tantum." [3] The clause italicized in the above quotation assumes a knowledge of the nature of God to which man has no legitimate claim. It is in vain for us to presume to understand the Almighty to perfection. We know that God is immutable in his being, his perfections, and his purposes; and we know that He is perpetually active. And, therefore, activity and immutability must be compatible; and no explanation of the latter inconsistent with the former ought to be admitted.

The Absolute Attributes of God not inconsistent with Personality.

These attributes of infinity, eternity, and immutability, are freely admitted by the modern philosophy to belong to the absolute Being. But it is maintained that such a Being cannot be a person. Personality implies self-consciousness. Self-consciousness necessarily implies limitation, a distinction between the self and the not-self. Ohne Du kein Ich, — unless there be something objective

---

[1] *In Joannis Evangelium Tractatus*, xxiii. 9, edit. Benedictines, vol iii. p. 1952, b, c.

[2] *Theologia*, i. viii. § i. xx. p. 414.

[3] Locus iii. xi. 9, edit. Edinburgh, 1847, vol. i. p. 186

and independent to which we stand opposed, as subject and object, there can be no consciousness of self. But nothing can be thus objective and independent in relation to the Absolute; and, therefore, the Absolute cannot have any consciousness of self, and consequently cannot be a personal Being. We have already seen (chap. iv.) that this objection is founded on an arbitrary definition of the Infinite and Absolute. It assumes that the Infinite must be all, and that the Absolute must be alone, without relation to anything out of itself. It is here only necessary to remark, in reference to the objection, (1.) That it may be admitted as a fact that the slumbering consciousness of self in the human soul is awakened and developed by contact with what is not only external to itself but also independent of it. But God is not subject to that law. He is eternally perfect and immutable; having in Himself the plenitude of life. There is, therefore, no analogy between the cases, and no ground for inferring in this case that what is true in us, who begin life as an undeveloped germ, must be true in relation to God. (2.) In the second place, we have no right to assume that even with regard to a finite intelligence created in the perfection of its being, self-consciousness is dependent on what is independent of itself. Such a being would of necessity be conscious of its own thoughts and feelings; for thought is a state of consciousness in an intelligent being. If God, therefore, can make an intelligent being in the perfection of its limited nature, it would be self-conscious even were it left alone in the universe. (3.) Admitting it to be true that " without a Thou there can be no I," we know that, according to the Scriptures and the faith of the Church universal, there are in the unity of the Godhead three distinct persons, the Father, the Son, and the Spirit; so that from eternity the Father can say I, and the Son Thou.

We must abide by the teachings of Scripture, and refuse to subordinate their authority and the intuitive convictions of our moral and religious nature to the arbitrary definitions of any philosophical system. The Bible everywhere teaches that God is an absolute Being, in the sense of being self-existent, necessary, independent, immutable, eternal, and without limitation or necessary relation to anything out of Himself. It teaches moreover that He is infinite; not in the sense of including all being, all power, all knowledge in Himself, to the exclusion of all other intelligent agents; but in the sense that no limit can be assigned to his being or perfections, other than that which arises out of his own perfection itself. He would cease to be infinite could He be unwise or untrue. It is to be remembered that God is infinite and absolute as a spirit, and a spirit from its nature is living, active, intelligent, self-conscious, and personal.

§ 8. *Knowledge.*

A. *Its Nature.*

By knowledge is meant the intellectual apprehension of truth. It supposes a subject and object; an intelligent subject that apprehends, and something true that is apprehended.

So far as we are concerned, knowledge is either intuitive or discursive. Our senses give us immediate knowledge of their appropriate objects; the understanding perceives intuitively primary truths; our moral and æsthetic nature gives us the immediate cognition of things right or wrong, and beautiful or deformed. Most of our knowledge, however, is derived *ab extra*, by instruction, observation, comparison, deduction, etc. In all cases there is the distinction between the mind which perceives and the object which is perceived.

Such being the nature of knowledge, can there be knowledge in God? Can there be this distinction between subject and object in an absolute and infinite Being? Not only are the wicked and the worldly disposed to think that God cannot know; that either He is too exalted to take cognizance of earthly things; or that it is impossible even for an infinite mind to embrace the universe and all its perpetual changes in his mental vision; but the possibility of knowledge, in the ordinary and proper sense of the word, is expressly denied to God by a large class of philosophers, and virtually even by many theologians of the highest rank in the history of the Church.

The Pantheistic Theory precludes the possibility of Knowledge in God.

1. As, according to the pantheistic theory, the universe is the existence form of God, as the infinite comes to intelligent consciousness and life only in the finite, there is and can be no knowledge in the infinite as distinguished from the finite. God lives only so far as finite beings live; He thinks and knows only so far as they think and know. Omniscience is only the sum or aggregate of the intelligence of the transient forms of finite beings. All this, as even Hamilton and Mansel admit, necessarily flows from the idea of an absolute Being which precludes the possibility of any such

conditions or relations as are involved in consciousness or intelligence. Strauss therefore says:[1] "Not in Himself, but in finite intelligences is God omniscient, which together constitute the fulness or completeness of all the possible forms or degrees of knowledge." And Spinoza says:[2] "Intellectus et voluntas, qui Dei essentiam constituerent, a nostro intellectu et voluntate toto cœlo differe deberent, nec in ulla re, præterquam in nomine, convenire possent; non aliter scilicet, quam inter se conveniunt canis, signum cœleste, et canis, animal latrans." This subject was considered in the chapter on Pantheism.

Knowledge and Power not to be confounded.

2. The possibility of knowledge in God is virtually denied by those who deny any distinction between knowledge and power. Knowledge, which is power, ceases to be knowledge; and therefore if omniscience is only a different name for omnipotence, it ceases to be a distinct attribute of God. It makes little difference whether we expressly deny a given perfection to God, or whether we so determine it as to make it mean nothing distinctive. It is deeply to be regretted that not only the Fathers, but also the Lutheran and Reformed theologians, after renouncing the authority of the schoolmen, almost immediately yielded themselves to their speculations. Instead of determining the nature of the divine attributes from the representations of Scripture and from the constitution of man as the image of God, and from the necessities of our moral and religious nature, they allowed themselves to be controlled by *à priori* speculations as to the nature of the infinite and absolute. Even Augustine, as before stated, says: "Nos ista, quæ fecisti videmus, quia sunt: tu autem quia vides ea, sunt."[3] And Scotus Erigena says,[4] "Voluntas illius et visio et essentia unum est."[5] . . . . "Visio Dei totius universitatis est conditio. Non enim aliud est ei videre, aliud facere; sed visio illius voluntas ejus est, et voluntas operatio." Thomas Aquinas also says,[6] "Deus per intellectum suum causat res, cum suum esse sit suum intelligere. Unde necesse est, quod sua scientia sit causa rerum."

The Lutheran and Reformed theologians represent God as *simplicissima simplicitas*, admitting of no distinction between faculty and act, or between one attribute and another. Thus Gerhard

---

1 *Dogmatik*, i. p. 575.
2 *Ethices*, i. xvii. Scholium, edit. Jena, 1803, vol. ii. p. 53.
3 *Confessiones*, xiii. xxxviii. 53, edit. Benedictines, vol. i. p. 410, b.
4 *De Divisione Naturæ*, iii. 17, p. 235.
5 *Ibid.* 29, p. 264.   6 *Summa*, i. xiv. 8, edit. Cologne, 1640, p. 36.

says: "Deus est ipsum esse subsistens, omnibus modis indetermi-
natum."[1] "Solus Deus summe simplex est, ut nec actus et poten-
tiæ, nec esse et essentiæ compositio ipsi competat."[2] "Essentia,
bonitas, potentia, sapientia, justitia, et reliqua attributa omnia sunt
in Deo realiter unum.[3] He also says: "In Deo idem est esse et
intelligere et velle." In like manner the Reformed theologian
Heidegger[4] says: "Voluntas ab intellectu non differt, quia intelli-
gendo vult et volendo intelligit. Intelligere et velle ejus idemque
perpetuus indivisus actus." This does not mean simply that in an
intelligent being, every act of the will is an intelligent act. He
knows while he wills, and knows what he wills. The meaning is,
that knowledge and power in God are identical. To know a thing
is, and to will it, are the same undivided and perpetual act. From
this it would seem to follow, that as God knows from eternity He
creates from eternity ; and that "all He knows, is." We are thus
led, by these speculations, into pantheistical views of the nature
of God and of his relation to the world.

This mode of representation is carried still further by the modern philosophical theologians. With Schleiermacher, all the attributes of God are virtually merged into the idea of causality. With
him God is *ens summum prima causa*.[5] He says that God's thinking and willing are the same, and that his omnipotence and omniscience are identical. When we say that He is omnipotent, we
only mean that He is the cause of all that is. And when we say
that He is omniscient, we only mean that He is an intelligent
cause. His power and knowledge are limited to the actual. The
possible is nothing ; it is the object neither of knowledge nor of
power. "Gott," says Schleiermacher, "weiss Alles was ist; und
Alles ist, was Gott weiss und dieses beides ist nicht zweierlei sondern einerlei, weil sein Wissen und sein allmächtiges Wollen eines
und dasselbe ist," *i. e.*, God knows all that is, and all is that God
knows. God, therefore, is limited to the world, which is the phenomenon of which He is the substance.

Another philosophical view of this subject, adopted even by
those who repudiate the pantheistic system and maintain that God
and the world are distinct, is, that as God is immanent in the
world, there is in Him no difference between self-consciousness and
world-consciousness, as they express it, *i. e.*, between God's knowledge of Himself and his knowledge of the world. They therefore

---

[1] Tom. i. loc. iii. cap. vi. § 43, p. 106, edit. Tübingen, 1762.
[2] *Ibid.* cap. x. § 80, p. 119.　　　　　　[3] *Ibid.* chap. vii. § 47, p. 108.
[4] *Corpus Theologiæ Christianæ,* Tiguri, 1732.
[5] *Christliche Glaube,* i. § 55, *Werke,* edit. Berlin, 1842, vol. iii. p. 295.

define omniscience by saying, " Insofern Gott gedacht wird als die Welt mit seinem Bewusstseyn umfassend, nennen wir ihn den Allwissenden." [1]   That is, " So far as we conceive of God as embracing the world in his consciousness, we call him omniscient." Whatever such language may mean to those who use it, to the ordinary mind it conveys the revolting idea that all the sins of men enter into the consciousness of God.

The Doctrine of the Scriptures on this Subject.

The Scriptural view of this subject, which distinguishes the attributes in God as distinct, and assumes that knowledge in Him, in its essential nature, is what knowledge is in us, does not conflict with the unity and simplicity of God as a spiritual being.   There is a sense in which knowledge and power, intellect and will, may be said to be identical in man.   They are not different substances. They are different modes in which the life or activity of the soul manifests itself.   So in God when we conceive of Him as a spirit, we do not think of Him as a compound being, but as manifesting his infinite life and activity, in knowing, willing, and doing.   What, therefore, we must hold fast to, if we would hold fast to God, is, that knowledge in God is knowledge, and not power or eternity ; that it is what knowledge is in us, not indeed in its modes and objects, but in its essential nature.   We must remove from our conceptions of the divine attributes all the limitations and imperfections which belong to the corresponding attributes in us ; but we are not to destroy their nature.   And in determining what is, and what is not, consistent with the nature of God as an infinitely perfect being, we are to be controlled by the teachings of the Scriptures, and by the necessities (or laws) of our moral and religious nature, and not by our speculative notions of the Infinite and Absolute. God, therefore, does and can know in the ordinary and proper sense of that word.   He is an ever present eye, to which all things are perfectly revealed.   " All things," says the Apostle, " are naked and opened unto the eyes of Him with whom we have to do." (Heb. iv. 13.)   " The darkness and the light are both alike " to Him.   (Ps. cxxxix. 12.)   " He that planted the ear, shall he not hear ? He that formed the eye, shall he not see ? " (Ps. xciv. 9.)   " O Lord thou hast searched me, and known me.   Thou knowest my down-sitting and my up-rising, thou understandest my thought afar off." (Ps. cxxxix. 1, 2.)   " The eyes of the LORD are in every place, beholding the evil and the good."

---

[1] Bruch, *Die Lehre von den göttlichen Eigenschaften*, p. 162.

(Prov. xv. 3.) " Hell and destruction are before the Lord: how much more then the hearts of the children of men ? " (Prov. xv. 11.) " Great is our Lord and of great power : his understanding is infinite." (Ps. cxlvii. 5.) " O house of Israel, ... I know the things that come into your mind, every one of them." (Ezek. xi. 5.) " Known unto God are all his works from the beginning of the world." (Acts. xv. 18.) " The very hairs of your head are all numbered." (Matt. x. 30.)

This knowledge of God is not only all-comprehending, but it is intuitive and immutable. He knows all things as they are, being as being, phenomena as phenomena, the possible as possible, the actual as actual, the necessary as necessary, the free as free, the past as past, the present as present, the future as future. Although all things are ever present in his view, yet He sees them as successive in time. The vast procession of events, thoughts, feelings, and acts, stands open to his view.

This infinite knowledge of God is not only clearly and constantly asserted in Scripture, but is also obviously included in the idea of an absolutely perfect being. Such a being cannot be ignorant of anything ; his knowledge can neither be increased nor diminished. The omniscience of God follows also from his omnipresence. As God fills heaven and earth, all things are transacted in his presence. He knows our thoughts far better than they are known to ourselves. This plenitude of divine knowledge is taken for granted in all acts of worship. We pray to a God who, we believe, knows our state and wants, who hears what we say, and who is able to meet all our necessities. Unless God were thus omniscient, He could not judge the world in righteousness. Faith in this attribute in its integrity is, therefore, essential even to natural religion.

B. *The Objects of Divine Knowledge.*

Various distinctions are made by theologians as to the objects of the divine knowledge.

1. God is said to know Himself and all things out of Himself. This is the foundation of the distinction between the *scientia necessaria* and the *scientia libera.* God knows Himself by the necessity of his nature ; but as everything out of Himself depends for its existence or occurrence upon his will, his knowledge of each thing as an actual occurrence is suspended on his will, and in that sense is free. Creation not being necessary, it depended on the will of God whether the universe as an object of knowledge should exist or not. This distinction is not of much importance. And it is

liable to the objection that it makes the knowledge of God dependent. Being the cause of all things, God knows everything by knowing Himself; all things possible, by the knowledge of his power, and all things actual, by the knowledge of his own purposes.

2. This distinction between the possible and actual, is the foundation of the distinction between the knowledge of simple intelligence and the knowledge of vision. The former is founded on God's power, and the latter upon his will. This only means that, in virtue of his omniscient intelligence, He knows whatever infinite power can effect; and that from the consciousness of his own purposes, He knows what He has determined to effect or to permit to occur. This is a distinction which the modern philosophical theologians ignore. Nothing, according to their philosophy is possible, but the actual. All that can be, either is, or is to be. This follows from the idea of God as mere cause. He produces all that can be; and there is in Him no causality for what does not exist.

The Actual and the Possible.

It seems to be an inconsistency in those orthodox theologians who deny the distinction in God between knowledge and power, to admit, as they all do, the distinction between the actual and possible. For if God creates by thinking or knowing, if in Him, as they say, *intelligere et facere idem est,* then all He knows must be, and must be as soon as He knows or thinks it, *i. e.,* from eternity. If, however, we retain the Scriptural idea of God as a spirit, who can do more than He does; if we ascribe to Him what we know to be a perfection in ourselves, namely, that our power exceeds our acts, that a faculty and the exercise of that faculty are not identical, then we can understand how God can know the possible as well as the actual. God is not limited to the universe, which of necessity is finite. God has not exhausted Himself in determining to cause the present order of things to be.

C. *Scientia Media.*

Intermediate between things possible and actual, some theologians assume a third class of events, namely, the conditionally future. They do not actually occur, but they would occur provided something else should occur. Had Christ come a thousand years sooner than the date of his actual advent, the whole history of the world would have been different. This is a popular mode of regarding the concatenation of events. It is constantly said, that if Cromwell had been permitted to leave England; or, if Napoleon had failed to escape from Elba, the state of Europe would have been very different from what it is at present. God, it is assumed, knows what would have been the sequence of events on any or every possible hypothesis. It is therefore said that there must be in God, besides the knowledge of simple intelligence by which He knows the possible, and the knowledge of vision by which He knows the actual, a *scientia media*, by which He knows the conditionally future. Illustrations of this form of knowledge, it is thought, are found in Scripture. In 1 Samuel xxiii. 11, it is said that David inquired of the Lord whether the men of Keilah would deliver him, should he remain among them, into the hands of Saul ; and was answered that they would. Here, it is argued, the event was not merely possible, but conditionally certain. If David remained in Keilah, he certainly would have been delivered up. Thus our Lord said, that if his mighty works had been done in Tyre and Sidon, the people of those cities would have repented. Here again is declared what would have happened, if something else had happened.

The Origin of this Distinction.

This distinction was introduced into theology by the Jesuit theologians Fonseca and Molina ; by the latter in his work " De Concordia Providentiæ et Gratiæ Divinæ cum Libero Arbitrio Hominis." Their object was to reconcile the foreordination of God with the freedom of man, and to explain the reason why some, and not others, were elected to eternal life. God foresaw who would repent and believe, if they received the knowledge of the Gospel and the gift of the Spirit, and these He elected to salvation. This theory of a *scientia media* was, for a like purpose, adopted by the Lutheran and Remonstrant theologians, but was strenuously opposed by the Reformed or Augustinians. (1.) Because all events are included under the categories of the actual and possible ; and, therefore, there is no room for such a class as events conditionally future. It is only possible, and not certain, how men would act under certain conditions, if their conduct be not predetermined, either by the purpose of God, or by their own decision already formed. Besides, it is the fundamental principle of the theologians who adopt this theory, or at least of many of them, that a free act must from its nature be uncertain as to its occurrence. A free agent, it is said, can always act contrary to any amount of influence brought to bear upon him, consistent with his free agency. But if free acts must be uncertain, they cannot be foreseen as certain under any conditions. (2.) The futurition of events, according to the Scriptures, depends on the foreordination of God, who foreordains whatever comes to pass. There is no certainty, therefore, which does not depend on the divine purpose. (3.) The kind of knowledge which this theory supposes cannot belong to God, because it is inferential. It is deduced from a consideration of second causes and their influence, and therefore is inconsistent with the perfection of God, whose knowledge is not discursive, but independent and intuitive. (4.) This theory is inconsistent with the Scriptural doctrine of God's providential government, as it assumes that the free acts of men are not under his control. (5.) It is contrary to the Scriptural doctrine, inasmuch as it supposes that election to salvation depends on the foresight of faith and repentance, whereas it depends on the good pleasure of God. (6.) The examples quoted from the Bible do not prove that there is a *scientia media* in God. The answer of God to David, about the men of Keilah, was simply a revelation of the purpose which they had already formed. Our Lord's declaration concerning Tyre and Sidon was only a figurative mode of stating the fact that the men of his generation were more hardened than the inhabitants of those ancient cities. It is not denied that God knows all events in all possible combinations and connections, but as nothing is certain but what He ordains to effect or permit, there can be no class of events conditionally future, and therefore there can be no *scientia media*. By conditionally future is meant what is suspended on a condition undetermined by God.

D. *Foreknowledge.*

Among the objects of the divine knowledge are the free acts of men. The Scriptures abundantly teach that such acts are foreknown. Such knowledge is involved in the prediction of events which either concern the free acts of men, or are dependent on them. If God be ignorant of how free agents will act, his knowledge must be limited, and it must be constantly increasing, which is altogether inconsistent with the true idea of his nature. His government of the world also, in that case, must be precarious, dependent, as it would then be on the unforeseen conduct of men. The Church, therefore, in obedience to the Scriptures, has, almost with one voice, professed faith in God's foreknowledge of the free acts of his creatures.

The Socinians, however, and some of the Remonstrants, unable to reconcile this foreknowledge with human liberty, deny that free acts can be foreknown. As the omnipotence of God is his ability to do whatever is possible, so his omniscience is his knowledge of everything knowable. But as free acts are in their nature uncertain, as they may or may not be, they cannot be known before they occur. Such is the argument of Socinus. This whole difficulty arises out of the assumption that contingency is essential to free agency. If an act may be certain as to its occurrence, and yet free as to the mode of its occurrence, the difficulty vanishes. That free acts may be absolutely certain, is plain, because they have in a multitude of cases been predicted. It was certain that the acts of Christ would be holy, yet they were free. The continued holiness of the saints in heaven is certain, and yet they are perfectly free. The foreknowledge of God is inconsistent with a false theory of free agency, but not with the true doctrine on that subject.

After Augustine, the common way of meeting the difficulty of reconciling foreknowledge with liberty, was to represent it as merely subjective. The distinction between knowledge and foreknowledge is only in us. There is no such difference in God. " Quid est præscientia," asks Augustine, " nisi scientia futurorum ? Quid autem futurum est Deo, qui omnia supergreditur tempora ? Si enim scientia Dei res ipsas habet, non sunt ei futuræ, sed præsentes, ac per hoc non jam præscientia, sed tantum scientia dici potest." [1]

E. *The Wisdom of God.*

Wisdom and knowledge are intimately related. The former is manifested in the selection of proper ends, and of proper means for the accomplishment of those ends. As there is abundant evidence of design in the works of nature, so all the works of God declare his wisdom. They show, from the most minute to the greatest, the most wonderful adaptation of means to accomplish the high end of the good of his creatures and the manifestation of his own glory. So also, in the whole course of history, we see evidence of the controlling power of God making all things work together for the best interests of his people, and the promotion of his kingdom upon earth. It is, however, in the work of redemption that this divine attribute is specially revealed. It is by the Church, that God has determined to manifest, through all ages, to principalities and powers, his manifold wisdom.

Of course those who deny final causes deny that there is any such attribute as wisdom in God. It is also said that the use of

---

[1] *De Diversis Quæstionibus ad Simplicianum*, II. ii. 2, edit. Benedictines, vol. vi. p. 195, a. Compare also what he says on this subject, *De Civitate Dei*, XI. xxi.: *Ibid.* vol. vii. p. 461.

means to attain an end is a manifestation of weakness. It is further urged that it is derogatory to God, as it supposes that He needs or desires what He does not possess. Even Schleiermacher says; " Bei Gott is Allwissenheit und Weisheit so gänzlich einerlei, dass die Unterscheidung keinen Werth hat, die Weisheit wäre nichts als auch wider absolute Lebendigkeit der Allmacht, also Alwissenheit." Wisdom is omniscience, omniscience is omnipotence, omnipotence is simply causality of all that is. Thus God sinks into the mere cause or ground of all things. It is not thus the Scriptures speak. We are called on to worship, " The only wise God." " O Lord, how manifold are thy works ! in wisdom hast Thou made them all," is the devout exclamation of the Psalmist. (Ps. civ. 24.) And in contemplation of the work of redemption the Apostle exclaims, " O the depth of the riches both of the wisdom and knowledge of God ! " (Rom. xi. 33.)

§ 9. *The Will of God.*
A. *The Meaning of the Term.*

If God is a spirit He must possess all the essential attributes of a spirit. Those attributes, according to the classification adopted by the older philosophers and theologians, fall under the heads of intelligence and will. To the former, are referred knowledge and wisdom ; to the latter, the power of self-determination, efficiency (in the case of God, omnipotence), and all moral attributes. In this wide sense of the word, the will of God includes: (1.) The will in the narrow sense of the word. (2.) His power. (3.) His love and all his moral perfections. In our day, generally but not always, the word " will " is limited to the faculty of self-determination. And even the older theologians in treating of the will of God treat only of his decrees or purposes. In their definitions, however, they take the word in its wide sense. Thus Calovius[1] says, " Voluntas Dei est, qua Deus tendit in bonum ab intellectu cognitum." And Quenstedt defines it as "ipsa Dei essentia cum connotatione inclinationis ad bonum concepta."[2] Turrettin says, the object of the intellect is the true; the object of the will, the good. Hence it is said, that God wills Himself necessarily, and all things out of Himself freely. Although the word seems to be taken in different senses in the same sentence, God's willing Himself means that He takes complacency in his own infinite excellence ; his willing things out of Himself, means his purpose that

---

[1] *Systema Socorum Theolog corum,* tom. ii. cap. 9; Wittenberg, 1655, p. 439.
[2] *Theologia,* i. viii. § 1, xxvii. p. 418.

they should exist. Although the theologians start with the wide definition of the word, yet in the prosecution of the subject they regard the will as simply the faculty of self-determination, and the determinations themselves. That is, the power to will, and volitions or purposes. It is altogether better to confine the word to this its proper meaning, and not make it include all the forms of feeling involving approbation or delight.

God then as a spirit is a voluntary agent. We are authorized to ascribe to Him the power of self-determination. This the Bible everywhere does. From the beginning to the end, it speaks of the will of God, of his decrees, purposes, counsels, and commands. The will is not only an essential attribute of our spiritual being, but it is the necessary condition of our personality. Without the power of rational self-determination we should be as much a mere force as electricity, or magnetism, or the principle of vegetable life. It is, therefore, to degrade God below the sphere of being which we ourselves occupy, as rational creatures, to deny to Him the power of self-determination ; of acting or not acting, according to his own good pleasure.

B. *The Freedom of the Divine Will.*

The will of God is free in the highest sense of the word. An agent is said to be free, (1.) When he is at liberty to act or not to act, according to his good pleasure. This is liberty in acting. (2.) He is free as to his volitions, when they are determined by his own sense of what is wise, right, or desirable.

Freedom is more than spontaneity. The affections are spontaneous, but are not free. Loving and hating, delighting in and abhorring, do not depend upon the will.

God is free in acting, as in creating and preserving, because these acts do not arise from the necessity of his nature. He was free to create or not create ; to continue the universe in existence or to cause it to cease to be. He is free also in keeping his promises, because his purpose so to do is determined by his own infinite goodness. It is indeed inconceivable that God should violate his word. But this only proves that moral certainty may be as inexorable as necessity.

C. *The Decretive and Preceptive Will of God.*

The decretive will of God concerns his purposes, and relates to the futurition of events. The preceptive will relates to the rule of duty for his rational creatures. He decrees whatever he purposes to effect or to permit. He prescribes, according to his own will, what his creatures should do, or abstain from doing. The decretive and preceptive will of God can never be in conflict. God never decrees to do, or to cause others to do, what He forbids. He may, as we see He does, decree to permit what He forbids. He permits men to sin, although sin is forbidden. This is more scholastically expressed by the theologians by saying, A positive decretive will cannot consist with a negative preceptive will; *i. e.*, God cannot decree to make men sin. But a negative decretive will may consist with an affirmative preceptive will; *e. g.*, God may command men to repent and believe, and yet, for wise reasons, abstain from giving them repentance.

The distinction between *voluntas beneplaciti et signi*, as those terms are commonly used, is the same as that between the decretive and preceptive will of God. The one referring to his decrees, founded on his good pleasure; the other to his commands, founded on what He approves or disapproves.

By the secret will of God, is meant his purposes, as still hidden in his own mind; by his revealed will, his precepts and his purposes, as far as they are made known to his creatures.

D. *Antecedent and Consequent Will.*

These terms, as used by Augustinians, have reference to the relation of the decrees to each other. In the order of nature the end precedes the means, and the purpose of the former is antecedent to the purpose of the latter. Thus it is said, that God by an antecedent will, determined on the manifestation of his glory; and by a consequent will, determined on the creation of the world as a means to that end.

By Lutherans and Remonstrants these terms are used in a very different sense. According to their views, God by an antecedent will determined to save all men; but, foreseeing that all would not repent and believe, by a subsequent will He determined to save those whom he foresaw would believe. That is, He first purposed one thing and then another.

E. *Absolute and Conditional Will.*

These terms, when employed by Augustinians, have reference not so much to the purposes of God, as to the events which are decreed. The event, but not the purpose of God, is conditional. A man reaps, if he sows. He is saved, if he believes. His reaping and salvation are conditional events. But the purpose of God is absolute. If He purposes that a man shall reap, He purposes that he shall sow ; if He purposes that he shall be saved, He purposes that he shall believe. Anti-Augustinians, on the other hand, regard the purposes of God as conditional. He purposes the salvation of a man, if he believes. But whether he believes or not, is left undetermined ; so that the purpose of God is suspended on a condition not under his control, or, at least, undecided. A father may purpose to give an estate to his son, if he be obedient ; but whether the son will fulfil the condition is undetermined, and therefore the purpose of the father is undecided. It is, however, manifestly inconsistent with the perfection of God, that He should first will one thing and then another ; nor can his purposes be dependent on the uncertainty of human conduct or events. These are questions, however, which belong to the consideration of the doctrine of decrees. They are mentioned here because these distinctions occur in all discussions concerning the Divine Will, with which the student of theology should be familiar.

In this place it is sufficient to remark, that the Greek word θέλω, and the corresponding English verb, *to will*, sometimes express feeling, and sometimes a purpose. Thus in Matt. xxvii. 43, the words εἰ θέλει αὐτόν are correctly rendered, " if he delight in him." Comp. Ps. xxii. 8. It is in this sense the word is used, when it is said that God wills all men to be saved. He cannot be said to purpose or determine upon any event which is not to come to pass. A judge may will the happiness of a man whom he sentences to death. He may will him not to suffer when he wills him to suffer. The infelicity in such forms of expression is that the word " will " is used in different senses. In one part of the sentence it means desire, and in the other purpose. It is perfectly consistent, therefore, that God, as a benevolent Being, should desire the happiness of all men, while he purposes to save only his own people.

F. *The Will of God as the Ground of Moral Obligation.*

The question on this subject is, Whether things are right or wrong, simply because God commands or forbids them ? Or, does He command or forbid them, because they are right or wrong for some other reason than his will ? According to some, the only reason that a thing is right, and therefore obligatory, is, that it tends to promote the greatest happiness, or the greatest good of the universe. According to others, a thing is right which tends to promote our own happiness ; and for that reason, and for that reason alone, it is obligatory. If vice would make us happier than virtue, we should be bound to be vicious. It is a more decorous mode of expressing substantially the same theory, to say that the ground of moral obligation is a regard to the dignity of our own nature. It makes little difference whether it be our own dignity, or our own happiness, which we are bound to regard. It is self, in either case, to whom our whole allegiance is due. Others, again, place the ground of moral obligation in the fitness of things, which they exalt above God. There is, they affirm, an eternal and necessary difference between right and wrong, to which God, it is said, is as much bound to be conformed as are his rational creatures.

The common doctrine of Christians on this subject is, that the will of God is the ultimate ground of moral obligation to all rational creatures. No higher reason can be assigned why anything is right than that God commands it. This means, (1.) That the divine will is the only rule for deciding what is right and what is wrong. (2.) That his will is that which binds us, or that to which we are bound to be conformed. By the word " will " is not meant any arbitrary purpose, so that it were conceivable that God should will right to be wrong, or wrong right. The will of God is the expression or revelation of his nature, or is determined by it; so that his will, as revealed, makes known to us what infinite wisdom and goodness demand. Sometimes things are right simply because God has commanded them; as circumcision, and other ritual institutions were to the Jews. Other things are right because of the present constitution of things which God has ordained; such as the duties relating to property, and the permanent relations of society. Others, again, are right because they are demanded by the immutable excellence of God. In all cases, however, so far as we are concerned, it is his will that binds us, and constitutes the difference between right and wrong ; his will, that is, as the expression of his infinite perfection. So that the ultimate foundation of moral obligation is the nature of God.

§ 10. *The Power of God.*

A. *The Nature of Power, or, The Origin of the Idea.*

We get the idea of power from our own consciousness. That is, we are conscious of the ability of producing effects. Power in man is confined within very narrow limits. We can change the current of our thoughts, or fix our attention on a particular object,

and we can move the voluntary muscles of our body.   Beyond this
our direct power does not extend.   It is from this small measure
of efficiency that all the stores of human knowledge and all the
wonders of human art are derived.   It is only our thoughts, volitions, and purposes, together with certain acts of the body, that are
immediately subject to the will.   For all other effects we must
avail ourselves of the use of means.   We cannot will a book, a
picture, or a house into existence.   The production of such effects
requires protracted labor and the use of diverse appliances.

B. *Omnipotence.*

It is by removing all the limitations of power, as it exists in us,
that we rise to the idea of the omnipotence of God.   We do not
thus, however, lose the idea itself.   Almighty power does not cease
to be power.   We can do very little.   God can do whatever He
wills.   We, beyond very narrow limits, must use means to accomplish our ends.   With God means are unnecessary.   He wills, and
it is done.   He said, Let there be light ; and there was light.   He,
by a volition created the heavens and the earth.   At the volition
of Christ, the winds ceased, and there was a great calm.   By an
act of the will He healed the sick, opened the eyes of the blind,
and raised the dead.   This simple idea of the omnipotence of God,
that He can do without effort, and by a volition, whatever He
wills, is the highest conceivable idea of power, and is that which
is clearly presented in the Scriptures.   In Gen. xvii. 1, it is said,
" I am the Almighty God."   The prophet Jeremiah exclaims,
" Ah Lord God! behold thou hast made the heavens and the earth
by thy great power, and stretched out arm ; and there is nothing
too hard for thee." (Jer. xxxii. 17.)   God is said to have created
all things by the breath of his mouth, and to uphold the universe
by a word.   Our Lord says, " With God all things are possible."
(Matt. xix. 26.)   The Psalmist long before had said, " Our God
is in the heavens ; He hath done whatsoever He pleased." (Ps.
cxv. 3.)   And again, " Whatsoever the Lord pleased, that did He
in heaven, and in earth, in the seas, and all deep places." (Ps.
cxxxv. 6.)   The Lord God omnipotent reigneth, and doeth his
pleasure among the armies of heaven and the inhabitants of the
earth, is the tribute of adoration which the Scriptures everywhere
render unto God, and the truth which they everywhere present as
the ground of confidence to his people.   This is all we know, and
all we need to know on this subject ; and here we might rest satisfied, were it not for the vain attempts of theologians to reconcile

these simple and sublime truths of the Bible with their philosophical speculations.

C. *The Negation of Power.*

The sensuous school of philosophers deny that there is any real efficiency or power in existence. Their principle is, that all knowledge is derived from the senses; and consequently, that, as we cannot know anything of which the senses do not take cognizance, it is unphilosophical or unreasonable to admit the existence of anything else. Our senses, however, do not take cognizance of efficiency. It cannot be felt, or seen, or heard, or tasted. Therefore it does not exist. A cause is not that to which an effect is due, but simply that which uniformly precedes it. All we can know, and all we can rationally believe, is the facts which affect our senses, and the order of their sequence; which order, being uniform and necessary, has the character of law. This is the doctrine of causation proposed by Hume, Kant, Brown, Mill, and virtually by Sir William Hamilton; and it is this principle which lies at the foundation of the Positive Philosophy of Comte. Of course, if there be no such thing as power, there is no such attribute in God as omnipotence.

It is sufficient to say, in this connection, in reference to this theory, (1.) That it is contrary to every man's consciousness. We are conscious of power, *i. e.,* of the ability to produce effects. And consciousness has the same authority, to say the least, when it concerns what is within, as when it concerns what affects the senses. We are not more certain that our hand moves, than we are that we have the power to move, or not to move it, at pleasure. (2.) This theory contradicts the intuitive and indestructible convictions of the human mind. No man believes, or can believe really and permanently, that any change or effect can occur without an efficient cause. The fact that one event follows another, is not the ultimate fact. It is intuitively certain that there must be an adequate reason for that sequence. Such is the universal judgment of mankind. (3.) The argument, if valid against the reality of power, is valid against the existence of substance, of mind, and of God. This is admitted by the consistent advocates of the principle in question. Substance, mind, and God, are as little under the cognizance of the senses as power; and, therefore, if nothing is to be admitted but on the testimony of the senses, the existence of substance, mind, and God, must be denied. This principle, therefore, cannot be admitted without doing violence to our whole rational, moral, and religious nature. In other words, it

cannot be admitted at all ; for men cannot, permanently, either believe or act contrary to the laws of their nature.

D. *Absolute Power*.

By absolute power, as understood by the schoolmen and some of
the later philosophers, is meant power free from all the restraints
of reason and morality. According to this doctrine, contradictions,
absurdities, and immoralities, are all within the compass of the divine power. Nay, it is said that God can annihilate Himself. On
this subject Des Cartes says, Deus " non voluit tres angulos trianguli æquales esse duobus rectis, quia cognovit aliter fieri non posse.
Sed contra . . . . quia voluit tres angulos trianguli necessario
æquales esse duobus rectis, idcirco jam hoc verum est, et fieri aliter non potest, atque ita de reliquis." [1] This " summa indifferen-
tia," he says, " in Deo, summum est ejus omnipotentiæ argumen-
tum." [2]

It is, however, involved in the very idea of power, that it has
reference to the production of possible effects. It is no more a
limitation of power that it cannot effect the impossible, than it is of
reason that it cannot comprehend the absurd, or of infinite goodness
that it cannot do wrong. It is contrary to its nature. Instead of
exalting, it degrades God, to suppose that He can be other than
He is, or that He can act contrary to infinite wisdom and love.
When, therefore, it is said that God is omnipotent because He can
do whatever He wills, it is to be remembered that his will is determined by his nature. It is certainly no limitation to perfection to
say that it cannot be imperfect.

In this view of the omnipotence of God, the great body of the
theologians, especially among the Reformed, agree. Thus Zwingle [3] says : " Summa potentia non est nisi omnia possit, quantum ad
legitimum posse attinet : nam malum facere aut se ipsum deponere
aut in se converti hostiliter aut sibi ipsi contrarium esse posse im-
potentia est, non potentia." Musculus, [4] " Deus omnipotens, quia
potest quæ vult, quæque ejus veritati, justitiæ conveniunt." Keckermann, [5] "Absolute possibilia sunt, quæ nec Dei naturæ, nec aliarum rerum extra Deum essentiæ contradicunt." This scholastic doctrine of absolute power Calvin [6] stigmatizes as profane, " quod . . . .
merito detestabile nobis esse debet."

[1] *Meditationes. Responsiones Sextæ*, vi. edit. Amsterdam, 1685, p. 160.   [2] *Ibid.* p. 161.
[3] *De Providentia Dei*, Epilogus. *Opera*, edit. Turici, 1841, vol. iv. p. 138.
[4] See *Soci Communes Theologici*, edit. Basle, 1573, pp. 402–408.
[5] *Systema Theologiæ*, lib. i., cap. v. 4 ; edit. Hanoviæ, 1603, p. 107.
[6] *Institutio*, iii. xxiii. 2, edit. Berlin, 1834, part ii. p. 148.

Potentia Absoluta and Potentia Ordinata.

There is a sense of the terms in which absolute power is generally recognized among theologians. A distinction is commonly made between the *potentia absoluta* and the *potentia ordinata* of God. By the latter is meant the efficiency of God, as exercised uniformly in the ordered operation of second causes; by the former, his efficiency, as exercised without the intervention of second causes. Creation, miracles, immediate revelation, inspiration, and regeneration, are to be referred to the *potentia absoluta* of God; all his works of providence to his *potentia ordinata*. This distinction is important, as it draws the line between the natural and supernatural, between what is due to the operation of natural causes, sustained and guided by the providential efficiency of God, and what is due to the immediate exercise of his power. This distinction, indeed, is rejected by the modern philosophy. God in creating and sustaining the world, does it as a whole. Nothing is isolated. There is no individual act, but only a general efficiency on the part of God; and, consequently, no particular event can be referred to his absolute power or immediate agency. Everything is natural. There can be no miracle, and no special providence.[1]

E. *Confounding Will and Power.*

Another perversion of the Scriptural doctrine on this subject is, that which denies any distinction between will and power, or faculty and act, in God. It is said that it is unphilosophical to say that God can do anything. We use the word "can" only in reference to difficulty to be overcome. When nothing stands in the way, when all opposition is precluded, then we no longer say, we can. It is, therefore, inconsistent with the nature of an absolute Being to say that He is able to do this or that.[2] It is further denied that *willing* can be ascribed to God, if any difference be assumed between willing and doing. The ordinary definition of omnipotence, *Potest quod vult*, is to be rejected. It is admitted, that the distinction between will and power is unavoidable, if we determine the nature of God from the analogy of our constitution. As will and power are distinct in us, we are disposed to think they are distinct in Him. But this method of determining the attributes of God leads to the destruction of the true idea of an absolute being. In such a being, no such distinction can be admitted; and

---

[1] Strauss, i. p. 592. Schleiermacher I. § 54. *Werke*, edit. Berlin, 1842, vol. iii. p. 285.
[2] Bruch, p. 155.

therefore, in relation to God there can be no distinction between the actual and the possible. Nothing is possible but the actual ; and all that is possible becomes actual. Strauss[1] says, after Schleiermacher,[2] that by the omnipotence of God is to be understood " not only that all that is has its causality in God, but that everything is and occurs for which any causality in God exists." Bruch[3] says, that by the omnipotence of God is meant nothing more than that He is the original ground and cause of all things. He quotes Nitsch[4] as saying, that " The idea of omnipotence is the repetition and application of the idea of God as creator of heaven and earth." Nitsch, however, does not understand the passage in the sense put upon it ; for he adds, in his note commenting on the dictum of Abelard, " Deus non potest facere aliquid præter ea quæ facit," that, if this means that the actual exhausts the resources of God, it is to be rejected. The words of Abelard, nevertheless, correctly express the doctrine of the modern German school of theologians on this subject. Schleiermacher's language on this point is explicit and comprehensive. "Alles ist ganz durch die göttliche Allmacht und ganz durch den Naturzusammenhang, nicht aber darf die erstere als Ergänzung der letztern angesehen werden. Die Gesammtheit des endlichen Seins ist als vollkommene Darstellung der Allmacht zu denken, so dass alles wirklich ist und geschieht, wozu eine Productivität in Gott ist. Damit fällt weg die Differenz des Wirklichen und Möglichen, des absoluten und hypothetischen Wollens oder Könnens Gottes ; denn dies führt auf einen wirksamen und unwirksamen Willen und letzterer kann bei Gott unmöglich statt finden ; so wenig als Können und Wollen getrennt sein können." That is, " Everything is entirely through the divine omnipotence, and everything is through the course of nature. The former, however, must not be regarded as supplementary to the latter. The aggregate of finite things is the complete revelation of God's omnipotence, so that everything is and occurs for which there is a productivity in God. Thus the difference between the actual and the possible, between the absolute and hypothetical willing and power of God, disappears, because this implies an operative and inoperative will, but the latter is impossible in God ; just as little as willing and power can be separated."[5] This passage is quoted by Schweizer,[6] who adopts the views which it presents.

[1] *Dogmatik*, vol. i. p. 587.   [2] *Glaubenslehre*, I. § 54.
[3] *Die Lehre von den göttlichen Eigenschaften*, p. 154.
[4] *Christliche Lehre*, p. 160.
[5] Gess, *Uebersicht über das System Schleiermacher's*, p. 88.
[6] *Glaubenslehre*, I. p. 263.

This Doctrine Destroys our Knowledge of God.

In reference to this doctrine, it may be remarked, —

1. That it utterly confounds all our ideas of God. It renders all knowledge of Him impossible. If will and power are identical, then those words lose for us their meaning. We cannot know what God is, if this doctrine be true ; and if we know not what He is, we cannot rationally worship, love, or trust Him.

2. The doctrine effectually destroys the personality of God. A person is a self-conscious, self-determining being. But in denying will to God, self-determination, and consequently personality, is denied to Him. This consequence is admitted by the advocates of this doctrine. " If in God," says Strauss, " willing and power are identical, then there can be no freedom of the will in God, in the sense of the Church theologians, who hold that it was possible for God not to create the world, or to have created it other than it is. If there be no ability in God to do what He does not do, there can be no freedom of will or power of choice." " Mit diesem Können fällt auch die Freiheit im Sinne eines Wahlvermögens hinweg." [1] This, however, it is said, is not the doctrine of fate ; for fate supposes an *ab extra* necessity to which God is subject. If it does not teach fate, it at least teaches inexorable necessity. Spinoza says, " Ea res libera dicetur, quæ ex sola suæ naturæ necessitate existit et a se sola ad agendum determinatur. Necessaria autem, vel potius coacta quæ ab alio determinatur ad existendum et operandum certa ac determinata ratione." [2] And again,[3] " Deum nullo modo fato subjicio, sed omnia inevitabili necessitate ex Dei natura sequi concipio." In this sense the sun is free in shining. It shines from the necessity of its nature. We think from a like necessity ; but we can think of one thing or another, changing the current of our thoughts at pleasure. And thus we are free in exercising the power of thought. This freedom is denied to God. He can think only in one way. And all his thoughts are creative. He does, therefore, what He does, from a necessity of his nature, and does all He is able to do. God, according to this doctrine, is not a personal Being.

3. The Scriptures constantly represent God as able to do whatever He wills. They recognize the distinction between the actual and the possible ; between ability and act ; between what God

---

[1] *Dogmatik,* vol. i. p. 587.
[2] *Ethices,* i. def. vii. edit. Jena, 1803, vol. ii. p. 36
[3] Epistola xxiii. *Ibid.* vol. i. 513.

does, and what He is able to do. With Him all things are possible. He is able of stones to raise up children unto Abraham.
He can send me, says our Lord, twelve legions of angels.

4. As this is the doctrine of the Bible, it is the instinctive judgment of the human mind. It is a perfection in us, that we can do
far more than we actually accomplish. With us the actual is not
the measure of the possible.

5. It is, therefore, a limitation of God, a denial of his omnipotence, to say that He can do only what He actually brings to pass.
There is infinitely more in God than simple causality of the actual.

It is consequently an erroneous definition of omnipotence to call
it All-power, meaning thereby that all the efficiency in the universe
is the efficiency of God ; which is not only a pantheistic doctrine,
but it makes the finite the measure of the infinite.

§ 11. *Holiness of God.*

This is a general term for the moral excellence of God. In 1
Sam. ii. 2, it is said, " There is none holy as the LORD ; " no other
Being absolutely pure, and free from all limitation in his moral
perfection. " Thou Holy One of Israel," is the form of address
which the Spirit puts into the lips of the people of God. " Exalt
the LORD our God, and worship at his holy hill; for the LORD our
God is Holy." (Ps. xcix. 9.) " Holy and reverend is his name."
(Ps. cxi. 9.) " Thou art of purer eyes than to behold evil, and
canst not look on iniquity." (Hab. i. 13.) " Who shall not fear
thee, O Lord, and glorify thy name? for Thou only art Holy."
(Rev. xv. 4.) Holiness, on the one hand, implies entire freedom
from moral evil ; and, upon the other, absolute moral perfection.
Freedom from impurity is the primary idea of the word. To sanctify is to cleanse ; to be holy, is to be clean. Infinite purity, even
more than infinite knowledge or infinite power, is the object of
reverence. Hence the Hebrew word קָדוֹשׁ, as used in Scripture,
is often equivalent to *venerandus.* " The Holy One of Israel," is
He who is to be feared and adored. Seraphim round about the
throne who cry day and night, Holy, Holy, Holy is the Lord of
hosts, give expression to the feelings of all unfallen rational creatures in view of the infinite purity of God. They are the representatives of the whole universe, in offering this perpetual homage
to the divine holiness. It is because of his holiness, that God is a
consuming fire. And it was a view of his holiness which led the
prophet to exclaim, " Woe is me ! for I am undone ; because I am
a man of unclean lips, and I dwell in the midst of a people of un-

clean lips: for mine eyes have seen the king, the LORD of hosts."
(Is. vi. 5.)

It is in their application to the moral attributes of God, that the
two methods of determining his nature come most directly into
conflict.   If we allow ourselves to be determined in answering the
question, What is God? by the teachings of his Word, and the constitution of our own nature; if we refer to Him, in an infinite degree,
every good we find in ourselves, then we can have no hesitation in
believing that He is holy, just, and good.   But if the philosophical
notion of the absolute and infinite is to decide every question concerning the divine nature, then we must give up all confidence in
our apprehensions of God, as an object of knowledge.   This
Strauss, the most candid of the recent philosophical theologians,
frankly admits.   He says: " The ideas of the absolute and of the
holy are incompatible.   He who holds to the former must give up
the latter, since holiness implies relation; and, on the other hand,
he who holds fast the idea of God as holy, must renounce the
idea of his being absolute; for the idea of absolute is inconsistent
with the slightest possibility of its being other than it is.   The impossibility of referring moral attributes to God had been admitted
by some of the fathers of the Church." [1]

The Reasons urged for denying Moral Attributes to God.

The grounds on which it is denied that moral attributes can be
predicated of God, are such as these: —

1. To assume that God can delight in good, and hate evil, takes
for granted that He is susceptible of impression *ab extra*, which is
inconsistent with his nature.

2. It is said that moral excellence implies subjection to a moral
law.   But an absolute and infinite Being cannot be thus subject to
law.   It is true that God is not subject to any law out of Himself.   He is *exlex*, absolutely independent.   He is a law unto
Himself.   The conformity of his will to reason is no subjection.
It is only the harmony of his nature.   God's being holy, implies nothing more than that He is not in conflict with Himself.
On this point even the rationalistic theologian Wegscheider says:
" Minime Deus cogitandus est tanquam pendens ex lege ethica

---

[1] " So wollen also die Begriffe des Absoluten und des Heiligen nicht zusammengehen:
sondern wer das Absolute festhält, der löst die Heiligkeit auf, welche nur an einem in Relation gestellten Wesen etwas ist; und wer es umgekehrt mit der Heiligkeit ernstlich nimmt,
der tritt der Idee der Absolutheit zu nahe, welche durch den leisesten Schatten der Möglichkeit, anders zu sein als sie ist, verunreinigt wird.   Diese Einsicht in die Unanwendbar-
keit moralischer Attribute auf Gott hatten schon einzelne Kirchenväter . . . erkannte."
— *Dogmatik*, vol. i. p. 595.

vel eidem subjectus tanquam potestati cuidam alienæ; sed Deus sanctus ipsa ea lex est, natura quidam hypostatica indutus." [1]

3. It is said that moral excellence must be free. A moral agent, to be holy, must voluntarily do right. But this implies that he is able to do wrong. There must, therefore, be at least a metaphysical possibility of God's being evil, or He cannot be good. But all possibility of the Absolute being other than it is, is inconsistent with its nature. To this it may be answered that the ideas of liberty and necessity are indeed antagonistic; but that liberty and absolute certainty are perfectly compatible. That an infinitely wise Being will not act irrationally, is as absolutely certain as that the self-contradictory cannot be true. The one is as inconceivable as the other. It is just as impossible that an infinitely holy Being should be unholy as that light should be darkness. The impossibility, however, is of a different kind. The former is what Augustine calls the *felix necessitas boni*, which is the highest idea of freedom.

4. Strauss says that those who attribute moral perfections to God, forget that a purely spiritual Being can have nothing of what we call reason, wisdom, goodness, wrath, righteousness, etc. " Strictly speaking," he adds " the ascription of moral attributes to God supposes that He is material; and the most abstract theological ideas on the subject are really founded on Materialism." This is founded on the assumption that spirit is impersonal, a generic force, which becomes individual and personal only by union with a material organization, just as the Realists define man to be generic humanity, individualized and rendered personal by union with a given corporeal organization.

It is surely most unreasonable to sacrifice to such speculations all religion, and all confidence in the intuitive judgments of the human mind, as well as all faith in God and in the Bible.

It is scarcely less destructive of the true doctrine, to define holiness in God as the causality of conscience in us. That we are moral beings is not admitted to be a proof that God has moral attributes. That the sun produces cheerfulness in us is no proof that the sun is cheerful. But if we know nothing of God except that He is the cause of all things, He is to us only an inscrutable force, and not a Father, and not a God.

[1] *Institutiones*, p. 273.

§ 12. *Justice.*

A. *Meaning of the Word.*

The word justice, or righteousness, is used in Scripture some-times in a wider and sometimes in a more restricted sense. In theology, it is often distinguished as *justitia interna*, or moral excellence, and *justitia externa*, or rectitude of conduct. In Hebrew צַדִּיק means, in a physical sense, *straight;* and in a moral sense, *right*, what is as it should be. And צְדָקָה means rightness, that which satisfies the demands of rectitude or law. The Greek word δίκαιος has the physical sense of *equal;* and the moral sense of, conformed to what is right; and δικαιοσύνη is either that which divides equally, *i. e.*, equity in the moral sense, or that which sat-isfies the demands of right. The Latin *justus* and *justitia* are commonly used in the wide sense for what is right, or as it should be. Cicero [1] defines *justitia* as "animi affectio suum cuique tri-buens." This definition he elsewhere amplifies, saying: " Justitia erga Deos religio, erga parentas pietas, creditis in rebus fides, in moderatione animadvertendi lenitas, amicitia in benevolentia nomi-natur." [2]

When we regard God as the author of our moral nature, we conceive of Him as holy ; when we regard Him in his dealings with his rational creatures, we conceive of Him as righteous. He is a righteous ruler; all his laws are holy, just, and good. In his moral government He faithfully adheres to those laws. He is im-partial and uniform in their execution. As a judge he renders unto every man according to his works. He neither condemns the in-nocent, nor clears the guilty ; neither does He ever punish with undue severity. Hence the justice of God is distinguished as *rectoral*, or that which is concerned in the imposition of righteous laws and in their impartial execution ; and *distributive*, or that which is manifested in the righteous distribution of rewards and punishment. The Bible constantly represents God as a righteous ruler and a just judge. These two aspects of his character, or of our relation to Him, are not carefully distinguished. We have the assurance which runs through the Scriptures, that " The judge of all the earth " must " do right." (Gen. xviii. 25.) " God is a righteous judge." (Ps. vii. 11, marginal reading.) " He shall judge the world with righteousness." (Ps. xcvi. 13.) " Clouds

---

[1] *De Finibus*, v. 23, 65, edit. Leipzig, 1850, p. 1042.
[2] *Partitiones Oratoriæ*, 22, 78, edit. *ut sup.* p. 194.

and darkness are round about Him : righteousness and judgment are the habitation of his throne." (Ps. xcvii. 2.) Notwithstanding all the apparent inequalities in the distribution of his favours; notwithstanding the prosperity of the wicked and the afflictions of the righteous, the conviction is everywhere expressed that God is just ; that somehow and somewhere He will vindicate his dealings with men, and show that He is righteous in all his ways and holy in all his works.

B. *Justice in its Relation to Sin.*

As the sense of guilt is universal among men, and as the manifestations of sin are so constant and pervading, it is mainly in its relation to sin that the justice of God is revealed. Hence many theologians define the justice of God as that attribute of his nature which is manifested in the punishment of sin. Goodness, it is said, is manifested in bestowing good, and justice in the infliction of punishment. Schleiermacher says, " Justice is that causality in God which connects suffering with actual sin." [1] Schweizer says, " We know God as just only through the punishment of sin." Hegel says, " The manifestation of the nothingness of the finite as power, is justice." This is the philosophical statement of the principle that " Might is Right," a principle which underlies the morals and religion of the modern philosophy.

C. *The Reformation of the Offender is not the Primary Object of Punishment.*

As the justice of God is specially manifested in the punishment of sin, it is of primary importance to determine why sin is punished.

One prevalent theory on this subject is, that the only legitimate end of punishment is the reformation of the offender.

It is of course to be admitted, that the good of the offender is often the ground or reason why evil is inflicted. A father chastises a child in love, and for its good. And God, our heavenly Father, brings suffering upon his children for their edification. But evil inflicted for the benefit of the sufferer, is chastisement, and not punishment. Punishment, properly speaking, is evil inflicted in satisfaction of justice.

That the good of the sufferer is not the primary end of the infliction of punishment, is proved : —

1. Because the punishment of the wicked is always, in the Scriptures, referred to the anger of God, and the chastisement of

---

[1] *Christliche Glaube*, § 84, *Works* Berlin, 1843, vol. iv. p. 465.

his people to his love. The cases, therefore, are not analogous. This difference of representation is designed to teach us that the wicked and the good do not stand in the same relation to God, as objects of benevolence ; but that the one He punishes to testify his disapprobation and satisfy his justice, and the other He chastises to bring them nearer to Himself.

2. In many cases the nature of the punishment precludes the possibility of the good of the offender being the ground of its infliction. The deluge, the destruction of the cities of the plain, and the overthrow of Jerusalem, were certainly not designed for the benefit of the men who suffered from those desolating inflictions. Much less can it be assumed that the punishment of the fallen angels, and of the finally impenitent, is intended to be reformatory.

3. Scripture and experience both teach that suffering, when of the nature of punishment, has no tendency to reform. When suffering is seen to come from a father's hand, and to be a manifestation of love, it has a sanctifying power ; but when it comes from the hand of God, as a judge and an avenger, and is the expression of displeasure and a proof of our alienation from God, its tendency is to harden and to exasperate. Hence the Apostle says, that so long as men are under condemnation, they bring forth fruit unto sin ; and that, only when reconciled to God and assured of his love, do they bring forth fruit unto God. The great New Testament prophet, in his vision of the world of woe, represents the lost as gnawing their tongues with pain and blaspheming God. The denunciation of punishment is addressed to fear, but fear is not the principle of genuine obedience.

4. On this subject, appeal may be fairly made to the common consciousness of men. Such is our moral hebetude that it is only glaring offences which awaken our moral sensibilities, and reveal their true nature. When any great crime is committed, there is an instinctive and universal demand for the punishment of the criminal. No man can pretend that the desire for his reformation is the feeling which prompts that demand. That is not so much as thought of. It is the instinctive judgment of the mind that he ought to suffer. It is not benevolence towards him which calls for the infliction of punishment.

D. *The Prevention of Crime is not the Primary End of Punishment.*

The doctrine that the only legitimate end of punishment is the prevention of crime, has had great prevalence in the Church and

the world.   It is the common doctrine of jurists.   It is, of course,
to be conceded that the good of society and of the moral government of God, is one important end of punishment in all govern-
ments, human or divine.   It is, however, rather an important collateral effect of the administration of justice, than its immediate
design.   The doctrine in question merges justice into benevolence.
According to this way of thinking, it is only because God has a
view to the happiness of his rational creatures, that He visits sin
with punishment.   This doctrine was adopted by some of the early
fathers.   In answer to the objection that the Bible represented
God as a vindictive being, because it speaks of his anger and of
his determination to punish, they said that He punished only out
of benevolence.   Thus Clemens Alexandrinus[1] says, "Men ask
how God can be good and kind if He is angry and punishes?
They should remember that punishment is for the good of the
offender and for the prevention of evil."   And Tertullian[2] says:
"Omne hoc justitiæ opus procuratio bonitatis est."   Origen,[3] also
to the same effect, says: "Ex quibus omnibus constat, unum eun-
demque esse justum et bonum legis et evangeliorum Deum, et
benefacere cum justitia et cum bonitate punire."

Many later theologians take the same view.   Leibnitz defines
justice to be benevolence guided by wisdom.   Wolf, who modified
the whole system of theology in accordance with the philosophy of
Leibnitz, adopted the same view.   So did Stapfer,[4] who says:
"Quando Deus ejusmodi malum triste ex peccato necessario se-
quens creaturæ accidere sinit, ... dicitur peccatorem punire,
et hoc sensu ipsi tribuitur justitia vindicativa.   In justitia punitiva
bonitas cum sapientia administratur.[5]   Notio justitiæ resolvitur in
notionem sapientiæ et bonitatis."   Grotius, the jurist, makes this
idea of justice the fundamental principle of his great work, "De
Satisfactione Christi."

The Optimist Theory.

In this country the same view has been extensively adopted,
and made, as it must of necessity be, the controlling principle of
those systems of theology in which it is incorporated.   It is assumed that happiness is the greatest good; and hence that the pur-

---

[1] *Pædagogus*, I. viii.; edit. Cologne, 1688, p. 114, c. and p. 115.
[2] *Adversus Marcionem*, II. 10; edit. Basel, 1562, p. 179, seu II. 13; edit. Leipzig, 1841, iii.
p. 90.   *Bibliotheca*, Gersdorf, vol. vi.
[3] *De Principiis*, II. v. 3; edit. Paris, 1733, vol. i. p. 88, a.
[4] *Institutiones*, i. 153; edit. Tiguri, 1743, p. 154.
[5] *Ibid.* i. 154.

pose and desire to promote happiness is the sum of all virtue. From this it follows, that this world, the work of a God of infinite benevolence, wisdom, and power, must be the best possible world for the production of happiness; and, therefore, the permission of sin, and its punishment, must be referred to the benevolence of God. They are the necessary means for securing the greatest amount of happiness. If happiness be not the greatest good; if holiness be a higher end than happiness; if expediency be not the ground and measure of moral obligation, it is obvious that this whole structure collapses.

Proof of the Scriptural Doctrine.

It is admitted that happiness is promoted by justice, and therefore that it is contrary to a wise benevolence that men should be allowed to sin with impunity. But justice cannot properly be merged into benevolence. And that the promotion of happiness by the prevention of crime is not the primary end of the infliction of punishment, is evident, —

1. From the testimony of every man's consciousness. Every man knows that benevolence and justice, as revealed in his own consciousness, are different sentiments. The one prompts to the promotion of happiness, the other involves the instinctive judgment, that a criminal ought to suffer for his crime. We do not stop to ask, or to think, what may be the collateral effect on others of the infliction of punishment. Anterior to such reflection, and independent of it, is the intuitive perception, that sin should be punished, for its own sake, or on account of its inherent ill-desert. These instinctive moral judgments are as clear and as trustworthy revelations of the nature of God as can possibly be made. They force conviction in spite of all speculative sophistries. Every man knows the righteous judgment of God, that those who sin are worthy of death. If justice and benevolence are distinct in us, they are distinct in God. If we, in obedience to the nature which He has given us, intuitively perceive or judge that sin ought to be punished for its own sake, and irrespective of the good effect punishment may have on others, then such also is the judgment of God. This is the principle which underlies and determines all our ideas of the Supreme Being. If moral perfection be not in Him what it is in us, then He is to us an unknown something, and we use words without meaning when we speak of Him as holy, just, and good.

Argument from the Religious Experience of Believers.

2. This sense of justice, which is indestructible in the nature of man, and which, in common with reason and conscience, has survived the Fall, is not only revealed in the ordinary experience of men, but still more distinctly in their religious consciousness. What is commonly called " conviction of sin," is only a modification, and higher form, of those inward experiences which are common to all men. All men know that they are sinners. They all know that sin, as related to the justice of God, is guilt, that which ought to be punished ; and that, as related to his holiness, it renders us polluted and offensive in his sight. They also know, intuitively, that God is just as well as holy ; and, therefore, that his moral perfection calls for the punishment of sin, by the same necessity by which He disapproves of and hates it. Under the pressure of these convictions, and the consciousness of their utter inability either to satisfy divine justice, or to free themselves from the defilement and power of sin, men either tremble in the constant looking for of judgment, or they look out of themselves for help. When, under either the common or saving operations of the Spirit of God, these sentiments are deepened, then their nature is more clearly revealed. A man, when thus convinced of sin, sees that not only would it be right that he should be punished, but that the justice, or moral excellence of God, demands his punishment. It is not that he ought to suffer for the good of others, or to sustain the moral government of God, but that he, as a sinner and for his sins, ought to suffer. Were he the only creature in the universe, this conviction would be the same, both in nature and degree. Such is the experience of men under the conviction of sin, as recorded in the Scriptures and in the history of the Church. In many cases criminals under the pressure of these feelings have delivered themselves to the officers of justice to be punished. More frequently they resort to self-inflicted tortures to satisfy the clamors of conscience. We have, therefore, an inward revelation, which can neither be suppressed nor perverted, that justice is not benevolence.

The Sense of Justice not due to Christian Culture.

3. That this sense of justice is not due to Christian culture, or to the influence of peculiar forms of doctrine, but belongs to the common consciousness of men, is plain. (*a.*) Because it is impressed upon all human languages as far as known or cultivated. All languages have different words for justice and benevolence.

There could not be this difference in the words, if the sentiments themselves were not different. Every one knows that when we say a man is just, we mean one thing ; and when we say he is benevolent, we mean another thing. (*b.*) All history as it records the workings of human nature, reveals this innate sense of justice. We everywhere hear men calling for the punishment of offenders, or denouncing those who allow them to escape with impunity. No mass of men ever witness a flagrant act of cruelty or wrong without an irrepressible manifestation of indignation. The voice of nature, which in such cases is the voice of God, demands the punishment of the wrong-doer. (*c.*) In all religions which reveal the inward convictions of men, there are expiatory rites. Every sacrifice for sin, the smoke from every altar, which has been going up through all ages and from every part of the world, are so many attestations to the truth of reason and of Scripture, that there is such an attribute as justice in God, distinct from his benevolence.

Argument from the Holiness of God.

4. The truth of this doctrine may also be inferred from the holiness of God. If He is infinitely pure, his nature must be opposed to all sin ; and as his acts are determined by his nature, his disapprobation of sin must manifest itself in his acts. But the disfavour of God, the manifestation of his disapprobation, is death, as his favour is life. It cannot be that this essential opposition between holiness and sin should be dependent for its manifestation on the mere *ab extra* consideration that evil would result from sin being allowed to go unpunished. It might as well be said that we should feel no aversion to pain, unless aware that it weakened our constitution. We do not approve of holiness simply because it tends to produce happiness ; neither do we disapprove of sin simply because it tends to produce misery. It is inevitable, therefore, that the perfection of the infinitely holy God should manifest its opposition to sin, without waiting to judge of the consequences of the expression of this divine repugnance.

5. The doctrine that the prevention of crime is the only legitimate end of punishment, or that there is no such attribute in God as justice, as distinguished from benevolence, rests on the assumption, before remarked upon, that all virtue consists in benevolence ; which again rests on the assumption that happiness is the highest good ; which makes expediency the ground of moral obligation, and the rule of moral conduct. It is indeed a solecism to use the word *moral* in such connections, for, on this theory, the word has no

meaning. A thing may be wise or unwise, expedient or inexpedient, but in no other sense right or wrong. Wrong becomes right, and right becomes wrong, as the greater amount of happiness flows from the one or from the other. As this utilitarian theory of morals has been banished from the schools of philosophy, it should be banished from systems of theology.

Argument from the Connection between Sin and Misery.

6. The inseparable connection between sin and misery is a revelation of the justice of God. That holiness promotes happiness is a revelation of the relation in which God stands to holiness ; and that sin produces misery is no less a revelation of the relation in which He stands to moral evil. This constitution of things depending on the nature and will of God, proves that sin is evil in its own nature, and is punished for its own sake. The law of God which includes a penalty as well as precepts, is in both a revelation of the nature of God. If the precepts manifest his holiness, the penalty as clearly manifests his justice. If the one is immutable, so also is the other. The wages of sin is death. Death is what is due to it in justice, and what without injustice cannot be withheld from it. If the prevention of crime were the primary end of punishment, then if the punishment of the innocent, the execution, for example, of the wife and children of a murderer, would have a greater restraining influence than the punishment of the guilty murderer, their execution would be just. But this would shock the moral sense of men.

Argument from the Scriptural Doctrines of Satisfaction and Justification.

7. The Scriptural doctrines of satisfaction and justification rest on the principle that God is immutably just, *i. e.*, that his moral excellence, in the case of sin, demands punishment, or expiation. The Bible clearly teaches the necessity of satisfaction to justice in order to the forgiveness of sin. Christ was set forth as a propitiation, in order that God might be just in justifying the ungodly. This assumes that it would be unjust, *i. e.*, contrary to moral rectitude, to pardon the guilty without such a propitiation. This necessity for a satisfaction is never referred to expediency or to governmental considerations. If sin could have been pardoned, without a satisfaction, the Apostle says, Christ is dead in vain. (Gal. ii. 21.) If there could have been a law which could have given life, salvation would have been by the law. (Gal. iii. 21.)

Moreover, if there is no such attribute in God as justice, as distinguished from benevolence, then there can be no such thing as justification. There may be pardon, as the act of a sovereign remitting a penalty and restoring an offender to favour; but no such thing as justification, as an act of a judge proceeding according to law and pronouncing the demands of justice satisfied. The Scriptures, however, according to the almost unanimous judgment of the Church, pronounce that justification is more than an act of executive clemency. Conscience is not satisfied with mere forgiveness. It is essential to peace with God, that the soul should see that justice is satisfied. This is the reason why the death of Christ, why his blood, is so inexpressibly precious in the eyes of his people. All the experience of the saints is a protest against the principle that expiation is unnecessary, that sin can be pardoned without a satisfaction of justice.

Paul's Argument.

The whole argument of the Apostle in his Epistle to the Romans is founded on the principle that justice is a divine attribute distinct from benevolence. His argument is: God is just. All men are sinners. All, therefore, are guilty, i. e., under condemnation. Therefore no man can be justified, i. e., pronounced not guilty, on the ground of his character or conduct. Sinners cannot satisfy justice. But what they could not do, Christ, the Eternal Son of God, clothed in our nature, has done for them. He has brought in everlasting righteousness, which meets all the demands of the law. All those who renounce their own righteousness, and trust to the righteousness of Christ, God justifies and saves. This is the gospel as preached by Paul. It all rests on the assumption that God is just.

The doctrine of the vindicatory justice, which has this clear evidence of its truth, in the moral nature of man, in the religious experience of believers, and in the teaching and doctrines of the Scriptures, has ever been considered as a turning point in theology.

E. *Philosophical Views of the Nature of Justice.*

The teachings of the Scriptures, and the faith of the Church, so far as the divine attributes are concerned, are founded on the assumption that God is a personal Being. It is involved in that assumption, not only that He possesses intelligence and moral character, but that he thinks, feels, wills, and acts. It is, moreover, involved in the idea of personality, that thinking, feeling, willing, and acting in God, are, in all that is essential, analogous to what those terms signify in us. The modern philosophy, however, teaches that, if God be an absolute Being, thinking, feeling, willing, and acting are inconsistent with his nature. Hence, —

1. Some teach that God is only the original ground of being, having in Himself no distinctive attributes. What we call the attributes of God are only the attributes of finite creatures having the ground of their being in God. That they are intelligent, moral, voluntary agents, is no proof that the same is true of God. That the sun produces the sensation of heat in us is no proof that it experiences the same sensation. The attributes of God, therefore, are only different aspects of the causality in Him which produces different effects. Justice, then, is not an attribute of God ; it is only the causality to which the connection between sin and suffering is to be referred.

2. Others, while insisting that personality, and all that it involves, are incompatible with the idea of an absolute Being, still maintain that we are constrained, and bound, to believe in the personality of God, on the authority of the Bible and of our own moral nature. But the Bible reveals, it is said, not absolute, but only regulative truth; not what He is, but what it is expedient for us to think He is. Justice in God, then, is for us what generosity in a fairy is for nursery children.

3. Others again, while they admit personality in God, make it a personality which precludes all willing, and all acting, except in the form of law, or general, uniform efficiency. Justice in God, therefore, is only a name for one form, or one mode, of the manifestation of the power of God. As it is to be referred to his ordination, or to his nature, that fire burns and acids corrode, so it is to be referred to his general efficiency that sin produces misery. There is no special intervention of God, when fire burns ; and there is no special decision, or judgment on his part, when a sinner is punished. Punishment is not the execution of a sentence pronounced by an intelligent being on the merits of the case, but the operation of a general law. Bruch (Professor of Theology in the Theological Seminary in Strasbourg) is a representative of this mode of thinking. He professes Theism, or faith in a personal God, but he teaches that the attributes of God are nothing else (als die Modalitäten seiner ewigen Wirksamkeit) " than the modes of his constant efficiency." Since among men justice is exercised in a succession of special acts, it is erroneously inferred that there is a like succession of acts of the will of God by which He approves or condemns. The great difficulty, he says, arises from judging

of God after the analogy of our own nature. He admits that the Bible does this; that it constantly speaks of God as a righteous judge, administering justice according to his will. In this case, however, he adds, it is important to separate the real truth from the imperfection of its Scriptural form. Penalties are not evils inflicted by a special act of the divine will, but the natural consequences of sin, which cannot fail to manifest themselves. There is an organic connection between sin and evil. All the activity or agency of God is in the form of laws having their foundation in his nature. Thus justice is simply that law, or uniform mode of divine operation, by which sin is made its own punishment.[1] Hence there is no distinction between natural and positive inflictions; the deluge was either no punishment, or it was the natural consequence of the sins of the antediluvians. Hence, there is no such thing as forgiveness. The only possible way to remove the suffering is to remove the sin. But how is the sin of theft or murder to be removed? We can understand how pride or envy may be subdued and the suffering they occasion be escaped: but how can a past act be removed? A man hardened in sin suffers little or nothing for a special offence; the morally refined suffer indescribably. Thus, according to this theory, the better a man is, the more severely he is punished for his sin. Strauss is consistent enough to carry the principle out, and discard altogether the ideas of reward and punishment, as belonging to a low form of thought. He quotes and adopts the *dictum* of Spinoza: "Beatitudo non est virtutis præmium, sed ipsa virtus."

4. Scarcely distinguished from the doctrine last mentioned, is that presented by Dr. John Young.[2] His doctrine is that there are certain eternal and immutable laws arising out of the nature of things, independent of the will or nature of God, to which He is as much subject as his creatures. One of these laws is, that virtue produces happiness, and vice misery. The one is, therefore, rewarded, and the other punished, by the necessary and immutable operation of that law, and not by the will of God. God, therefore, ceases to be the ruler of the world. He is Himself subordinate to eternal and necessary laws. That this doctrine is at variance with the whole tenor of the Bible cannot be doubted. It is no less opposed to the dictates of our own moral and religious nature. It is revealed in that nature that we are subject, not to necessary and

---

[1] See the section on the "Gerechtigkeit Gottes" in Bruch's *Lehre von den Göttlichen Eigenschaften*, pp. 275–296.

[2] *Light and Life of Men.*

self-acting laws, but to an intelligent, personal God, to whom we are accountable for our character and conduct, and who rewards and punishes his creatures according to their works.

As a philosophical theory, this doctrine is much below the standard of the German theologians. For they, as far as they are Theists, admit that these immutable laws are determined by the nature of God, and are the uniform modes of his operation. Indeed, as God and his creatures exhaust the whole category of being, the "nature of things," apart from the nature of God and of his creatures, seems to be a phrase without meaning. It is tantamount to the "nature of nonentity."

§ 13. *The Goodness of God.*

A. *The Scriptural Doctrine.*

Goodness, in the Scriptural sense of the term, includes benevolence, love, mercy, and grace. By benevolence is meant the disposition to promote happiness; all sensitive creatures are its objects. Love includes complacency, desire, and delight, and has rational beings for its objects. Mercy is kindness exercised towards the miserable, and includes pity, compassion, forbearance, and gentleness, which the Scriptures so abundantly ascribe to God. Grace is love exercised towards the unworthy. The love of a holy God to sinners is the most mysterious attribute of the divine nature. The manifestation of this attribute for the admiration and beatification of all intelligent creatures, is declared to be the special design of redemption. God saves sinners, we are told, " That in the ages to come He might show the exceeding riches of his grace in his kindness toward us, through Christ Jesus." (Eph. ii. 7.) This is the burden of that Epistle.

As all the modifications of goodness above mentioned are found even in our dilapidated nature, and commend themselves to our moral approbation, we know they must exist in God without measure and without end. In him they are infinite, eternal, and immutable.

Benevolence.

The goodness of God in the form of benevolence is revealed in the whole constitution of nature. As the universe teems with life, it teems also with enjoyment. There are no devices in nature for the promotion of pain for its own sake; whereas the manifestations of design for the production of happiness are beyond computation. The manifestation of the goodness of God in the

form of love, and specially of love to the undeserving, is, as just
stated, the great end of the work of redemption. " God so loved
the world, that He gave his only begotten Son, that whosoever
believeth in Him should not perish, but have everlasting life."
(John iii. 16.) " Herein is love, not that we loved God, but that
He loved us, and sent his Son to be the propitiation for our sins."
(1 John iv. 10.) The Apostle prays that believers might be able
to comprehend the height and depth, the length and breadth, of
that love which passes knowledge.   (Eph. iii. 19.)

Love.

Love in us includes complacency and delight in its object, with
the desire of possession and communion. The schoolmen, and
often the philosophical theologians, tell us that there is no feeling
in God. This, they say, would imply passivity, or susceptibility of
impression from without, which it is assumed is incompatible with
the nature of God. " We must exclude," says Bruch,[1] "passivity
from the idea of love, as it exists in God. For God cannot be the
subject of passivity in any form. Besides, if God experienced complacency in intelligent beings, He would be dependent on them :
which is inconsistent with his nature as an Absolute Being."
Love, therefore, he defines as that attribute of God which secures
the development of the rational universe ; or, as Schleiermacher
expresses it, " It is that attribute in virtue of which God communicates Himself." [2] According to the philosophers, the Infinite develops itself in the finite ; this fact, in theological language, is due
to love. The only point of analogy between love in us and love
in the Absolute and Infinite, is self-communication. Love in us
leads to self-revelation and communion ; in point of fact the Infinite is revealed and developed in the universe, and specially in
humanity. Bruch admits that this doctrine is in real contradiction
to the representations of God in the Old Testament, and in apparent contradiction to those of the New Testament. If love in God
is only a name for that which accounts for the rational universe ;
if God is love, simply because He develops himself in thinking and
conscious beings, then the word has for us no definite meaning ; it
reveals to us nothing concerning the real nature of God. Here
again we have to choose between a mere philosophical speculation
and the clear testimony of the Bible, and of our own moral
and religious nature. Love of necessity involves feeling, and if

[1] *Eigenschaften*, page 240.
[2] *Christliche Glaube*, § 166; *Works*, Berlin, 1843, vol. iv. p. 513.

there be no feeling in God, there can be no love. That He produces happiness is no proof of love. The earth does that unconsciously and without design. Men often render others happy from vanity, from fear, or from caprice. Unless the production of happiness can be referred, not only to a conscious intention, but to a purpose dictated by kind feeling, it is no proof of benevolence. And unless the children of God are the objects of his complacency and delight, they are not the objects of his love. He may be cold, insensible, indifferent, or even unconscious; He ceases to be God in the sense of the Bible, and in the sense in which we need a God, unless He can love as well as know and act. The philosophical objection against ascribing feeling to God, bears, as we have seen, with equal force against the ascription to Him of knowledge or will. If that objection be valid, He becomes to us simply an unknown cause, what men of science call force; that to which all phenomena are to be referred, but of which we know nothing. We must adhere to the truth in its Scriptural form, or we lose it altogether. We must believe that God is love in the sense in which that word comes home to every human heart. The Scriptures do not mock us when they say, "Like as a father pitieth his children, so the LORD pitieth them that fear Him." (Ps. ciii. 13.) He meant what He said when He proclaimed Himself as "The LORD, the LORD God, merciful and gracious, long-suffering and abundant in goodness and truth." (Ex. xxxiv. 6.) "Beloved," says the Apostle, "let us love one another: for love is of God; and every one that loveth is born of God, and knoweth God. He that loveth not, knoweth not God; for God is love. In this was manifested the love of God toward us, because that God sent his only-begotten Son into the world, that we might live through Him. Herein is love, not that we loved God, but that He loved us, and sent his Son to be the propitiation for our sins. Beloved, if God so loved us, we ought also to love one another." (1 John iv. 7–11.) The word love has the same sense throughout this passage. God is love; and love in Him is, in all that is essential to its nature, what love is in us. Herein we do rejoice, yea, and will rejoice.

B. *The Existence of Evil.*

How can the existence of evil, physical and moral, be reconciled with the benevolence and holiness of a God infinite in his wisdom and power? This is the question which has exercised the reason and tried the faith of men in all ages of the world. Such is the distance between God and man, such the feebleness of our powers, and such the limited range of our vision, it might seem reasonable to leave this question to be answered by God himself. If a child cannot rationally sit in judgment on the conduct of his parents, nor a peasant comprehend the affairs of an empire, we certainly are not competent to call God to account, or to ask of Him the reason of his ways. We might rest satisfied with the assurance that the Judge of all the earth must do right. These considerations, however, have not availed to prevent speculation on this subject. The existence of evil is constantly brought forward by sceptics as an argument against religion; and it is constantly in the minds of believers as a difficulty and a doubt. While it is our duty to obey the injunction, " Be still and know that I am God," it is no less our duty to protest against those solutions of this great problem which either destroy the nature of sin or the nature of God.

Theories which involve the Denial of Sin.

Most of the theories proposed to account for the existence of evil, come under one or the other of the three following classes : First, those which really or virtually deny the existence of evil in the world. What we call evil is distinguished as physical and moral, pain and sin. There is some plausibility in the argument to prove that pain is not necessarily an evil. It is necessary to the safety of sentient creatures. But pain exists far beyond the bounds of this necessity. Such is the amount and variety of suffering in the world, of the just and of the unjust, of infants and of adults, that no philosophy can smother the conviction that the misery which weighs so heavily on the children of men, is an appalling evil. There is no such trial to our faith, as to see an infant suffering excruciating pain. If, however, pain could be removed from the category of evil, sin is not so easily disposed of. The world lies in wickedness. The history of man is, to a large degree, the history of sin. If God be holy, wise, and omnipotent, how can we account for this widely extended and long-continued prevalence of sin ?

One solution is sought in the denial that sin is an evil. In other words, it is denied that there is any such thing as sin. What we so regard is, as some maintain, nothing more than limitation of being. To be free from sin, we must be free from limitation, *i. e.*, infinite. It is not an evil that one tree is smaller, less beautiful, or less valuable than others ; or that a plant has not the sensitive life of an animal ; or that all animals have not the rational powers of man. As in a forest, we see trees of every shape and size, perfectly and imperfectly developed, and this diversity is itself a good so among men there are some more, and some less conformed to the ideal standard of reason and right, but this is not an evil. It is only diversity of development; the manifold forms of an endless life.

Others say that what we call sin is the necessary condition of virtue. There can be no action without reaction; no strength without obstacles to be overcome; no pleasure without pain; and no virtue without vice. Moral goodness is mastery over moral evil. There cannot be one without the other. All would be dead and motionless, a stagnant sea, were it not for this antagonism.

Others again say that sin has only a subjective reality. It is analogous to pain. Some things affect us agreeably, others disagreeably; some excite self-approbation, some disapprobation. But that is simply our own concern. God no more participates in our judgments than He does in our sensations.

Others do not so expressly deny the existence of sin. They admit that it is not only evil to us, but that it involves guilt in the sight of God, and therefore should be punished. Nevertheless, they represent it as arising necessarily out of the constitution of our nature. All creatures are subject to the law of development — to a " Werden." Perfection is a goal to be reached by a gradual process. This law controls every sphere of life, vegetable, animal, intellectual, and moral. Every plant is developed from a seed. Our bodies begin in a germ; infancy is feeble and suffering. Our minds are subject to the same law. They are, of necessity, open to error. Our moral life is not an exception to this rule. Moral beings, at least those constituted as we are, cannot avoid sin. It is incident to their nature and condition. It is to be outlived and overcome. If the world be so constituted and so directed that there is a continued progress toward perfection; if all evil, and especially all sin, be eliminated by this progress, the wisdom, goodness, and holiness of God will be thereby vindicated. Bruch [1] asks, " Why has God (der heilige Urgeist) brought men into the world with only the potentiality of freedom (which with him includes perfection), and not with the actuality, but left that perfection to be attained by a long process of development? The only answer to that question," he says, is, " that development lies in the very nature of the finite. It must strive toward perfection by an endless

[1] *Eigenschaften*, p. 266.

process, without ever reaching it in its fulness.   We might as well
ask why God has ordained that the tree should be developed from
a germ? or why the earth itself has passed through so many
periods of change, ever from a lower to a higher state? or why
the universe is made up of things finite, and is itself finite?" He
adds the further consideration, "that God, with the possibility of
sin, has provided redemption by which it is to be overcome, banished, and swallowed up."   "The annihilation of sin is the design
of the whole work of redemption. ‘The Son of Man is come that
He might destroy the works of the devil.’   (1 John iii. 8.)   Sin,
however, will disappear only when not the individual alone, but
when the whole race of man has reached the goal of its destination, — and when," he asks, " will this happen?"[1] That question
he leaves unanswered.   On a following page, however, he quotes
Klaiber[2] as saying : " Divine revelation gives the only possible
and satisfactory answer to the question, how the existence of sin
can be reconciled with the holiness of God, an answer which satisfies not only our pious feelings, but our anthropological and theological speculations, in that it makes known the truth that God
determined on the creation of beings, who, as free agents, were
subject to the possibility of sin, and who were through their own
fault sunk in evil, in connection with redemption ; so that sin is
only a transient, vanishing phenomenon in the development of
finite beings.   This is the great idea which pervades the whole of
revelation ; yea, which is its essence and its goal."

It is obvious that all theories which make sin a necessary evil,
destroy its nature as revealed in Scripture, and in our own consciousness.

Sin considered as the Necessary Means of the Greatest Good.

A much more plausible theory, belonging to the class of those
which virtually, although not professedly, destroy the nature of
sin, is that which regards it as the necessary means of the greatest
good.   Sin, in itself, is an evil ; relatively, it is a good.   The universe is better with it than without it.   In itself, it is an evil that
the smaller animals should be devoured by the larger ; but as this
is necessary to prevent the undue development of animal life, and
as it ministers to the higher forms thereof, it becomes a benevolent
arrangement.   The amputation of a limb is an evil ; but if necessary to save life, it is a good.   Wars are dreadful evils, yet the

---

Eigenschaften, pp. 269, 270.   [2] *Von der Sünde und Erlösung,* p. 21, *Stud.*
d. *Ev. Geistl. Würtembergs,* vol. ii. part 2.   Stuttgart, 1835.

world is indebted to wars for the preservation of civil and religious liberty, for which they are a small price. Better have war than lose the liberty wherewith Christ has made us free. Thus, if sin be the necessary means of the greatest good, it ceases to be an evil, on the whole, and it is perfectly consistent with the benevolence of God to permit its occurrence. This has been a favorite method of solving the problem of evil in all ages. This is the idea which Leibnitz wrought out so elaborately in his "Théodicée." It has been adopted by many theologians who do not carry it on to its legitimate consequences. Thus Twesten [1] says: "If the world be absolutely dependent on the most perfect Being; if it be the work of the highest love, power, and wisdom; and if it be constantly controlled and governed by God, it must be absolutely perfect." Hence even sin, although like pain an evil in itself, must on the whole be a good. It is a necessary element in a perfect world. Twesten, therefore, says,[2] "If the world, with the sin and misery which it contains, produces a greater amount of good, and reveals the divine power and love more fully than could otherwise be possible, then the consistency of the existence of evil with the universal causality (or government) of God is thereby vindicated." The word good in this connection, according to the common doctrine of optimists, does not mean moral good, but happiness. The principle on which this theory is founded was propounded in a posthumous treatise of President Edwards, in which he taught that virtue consists in the love of being. This principle was adopted and carried out by Drs. Hopkins and Emmons in their systems of theology, which for many years had great influence in this country.

Objections to this Theory.

Plausible as this theory is, it is liable to many objections.

1. In the first place, we have no right to limit the infinite God. To say that this is the best possible world, is to say that God can make nothing greater or better; which, unless the world be infinite, is to say that God is finite. It is enough for us to believe that the world with its finite results, is what God in his wisdom saw fit to call into existence; but that it is the best He could make, is a gratuitous and derogatory assumption.

2. It is unscriptural, and contrary to our moral reason, to make happiness the end of creation. The Bible declares the glory of God, an infinitely higher end, to be the final cause for which all things exist. It is the instinctive judgment of men, that holiness

---

[1] *Dogmatik*, ii. p. 121.　　　　　　[2] *Ibid.* p. 130.

or moral excellence is a greater good than happiness. But, on this theory, holiness has no value except as a means of producing happiness. This cannot be believed, except under a protest from our moral nature. The theory in question, therefore, solves the problem of evil by denying its existence. Nothing is an evil which tends to the greatest happiness. Sin is the necessary means of the greatest good, and therefore is not an evil.

The Doctrine that God cannot prevent Sin in a Moral System.

The second general method of reconciling the existence of sin with the benevolence and holiness of God, is, not to deny that sin, even all things considered, is an evil ; but to affirm that God cannot prevent all sin, or even the present amount of sin, in a moral system. It assumes that certainty is inconsistent with free agency. Any kind or degree of influence which renders it certain how a free agent will act, destroys his liberty in acting. He must always be able to act contrary to any degree of influence brought to bear upon him, or he ceases to be free. God, therefore, of necessity limits Himself when He creates free agents. They are beyond his absolute control. He may argue and persuade, but He cannot govern.

This doctrine that God cannot effectually control the acts of free agents without destroying their liberty, is so contrary to the Scriptures, that it has never been adopted by any organized portion of the Christian Church. Some theologians avail themselves of it for an emergency, when treating of this subject, although it is utterly at variance with their general scheme. Twesten, for example, who, as we have seen, in one place teaches that God voluntarily permits sin as the necessary means of the greatest good, in another place [1] says that He cannot prevent it in a moral system. " Mit der Freiheit," he says, " war die Möglichkeit des Misbrauchs gegeben ; ohne jene zu vernichten, konnte Gott diesen nicht verhindern." That is, without destroying liberty, God cannot prevent its abuse. If this be so, then God cannot govern free agents. He cannot secure the accomplishment of his purposes, or the fulfilment of his promises. There is no security for the triumph of good in the universe. Angels and saints in heaven may all sin, and evil become dominant and universal. On this theory, all prayer that God would change our own hearts, or the hearts of others, becomes irrational. All this is so contrary to the teaching of the Bible, which everywhere asserts the sovereignty and supremacy of God,

1 *Dogmatik*, ii. p. 137.

declaring that the hearts of men are in his hand, and that He turns them as the rivers of water ; that He makes his people willing in the day of his power, working in them to will and to do, according to his good pleasure ; it is so inconsistent with the promise to give repentance and faith, with the assertion of his power to change the heart ; it is so incompatible with the hopes and confidence of the believer, that God can keep him from falling; and so subversive of the idea of God as presented in the Bible and revealed in our nature, that the Church has, almost with one accord, preferred to leave the mystery of evil unexplained, rather than to seek its solution in a principle which undermines the foundation of all religion.

The Scriptural Doctrine.

The third method of dealing with this question is to rest satisfied with the simple statements of the Bible. The Scriptures teach, (1.) That the glory of God is the end to which the promotion of holiness, and the production of happiness, and all other ends are subordinate. (2.) That, therefore, the self-manifestation of God, the revelation of his infinite perfection, being the highest conceivable, or possible good, is the ultimate end of all his works in creation, providence, and redemption. (3.) As sentient creatures are necessary for the manifestation of God's benevolence, so there could be no manifestation of his mercy without misery, or of his grace and justice, if there were no sin. As the heavens declare the glory of God, so He has devised the plan of redemption, " To the intent that now unto the principalities and powers in heavenly places, might be known by the Church the manifold wisdom of God." (Eph. iii. 10.) The knowledge of God is eternal life. It is for creatures the highest good. And the promotion of that knowledge, the manifestation of the manifold perfections of the infinite God, is the highest end of all his works. This is declared by the Apostle to be the end contemplated, both in the punishment of sinners and in the salvation of believers. It is an end to which, he says, no man can rationally object. " What if God, willing to shew his wrath (or justice), and to make his power known, endured with much long suffering the vessels of wrath fitted to destruction : and that He might make known the riches of his glory on the vessels of mercy, which He had afore prepared unto glory." (Rom. ix. 22, 23.) Sin, therefore, according the Scriptures, is permitted, that the justice of God may be known in its punishment, and his grace in its forgiveness. And the universe, without the knowledge of these attributes, would be like the earth without the light of the sun.

The glory of God being the great end of all things, we are not obliged to assume that this is the best possible world for the production of happiness, or even for securing the greatest degree of holiness among rational creatures.   It is wisely adapted for the end for which it was designed, namely, the manifestation of the manifold perfections of God.   That God, in revealing Himself, does promote the highest good of his creatures, consistent with the promotion of his own glory, may be admitted.   But to reverse this order, to make the good of the creature the highest end, is to pervert and subvert the whole scheme ; it is to put the means for the end, to subordinate God to the universe, the Infinite to the finite. This putting the creature in the place of the Creator, disturbs our moral and religious sentiments and convictions, as well as our intellectual apprehensions of God, and of his relation to the universe.

The older theologians almost unanimously make the glory of God the ultimate, and the good of the creature the subordinate end of all things.   Twesten, indeed, says [1] it makes no difference whether we say God proposes his own glory as the ultimate end, and, for that purpose, determined to produce the highest degree of good ; or that He purposed the highest good of his creatures, whence the manifestation of his glory flows as a consequence.   It, however, makes all the difference in the world, whether the Creator be subordinate to the creature, or the creature to the Creator ; whether the end be the means, or the means the end.   There is a great difference whether the earth or the sun be assumed as the centre of our solar system.   If we make the earth the centre, our astronomy will be in confusion.   And if we make the creature, and not God, the end of all things, our theology and religion will in like manner be perverted.   It may, in conclusion, be safely asserted that a universe constructed for the purpose of making God known, is a far better universe than one designed for the production of happiness.

§ 14. *The Truth of God.*

Truth, is a word of frequent occurrence and of wide signification in the Bible.   The primary meaning of the Greek word ἀλήθεια (from ἀ and λήθω) is openness ; what is not concealed.   But in the Hebrew, and therefore in the Bible, the primary idea of truth is, that which sustains, which does not fail, or disappoint our expectations.   The true, therefore, is, (1.) That which is real, as opposed to that which is fictitious or imaginary.   Jehovah is

the true God, because He is really God, while the gods of the
heathen are vanity and nothing, mere imaginary beings, having
neither existence nor attributes. (2.) The true is that which
completely comes up to its idea, or to what it purports to be. A
true man is a man in whom the idea of manhood is fully realized.
The true God is He in whom is found all that Godhead imports.
(3.) The true is that in which the reality exactly corresponds to the
manifestation. God is true, because He really is what He declares
Himself to be ; because He is what He commands us to believe Him
to be ; and because all his declarations correspond to what really
is. (4.) The true is that which can be depended upon, which
does not fail, or change, or disappoint. In this sense also God is
true as He is immutable and faithful. His promise cannot fail;
his word never disappoints. His word abideth forever. When
our Lord says, " Thy word is truth," He says that all that God has
revealed may be confided in as exactly corresponding to what
really is, or is to be. His word can never fail, though heaven and
earth pass away.

The truth of God, therefore, is the foundation of all religion. It
is the ground of our assurance, that what He has revealed of Himself and of his will, in his works and in the Scriptures, may be
relied upon. He certainly is, and wills, and will do, whatever He
has thus made known. It is no less the foundation of all knowledge. That our senses do not deceive us ; that consciousness is
trustworthy in what it teaches; that anything is what it appears
to us to be; that our existence is not a delusive dream, has no
other foundation than the truth of God. In this sense, all knowledge is founded on faith, *i. e.*, the belief that God is true.

The theologians are accustomed to say : (1.) " Veritas Dei in
essentia, est convenientia omnium eorum, quæ ad naturam perfec-
tissimi pertinent eamque totam constituunt ; qua ratione Deus verus
opponitur fictis et commentitiis." (Jer. x. 8, 10, 11 ; John v. 20,
21.) (2.) " Veritas Dei in intellectu, est convenientia cogitationum
cum objecto." . . . . (Job xi. 7; Acts xv. 18.) (3.) " Veritas
Dei in voluntate est convenientia decreti ac propositi efficacis
cujusque cum rationibus in intellectu probe cognitis et judicatis."
(Rom. xi. 33.) (4.) " Veritas Dei in factis, est convenientia actionum cum proposito." (Ps. xxv. 10, ...) (5.) " Veritas
Dei in dictis, quæ singulatim vocari solet veracitas, est convenientia verborum omnium cum recta cogitatione animique sententia, et
efficaci voluntatis proposito." (Num. xxiii. 19 ; 1 Sam. xv. 29 ;
Tit. i. 2 ; Heb. vi. 18.) " Hæc cernitur (*a*), in doctrinis (Is. xvii.

17) ; (*b*), in prædictionibus, promissionibus, ut et comminationibus. (Num. xxiii. 19.) " [1]

To the same effect the Reformed theologian Endemann, says, "Veracitas Deo duplici sensu recte adscribitur, (1.) Quatenus nunquam errat, quia est omniscius, nunquam errorem aliis significat, quia id repugnat bonitati ejus. . . . . (2.) Quatenus Deus ea actu sentit, quæ verbis vel factis entibus intelligentibus significat. Deus actionibus et sermonibus suis eum intendit finem, ut sibi homines credant, confidant, etc., quem finem everteret si semel a veritate discederet.   Scriptura docet idem *scil.* quod Deus . . . . [est] verax, immunis ab omni errore et mendacio. . . . . Fidelis est Deus, quatenus ingenue aliquid promittit ; atque promissum certissimo complet. . . . . Severitatem Deo tribuimus quatenus comminationes suas implet." [2]

The philosophical theologians virtually deny that there is any such attribute in God as truth.   They say that what is intended by that term is only the uniformity of law.   The efficiency of God is always exercised in such a way that we may confide in the regular sequence of events.   In this respect it may be said that God is true.   Bruch[3] admits "That this idea arises necessarily out of our religious consciousness, inasmuch as we embrace with full confidence what we regard as a divine revelation, and are persuaded that God in due time will fulfil whatever He has purposed, promised, or threatened.   This confidence is in the strongest terms often expressed in the sacred writings, and is the source of the firm faith by which the Christian receives the revelation made in Christ ; and of the unshaken confidence with which he anticipates the fulfilment of the divine promises."   Nevertheless, although this idea of the truth of God has its foundation in our own nature, and is so clearly recognized in Scripture, and although it enters so deeply into the religious experience and hopes of the believer, it is a delusion.   There is no such attribute in God.   It is unphilosophical, and therefore impossible that there should be the distinction, which must then be assumed, between purpose and act in the divine mind. The ascription of truth or veracity to God rests, says Bruch, "on the assumption of a distinction in Him between thought and its manifestation, between his promises and threatenings, and their accomplishment, which not only destroys the unity of the divine essence, but reduces Him to the limitations and changes of time.

---

[1] Hollaz, *Examen Theologicum*, edit. Leipzig, 1763, pp. 243, 244.

[2] *Compendium Theologicum*, I. § 33; edit. Hanoviæ, 1777, pp. 97, 99

[3] *Eigenschaften*, p. 250.

. . . . As the ascription of veracity to God arises out of what we observe in ourselves, it bears the impress of anthropomorphism, and has no claim to scientific recognition." [1] He further objects to the ascription of truth to God, in the ordinary sense of that term, because God works uniformly according to law, and therefore, "properly speaking, there can be no such thing as promises or threatenings with Him." [2] The idea is, that as God has established certain physical laws, and if men comply with them they are well, if they violate them, they suffer for it; so there are laws which determine the well-being of rational creatures: if we observe those laws, we are happy; if we disregard them, we are miserable. God has nothing to do with it, except as He established those laws and carries them out. The philosophical idea, therefore, of the truth of God, is the immutability of law, physical and moral. This view is still more definitely presented by Schweizer.[3] God from the beginning to the end of the world is one and the same causality; this, in reference to the moral world, is his truth, *veracitas*, *fidelitas*, in so far as the later revelations, or manifestations of this causality, correspond to what the earlier manifestations would lead us to expect. God, according to this view, is not so much a person, as a name for the moral order of the universe. There is, of course, some truth in this mode of representation. The laws of God, by which He governs his creatures, rational and irrational, are uniform. It is true that a man reaps what he sows; that he receives here and hereafter the natural consequences of his conduct. If he sows to the flesh, he reaps corruption; if he sows to the spirit, he reaps life everlasting. But these laws are administered by a personal God, who, as He controls physical laws so as to produce plenty or famine, health or pestilence, as to Him seems fit, so also He controls all the laws which determine the well-being of the souls of men, so as to accomplish his designs and to secure the fulfilment of his promises and threatenings. The laws of a well-ordered human government are uniform and impartial, but that is not inconsistent with their human administration.

It is a great mercy that, at least in some cases, those whose philosophy forbids their believing in the personality of God, believe in the personality of Christ, whom they regard as a man invested with all the attributes of the Godhead, and whom they love and worship accordingly.

---

[1] *Eigenschaften*, p. 250.   [2] *Ibid.* p. 252.
[3] *Glaubenslehre*, vol. i. p. 443.

§ 15. *Sovereignty.*

Sovereignty is not a property of the divine nature, but a prerogative arising out of the perfections of the Supreme Being. If God be a Spirit, and therefore a person, infinite, eternal, and immutable in his being and perfections, the Creator and Preserver of the universe, He is of right its absolute sovereign. Infinite wisdom, goodness, and power, with the right of possession, which belongs to God in all his creatures, are the immutable foundation of his dominion. " Our God is in the heavens ; He hath done whatsoever He pleased." (Ps. cxv. 3.) " All the inhabitants of the earth are reputed as nothing: and He doeth according to his will in the army of heaven, and among the inhabitants of the earth : and none can stay his hand, or say unto him, What doest thou ? " (Dan. iv. 35.) " All that is in the heaven and in the earth is thine." (1 Chron. xxix. 11.) " The earth is the Lord's, and the fulness thereof; the world, and they that dwell therein." (Ps. xxiv. 1.) " Thine is the kingdom, O Lord, and thou art exalted as head above all." (1 Chron. xxix. 11.) " Behold, all souls are mine ; as the soul of the father, so also the soul of the son is mine." (Ez. xviii. 4.) " Woe unto him that striveth with his Maker ! Let the potsherd strive with the potsherds of the earth. Shall the clay say to him that fashioned it, What makest thou ? or thy work, He hath no hands ? " (Is. xlv. 9.) " Is it not lawful for me to do what I will with mine own ? " (Matt. xx. 15.) He " worketh all things after the counsel of his own will." (Eph. i. 11.) " Of Him, and through Him, and to Him are all things : to whom be glory forever. Amen." (Rom. xi. 36.)

From these and similar passages of Scriptures it is plain, (1.) That the sovereignty of God is universal. It extends over all his creatures from the highest to the lowest. (2.) That it is absolute. There is no limit to be placed to his authority. He doeth his pleasure in the armies of heaven and among the inhabitants of the earth. (3.) It is immutable. It can neither be ignored nor rejected. It binds all creatures, as inexorably as physical laws bind the material universe.

This sovereignty is exercised, (1.) In establishing the laws, physical and moral, by which all creatures are to be governed. (2.) In determining the nature and powers of the different orders of created beings, and in assigning each its appropriate sphere. (3.) In appointing to each individual his position and lot. It is the Lord who fixes the bounds of our habitation. Our times are in his hands. He determines when, where, and under what circumstances each individual of our race is to be born, live, and die. Nations, no less than individuals, are thus in the hands of God, who assigns them their heritage in the earth, and controls their destiny. (4.) God is no less sovereign in the distribution of his favours. He does what He wills with his own. He gives to some riches, to others, honour; to others, health; while others are poor, unknown, or the victims of disease. To some, the light of the gospel is sent; others are left in darkness. Some are brought through faith unto salvation; others perish in unbelief. To the question, Why is this? the only answer is that given by our Lord. "Even so, Father, for so it seemeth good in thy sight."

Although this sovereignty is thus universal and absolute, it is the sovereignty of wisdom, holiness, and love. The authority of God is limited by nothing out of Himself, but it is controlled, in all its manifestations, by his infinite perfections. If a man is free and exalted, in proportion as he is governed by enlightened reason and a pure conscience, so is he supremely blessed who cheerfully submits to be governed by the infinite reason and holiness of God. This sovereignty of God is the ground of peace and confidence to all his people. They rejoice that the Lord God omnipotent reigneth; that neither necessity, nor chance, nor the folly of man, nor the malice of Satan controls the sequence of events and all their issues. Infinite wisdom, love, and power, belong to Him, our great God and Saviour, into whose hands all power in heaven and earth has been committed.

CHAPTER VI.

THE TRINITY.

§ 1. *Preliminary Remarks.*

THE doctrine of the Trinity is peculiar to the religion of the Bible. The Triad of the ancient world is only a philosophical statement of the pantheistic theory which underlies all the religions of antiquity. With the Hindus, simple, undeveloped, primal being, without consciousness or attributes, is called Brahm. This being, as unfolding itself in the actual world, is Vishnu; as returning into the abyss of unconscious being, it is Shiva. In Buddhism we find essentially the same ideas, in a more dualistic form. Buddhism makes more of a distinction between God, or the spiritual principle of all things, and nature. The soul of man is a part, or an existence-form, of this spiritual essence, whose destiny is, that it may be freed from nature and lost in the infinite unknown. In Platonism, also, we find a notional Trinity. Simple being ($\tau\grave{o}$ $\check{o}\nu$) has its $\lambda\acute{o}\gamma os$, the complex of its ideas, the reality in all that is phenomenal and changing. In all these systems, whether ancient or modern, there is a Thesis, Antithesis, and Synthesis; the Infinite becomes finite, and the finite returns to the Infinite. It is obvious, therefore, that these trinitarian formulas have no analogy with the Scriptural doctrine of the Trinity, and serve neither to explain nor to confirm it.

The design of all the revelations contained in the Word of God is the salvation of men. Truth is in order to holiness. God does not make known his being and attributes to teach men science, but to bring them to the saving knowledge of Himself. The doctrines of the Bible are, therefore, intimately connected with religion, or the life of God in the soul. They determine the religious experience of believers, and are presupposed in that experience. This is specially true of the doctrine of the Trinity. It is a great mistake to regard that doctrine as a mere speculative or abstract truth, concerning the constitution of the Godhead, with which we have no practical concern, or which we are required to believe simply because it is revealed. On the contrary, it underlies the whole plan of salvation, and determines the character of the religion (in the subjective sense of that word) of all true Christians. It is the unconscious, or unformed faith, even of those of God's people who are unable to understand the term by which it is expressed. They all believe in God, the Creator and Preserver against whom they have sinned, whose justice they know they cannot satisfy, and whose image they cannot restore to their apostate nature. They, therefore, as of necessity, believe in a divine Redeemer and a divine Sanctifier. They have, as it were, the factors of the doctrine of the Trinity in their own religious convictions. No mere speculative doctrine, especially no doctrine so mysterious and so out of analogy with all other objects of human knowledge, as that of the Trinity, could ever have held the abiding control over the faith of the Church, which this doctrine has maintained. It is not, therefore, by any arbitrary decision, nor from any bigoted adherence to hereditary beliefs, that the Church has always refused to recognize as Christians those who reject this doctrine. This judgment is only the expression of the deep conviction that Antitrinitarians must adopt a radically and practically different system of religion from that on which the Church builds her hopes. It is not too much to say with Meyer,[1] that " the Trinity is the point in which all Christian ideas and interests unite; at once the beginning and the end of all insight into Christianity."

This great article of the Christian faith may be regarded under three different aspects: (1.) The Biblical form of the doctrine. (2.) The ecclesiastical form, or the mode in which the statements of the Bible have been explained in the symbols of the Church and the writings of theologians. (3.) Its philosophical form, or the attempts which have been made to illustrate, or to prove, the doctrine on philosophical principles. It is only the doctrine as presented in the Bible, which binds the faith and conscience of the people of God.

§ 2. *Biblical Form of the Doctrine.*

A. *What that Form is.*

The form in which this doctrine lies in the Bible, and in which it enters into the faith of the Church universal, includes substantially the following particulars.

1. There is one only living and true God, or divine Being. The religion of the Bible stands opposed not only to Atheism, but to all forms of polytheism. The Scriptures everywhere assert that

[1] *Lehre von der Trinität*, vol. i. p. 42.

Jehovah alone is God. (Deut. vi. 4.) " The Lord our God is one
Lord." " I am the first, and I am the last; and besides me there
is no God." (Is. xliv. 6.) "Thou believest that there is one
God; thou doest well." (James ii. 19.) The Decalogue, which
is the foundation of the moral and religious code of Christianity,
as well as of Judaism, has as its first and greatest commandment,
"Thou shalt have no other God before me." No doctrine, therefore, can possibly be true which contradicts this primary truth of
natural as well as of revealed religion.

2. In the Bible all divine titles and attributes are ascribed
equally to the Father, Son, and Spirit. The same divine worship
is rendered to them. The one is as much the object of adoration,
love, confidence, and devotion as the other. It is not more evident that the Father is God, than that the Son is God; nor is the
deity of the Father and Son more clearly revealed than that of the
Spirit.

3. The terms Father, Son, and Spirit do not express different relations of God to his creatures. They are not analogous
to the terms Creator, Preserver, and Benefactor, which do express
such relations. The Scriptural facts are, (a.) The Father says
I; the Son says I; the Spirit says I. (b.) The Father says Thou
to the Son, and the Son says Thou to the Father; and in like
manner the Father and the Son use the pronouns He and Him in
reference to the Spirit. (c.) The Father loves the Son; the Son
loves the Father; the Spirit testifies of the Son. The Father,
Son, and Spirit are severally subject and object. They act and
are acted upon, or are the objects of action. Nothing is added
to these facts when it is said that the Father, Son, and Spirit are
distinct persons; for a person is an intelligent subject who can
say I, who can be addressed as Thou, and who can act and can be
the object of action. The summation of the above facts is expressed
in the proposition, The one divine Being subsists in three persons,
Father, Son, and Spirit. This proposition adds nothing to the
facts themselves; for the facts are, (1.) That there is one divine
Being. (2.) The Father, Son, and Spirit are divine. (3.) The
Father, Son, and Spirit are, in the sense just stated, distinct
persons. (4.) Attributes being inseparable from substance,
the Scriptures, in saying that the Father, Son, and Spirit possess
the same attributes, say they are the same in substance; and, if
the same in substance, they are equal in power and glory.

4. Notwithstanding that the Father, Son, and Spirit are the
same in substance, and equal in power and glory, it is no less true,

according to the Scriptures, (*a.*) That the Father is first, the Son second, and the Spirit third. (*b.*) The Son is of the Father (ἐκ θεοῦ, the λόγος, εἰκὼν, ἀπαύγασμα, τοῦ θεοῦ) ; and the Spirit is of the Father and of the Son. (*c.*) The Father sends the Son, and the Father and Son send the Spirit. (*d.*) The Father operates through the Son, and the Father and Son operate through the Spirit. The converse of these statements is never found. The Son is never said to send the Father, nor to operate through Him; nor is the Spirit ever said to send the Father, or the Son, or to operate through them. The facts contained in this paragraph are summed up in the proposition : In the Holy Trinity there is a subordination of the Persons as to the mode of subsistence and operation. This proposition again adds nothing to the facts themselves.

5. According to the Scriptures, the Father created the world, the Son created the world, and the Spirit created the world. The Father preserves all things ; the Son upholds all things; and the Spirit is the source of all life. These facts are expressed by saying that the persons of the Trinity concur in all acts *ad extra*. Nevertheless there are some acts which are predominantly referred to the Father, others to the Son, and others to the Spirit. The Father creates, elects, and calls; the Son redeems; and the Spirit sanctifies. And, on the other hand, there are certain acts, or conditions, predicated of one person of the Trinity, which are never predicated of either of the others. Thus, generation belongs exclusively to the Father, filiation to the Son, and procession to the Spirit. This is the form in which the doctrine of the Trinity lies in the Bible. The above statement involves no philosophical element. It is simply an arrangement of the clearly revealed facts bearing on this subject. This is the form in which the doctrine has always entered into the faith of the Church, as a part of its religious convictions and experience.

To say that this doctrine is incomprehensible, is to say nothing more than must be admitted of any other great truth, whether of revelation or of science. To say that it is impossible that the one divine substance can subsist in three distinct persons, is certainly unreasonable, when, according to that form of philosophy which has been the most widely diffused, and the most persistent, everything that exists is only one of the innumerable forms in which one and the same infinite substance subsists ; and when, according to the Realists, who once controlled the thinking world, all men are the individualized forms of the numerically same substance called generic humanity.

B. *Scriptural Proof of the Doctrine.*

No such doctrine as that of the Trinity can be adequately proved by any citation of Scriptural passages. Its constituent elements are brought into view, some in one place, and some in another. The unity of the Divine Being; the true and equal divinity of the Father, Son, and Spirit; their distinct personality; the relation in which they stand one to the other, and to the Church and the world, are not presented in a doctrinal formula in the Word of God, but the several constituent elements of the doctrine are asserted, or assumed, over and over, from the beginning to the end of the Bible. It is, therefore, by proving these elements separately, that the whole doctrine can be most satisfactorily established. All that is here necessary is, a reference to the general teachings of Scripture on the subject, and to some few passages in which everything essential to the doctrine is included.

The Progressive Character of Divine Revelation.

1. The progressive character of divine revelation is recognized in relation to all the great doctrines of the Bible. One of the strongest arguments for the divine origin of the Scriptures is the organic relation of its several parts. They comprise more than sixty books written by different men in different ages, and yet they form one whole; not by mere external historical relations, nor in virtue of the general identity of the subjects of which they treat, but by their internal organic development. All that is in a full-grown tree was potentially in the seed. All that we find unfolded in the fulness of the gospel lies in a rudimental form in the earliest books of the Bible. What at first is only obscurely intimated is gradually unfolded in subsequent parts of the sacred volume, until the truth is revealed in its fulness. This is true of the doctrines of redemption; of the person and work of the Messiah, the promised seed of the woman; of the nature and office of the Holy Spirit; and of a future state beyond the grave. And this is specially true of the doctrine of the Trinity. Even in the book of Genesis there are intimations of the doctrine which receive their true interpretation in later revelations. That the names of God are in the plural form; that the personal pronouns are often in the first person plural ("Let us make man in our image"); that the form of benediction is threefold, and other facts of like nature, may be explained in different ways. But when it becomes plain, from the progress of the revelation, that there are three persons in the God-

head, then such forms of expression can hardly fail to be recognized as having their foundation in that great truth.

2. Much more important, however, is the fact, that not only in Genesis, but also in all the early books of Scripture, we find a distinction made between Jehovah and the angel of Jehovah, who himself is God, to whom all divine titles are given, and divine worship is rendered. As the revelation is unfolded, such distinction becomes more and more manifest. This messenger of God is called the word, the wisdom, the Son of God. His personality and divinity are clearly revealed. He is of old, even from everlasting, the Mighty God, the Adonai, the Lord of David, Jehovah our Righteousness, who was to be born of a virgin, and bear the sins of many.

3. In like manner, even in the first chapter of Genesis, the Spirit of God is represented as the source of all intelligence, order, and life in the created universe; and in the following books of the Old Testament He is represented as inspiring the prophets, giving wisdom, strength, and goodness to statesmen and warriors, and to the people of God. This Spirit is not an agency, but an agent, who teaches and selects; who can be sinned against and grieved; and who, in the New Testament, is unmistakably revealed as a distinct person. When John the Baptist appeared, we find him speaking of the Holy Spirit as of a person with whom his countrymen were familiar, as an object of divine worship and the giver of saving blessings. Our divine Lord also takes this truth for granted, and promised to send the Spirit, as a Paraclete, to take his place; to instruct, comfort, and strengthen them; whom they were to receive and obey. Thus, without any violent transition, the earliest revelations of this mystery were gradually unfolded, until the Triune God, Father, Son, and Spirit, appears in the New Testament as the universally recognized God of all believers.

The Formula of Baptism.

4. In the formulas of Baptism and of the Apostolic Benediction, provision was made to keep this doctrine constantly before the minds of the people, as a cardinal article of the Christian faith. Every Christian is baptized in the name of the Father, of the Son, and of the Holy Ghost. The personality, the divinity, and consequently the equality of these three subjects, are here taken for granted. The association of the Son and Spirit with the Father; the identity of relation, so far as dependence and obedience are concerned, which we sustain to the Father, Son, and Spirit re-

spectively; the confession and profession involved in the ordinances; all forbid any other interpretation of this formula than that which it has always received in the Church. If the expression, " In the name of the Father," implies the personality of the Father, the same implication is involved when it is used in reference to the Son and Spirit. If we acknowledge our subjection and allegiance to the one, we acknowledge the same subjection and allegiance to the other divine persons here named.

The Apostolic Benediction.

In the apostolic benediction a prayer is addressed to Christ for his grace, to the Father for his love, and to the Spirit for his fellowship. The personality and divinity of each are therefore solemnly recognized every time that this benediction is pronounced and received.

5. In the record of our Lord's baptism, the Father addresses the Son, and the Spirit descends in the form of a dove. In the discourse of Christ, recorded in the 14th, 15th, and 16th chapters of John's Gospel, our Lord speaks to and of the Father, and promises to send the Spirit to teach, guide, and comfort his disciples. In that discourse the personality and divinity of the Father, Son, and Spirit are recognized with equal clearness. In 1 Cor. xii. 4–6, the Apostle speaks of diversity of gifts, but the same Spirit; of diversity of administration, but the same Lord; and of diversities of operations, but the same God.

It is not to be forgotten, however, that the faith of the Church in the doctrine of the Trinity, does not rest exclusively or principally on such arguments as those mentioned above. The great foundation of that faith is what is taught everywhere in the Bible of the unity of the Divine Being; of the personality and divinity of the Father, Son, and Spirit; and of their mutual relations.

§ 3. The Transition Period.

A. *The Necessity for a more Definite Statement of the Doctrine.*

The Biblical form of the doctrine of the Trinity, as given above, includes everything that is essential to the integrity of the doctrine, and all that is embraced in the faith of ordinary Christians. It is not all, however, that is included in the creeds of the Church. It is characteristic of the Scriptures, that the truths therein presented are exhibited in the form in which they address themselves to our religious consciousness. To this feature of the Word of

God, its adaptation to general use is to be attributed. A truth often lies in the mind of the Church as an object of faith, long before it is wrought out in its doctrinal form; that is, before it is analyzed, its contents clearly ascertained, and its elements stated in due relation to each other. When a doctrine so complex as that of the Trinity is presented as an object of faith, the mind is forced to reflect upon it, to endeavour to ascertain what it includes, and how its several parts are to be stated, so as to avoid confusion or contradiction. Besides this internal necessity for a definite statement of the doctrine, such statement was forced upon the Church from without. Even among those who honestly intended to receive what the Scriptures taught upon the subject, it was inevitable that there should arise diversity in the mode of statement, and confusion and contradiction in the use of terms. As the Church is one, not externally merely, but really and inwardly, this diversity and confusion are as much an evil, a pain, and an embarrassment, troubling its inward peace, as the like inconsistency and confusion would be in an individual mind. There was, therefore, an inward and outward necessity, in the Church itself, for a clear, comprehensive, and consistent statement of the various elements of this complex doctrine of Christian faith.

B. *Conflict with Error.*

Besides this necessity for such a statement of the doctrine as would satisfy the minds of those who received it, there was a further necessity of guarding the truth from the evil influence of false or erroneous exhibitions of it. The conviction was deeply settled in the minds of all Christians that Christ is a divine person. The glory which He displayed, the authority which He assumed, the power which He exhibited, the benefits which He conferred, necessitated the recognition of Him as the true God. No less strong, however, was the conviction that there is only one God. The difficulty was, to reconcile these two fundamental articles of the Christian faith. The mode of solving this difficulty, by rejecting one of these articles to save the other, was repudiated by common consent. There were those who denied the divinity of Christ, and endeavoured to satisfy the minds of believers by representing Him as the best of men; as filled with the Spirit of God; as the Son of God, because miraculously begotten; or as animated and conrolled by the power of God; but, nevertheless, merely a man. This view of the person of Christ was so universally rejected in the early Church, as hardly to occasion controversy. The errors with which the advocates of the doctrine of the Trinity had to contend were of a higher order. It was of course unavoidable that both parties, the advocates and the opponents of the doctrine, availed themselves of the current philosophies of the age. Consciously or unconsciously, all men are more or less controlled in their modes of thinking on divine subjects by the metaphysical opinions which prevail around them, and in which they have been educated. We accordingly find that Gnosticism and Platonism coloured the views of both the advocates and the opponents of the doctrine of the Trinity during the Ante-Nicene period.

The Gnostics.

The Gnostics held that there was a series of emanations from the primal Being, of different orders or ranks. It was natural that those addicted to this system, and who professed to be Christians, should represent Christ as one of the highest of these emanations, or Eons. This view of his person admitted of his being regarded as consubstantial with God, as divine, as the creator of the world, as a distinct person, and of his having at least an apparent or docetic union with humanity. It therefore suited some of the conditions of the complicated problem to be solved. It, however, represented Christ as one of a series of emanations, and reduced Him to the category of dependent beings, exalted above others of the same class in rank, but not in nature. It moreover involved the denial of his true humanity, which was as essential to the faith of the Church, and as dear to his people as his divinity. All explanations of the Trinity, therefore, founded on the Gnostic philosophy were rejected as unsatisfactory and heretical.

The Platonizers.

The Platonic system as modified by Philo, and applied by him to the philosophical explanation of the theology of the Old Testament, had far more influence on the speculations of the early Fathers than Gnosticism. According to Plato, God formed, or had in the divine reason, the ideas, types, or models of all things, which ideas became the living, formative principles of all actual existences. The divine reason, with its contents, was the Logos. Philo, therefore, in explaining creation, represents the Logos as the sum of all these types or ideas, which make up the κόσμος νοητός, or ideal world. In this view the Logos was designated as ἐνδιάθετος (*mente conceptus*). In creation, or the self-manifestation of God in nature, this divine reason or Logos is born, sent forth, or projected, becoming the λόγος προφορικός, giving life and form to all things. God, as thus manifested in the world, Philo called not only λόγος, but also υἱός, εἰκών, υἱὸς μονογενής, πρωτόγονος, σκία, παράδειγμα, δόξα, ἐπιστήμη, θεοῦ, and δεύτερος Θεός. In the application of this philosophy to the doctrine of Christ, it was easy to make him the λόγος προφορικός, to assume and assert his personality, and to represent him as specially manifested or incarnate in Jesus of Nazareth. This attempt was made by Justin Martyr, Tatian, and Theophilus. It succeeded so far as it exalted Christ above all creatures; it made him the creator and preserver of all things, the light and life of the world. It did not satisfy the consciousness of the Church, because it represented the divinity of Christ as essentially subordinate; it made his generation antemundane, but not eternal; and especially because the philosophy, from which this theory of the Logos was borrowed, was utterly opposed to the Christian system. The Logos of Plato and Philo was only a collective term for the ideal world, the ἰδέα τῶν ἰδεῶν; and therefore the real distinction between God and the Logos, was that between God as hidden and God as revealed. God in himself was ὁ θεός; God in nature was the Logos. This is, after all, the old heathen, pantheistic doctrine, which makes the universe the manifestation, or existence form of God.

Origen's Doctrine.

Origen presented the Platonic doctrine of the generation and nature of the Logos in a higher form than that in which it had been exhibited in the speculations of others among the fathers. He not only insisted, in opposition to the Monarchians or Unitarians, upon the distinct personality of the Son, but also upon his eternal, as opposed to his antemundane, generation. Nevertheless, he referred this generation to the will of the Father. The Son was thus reduced to the category of creatures, for according to Origen, creation is from eternity. Another unsatisfactory feature of all these speculations on the Logos-theory was, that it made no provision for the Holy Spirit. The Logos was the Word, or Son of God, begotten before creation in order to create, or, according to Origen, begotten from eternity; but what was the Holy Spirit? He appears in the baptismal service and in the apostolic benediction as a distinct person, but the Logos-theory provided only for a Dyad, and not a Triad. Hence the greatest confusion appears in the utterances of this class of writers concerning the Holy Ghost. Sometimes, He is identified with the Logos; sometimes, He is represented as the substance common to the Father and the Son: sometimes, as the mere power or efficiency of God; sometimes, as a distinct person subordinate to the Logos, and a creature.

The Sabellian Theory.

Another method of solving this great problem and of satisfy-
ing the religious convictions of the Church, was that adopted by
the Monarchians, Patripassians, or Unitarians, as they were in-
differently called. They admitted a modal trinity. They acknowledged the true divinity of Christ, but denied any personal distinctions in the Godhead. The same person is at once Father, Son,
and Holy Spirit; these terms expressing the different relations in
which God reveals Himself in the world and in the Church.
Praxeas, of Asia Minor, who taught this doctrine in Rome, A. D.
200; Noetus, of Smyrna, A. D. 230; Beryll, bishop of Bostra, in
Arabia, A. D. 250; and especially Sabellius, a presbyter of Ptole-
mais, A. D. 250, after whom this doctrine was called Sabellianism,
were the principal advocates of this theory. The only point as to
which this doctrine satisfied the religious convictions of Christians,
was the true divinity of our Lord. But as it denied the distinct
personality of the Father and of the Spirit, to whom every believer
felt himself to stand in a personal relation, to whom worship and
prayers were addressed, it could not be received by the people of
God. Its opposition to Scripture was apparent. In the Bible the
Father is represented as constantly addressing the Son as " Thou,"
as loving Him, as sending Him, as rewarding and exalting Him;
and the Son as constantly addresses the Father and refers everything to his will, so that their distinct personality is one of the most
clearly revealed doctrines of the Word of God. Sabellianism was,
therefore, soon almost universally rejected.

Arianism.

Although Origen had insisted on the distinct personality of the
Son, and upon his eternal generation, and although he freely called
him God, nevertheless he would not admit his equality with God.
The Father, alone, according to him was ὁ θεός, the Son was simply θεός. The Son was θεὸς ἐκ θεοῦ and not αὐτο-θεός. And this
subordination was not simply as to the mode of subsistence and
operation, but as to nature; for Origen taught that the Son was of
a different essence from the Father, ἕτερος κατ' οὐσίαν, and owed his
existence to the will of the Father. His disciples carried out his
doctrine and avowedly made Christ a creature. This was done by
Dionysius of Alexandria, a scholar of Origen, who spoke of the
Son as ποίημα and κτίσμα, a mode of representation, however, which
he subsequently retracted or explained away. It is plain, however,

that the principles of Origen were inconsistent with the true divinity of Christ. It was not long, therefore, before Arius, another presbyter of Alexandria, openly maintained that the Son was not eternal, but was posterior to the Father ; that He was created not from the substance of God, but ἐκ οὐκ ὄντων, and therefore was not ὁμοούσιος with the Father. He admitted that the Son existed before any other creature, and that it was by Him God created the world.

It is to be constantly remembered that these speculations were the business of the theologians. They neither expressed nor affected to express the mind of the Church. The great body of the people drew their faith, then, as now, immediately from the Scriptures and from the services of the sanctuary. They were baptized in the name of the Father, and of the Son, and of the Holy Ghost. They addressed themselves to the Father as the creator of heaven and earth, and as their reconciled God and Father, and to Jesus Christ as their Redeemer, and to the Holy Ghost as their sanctifier and comforter. They loved, worshipped, and trusted the one as they did the others. This was the religious belief of the Church, which remained undisturbed by the speculations and controversies of the theologians, in their attempts to vindicate and explain the common faith. This state of confusion was, however, a great evil, and in order to bring the Church to an agreement as to the manner in which this fundamental doctrine of Christianity should be stated, the Emperor Constantine summoned the First Ecumenical Council, to meet at Nice, in Nicomedia, A. D. 325.

§ 4. *The Church Doctrine as presented by the Council of Nice.*

A. *The Objects for which that Council was convened.*

The object for which the Council was called together was threefold. (1.) To remedy the confusion which prevailed in the use of several important words employed in discussions on the doctrine of the Trinity. (2.) To condemn errors which had been adopted in different parts of the Church. (3.) To frame such a statement of the doctrine as would include all its Scriptural elements, and satisfy the religious convictions of the mass of believers. This was an exceedingly difficult task.

1. Because the *usus loquendi* of certain important terms was not then determined. The word ὑπόστασις, for example, was used in two opposite senses. It was often taken, in its etymological sense, for substance, and is used by the Council itself as synonymous with οὐσία. But it had already begun to be used in the sense of person.

As it expresses reality, as opposed to what is phenomenal or apparent, or mode of manifestation, it came to be universally used in the Greek Church, in the latter sense, as a safeguard against the idea of a mere modal Trinity. It will be admitted that great confusion must prevail, if one man should say there is only one ὑπόστασις in the Godhead, and another affirm that there are three, when both meant the same thing, the one using the word in the sense of substance, and the other in that of person.

In the Latin Church the same difficulty was experienced in the use of the words *substantia* and *subsistentia*. These words were often interchanged as equivalent, and both were used, sometimes in the sense of substance, and sometimes in that of *suppositum*. Usage finally determined the former to mean substance or essence, and the latter a mode in which substance exists, *i. e.*, *suppositum*. According to established usage, therefore, there is one substance, and there are three subsistences in the Godhead.

To express the idea of a *suppositum intelligens*, or self-conscious agent, the Greeks first used the word πρόσωπον. But as that word properly means *the face, the aspect*, and as it was used by the Sabellians to express their doctrine of the threefold aspect under which the Godhead was revealed, it was rejected, and the word ὑπόστασις adopted. The Latin word *persona* (from *per* and *sono*) properly means a mask worn by an actor and through which he spoke ; and then the role or character which the actor sustained. On this account the word had a struggle before it was adopted in the terminology of theology.

The celebrated term ὁμοούσιος, so long the subject of controversy, was not free from ambiguity. It expressed plainly enough sameness of substance, but whether that sameness was specific or numerical, the usage of the word left undecided. Porphyry is quoted as saying, that the souls of men and of irrational animals are ὁμοούσιοι, and Aristotle as saying that the stars are ὁμοούσιοι, and men and brutes are said to be ὁμοούσιοι as to their bodies ; and in like manner angels, demons, and human souls, are said to be all ὁμοούσιοι. In this sense, Peter, James, and John are ὁμοούσιοι, as having the same nature in kind. On this account the use of the word was objected to, as admitting of a Tritheistic interpretation. The Council, however, determined the sense in which it was to be understood in their decisions, by saying that the Son was begotten ἐκ τῆς οὐσίας τοῦ πατρός, and by denying that He was created. As God is a spirit, and as we are spirits, we are said, in Scripture, to be like Him, and to be his children, to be of the same nature. But with regard to the Son it was declared that He was of the same numerical essence with the Father; He is truly God, possessing the same attributes and entitled to the same homage. Thus explained, the word became an insuperable barrier against the adoption of the Nicene Creed by any who denied the true divinity of the Son of God.

Difference of Opinion among the Members of the Council.

2. A second difficulty with which the Council had to contend, was diversity of opinion among its own members. All the conflicting views which had agitated the Church were there represented. The principal parties were, first, the Arians, who held, (1.) That the Son owed his existence to the will of the Father. (2.) That He was not eternal; but that there was a time when He was not. (3.) That He was created ἐξ οὐκ ὄντων, out of nothing, and was therefore κτίσμα καὶ ποίημα. (4.) That He was not immutable, but τρεπτὸς φύσει. (5.) That his preëminence consisted in the fact that He alone was created immediately by God, whereas all other creatures were created by the Son. (6.) He was not God of Himself, but was made God, ἐθεοποιήθη; that is, on account of his exalted nature, and the relation in which He stands to all other creatures, as Creator and Governor, He was entitled to divine worship.

One of the passages of Scripture on which the Arians principally relied was Prov. viii. 22, which in the Septuagint is rendered: ἔκτισέ με ἀρχὴν ὁδῶν αὐτοῦ (He created me in the beginning of his ways). As Wisdom, there spoken of, was universally understood to be the Logos, and as the Septuagint was regarded as authoritative, this passage seemed to prove, beyond dispute, that the Logos or Son was created. The Orthodox were forced to explain away this passage by saying that κτίζειν was here to be taken in the sense of γεννᾶν, the word elsewhere used to express the relation between the Father and the Son. Ignorance, or neglect of the Hebrew, prevented their answering the argument of the Arians by showing that the word קָנָה here rendered by the Septuagint ἔκτισε, means not only to establish, but to possess. The Vulgate, therefore, correctly renders the passage, " Dominus possidet me ; " and the English version also reads, " The Lord possessed me." The Arians proper constituted a small minority of the Council.

The Semi-Arians.

The second party included the Semi-Arians and the disciples of Origen. These held with the Arians, (1.) That the Son owed his existence to the will of the Father.   (2.) That He was not of the same essence, but ἕτερος κατ' οὐσίαν.   They seemed to hold that there was an essence intermediate between the divine substance and created substances.   It was in reference to this form of opinion that Augustine afterwards said,[1] "Unde liquido apparet ipsum factum non esse per quem facta sunt omnia.   Et si factus non est, creatura non est: si autem creatura non est, ejusdem cum Patre substantiæ est.   Omnis enim substantia quæ Deus non est, creatura est; et quæ creatura non est, Deus est."

(3.) The Son was, therefore, subordinate to the Father, not merely in rank or mode of subsistence, but in nature.   He belonged to a different order of beings.   He was not αὐτόθεος, ὁ Θεός, or, ὁ ἀληθινὸς θεός; but simply θεός, a term which, according to Origen, could be properly applied to the higher orders of intelligent creatures.

(4.) The Son, although thus inferior to the Father, having life in Himself, was the source of life, i. e., the Creator.

(5.) The Holy Spirit, according to most of the Arians and to Origen, was created by the Son, — the first and highest of the creatures called into being by his power.

The Orthodox.

The third party in the Council were the Orthodox, who constituted the great majority.   All Christians were the worshippers of Christ.   He was to them the object of supreme love and the ground of their confidence; to Him they were subject in heart and life.   They looked to Him for everything.   He was their God in the highest sense of the word.   He was, moreover, in their apprehension, a distinct person, and not merely another name for the Father. But as the conviction was no less deeply rooted in the minds of Christians, that there is only one God or divine Being, the problem which the Council had to solve was to harmonize these apparently incompatible convictions, namely, that there is only one God, and yet that the Father is God, and the Son, as a distinct person, is God, the same in substance and equal in power and glory.   The only thing to be done was, to preserve the essential elements of the doctrine, and yet not make the statement of it self-contradictory.   To meet these conditions, the Council framed the following Creed, namely, "We believe in one God, the Father almighty, the maker of all things visible and invisible; and in one Lord Jesus Christ, the Son of God, only begotten, begotten of the Father, that

[1] *De Trinitate*, I. vi. 9, edit. Benedictines, vol. viii. p. 1161, c.

is, of the essence of the Father, God of God, Light of Light, very God of very God, begotten and not made, consubstantial with the Father, by whom all things were made whether in heaven or on earth; who for us men and our salvation came down from heaven; and was incarnate and became man, suffered and rose again on the third day; ascended into heaven, and will come to judge the living and the dead. And we believe in the Holy Ghost. But those who say, that there was a time when He (the Son) was not, that He was not before He was made, or was made out of nothing, or of another or different essence or substance, that He was a creature, or mutable, or susceptible of change, the Holy Catholic Church anathematizes."

B. *Council of Constantinople. The so-called Athanasian Creed.*

The most obvious deficiency in the Nicene Creed is the omission of any definite statement concerning the Holy Spirit. This is to be accounted for by the fact that the doctrine concerning the Son, and his relation to the Father, was then the absorbing subject of controversy. Athanasius, however, and other expounders and defenders of the Nicene Creed, insisted that the Spirit is consubstantial with the Father and the Son, and that such was the mind of the Council. As this, however, was disputed, it was distinctly asserted in several provincial Councils, as in that of Alexandria, A. D. 362, and that of Rome, A. D. 375. It was opposition to this doctrine which led to the calling of the Second Ecumenical Council, which met in Constantinople, A. D. 381. In the modification of the Nicene Creed, as issued by that Council, the following words were added to the clause, " We believe in the Holy Ghost," namely : " Who is the Lord and giver of life, who proceedeth from the Father, who with the Father and the Son together is worshipped and glorified, who spoke by the prophets." Some of the Greek and the great body of the Latin fathers held that the Spirit proceeded from the Son as well as from the Father, and by the Synod of Toledo, A. D. 589, the words *filioque* were added to the creed. This addition was one of the causes which led to the separation of the Eastern and Western Churches.

The Athanasian Creed.

After the Council of Constantinople, A. D. 381, the controversies which agitated the Church had reference to the constitution of the person of Christ. Before the questions involved in those controversies were authoritatively decided, the so-called Athanasian

Creed, an amplification of those of Nice and of Constantinople, came to be generally adopted, at least, among the Western Churches. That creed was in these words, namely: "Whoever would be saved, must first of all take care that he hold the Catholic faith, which, except a man preserve whole and inviolate, he shall without doubt perish eternally. But this is the Catholic faith, that we worship one God in trinity, and trinity in unity. Neither confounding the persons nor dividing the substance. For the person of the Father is one; of the Son, another; of the Holy Spirit, another. But the divinity of the Father, and of the Son, and of the Holy Spirit, is one, the glory equal, the majesty equal. Such as is the Father, such also is the Son, and such the Holy Spirit. The Father is uncreated, the Son is uncreated, the Holy Spirit is uncreated. The Father is infinite, the Son is infinite, the Holy Spirit is infinite. The Father is eternal, the Son is eternal, the Holy Spirit is eternal. And yet there are not three eternal Beings, but one eternal Being. As also there are not three uncreated Beings, nor three infinite Beings, but one uncreated and one infinite Being. In like manner, the Father is omnipotent, the Son is omnipotent, and the Holy Spirit is omnipotent. And yet, there are not three omnipotent Beings, but one omnipotent Being. Thus the Father is God, the Son, God, and the Holy Spirit, God. And yet there are not three Gods, but one God only. The Father is Lord, the Son, Lord, and the Holy Spirit, Lord. And yet there are not three Lords, but one Lord only. For as we are compelled by Christian truth to confess each person distinctively to be both God and Lord, we are prohibited by the Catholic religion to say that there are three Gods, or three Lords. The Father is made by none, nor created, nor begotten. The Son is from the Father alone, not made, not created, but begotten. The Holy Spirit is not created by the Father and the Son, nor begotten, but proceeds. Therefore, there is one Father, not three Fathers; one Son, not three Sons; one Holy Spirit, not three Holy Spirits. And in this Trinity there is nothing prior or posterior, nothing greater or less, but all three persons are coeternal, and coequal to themselves. So that through all, as was said above, both unity in trinity, and trinity in unity is to be adored. Whoever would be saved, let him thus think concerning the Trinity."

It is universally agreed that Athanasius was not the author of this creed. It appears only in the Latin language in its original form; and it has modes of expression borrowed from the writings of Augustine, and of Vincent of Lerins, A. D. 434. As it also contains allusions to subsequent controversies concerning the person of Christ, it is naturally referred to some period between the middle of the fifth and the middle of the sixth centuries. Although not issued with the authority of any Council, it was soon universally admitted in the West, and subsequently in the East, and was everywhere regarded as an ecumenical symbol.

The Doctrine of the Trinity as set forth in these three ancient creeds, — the Nicene, the Constantinopolitan, and Athanasian (so-called), — is the Church Form of that fundamental article of the Christian faith. There is no difference, except as to amplification, between these several formulas.

§ 5. *Points decided by these Councils.*
A. *Against Sabellianism.*

These Councils decided that the terms Father, Son, and Spirit, were not expressive merely of relations *ad extra*, analogous to the terms, Creator, Preserver, and Benefactor. This was the doctrine known as Sabellianism, which assumed that the Supreme Being is not only one in essence, but one in person. The Church doctrine asserts that Father, Son, and Spirit express internal, necessary, and eternal relations in the Godhead; that they are personal designations, so that the Father is one person, the Son another person, and the Spirit another person. They differ not as ἄλλο καὶ ἄλλο, but as ἄλλος καὶ ἄλλος; each says I, and each says Thou, to either of the others. The word used in the Greek Church to express this fact was first πρόσωπον, and afterwards, and by general consent, ὑπόστασις; in the Latin Church, "*persona*," and in English, person. The idea expressed by the word in its application to the distinctions in the Godhead, is just as clear and definite as in its application to men.

B. *Against the Arians and Semi-Arians.*

The Councils held that the Father, Son, and Spirit are the same in substance, and equal in power and glory. Whatever divine perfection, whether eternity, immutability, infinity, omnipotence, or holiness, justice, goodness, or truth, can be predicated of the one, can in the same sense and measure be predicated of the others. These attributes belonging to the divine essence, and that essence being common to the three persons, the attributes or perfections are in like manner common to each. It is not the Father as such, nor the Son as such, who is self-existent, infinite, and eternal, but the Godhead, or divine essence, which subsists in the three persons. The Greek words used to express that which was common to the three persons of the Trinity were, as we have seen, οὐσία, φύσις, and at first, ὑπόστασις; to which correspond the Latin words *substantia*, or *essentia*, and *natura;* and the English, substance, essence, and nature. The word selected by the Nicene fathers to express the idea of community of substance, was, ὁμοού- σιος. But this word, as we have already seen, may express either specific sameness, or numerical identity. In the former sense, all spirits, whether God, angels, or men, are ὁμοούσιοι. They are similar in essence, *i. e.*, they are rational intelligences. That the Council intended the word to be taken in the latter sense, as expressing numerical identity, is plain, (1.) Because in its wider sense ὁμοούσιος does not differ from ὁμοιούσιος, which word the Council refused to adopt. The Arians were willing to admit that the Father, Son, and Spirit were ὁμοιούσιοι, but refused to admit that they were ὁμοούσιοι. This proves that the words were used in radically different senses. (2.) Because this Council declares that the Son was eternal; that He was not created or made, but begotten ἐκ τῆς οὐσίας τοῦ πατρός, " of the very essence of the Father." (3.) This is implied in the explanation of " eternal generation " universally adopted by the Nicene fathers, as " the eternal communication of the same numerical essence whole and entire, from the Father to the Son." (4.) If the term ὁμοούσιος be taken in the sense of specific sameness, then the Nicene Creed teaches Tritheism. The Father, Son, and Spirit are three Gods in the same sense that Abraham, Isaac, and Jacob are three men, for all men in that sense of the term are ὁμοούσιοι. It is the clear doctrine of these Councils that the same numerical, infinite, indivisible essence subsists in the three persons of the Trinity. This is still further evident from the inadequate illustrations of this great mystery which the early fathers sought for in nature; as of the light, heat, and splendor of the sun; the fountain and its streams; and especially from memory, intelligence, and will in man. In all these illustrations, however inadequate, the point of analogy was unity (numerical identity) of essence with triplicity.

C. *The Mutual Relation of the Persons of the Trinity.*

On this subject the Nicene doctrine includes, —

1. The principle of the subordination of the Son to the Father, and of the Spirit to the Father and the Son. But this subordination does not imply inferiority. For as the same divine essence with all its infinite perfections is common to the Father, Son, and

Spirit, there can be no inferiority of one person to the other in the Trinity. Neither does it imply posteriority; for the divine essence common to the several persons is self-existent and eternal. The subordination intended is only that which concerns the mode of subsistence and operation, implied in the Scriptural facts that the Son is of the Father, and the Spirit is of the Father and the Son, and that the Father operates through the Son, and the Father and the Son through the Spirit.

2. The several persons of the Trinity are distinguished by a certain "property," as it is called, or characteristic. That characteristic is expressed by their distinctive appellations. The first person is characterized as Father, in his relation to the second person; the second is characterized as Son, in relation to the first person; and the third as Spirit, in relation to the first and second persons. Paternity, therefore, is the distinguishing property of the Father; filiation of the Son; and procession of the Spirit. It will be observed that no attempt at explanation of these relations is given in these ecumenical creeds, namely, the Nicene, that of Constantinople, and the Athanasian. The mere facts as revealed in Scripture are affirmed.

3. The third point decided concerning the relation of the persons of the Trinity, one to the other, relates to their union. As the essence of the Godhead is common to the several persons, they have a common intelligence, will, and power. There are not in God three intelligences, three wills, three efficiencies. The Three are one God, and therefore have one mind and will. This intimate union was expressed in the Greek Church by the word περιχώρησις, which the Latin words *inexistentia, inhabitatio*, and *intercommunio*, were used to explain. These terms were intended to express the Scriptural facts that the Son is in the Father, and the Father in the Son; that where the Father is, there the Son and Spirit are; that what the one does the others do (the Father creates, the Son creates, the Spirit creates), or, as our Lord expresses it, "What things soever" the Father "doeth, these also doeth the Son likewise." (John v. 19.) So also what the one knows, the others know. "The Spirit searcheth all things, yea, the deep things of God. For what man knoweth the things of a man, save the spirit of man which is in him? even so the things of God knoweth no man, but the Spirit of God." (1 Cor. ii. 10, 11.) A common knowledge implies a common consciousness. In man the soul and body are distinct, yet, while united, they have a common life. We distinguish between acts of the intellect, and acts of the

will, and yet in every act of the will there is an exercise of the intelligence ; as in every act of the affections there is a joint action of the intelligence and will.   These are not illustrations of the relations of the persons of the Trinity, which are ineffable, but of the fact that in other and entirely different spheres there is this community of life in different subsistences, — different subsistences, at least so far as the body and soul are concerned.

This fact — of the intimate union, communion, and inhabitation of the persons of the Trinity — is the reason why everywhere in Scripture, and instinctively by all Christians, God as God is addressed as a person, in perfect consistency with the Tripersonality of the Godhead.   We can, and do pray to each of the Persons separately ; and we pray to God as God ; for the three persons are one God ; one not only in substance, but in knowledge, will, and power.   To expect that we, who cannot understand anything, not even ourselves, should understand these mysteries of the Godhead, is to the last degree unreasonable.   But as in every other sphere we must believe what we cannot understand ; so we may believe all that God has revealed in his Word concerning Himself, although we cannot understand the Almighty unto perfection.

§ 6.   *Examination of the Nicene Doctrine.*
A. *Subordination.*

A distinction must be made between the Nicene Creed (as amplified in that of Constantinople) and the doctrine of the Nicene fathers.   The creeds are nothing more than a well-ordered arrangement of the facts of Scripture which concern the doctrine of the Trinity.   They assert the distinct personality of the Father, Son, and Spirit ; their mutual relation as expressed by those terms ; their absolute unity as to substance or essence, and their consequent perfect equality ; and the subordination of the Son to the Father, and of the Spirit to the Father and the Son, as to the mode of subsistence and operation.   These are Scriptural facts, to which the creeds in question add nothing ; and it is in this sense they have been accepted by the Church universal.

But the Nicene fathers did undertake, to a greater or less degree, to explain these facts.   These explanations relate principally to the subordination of the Son and Spirit to the Father, and to what is meant by generation, or the relation between the Father and the Son.   These two points are so intimately related that they cannot be considered separately.   Yet as the former is more comprehensive than the latter, it may be expedient to speak of them in order, although what belongs to the one head, in a good degree belongs also to the other.

The ambiguity of the word ὁμοούσιος has already been remarked upon. As οὐσία may mean generic nature common to many individuals, not *unum in numero*, but *ens unum in multis*, so ὁμοούσιος (consubstantial) may mean nothing more than sameness of species or kind. It is therefore said, that "the term *homoousion*, in its strict grammatical sense differs from *monoousion* or *toutoousion*, as well as from *heteroousion*, and signifies not numerical identity, but equality of essence or community of nature among several beings." [1] "The Nicene Creed," Dr. Schaff adds, "does not expressly assert the singleness or numerical unity of the divine essence (unless it be in the first article : 'we believe in *one* God '), and the main point with the Nicene fathers was to urge against Arianism the strict divinity and essential equality of the Son and Holy Ghost with the Father. If we press the difference of *homoousion* from *monoousion*, and overlook the many passages in which they assert with equal emphasis the *monarchia* or numerical unity of the Godhead, we must charge them with tritheism."

Gieseler goes much further, and denies that the Nicene fathers held the numerical identity of essence in the persons of the Trinity. The Father, Son. and Spirit were the same in substance as having the same nature, or same kind of substance. This he infers was their doctrine not only from the general style of their teaching, and from special declarations, but from the illustrations which they habitually employed. The Father and the Son are the same in substance as among men father and son have the same nature ; or as Basil says, Father and Son differ in rank, as do the angels, although they are the same in nature. Gieseler says that the numerical sameness of nature in the three divine persons, was first asserted by Augustine. It was he, according to Gieseler, who first excluded all idea of subordination in the Trinity.[2] "Athanasius and Hilary understood the proposition, 'There is one God' of the Father. Basil the Great and the two Gregories understood by the word God a generic idea (Gattungsbegriff), belonging equally to the Father and the Son. Basil in the ' Apologia ad Cæsarienses,' says, ἡμεῖς ἕνα θεὸν, οὐ τῷ ἀριθμῷ, ἀλλὰ τῇ φύσει ὁμολογοῦμεν, and endeavours to show that there can be no question of number in reference to God, as numerical difference pertains only to material

---

[1] Schaff's *History of the Christian Church*, vol. iii. p. 672.
[2] *Kirchengeschichte*, vol. vi. § 60, p. 323. Bonn, 1855.

things. Augustine on the contrary expressly excludes the idea of generic unity,[1] and understands the proposition ' there is one God ' not of the Father alone, but of the whole Trinity,[2] and, therefore, taught that there is one God in three persons." This, however, is the precise doctrine of the Nicene Creed itself, which affirms faith " in one God," and not in three. Basil in the place quoted is refuting the charge of Tritheism. His words are, πρὸς δὲ τοὺς ἐπηρεάζοντας ἡμῖν τὸ τρίθεον, ἐκεῖνο λεγέσθω ὅτιπερ ἡμεῖς ἕνα θεὸν, etc.[3] On page 460 reasons have already been given for assuming that the sameness of substance taught by the Nicene fathers was not simply generic but numerical. On this subject Pearson, a thorough advocate of the Nicene Creed, says, " As it (the divine nature) is absolutely immaterial and incorporeal, it is also indivisible ; Christ cannot have any part of it only communicated unto Him, but the whole, by which He must be acknowledged co-essential, of the same substance with the Father; as the Council of Nice determined, and the ancient fathers before them taught." [4] If the whole divine essence belongs equally to the several persons of the Trinity, there is an end to the question, whether the sameness be specific or numerical. Accordingly the Bishop says : " The Divine essence being by reason of its simplicity not subject to division, and in respect of its infinity uncapable of multiplication, is so communicated as not to be multiplied ; insomuch that He which proceedeth by that communication hath not only the same nature, but is also the same God. The Father God, and the Word God ; Abraham man, and Isaac man : but Abraham one man, Isaac another man ; not so the Father one God, and the Word another, but the Father and the Word both the same God." [5]

Gieseler says that Augustine effectually excluded all idea of subordination in the Trinity by teaching the numerical sameness of essence in the persons of the Godhead. This does indeed preclude all priority and all superiority as to being and perfection. But it does not preclude subordination as to the mode of subsistence and operation. This is distinctly recognized in Scripture, and was as fully taught by Augustine as by any of the Greek fathers, and is even more distinctly affirmed in the so-called Athanasian Creed, representing the school of Augustine, than in the Creed of the Council of Nice. There is, therefore, no just ground of objection to the

1 De Trinitate, vii. vi. edit. Benedictines, vol. viii. p. 1314, d.
2 Epistola ccxxxviii. iii. 18, vol. ii. p. 1304, a.
3 Epistola viii. edit. Migne, vol. iii. p. 115, e.
4 Pearson, On Creed, seventh edition, 1701, p. 135.   5 Pearson, p. 138.

Nicene Creed for what it teaches on that subject. It does not go beyond the facts of Scripture. But the fathers who framed that creed, and those by whom it was defended, did go beyond those facts. They endeavoured to explain what was the nature of that subordination. While denying to the Father any priority or superiority to the other persons of the Trinity, as to being or perfection, they still spoke of the Father as the Monas, as having in order of thought the whole Godhead in Himself; so that He alone was God of Himself (αὐτόθεος, in that sense of the word), that He was the fountain, the cause, the root, *fons, origo, principium*, of the divinity as subsisting in the Son and Spirit; that He was greater than the other divine persons. They understood many passages which speak of the inferiority of the Son to the Father, of the Logos as such; and not of the historical Son of God clothed in our nature. Thus Waterland[1] says of these fathers, " The title of ὁ Θεὸς, being understood in the same sense with αὐτόθεος, was, as it ought to be, generally reserved to the Father, as the distinguishing personal character of the first person of the Holy Trinity. And this amounts to no more than the acknowledgment of the Father's prerogative as Father. But as it might also signify any Person who is truly and essentially God, it might properly be applied to the Son too : and it is so applied sometimes, though not so often as it is to the Father."

Hilary of Poictiers expresses the general idea of the Nicene fathers on this point, when he says : " Et quis non Patrem potiorem confitebitur, ut ingenitum a genito, ut patrem a filio, ut eum qui miserit ab eo qui missus est, ut volentem ab ipso qui obediat ? Et ipse nobis erit testis : *Pater major me est.* Hæc ita ut sunt, intelligenda sunt, sed cavendum est, ne apud imperitos gloriam Filii honor Patris infirmet."[2]

Bishop Pearson[3] says the preëminence of the Father " undeniably consisteth in this : that He is God not of any other but of Himself, and that there is no other person who is God, but is God of Himself. It is no diminution to the Son, to say He is from another, for his very name imports as much ; but it were a diminution to the Father to speak so of Him ; and there must be some preëminence, where there is place for derogation. What the Father is, He is from none ; what the Son is, He is from Him ; what

---

[1] *Works*, vol. i. p. 315.

[2] *De Trinitate*, III., *Works*, Paris, 1631, p. 23, a. See on this point Schaff's *History of the Christian Church*, vol. iii. § 130. Gieseler's *Kirchengeschichte*, vol. vi. § 60. Pearson *On the Creed*, and especially, Bull's *Defence of the Nicene Creed*, fourth section.

[3] Page 35.

the first is, He giveth ; what the second is, He receiveth. The First
is Father indeed by reason of his Son, but He is not God by reason
of Him ; whereas the Son is not so only in regard of the Father,
but also God by reason of the same." Among the patristical
authorities quoted by Pearson, are the following from Augustine : [1]
" Pater de nullo patre, Filius de Deo Patre. Pater quod est, a
nullo est : quod autem Pater est, propter Filium est. Filius vero
et quod Filius est, propter Patrem est ; et quod est, a Patre est."
" Filius non hoc tantum habet nascendo, ut Filius sit, sed omnino
ut sit. . . . . Filius non tantum ut sit Filius, quod relative dicitur, sed omnino ut sit, ipsam substantiam nascendo habet." [2]

The Reformers themselves were little inclined to enter into these
speculations. They were specially repugnant to such a mind as
Luther's. He insisted on taking the Scriptural facts as they were,
without any attempt at explanation. He says : " We should, like
the little children, stammer out what the Scriptures teach : that
Christ is truly God, that the Holy Ghost is truly God, and yet
that there are not three Gods, or three Beings, as there are three
Men, three Angels, three Suns, or three Windows. No, God is
not thus divided in his essence ; but there is one only divine Being
or substance. Therefore, although there are three persons, God
the Father, God the Son, and God the Holy Ghost, yet the Being
is not divided or distinguished ; since there is but one God in one
single, undivided, divine substance." [3]

Calvin also was opposed to going beyond the simple statement
of the Scriptures.[4] After saying that Augustine devotes the fifth
book on the Trinity to the explanation of the relation between the
Father and the Son, he adds : " Longe vero tutius est in ea quam
tradit relatione subsistere, quam subtilius penetrando ad sublime
mysterium, per multas evanidas speculationes evagari. Ergo quibus
cordi erit sobrietas et qui fidei mensura contenti erunt, breviter
quod utile est cognitu accipiant : nempe quum profitemur nos credere in unum Deum, sub Dei nomine intelligi unicam et simplicem
essentiam, in qua comprehendimus tres personas vel hypostaseis :
ideoque quoties Dei nomen indefinite ponitur, non minus Filium
et Spiritum, quam Patrem designari : ubi autem adjungitur Filius
Patri, tunc in medium venit relatio : atque ita distinguimus inter personas. Quia vero proprietates in personis ordinem secum ferunt,

[1] In *Joannis Evangelium Tractatus*, xix. 13, edit. Benedictines, vol. iii. p. 1903, a
[2] *De Trinitate*, v. xv. 16, vol. viii. p. 1286, c, d.
[3] *Walch*, xiii. p. 1510. *Die Dritte Predigt a. Tage d. heil. Dreifaltigk.* 5; *Works*,
edit. Walch, vol. xiii. p. 1510.
[4] *Institutio*, I. xiii. 19, 20, edit. Berlin, 1834, part i. pp. 100, 101.

ut in Patre sit principium et origo: quoties mentio sit Patris et Filii simul, vel Spiritus, nomen Dei peculiariter Patri tribuitur. Hoc modo retinetur unitas essentiæ et habetur ratio ordinis, quæ tamen ex Filii et Spiritus deitate nihil minuit : et certe quum ante visum fuerit Apostolos asserere Filium Dei illum esse, quem Moses et Prophetæ testati sunt esse Jehovam, semper ad unitatem essentiæ venire necesse est." We have here the three essential facts involved in the doctrine of the Trinity, namely, unity of essence, distinction of persons, and subordination without any attempt at explanation.

Calvin was accused by some of his contemporaries of teaching the incompatible doctrines of Sabellianism and Arianism. In a letter to his friend Simon Grynée, rector of the Academy of Basle, dated May, 1537, he says the ground on which the charge of Sabellianism rested, was his having said that Christ was " that Jehovah, who of Himself alone was always self-existent, which charge," he says, " I was quite ready to meet." His answer is : " If the distinction between the Father and the Word be attentively considered, we shall say that the one is from the other. If, however, the essential quality of the Word be considered, in so far as He is one God with the Father, whatever can be said concerning God may also be applied to Him the Second Person in the glorious Trinity. Now, what is the meaning of the name Jehovah ? What did that answer imply which was spoken to Moses ? I AM THAT I AM. Paul makes Christ the author of this saying." [1] This argument is conclusive. If Christ be Jehovah, and if the name Jehovah implies self-existence, then Christ is self-existent. In other words, self-existence and necessary existence, as well as omnipotence and all other divine attributes, belong to the divine essence common to all the persons of the Trinity, and therefore it is the Triune God who is self-existent, and not one person in distinction from the other persons. That is, self-existence is not to be predicated of the divine essence only, nor of the Father only, but of the Trinity, or of the Godhead as subsisting in three persons. And, therefore, as Calvin says, when the word God is used indefinitely it means the Triune God, and not the Father in distinction from the Son and Spirit.

---

[1] *Calvin's Letters.* vol. i. pp. 55, 56, edit. Presbyterian Board, Philadelphia.

B. *Eternal Generation.*

As in reference to the subordination of the Son and Spirit to the Father, as asserted in the ancient creeds, it is not to the fact that exception is taken, but to the explanation of that fact, as given by the Nicene fathers, the same is true with regard to the doctrine of Eternal Generation. It is no doubt a Scriptural fact that the relation between the First and Second persons of the Trinity is expressed by the relative terms Father and Son. It is also said that the Son is begotten of the Father; He is declared to be the only begotten Son of God. The relation, therefore, of the Second Person to the First is that of filiation or sonship. But what is meant by the term, neither the Bible nor the ancient creeds explain. It may be sameness of nature; as a son is of the same nature as his father. It may be likeness, and the term Son be equivalent to εἰκών, ἀπαύγασμα, χαρακτήρ, or λόγος, or revealer. It may be derivation of essence, as a son, in one sense, is derived from his father. Or, it may be something altogether inscrutable and to us incomprehensible.

The Nicene fathers, instead of leaving the matter where the Scriptures leave it, undertake to explain what is meant by sonship, and teach that it means derivation of essence. The First Person of the Trinity is Father, because He communicates the essence of the Godhead to the Second Person; and the Second Person is Son, because He derives that essence from the First Person. This is what they mean by Eternal Generation. Concerning which it was taught, —

1. That it was the person not the essence of the Son that was generated. The essence is self-existent and eternal, but the person of the Son is generated (*i. e.*, He becomes a person) by the communication to Him of the divine essence. This point continued to be insisted upon through the later periods of the Church. Thus Turrettin[1] says, " Licet Filius sit a Patre, non minus tamen αὐτόθεος dicitur, non ratione Personæ, sed ratione Essentiæ; non relate qua Filius, sic enim est a Patre, sed absolute qua Deus, quatenus habet Essentiam divinam a se existentem, et non divisam vel productam ab alia essentia, non vero qua habens essentiam illam a seipso. Sic Filius est Deus a seipso, licet non sit a seipso Filius."

Again,[2] "Persona bene dicitur generare Personam, quia actiones sunt suppositorum; sed non Essentia Essentiam, quia quod gignit et gignitur necessario multiplicatur, et sic via sterneretur ad Tri-

---

[1] Locus III. xxviii. 40, edit. Edinburgh, 1847, vol. i. p. 260.
[2] *Ibid.* xxix. 6, p. 262.

theismum. Essentia quidem generando communicatur; sed generatio, ut a Persona fit originaliter, ita ad Personam terminatur." This is the common mode of representation.

2. This generation is said to be eternal. "It is an eternal movement in the divine essence."

3. It is by necessity of nature, and not by the will of the Father.

4. It does not involve any separation or division, as it is not a part, but the whole and complete essence of the Father that is communicated from the Father to the Son.

5. It is without change.

The principal grounds urged in support of this representation. are the nature of sonship among men, and the passage in John v. 26, where it is said, " As the Father hath life in Himself, so hath He given to the Son to have life in Himself."

It is admitted that the relation between the First and Second persons in the Trinity is expressed by the words Father and Son, and therefore while everything in this relation as it exists among men, implying imperfection or change, must be eliminated, yet the essential idea of paternity must be retained. That essential idea is assumed to be the communication of the essence of the parent to his child; and, therefore, it is maintained that there must be a communication of the essence of the Godhead from the Father to the Son in the Holy Trinity. But, in the first place, it is a gratuitous assumption that, so far as the soul is concerned, there is even among men any communication of the essence of the parent to the child. Traducianism has never been the general doctrine of the Christian Church. As, therefore, it is, to say the least, doubtful, whether there is any communication of the essence of the soul in human paternity, it is unreasonable to assume that such communication is essential to the relation of Father and Son in the Trinity.

In the second place, while it is admitted that the terms Father and Son are used to give us some idea of the mutual relation of the First and Second persons of the Trinity, yet they do not definitely determine what that relation is. It may be equality and likeness. Among men Father and Son belong to the same order of beings. The one is not inferior in nature, although he may be in rank, to the other. And the son is like his father. In the same manner in the Holy Trinity the Second Person is said to be the εἰκών, the ἀπαύγασμα, the χαρακτήρ, the λόγος, the Word or Revealer of the Father, so that he who hears the Son hears the Father, he who hath seen the one has seen the other. Or the relation may be that of affection. The reciprocal love of father and son is peculiar. It is, so to speak, necessary; it is unchangeable, it is unfathomable; it leads, or has led, to every kind and degree of self-sacrifice. It is not necessary to assume in reference to the Trinity that these relations are all that the relative terms Father and Son are intended to reveal. These may be included, but much more may be implied which we are not now able to comprehend. All that is contended for is, that we are not shut up to the admission that derivation of essence is essential to sonship.

As to the passage in John v. 26, where it is said the Father hath given to the Son to have life in Himself, everything depends on the sense in which the word Son is to be taken. That word is sometimes used as a designation of the λόγος, the Second Person of the Trinity, to indicate his eternal relation to the First Person as the Father. It is, however, very often used as a designation of the incarnate λόγος, the Word made flesh. Many things are in Scripture predicated of the Godman, which cannot be predicated of the Second Person of the Trinity as such. If in this passage the Son means the Logos, then it does teach that the First Person of the Trinity communicated life, and therefore the essence in which that life inheres, to the Second Person. But if Son here designates the Theanthropos, then the passage teaches no such doctrine. That it is the historical person, Jesus of Nazareth here spoken of, may be argued not only from the fact that He is elsewhere so frequently called the Son of God, as in the comprehensive confession required of every Christian in the apostolic age, " I believe that Jesus is the Son of God ; " but also from the context. Our Lord had healed an impotent man on the Sabbath. For this the Jews accused Him of breaking the Sabbath. He vindicated Himself by saying that He had the same right to work on the Sabbath that God had, because He was the Son of God, and therefore equal with God. That He had power not only to heal but to give life, for as the Father had life in Himself, so had He given to the Son to have life in Himself. He had also given Him authority to execute judgment. He was to be the judge of the quick and dead, because He is the Son of man, i. e., because He had become man for us and for our salvation. His accusers need not be surprised at what He said, because the hour was coming when all who are in the grave shall hear his voice, and shall come forth, they who have done good, unto the resurrection of life, and they who had done evil, unto the resurrection of damnation. The subject of discourse, therefore, in the context, is the historical

person who had healed the impotent man, and who with equal propriety could be called God or man, because He was both God and
man. What the passage teaches, therefore, concerns the constitution of Christ's person as He appeared on earth, and not the
nature of the relation of the Father and Son in the Godhead.

C. *Eternal Sonship.*

There is, therefore, a distinction between the speculations of the
Nicene fathers, and the decisions of the Nicene Council. The
latter have been accepted by the Church universal, but not the
former. The Council declared that our Lord is the Eternal Son
of God, *i. e.*, that He is from eternity the Son of God. This
of course involves the denial that He became the Son of God
in time ; and, consequently, that the primary and essential reason for his being called Son is not his miraculous birth, nor his
incarnation, nor his resurrection, nor his exaltation to the right
hand of God. The Council decided that the word Son as applied to Christ, is not a term of office but of nature ; that it
expresses the relation which the Second Person in the Trinity from
eternity bears to the First Person, and that the relation thus indicated is sameness of nature, so that sonship, in the case of Christ,
includes equality with God. In other words, God was in such a
sense his Father that He was equal with God. And consequently
every time the Scriptures call Jesus the Son of God, they assert
his true and proper divinity. This does not imply that every time
Christ is called the Son of God, what is said of Him is to be understood of his divine nature. The fact is patent, and is admitted
that the person of our Lord may be designated from either nature. He may be called the Son of David and the Son of God.
And his person may be designated from one nature when what is
predicated of Him is true only of the other nature. Thus, on
the one hand, the Lord of Glory was crucified ; God purchased the
Church with his blood ; and the Son is said to be ignorant ; and,
on the other hand, the Son of Man is said to be in heaven when He
was on earth. This being admitted it remains true that Christ is
called the Son of God as to his divine nature. The Logos, the
Second Person of the Trinity as such and because of his relation
to the First Person, is the Son of God. Such is the doctrine of
the Nicene Council, and that it is no less the doctrine of the Scriptures, is plain from the following considerations : —

1. The terms Father, Son, and Spirit, as applied to the persons
of the Trinity, are relative terms. The relations which they ex-

press are mutual relations, *i. e.*, relations in which the different persons stand one to another. The First Person is called Father, not because of his relation to his creatures, but because of his relation to the Second Person. The Second Person is called Son, not because of any relation assumed in time, but because of his eternal relation to the First Person. And the Third Person is called Spirit because of his relation to the First and Second.

2. If, as the whole Christian Church believes, the doctrine of the Trinity is a Scriptural doctrine, and if, as is also admitted by all the parties to this discussion, it was the purpose of God to reveal that doctrine to the knowledge and faith of his people, there is a necessity for the use of terms by which the persons of the Trinity should be designated and revealed. But if the terms Father, Son, and Spirit do not apply to the persons of the Trinity as such, and express their mutual relations, there are no such distinctive terms in the Bible by which they can be known and designated.

3. There are numerous passages in the Scriptures which clearly prove that our Lord is called Son, not merely because He is the image of God, or because He is the object of peculiar affection, nor because of his miraculous conception only; nor because of his exaltation, but because of the eternal relation which He sustains to the First Person of the Trinity. These passages are of two kinds. First, those in which the Logos is called Son, or in which Christ as to his divine nature and before his incarnation is declared to be the Son of God; and secondly, those in which the application of the term Son to Christ involves the ascription of divinity to Him. He is declared to be the Son of God in such a sense as implies equality with God. To the former of these classes belong such passages as the following: Rom. i. 3, 4, where Christ is declared to be κατὰ σάρκα, the Son of David, and κατὰ πνεῦμα ἁγιοσύνης, the Son of God. That πνεῦμα ἁγιοσύνης does not here mean the Holy Spirit, much less a pneumatic state, but the higher or divine nature of Christ, is evident from the antithesis. As to his human nature, He is the Son of David; as to his divine nature, He is the Son of God. As to his humanity, He is consubstantial with man; as to his divinity, He is consubstantial with God. If his being the Son of David proves He was a man, his being the Son of God proves that He is God. Hence Christ was called Son before his incarnation, as in Gal. iv. 4, " God sent forth his Son, made of a woman." It was the Logos that was sent, and the Logos was Son. Thus in John i. 1–14, we are taught that the Logos was in the beginning with God, that He was God, that He made all things, that He was

the light and life of men, and that He became flesh, and revealed his glory as the Son of God. Here it is plain that the Logos or Word is declared to be the Son. And in the eighteenth verse of that chapter it is said, " No man hath seen God at any time ; the only begotten Son, which is in the bosom of the Father (ὁ ὢν εἰς τὸν κόλπον τοῦ πατρός), He hath declared Him." Here the present tense, ὁ ὤν, expresses permanent being ; He who is, was, and ever shall be, in the bosom of the Father, *i. e.*, most intimately united with Him, so as to know Him, as He knows Himself, is the Son. According to Chrysostom, this language implies the συγγένεια καί ἑνότης τῆς οὐσίας of the Father and the Son, which were not interrupted by his manifestation in the flesh. To the latter class belong such passages as the following : John v. 18–25, where Christ calls God his Father in a sense which implied equality with God. If sonship implies equality with God, it implies participation of the divine essence. It was for claiming to be the Son of God in this sense, that the Jews took up stones to stone Him. Our Lord defended Himself by saying that He had the same power God had, the same authority, the same life-giving energy, and therefore was entitled to the same honour. In John x. 30–38 there is a similar passage, in which Christ says that God is his Father in such a sense that He and the Father are one. In the first chapter of the Epistle to the Hebrews, it is argued that Christ does not belong to the category of creatures ; that all angels (*i. e.*, all intelligent creatures higher than man) are subject to Him, and are required to worship Him because He is the Son of God. As Son He is the brightness of the Father's glory, the express image of his person, upholding all things by the word of his power. Because He is the Son of God, He is the God who in the beginning laid the foundations of the earth, and the heavens are the work of his hands. They are mutable, but He is unchangeable and eternal.

There can, therefore, be no reasonable doubt that according to the Scriptures, the term Son as applied to Christ expresses the relation of the Second to the First Person in the adorable Trinity. In other words, it is not merely an official title, but designates the Logos and not exclusively the Theanthropos.

4. Another argument in proof of this doctrine is derived from the fact that Christ is declared to be " the only-begotten Son of God," "his own Son," *i. e.*, his Son in a peculiar and proper sense. Angels and men are called the sons of God, because He is the Father of all spirits. Holy men are his sons because partakers of his moral nature, as wicked **men** are called children of the devil.

God's people are his sons and daughters by regeneration and adoption. It is in opposition to all these kinds of sonship that Christ is declared to be God's only Son, the only person in the universe to whom the word can be applied in its full sense as expressing sameness of essence.

Objections to the Doctrine.

The speculative objections to this doctrine of eternal sonship have already been considered. If Christ is Son, if He is God of God, it is said He is not self-existent and independent. But self-existence, independence, etc., are attributes of the divine essence, and not of one person in distinction from the others. It is the Triune God who is self-existent and independent. Subordination as to the mode of subsistence and operation, is a Scriptural fact ; and so also is the perfect and equal Godhead of the Father and the Son, and therefore these facts must be consistent. In the consubstantial identity of the human soul there is a subordination of one faculty to another, and so, however incomprehensible to us, there may be a subordination in the Trinity consistent with the identity of essence in the Godhead.

Psalm ii. 7.

More plausible objections are founded on certain passages of the Scriptures. In Ps. ii. 7, it is said, " Thou art my Son ; this day have I begotten thee." From this it is argued that Christ or the Messiah was constituted or made the Son of God in time, and therefore was not the Son of God from eternity. To this it may be answered, —

1. That the term Son, as used in the Scriptures, expresses different relations, and therefore may be applied to the same person for different reasons ; or, have one meaning, i. e., express one relation in one place, and a different one in another. It may refer or be applied to the Logos, or to the Theanthropos. One ground for the use of the designation does not exclude all the others. God commanded Moses to say unto Pharaoh, " Israel is my son, even my first-born." (Ex. iv. 22.) And He said of Solomon, " I will be his father and he shall be my son." (2 Sam. vii. 14.) The word son here expresses the idea of adoption, the selection of one people or of one man out of many to stand to God in a peculiar relation of intimacy, affection, honour, and dignity. If for these reasons the theocratic people, or a theocratic king, may be called the Son of God, for the same reasons, and preëminently, the Messiah may be

so designated. But this is no argument to prove that the Logos may not in a far higher sense be called the Son of God.

2. The passage in question, however, need not be understood of an event which occurred in time. Its essential meaning is, " Thou art my Son, now art thou my Son." The occasion referred to by the words " this day " was the time when the Sonship of the king of Zion should be fully manifested. That time, as we learn from Rom. i. 4, was the day of his resurrection. By his rising again from the dead, He was clearly manifested to be all that He claimed to be, — the Son of God and the Saviour of the world.

3. There is another interpretation of the passage which is essentially the same as that given by many of the fathers, and is thus presented by Dr. Addison Alexander in his commentary on Acts xiii. 33, " The expression in the Psalm, ' I have begotten thee,' means, I am He who has begotten thee, *i. e.*, I am thy father. ' To-day ' refers to the date of the decree itself (Jehovah said, To-day, etc.) ; but this, as a divine act, was eternal, and so must be the Sonship which it affirms."

Acts xiii. 32, 33.

It may be urged, however, that in Acts xiii. 32, 33, this passage is quoted in the proof of the resurrection of Christ, which shows that the Apostle understood the passage to teach that Christ was begotten or made the Son of God when He rose from the dead. The passage in Acts reads thus in our version : " We declare unto you glad tidings, how that the promise which was made unto the fathers, God hath fulfilled the same unto us their children, in that He hath raised up Jesus again (ἀναστήσας) ; as it is also written in the second psalm, Thou art my Son, this day have I begotten thee." Here there is no reference to the resurrection. The glad tidings which the Apostle announced was not the resurrection, but the advent of the Messiah. That was the promise made to the fathers, which God had fulfilled by raising up, *i. e.*, bringing into the world the promised deliverer. Compare Acts ii. 30 ; iii. 22, 26 ; vii. 37, in all which passages where the same word is used, the " raising up" refers to the advent of Christ; as when it is said, " A prophet shall the Lord your God raise up unto you of your brethren, like unto me." The word *is* never used absolutely in reference to the resurrection unless, as in Acts ii. 32, where the resurrection is spoken of in the context. Our translators have obscured the meaning by rendering ἀναστήσας " having raised up *again*," instead of simply " having raised up," as they render it elsewhere.

That this is the true meaning of the passage is clear from the succeeding verses. Paul having said that God had fulfilled his promise to the fathers by raising up Christ, agreeably to Psalm ii. 7, immediately adds as an additional fact, " And as concerning that He raised Him up from the dead, now no more to return to corruption, He said on this wise, I will give you the sure mercies of David. Wherefore he saith also in another psalm, Thou shalt not suffer thine Holy One to see corruption." (Acts xiii. 34, 35.) The Apostle, therefore, does not teach that Christ was made the Son of God by his resurrection. But even, as just remarked, if He did teach that the Theanthropos was in one sense made the Son of God, that would not prove that the Logos was not Son in another and higher sense.

Luke i. 35.

The same remark is applicable to Luke i. 35 : " The Holy Ghost shall come upon thee, and the power of the Highest shall overshadow thee ; therefore also that holy thing which shall be born of thee, shall be called the Son of God." Bishop Pearson, one of the most strenuous defenders of " eternal generation," and of all the peculiarities of the Nicene doctrine of the Trinity, gives four reasons why the Theanthropos or Godman is called the Son of God. (1.) His miraculous conception. (2.) The high office to which he was designated. (John x. 34, 35, 36.) (3.) His resurrection, according to one interpretation of Acts xiii. 33. " The grave," he says, " is as the womb of the earth ; Christ, who is raised from thence, is as it were begotten to another life, and God, who raised him, is his Father." [1] (4.) Because after his resurrection He was made the heir of all things. (Heb. i. 2–5.) Having assigned these reasons why the Godman is called Son, he goes on to show why the Logos is called Son. There is nothing, therefore, in the passages cited inconsistent with the Church doctrine of the eternal Sonship of our Lord. The language of the angel addressed to the Virgin Mary, may, however, mean no more than this, namely, that the assumption of humanity by the eternal Son of God was the reason why He should be recognized as a divine person. It was no ordinary child who was to be born of Mary, but one who was, in the language of the prophets, to be the Wonderful, the Counsellor, the Mighty God, the Everlasting Father, the Son of the Highest. It was because the Eternal Son was made of a woman, that that Holy Thing born of the virgin was to be called the Son of God.

[1] Pearson on *Creed*, p. 106.

It need hardly be remarked that no valid objection to the doctrine of the eternal Sonship of Christ, or, that He is Son as to his divine nature, can be drawn from such passages as speak of the Son as being less than the Father, or subject to Him, or even ignorant. If Christ can be called the Lord of glory, or God, when his death is spoken of, He may be called Son, when other limitations are ascribed to Him. As He is both God and man, everything that is true either of his humanity or of his divinity, may be predicated of Him as a person ; and his person may be denominated from one nature, when the predicate belongs to the other nature. He is called the Son of Man when He is said to be omnipresent; and He is called God when He is said to have purchased the Church with his blood.

D. *The Relation of the Spirit to the other Persons of the Trinity.*

As the councils of Nice and Constantinople were fully justified by Scripture in teaching the eternal Sonship of Christ, so what they taught of the relation of the Spirit to the Father and the Son, has an adequate Scriptural foundation.

That relation is expressed by the word procession, with regard to which the common Church doctrine is, (1.) That it is incomprehensible, and therefore inexplicable. (2.) That it is eternal. (3.) That it is equally from the Father and the Son. At least such is the doctrine of the Latin and all other Western churches. (4.) That this procession concerns the personality and operations of the Spirit, and not his essence.

The Scriptural grounds for expressing this relation by the term procession, are (1.) The signification of the word spirit. It means breath, that which proceeds from, and which gives expression and effect to our thoughts. Since Father and Son, as applied to the First and Second persons of the Trinity, are relative terms, it is to be assumed that the word Spirit as the designation of the Third Person, is also relative. (2.) This is further indicated by the use of the genitive case in the expressions πνεῦμα τοῦ πατρός, τοῦ υἱοῦ, which is explained by the use of the preposition ἐκ, as πνεῦμα ἐκ τοῦ πατρός. The revealed fact is that the Spirit is of the Father, and the Church in calling the relation, thus indicated, a procession, does not attempt to explain it. (3.) In John xv. 26, where the Spirit is promised by Christ, He is said to proceed from the Father.

That the Latin and Protestant churches, in opposition to the Greek Church, are authorized in teaching that the Spirit proceeds not from the Father only, but from the Father and the Son, is evident, because whatever is said in Scripture of the relation of the Spirit to the Father, is also said of his relation to the Son.   He is said to be the " Spirit of the Father," and " Spirit of the Son ; " He is given or sent by the Son as well as by the Father ; the Son is said to operate through the Spirit.   The Spirit is no more said to send or to operate through the Son, than to send or operate through the Father.   The relation, so far as revealed, is the same in the one case as in the other.

When we consider the incomprehensible nature of the Godhead, the mysterious character of the doctrine of the Trinity, the exceeding complexity and difficulty of the problem which the Church had to solve in presenting the doctrine that there are three persons and one God, in such a manner as to meet the requirements of Scripture and the convictions of believers, and yet avoid all contradiction, we can hardly fail to refer the Church creeds on this subject, which have for ages secured assent and consent, not to inspiration, strictly speaking, but to the special guidance of the Holy Spirit.

§ 7. *Philosophical Form of the Doctrine of the Trinity.*

The philosophical statements of the doctrine of the Trinity have been intended by their authors either to prove it, or to illustrate it, or to explain it away and substitute some speculative theory as to the constitution of the universe for the Scriptural doctrine of the Triune God.   The two former of these classes, those designed for proof, and those designed for illustration, need not be discriminated.   It may be remarked in reference to them all that they are of little value.   They do not serve to make the inconceivable intelligible.   The most they can do, is to show that in other spheres and in relation to other subjects, we find a somewhat analogous triplicity in unity.   In most cases, however, these illustrations proceed on the assumption that there are mysteries in the Godhead which have no counterpart in the constitution of our nature, or in anything around us in the present state of our existence.

We have already seen that the fathers were accustomed to refer to the union of light, heat, and radiance in the one substance of the sun ; to a fountain and its streams ; to the root, stem, and flower of a plant ; to the intellect, will, and affections in the soul ; as examples of at least a certain kind of triplicity in unity, elsewhere than in the Godhead.   The last-mentioned analogy, especially, was frequently presented, and that in different forms.   Augustine said, that as man was made in the image of the Triune God, we have

reason to expect something in the constitution of our nature answering to the Trinity in the Godhead. He refers to the memory,
intelligence, and will, as co-existing in one mind, so that the operations of the one are involved in the operations of the others. Gregory of Nyssa refers for his illustration to the soul, the reason, and
the living power, united in one spiritual substance in man. It was
admitted, however, that these analogies did not hold as to the main
point, for these different powers in man are not different subsistences, but different modes of activity of one and the same personal essence, so that these illustrations lead rather to the Sabellian,
than to the Scriptural view of the doctrine of the Trinity.

By far the most common illustration was borrowed from the
operations of our consciousness. We conceive of ourselves as
objective to ourselves, and are conscious of the identity of the subject and object. We have thus the subjective Ego, the objective
Ego, and the identity of the two; the desired Thesis, Analysis,
and Synthesis. In one form or another, this illustration has come
down from the fathers, through the schoolmen and reformers, to
theologians of our own day. Augustine[1] says, "Est quædam imago
Trinitatis, ipsa mens, et notitia ejus, quod est proles ejus ac de seipsa
verbum ejus, et amor tertius, et hæc tria unum atque una substantia." Again,[2] "Hæc — tria, memoria, intelligentia, voluntas, quoniam non sunt tres vitæ, sed una vita; nec tres mentes, sed una
mens: consequenter utique nec tres substantiæ sunt, sed una substantia." And,[3] "Mens igitur quando cogitatione se conspicit,
intelligit se et recognoscit: gignit ergo hunc intellectum et cognitionem suam. . . . . Hæc autem duo, gignens et genitum,
dilectione tertia copulantur, quæ nihil est aliud quam voluntas fru-
endum aliquid appetens vel tenens." Anselm[4] has the same idea:
"Habet mens rationalis, quum se cogitando intelligit, secum imaginem suam ex se natam, id est cogitationem sui ad suam similitudinem, quasi sua impressione formatam, quamvis ipsa se a sua
imagine, non nisi ratione sola, separare possit, quæ imago ejus
verbum ejus est. Hoc itaque modo, quis neget, summam sapien-
tem, quum se dicendo intelligit, gignere consubstantialem sibi similitudinem suam, id est Verbum suum." Melancthon[5] adopts and
carries out the same idea: "Filius dicitur imago et λόγος: est igitur

[1] De Trinitate, IX. xii. 18, edit. Benedictines, Paris, 1837, vol. viii. p. 1352, b.
[2] Ibid. x. xi. 18, p. 1366, a.
[3] Ibid. xiv. vi. 8, pp. 1443, d, 1444, a.
[4] Monologium, xxxiii., edit. Migne, p. 188, b. See also Thomas Aquinas, I. xxvii. 3, edit
Cologne, 1640, p. 56.
[5] Loci Communes, De Filio, edit. Erlangen, 1828, vol. i. pp. 19, 21.

imago cogitatione Patris genita; quod ut aliquo modo considerari possit, a nostra mente exempla capiamus. Voluit enim Deus in homine conspici vestigia sua. . . . . Mens humana cogitando mox pingit imaginem rei cogitatæ, sed nos non transfundimus nostram essentiam in illas imagines, suntque cogitationes illæ subitæ et evanescentes actiones. At Pater æternus sese intuens gignit cogitationem sui, quæ est imago ipsius, non evanescens, sed subsistens, communicata ipsi essentia. Hæc igitur imago est secunda persona. . . . . Ut autem Filius nascitur cogitatione, ita Spiritus Sanctus procedit a voluntate Patris et Filii; voluntatis enim est agitare, diligere, sicut et cor humanam non imagines, sed spiritus seu halitus gignit." Leibnitz,[1] says " Je ne trouve rien dans les créatures de plus propre à illustrer ce sujet, que la réflexion des esprits, lorsqu'un même esprit est son propre objet immediat, et agit sur soi-même en pensant à soi-même et à ce qu'il fait. Car le redoublement donne une image ou ombre de deux substances respectives dans une même substance absolue, savoir de celle qui entend, et de celle qui est entendue; l'un et l'autre de ces êtres est substantiel, l'un et l'autre est un concret individu, et ils différent par des rélations mutuelles, mais ils ne sont qu'une seule et même substance individuelle absolue."

Of the theologians of the seventeenth century belonging to the Reformed Church, Keckermann was the most disposed to present the doctrines of the Bible in a philosophical form. We find, therefore, with him a similar attempt to make the mystery of the Trinity intelligible. He regards the existence of God as consisting in self-conscious thought. As thought is eternal, it must have an eternal absolute, and perfect object. That object must, therefore, itself be God. The unity of the divine essence demands that this object should be in God himself, and therefore, it eternally returns to Him.[2]

The modern theologians of Germany, who profess allegiance to the Scriptures, have, in many cases, taken the ground that absolute unity in the divine essence would be inconsistent with self-consciousness. We become self-conscious by distinguishing ourselves from what is not ourselves, and especially from other persons of like nature with ourselves. If, therefore, there were no person objective to God, to whom He could say Thou, He could not say I. Thus Martensen[3] says: Although the creature can have no adequate comprehension of the divine nature, we have a semblance

---

[1] *Remarque sur le Livre d'un Antitrinitaire Anglois*, edit. Geneva, 1768, vol. i. p. 27.

[2] *Systema Theologiæ, Opera*, ii. p. 72. *Opera*, edit. Cologne, 1614, vol. ii. *Systema Theologiæ* (tract at end of vol.), p. 72, the last of three pages marked 72.

[3] *Dogmatik*, pp. 129, 130.

of the Trinity in ourselves; as we are formed in the image of God,
we have the right to conceive of God according to the analogy of
our own nature. As distinction of persons is necessary to self-
consciousness in us, so also in God. Therefore, if God be not a
Trinity, He cannot be a person. How, he asks, can God from
eternity be conscious of Himself as Father, without distinguishing
Himself from Himself as Son? In other words, how can God be
eternally self-conscious, without being eternally objective to Himself? That with us the objective Ego is merely ideal and not a
different person from the subjective Ego, arises from our nature as
creatures. With God, thinking and being are the same. In thinking Himself his thought of Himself is Himself in a distinct hypos-
tasis. Dr. Shedd[1] has given a similar exposition, "in proof that
the necessary conditions of self-consciousness in the finite spirit,
furnish an analogue to the doctrine of the Trinity, and go to prove
that trinity in unity is necessary to self-consciousness in the Godhead."

Pantheistic Trinitarianism.

In all that precedes, reference has been made to those who have
had for their object to vindicate the doctrine of the Trinity, by
showing that it is not out of analogy with other objects of human
thought. There are, however, many modern systems which profess to be Trinitarian, which are in fact mere substitutions of the
formulas of speculation for the doctrine of the Bible. Men speak
of the Trinity, of the Father, Son, and Spirit, when they mean by
those terms something which has not the least analogy with the
doctrine of the Christian Church. Many by the Trinity do not
mean a Trinity of persons in the Godhead, but either three radical
forces, as it were, in the divine nature, which manifest themselves
in different ways; or three different relations of the same subject;
or three different states or stages of existence. Thus with some,
the absolute power or efficiency of the Supreme Being considered
as creating, upholding, and governing the world, is the Father; as
illuminating rational creatures, is the Son; and, as morally educat-
ing them, is the Spirit. According to Kant, God as creator is the
Father; as the preserver and governor of men, He is the Son; and
as the administrator of law, as judge and rewarder, He is the Spirit.
With DeWette, God in Himself is the Father; as manifested in the
world, the Son; and as operating in nature, the Spirit. Schleiermacher says, God in Himself is the Father; God in Christ is the Son;
God in the Church, is the Holy Spirit. The avowed Pantheists

[1] *History of Christian Doctrine*, vol. i. p. 366.

also use the language of Trinitarianism. God as the infinite and absolute Being is the Father ; as coming to consciousness and existence in the world, He is the Son ; as returning to Himself, the Spirit. Weisse attempts to unite Theism and Pantheism. He pronounces the Nicene doctrine of the Trinity the highest form of philosophical thought. He professes to adopt that doctrine *ex animo* in its commonly admitted sense. There is a threefold personality (Ichheit) in God necessary to the constitution of his nature. When the world was created the second of these persons became its life, merging his personality in the world and became impersonal, in order to raise the world into union and identity with God. When the curriculum of the world is accomplished, the Son resumes his personality.[1]

[1] C. H. Weisse, *Idee der Gottheit;* Dresden, 1833, pp. 257 ff., 273.

The Literature of the doctrine of the Trinity would fill a volume. Bull's *Defence of the Nicene Creed*, Pearson *On the Creed*, Waterland *On the Trinity*, Meier's *Geschichte der Lehre von der Trinität*, Baur's *Geschichte der Lehre von der Trinität*, Dorner's *History of the Person of Christ*, in five volumes, one of the series of Clark's *Foreign Theological Library*, a very valuable collection of important modern works, Shedd's *History of Christian Doctrine*, and the other historical works on the doctrines of the Church, open the whole field for the theological student.

CHAPTER VII.

THE DIVINITY OF CHRIST

§ 1. *Testimony of the Old Testament.*

THE doctrine of redemption is the distinguishing doctrine of the Bible. The person and work of the Redeemer is therefore the great theme of the sacred writers. From the nature of the work which He was to accomplish, it was necessary that He should be at once God and man. He must participate in the nature of those whom He came to redeem ; and have power to subdue all evil, and dignity to give value to his obedience and sufferings. From the beginning to the end, therefore, of the sacred volume, from Genesis to Revelation, a Godman Redeemer is held up as the object of supreme reverence, love, and confidence to the perishing children of men. It is absolutely impossible to present a tithe of the evidence which the Scriptures contain of the truth of this doctrine. It is to the Bible what the soul is to the body — its living and all-pervading principle, without which the Scriptures are a cold, lifeless system of history and moral precepts. It seems, therefore, to be a work of supererogation to prove to Christians the divinity of their Redeemer. It is like proving the sun to be the source of light and heat to the system of which it is the centre. Still as there are men, professing to be Christians, who deny this doctrine, as there have been, and still are men, who make the sun a mere satellite of the earth, it is necessary that a part at least of the evidence by which this great truth is proved should be presented, and should be at command to resist the gainsayers.

The Protevangelium.

Immediately after the apostasy of our first parents it was announced that the seed of the woman should bruise the serpent's head. The meaning of this promise and prediction is to be determined by subsequent revelations. When interpreted in the light of the Scriptures themselves, it is manifest that the seed of the woman means the Redeemer, and that bruising the serpent's head means his final triumph over the powers of darkness. In this protevangelium, as it has ever been called, we have the dawning revelation of the humanity and divinity of the great deliverer. As seed of the woman his humanity is distinctly asserted, and the nature of the triumph which he was to effect, in the subjugation of Satan, proves that he was to be a divine person. In the great conflict between good and evil, between the kingdom of light and the kingdom of darkness, between Christ and Belial, between God and Satan, he that triumphs over Satan, is, and can be nothing less than divine. In the earliest books of Scripture, even in Genesis, we have therefore clear intimations of two great truths; first, that there is a plurality of persons in the Godhead; and secondly, that one of those persons is specially concerned in the salvation of men, — in their guidance, government, instruction, and ultimate deliverance from all the evils of their apostasy. The language employed in the record of the creation of man, " Let us make man, in our image, after our likeness," admits of no satisfactory explanation other than that furnished by the doctrine of the Trinity.

Jehovah and the Angel Jehovah.

On this primary and fundamental revelation of this great truth all the subsequent revelations of Scripture are founded. As there is more than one person in the Godhead, we find at once the distinction between Jehovah as the messenger, a mediator, and Jehovah as He who sends, between the Father and the Son, as co-equal, co-eternal persons, which runs through the Bible, with ever-increasing clearness. This is not an arbitrary or unauthorized interpretation of the Old Testament scriptures. In Luke xxiv. 27, it is said of our Lord, that " beginning at Moses, and all the prophets, He expounded unto them in all the Scriptures the things concerning Himself." Moses therefore did testify of Christ; and we have a sure ground on which to rest in interpreting the passages of the Old Testament, which set forth the person and work of the great deliverer, as referring to Christ.

He who was promised to Adam as the seed of the woman, it was next declared should be the seed of Abraham. That this does not refer to his descendants collectively, but to Christ individually, we know from the direct assertion of the Apostle (Gal. iii. 16), and from the fulfilment of the promise. It is not through the children of Abraham as a nation, but through Christ, that all the nations of the earth are blessed. And the blessing referred to, the promise to Abraham, which, as the Apostle says, has come upon us, is the promise of redemption. Abraham therefore saw the day of Christ and was glad, and as our Lord said, Before Abraham was I am. This proves that the person predicted as the seed of the woman and as the seed of Abraham, through whom redemption was to be effected, was to be both God and man. He could not be the seed of Abraham unless a man, and he could not be the Saviour of men unless God.

We accordingly find throughout the Old Testament constant mention made of a person distinct from Jehovah, as a person, to whom nevertheless the titles, attributes, and works of Jehovah are ascribed. This person is called the אֲדֹנָי, מַלְאַךְ יְהֹוָה, מַלְאַךְ אֱלֹהִים, אֱלֹהִים, יְהֹוָה. He claims divine authority, exercises divine prerogatives, and receives divine homage. If this were a casual matter, if in one or two instances the messenger spoke in the name of him who sent him, we might assume that the person thus designated was an ordinary angel or minister of God. But when this is a pervading representation of the Bible; when we find that these terms are applied, not first to one, and then to another angel indiscriminately, but to one particular angel; that the person so designated is also called the Son of God, the Mighty God; that the work attributed to him is elsewhere attributed to God himself; and that in the New Testament, this manifested Jehovah, who led his people under the Old Testament economy, is declared to be the Son of God, the λόγος, who was manifested in the flesh, it becomes certain that by the angel of Jehovah in the early books of Scripture, we are to understand a divine person, distinct from the Father.

A. *The Book of Genesis.*

Thus as early as Gen. xvi. 7, the angel of Jehovah appears to Hagar and says, "I will multiply thy seed exceedingly, that it shall not be numbered for multitude." And Hagar, it is said, " called the name of Jehovah that spake unto her [*Attah el Roi*] Thou God seest me" (ver. 13). This angel therefore is declared to be Jehovah, and promises what God only could perform. Again, in Gen. xviii. 1, it is said, Jehovah appeared to Abraham in the plains of Mamre, who promised to him the birth of Isaac. In ver. 13, he is again called Jehovah. Jehovah said, "Is anything too hard for Jehovah? At the time appointed I will return unto thee . . . . and Sarah shall have a son." As the angels turned toward Sodom, one of them, called Jehovah, said, "Shall I hide from Abraham that thing which I do?" and, "Jehovah said, Because the cry of Sodom and Gomorrah is great, and because their

sin is very grievous, I will go down now and see," etc., and
Abraham, it is added, stood before Jehovah. Through the whole
of Abraham's intercession in behalf of the cities of the plain, the
angel is addressed as Adonai, a title given only to the true God,
and speaks as Jehovah, and assumes the authority of God, to
pardon or punish as to him seems fit. When the execution of the
sentence pronounced on Sodom is mentioned, it is said, " Jehovah
rained . . . . brimstone and fire from Jehovah out of heaven."
With regard to this and similar remarkable expressions, the question is not, What may they mean? but, What do they mean? Taken
by themselves they may be explained away, but taken in the light
of the connected revelations of God on the subject, it becomes apparent that Jehovah is distinguished as a person from Jehovah ;
and therefore that in the Godhead there is more than one person to
whom the name Jehovah belongs. In this case, the words " brimstone and fire " may be connected with the words "from Jehovah,"
in the sense of " fire of God " as a figurative expression for the
lightning. The passage would then mean simply, " Jehovah rained
lightning on Sodom and Gomorrah." But this is not only against
the authorized punctuation of the passage as indicated by the
accents, but also against the analogy of Scripture. That is, it is
an unnatural interpretation, and brings this passage into conflict
with those in which the distinction between the angel of Jehovah
and Jehovah, i. e., between the persons of the Godhead, is clearly
indicated.

In Gen. xxii. 2, God commands Abraham to offer up Isaac as a
sacrifice. The angel of Jehovah arrests his hand at the moment
of immolation, and says (ver. 12), " Now I know that thou fearest
God, seeing thou hast not withheld thy son, thine only son, from
me." And in ver. 16, the angel of the Lord said, " By myself
have I sworn, saith Jehovah . . . . that in blessing I will bless
thee, and in multiplying I will multiply thy seed." And Abraham
called the name of that place " Jehovah-jireh." Here God, the
angel of Jehovah, and Jehovah are names given to the same person, who swears by Himself and promises the blessing of a numerous posterity to Abraham. The angel of Jehovah must therefore
be a divine person.

In Jacob's vision, recorded Gen. xxviii. 11–22, he saw a ladder
reaching to heaven, " and behold Jehovah stood above it, and said,
I am the Lord God of Abraham thy father, and the God of Isaac :
the land whereon thou liest, to thee will I give it, and to thy seed.
And thy seed shall be as the dust of the earth." Here the person

elsewhere called the angel of Jehovah, and who had given the same promise to Abraham, is called the Lord God of Abraham and the God of Israel. In Gen. xxxii. 24–32, Jacob is said to have wrestled with an angel, who blessed him, and in seeing whom Jacob said, " I have seen God face to face." The prophet Hosea, xii. 4, in referring to this event, says, " Jacob had power over the angel, and prevailed : he wept, and made supplication unto him : he found him in Beth-el, and there he spake with us; even Jehovah God of Hosts ; Jehovah is his memorial." The angel with whom Jacob wrestled, was the Lord God of Hosts.

B. *The other Historical Books of the Old Testament.*

In Exodus iii. we have the account of the revelation of God to Moses on Mount Horeb. " The angel of the LORD," it is said, " appeared unto him in a flame of fire out of the midst of a bush." And Moses turned to see this great sight, " and when Jehovah saw that he turned aside to see, God called unto him, out of the midst of the bush . . . . and said, Draw not nigh hither: put off thy shoes from off thy feet, for the place whereon thou standest is holy ground. Moreover he said, I am the God of thy father, the God of Abraham, the God of Isaac, and the God of Jacob. And Moses hid his face ; for he was afraid to look upon God." Here the angel of Jehovah is identical with Jehovah, and is declared to be the God of Abraham, Isaac, and Jacob. The personal distinction between Jehovah and the angel of Jehovah (*i. e.*, between the Father and the Son, as these persons are elsewhere, and usually in the later Scriptures, designated), is clearly presented in Ex. xxiii. 20, where it is said, ": Behold, I send an angel before thee, to keep thee in the way, and to bring thee into the place which I have prepared. Beware of him, and obey his voice, provoke him not ; for he will not pardon your transgressions : for my name is in him." The last phrase is equivalent to, " I am in him." By the name of God, is often meant God himself as manifested. Thus it is said of the temple, 1 Kings viii. 29, " My name shall be there," *i. e.*, " There will I dwell." As in the New Testament the Father is said to send the Son, and to be in Him; so here Jehovah is said to send the angel of Jehovah and to be in him. And as the Son of Man had power on earth to forgive sin, so the angel of Jehovah had authority to forgive or punish at his pleasure. Michaelis, in his marginal annotations to his edition of the Hebrew Bible, says in reference to this passage (Ex. xxiii. 20) : " *Bechai* ex Kabbala docet, hunc angelum non esse ex numero creatorum existentium extra Dei essentiam, sed ex emanationibus, quæ intra Dei essentiam subsistunt, sic in *Tanchuma* explicari, quod sit *Metatron*, Princeps faciei, John vi. 46." That the angel of Jehovah is a divine person, is further manifest from the account given in Exodus xxxii. and xxxiii. of what God said to Moses after the people had sinned in worshipping the golden calf.   In punishment of that offence God threatened no longer personally to attend the people.   In consequence of this manifestation of the divine displeasure the whole congregation were assembled before the door of the Tabernacle, and humbled themselves before God.   And Jehovah descended and spake unto Moses face to face as a man speaketh unto his friend.   And Moses interceded for the people and said, If thy presence go not with *us* carry us not up hence.   And Jehovah said, My presence (*i. e.*, I myself) shall go with thee and I will give thee rest.   This shows that a divine person, Jehovah, had previously guided the people, and that on their repentance, He promised to continue with them. This person, called the angel of Jehovah, Jehovah himself, is in Is. lxiii. 9, called "the angel of the face of Jehovah," *i. e.*, the angel or the messenger, who is the image of God.   It can hardly be doubted, therefore, that this angel was the Son of God, sent by Him and therefore called his angel; who in Is. lxiii. is designated as the Saviour of Israel and the Redeemer of Jacob; who came to reveal God, as He was the brightness of his glory and the express image of his person, in whom was his name, or, as it is expressed in the New Testament, the fulness of the Godhead; who in the fulness of time, for us men and for our salvation, became flesh, and revealed his glory as the only begotten Son full of grace and truth.

In subsequent periods of the history of God's people this same divine person appears as the leader and God of Israel.   He manifested himself to Joshua (v. 14) as "Prince of the host of the Lord"; to Gideon (Judges vi. 11), as the angel of Jehovah, and spake to him, saying, *i. e.*, Jehovah said to him, Go in this thy might and thou shalt save Israel from the hand of the Midianites. In verse 16 it is again said, "Jehovah said unto him surely I will be with thee, and thou shalt smite the Midianites as one man." When Gideon became aware who it was that spoke to him he exclaimed, "Alas, O Lord God, for because I have seen the angel of Jehovah face to face.   And Jehovah said unto him, Peace be unto thee; fear not: thou shalt not die."   The same angel appeared to Manoah and promised him a son, and revealed himself as he had done to Gideon by causing fire to issue from a rock and consume the sacrifice which had been placed upon it. When Manoah knew that it was the angel of Jehovah, he said unto his wife, " We shall surely die, because we have seen God."

C. *Different Modes of explaining these Passages.*

There are only three methods on which these and similar passages in the Old Testament can with any regard to the divine authority of the Scriptures be explained. The one is that the angel of Jehovah is a created angel, one of the spirits who wait continually on God and do his will. The fact that he assumes divine titles, claims divine prerogatives, and accepts divine homage, is explained on the principle, that the representative has a right to the titles and honours of the Being, or person whom he represents. He speaks as God because God speaks through him. This hypothesis, which was early and extensively adopted, might be admitted if the cases of the kind were few in number, and if the person designated as the angel of Jehovah did not so obviously claim to be himself Jehovah. And what is a more decisive objection to this mode of interpretation, is the authority of the subsequent parts of the Word of God. These passages do not stand alone. The Church might well hesitate on the ground of these early revelations to admit the doctrine of a plurality of persons in the Godhead. If everywhere else in Scripture God were revealed as only one person, almost any degree of violence of interpretation might be allowed to bring these passages into harmony with that revelation. But as the reverse is true; as with ever increasing clearness the existence of three persons in the Godhead is made known in Scripture, it becomes in the highest degree unnatural to explain these passages otherwise than in accordance with that doctrine. Besides this we have the express testimony of the inspired writers of the New Testament, that the angel of the Lord, the manifested Jehovah who led the Israelites through the wilderness, and who dwelt in the temple, was Christ; that is, was the λόγος, or Eternal Son of God, who became flesh and fulfilled the work which it was predicted the Messiah should accomplish. The Apostles do not hesitate to apply to Christ the language of the Old Testament used to set forth the majesty, the works, or the kingdom of the Jehovah of the Hebrew Scriptures. (John xii. 41; Rom. xiv. 11; 1 Cor. x. 4; Heb. i. 10–13, and often elsewhere.) The New Testament, therefore, clearly identifies the Logos or Son of God with the Angel of Jehovah, or Messenger of the Covenant, of the Old Testament.

The second hypothesis on which these passages have been explained, admits that the angel of the Lord is a really divine person, but denies that he is personally distinguished from Jehovah. It was one and the same person who sent and was sent, was the speaker and the one spoken to. But this assumption does such violence to all just rules of interpretation, and is so inconsistent with the subsequent revelations of the Word of God, that it has found little favour in the Church. We are, therefore, shut up to the only other mode of explaining the passages in question, which has been almost universally adopted in the Church, at least since the Reformation. This assumes the progressive character of divine revelation, and interprets the obscure intimations of the early Scriptures by the clearer light of subsequent communications. The angel, who appeared to Hagar, to Abraham, to Moses, to Joshua, to Gideon, and to Manoah, who was called Jehovah and worshipped as Adonai, who claimed divine homage and exercised divine power, whom the psalmists and prophets set forth as the Son of God, as the Counsellor, the Prince of Peace, the mighty God, and whom they predicted was to be born of a virgin, and to whom every knee should bow and every tongue confess, of things in heaven and things on earth, and things under the earth, is none other than He whom we now recognize and worship as our God and Saviour Jesus Christ. It was the Λόγος ἄσαρκος whom the Israelites worshipped and obeyed ; and it is the Λόγος ἔνσαρκος whom we acknowledge as our Lord and God.

It is universally admitted that the Old Testament does predict a Messiah, one who was to appear in the fulness of time to effect the redemption of his people, and through whom the knowledge of the true religion was to be extended throughout the world. While it is clearly revealed that this Redeemer was to be the seed of the woman, the seed of Abraham, of the tribe of Judah, and of the house of David, it was no less clearly revealed that He was to be a divine person. He is presented under the different aspects of a triumphant king, a suffering martyr, and a divine person. Sometimes these representations are all combined in the descriptions given of the coming Deliverer ; sometimes the one, and sometimes the other view of his character is held up either exclusively or most prominently in the prophetic writings. They, however, are all exhibited in the Hebrew Scriptures, as they all combine and harmonize in the person and work of our Lord and Saviour.

D. *The Psalms.*

In the second Psalm, the heathen are represented as combining against the Messiah, verses 1–3. God derides their efforts, verses 4, 5. He declares his purpose to constitute the Messiah king in Zion. That this Messiah is a divine person is plain: (1.) Because He is called the Son of God, which, as has been shown, implies equality with God. (2.) He is invested with universal and absolute dominion. (3.) He is the Jehovah whom the people are commanded in verse 11 to worship. (4.) Because all are required to acknowledge his authority and do Him homage. (5.) Because those are pronounced blessed who put their trust in Him, whereas the Scriptures declared them to be cursed who put their trust in princes.

In the twenty-second Psalm, a sufferer is described whose words our Lord upon the cross appropriates to Himself, verses 1–19. He prays for deliverance, verses 19–21. The consequences of that deliverance are such as prove that the subject of the psalm must be a divine person. His sufferings render it certain, (1.) That all good men will fear and love God because He rescued this sufferer from his enemies. (2.) That provision will be made for the wants of all men. (3.) That all nations will be converted unto God. (4.) That the blessings which He secures will last forever.

In the forty-fifth Psalm a king is described who must be a divine person. (1.) Because his perfect excellence is the ground of the praise rendered to Him. (2.) Because his kingdom is declared to be righteous and everlasting. (3.) He is addressed as God, " Thy throne O God is for ever and ever," which is quoted Heb. i. 8, and applied to Christ for the very purpose of proving that He is entitled to the worship of all intelligent creatures. (4.) The Church is declared to be his bride, which implies that He is to his people the object of supreme love and confidence.

The seventy-second Psalm contains a description of an exalted king, and of the blessings of his reign. These blessings are of such a nature as to prove that the subject of the psalm must be a divine person. (1.) His kingdom is to be everlasting. (2.) Universal. (3.) It secures perfect peace with God and good-will among men. (4.) All men are to be brought to submit to Him through love. (5.) In Him all the nations of the earth are to be blessed ; *i. e.*, as we are distinctly taught in Gal. iii. 16, it is in Him that all the blessings of redemption are to come upon the world.   The subject of this psalm, is therefore, the Redeemer of the world.

The hundred and tenth Psalm is repeatedly quoted and expounded in the New Testament, and applied to Christ to set forth the dignity of his person and the nature of his work.   (1.) He is David's Lord.   But if David's Lord, how can He be David's Son ? This was the question which Christ put to the Pharisees, in order to convince them that their ideas of the Messiah fell far below the doctrine of their own Scriptures.   He was indeed to be David's Son, as they expected, but at the same time He was to be possessed of a nature which made Him David's Lord.   (2.) In virtue of this divine nature He was to sit at God's right hand ; that is, to be associated with Him on terms of equality as to glory and dominion. Such is the Apostle's exposition of this passage in Heb. i. 13.   To no angel, *i. e.*, to no creature, has God ever said, " Sit on my right hand."   The subject of this psalm is no creature ; and if not a creature, He is the Creator.   (3.) This person, who is at once David's Son and David's Lord, is eternally both priest and king. This again is referred to in Heb. vii. 17, to prove that He must be a divine person.   It is only because He is possessed of "an endless life," or, as it is elsewhere said, because He has life in Himself even as the Father has life in Himself, that it is possible for Him to be a perpetual priest and king.   (4.) In verse 5, He is declared to be the supreme Lord, for He is called Adonai, a title never given to any but the true God.

E.   *The Prophetical Books.*

In Isaiah iv. 2, the appearance of the Branch of Jehovah is predicted, to whose advent such effects are ascribed as prove Him to be a divine person.   Those effects are purification, the pardon of sin, and perfect security.

Chapter vi. contains an account of the prophet's vision of Jehovah in his holy temple, surrounded by the hosts of adoring angels, who worship Him day and night.   The person thus declared to be Jehovah, the object of angelic worship, the Apostle John tells us, xii. 41, was none other than Christ, whom all Christians and all angels now worship.

In chapters vii.–ix. the birth of a child whose mother was a virgin, is predicted.   That this child was the eternal Son of God, equal with the Father, is proved, (1.) From his name Immanuel, which means God with us, *i. e.*, God in our nature.   (2.) The land of Israel is said to be his land.   (3.) He is called Wonderful, Counsellor, the Mighty God, Father of Eternity, and Prince of Peace. (4.) His kingdom is everlasting and universal. (5.) The consequences of his advent and dominion are such as flow only from the dominion of God. In the eleventh chapter we have another description of the perfection of his person and of his kingdom, which is applicable only to the person and kingdom of God. It is only where God reigns that the peace, holiness, and blessedness which attend the coming of the predicted deliverer, are ever found. The same argument may be drawn from the prophetic account of the Messiah and of his kingdom contained in the latter part of Isaiah, from the fortieth chapter to the sixty-sixth. This Messiah was to effect the redemption of his people, not merely from the Babylonish captivity, but from all evil; to secure for them the pardon of sin, and reconciliation with God; the prevalence of true religion to the ends of the earth; and, finally, the complete triumph of the kingdom of light over the kingdom of darkness. This is a work which none other than a divine person could effect.

The prophet Micah (v. 1–5) predicted that one was to be born in Bethlehem, who was to be, (1.) The Ruler of Israel, *i. e.*, of all the people of God. (2.) Although to be born in time and made of a woman, his " goings forth have been from of old, from everlasting." (3.) He shall rule in the exercise of the strength and majesty of God, *i. e.*, manifest in 'his government the possession of divine attributes and glory. (4.) His dominion shall be universal; and (5.) Its effects peace; *i. e.*, perfect harmony, order, and blessedness.

The prophet Joel does not bring distinctly into view the person of the Redeemer, unless it be in the doubtful passage in ii. 23. He goes through the usual round of Messianic predictions; foretells the apostasy of the people, reproves them for their sins, threatens divine judgments, and then promises deliverance through a " teacher of righteousness " (according to one interpretation of ii. 23), and then the effusion of the Holy Spirit upon all fl sh. The gift of the Holy Ghost is everywhere represented as the characteristic blessing of the Messianic period, because secured by the merit of the Redeemer's death. That He thus gives the Holy Spirit is the highest evidence of his being truly God.

In Jere niah xxiii., the restoration or redempti n of God's people is fo.etold. This redemption was to be effected by one who is declared to be, (1.) A descendant of David. (2.) He is called the Branch, a designation which connects this prophecy with those of Isaiah in which the Messiah receives the same title. (3.) He was to be a king. (4.) His reign was to be prosperous, Judah and Israel were to be again united: *i. e.*, perfect harmony and peace were to be secured. (5.) This deliverer is called Jehovah, our Righteousness. In the thirty-third chapter, the same deliverance is predicted, and the same name is here given to Jerusalem which in the former passage was given to the Messiah. In the one case it is symbolical, in the other significant.

In Daniel ii. 44, it is foretold that the kingdom of the Messiah is to be everlasting, and is destined to supersede and absorb all other kingdoms. In vii. 9–14, it is said that one like unto the Son of Man was brought unto the Ancient of Days; and a dominion, glory, and kingdom given unto Him; that all people, nations, and languages should serve Him; his dominion is to be an everlasting dominion, which shall not pass away, and his kingdom that which shall not be destroyed. In ix. 24–27, is recorded the prediction concerning the seventy weeks, and the coming and work of the Messiah, which work is truly divine.

The first six chapters of the prophecies of Zechariah are a series of visions, foreshadowing the return of the Jews from Babylon, the restoration of the city, and the rebuilding of the temple; the subsequent apostasy of the people; the advent of the Messiah; the establishment of his kingdom, and the dispersion of the Jews. From the ninth chapter to the end of the book, the same events are predicted in ordinary prophetic language. Jerusalem is called upon to rejoice at the advent of her king. He was to be meek and lowly, unostentatious and peaceful, and his dominion universal. In chapter xi. He is represented as a shepherd who makes a last attempt to gather his flock. He is to be rejected by those whom He came to save, and sold for thirty pieces of silver. For this enormity the people are to be given up to long desolation; but at last God will pour upon them the Spirit of grace and supplication, and they shall look upon me, saith Jehovah, whom they have pierced, and mourn. This shepherd is declared to be God's fellow, associate, or equal. His kingdom shall triumph, shall become universal, and holiness shall everywhere prevail.

In Malachi iii. 1–4, it is predicted (1.) That a messenger should appear to prepare the way of the Lord. (2.) That the Lord, *i. e.*, Jehovah, the messenger of the covenant, *i. e.*, the Messiah, should come to his temple. (3.) At his advent the wicked shall be destroyed, and the Church saved.[1]

---

[1] On this subject see Hengstenberg's *Christology*; Smith's *Messiah*; Allix's *Judgment of the Jewish Church.*

It is plain, even from this cursory review, that the Old Testament clearly predicts the advent of a divine person clothed in our nature, who was to be the Saviour of the world. He was to be the seed of the woman, the seed of Abraham, of the tribe of Judah, of the house of David; born of a virgin; a man of sorrows; and to make " his soul an offering for sin." He is, however, no less clearly declared to be the Angel of Jehovah, Jehovah, Elohim, Adonai, the Mighty God, exercising all divine prerogatives, and entitled to divine worship from men and angels. Such is the doctrine of the Old Testament as to what the Messiah was to be; and this is the doctrine of the New Testament, as to what Jesus of Nazareth in fact is.

§ 2. *General Characteristics of the New Testament Teaching concerning Christ.*

A. *The Sense in which Christ is called Lord.*

The first argument from the New Testament in proof of the divinity of Christ, is derived from the fact that He is everywhere called Lord; the Lord; our Lord. It is admitted that the Greek word κύριος means owner, and one who has the authority of an owner, whether of men or things. The Lord of a vineyard is the owner of the vineyard, and the Lord of slaves is the owner of slaves. It is also admitted that the word is used with all the latitude of the Latin word *Dominus*, or the English Master or Mister. It is applied as a title of respect, not only to magistrates and princes, but to those who are not invested with any official authority. It is, therefore, not merely the fact that Jesus is called Lord, that proves that He is also God; but that He is called Lord in such a sense and in such a way as is consistent with no other hypothesis. In the first place, Christ is called Lord in the New Testament with the same constancy and with the same preëminence that Jehovah is called Lord in the Old Testament. This was the word which all the readers, whether of the Hebrew or Greek Scriptures, under the old economy were accustomed to use to express their relation to God. They recognized Him as their owner, as their Supreme Sovereign, and as their protector. He was in that sense their Lord. The Lord is on our side. The Lord be with you. The Lord He is God. Blessed is the nation whose God is the Lord. Thou Lord art good. Thou Lord art most high forever. O Lord, there is none like unto thee. I will praise the Lord. Have mercy upon me, O Lord. O Lord, thou art my God. The religious ear of the people was educated in the use of this language from their infancy. The Lord was their God. They worshipped and praised Him, and invoked his aid in calling him Lord. The same feelings of reverence, adoration, and love, the same sense of dependence and desire of protection are expressed throughout the New Testament in calling Jesus Lord. Lord, if thou wilt, thou canst make me clean. Lord, save me. Joy of thy Lord. Lord, when saw we thee a hungered? He that judgeth me is the Lord. If the Lord will. To be present with the Lord. Them that call on the Lord. Which the Lord shall give me in the last day. Blessed are the dead who die in the Lord. Thou art worthy, O Lord, to receive glory and honour.

Jesus Christ, therefore, is Lord to Christians in the same sense that Jehovah was Lord to the Hebrews. The usage referred to is altogether peculiar; no man — not Moses, nor Abraham, nor David, nor any of the prophets or Apostles, is ever thus prevailingly addressed or invoked as Lord. We have but one Lord; and Jesus Christ is Lord. This is an argument which addresses itself to the inward experience, rather than to the mere understanding. Every believer knows in what sense he calls Jesus Lord; and he knows that in thus recognizing Him as his owner, as his absolute sovereign, to whom the allegiance of his soul, and not merely of his outward life, is due; and as his protector and Saviour, he is in communion with the Apostles and martyrs. He knows that it is from the New Testament he has been taught to worship Christ in calling him Lord.

But in the second place, Jesus Christ is not only thus called Lord by way of eminence, but He is declared to be the Lord of lords; to be the Lord of glory; the Lord of all; the Lord of the living and the dead; the Lord of all who are in heaven and on earth, and under the earth. All creatures, from the highest to the lowest, must bow the knee to Him, and acknowledge his absolute dominion. He is in such a sense Lord as that no man can truly call Him Lord but by the Holy Ghost. If his Lordship were merely the supremacy which one creature can exercise over other creatures, there would be no necessity for a divine illumination to enable us to recognize his authority. But if He is Lord in the absolute sense in which God alone is Lord; if He has a right in us, and an authority over us, which belong only to our Maker and Redeemer, then it is necessary that the Holy Spirit should so reveal to us the glory of God in the face of Jesus Christ, as to lead us to prostrate ourselves before Him as our Lord and our God.

In the third place, Christ is called Lord, when that word is used

for the incommunicable divine names and titles Jehovah and
Adonai.   It is well known that the Jews from an early period
had a superstitious reverence, which prevented their pronouncing
the word Jehovah.   They therefore, in their Hebrew Scriptures,
gave it the vowel points belonging to the word Adonai, and so pronounced it whenever they read the sacred volume.   When they
translated their Scriptures into Greek, they uniformly substituted
κύριος, which answers to *Adon*, for Jehovah.   In like manner,
under the influence of the LXX., the Latin Christians in their
version used *Dominus ;* and constrained by the same wide spread
and long-continued usage, the English translators have, as a general thing, put Lord (in small capitals) where the Hebrew has Jehovah.   In very many cases we find passages applied to Christ as
the Messiah, in which He is called Lord, when *Lord* should be
Jehovah or Adonai.   In Luke i. 76, it is said of John the Baptist,
the forerunner of Christ, that he should go before the face of the
Lord ; but in Malachi iii. 1, of which this passage declares the fulfilment, the person speaking is Jehovah.   The day of Christ, in
the New Testament, is called " the day of the Lord ; " in the Old
Testament it is called " the day of Jehovah, the great day."
יוֹם יְהוָֹה הַגָּדוֹל.   Romans x. 13, quotes Joel ii. 32, which speaks
of Jehovah, and applies it to Christ, saying, " Whosoever shall
call upon the name of the Lord shall be saved."   Rom xiv. 10, 11,
quotes Isaiah xlv. 23, " We shall all stand before the judgment
seat of Christ.   For it is written, As I live, saith the Lord (Jehovah), every knee shall bow to me," etc.   This is common throughout the New Testament, and therefore Christ is there set forth as
Lord in the same sense in which the Supreme God is Lord.   The
meaning of the word as applied to Christ being thus established, it
shows how constant and familiar is the recognition of his divinity
by the sacred writers.   They acknowledge Him to be God every
time they call Him Lord.

B. *Christ presented as the Object of our Religious Affections.*

Another general feature of the New Testament, intimately connected with the one just mentioned, and consequent upon it, is,
that Christ is everywhere recognized as the proper object of all the
religious affections.   As He is our Lord, in the sense of being our
absolute proprietor, our maker, preserver, and redeemer, and our
sovereign, having the right to do with us as seems good in his sight,
we are called upon to make Him the supreme object of our love,
his will the highest rule of duty, and his glory the great end of our

being. We are to exercise the same faith and confidence in Him that we do in God; yield Him the same obedience, devotion, and homage. We find, therefore, that such is the case from the beginning to the end of the New Testament writings. Christ is the God of the Apostles and early Christians, in the sense that He is the object of all their religious affections. They regarded Him as the person to whom they specially belonged; to whom they were responsible for their moral conduct; to whom they had to account for their sins; for the use of their time and talents; who was ever present with them, dwelling in them, controlling their inward, as well as their outward life; whose love was the animating principle of their being; in whom they rejoiced as their present joy and as their everlasting portion. This recognition of their relation to Christ as their God, is constant and pervading, so that the evidence of it cannot be gathered up and stated in a polemic or didactic form. But every reader of the New Testament to whom Christ is a mere creature, however exalted, must feel himself to be out of communion with the Apostles and apostolic Christians, who avowed themselves and were universally recognized by others as being the worshippers of Christ. They knew that they were to stand before his judgment seat; that every act, thought, and word of theirs, and of every man who shall ever live, was to lie open to his omniscient eye; and that on his decision the destiny of every human soul was to depend. Knowing therefore the terror of the Lord, they persuaded men. They enforced every moral duty, not merely on the grounds of moral obligation, but by considerations drawn from the relation of the soul to Christ. Children are to obey their parents, wives their husbands, servants their masters, not as pleasing men, but as doing the will of Christ. True religion in their view consists not in the love or reverence of God, merely as the infinite Spirit, the creator and preserver of all things, but in the knowledge and love of Christ. Whoever believes that Jesus is the Son of God, i. e., whoever believes that Jesus of Nazareth is God manifested in the flesh, and loves and obeys Him as such, is declared to be born of God. Any one who denies that truth, is declared to be antichrist, denying both the Father and the Son, for the denial of the one is the denial of the other. The same truth is expressed by another Apostle, who says, "If our gospel be hid it is hid to them that are lost, in whom the god of this world hath blinded the minds of them which believe not, lest they should see the glory of God as it shines in the face of Jesus Christ." They are lost, according to this Apostle, who do not see, as well as believe, Jesus to be God dwelling in the flesh. Hence such effects are ascribed to the knowledge of Christ, and to faith in Him ; such hopes are entertained of the glory and blessedness of being with Him, as would be impossible or irrational if Christ were not the true God. He is our life. He that hath the Son hath life. He that believes on Him shall live forever. It is not we that live, but Christ that liveth in us. Our life is hid with Christ in God. We are complete in Him, wanting nothing. Though we have not seen Him, yet believing in Him, we rejoice in Him with joy unspeakable. It is because Christ is God, because He is possessed of all divine perfections, and because He loved us and gave Himself for us, and hath redeemed us and made us kings and priests unto God, that the Spirit of God says, " If any man love not the Lord Jesus Christ, let him be anathema maranatha." The denial of the divinity of the Son of God, the refusal to receive, love, trust, worship, and serve Him as such, is the ground of the hopeless condemnation of all who hear and reject the gospel. And to the justice of this condemnation all rational creatures, holy and unholy, justified or condemned, will say, Amen. The divinity of Christ is too plain a fact, and too momentous a truth, to be innocently rejected. Those are saved who truly believe it, and those are already lost who have not eyes to see it. He that believeth not is condemned already, because he hath not believed in the name of the only begotten Son of God. He that believeth on the Son hath everlasting life ; and he that believeth not the Son shall not see life, but the wrath of God abideth on him. It is the doctrine of the New Testament, therefore, that the spiritual apprehension and the sincere recognition of the Godhead of the Redeemer constitutes the life of the soul. It is in its own nature eternal life ; and the absence or want of this faith and knowledge is spiritual and eternal death. Christ is our life ; and therefore he that hath not the Son hath not life.

C. *The Relations which Christ bears to his People and to the World.*

As the relation which believers consciously bear to Christ is that we can sustain to God only, so the relation which He assumes to us, which He claims as belonging to him in virtue of his nature as well as of his work, is that which God only can sustain to rational creatures.

His Authority as a Teacher.

This is plain as to the authority He assumes as a teacher both of truth and duty. Everything which He declared to be true, all

Christians have ever felt bound to believe, without examination; and all that He commanded them to do or to avoid, they have ever regarded as binding the conscience. His authority is the ultimate and highest ground of faith and moral obligation. As the infinite and absolute reason dwelt in Him bodily, his words were the words of God. He declared himself to be the Truth, and therefore to question what He said was to reject the truth; to disobey Him was to disobey the truth. He was announced as the Λόγος, the personal and manifested Reason, which was and is the light of the world, — the source of all reason and of all knowledge to rational creatures. Hence He spake as never man spake. He taught with authority. He did not do as Moses and the prophets did, speak in the name of God, and say, Thus saith the Lord, referring to an authority out of themselves. But He spoke in his own name, and the Apostles in the name of Christ. He was the ultimate authority. He uniformly places Himself in the relation of God to his people. Ye shall be saved "if ye do whatsoever I command you." He that heareth me heareth God. I and the Father are one; He in me and I in Him. Heaven and earth shall pass away, but my words shall never pass away. Moses said unto you thus and so, but I say unto you. He did not deny the divine mission of Moses, but He assumed the right to modify or repeal the laws which God had given to his people under the old economy. The whole of revealed truth in the Old as well as in the New Testament is referred to Him as its source. For the ancient prophets taught nothing but what "the Spirit of Christ which was in them did signify," which is equivalent to saying that they spake "as they were moved by the Holy Ghost;" or "that all Scripture is given by inspiration of God." And the Apostles presented themselves simply as witnesses of what Christ had taught. Paul declared that he received all his knowledge "by the revelation of Jesus Christ." And in his Epistle to the Corinthians he expresses the same truth by saying negatively, that his knowledge was not derived from human reason (the spirit that is in men), but from the Spirit of God. Nothing is more obvious to the reader of the New Testament than this divine authority as a teacher everywhere claimed by Christ and for Him. To disbelieve Him is to disbelieve God; and to disobey Him is to disobey God. This is entirely different from the authority claimed by the prophets and Apostles. They assumed nothing for themselves. Paul disclaimed all authority over the faith of God's people, except on the ground of the proof which he gave that it was "Christ speaking in" him. (2 Cor. xiii. 3.)

His Control over all Creatures.

The divine authority of Christ is manifest in the control which He claimed over all his people and over all creatures. All power was and is in his hands. His ministers are under his direction; He sends one here and another there. All Paul's labors and journeyings were performed under his continued guidance. This is but an illustration of the universal and absolute control which He constantly exercises over the whole universe. The angels in heaven are his messengers, and the course of human history, as well as the circumstances of every individual man, is determined by Him. So also is the eternal destiny of all men in his hands. I will reward every man, He says, according to his works. (Matt. xvi. 27, and Rev. xxii. 12.) " Many will say to me in that day, Lord, Lord, have we not prophesied in thy name? and in thy name have cast out devils? and in thy name done many wonderful works? And then will I profess unto them, I never knew you: depart from me, ye that work iniquity." (Matt. vii. 22, 23.) In the last day, at the " time of harvest, I will say to the reapers, Gather ye together first the tares, and bind them in bundles to burn them: but gather the wheat into my barn." (Matt. xiii. 30.) And in ver. 41, " The Son of Man shall send forth his angels, and they shall gather out of his kingdom all things that offend, and them which do iniquity; and shall cast them into a furnace of fire: there shall be wailing and gnashing of teeth." The king in that day will say, " Depart from me, ye cursed, into everlasting fire prepared for the devil and his angels: for I was a hungered, and ye gave me no meat: I was thirsty, and ye gave me no drink:" for " inasmuch as ye did it not to one of the least of these, ye did it not unto me." It is the attitude, therefore, in which men stand to Christ (provided they have heard his name), which is to determine their destiny in the last day. Sinning against Christ, denying or rejecting Him, is denying or rejecting God. Our Lord therefore uniformly places Himself in the relation of God to the souls of men, claiming the same authority over them, the same right to decide their destiny, and representing all sin as committed against Himself. Thus also He says, that it were better for a man to have a millstone hung about his neck, and he cast into the midst of the sea, than to offend one of the little ones who believe on Him. " Whosoever shall confess me before men, him shall the Son of Man also confess before the angels of God: but he that denieth me before men, shall be denied before the angels of God." (Luke xii. 8, 9.) " He that loveth father or mother, ... son or daughter more than me is not worthy of me." Such supreme love is due to God alone, and Christ in claiming this love from us, places Himself before us as God.

D. *The Nature of his Promises.*

The same is plain from the nature of his promises. Christ promises to his people blessings which none but God has either the right or the power to bestow. He promises to forgive sin. It is intuitively certain that God only can forgive sin ; He is our moral governor ; it is against Him that all sin is committed, and He only has the right to remit its penalty. When therefore Christ says to the soul, Thy sins are forgiven, He exercises a divine prerogative. Even the Man of Sin, who sitteth in the temple of God and exalteth himself above all that is called God, claims no more than the judicial authority of deciding when the conditions of pardon at the bar of God have been fulfilled. He assumes, in relation to the divine law, the relation which a human judge sustains to the law of the land. A judge does not acquit or condemn on his own authority. The authority is in the state or sovereign power. The judge merely determines whether the grounds of condemnation are present or not. But as the sovereign against whom sin is committed, Christ has the right to pardon or to punish. Again, He promises the Holy Spirit. John the Baptist announced his approach as one who was to baptize the people with fire and with the Holy Ghost. And accordingly it is recorded that He did send down on his disciples, especially on the day of Pentecost, power from on high. It had been predicted that God would pour out his Spirit on all flesh ; and that prophecy the Apostle Peter teaches was fulfilled when Christ, exalted at the right hand of God, shed forth his gifts on his waiting disciples. In his farewell discourse to the Apostles, He said, I will send you another Comforter, even the Spirit of truth, who shall abide with you forever. All the sanctifying influences, as well as all the gifts of teaching and of miracles which the Church has ever enjoyed, come from the Lord Jesus Christ. He gives the Spirit to every one severally as He will. " Unto every one of us," says Paul, " is given grace according to the measure of the gift of Christ." (Eph. iv. 7.) He promises to hear and answer the prayers of his people in all ages and in all parts of the world. " Whatsoever ye shall ask in my name, I will do it." " Wherever two or three are gathered together in my name, there am I in the midst of them." " Lo I am with you alway, even unto the end of the world." He thus promises his continued presence to his disciples wherever they may be. He also promises to all who believe on Him, eternal life. He has power to quicken or to give life to as many as He will. "My sheep follow me, and I give unto them eternal life." "I will raise them up at the last day." "To him that overcometh will I give to eat of the tree of life." "Be thou faithful unto death, and I will give thee a crown of life." "A crown of righteousness, which the Lord, the righteous judge, shall give me in that day." "Peace I leave with you, my peace I give unto you: not as the world giveth, give I unto you." "Ye believe in God, believe also in me." "I go to prepare a place for you." "I will come again and receive you unto myself; that where I am, there ye may be also." "Come unto me, all ye that labour and are heavy laden, and I will give you rest." It is obvious that the infinite God himself can neither promise nor give anything greater or higher than Christ gives his people. To Him they are taught to look as the source of all blessings, the giver of every good and every perfect gift. There is no more comprehensive prayer in the New Testament than that with which Paul closes his Epistle to the Galatians: "The grace of our Lord Jesus Christ be with your spirit." His favour is our life, which it could not be if He were not our God.

E. *His Control over Nature.*

A fourth general feature of the New Testament teaching concerning Christ, relates to the control attributed to Him over the external world. The laws of nature are ordained by God. They can be changed or suspended by Him alone. A miracle, therefore, or any event which involves such change or suspension, is an evidence of the immediate operation of divine power. The efficient agent, therefore, in working a miracle, must possess divine power. When Moses, the prophets, or the Apostles wrought miracles, they expressly disclaimed the idea that it was by their own efficiency. Why look ye on us, says the Apostle Peter, as though by our own power we had made this man whole? When Moses divided the Red Sea, the efficiency by which that effect was produced was no more in him than in the rod with which he smote the waters. Christ, however, wrought miracles by his own inherent power; and it was to his efficiency the Apostles attributed the miracles wrought through them. It was his name, or faith in Him, as Peter taught the people, which effected the instantaneous healing of the lame man. Christ never referred this miraculous power to any source out of Himself; He claimed it as his own prerogative; and

He conferred the power upon others.   He said of Himself that He
had power to lay down his life and power to take it again ; that He
had life in Himself and could give life to as many as He pleased ;
I will give you, He said to his disciples, power to tread on serpents
and scorpions, and over all the power of the adversary.   Every
miracle of Christ, therefore, was a visible manifestation of his divinity.   When He healed the sick, opened the eyes of the blind,
restored the lame, raised the dead, fed thousands with a few loaves
of bread, and calmed the raging of the sea, it was by a word, by
the effortless exercise of his will.   He thus manifested forth his
glory, giving ocular demonstration to those who had eyes to see,
that He was God in fashion as a man.   He therefore appealed
directly to his works, "Though ye believe not me, believe the
works; that ye may know, and believe, that the Father is in me,
and I in Him."   "If I do not the works of my Father, believe me
not."   (John x. 37, 38.)   "If I had not done among them the
works which none other man did, they had not had sin : but now
have they both seen and hated both me and my Father."   (John
xv. 24.)

It is only a small part of the evidence of the divinity of our Lord
that can thus be gathered up from the general teaching of the New
Testament.   It is important to bear in mind that faith in this doctrine rests not on this or that passage, or on this or that mode of
representation, but upon the whole revelation of God concerning
his Son.   The divinity of the Lord Jesus Christ is wrought into
the texture of the Scriptures, and is everywhere asserted or assumed.   There are, however, many passages in which the doctrine
is so clearly presented, that they should not be passed by in any
formal discussion of this subject.

§ 3. Particular Passages which Teach the Divinity of Christ.

A. The Writings of St. John.

John i. 1–14. Why the higher nature of Christ is called ὁ λόγος,
and why John used that designation, are different questions. As
the word λόγος does not occur in Scripture in the sense of reason,
it should be taken in its ordinary meaning. The question why the
Son is called "The Word" may be answered by saying that the
term expresses both his nature and his office. The word is that
which reveals. The Son is the εἰκών and ἀπαύγασμα of God, and
therefore his word. It is his office to make God known to his
creatures. No man hath seen God at any time ; the only begotten

Son who is in the bosom of the Father, He hath declared Him. The
Son, therefore, as the revealer of God, is the Word. The reason
why John selected this designation of the divine nature of Christ,
is not so easy to determine. It may indeed be said that there is
ground for the use of the term in the usage of the Old Testament
and of the Jews who were contemporaries with the Apostle. In
the Hebrew Scriptures the manifested Jehovah is called the Word
of God, and to Him individual subsistence and divine perfections
are ascribed. (Ps. xxxiii. 6; cxix. 89; Is. xl. 8; Ps. cvii. 20;
cxlvii. 18.) This is more frequently done in the apocryphal books
and in the Targums. It was not therefore an unusual or unknown
term introduced by the Apostle John. Still as he only, of the New
Testament writers, thus employs the word, there must have been
some special reason for his doing so. That reason may have been
to counteract the erroneous views concerning the nature of God
and his Word, which had begun to prevail, and which had some
support from the doctrines of Philo and other Alexandrian Jews.
It is, however, of less importance to determine why John calls the
Son λόγος, than to ascertain what he teaches concerning Him.
He does teach (1.) That He is eternal. He was in the beginning;
i. e., was before the creation; before the foundation of the world;
before the world was. Compare Prov. viii. 23; John xvii. 5, 24;
Eph. i. 4. These are all Scriptural forms of expressing the idea
of eternity. The Word then *was* (ἦν), He did not begin to be but
already was. The ἦν of ver. 1 stands opposed to ἐγένετο ver. 14.
" He *was* the Word, and *became* flesh." (2.) The eternal Word existed in intimate union with God. " The Word was with God; " as
Wisdom is said to have been with Him in the beginning. (Prov.
viii. 30; John i. 18.) (3.) He was God. The word θεός is clearly
the predicate, as it is without the article (compare John iv. 24,
πνεῦμα ὁ θεός, God is a Spirit), and because λόγος is the subject in
the whole context. That θεός is neither to be taken for θεῖος, nor
rendered *a God*, is plain from what is immediately said of the λόγος
in the following verses, and from the analogy of Scripture, which
proves that the λόγος is θεός in the highest sense of the word. In
this connection ὁ θεὸς ἦν ὁ λόγος would be equivalent to saying, " The
Son is the Father." Θεός without the article occurs frequently in
the New Testament when it refers to the supreme God. (4.) The
λόγος is the creator of all things. All things were made by Him,
δι' αὐτοῦ. The διά here does not necessarily express subordinate
instrumentality. All things are said to be διὰ θεοῦ as well as ἐκ θεοῦ.
The Father operates through the Son and the Son through the

Spirit.   All that the preposition indicates is subordination as to the mode of operation, which is elsewhere taught in relation to the persons of the Trinity.   That all creatures owe their being to the Word, is made the more prominent by saying, " Without him was not anything made that was made ; " πᾶν ὁ γέγονεν is through Him.   He therefore cannot be a creature.   He was not only before all creatures, but everything created was by Him caused to be.   (5.) The λόγος is self-existent.   He is underived.   " In him was life."   This is true only of God.   The Godhead subsisting in the Father, Word, and Spirit, alone is self-existent, having life in itself.   (6.) The life of the Word " is the light of men."   Having life in Himself, the Word is the source of life in all that lives, and especially of the intellectual and spiritual life of man ; and therefore He is said to be the light of men ; i. e., the source of intellectual life and knowledge in all their forms.   (7.) The λόγος, as the true or real light, shineth in darkness (ἐν τῇ σκοτίᾳ = ἐν τοῖς ἐσκοτισμένοις) in the midst of a world alienated from God.   The men of the world, the children of darkness, do not comprehend the light ; they do not recognize the Word as God, the creator of all things, and the source of life and knowledge.   To those who do thus recognize Him, He gives power to become the sons of God, that is, He raises them to the dignity and blessedness of God's children.   (8.) This Word became flesh ; that is, became a man.   This use of the word *flesh* is explained by such passages as 1 Tim. iii. 16 ; Heb. ii. 14 ; Rom. viii. 3, in connection with Luke i. 35 ; Gal. iv. 4 ; Phil. ii. 7.   As to the glory of the incarnate λόγος, the Apostle says of himself and of his fellow disciples, " We beheld his glory, the glory as of the only begotten of the Father ; " such as could belong to none other than to Him who is the eternal Son of God, consubstantial with the Father.

Other Passages in St. John's Gospel.

This introduction, which thus unmistakably sets forth the divine nature of Christ, is the key-note of John's Gospel, and of all his other writings.   His main object is to convince men that Jesus is God manifest in the flesh, and that the acknowledgment of Him as such is necessary to salvation.   This Apostle was, therefore, in the early Church called the Θεολόγος, because he taught so clearly and earnestly that the λόγος is God.   In verse 18 of this chapter he says that the Son alone has the knowledge of God, and is the source of that knowledge to others.   He showed Nathanael that He knew his character, being the searcher of hearts.   In his discourse with Nicodemus, He spoke with divine authority ; revealing the things of heaven, because He came from heaven and was even then in heaven. His coming into the world was the highest evidence of divine love, and the salvation of all men depends on faith in Him ; that is, on their believing that He is what He declared Himself to be, and trusting Him and obeying Him accordingly. When the Jews censured Him for healing a lame man on the Sabbath, He defended Himself by saying that God worked on the Sabbath ; that He and the Father were one ; that He did whatever God did ; that He could give life to whom He willed; that all judgment was committed to Him, and that He was entitled to the same honour as the Father. In the sixth chapter He sets Himself forth as the source of life, first under the figure of bread, and then under that of a sacrifice. In the eighth chapter He declares Himself to be the light of the world. " He that followeth me shall not walk in darkness, but shall have the light of life." He alone could give true freedom, freedom from the condemnation and power of sin. He had been the only Saviour from the beginning as He was the object of faith to Abraham, who saw his day, and rejoiced, for he says, " Before Abraham was I am," thereby asserting not only his preëxistence, but his eternity, as He declares himself to be the " I am," that is, the self-existing and immutable Jehovah.

In chapter x., under the character of a shepherd, He represents Himself as the head of all God's people, whose voice they hear, whose steps they follow, and in whose care they trust. For them He lays down his life, and takes it again. To them He gives eternal life, and their salvation is certain, for no one is able to pluck them out of his hands ; and He and the Father are one. The eleventh chapter contains the history of the resurrection of Lazarus, on which it may be remarked, (1.) That his disciples had full confidence that Christ could deliver from death whom He pleased. (2.) That He claims to be the resurrection and the life. To all that believe on Him He is the source of spiritual life to the soul, and of a resurrection to the body. (3.) In illustration and proof of his divine power, He called Lazarus from the grave.

Our Lord's Last Discourse.

The discourse recorded in the 14th, 15th, and 16th, and the prayer recorded in the 17th chapter, are the words of God to men. No created being could speak as Christ here speaks. He begins by exhorting his disciples to have the same faith in Him which they had in God. He went to prepare heaven for them, and would return and take them to Himself. The knowledge of Him is the knowledge of God. He who had seen Him had seen the Father also ; for He and the Father are one. He promised to send them the Holy Ghost to abide with them permanently; and that He would manifest Himself to them as God manifests Himself to the saints, revealing to them his glory and love, and making them sensible of his presence. He would continue to be to his Church the source of life ; union with Him is as necessary as the union of a branch to the vine. The Holy Spirit sent by Him would reveal the things of Christ, rendering the Apostles infallible as teachers, and giving divine illumination to all believers. It was necessary that He should leave them in order to send the Spirit, who would convince the world of the sin of not believing Him to be all He claimed to be ; of the righteousness of his assumption to be the Son of God and Saviour of the world, of which his going to the Father (i. e., resurrection) was the decisive proof; and also of the certainty of a future judgment, inasmuch as the prince of this world was already judged. The Spirit was to glorify Christ, i. e., to reveal Him as possessing all divine perfections, for whatsoever the Father hath the Son hath likewise. His intercessory prayer could proceed from the lips of none but a divine person. He speaks as one who had power over all flesh, and who could give eternal life to all whom God the Father had given Him. Eternal life consists in the knowledge of God, and of Him whom God had sent. He prays that He, clothed in our nature, might be glorified with the glory which He had before the foundation of the world ; that his people might be sanctified ; that they might be one by his dwelling in them, and that they might be made partakers of his glory.

He was condemned by the Jews for claiming to be the Son of God, and by Pilate for claiming to be a king. When He was crucified the heavens were darkened, the earth trembled, the dead arose, and the vail of the temple was rent. By his resurrection his claim to be the Son of God and Saviour of men was authenticated. Thomas, not being present at the first interview between Christ and his disciples, doubted the fact of his resurrection ; but when he saw Him he was fully convinced, and owned Him as his Lord and God. (John xx. 28.) That ὁ κύριός μου καὶ ὁ θεός μου is an address to Christ, and not an exclamation, is evident, (1.) From the words ἀπεκρίθη καὶ εἶπεν, *he responded and said*, which would be out of place before an exclamation. They introduce a reply to what Christ had said. Thomas answered that he was fully satisfied and firmly convinced that Christ was Lord and God. The word εἰπεῖν never means to exclaim. (2.) Such an exclamation

would be abhorrent to a Jew, who had even a superstitious reverence for the name of God, especially for the name Jehovah, and
ὁ κύριος ὁ θεός is equivalent to יְהֹוָה אֱלֹהִים. (3.) The repetition of
the pronoun μοῦ also requires the passage to be considered as an
address to Christ.

The Epistles of St. John.

In his epistles the Apostle John presents the divinity of Christ
with equal prominence. The great design of those epistles was to
establish the faith of believers in the midst of the errors which had
begun to prevail. The chief of those errors was denial, in some
form, of the incarnation of the Son of God. Hence the Apostle
not only insists so strenuously on the acknowledgment that Jesus
Christ had come in the flesh, but makes that the one great fundamental doctrine of the gospel. " Whosoever shall confess that
Jesus is the Son of God, God dwelleth in him, and he in God."
He begins his epistles by reminding his readers that the Apostles
had enjoyed the clearest possible evidence that the Λόγος τῆς ζωῆς
(He who has life and gives life) was manifest in the flesh. They
had seen, looked upon, and handled Him. John gave believers this
assurance in order that they might have fellowship with God and
with his Son Jesus Christ. Many had already apostatized and
denied the doctrine of the incarnation. To deny that doctrine,
however, was to deny God ; for whosoever denies the Son, rejects
the Father also. He exhorts them, therefore, to abide in the Son
as the only means of abiding in God and attaining eternal life.
The tests by which they were to try those who professed to be
inspired teachers, were, (1.) Whether they acknowledged the doctrine of the incarnation, *i. e.*, of the true divinity and humanity of
Christ. (iv. 2, 3, 15.) (2.) Conformity of doctrine with the
teachings of the Apostles. (3.) Love to God, founded on his
redeeming love to us, and love to the brethren, springing from this
love to God. In chapter v. he tells his readers that the great truth
to be believed is that Jesus is the Son of God. This is the faith
which overcomes the world. This great truth is established by the
testimony of God, both external and internal, for he that believeth
on the Son of God hath the witness in himself ; he that believeth
not this testimony makes God a liar, because he believeth not the
record which God has given of his Son. In Him is eternal life, so
that he that hath the Son, hath life. He closes his epistle by saying: " We know that the Son of God is come, and hath given us
an understanding, that we may know Him that is true (*i. e.*, that

we may know the true God); and we are in Him that is true (*i. e.*, the true God), even in his Son Jesus Christ. This (*i. e.*, this person Jesus Christ) is the true God and eternal life." That this passage is to be referred to Christ, is plain. (1.) Because He is the subject of discourse in the context, and throughout the epistle. The great design of the Apostle is to tell us who and what Christ is. (2.) In the immediately preceding clauses he had called Him the true, " we are in Him that is true," even in Jesus Christ. " The true " and " the true God," are used as convertible expressions. (3.) Christ is repeatedly called " eternal life," by this Apostle, and "eternal life" is said to be in Him, which language is not used of God as such, nor of the Father. (4.) Χριστός is the natural antecedent of οὗτος, not only because the nearest, but because it is the prominent subject. (5.) This has been the received interpretation in the Church, at least since the Arian controversy ; and the objections urged against it are mainly theological, rather than exegetical. It is to be remarked that Christ is here called not merely θεός but ὁ θεός, as in John xx. 28.

The Apocalypse.

The Book of Revelation is one continued hymn of praise to Christ, setting forth the glory of his person and the triumph of his kingdom ; representing Him as the ground of confidence to his people, and the object of worship to all the inhabitants of heaven. He is declared to be the ruler of the kings of the earth. He has made us kings and priests unto God. He is the First and the Last, language never used but of God, and true of Him alone. Compare Is. xliv. 6. In the epistles to the seven churches, Christ assumes the titles and prerogatives of God. He calls Himself, He who holds the seven stars in his right hand ; the First and the Last ; He who has the sharp sword and eyes of fire, from which nothing can be hid. He has the seven spirits. He is the Holy and the True. He has the keys of David ; He opens and no man shuts, and shuts and no man opens ; his decision on the destiny of men admits of no appeal. He is the supreme arbiter ; the faithful and true witness ; the ἀρχὴ τῆς κτίσεως τοῦ θεοῦ, the principle, *i. e.*, both the head and source, of the whole creation. He reproves the churches for their sins, or praises them for their fidelity, as their moral ruler against whom sin is committed and to whom obedience is rendered. He threatens punishments and promises blessings which God alone can inflict or bestow. In chapter v. the Apostle represents all the inhabitants of heaven as prostrate at the feet of Christ, ascribing blessings and honour and glory and power to Him that sitteth upon the throne and unto the Lamb forever and ever. The New Jerusalem is the seat of his kingdom. He is its light, glory, and blessedness. He again and again declares himself to be the Alpha and Omega, the First and the Last (*i. e.*, the immutable and eternal), the Beginning and the End, for whose second coming the whole Church is in earnest expectation.

B. *The Epistles of St. Paul.*

In the epistles of Paul, the same exalted exhibition is made of the person and work of Christ. In the Epistle to the Romans, Christ is declared to be the Son of God, the object of faith, the judge of the world, the God of providence, the giver of the Holy Spirit, and what in the Old Testament is said of Jehovah, the Apostle applies to Christ. In chapter ix. 5, He is expressly declared to be "over all, God blessed forever." The text here is beyond dispute. The only method to avoid the force of the passage is by changing the punctuation. Erasmus, who has been followed by many modern interpreters, placed a full stop after κατὰ σάρκα, or after πάντων. In the former case the passage would read, "Of whom is Christ concerning the flesh. The God who is over all be blessed forever;" in the latter, "Of whom Christ came concerning the flesh, who is above all," *i. e.*, higher than the patriarchs. It is frankly admitted by the advocates of these interpretations that the reason for adopting them is to avoid making the Apostle assert that Christ is God over all. As they do not admit that doctrine, they are unwilling to admit that the Apostle teaches it. It was universally referred to Christ in the ancient Church, by all the Reformers, by all the older theologians, and by almost all of the modern interpreters who believe in the divinity of Christ. This uniformity of assent is itself a decisive proof that the common interpretation is the natural one. We are bound to take every passage of Scripture in its obvious and natural sense, unless the plainer declarations of the Word of God show that a less obvious meaning must be the true one. That the common interpretation of this passage is correct is plain, —

1. Because Christ is the subject of discourse ; God is not mentioned in the context. The Apostle is mentioning the distinguishing blessings of the Jewish nation. To them were given the law, the glory, the covenant, and the promises, and above all, from them "as concerning the flesh (*i. e.*, as far as his humanity is concerned), Christ came, who is over all, God blessed forever." Here every-

thing is natural and to the point.   It shows how preëminent was
the distinction of the Jews that from them the Messiah, God manifest in the flesh, should be born.   Compared to this all the other
prerogatives of their nation sink into insignificance.

2. The words κατὰ σάρκα demand an antithesis.   There would be
no reason for saying that Christ, *as far as He was a man*, was descended from the Jews, if He was not more than man, and if there
were not a sense in which He was not descended from them.   As
in Rom. i. 3, 4, it is said that κατὰ σάρκα He was the Son of David,
but κατὰ πνεῦμα the Son of God ; so here it is said, that κατὰ σάρκα
He was descended from the patriarchs, but that in his higher nature He is God over all, blessed forever.

3. The usage of the language demands the common interpretation.   In all exclamations and benedictions, in distinction from
mere narration, the predicate uniformly stands before the subject,
if the copula εἶναι be omitted.   This usage is strictly observed in
the Septuagint, in the Apocrypha, and in the New Testament.
We therefore always read in such doxologies εὐλογητὸς ὁ θεός, and
never ὁ θεὸς εὐλογητός.   In the Hebrew Scriptures, בָּרוּךְ occurs forty
times in doxologies and formulas of praise before the subject.   It
is always " Blessed be God," and never " God be blessed."   In the
Septuagint, Psalm lxviii. 20 (19), κύριος ὁ θεὸς εὐλογητός is the only
apparent exception to this rule.   And there the Hebrew adheres
to the common form, and the Greek version is a rhetorical para-
phrase of the original.   The Hebrew is simply בָּרוּךְ אֲדֹנָי, for which
the LXX. have, Κύριος ὁ θεὸς εὐλογητός, εὐλογητὸς κύριος.   Every consideration, therefore, is in favour of the interpretation which has
been accepted by the Church as giving the true meaning of this
passage.   Christ is God over all, blessed forever.

The Epistles to the Corinthians.

In the Epistles to the Corinthians, Christ is represented, (1.)
As the proper object of religious homage.   All believers are represented as his worshippers.   (1 Cor. i. 2.)   (2.) As the source
of spiritual life.   (1 Cor. i. 4–9, 30, 31.)   (3.) As the Lord of
all Christians and the Lord of glory.   (1 Cor. ii. 8.)   (4.) As
creator of the universe (1 Cor. viii. 6), δἰ οὖ τὰ πάντα.   (5.) As
the Jehovah of the Old Testament, who led the Israelites through
the wilderness.   (1 Cor. x. 1–13.)   (6.) As the giver of spiritual
gifts.   (1 Cor. xii.)   (7.) As the Lord from heaven to whom the
universe (τὰ πάντα) is subject.   (1 Cor. xv. 25.)   (8.) A life·giv-

ing Spirit (πνεῦμα ζωοποιοῦν), *i. e.*, a Spirit having life in Himself, and a source of life to others. (1 Cor. xv. 45.) (9.) The proper object of supreme love, whom not to love, justly subjects the soul to eternal death. (1 Cor. xvi. 22.) (10.) The object of prayer (1 Cor. xvi. 23), from whom grace is to be sought. (11.) He gives success in preaching the gospel, causing his ministers to triumph. (2 Cor. ii. 14.) (12.) The vision of his glory transforms the soul into his likeness. (2 Cor. iii. 17, 18.) (13.) In his face is the glory of God, to which those only are blind who are lost. (2 Cor. iv. 3–6.) (14.) His presence, or being with Him, constitutes the believer's heaven. (2 Cor. v. 1–8.) (15.) Before his judgment-seat all men are to be arraigned. (2 Cor. v. 10.) (16.) His love is the highest motive to action. (2 Cor. v. 14.)

Galatians.

(1.) Paul says that he was an Apostle not by the will of man, but by Jesus Christ. (i. 1.) (2.) The conversion of the soul is effected by the knowledge of Christ as the Son of God. (ii. 16.) (3.) Spiritual life is maintained by faith of which Christ is the object. (ii. 20, 21.) (4.) Christ lives in us, as God is said to dwell in his people. (ii. 20.) (5.) He was the object of Abraham's faith. (iii. 6–9.) (6.) He was Abraham's seed in whom all nations are blessed. (iii. 16.) (7.) By faith in Him we become the sons of God. (iii. 26.) (8.) The Holy Ghost is the Spirit of Christ. (iv. 6.) (9.) His will is our law. (vi. 2.) (10.) His grace or favour the source of all good. (vi. 18.)

Ephesians.

(1.) In Christ and under Him all the objects of God's redeeming love are to be united in one harmonious whole. (i. 10.) (2.) In Him we have eternal life, or are made the heirs of God. (i. 11–14.) (3.) He is exalted above all principality, and power, and might, and dominion, *i. e.*, above all rational creatures. (i. 21.) (4.) In Him we are quickened, or raised from the death of sin, made partakers of spiritual life, and exalted to heaven. (ii. 1–6.) (5.) In iii. 9, God is said to have created all things by Jesus Christ. (The text, however, in that passage is somewhat doubtful.) (6.) He fills the universe. (i. 23, and iv. 10.) (7.) He is the head of the Church, from whom it derives its life. (iv. 16.) (8.) He sanctifies the Church. (v. 26.) (9.) The discharge of all social duties is enforced by the consideration of the authority of Christ. We are to serve men as doing service to Him. (vi. 1–9.)

Philippians.

In Philippians, besides the usual recognition of Christ as the source and giver of grace and peace, which comprehend all spiritual blessings, and the acknowledgment of Him as the end of our being (i. 21, 22), we have in ii. 6–11 the clearest declaration of the divinity of Christ. It is said, (1.) That He " was (or existed, $\dot{v}\pi\acute{a}\rho\chi\omega\nu$) in the form of God," *i. e.*, was God both as to nature and manifestation. He could not be the one without being the other. The word $\mu o\rho\phi\acute{\eta}$ may mean either the mode of manifestation, that which appears, as when it is said " the king of heaven appeared on earth $\dot{\epsilon}\nu$ $\mu o\rho\phi\hat{\eta}$ $\dot{a}\nu\theta\rho\acute{\omega}\pi o\nu$; " or the nature or essence ($\phi\acute{v}\sigma\iota s$ or $o\dot{v}\sigma\acute{\iota}a$) itself. The latter view is adopted by most of the fathers. The former, however, is more in accordance with the common usage of the word, and with the immediate context. He who existed in the form of God, took upon Him the form of a servant ($\mu o\rho\phi\acute{\eta}\nu$ $\delta o\acute{v}\lambda o\nu$), *i. e.*, the real condition of a servant. (2.) He is declared to be equal with God. The $\check{\iota}\sigma a$ $\epsilon\hat{\iota}\nu a\iota$ $\theta\epsilon\hat{\omega}$ he did not, considered as an $\dot{a}\rho\pi a\gamma\mu\acute{o}\nu$, *i. e.*, an act of robbery, or an unjust assumption. He was fully entitled to claim equality with God. (3.) This truly divine person assumed the fashion of a man, which is explained by saying He was found " in the likeness of men." He appeared in form, carriage, language, mode of thinking, speaking, feeling, and acting, like other men. He was not *purus putus homo*, a mere man, but " God incarnate," God manifest in the flesh. (4.) This divine person, clothed in man's nature, humbled Himself even unto death, even to the death of the cross. (5.) Therefore He (not God, or the divine nature in Christ, but the Theanthropos), is exalted above every name that is named, " that at the name of Jesus (*i. e.*, the name of the Theanthropos, as it is He as a divine person clothed in the nature of man, who is the object of worship), every knee should bow, of things in heaven, and things in earth, and things under the earth." This is an exhaustive amplification. It includes the whole rational creation, from the highest archangel to the weakest saint ; all, all that have life acknowledge Christ to be what God alone can be, their supreme and absolute Lord. It is because Christ is and has done what is represented, that the Apostle says, in the following chapter, that He counted all things as nothing for the knowledge of Christ, and that his only desire was to be found in Him and clothed in his righteousness. This divine Redeemer is to come again, and " shall change our vile body, that it may be fashioned like unto his glorious body, according to the working whereby He is able even to subdue all things unto Himself.   (iii. 21.)

Colossians.

Colossians i. 15–20, is expressly designed to set forth the true Godhead of Christ in opposition to the errors springing from the emanation theory, which had already begun to prevail in the churches of Asia Minor.   This passage sets forth the relation of Christ, first to God, and secondly to the universe, and thirdly to the Church.   Here, as in so many other places of Scripture, the predicates of the Λόγος ἄσαρκος and of the Λόγος ἔνσαρκος, are mingled together.   As in Heb. i. 2, 3, the Son is said to have created all things, and to be the brightness of the Father's glory, and also to have made purification for sin ; so here part of what is said belongs to the Logos as existing from eternity, and part belongs to Him as clothed in our nature.   It was the Λόγος ἄσαρκος who is declared to be the image of the invisible God and creator of all things ; and it is the Λόγος ἔνσαρκος who is declared to be the head of the Church. The relation of Christ to God, in this passage is expressed, (1.) By the words just quoted, " He is the image of the invisible God." He is so related to God that He reveals what God is, so that those who see Him, see God, those who know Him, know God, and those who hear Him, hear God.   He is the brightness of God's glory, and his express image.   (2.) His relation to God is also expressed by saying that He is begotten from eternity, or the only begotten Son.   The words πρωτότοκος πάσης κτίσεως are indeed variously explained.   By Socinians they are made to mean that He was the head of the new dispensation; by Arians that He was the first created of all rational creatures ; by many orthodox interpreters πρωτότοκος is taken in its secondary sense, of head or chief.   They therefore understand the Apostle to say that Christ is the ruler or head over the whole creation.   All these interpretations, however, are inconsistent with the proper meaning of the words, with the context, and with the analogy of Scripture.   Πρωτότοκος means *born before*.   What Christ is said to have been born before, is expressed by πάσης κτίσεως.   He was born (or begotten) before any or every creature, *i. e.*, before creation, or from eternity.   All the arguments adduced in a preceding chapter in proof of the eternal generation of the Son, are arguments in favour of this interpretation.   Besides, the Arian interpretation is inconsistent with the meaning of the words.   That interpretation assumes that the genitive πάσης κτίσεως is to be taken partitively, so that Christ is said to be a part of the creation, the first of creatures, as He is said to be the first of those who rose from the dead, when He is called πρωτό-τοκος τῶν νεκρῶν. But πᾶσα κτίσις does not mean the whole creation, as indicating the class or category to which Christ belongs, but *every creature*, as indicating a relation or comparison ; Christ is the first begotten as to every creature, *i. e.*, begotten before any crea-ture (*i. e.*, eternally, according to the constant usage of Scripture, for what is before creation is eternal.) Besides, the connection re-quires this interpretation. The Apostle proves that Christ is the image of the invisible God, and the πρωτότοκος πάσης κτίσεως by an argument which proves that He cannot be a creature ; and therefore the birth of which he speaks must be before time. Secondly, the re-lation of Christ to the universe is expressed in this passage by say-ing, (1.) That He is the Creator of all things. This is amplified, as the all things are declared to include all that are in heaven and earth, visible and invisible, rational and irrational, however exalted, even thrones, dominions, principalities, and powers ; that is, the whole hierarchy of the spiritual world. (2.) He is not only the author but the end of the creation, for all things were not only created by Him, but for Him. (3.) He upholds all things ; by Him all things consist, *i. e.*, are preserved in being, life, and order. Thirdly, Christ is the head of the Church, the source of life and grace to all its members. For in Him " all fulness," the plenitude of divine blessings dwells. In chapter ii. 3, all the treasures of wisdom and knowledge (*i. e.*, all knowledge or omniscience) are said to dwell in Christ ; and in ii. 9, that He is filled with " the fulness of the Godhead." This is very different from the πλήρωμα mentioned in i. 19, where the Apostle is speaking of what Beza calls " cumulatissima omnium divinarum rerum copia, ex qua, tan-quam inexhausto fonte, omnes gratiæ in corpus pro cujusque mem-bri modulo deriventur ; " [1] but here the reference is to the divine being, nature, or essence itself, τὸ πλήρωμα τῆς θεότητος. The word θεότης is abstract of θεός as θειότης is of θεῖος ; the former means God-head, that which makes God, God ; the latter means divinity, that which renders divine. The entire plenitude of the divine essence (not a mere emanation of that essence as the rising sect of the Gnostics taught), dwells (κατοικεῖ permanently abides, it is no tran-sient manifestation) in Him *bodily*, σωματικῶς, invested with a body. The Godhead in its fulness is incarnate in Christ. He is, therefore, not merely θεός but ὁ θεός in the highest sense. More than Paul says cannot be said.

[1] *In loc.* edit. Geneva, 1565, p. 423.

The Pastoral Epistles.

In Paul's pastoral epistles to Timothy and Titus, besides the ordinary recognition of the divinity of Christ found in almost every page of the New Testament, there are four passages in which, at least according to the common text and the most natural interpretation, he is directly called God. Even 1 Tim. i. 1, κατ᾿ ἐπιταγὴν Θεοῦ σωτῆρος ἡμῶν καὶ Κυρίου Ἰησοῦ Χριστοῦ, may be naturally rendered, "according to the command of God our Saviour, *even* our Lord Jesus Christ." This is in accordance with the parallel passages in Titus i. 3, "according to the commandment of God our Saviour;" and Titus ii. 13, "of the great God our Saviour Jesus Christ." In this latter passage there is no reason, as Winer and De Wette acknowledge, for questioning that Christ is called the great God, except what they regard as the Christology of the New Testament. They do not admit that Christ is the great God according to the doctrine of Paul, and therefore they are unwilling to admit that this passage contains that declaration. But if, as we have seen, and as the whole Church believes, not only Paul but all the Apostles and prophets, abundantly teach that the Messiah is truly God as well as truly man, there is no force in this objection. Violence must be done to the ordinary rules of language if τοῦ μεγάλου θεοῦ καὶ σωτῆρος are not referred to the same subject; inasmuch as θεοῦ has the article and σωτῆρος is without it. The fair meaning of the words is, "The Great God who is our Saviour Jesus Christ." This interpretation is also demanded, (1.) By the context. Jesus Christ is the subject of discourse. Of Him it is said that He is the great God our Saviour, who gave Himself for us. (2.) Because the ἐπιφανεία, *appearance* (here in reference to the second advent), is repeatedly used in the New Testament of Christ, but never of God as such, or of God the Father. See 2 Tim. i. 10; 2 Thess. ii. 8; 1 Tim. vi. 14; 2 Tim. iv. 1, 8. (3.) The position of the words σωτῆρος ἡμῶν before Ἰησοῦ Χριστοῦ. If "God" and "Saviour" referred to different persons the natural order of the words would be, "The appearance of the great God and Jesus Christ our Saviour;" and not as it is, "The appearance of the great God and our Saviour Jesus Christ." Great God and Saviour obviously belong to the same person in 1 Tim. i. 1. "The command of God our Saviour," and in Titus i. 3, "God our Saviour;" and in this place (Tit. ii. 13) that God and Saviour is declared to be Jesus Christ.

The most important passage, however, in these pastoral epistles, is 1 Tim. iii. 16. With regard to that passage it may be remarked,

(1.) That it admits of two interpretations. According to the one, the Church is declared to be the pillar and ground of truth ; according to the other, the pillar and ground of truth is the great mystery of godliness. The latter is greatly to be preferred as equally consistent with the grammatical structure of the passage, and as far more in harmony with the analogy of Scripture. The pillar and ground of truth, the great fundamental doctrine of the Gospel, is often elsewhere declared to be the doctrine of the manifestation of God in the flesh. On this doctrine all our hopes of salvation rest. (2.) Whatever reading be adopted, whether θεός, ὅς, or ὁ, all of which appear in different manuscripts, the passage must refer to Christ. He it was who was manifest in the flesh, justified by the Spirit, and received up into glory. (3.) Whatever reading be adopted, the passage assumes or asserts the divinity of our Lord. With the apostolic writers, the doctrine of the incarnation is expressed by saying, that the λόγος " became flesh " (John i. 14) ; or, " Christ is come in the flesh " (1 John iv. 2) ; or, " He who is the brightness of God's glory " took part of flesh and blood " (Heb. ii. 14) ; or, He that was " equal with God " was " found in fashion as a man." (Phil. ii. 8.) The same truth, therefore, is expressed, whether we say, " God was manifest in the flesh ; " or, " He who was manifest in the flesh ; " or, that " the mystery of godliness was manifest in the flesh." (4.) The external authorities are so divided that the most competent editors and critics differ as to what is the original text. For θεός we find the great body of the cursive Greek manuscripts and almost all the Greek Fathers. The authority of the Codex Alexandrinus is claimed on both sides. The question there is, whether the letter is Θ or O ; some say they see distinct traces of the line in the Theta, others say they do not. For ὅς C, F, G, of the uncial manuscripts, only two of the cursive manuscripts, and the Coptic and Sahidic versions, are quoted. To this must be added the testimony of the very ancient manuscript recently discovered by Tischendorf, the text of which has been published under his auspices at St. Petersburg. For ὁ the uncial manuscript D, the Latin Vulgate and the Latin Fathers are the witnesses. In view of this state of the question, Wetstein, Griesbach, Lachmann, Tischendorf, and Tregelles, among the editors, decide for ὅς. Mill, Matthies, as well as the older editors Erasmus, Beza, the Complutensian, and the later ones, as Knapp and Hahn, retain θεός.[1] (5.) The internal evidence, so far as the per-

[1] Dr. Henderson has ably vindicated the reading θεός in his *Critical Examination of the Various Readings in 1 Tim. iii.* 16

spicuity of the passage and the analogy of Scripture are concerned, are decidedly in favour of the common text. There is something remarkable in the passage ; it is brought in apparently as a quotation from a hymn, as some think, or from a confession of faith, as others suppose, at least, as a familiar formula in which the leading truths concerning the manifestation of Christ are concisely stated. (1.) He is God. (2.) He was manifest in the flesh, or became man. (3.) He was justified, *i. e.*, his claims to be regarded as God manifest in the flesh were proved to be just, by the Spirit (*i. e.*, either by the Holy Ghost, or by the πνεῦμα or divine nature revealing itself in Him. Comp. John i. 14). (4.) He was seen of angels. They recognized and served Him. (5.) He was preached unto the Gentiles, as He came to be the Saviour of all men, and not of the Jews only. (6.) He was believed upon as God and Saviour ; and (7.) He was received up into glory, where He now lives, reigns, and intercedes.

Epistle to the Hebrews.

The doctrines of the Bible are generally stated with authority ; announced as facts to be received on the testimony of God. It is seldom that the sacred writers undertake to prove what they teach. The first chapter of the Epistle to the Hebrews is an exception to this general rule. The divinity of Christ is here formally proved. As the design of the Apostle was to persuade the Hebrew Christians to adhere to the gospel, and to guard them from the fatal sin of apostatizing to Judaism, he sets before them the immeasurable superiority of the gospel to the Mosaic economy. The first point of that superiority, and that on which all the others depend, is the superior dignity of Christ as a divine person, to Moses and all the prophets. To set forth that superiority, he first asserts that Christ, the Son of God, is the possessor of all things ; that through Him God made the world; that He is the brightness of God's glory, the express image of his nature, upholding all things by the word of his power ; and that because He has by Himself made purification for sin, He is now, as the Theanthropos, set down at the right hand of the majesty on high. The true divinity of Christ being thus asserted, the Apostle proceeds to prove that this is the doctrine of the Scriptures. (1.) Because He is in the Bible called the Son of God, a title which cannot be given in its true sense to any creature. Christ, therefore, is higher than the angels ; and as the word angels in the Bible includes all intelligent creatures higher than man, Christ is higher than all creatures, and therefore cannot Himself be a creature. He belongs to a different category of being. (2.) All angels (*i. e.*, all the higher intelligences) are commanded to worship Him (*i. e.*, to prostrate themselves before Him). (3.) While the angels are addressed as mere instruments by which God effects his purposes, the Son is addressed as God. "Thy throne O God is for ever and ever." (4.) He laid the foundations of the earth, and the heavens are the work of his hands. (5.) They are mutable, but He is immutable and eternal. (6.) He is associated with God in glory and dominion. On this great truth, thus established, the Apostle grounds all the duties and doctrines which he urges on the faith and obedience of his readers. It is on this ground that there is no escape for those who reject the salvation which He has provided. (ii. 1–5.) It is on this ground also that He has a dominion never granted to angels, all things being made subject to Him. (ii. 5–10.) As it was a divine person, the eternal Son of God, who assumed our nature, and became a high priest for us, his sacrifice is efficacious, and need not be repeated; and He is a perpetual priest, higher than the heavens, who can save to the uttermost all who come unto God by Him. This Saviour is the same yesterday, to-day, and forever. Faith in Him will enable us to overcome the world, as faith in the promises concerning Christ enabled the ancient worthies to witness a good confession under the greatest trials and sufferings.

The other Sacred Writers of the New Testament.

The same testimony to the divinity of our Lord is borne by the Apostles James and Peter. The former calls Him the Lord of glory, the latter in his First Epistle represents Him as the proper object of supreme love. Faith in Him secures salvation. His spirit dwelt in the ancient prophets. He is the foundation of the Church. (ii. 6.) Having suffered the just for the unjust to bring us unto God, He is now exalted at the right hand of God, the whole universe of intelligent creatures being subject to Him. (iii. 18.) In his Second Epistle he speaks of the knowledge of Christ as the source of grace and peace (i. 2.), and of holiness (ver. 8). At death believers enter into his everlasting kingdom (ver. 11). Peter was an eyewitness of his divine majesty when he was with Him in the holy mount. Lord and Saviour, equivalent in the lips of a Jew, to Jehovah Saviour, is his common designation of Christ. True religion, according to this Apostle, consists in the knowledge of Christ as the Son of God, to whom, therefore, he ascribes eternal glory.

Imperfect and unsatisfactory as this survey necessarily is, it is enough to prove not only that the Scriptures teach the divinity of Christ, but that Christianity as a religion consists in the love, worship, and service of the Lord Jesus, whose creatures we are, and to whom we belong by the still dearer relation of those whom He hath purchased with his own precious blood.

CHAPTER VIII.

THE HOLY SPIRIT.

§ 1. *His Nature.*

THE words רוּחַ and πνεῦμα are used in different senses, both literal and figurative, in the sacred Scriptures. They properly mean wind, as when our Lord says, " The πνεῦμα bloweth where it listeth ; " then any invisible power ; then immaterial, invisible agents, as the soul and angels ; then God himself, who is said to be a Spirit, to express his nature as an immaterial, intelligent being ; and finally, the Third Person of the Trinity is called " The Spirit " by way of eminence, probably, for two reasons. First, because He is the power or efficiency of God, *i. e.*, the person through whom the efficiency of God is directly exercised ; and secondly, to express his relation to the other persons of the Trinity. As Father and Son are terms expressive of relation, it is natural to infer that the word Spirit is to be understood in the same way. The Son is called the Word, as the revealer or image of God, and the Third Person is called Spirit as his breath or power. He is also predominantly called the Holy Spirit, to indicate both his nature and operations. He is absolutely holy in his own nature, and the cause of holiness in all creatures. For the same reason He is called the Spirit of Truth, the Spirit of Wisdom, of Peace, of Love, and of Glory.

A. *His Personality.*

The two points to be considered in reference to this subject, are, first the nature, and second the office or work of the Holy Spirit. With regard to his nature, is He a person or a mere power ? and if a person, is He created or divine, finite or infinite ? The personality of the Spirit has been the faith of the Church from the beginning. It had few opponents even in the chaotic period of theology ; and in modern times has been denied by none but Socinians, Arians, and Sabellians. Before considering the direct proof of the Church doctrine that the Holy Spirit is a person, it may be well to remark, that the terms " The Spirit," " The Spirit of God," " The Holy Spirit," and when God speaks, " My Spirit," or, when God is spoken of "His Spirit," occur in all parts of Scripture from Genesis to Revelation. These and equivalent terms are evidently to be understood in the same sense throughout the Scriptures. If the Spirit of God which moved on the face of the waters, which strove with the antediluvians, which came upon Moses, which gave skill to artisans, and which inspired the prophets, is the power of God; then the Spirit which came upon the Apostles, which Christ promised to send as a comforter and advocate, and to which the instruction, sanctification, and guidance of the people of God are referred, must also be the power of God. But if the Spirit is clearly revealed to be a person in the later parts of Scripture, it is plain that the earlier portions must be understood in the same way. One part of the Bible, and much less one or a few passages must not be taken by themselves, and receive any interpretation which the isolated words may bear, but Scripture must interpret Scripture. Another obvious remark on this subject is, that the Spirit of God is equally prominent in all parts of the word of God. His intervention does not occur on rare occasions, as the appearance of angels, or the Theophanies, of which mention is made here and there in the sacred volume; but He is represented as everywhere present and everywhere operative. We might as well strike from the Bible the name and doctrine of God, as the name and office of the Spirit. In the New Testament alone He is mentioned not far from three hundred times. It is not only, however, merely the frequency with which the Spirit is mentioned, and the prominence given to his person and work, but the multiplied and interesting relations in which He is represented as standing to the people of God, the importance and number of his gifts, and the absolute dependence of the believer and of the Church upon Him for spiritual and eternal life, which render the doctrine of the Holy Ghost absolutely fundamental to the gospel. The work of the Spirit in applying the redemption of Christ is represented to be as essential as that redemption itself. It is therefore indispensable that we should know what the Bible teaches concerning the Holy Ghost, both as to his nature and office.

Proof of his Personality.

The Scriptures clearly teach that He is a person. Personality includes intelligence, will, and individual subsistence. If, therefore, it can be proved that all these are attributed to the Spirit, it is thereby proved that He is a person. It will not be necessary or advisable to separate the proofs of these several points, and cite passages which ascribe to Him intelligence; and then others, which attribute to Him will; and still others to prove his individual subsistence, because all these are often included in one and the same passage; and arguments which prove the one, in many cases prove also the others.

1. The first argument for the personality of the Holy Spirit is derived from the use of the personal pronouns in relation to Him. A person is that which, when speaking, says I; when addressed, is called thou; and when spoken of, is called he, or him. It is indeed admitted that there is such a rhetorical figure as personification; that inanimate or irrational beings, or sentiments, or attributes, may be introduced as speaking, or addressed as persons. But this creates no difficulty. The cases of personification are such as do not, except in rare instances, admit of any doubt. The fact that men sometimes apostrophize the heavens, or the elements, gives no pretext for explaining as personification all the passages in which God or Christ is introduced as a person. So also with regard to the Holy Spirit. He is introduced as a person so often, not merely in poetic or excited discourse, but in simple narrative, and in didactic instructions; and his personality is sustained by so many collateral proofs, that to explain the use of the personal pronouns in relation to Him on the principle of personification, is to do violence to al. the rules of interpretation. Thus in Acts xiii. 2, " The Holy Ghost said, Separate me Barnabas and Saul, for the work whereunto I have called them." Our Lord says (John xv. 26), " When the Comforter (ὁ παράκλητος) is come whom I will send unto you from the Father, even the Spirit of truth (τὸ πνεῦμα τῆς ἀληθείας) which (ὅ) proceedeth from the Father, *He* (ἐκεῖνος) shall testify of me." The use of the masculine pronoun *He* instead of *it*, shows that the Spirit is a person. It may indeed be said that as παράκλητος is masculine, the pronoun referring to it must of course be in the same gender. But as the explanatory words τὸ πνεῦμα intervene, to which the neuter ὅ refers, the following pronoun would naturally be in the neuter, if the subject spoken of, the πνεῦμα, were not a person. In the following chapter (John xvi. 13, 14) there is no ground for this objection. It is there said, " When *He* (ἐκεῖνος), the Spirit of truth, is come, He will guide you into all truth: for He shall not speak of Himself; but whatsoever He shall hear, that shall He speak, and He will show you things to come. *He* shall glorify me (ἐκεῖνος ἐμὲ δοξάσει): for He shall receive of mine, and shall show it unto you." Here there is no possibility of accounting for the use of the personal pronoun He (ἐκεῖνος) on any other ground than the personality of the Spirit.

2. We stand in relations to the Holy Spirit which we can sustain only to a person. He is the object of our faith. We believe on the Holy Ghost. This faith we profess in baptism. We are baptized not only in the name of the Father and of the Son, but also of the Holy Ghost. The very association of the Spirit in such a connection, with the Father and the Son, as they are admitted to be distinct persons, proves that the Spirit also is a person. Besides the use of the word εἰς τὸ ὄνομα, *unto the name*, admits of no other explanation. By baptism we profess to acknowledge the Spirit as we acknowledge the Father and the Son, and we bind ourselves to the one as well as to the others. If when the Apostle tells the Corinthians that they were not baptized εἰς τὸ ὄνομα Παύλου, and when he says that the Hebrews were baptized unto Moses, he means that the Corinthians were not, and that the Hebrews were made the disciples, the one of Paul and the others of Moses ; then when we are baptized unto the name of the Spirit, the meaning is that in baptism we profess to be his disciples ; we bind ourselves to receive his instructions, and to submit to his control. We stand in the same relation to Him as to the Father and to the Son ; we acknowledge Him to be a person as distinctly as we acknowledge the personality of the Son, or of the Father. Christians not only profess to believe on the Holy Ghost, but they are also the recipients of his gifts. He is to them an object of prayer. In the apostolic benediction, the grace of Christ, the love of the Father, and the fellowship of the Holy Ghost, are solemnly invoked. We pray to the Spirit for the communication of Himself to us, that He may, according to the promise of our Lord, dwell in us, as we pray to Christ that we may be the objects of his unmerited love. Accordingly we are exhorted not " to sin against," " not to resist," not " to grieve " the Holy Spirit. He is represented, therefore, as a person who can be the object of our acts ; whom we may please or offend ; with whom we may have communion, *i. e.*, personal intercourse ; who can love and be loved ; who can say " thou " to us ; and whom we can invoke in every time of need.

3. The Spirit also sustains relations to us, and performs offices which none but a person can sustain or perform. He is our teacher, sanctifier, comforter, and guide. He governs every believer who is led by the Spirit, and the whole Church. He calls, as He called Barnabas and Saul, to the work of the ministry, or to some special field of labour. Pastors or bishops are made overseers by the Holy Ghost.

4. In the exercise of these and other functions, personal acts are constantly attributed to the Spirit in the Bible; that is, such acts as imply intelligence, will, and activity or power. The Spirit searches, selects, reveals, and reproves. We often read that " The Spirit said." (Acts xiii. 2; xxi. 11; 1 Tim. iv. 1, etc., etc.) This is so constantly done, that the Spirit appears as a personal agent from one end of the Scriptures to the other, so that his personality is beyond dispute. The only possible question is whether He is a distinct person from the Father. But of this there can be no reasonable doubt, as He is said to be the Spirit of God and the Spirit which is of God (ἐκ θεοῦ); as He is distinguished from the Father in the forms of baptism and benediction; as He proceeds from the Father; and as He is promised, sent, and given by the Father. So that to confound the Holy Spirit with God would be to render the Scriptures unintelligible.

5. All the elements of personality, namely, intelligence, will, and individual subsistence, are not only involved in all that is thus revealed concerning the relation in which the Spirit stands to us and that which we sustain to Him, but they are all distinctly attributed to Him. The Spirit is said to know, to will, and to act. He searches, or knows all things, even the deep things of God. No man knoweth the things of God, but the Spirit of God. (1 Cor. ii. 10, 12.) He distributes " to every man severally as he will." (1 Cor. xii. 11.) His individual subsistence is involved in his being an agent, and in his being the object on which the activity of others terminates. If He can be loved, reverenced, and obeyed, or offended and sinned against, He must be a person.

6. The personal manifestations of the Spirit, when He descended on Christ after his baptism, and upon the Apostles at the day of Pentecost, of necessity involve his personal subsistence. It was not any attribute of God, nor his mere efficiency, but God himself, that was manifested in the burning bush, in the fire and clouds on Mount Sinai, in the pillar which guided the Israelites through the wilderness, and in the glory which dwelt in the Tabernacle and in the Temple.

7. The people of God have always regarded the Holy Spirit as a person. They have looked to Him for instruction, sanctification, direction, and comfort. This is part of their religion. Christianity (subjectively considered) would not be what it is without this sense of dependence on the Spirit, and this love and reverence for his person. All the liturgies, prayers, and praises of the Church, are filled with appeals and addresses to the Holy Ghost.

This is a fact which admits of no rational solution if the Scriptures do not really teach that the Spirit is a distinct person. The rule *Quod semper, quod ubique, quod ab omnibus*, is held by Protestants as well as by Romanists. It is not to the authority of general consent as an evidence of truth, that Protestants object, but to the applications made of it by the Papal Church, and to the principle on which that authority is made to rest. All Protestants admit that true believers in every age and country have one faith, as well as one God and one Lord.

B. *Divinity of the Holy Spirit.*

On this subject there has been little dispute in the Church. The Spirit is so prominently presented in the Bible as possessing divine attributes, and exercising divine prerogatives, that since the fourth century his true divinity has never been denied by those who admit his personality.

1. In the Old Testament, all that is said of Jehovah is said of the Spirit of Jehovah ; and therefore, if the latter is not a mere periphrase for the former, he must of necessity be divine. The expressions, Jehovah said, and, the Spirit said, are constantly interchanged ; and the acts of the Spirit are said to be acts of God.

2. In the New Testament, the language of Jehovah is quoted as the language of the Spirit. In Is. vi. 9, it is written, Jehovah said, " Go and tell this people," etc. This passage is thus quoted by Paul, Acts xxviii. 25, " Well spake the Holy Ghost by Esaiàs the prophet," etc. In Jeremiah xxxi. 31, 33, 34, it is said, " Behold the days come, saith Jehovah, that I will make a new covenant with the house of Israel ; " which is quoted by the Apostle in Heb. x. 15, saying, " Whereof the Holy Ghost also is a witness to us : for after that He had said before, This is the covenant that I will make with them after those days, saith the Lord ; I will put my laws into their hearts," etc. Thus constantly the language of God is quoted as the language of the Holy Ghost. The prophets were the messengers of God ; they uttered his words, delivered his commands, pronounced his threatenings, and announced his promises, because they spake as they were moved by the Holy Ghost. They were the organs of God, because they were the organs of the Spirit. The Spirit, therefore, must be God.

3. In the New Testament the same mode of representation is continued. Believers are the temple of God, because the Spirit dwells in them. Eph. ii. 22 : Ye are " a habitation of God through the Spirit." 1 Cor. vi. 19 : " Know ye not that your

body is the temple of the Holy Ghost which is in you, which ye have of God?" In Rom. viii. 9, 10, the indwelling of Christ is said to be the indwelling of the Spirit of Christ, and that is said to be the indwelling of the Spirit of God. In Acts v. 1–4, Ananias is said to have lied unto God because he lied against the Holy Ghost.

4. Our Lord and his Apostles constantly speak of the Holy Spirit as possessing all divine perfections. Christ says, "All manner of sin and blasphemy shall be forgiven unto men: but the blasphemy against the Holy Ghost shall not be forgiven unto men." (Matt. xii. 31.) The unpardonable sin, then, is speaking against the Holy Ghost. This could not be unless the Holy Ghost were God. The Apostle, in 1 Cor. ii. 10, 11, says that the Spirit knows all things, even the deep things (the most secret purposes) of God. His knowledge is commensurate with the knowledge of God. He knows the things of God as the spirit of a man knows the things of a man. The consciousness of God is the consciousness of the Spirit. The Psalmist teaches us that the Spirit is omnipresent and everywhere efficient. "Whither," he asks, "shall I go from thy Spirit? or whither shall I flee from thy presence?" (Ps. cxxxix. 7.) The presence of the Spirit is the presence of God. The same idea is expressed by the prophet when he says, "Can any hide himself in secret places that I shall not see him? saith Jehovah. Do not I fill heaven and earth? saith Jehovah." (Jer. xxiii. 24.)

5. The works of the Spirit are the works of God. He fashioned the world. (Gen. i. 2.) He regenerates the soul: to be born of the Spirit is to be born of God. He is the source of all knowledge; the giver of inspiration; the teacher, the guide, the sanctifier, and the comforter of the Church in all ages. He fashions our bodies; He formed the body of Christ, as a fit habitation for the fulness of the Godhead; and He is to quicken our mortal bodies. (Rom. viii. 11.)

6. He is therefore presented in the Scriptures as the proper object of worship, not only in the formula of baptism and in the apostolic benediction, which bring the doctrine of the Trinity into constant remembrance as the fundamental truth of our religion, but also in the constant requirement that we look to Him and depend upon Him for all spiritual good, and reverence and obey Him as our divine teacher and sanctifier.

Relation of the Spirit to the Father and to the Son.

The relation of the Spirit to the other persons of the Trinity has been stated before. (1.) He is the same in substance and equal in power and glory. (2.) He is subordinate to the Father and Son, as to his mode of subsistence and operation, as He is said to be of the Father and of the Son; He is sent by them, and they operate through Him. (3.) He bears the same relation to the Father as to the Son; as He is said to be of the one as well as of the other, and He is given by the Son as well as by the Father. (4.) His eternal relation to the other persons of the Trinity is indicated by the word Spirit, and by its being said that he is ἐκ τοῦ θεοῦ, out of God, *i. e.*, God is the source whence the Spirit is said to proceed.

§ 2. *The Office of the Holy Spirit.*

A. *In Nature.*

The general doctrine of the Scriptures on this subject is that the Spirit is the executive of the Godhead. Whatever God does, He does by the Spirit. Hence in the creed of Constantinople, adopted by the Church universal, He is said to be τὸ Πνεῦμα, τὸ κύριον, τὸ ζωοποιόν. He is the immediate source of all life. Even in the external world the Spirit is everywhere present and everywhere active. Matter is not intelligent. It has its peculiar properties, which act blindly according to established laws. The intelligence, therefore, manifested in vegetable and animal structures, is not to be referred to matter, but to the omnipresent Spirit of God. It was He who brooded over the waters and reduced chaos into order. It was He who garnished the heavens. It is He that causes the grass to grow. The Psalmist says of all living creatures, " Thou hidest thy face, they are troubled: thou takest away their breath, they die, and return to their dust. Thou sendest forth thy Spirit, they are created: and thou renewest the face of the earth." (Ps. civ. 29, 30.) Compare Is. xxxii. 14, 15. Job, speaking of his corporeal frame, says, " The Spirit of God hath made me." (Job xxxiii. 4.) And the Psalmist, after describing the omnipresence of the Spirit, refers to his agency the wonderful mechanism of the human body. "I am fearfully and wonderfully made . . . . my substance was not hid from thee, when I was made in secret, and curiously wrought in the lowest parts of the earth. Thine eyes did see my substance, yet being unperfect; and in thy book all my members were written, which in continuance were fashioned, when as yet there was none of them." (Ps. cxxxix. 14–16.) Cyprian (or the author of the Tract " De Spiritu Sancto," included in his works) says, " Hic Spiritus Sanctus ab ipso mundi initio aquis legitur superfusus; non materialibus aquis quasi vehiculo egens,

I.   34

quas potius ipse ferebat et complectentibus firmamentum dabat congruum motum et limitem præfinitum. . . . [Hic est] spiritus vitæ cujus vivificus calor animat omnia et fovet et provehit et fœcundat. Hic Spiritus Sanctus omnium viventium anima, ita largitate sua se omnibus abundanter infundit, ut habeant omnia rationabilia et irrationabilia secundum genus suum ex eo quod sunt et quod in suo ordine suæ naturæ competentia agunt. Non quod ipse sit substantialis anima singulis, sed in se singulariter manens, de plenitudine sua distributor magnificus proprias efficientias singulis dividit et largitur ; et quasi sol omnia calefaciens, subjecta omnia nutrit, et absque ulla sui diminutione, integritatem suam de inexhausta abundantia, quod satis est, et sufficit omnibus, commodat et impartit." [1]

The Spirit the Source of all Intellectual Life.

The Spirit is also represented as the source of all intellectual life. When man was created it is said God "breathed into his nostrils the breath of life ; and man became (נֶפֶשׁ חַיָּה) a living soul." (Gen. ii. 7.)   Job xxxii. 8, says, The inspiration of the Almighty giveth men understanding, i. e., a rational nature, for it is explained by saying, He "teacheth us more than the beasts of the earth, and maketh us wiser than the fowls of heaven." (Job xxxv. 11.) The Scriptures ascribe in like manner to Him all special or extraordinary gifts. Thus it is said of Bezaleel, "I have called" him, "and I have filled him with the Spirit of God, in wisdom, in understanding, and in knowledge, and in all manner of workmanship, to devise cunning works, to work in gold, and in silver, and in brass." (Ex. xxxi. 2, 3, 4.) By his Spirit God gave Moses the wisdom requisite for his high duties, and when he was commanded to devolve part of his burden upon the seventy elders, it was said, "I will take of the Spirit which is upon thee, and will put it upon them." (Num. xi. 17.) Joshua was appointed to succeed Moses, because in him was the Spirit. (Num. xxvii. 18.) In like manner the Judges, who from time to time were raised up, as emergency demanded, were qualified by the Spirit for their peculiar work, whether as rulers or as warriors. Of Othniel it is said, "The Spirit of the Lord came upon him, and he judged Israel and went out to war." (Judges iii. 10.) So the Spirit of the Lord is said to have come upon Gideon and on Jephthah and on Samson. When Saul offended God, the Spirit of the Lord is said to have departed from him. (1 Sam. xvi. 14.) When Samuel anointed David, "The Spirit of the Lord came upon" him "from that day forward." (1 Sam. xvi. 13.) In like

---

[1] *Works*, edit. Bremæ, 1690, on p. 61 of the second set in the Opuscula.

manner under the new dispensation the Spirit is represented as not only the author of miraculous gifts, but also as the giver of the qualifications to teach and rule in the Church. All these operations are independent of the sanctifying influences of the Spirit. When the Spirit came on Samson or upon Saul, it was not to render them holy, but to endue them with extraordinary physical and intellectual power ; and when He is said to have departed from them, it means that those extraordinary endowments were withdrawn.

B. *The Spirit's Office in the Work of Redemption.*

With regard to the office of the Spirit in the work of redemption, the Scriptures teach, —

1. That He fashioned the body, and endued the human soul of Christ with every qualification for his work. To the Virgin Mary it was said, " The Holy Ghost shall come upon thee, and the power of the Highest shall overshadow thee : therefore also that holy thing which shall be born of thee, shall be called the Son of God." (Luke i. 35.) The prophet Isaiah predicted that the Messiah should be replenished with all spiritual gifts. " Behold my servant whom I uphold ; mine elect in whom my soul delighteth ; I have put my Spirit upon him : he shall bring forth judgment to the Gentiles." (Is. xlii. 1.) " There shall come forth a rod out of the stem of Jesse, and a branch shall grow out of his roots : and the Spirit of the LORD shall rest upon him, the spirit of wisdom and understanding, the spirit of counsel and might, the spirit of knowledge and of the fear of the LORD." (Is. xi. 1, 2.) When our Lord appeared on earth, it is said that the Spirit without measure was given unto Him. (John iii. 34.) " And John bare record, saying, I saw the Spirit descending from heaven like a dove, and it abode upon him." (John i. 32.) He was, therefore, said to have been full of the Holy Ghost.

2. That the Spirit is the revealer of all divine truth. The doctrines of the Bible are called the things of the Spirit. With regard to the writers of the Old Testament, it is said they spake as they were moved by the Holy Ghost. The language of Micah is applicable to all the prophets, " Truly I am full of power by the Spirit of the LORD, and of judgment, and of might, to declare unto Jacob his transgression and to Israel his sin." (Micah iii. 8.) What David said, the Holy Ghost is declared to have said. The New Testament writers were in like manner the organs of the Spirit. The doctrines which Paul preached he did not receive from men,

" but God," he says, " hath revealed them unto us by his Spirit."
(1 Cor. ii. 10.) The Spirit also guided the utterance of those
truths ; for he adds, " Which things also we speak, not in the
words which man's wisdom teacheth, but which the Holy Ghost
teacheth ; communicating the things of the Spirit in the words of
the Spirit " (πνευματικοῖς πνευματικὰ συγκρίνοντες). The whole Bible,
therefore, is to be referred to the Spirit as its author.

3. The Spirit not only thus reveals divine truth, having guided
infallibly holy men of old in recording it, but He everywhere attends it by his power. All truth is enforced on the heart and conscience with more or less power by the Holy Spirit, wherever that
truth is known. To this all-pervading influence we are indebted
for all there is of morality and order in the world. But besides
this general influence, which is usually called common grace, the
Spirit specially illuminates the minds of the children of God, that
they may know the things freely given (or revealed to them) by
God. The natural man does not receive them, neither can he
know them, because they are spiritually discerned. All believers
are therefore called (πνευματικοί) spiritual, because thus enlightened
and guided by the Spirit.

4. It is the special office of the Spirit to convince the world of
sin ; to reveal Christ, to regenerate the soul, to lead men to the
exercise of faith and repentance ; to dwell in those whom He thus
renews, as a principle of a new and divine life. By this indwelling
of the Spirit, believers are united to Christ, and to one another, so
that they form one body. This is the foundation of the communion
of saints, making them one in faith, one in love, one in their inward
life, and one in their hopes and final destiny.

5. The Spirit also calls men to office in the Church, and endows
them with the qualifications necessary for the successful discharge
of its duties. The office of the Church, in this matter, is simply
to ascertain and authenticate the call of the Spirit. Thus the
Holy Ghost is the immediate author of all truth, of all holiness, of
all consolation, of all authority, and of all efficiency in the children
of God individually, and in the Church collectively.

§ 3. *History of the Doctrine concerning the Holy Spirit.*

During the Ante-Nicene period, the Church believed concerning
the Holy Ghost what was revealed on the surface of Scripture, and
what was involved in the religious experience of all Christians.
There is to them one God, the Father, whose favour they had forfeited by sin, and to whom they must be reconciled ; one Lord

Jesus Christ, the only begotten Son of God, through whom this reconciliation is effected ; and one Holy Spirit, by whom they are, through Christ, brought near to God. This all Christians believed, as they professed in their baptism, and in repeating and receiving the apostolic benediction. With this simple faith underlying and sustaining the life of the Church, there coexisted among theologians great obscurity, indistinctness, and inconsistency of statement, especially in reference to the nature and office of the Holy Ghost. This ought not to be a matter of surprise, because in the Scriptures themselves the same work is often ascribed to God and to the Spirit of God, which led some at times to assume that these terms expressed one and the same thing; as the spirit of a man is the man himself. In the Scriptures, also, the terms Word and Breath (or Spirit) are often interchanged ; and what in one place is said to be done by the Word, in another is said to be done by the Spirit. The Λόγος is represented as the life of the world and the source of all knowledge, and yet the same is said of the Spirit. Paul declares in one place (Gal. i. 12) that he received the doctrines which he taught, by the revelation of Jesus Christ; in another (1 Cor. ii. 10), that he was taught them by the Spirit. Misled by such representation, some of the fathers identified the Son and Spirit. Even Tertullian, in one place says, " Spiritus substantia est Sermonis, et Sermo operatio Spiritus, et duo unum sunt." [1] Finally, as it is plain from the Scripture that the Spirit is of the Son, as the Son is of the Father (the difference between generation and procession being perfectly inscrutable), all the Arians and semi-Arians who taught that the Son was created by the Father, held that the Spirit was created by the Son.   This roused so much controversy and agitation, that first the Council of Nice, A. D. 325, and then that of Constantinople, A. D. 381, were called to frame a satisfactory statement of the Scriptural doctrine on this subject. In the Creed of the Apostles, as it is called, which is so ancient that Rufinus and Ambrose referred it to the Apostles themselves, it is simply said, " I believe on the Holy Ghost."   The same words without addition are repeated in the Nicene Creed, but in the Creed of Constantinople it is added, " I believe in the Holy Ghost, the divine (τὸ κύριον), the life-giving, who proceedeth from the Father, who is to be worshipped and glorified with the Father and the Son, and who spake through the prophets." In the Athanasian Creed (so-called), it is said that the Spirit is consubstantial with the Father and the Son ; that He is uncreated, eternal, and omnipotent, equal in

[1] *Adversus Praxean*, 15, *Works*, edit. Basle, 1562, p. 426

majesty and glory, and that He proceeds from the Father and the Son. These creeds are Catholic, adopted by the whole Church. Since they were framed there has been no diversity of faith on this subject among those recognized as Christians.

Those who, since the Council of Constantinople have denied the common Church doctrine, whether Socinians, Arians, or Sabellians, regard the Holy Spirit not as a creature, but as the power of God, *i. e.*, the manifested divine efficiency. The modern philosophical theologians of Germany do not differ essentially from this view. De Wette, for example, says, that the Spirit is God as revealed and operative in nature ; Schleiermacher says the term designates God as operative in the Church, *i. e.*, " der Gemeingeist der Kirche." This, however, is only a name. God with Schleiermacher is only the unity of the causality manifested in the world. That causality viewed in Christ we may call Son, and viewed in the Church we may call the Spirit. God is merely cause, and man a fleeting effect. Happily Schleiermacher's theology and Schleiermacher's religion were as different as the speculations and the every day faith of the idealist.

CHAPTER IX.

THE DECREES OF GOD.

§ 1. *The Nature of the Decrees.*

IT must be remembered that theology is not philosophy. It does not assume to discover truth, or to reconcile what it teaches as true with all other truths. Its province is simply to state what God has revealed in his Word, and to vindicate those statements as far as possible from misconceptions and objections. This limited and humble office of theology it is especially necessary to bear in mind, when we come to speak of the acts and purposes of God. " The things of God knoweth no man ; but the Spirit of God." (1 Cor. ii. 11.) In treating, therefore, of the decrees of God, all that is proposed is simply to state what the Spirit has seen fit to reveal on that subject.

" The decrees of God are his eternal purpose, according to the counsel of his will, whereby for his own glory He hath foreordained whatsoever comes to pass." [1] Agreeably to this statement: (1.) The end or final cause contemplated in all God's decrees, is his own glory. (2.) They are all reducible to one eternal purpose. (3.) They are free and sovereign, determined by the counsel of his own will. (4.) They comprehend all events.

A. *The Glory of God the Final Cause of all his Decrees.*

The final cause of all God's purposes is his own glory. This is frequently declared to be the end of all things. " Thou art worthy," say the heavenly worshippers, " O Lord, to receive glory, and honour, and power: for thou hast created all things, and for thy pleasure they are and were created." (Rev. iv. 11.) All things are said to be not only of God and through Him, but for Him. He is the beginning and the end. The heavens declare his glory ; that is the purpose for which they were made. God frequently announces his determination to make his glory known. " As truly as I live, all the earth shall be filled with the glory of the Lord." (Num. xiv. 21.) This is said to be the end of all the dispensations of his providence, whether beneficent or punitive. " For mine own

---

[1] *Westminster Shorter Catechism.* 7.

sake, even for mine own sake, will I do it; for how should my name be polluted? and I will not give my glory unto another." (Is. xlviii. 11.) "I wrought for my name's sake, that it should not be polluted before the heathen." (Ezek. xx. 9.) In like manner the whole plan of redemption and the dispensations of his grace, are declared to be designed to reveal the glory of God. (1 Cor. i. 26–31; Eph. ii. 8–10.) This is the end which our Lord proposed to Himself. He did everything for the glory of God; and for this end all his followers are required to live and act. As God is infinite, and all creatures are as nothing in comparison with Him, it is plain that the revelation of his nature and perfections must be the highest conceivable end of all things, and the most conducive to secure all other good subordinate ends. Order and truth, however, depend on things being put in their right relations. If we make the good of the creature the ultimate object of all God's works, then we subordinate God to the creature, and endless confusion and unavoidable error are the consequence. It is characteristic of the Bible that it places God first, and the good of the creation second. This also is the characteristic feature of Augustinianism as distinguished from all other forms of doctrine. And when the Protestants were divided at the time of the Reformation, it was mainly on this point. The Lutheran and Reformed churches are distinguished in all that characterizes their theological systems, by the fact that the latter allow the supremacy and sovereignty of God in the workings of his providence and grace to determine everything for his own glory, while the former lean more or less to the error of restraining God's liberty of action by the assumed powers and prerogatives of man. The Bible, Augustine, and the Reformed, give one answer to all such questions as the following: Why did God create the world? Why did He permit the occurrence of sin? Why was salvation provided for men and not for angels? Why was the knowledge of that salvation so long confined to one people? Why among those who hear the gospel, do some receive, and others reject it? To all these, and similar questions, the answer is, not because the happiness of creatures would be secured in a higher degree by the admission of sin and misery, than by their entire exclusion; some men are saved and others perish not because some of their own will believe and others do not believe, but simply because, Thus it seemed good in the eyes of God. Whatever He does or permits to be done, is done or permitted for the more perfect revelation of his nature and perfections. As the knowledge of God is the ground and sum of all good, it of course follows that the more perfectly God is known, the more fully the highest good (not merely nor necessarily the highest happiness) of the intelligent universe is promoted. But this is a subordinate effect, and not the chief end. It is therefore in accordance with the whole spirit and teachings of the Bible, and with the essential character of Augustinianism, that our standards make the glory of God the end of all his decrees.

B. *The Decrees Reducible to one Purpose.*

The second point included in this doctrine is, that the decrees of God are all reducible to one purpose. By this is meant that from the indefinite number of systems, or series of possible events, present to the divine mind, God determined on the futurition or actual occurrence of the existing order of things, with all its changes, minute as well as great, from the beginning of time to all eternity. The reason, therefore, why any event occurs, or, that it passes from the category of the possible into that of the actual, is that God has so decreed. The decrees of God, therefore, are not many, but one purpose. They are not successively formed as the emergency arises, but are all parts of one all-comprehending plan. This view of the subject is rendered necessary by the nature of an infinitely perfect Being. It is inconsistent with the idea of absolute perfection, that the purposes of God are successive, or that He ever purposes what He did not originally intend ; or that one part of his plan is independent of other parts. It is one scheme, and therefore one purpose. As, however, this one purpose includes an indefinite number of events, and as those events are mutually related, we therefore speak of the decrees of God as many, and as having a certain order. The Scriptures consequently speak of the judgments, counsels, or purposes of God, in the plural number, and also of his determining one event because of another. When we look at an extensive building, or a complicated machine, we perceive at once the multiplicity of their parts, and their mutual relations. Our conception of the building or of the machine is one, and yet it comprehends many distinct perceptions, and the apprehension of their relations. So also in the mind of the architect or mechanist, the whole is one idea, though he intends many things, and one in reference to another. We can, therefore, in a measure, understand how the vast scheme of creation, providence, and redemption, lies in the divine mind as one simple purpose, although including an infinite multiplicity of causes and effects.

C. *The Decrees of God are Eternal.*

That the decrees of God are eternal, necessarily follows from the perfection of the divine Being. He cannot be supposed to have at one time plans or purposes which He had not at another. He sees the end from the beginning; the distinctions of time have no reference to Him who inhabits eternity. The Scriptures therefore always speak of events in time as revelations of a purpose formed in eternity. The salvation of men, for example, is said to be " according to the eternal purpose which He purposed in Christ Jesus." (Eph. iii. 11.) What is revealed in time was hidden for ages, *i. e.*, from eternity in the mind of God. (Eph. iii. 9.) Believers were chosen in Christ before the foundation of the world. (Eph. i. 4.) "Who hath saved us, and called us . . . . according to his own purpose and grace, which was given us in Christ Jesus, πρὸ χρόνων αἰωνίων, before eternal ages." (2 Tim. i. 9.) Christ as a sacrifice was " foreordained before the foundation of the world, but was manifest in these last times for you, who by Him do believe in God." (1 Pet. i. 20, 21 ; Rom. xi. 33–36 ; Acts ii. 23.) This is the constant representation of Scripture. History in all its details, even the most minute, is but the evolution of the eternal purposes of God. It is no objection to this doctrine that the Scriptures often represent one purpose of God as consequent upon another, or that they speak of his purposes as determined by the conduct of men. The language of Scripture is founded on apparent truth; they speak, as men always do, as things appear, not as they themselves know or believe them to be. We speak of the concave heavens, or of the firm foundation of the heavens, although we know that it is not concave, and that it does not rest on any foundation. So the Bible speaks of the decrees of God as they appear to us in their successive revelation and in their mutual relations, and not as they exist from eternity in the divine mind. Neither is there any force in the objection that the agent must be before his acts. The sun is not before his brightness, nor the mind before thought, nor life before consciousness, nor God before his purposes. These objections are founded on the assumption that God is subject to the limitations of time. To Him there is neither past nor future, neither before nor after.

D. *The Decrees of God are Immutable.*

Change of purpose arises either from the want of wisdom or from the want of power. As God is infinite in wisdom and power, there can be with Him no unforeseen emergency and no inadequacy of means, and nothing can resist the execution of his original intention. To Him, therefore, the causes of change have no existence. With God there is, as the Scriptures teach, " no variableness, neither shadow of turning." (James i. 17.) " The counsel of the LORD standeth for ever, the thoughts of his heart to all generations." (Ps. xxxiii. 11.) " The LORD of hosts hath sworn, saying, Surely as I have thought, so shall it come to pass; and as I have purposed, so shall it stand." (Is. xiv. 24.) "I am God . . . . declaring the end from the beginning, and from ancient times the things that are not yet done, saying, My counsel shall stand, and I will do all my pleasure." (Is. xlvi. 9, 10.) The uniformity of the laws of nature is a constant revelation of the immutability of God. They are now what they were at the beginning of time, and they are the same in every part of the universe. No less stable are the laws which regulate the operations of the reason and conscience. The whole government of God, as the God of nature and as moral governor, rests on the immutability of his counsels.

E. *The Decrees of God are Free.*

This includes three ideas, —

1. They are rational determinations, founded on sufficient reasons. This is opposed to the doctrine of necessity, which assumes that God acts by a mere necessity of nature, and that all that occurs is due to the law of development or of self-manifestation of the divine being. This reduces God to a mere *natura naturans,* or *vis formativa,* which acts without design. The true doctrine is opposed also to the idea that the only cause of events is an intellectual force analogous to the instincts of irrational animals. The acts performed under the guidance of instinct are not free acts, for liberty is a *libentia rationalis,* spontaneity determined by reason. It is therefore involved in the idea of God as a rational and personal being that his decrees are free. He was free to create or not to create; to create such a world as now is, or one entirely different. He is free to act or not act, and when He purposes, it is not from any blind necessity, but according to the counsel of his own will.

2. Our purposes are free, even when formed under the influence of other minds. We may be argued or persuaded into certain courses of action, or induced to form our designs out of regard to the wishes or interests of others. God is infinitely exalted above all *ab extra* influence. " Who hath known the mind of the Lord ? or who hath been his counsellor? " (Rom. xi. 34.) " Behold,

God exalteth by his power : who teacheth like Him ? Who hath enjoined Him his way ? " (Job xxxvi. 22, 23.) " Who hath directed the Spirit of the Lord ? or being his counsellor hath taught Him ? With whom took He counsel, and who instructed Him, and taught Him in the path of judgment ? " (Is. xl. 13, 14.) " Who hath known the mind of the Lord, that he may instruct Him ? " (1 Cor. ii. 16.) God adopted the plan of the universe on the ground of his own good pleasure, for his own glory, and every subordinate part of it in reference to the whole. His decrees are free, therefore, in a far higher sense than that in which the ordinary purposes of men are free. They were formed purely on the counsel of his own will. He purposes and does what seemeth good in his sight.

3. The decrees of God are free in the sense of being absolute or sovereign. The meaning of this proposition is expressed negatively by saying that the decrees of God are in no case conditional. The event decreed is suspended on a condition, but the purpose of God is not. It is inconsistent with the nature of God to assume suspense or indecision on his part. If He has not absolutely determined on what is to occur, but waits until an undetermined condition is or is not fulfilled, then his decrees can neither be eternal nor immutable. He purposes one thing if the condition be fulfilled, and another if it be not fulfilled, and thus everything must be uncertain not only in the divine mind, but also in the event. The Scriptures, therefore, teach that He doeth whatsoever He pleaseth. (Ps. cxv. 3.) He doeth his pleasure in the army of heaven, and among the inhabitants of the earth. (Dan. iv. 35 ; Ps. cxxxv. 6.) Of Him, and through Him, and to Him are all things. (Rom. xi. 36.) It is expressly taught that the purposes of God, even as to the future destiny of men, are founded on his own good pleasure. As all have sinned and come short of the glory of God, He has mercy upon whom He will have mercy. It is not according to our works, but of his grace that He saves us. It is of Him that we are in Christ Jesus, that those who glory should glory in the Lord. (Matt. xi. 26 ; Rom. viii. 29, 30 ; ix. 15–18 ; Eph. i. 5, etc., etc.)

F. *The Decrees of God are certainly Efficacious.*

The decrees of God are certainly efficacious, that is, they render certain the occurrence of what He decrees. Whatever God foreordains, must certainly come to pass. The distinction between the efficient (or efficacious) and the permissive decrees of God, although important, has no relation to the certainty of events. All events embraced in the purpose of God are equally certain, whether He has determined to bring them to pass by his own power, or simply to permit their occurrence through the agency of his creatures. It was no less certain from eternity that Satan would tempt our first parents, and that they would fall, than that God would send his Son to die for sinners. The distinction in question nas reference only to the relation which events bear to the efficiency of God. Some things He purposes to do, others He decrees to permit to be done. He effects good, He permits evil. He is the author of the one, but not of the other. With this explanation, the proposition that the decrees of God are certainly efficacious, or render certain all events to which they refer, stands good. This is proved, —

1. From the perfection of God, which forbids the ascription to Him of purposes uncertain as to their accomplishment. No man fails to execute what he purposes, except through the want of wisdom or power to secure the end proposed, or through some vacillation in his own mind. It would be to reduce God to the level of his creatures, to assume that what He decrees, should fail to come to pass.

2. From the unity of God's plan. If that plan comprehends all events, all events stand in mutual relation and dependence. If one part fails, the whole may fail or be thrown into confusion.

3. From the evident concatenation of events in the progress of history, which proves that all things are intimately connected, the most important events often depending on the most trivial, which shows that all must be comprehended in the plan of God.

4. From the providential and moral government of God. There could be no certainty in either if the decrees of God were not efficacious. There could be no assurance that any divine prophecy, promise, or threatening, would be accomplished. All ground of confidence in God would thus be lost, and chance and not God would become the arbiter of all events. The Scriptures variously and constantly teach this doctrine, (a.) By all those passages which assert the immutability and sovereignty of the divine decrees. (b.) By those which affirm that He fixes the bounds of our habitations, that our days are all numbered, and that even a hair from our heads cannot perish without his notice. (c.) By those which declare that nothing can counteract his designs. "The LORD of hosts," says the prophet, "hath purposed, who shall disannul it? And his hand is stretched out, and who shall turn it back." (Is. xiv. 27.) "I will work, and who shall

let it ? "   (xliii. 13.)   (d.) By those which teach doctrines that
necessarily assume the certainty of all God's decrees.   The whole
plan of redemption rests on that foundation.   It is inconceivable
that God should devise such a scheme, and not secure its execution,
and that He should send his Son into the world, and leave the
consequences of that infinite condescension undetermined.   It is,
therefore, the doctrine of reason as well as of Scripture, that God
has a plan or end for which the universe was created, that the
execution of that plan is not left contingent, and that whatever
is embraced in the decrees of God must certainly come to pass.

G. *The Decrees of God relate to all Events.*

God foreordains whatsoever comes to pass.   Some events are
necessary, that is, are brought about by the action of necessary
causes; others are contingent or free, or are acts of free agents;
some are morally good, others are sinful.   The doctrine of the
Bible is, that all events, whether necessary or contingent, good or
sinful, are included in the purpose of God, and that their futurition or actual occurrence is rendered absolutely certain.   This is
evident, —

1. From the unity of the divine purposes.   That unity supposes
that the whole scheme of creation, providence, and redemption,
was fixed by the divine decree.   It was formed from ages in the
divine mind, and is gradually unfolded by the course of events.   It
is therefore inconsistent with this sublime and Scriptural representation, to suppose that any class of actual events, and especially
that class which is most influential and important, should be omitted from the divine purpose.   He who purposes a machine, purposes all its parts.   The general who plans a campaign, includes all
the movements of every corps, division, and brigade in his army,
and if his foresight were perfect, and his control of events absolute,
his foreordination would extend to every act of every soldier.
Whatever is wanting in his foreordination is due to the limitation
of human power.   As God is infinite in knowledge and resources,
his purpose must include all events.

2. It is therefore inconsistent with the perfection of God to suppose either that He could not form a plan comprehending all
events, or that He could not carry it into execution, without doing
violence to the nature of his creatures.

3. The universality of the decree follows from the universal dominion of God.   Whatever He does, He certainly purposed to do.
Whatever He permits to occur, He certainly purposed to permit.

Nothing can occur that was not foreseen, and if foreseen it must have been intended. As the Scriptures teach that the providential control of God extends to all events, even the most minute, they do thereby teach that his decrees are equally comprehensive.

4. Another argument is derived from the certainty of the divine government. As all events are more or less intimately connected, and as God works by means, if God does not determine the means as well as the event, all certainty as to the event itself would be destroyed. In determining the redemption of man, He thereby determined on the mission, incarnation, sufferings, death, and resurrection of his Son, on the gift of the Spirit, upon the faith, repentance, and perseverance of all his people. The prediction of future events, which often depend on the most fortuitous occurrences, or which include those that appear to us of no account, proves that the certainty of the divine administration rests on the foreordination of God extending to all events both great and small.

The Scriptures in various ways teach that God foreordains whatever comes to pass.

1. They teach that God works all things according to the counsel of his will. There is nothing to limit the words "all things," and therefore they must be taken in the fullest extent.

2. It is expressly declared that fortuitous events, that is, events which depend on causes so subtle and so rapid in their operation as to elude our observation, are predetermined; as the falling of the lot, the flight of an arrow, the falling of a sparrow, the number of the hairs of our heads.

Free Acts are Foreordained.

3. The Bible especially declares that the free acts of men are decreed beforehand. This is involved in the doctrine of prophecy, which assumes that events involving the free acts of a multitude of men are foreseen and foreordained. God promises to give faith, a new heart, to write his law upon the minds of his people, to work in them to will and to do, to convert the Gentiles, to fill the world with the true worshippers of Christ, to whom every knee is gladly to bow. If God has promised these things, He must of course purpose them, but they all involve the free acts of men.

4. The Scriptures teach that sinful acts, as well as such as are holy, are foreordained. In Acts ii. 23, it is said, " Him, being delivered by the determinate counsel and foreknowledge of God, ye have taken, and by wicked hands have crucified and slain; " iv. 27, " For of a truth against thy holy child Jesus, whom thou

hast anointed, both Herod and Pontius Pilate, with the Gentiles and the people of Israel were gathered together, for to do whatsoever thy hand and thy counsel determined before to be done." "Truly the Son of Man goeth as it was determined ; but woe unto that man by whom He is betrayed." (Luke xxii. 22.) It was foreordained that He should be betrayed ; but woe to him who fulfilled the decree. Here foreordination and responsibility are by our Lord Himself declared to coexist and to be consistent. In Rev. xvii. 17, it is said, "God hath put in their hearts to fulfil his will, and to agree, and give their kingdom unto the beast, until the words of God shall be fulfilled." The crucifixion of Christ was beyond doubt foreordained of God. It was, however, the greatest crime ever committed. It is therefore beyond all doubt the doctrine of the Bible that sin is foreordained.

5. Besides this, the conquests of Nebuchadnezzar, the destruction of Jerusalem, and many other similar events, were predicted, and therefore predetermined, but they included the commission of innumerable sins, without which the predictions, and consequently the revealed purposes of God, could not have been accomplished.

6. The whole course of history is represented as the development of the plan and purposes of God ; and yet human history is little else than the history of sin. No one can read the simple narrative concerning Joseph, as given in the book of Genesis, without seeing that everything in his history occurred in execution of a preconceived purpose of God. The envy of his brethren, their selling him into Egypt, and his unjust imprisonment, were all embraced in God's plan. "God," as Joseph himself said to his brethren, "sent me before you, to preserve you a posterity in the earth, and to save your lives by a great deliverance. So now it was not you that sent me hither, but God." (Gen. xlv. 7, 8.) This is but an illustration. What is true of the history of Joseph, is true of all history. It is the development of the plan of God. God is in history, and although we cannot trace his path step by step, yet it is plain in the general survey of events, through long periods, that they are ordered by God to the accomplishment of his divine purposes. This is obvious enough in the history of the Jewish nation, as recorded in the Scripture, but it is no less true in regard to all history. The acts of the wicked in persecuting the early Church, were ordained of God as the means for the wider and more speedy proclamation of the Gospel. The sufferings of the martyrs were the means not only of extending but of purifying the Church. The apostasy of the man of sin being predicted, was predetermined. The

destruction of the Huguenots in France, the persecution of the Puritans in England, laid the foundation for the planting of North America with a race of godly and energetic men, who were to make this land the land of refuge for the nations, the home of liberty, civil and religious. It would destroy the confidence of God's people could they be persuaded that God does not foreordain whatsoever comes to pass. It is because the Lord reigns, and doeth his pleasure in heaven and on earth, that they repose in perfect security under his guidance and protection.

§ 2. *Objections to the Doctrine of Divine Decrees.*

A. *Foreordination inconsistent with Free Agency.*

It is urged that the foreordination of all events is inconsistent with the free agency of man. The force of this objection depends on what is meant by a free act. To decide whether two things are inconsistent, the nature of each must be determined. By the decrees of God are to be understood the purpose of God rendering certain the occurrence of future events. By a free act is meant an act of rational self-determination by an intelligent person. If such an act is from its very nature contingent, or uncertain, then it is clear that foreordination is inconsistent with free agency. This theory of liberty has been adopted by a large body of philosophers and theologians, and is for them an insuperable objection to the doctrine of the divine decrees. In answer to the objection, it may be remarked, (1.) That it bears with equal force against foreknowledge. What is foreknown must be certain, as much as what is foreordained. If the one, therefore, be inconsistent with liberty, so also is the other. This is sometimes candidly admitted. Socinus argues that the knowledge of God embraces all that is knowable. Future free actions being uncertain, are not the objects of knowledge, and therefore it is no impeachment of the divine omniscience to say that they cannot be known. But then they cannot be predicted. We find, however, that the Scriptures are filled with such predictions. It is, therefore, evident that the sacred writers fully believed that free acts are foreknown by the divine mind, and therefore are certain as to their occurrence. Besides, if God cannot foreknow how free agents will act, He must be ignorant of the future, and be constantly increasing in knowledge. This is so incompatible with all proper ideas of the infinite mind, that it has been almost universally rejected, both by philosophers and by Christian theologians. A still weaker evasion is that proposed by some Ar-

minian writers, who admit that God's knowledge is not limited by
anything out of Himself, but hold that it may be limited by his own
will.   In creating free agents, He willed not to foreknow how
they would act, in order to leave their freedom unimpaired.   But
this is to suppose that God wills not to be God; that the Infinite
wills to be finite.   Knowledge with God is not founded on his will,
except so far as the knowledge of vision is concerned, *i. e.*, his
knowledge of his own purposes, or of what He has decreed shall
come to pass.   If not founded on his will, it cannot be limited by it.
Infinite knowledge must know all things, actual or possible.   It may,
however, be said that there is a difference between foreknowledge
and foreordination, in so far that the former merely assumes the
certainty of future events, whereas the latter causes their futurition.   But as the certainty of occurrence is the same in both cases,
it makes no difference as to the matter in hand.   The decree only
renders the event certain ; and therefore if certainty be not inconsistent with liberty, then foreordination is not.   That an event may
be free and yet certain, may be easily proved.   (1.) It is a matter of consciousness.   We are often absolutely certain how we
shall act, so far as we are free to act at all, and conscious that we
act freely.   A parent may be certain that he will succor a child in
distress, and be conscious that his free agency is not thereby impaired.   The more certain, in many cases, the more perfectly are
we self-controlled.   (2.) Free acts have been predicted, and
therefore their occurrence was certain.   (3.) Nothing was more
certain than that our Lord would continue holy, harmless, and un-
defiled, yet his acts were all free.   (4.) It is certain that the people of God will repent, believe, and persevere in holiness forever
in heaven, yet they do not cease to be free agents.   The decrees
of God, therefore, which only secure the certainty of events, are
not inconsistent with liberty as to the mode of their occurrence.
Although his purpose comprehends all things, and is immutable,
yet thereby " no violence is offered to the will of the creatures,
nor is the liberty or contingency of second causes taken away, but
rather established."

B. *Foreordination of Sin inconsistent with Holiness.*

It is further objected that it is inconsistent with the holiness of
God that He should foreordain sin.   There are two methods of
dealing with this and all similar objections.   The one may be
called the Scriptural method, as it is the one often adopted by the
sacred writers.   It consists in showing that the objection bears

against the plain declarations of Scripture, or against the facts of experience. In either case, it is for us sufficiently answered. It is vain to argue that a holy and benevolent God cannot permit sin and misery, if sin and misery actually exist. It is vain to say that his impartiality forbids that there should be any diversity in the endowments, advantages, or happiness of his rational creatures. It is vain to insist that a holy God cannot permit children to suffer for the sins of their parents, when we constantly see that they do thus suffer. So it is utterly irrational to contend that God cannot foreordain sin, if He foreordained (as no Christian doubts) the crucifixion of Christ. The occurrence of sin in the plan adopted by God, is a palpable fact; the consistency, therefore, of foreordination with the holiness of God cannot rationally be denied. The second method of dealing with such objections is to show that the principle on which they are founded is unsound. The principle on which the objection under consideration rests, is that an agent is responsible for all the necessary or certain consequences of his acts. The objection is, that a holy God cannot decree the occurrence of sin, because his decree renders that occurrence certain. That is, an agent is responsible for whatever his act renders certain. That principle, however, is utterly untenable. A righteous judge, in pronouncing sentence on a criminal, may be sure that he will cause wicked and bitter feelings in the criminal's mina, or in the hearts of his friends, and yet the judge be guiltless. A father, in excluding a reprobate son from his family, may see that the inevitable consequence of such exclusion will be his greater wickedness, and yet the father may do right. It is the certain consequence of God's leaving the fallen angels and the finally impenitent to themselves, that they will continue in sin, and yet the holiness of God remain untarnished. The Bible clearly teaches that God judicially abandons men to their sins, giving them up to a reprobate mind, and He therein is most just and holy. It is not true, therefore, that an agent is responsible for all the certain consequences of his acts. It may be, and doubtless is, infinitely wise and just in God to permit the occurrence of sin, and to adopt a plan of which sin is a certain consequence or element; yet as he neither causes sin, nor tempts men to its commission, He is neither its author nor approver. He sees and knows that higher ends will be accomplished by its admission than by its exclusion, that a perfect exhibition of his infinite perfections will be thereby effected, and therefore for the highest reason decrees that it shall occur through the free choice of responsible agents. Our great ground of confidence, however, is the assurance that the judge of all the earth must do right. Sin is, and God is; therefore the occurrence of sin must be consistent with his nature; and as its occurrence cannot have been unforeseen or undesigned, God's purpose or decree that it should occur must be consistent with his holiness.

C. *The Doctrine of Decrees destroys all Motive to Exertion.*

A third objection is, that the doctrine of foreordination, which supposes the certainty of all events, tends to the neglect of all use of means. If everything will happen just as God has predetermined, we need give ourselves no concern, and need make no effort. (1.) This objection supposes that God has determined the end without reference to the means. The reverse, however, is true. The event is determined in connection with the means. If the latter fail, so will the former. God has decreed that men shall live by food. If any man refuses to eat, he will die. He has ordained that men shall be saved through faith. If a man refuses to believe, he will perish. If God has purposed that a man shall live, He has also purposed to preserve him from the suicidal folly of refusing to eat. (2.) There is another fallacy included in this objection. It supposes that the certainty that an event will happen, acts as a motive to neglect the means of its attainment. This is not according to reason or experience. The stronger the hope of success, the greater the motive to exertion. If sure of success in the use of the appropriate means, the incentive to effort becomes as strong as it can be. On the other hand, the less hope, the less disposition there is to exert ourselves; and where there is no hope, there will be no exertion. The rational and Scriptural foundation for the use of means, and the proper motives to avail ourselves of them, are, (1.) The command of God. (2.) Their adaptation to produce the effect. (3.) The divine ordination which makes the means necessary to the attainment of the end. And (4.) The promise of God to give his blessing to those who obediently avail themselves of the means of his appointment.

D. *It is Fatalism.*

It is objected, in the fourth place, that the doctrine of decrees amounts to the heathen doctrine of fate. There is only one point of agreement between these doctrines. They both assume absolute certainty in the sequence of all events. They differ, however, not only as to the ground of that certainty, the nature of the influence by which it is secured, and the ends therein contemplated, but also in their natural effects on the reason and conscience of men.

The word Fatalism has been applied to different systems, some of which admit, while others deny or ignore the existence of a supreme intelligence. But in common usage it designates the doctrine that all events come to pass under the operation of a blind necessity. This system differs from the Scriptural doctrine of foreordination, (1.) In that it excludes the idea of final causes. There is no end to which all things tend, and for the accomplishment of which they exist. According to the Scriptural doctrine, all things are ordained and controlled to accomplish the highest conceivable or possible good. (2.) In that according to Fatalism the sequence of events is determined by an unintelligent concatenation of causes and effects. According to the doctrine of decrees, that sequence is determined by infinite wisdom and goodness. (3.) Fatalism admits of no distinction between necessary and free causes. The acts of rational agents are as much determined by a necessity out of themselves as the operations of nature. According to the Scriptures, the freedom and responsibility of man are fully preserved. The two systems differ, therefore, as much as a machine differs from a man; or as the actions of infinite intelligence, power, and love differ from the law of gravitation. (4.) The one system, therefore, leads to the denial of all moral distinctions, and to stolid insensibility or despair. The other to a sedulous regard to the will of an infinitely wise and good ruler, all whose acts are determined by a sufficient reason; and to filial confidence and submission.

CHAPTER X.

CREATION.

§ 1. *Different Theories concerning the Origin of the Universe.*

THE question concerning the origin of the universe has forced itself on the minds of men in all ages. That the mutable cannot be eternal, would seem to be self-evident. As everything within the sphere of human observation is constantly changing, men have been constrained to believe that the world as it now is had a beginning. But if it began to be, whence did it come? Without the light of a divine revelation, this question is unanswerable. The data for the solution of the problem do not lie within the sphere either of experience or of reason. All human theories on this subject are nothing more than conjectures more or less ingenious.

Apart from the pantheistic doctrine which makes the universe the existence form, or, as Goethe calls it, "das lebendiges Kleid" (the living garment) of God, the most prevalent views on this subject are, First, those theories which exclude mind from the causative origin of the world; Secondly, those which admit of mind, but only as connected with matter; and Thirdly, the Scriptural doctrine which assumes the existence of an infinite extramundane mind to whose power and will the existence of all things out of God is to be referred.

It is a self-evident truth that existence cannot spring spontaneously from non-existence. In this sense *ex nihilo nihil fit* is an universally admitted axiom. Those, therefore, who deny the existence of an extramundane mind, are forced to admit that as the universe now is, it must have always been. But as it is in a state of perpetual change it has not always been as it now is. There was a primordial state out of which the present order of things has arisen. The question is, How?

The purely Physical Theory.

According to the first hypothesis just mentioned, the primordial condition of the universe was that of universally diffused matter in a highly attenuated state. This matter had the properties, or forces, which it now everywhere exhibits ; and under the operation of these forces and in accordance with the laws of heat, motion, etc., not only the great cosmical bodies were formed and arranged themselves in their present harmonious relations, but also all the organisms, vegetable and animal, on this globe and elsewhere, were fashioned and sustained. Every man knows enough of physical laws to be able to predict with certainty that on a cold day in the open air the moisture of his breath will be condensed ; so, according to Professor Huxley, on this hypothesis, with adequate knowledge of those laws, it would have been easy from the beginning to predict, not only the mechanism of the heavens, but the fauna and flora of our globe in all the states and stages of its existence.

The Nebular hypothesis, as first proposed by La Place, was the application of this theory to the explanation of the origin and order of the heavenly bodies. This hypothesis may be thus stated, "Suppose that the matter composing the entire solar system once existed in the condition of a single nebulous mass, extending beyond the orbit of the most remote planet. Suppose that this nebula has a slow rotation upon an axis, and that by radiation it gradually cools, thereby contracting in its dimensions. As it contracts in its dimensions, its velocity of rotation, according to the principles of Mechanics, must necessarily increase, and the centrifugal force thus generated in the exterior portion of the nebula would at length become equal to the attraction of the central mass. This exterior portion would thus become detached, and revolve independently as an immense zone or ring. As the central mass continued to cool and contract in its dimensions, other zones would in the same manner become detached, while the central mass continually decreases in size and increases in density. The zones thus successively detached would generally break up into separate masses revolving independently about the sun ; and if their velocities were slightly unequal, the matter of each zone would ultimately collect in a single planetary, but still gaseous, mass, having a spheroidal form, and also a motion of rotation about an axis. As each of these planetary masses became still farther cooled, it would pass through a succession of changes similar to those of the first solar nebula ; rings of matter would be formed surrounding the planetary nucleus, and these rings, if they broke up into separate masses, would ultimately form satellites revolving about their primaries." [1] We thus have an ordered uni-

[1] Loomis, *Treatise on Astronomy*, New York, 1865, p. 314.

verse without the intervention of mind.   Every one knows, however, that there is a form in which the nebular hypothesis is held
by many Christian theists.

Theories which assume Intelligence in Nature itself.

The obvious impossibility of blind causes acting intelligently, or
of necessary causes being elective in their operation, has led many
who deny the existence of an extramundane Mind to hold, that
life and intelligence pertain to matter itself in some at least of its
combinations.   A plant lives.   There is something in the seed
which secures its development, each after its kind.   There is,
therefore, something in the plant, which according to this theory is
not external to the plant itself, which does the work of mind.
That is, it selects or chooses from the earth and air the elements
needed for its support and growth.   It moulds these elements into
organic forms, intended to answer a purpose, and adapted with
wonderful skill to accomplish a given object.   With regard to this
principle of life, this vital force, it is to be remarked that it is in
the plant; that it is never manifested, never acts, except in union
with the matter of which the plant is composed; when the plant
dies, its vitality is extinguished.   It ceases to exist in the same
sense in which light ceases when darkness takes its place.

What is true of the vegetable, is no less true of the animal
world.   Every animal starts in an almost imperceptible germ.
But that germ has something in it which determines with certainty
the genus, species, and variety of the animal.   It fashions all his
organs; prepares the eye for the light yet to be seen; the ear for
sounds yet to be heard; the lungs for air yet to be breathed.
Nothing more wonderful than this is furnished by the universe in
any of its phenomena.

If, therefore, vegetable and animal life work all these wonders,
what need have we to assume an extramundane mind to account
for any of the phenomena of the universe?   All that is necessary
is, that nature, *natura naturans*, the *vis in rebus insita*, should
act just as we see that the vital principle does act in plants and
animals.   This is Hylozoism; the doctrine that matter is imbued
with a principle of life.

Another form of this theory is more dualistic.   It admits the
existence of mind and matter as distinct substances, but always existing in combination, as soul and body in man in our present stage
of being.   The advocates of this doctrine, therefore, instead of
speaking of nature as the organizing force, speak of the soul of
the world; the *anima mundi*, etc.

It is enough to remark concerning these theories, (1.) That they leave the origin of things unaccounted for. Whence came the matter, which the theory in one form assumes? Whence came its physical properties, to which all organization is referred? And as to the other doctrine, it may be asked, Whence came the living germs of plants and animals? To assume that matter in a state of chaos is eternal; or that there has been an endless succession of living germs; or that there has been an eternal succession of cycles in the history of the universe, chaos unfolding itself into cosmos, during immeasurable ages, are all assumptions which shock the reason, and must of necessity be destitute of proof.

(2.) These theories are atheistic. They deny the existence of a personal Being to whom we stand in the relation of creatures and children. The existence of such a Being is an innate, intuitive truth. It cannot be permanently disbelieved. And, therefore, any theory which denies the existence of God must be not only false but short-lived.

The Scriptural Doctrine.

The Scriptural doctrine on this subject is expressed in the first words of the Bible: "In the beginning God created the heaven and the earth." The heavens and the earth include all things out of God. Of which things the Scriptures teach that they owe their existence to the will and power of God. The Scriptural doctrine therefore is, (1.) That the universe is not eternal. It began to be. (2.) It was not formed out of any preëxistence or substance; but was created *ex nihilo*. (3.) That creation was not necessary. It was free to God to create or not to create, to create the universe as it is, or any other order and system of things, according to the good pleasure of his will.

The doctrine of an eternal creation has been held in various forms. Origen, although he referred the existence of the universe to the will of God, still held that it was eternal. We speak of the divine decrees as free and yet as from everlasting. So Origen held that this was not the first world God made; that there never was a first, and never will be a last. " Quid ante faciebat Deus," he asks, " quam mundus inciperet? Otiosam enim et immobile͏ dicere naturam Dei, impium est simul et absurdum, vel putare, quod bonitas aliquando bene non fecerit, et omnipotentia aliquando non egerit potentatum. Hoc nobis objicere solent dicentibus mundum hunc ex certo tempore cœpisse, et secundum scripturæ fidem annos quoque ætatis ipsius numerantibus. . . . . Nos vero consequenter respondimus observantes regulam pietatis, quoniam non tunc primum cum visibilem istum mundum fecit Deus, cœpit operari, sed sicut post corruptionem hujus erit alius mundus, ita et antequam hic esset, fuisse alios credimus." [1]

Of course those of the schoolmen who made the thoughts of God creative, or identified purpose with act, or who said with Scotus Erigena, "Non aliud Deo esse et velle et facere," must regard the universe as coeternal with God. This was done by Scotus in a pantheistic sense, but others who regarded the universe as distinct from God and dependent upon Him, still held that the world is eternal. The influence of the modern Monistic philosophy, even upon theologians who believe in an extramundane personal God, has been such as to lead many of them to assume that the relation between God and the world is such that it must have always existed. The common doctrine of the Church has ever been, in accordance with the simple teaching of the Bible, that the world began to be.

The second point included in the Scriptural doctrine of creation is, that the universe was not formed out of any preëxistent matter, nor out of the substance of God. The assumption that any thing existed out of God and independent of his will, has ever been rejected as inconsistent with the perfection and absolute supremacy of God. The other idea, however, namely, that God fashioned the world out of his own substance, has found advocates, more or less numerous, in every age of the Church. Augustine, referring to this opinion, says, " Fecisti cœlum et terram ; non de te : nam esset æquale unigenito tuo, ac per hoc et tibi, ... et aliud præter te non erat, unde faceres ea ; . . . . et ideo de nihilo fecisti cœlum et terram." [2]

Not only those of the schoolmen and of the modern theologians who are inclined to the Monistic theory, made all things to be modifications of the substance of God, but many Theistic and even Evangelical writers of our day hold the same doctrine.[3] Sir William Hamilton also held that it is impossible to conceive the complement of existence being either increased or diminished. When anything new appears we are forced to regard it as something which had previously existed in another form. "We are unable, on the one hand, to conceive nothing becoming something; or,

---

[1] *De Principiis*, III. v. 3. *Works*, edit. Paris, 1733, vol. i. p. 149, c, d.

[2] *Confessiones*, XII. 7. *Works*, edit. Benedictines, Paris, 1836, vol. i. p. 356, c, d.

[3] The writer was dining one day with Tholuck and five or six of his students, when he took up a knife from the table, and asked, " Is this knife of the substance of God ? " and they all answered, " Yes."

on the other, something becoming nothing. When God is said to create out of nothing, we construe this to thought by supposing that He evolves existence out of Himself; we view the Creator as the cause of the Universe. ' *Ex nihilo nihil, in nihilum nil posse reverti,*' expresses, in its purest form, the whole intellectual phenomenon of causality." [1] To this he elsewhere adds, " In like manner, we conceive annihilation, only by conceiving the Creator to withdraw his creation from actuality into power. . . . The mind is thus compelled to recognize an absolute identity of existence in the effect and in the complement of its causes — between the *causatum* and the *causa*," [2] and therefore, " an absolute identity of existence " between God and the world. This doctrine the fathers, and the Church generally, strenuously resisted as inconsistent with the nature of God. It supposes that the substance of God admits of partition or division; that the attributes of God can be separated from his substance; and that the divine substance can become degraded and polluted.

The third point included in the Scriptural doctrine of creation is, that it was an act of God's free will. He was free to create or not to create. This is opposed to the doctrine of necessary creation, which has been set forth in different forms. Some regard the phenomenal universe as a mere evolution of absolute being by a necessary process, as a plant is developed from a seed. Others, regarding God as a Spirit, make life and thought essential and coeternal with Him, and this life and power are of necessity creative. God's "essence," says Cousin, "consists precisely in his creative power." [3] Again, he says, [4] " He cannot but produce ; so that the creation ceases to be unintelligible ; and God is no more without a world than a world without God." As, however, thought is spontaneous, Cousin, when called to account for such utterances, maintained that he did not deny that creation was free.

Some who do not admit that God is under any natural or metaphysical necessity to give existence to the universe, still assert a moral necessity for the creation of sensitive and rational creatures. God, it is said, is love; but it is the nature of love to long to communicate itself, and to hold fellowship with others than itself. Therefore God's nature impels Him to call into existence creatures in whom and over whom He can rejoice. Others say, that God is

---

[1] *Lectures on Metaphysics.* Boston, edit. 1859, lecture xxxix. p. 533.

[2] *Discussions on Philosophy and Literature*, etc. By Sir William Hamilton. New York, édit. 1853, p. 575.

[3] Cousin's *Psychology*, New York, edit. 1856, p. 443.   [4] *Ibid.* p. 447

benevolence, and therefore is under a moral necessity of creating beings whom He can render happy. Thus Leibnitz says : " Dieu n'est point nécessité, métaphysiquement parlant, à la création de ce monde. . . . . Cependant Dieu est obligé, par une nécessité morale, à faire les choses en sorte qu'il ne se puisse rien de mieux."

According to the Scriptures God is self-sufficient. He needs nothing out of Himself for his own well-being or happiness. He is in every respect independent of his creatures ; and the creation of the universe was the act of the free will of that God of whom the Apostle says in Rom. xi. 36, " Of Him, and through Him, and to Him are all things."

The common faith of the Church on this subject is clearly and beautifully expressed by Melancthon : [2] " Quod autem res ex nihilo conditæ sint, docet hæc sententia : ipse dixit et facta sunt ; ipse mandavit, et creata sunt, id est dicente seu jubente Deo, res exortæ sunt : non igitur ex materia priore exstructæ sunt, sed Deo dicente, cum res non essent, esse cœperunt ; et cum Joannes inquit : Omnia per ipsum facta esse, refutat Stoicam imaginationem, quæ fingit materiam non esse factam."

§ 2. Mediate and Immediate Creation.

But while it has ever been the doctrine of the Church that God created the universe out of nothing by the word of his power, which creation was instantaneous and immediate, i. e., without the intervention of any second causes ; yet it has generally been admitted that this is to be understood only of the original call of matter into existence. Theologians have, therefore, distinguished between a first and second, or immediate and mediate creation. The one was instantaneous, the other gradual ; the one precludes the idea of any preëxisting substance, and of coöperation, the other admits and implies both. There is evident ground for this distinction in the Mosaic account of the creation. God, we are told, " created the heaven and the earth. And the earth was without form and void ; and darkness was upon the face of the deep. And the Spirit of God moved upon the face of the waters." Here it is clearly intimated that the universe, when first created, was in a state of chaos, and that by the life-giving, organizing power of the Spirit of God, it was gradually moulded into the wonderful cosmos which we now behold. The whole of the first chapter of Genesis, after the first verse, is an account of the progress of creation ; the

---

[1] Théodicée, ii. 201 ; Works, Berlin, 1840, p. 566.
[2] Loci Communes. de Creatione, edit. Erlangen, 1828, p. 48.

production of light; the formation of an atmosphere; the separation of land and water; the vegetable productions of the earth; the animals of the sea and air; then the living creatures of the earth; and, last of all, man. In Gen. i. 27, it is said that God created man male and female; in chapter ii. 7, it is said, that " the Lord God formed man of the dust of the ground." It thus appears that forming out of preëxisting material comes within the Scriptural idea of creating. We all recognize God as the author of our being, as our Creator, as well as our Preserver. He is our Creator, not merely because He is the maker of heaven and earth, and because all they contain owe their origin to his will and power, but also because, as the Psalmist teaches us, He fashions our bodies in secret. " Thine eyes," says the sacred writer, " did see my substance, yet being unperfect; and in thy book all my members were written, which in continuance were fashioned, when as yet there was none of them." (Ps. cxxxix. 16.) And the Bible constantly speaks of God as causing the grass to grow, and as being the real author or maker of all that the earth, air, or water produces. There is, therefore, according to the Scriptures, not only an immediate, instantaneous creation *ex nihilo* by the simple word of God, but a mediate, progressive creation; the power of God working in union with second causes.

Augustine clearly recognizes this idea. " Sicut in ipso grano invisibiliter erant omnia simul quæ per tempora in arborem surgerent; ita ipse mundus cogitandus est, cum Deus simul omnia creavit, habuisse simul omnia quæ in illo et cum illo facta sunt quando factus est dies : non solum cœlum cum sole et luna et sideribus, quorum species manet motu rotabili, et terram et abyssos, quæ velut inconstantes motus patiuntur, atque inferius adjuncta partem alteram mundo conferunt ; sed etiam illa quæ aqua et terra produxit potentialiter atque causaliter, priusquam per temporum moras ita exorirentur, quomodo nobis jam nota sunt in eis operibus, quæ Deus usque nunc operatur." [1]

Thus far there is little room for diversity of opinion. But when the question is asked, How long was the universe in passing from its chaotic to its ordered state? such diversity is at once manifested. According to the more obvious interpretation of the first chapter of Genesis, this work was accomplished in six days. This therefore has been the common belief of Christians. It is a belief founded on a given interpretation of the Mosaic record, which interpreta-

---

[1] *De Genesi ad Literam*, v. 45; *Works*, edit. Benedictines, Paris, 1836, vol. iii. pp. 321 d

tion, however, must be controlled not only by the laws of language, but by facts. This is at present an open question. The facts necessary for its decision have not yet been duly authenticated. The believer may calmly await the result.

The theistical advocates of the Nebular Hypothesis assume that the universe was an indefinitely long period in coming to its present state. God, intending to produce just such a universe as we see around us, instead of by a fiat calling the sun, moon, and stars, with all their marshalled hosts, into existence, created simply nebulous matter diffused through space; invested it with certain properties or forces; gave it a rotatory motion, and then allowed these physical laws under his guidance to work out the harmonious system of the heavens. As He is as truly the maker of the oak evolved from the acorn, according to the laws of vegetable life, as though He had called it into existence in its maturity by a word; so, it is maintained, He is as truly the creator of heaven and earth, on the nebular hypothesis, as on the assumption of instantaneous creation. This, however, is merely a hypothesis which has never commanded general assent among scientific men. It is, therefore, of no authority as a norm for the interpretation of Scripture.

The same theory of gradual, or mediate creation, has been applied to account for all the phenomena of the vegetable and animal kingdoms. This has been done in different forms. According to all these theories there must be something to begin with. There must be matter and its forces. There must even be life, and living organisms. To account for these we are forced to accept of the Scriptural doctrine of an immediate creation *ex nihilo* by the power of God.

§ 3. *Proof of the Doctrine.*

The proof of the doctrine of a creation *ex nihilo* does not rest on the usage of the words בָּרָא or κτίζειν, which are interchanged with עָשָׂה and ποιεῖν. God is said to have created the world, and also to be the maker of the heavens and the earth. Plants and animals are said to be created, although formed out of the dust of the earth. That, however, the Scriptures do teach this great doctrine of natural and revealed religion, is plain, —

1. From the fact that no mention is ever made of any preëxisting substance out of which the world was made. The original creation is never represented as a moulding of matter into form and imbuing it with life. Nor do the Scriptures ever represent the world as an emanation from God, proceeding from Him by a necessity of his nature. Much less does the Bible ever identify

God and the world. In thus ignoring all other doctrines, the Scriptures leave us under the necessity of believing that God created the world out of nothing.

2. The descriptions of the work of creation given in the Bible, preclude the idea of emanation or mere formation. God said, " Let there be light, and there was light." In Ps. xxxiii. 6, it is said, " By the word of the LORD were the heavens made ; and all the host of them by the breath of his mouth." And in verse 9 : " He spake and it was done ; he commanded and it stood fast." It was, therefore, in the words of Melancthon, already quoted, *Dicente seu jubente Deo*, that the universe was called into existence. " Nam quid est aliud tota creatura," Luther asks, " quam verbum Dei a Deo prolatum, seu productum foras ? . . . . Mundum et omnia creavit facillimo opere, dicendo scilicet, ut non plus negotii Deo sit in creatione, quam nobis in appellatione." [1]

3. The same doctrine is involved in the absolute dependence of all things on God, and in his absolute sovereignty over them. "Thou, even thou, art Jehovah alone ; thou hast made heaven, the heaven of heavens, with all their host, the earth, and all things that are therein, the seas, and all that is therein, and thou preservest them all." (Neh. ix. 6.) " By Him were all things created, that are in heaven, and that are in earth, visible and invisible, whether they be thrones, or dominions, or principalities, or powers : all things were created by Him, and for Him : and He is before all things, and by Him all things consist." (Col. i. 16, 17.) " Thou hast created all things, and for thy pleasure they are and were created." (Rev. iv. 11.) The all things spoken of in these passages is made to include everything out of God. There can, therefore, be no preëxisting matter, existing independently of his will. Everything out of God is said to owe its existence to his will.

4. The same doctrine is included in the Scripture doctrine that the universe (τὰ πάντα) is ἐκ θεοῦ, of God ; that He is its source, not in the Gnostic sense, but in the sense consistent with other representations of the Bible, which refer the existence of all things to the command of God. The universe, therefore, is " of Him " as its efficient cause.

5. The Apostle in Heb. xi. 3, begins his illustration of the nature and power of faith by referring to the creation as the great fundamental truth of all religion. If there be no creation, there is no God. If the universe was called into being out of nothing, then there must be an extramundane Being to whom it owes its exist-

---

[1] *Genesis*, i. 5; *Works*, Wittenberg edit. 1555 (Latin), vol. vi. leaf 5, p. 2.

ence. The creation is a fact which we know only by revelation. What the sacred writer here asserts is, First, that the worlds (αἰῶνες, all contained in time and space) were created, set in order, and established, by the simple word or command of God. Compare Ps. lxxiv. (lxxiii.) 16, in the Septuagint, σὺ κατηρτίσω ἥλιον καὶ σελήνην. Secondly, this being the case, it follows that the universe was not formed out of any preëxisting substance. Thirdly, God is not a mere former, but the creator of the ordered universe. The difference among commentators in the interpretation of this passage does not affect its general sense. The words are εἰς τὸ μὴ ἐκ φαινομένων τὰ βλεπόμενα γεγονέναι. The first question is whether εἰς τὸ expresses the design, or simply the consequence. In the former case, the meaning is that God created the worlds by a word *in order that;* i. e., in order that men might know that the things seen were not made of what already existed. In the latter, it is simply stated as a fact, that as creation was by a word, it was not out of any preëxisting substance. The other doubtful point in the passage is the construction of the negative particle μή. It may be connected with φαινομένων. This passage is then parallel with 2 Macc. vii. 28, ἐξ οὐκ ὄντων ἐποίησεν αὐτὰ ὁ θεός; in the Latin, " Peto, nate, ut aspicias ad cœlum, et terram, et ad omnia, quæ in eis sunt; et intelligas, quia ex nihilo fecit illa Deus, et hominum genus." Delitzsch, in his commentary on this Epistle, shows that neither the position of the negative before the preposition, nor the use of μή instead of οὐ is any valid objection to this interpretation. Others, however, prefer to connect the μή with γεγονέναι, i. e., " the worlds were not made out of the phenomenal." The sense in either case is substantially the same. But the question arises, What is the implied antithesis to the phenomenal? Some say the real, the ideal, the thoughts of God. Delitzsch says we must supply to μὴ ἐκ φαινομένων, ἀλλ᾽ ἐκ νοητῶν, " and these νοητά are the eternal invisible types, out of which, as their ideal ground and source, visible things by the fiat of God have proceeded." This is Platonism, and foreign to the Scriptural mode of thinking and teaching. Whatever is real is phenomenal; that is, every substance, everything which really exists manifests itself somewhere and somehow. The proper antithesis, therefore, to φαινομένων is οὐκ ὄντων. " The worlds were not made out of anything which reveals itself as existing even in the sight of God, but out of nothing."

In Rom. iv. 17, God is described as He " who quickeneth the dead, and calleth those things which be not, as though they were." *To call* may here be taken in the sense of commanding, controlling

by a word. The passage then expresses the highest idea of omnipotence. The actual and the possible are equally subject to his
will; the non-existing, the merely possible, is as much obedient to
Him as the actually existing. Or *to call* may as elsewhere mean,
as De Wette explains it, to call into existence. " Der das Nicht-
seiende als Seiendes hervorruft." *Who calls the* non-existing into
existence; " the ὡς ὄντα being for ὡς ἐσόμενα or for εἰς τὸ εἶναι ὡς ὄντα.
On this text Bengel says, "Cogita frequens illud יהי Gen. i. ex-
primitur transitus a *non esse* ad *esse*, qui sit *vocante* Deo. Conf. Ez.
xxxvi. 29." [1]

6. The Scriptural doctrine on this subject is confirmed by all
those passages which ascribe a beginning to the world. By the
world is not meant the κόσμος as distinguished from chaos, the form
as distinguished from the substance, but both together. According
to the Bible there is nothing eternal but God. He, and He alone
is The Eternal. This is his distinguishing title, — He who is and
was and ever shall be. As the world therefore began to be, and
as the world includes everything out of God, there was nothing of
which the world could be made. It was therefore created *ex nihilo*.
This is taught in the first chapter of Genesis, " In the beginning
(before anything was) God created the heaven and the earth."
In many other parts of Scripture a beginning is ascribed to the
world, as in Ps. xc. 2, " Before the mountains were brought forth,
or ever thou hadst formed the earth and the world, even from everlasting to everlasting, thou art God." Ps. cii. 25, " Of old hast
thou laid the foundation of the earth." In John xvii. 5, our Lord
speaks of the glory which he had with the Father before the world
was. The foundation of the world is an epoch. Then time began.
What was before the foundation of the world is eternal. The
world, therefore, is not eternal, and if not eternal it must have had
a beginning, and if all things had a beginning, then there must have
been a creation *ex nihilo*.

7. The doctrine of creation flows from the infinite perfection of
God. There can be but one infinite being. If anything exists
independent of his will, God is thereby limited. The idea of the
absolute dependence of all things on God pervades the Scripture
and is involved in our religious consciousness. The God of the
Bible is an extramundane God, existing out of, and before the
world, absolutely independent of it, its creator, preserver, and governor. So that the doctrine of creation is a necessary consequence
of Theism. If we deny that the world owes its existence to the

---

[1] *Gnomon*, edit. Tubingen, 1759, p. 614.

will of God, then Atheism, Hylozoism, or Pantheism would seem to be the logical consequence. Hence, on the one hand, the Scriptures make that doctrine so prominent, presenting it on the first page of the Bible as the foundation of all subsequent revelations concerning the nature of God and his relation to the world, and appointing from the beginning one day in seven to be a perpetual commemoration of the fact that God created the heaven and earth. And, on the other, the advocates of Atheism or Pantheism contend against the doctrine of creation as the primary error of all false philosophy and religion. "Die Annahme einer Schöpfung ist der Grund-Irrthum aller falschen Metaphysik und Religionslehre, und insbesondere das Ur-Princip des Juden- und Heidenthums." [1]

§ 4. *Objections to the Doctrine.*

1. It has in all ages been urged as an objection to the doctrine of creation that it is inconsistent with an axiom, *ex nihilo nihil fit.* That aphorism may, however, have two meanings. It may mean that no effect can be without a cause, — that nothing can produce nothing. In that sense it expresses a self-evident truth with which the doctrine of creation is perfectly consistent. That doctrine does not suppose that the world exists without a cause, or comes from nothing. It assigns a perfectly adequate cause for its existence in the will of an Almighty intelligent Being. In the other sense of the phrase it means that a creation *ex nihilo* is impossible, that God cannot cause matter, or anything else, to begin to be. In this sense it is not a self-evident truth, but an arbitrary assumption, and consequently without force or authority. It is indeed inconceivable; but so also are the ordinary operations of the human will inconceivable. No man can understand how mind acts on matter. As the world actually exists, we must admit either that it began to be, or that it is eternal. But the difficulties connected with this last assumption are, as we saw when arguing for the existence of God, far greater than those which attend the admission of a creation *ex nihilo*. It was partly the difficulty of conceiving of the non-existing passing into existence, and partly the need for a solution of the question concerning the origin of evil, that led Plato and other Greek philosophers to adopt the theory of the eternity of matter, which they regarded as the source of evil; a theory which passed over to Philo and to the Platonizing fathers. The Scriptural theory, or rather doctrine of the origin of evil, refers it to the free agency of rational creatures, and dispenses with the preëxistence of anything independent of God.

[1] Fichte, *Von seligen Leben,* Berlin, 1806, p. 160.

2. A more formidable objection, at least one which has had far more power, is that the doctrine of a creation in time is inconsistent with the true idea of God. This objection is presented in two forms. First, it is said, that the doctrine of creation supposes a distinction between will and power, or efficiency and purpose in the divine mind. Scotus Erigena [1] says, " Non aliud est Deo esse et facere, sed ei esse id ipsum est et facere. Coæternum igitur est Deo suum facere et coessentiale." This was the common doctrine of the scholastic theology which defined God to be *actus purus*, and denied any distinction in Him between essence and attributes, power and act. If this view of the nature of God be correct, then the doctrine that supposes that God's eternal purpose did not take effect from eternity, must be false. If God creates by thinking, He formed the world when He purposed it. Secondly, it is said that the doctrine of creation is inconsistent with the nature of God, inasmuch as it assumes a change in Him from inaction to activity. What was God doing, it is asked, from eternity before He created the world? If He is Creator and Lord, He must always have been such, and hence there must always have been a universe over which He ruled. These difficulties have led to different theories designed to avoid them. Origen, as before mentioned, taught that there has been an eternal succession of worlds. Others say that creation is eternal, although due to the will of God. He did from the beginning what the Scriptures say He did in the beginning. A foot from eternity standing in the dust, or a seal from eternity impressed upon wax, would be the cause of the impression, although the impression would be coeternal with the foot or seal. Pantheists make the world essential to God. He *exists* only in the world. " Das gottgleiche All ist nicht allein das ausgesprochene Wort Gottes (*natura naturata*) sondern selbst das sprechende (*natura naturans*); nicht das erschaffene, sondern das selbst schaffende und sich selbst offenbarende auf unendliche Weise." [2] That is, " The universe is not merely the outspoken word of God, but also that which speaks; not the created, but the self-creating and self-revealing in unending forms."

Answer to the above Objections.

With regard to the objections above mentioned, it may be remarked, —

1. That they are drawn from a region which is entirely beyond

---

[1] *De Divisione Naturæ*, i. 74.
[2] *Schelling*, by Strauss, Dogmatik, vol. i. p. 658.

our comprehension. They assume that we can understand the Almighty unto perfection and search out all his ways; whereas it is obvious that with regard to a Being who is eternal and not subject to the limitations of time, we are using words without meaning when we speak of successive duration in reference to Him. If with God there is no past or future, it is vain to ask what He was doing before creation. It was stated, when treating of the attributes of God, that there are two methods of determining our conceptions of the divine nature and operations. The one is to start with the idea of the Absolute and Infinite and make that idea the touchstone; affirming or denying what is assumed to be consistent or inconsistent therewith. Those who adopt this method, refuse to submit to the teachings of their moral nature or the revelations of the Word of God, and make Him either an absolutely unknown cause, or deny to Him all the attributes of a person. The other method is to start with the revelation which God has made of Himself in the constitution of our own nature and in his holy Word. This method leads to the conclusion that God can think and act, that in Him essence and attributes are not identical, that power and wisdom, will and working in Him, are not one and the same, and that the distinction between *potentia* (inherent power) and act applies to Him as well as to us. In other words, that God is infinitely more than pure activity, and consequently that it is not inconsistent with his nature that He should do at one time what He does not do at another.

2. A second remark to be made on these objections is that they prove too much. If valid against a creation in time, they are valid against all exercise of God's power in time. Then there is no such thing as providential government, or gracious operations of the Spirit, or answering prayer. If whatever God does He does from eternity, then, so far as we are concerned, He does nothing. If we exalt the speculative ideas of the understanding above our moral and religious nature, and above the authority of the Scriptures, we give up all ground both of faith and knowledge, and have nothing before us but absolute skepticism or atheism. These objections, therefore, are simply of our own making. We form an idea of the Absolute Being out of our own heads, and then reject whatever does not agree with it. They have, consequently, no force except for the man who makes them.

3. The scholastic theologians, who themselves were in the trammels of such philosophical speculations, were accustomed to answer these cavils by counter subtleties. Even Augustine says that God

did not create the world in time, because before creation time was not. " Si literæ sacræ maximeque veraces ita dicunt, in principio fecisse Deum cœlum et terram, ut nihil antea fecisse intelligatur, quia hoc potius in principio fecisse diceretur, si quid fecisset ante cœtera cuncta quæ fecit ; procul dubio non est mundus factus in tempore, sed cum tempore." [1] This is true enough. If time be duration measured by motion or succession, it is plain that before succession there can be no time. It is hard, however, to see how this relieves the matter. The fact remains that the world is not eternal, and therefore, in our mode of conception, there were infinite ages during which the world was not. Still the difficulty is purely subjective, arising from the limitations of our nature, which forbid our comprehending God, or our understanding the relation of his activity to the effects produced in time. All we know is that God does work and act, and that the effects of his activity take place successively in time.

4. As to the objection that the doctrine of creation supposes a change in God, the theologians answer that it does not suppose any change in his will or purpose, for he purposed from eternity to create. On this point Augustine [2] says, " Una eademque sempiterna et immutabili voluntate res quas condidit et ut prius non essent egit, quamdiu non fuerunt, et ut posterius essent, quando esse cœperunt." In other words, God did not purpose to create from eternity ; but from eternity he had the purpose to create. As there is no change of purpose involved in creation, so there is no change from inaction to activity involved in the doctrine. God is essentially active. But it does not follow that his activity is always the same, *i. e.*, that it must always produce the same effects. The eternal purpose takes effect just as was intended from the beginning. These objections, however, are mere cobwebs ; but they are cobwebs in the eye ; the eye of our feeble understanding. They are best got rid of by closing that eye, and opening what the Scriptures call " the eyes of the heart." That is, instead of submitting ourselves to the guidance of the speculative understanding, we should consent to be led by the Spirit as He reveals the things of God in his Word, and in our own moral and religious nature.

§ 5. *Design of the Creation.*

Men have long endeavoured to find a satisfactory answer to the question, Why God created the world ? What end was it designed to accomplish ? Answers to this question have been sought from

---

[1] *De Civitate Dei*, xi. 6, edit. *Benedictines*, vol. vii. p. 444, c, d.
[2] *De Civitate Dei*, xii. 17, edit. *Benedictines*, vol. vii. p. 508, b.

the following sources, — (1.) The nature of God himself. (2.) From the nature of his works and the course of history. (3.) From the declarations of the Scriptures. As to the first source, it is to be remarked that the systems which preclude the admission of final causes, as Materialism and Pantheism in all their forms, of course preclude any question as to the design of the creation. The world is the evolution of an unconscious, unintelligent force, which has no design out of itself. To ask what is the design of the world is, in these systems, equivalent to asking what is the design of the being of God ; for God is the world and the world is God. ,Those who admit the existence of an intelligent extramundane God, and who endeavour from his nature to determine the end for which He created the world, have pursued different courses and come to different conclusions. From the absolute self-sufficiency of God it follows that the creation was not designed to meet or satisfy any necessity on his part. He is neither more perfect nor more happy because of the creation. Again it follows from the nature of an infinite Being that the ground (i. e., both the motive and the end) of the creation must be in Himself. As all things are from Him and through Him, so also they are for Him. Some infer from his holiness that the purpose to create arose, so to speak, from the desire to have a field for the development of moral excellence in rational creatures. By far the most common opinion from the beginning has been that the creation is to be referred to the bonitas, goodness, benevolence, or, as the modern Germans at least generally express it, the love of God. As God is love, and the nature of love is to communicate itself, as it must have an object to be enjoyed and rendered blessed, so God created the world that He might rejoice in it and render it blessed. From the time of Leibnitz, who made this idea the foundation of his " Théodicée," this theory has assumed a more contracted form. He reduced love to mere benevolence, or the desire to promote happiness. Hence the end of the creation was assumed to be the production of happiness. And as God is infinite, not only in benevolence, but also in wisdom and power, this world is necessarily the best possible world for the production of happiness. This theory is very fruitful of consequences. (1.) As all virtue consists in benevolence, happiness must be the highest good. Holiness is good only because it tends to happiness. It has no virtue of its own. (2.) Whatever tends to promote happiness is right. There is no such thing as sin. What we call sin, if a necessary means of the greatest good, becomes virtue. It is evil only so far as it has a contrary tendency. And as under the government of God all sin, past or present, does secure a greater amount of happiness than would otherwise be possible, there is really no sin in the universe. (3.) This is generalized into the principle that it is right to do evil that good may come. This is the principle on which God acts, according to this theory, and it is the principle on which men are entitled and bound to act; and on which in point of fact they do act. The question which on every occasion their doctrine presents for decision is necessarily, What will be the consequence of a certain act or course of conduct? Will it promote happiness or the reverse? and the answer decides the course to be pursued. The Jesuits have worked out this theory into a science, and are enabled to determine beforehand when murder, perjury, and blasphemy become virtues. As this doctrine revolts the moral sense, its adoption is necessarily degrading. Few principles, therefore, have been so productive of false doctrine and immorality as the principle that all virtue consists in benevolence, that happiness is the highest good, and that whatever promotes happiness is right.

The Scriptural Doctrine as to the Design of Creation.

It is obviously in vain for man to attempt to determine the design of the creation from the nature of God's works and from the course of his providence. That would require a knowledge of the whole universe and of its history to its consummation. The only satisfactory method of determining the question is by appealing to the Scriptures. There it is explicitly taught that the glory of God, the manifestation of his perfections, is the last end of all his works. This is, (1.) The highest possible end. The knowledge of God is eternal life. It is the source of all holiness and all blessedness to rational creatures. (2.) This in the Bible is declared to be the end of the universe as a whole; of the external world or works of nature; of the plan of redemption; of the whole course of history; of the mode in which God administers his providence and dispenses his grace; and of particular events, such as the choice of the Israelites and all the dealings of God with them as a nation. It is the end which all rationa. creatures are commanded to keep constantly in view; and it comprehends and secures all other right ends. The common objection, that this doctrine represents God as self-seeking, has already been answered. God, as infinitely wise and good, seeks the highest end; and as all creatures are as the dust of the balance compared to Him, it follows that his glory is an infinitely higher end than anything that concerns them exclusively. For a creature to seek his own glory or happiness in preference to that of God, is folly and sin, because he is utterly insignificant. He prefers a trifle to what is of infinite importance. He sacrifices, or endeavours to sacrifice, an end which involves the highest excellence of all creatures, to his own advantage. He serves the creature more than the Creator. He prefers himself to God. Many theologians endeavour to combine these different views as to the design of the creation. They say that the highest end is the glory of God, and the subordinate end the good of his creatures. Or, they say that the two are the same. God purposes to glorify Himself in the happiness of his creatures; or to promote the happiness of his creatures as a means of manifesting his glory. But this is only to confuse and confound the matter. The end is one thing; the consequences another. The end is the glory of God; the consequences of the attainment of that end are undoubtedly the highest good (not necessarily the greatest amount of happiness), and that highest good may include much sin and much misery so far as individuals are concerned. But the highest good is that God should be known.

§ 6. *The Mosaic Account of the Creation.*

There are three methods of interpreting this portion of the Bible. (1.) The historical. (2.) The allegorical. (3.) The mythical. The first assumes it to be a veritable history. The second has two forms. Many of the Fathers who allegorized the whole of the Old Testament without denying its historical verity, allegorized in like manner the history of the creation. That is, they sought for a hidden moral or spiritual sense under all historical facts. Others regarded it as purely an allegory without any historical basis, any more than the parables of our Lord. The mythical theory, as the name imports, regards the record of the creation as a mere fable, or fabulous cosmogony, designed to express a theory as to the origin of the universe, of man, and of evil, of no more value than the similar cosmogonies which are found in the early literature of all nations. In favour of the historical character of the record are the following considerations, — (1.) It purports to be a veritable history. (2.) It is the appropriate and necessary introduction of an acknowledged history. (3.) It is referred to and quoted in other parts of the Bible as the true account of the creation of the world; especially in the fourth commandment, where, as well as in other parts of Scripture, it is made the foundation of the institution of the Sabbath. (4.) The facts here recorded, including as they do the creation and probation of man, lie at the foundation

of the whole revealed plan of redemption. The whole Bible, therefore, rests upon the record here given of the work of creation, and
consequently all the evidence which goes to support the divine
authority of the Bible, tends to sustain the historical verity of that
record.

Objections to the Mosaic Account of the Creation.

The principal objections to the Mosaic account of the creation
are either critical, astronomical, or geological. Under the first
head it is objected that the account is inconsistent with itself, especially in what is said of the creation of man ; and that it is evidently
composed of independent documents, in one of which God is called
אֱלֹהִים, and in the other יְהוָֹה. The former of these objections is
answered by showing that the two accounts of the creation are not
inconsistent ; the one is a concise statement of the fact, the other
a fuller account of the manner of its occurrence. As to the second
objection, it is enough to say that, admitting the fact on which it is
founded, it creates no difficulty in the way of acknowledging the
historical character of the record. It is of no importance to us
whence Moses derived his information, whether from one or more
historical documents, from tradition, or from direct revelation. We
receive the account on his authority and on the authority of the
Book of which it is a recognized and authentic portion.

The astronomical objections are, (1.) That the whole account
evidently assumes that our earth is the centre of the universe, and
that the sun, moon, and stars are its satellites. (2.) That light is
said to have been created and the alternation between day and
night established before the creation of the sun ; and (3.) That
the visible heavens are represented as a solid expanse. The first
of these objections bears with as much force against all the representations of the Bible and the language of common life. Men
instinctively form their language according to apparent, and not
absolute or scientific truth. They speak of the sun as rising and
setting ; of its running its course through the heavens, although
they know that this is only apparently and not really true. The
language of the Bible on this, as well as on all other subjects, is
framed in accordance with the common usage of men. The
second objection is founded on the assumption that the fourteenth
verse speaks of the creation of the sun and other heavenly bodies.
This is not its necessary meaning. The sense may be that God
then appointed the sun and moon to the service of measuring and
regulating times and seasons. But even if the other interpretation
be adopted, there need be no conflict between the record and the

astronomical fact that the sun is now the source of light to the world. The narrative makes a distinction between the cosmical light mentioned in the earlier part of the chapter, and the light emanating from the sun, specially designed for our globe. The third objection is met by the remark already made. If we speak of the concave heavens, why might not the Hebrews speak of the solid heavens? The word firmament applied to the visible heavens is as familiar to us as it was to them. Calvin well remarks, " Moses vulgi ruditati se accommodans, non alia Dei opera com-memorat in historia creationis, nisi quæ oculis nostris occurrunt."[1]

Geology and the Bible.

The geological objections to the Mosaic record are apparently the most serious. According to the commonly received chronology, our globe has existed only a few thousand years. According to geologists, it must have existed for countless ages. And again, according to the generally received interpretation of the first chapter of Genesis, the process of creation was completed in six days, whereas geology teaches that it must have been in progress through periods of time which cannot be computed.

Admitting the facts to be as geologists would have us to believe, two methods of reconciling the Mosaic account with those facts have been adopted. First, some understand the first verse to refer to the original creation of the matter of the universe in the indefinite past, and what follows to refer to the last reorganizing change in the state of our earth to fit it for the habitation of man. Second, the word day as used throughout the chapter is understood of geological periods of indefinite duration.

In favour of this latter view it is urged that the word day is used in Scripture in many different senses; sometimes for the time the sun is above the horizon; sometimes for a period of twenty-four hours; sometimes for a year, as in Lev. xxv. 29, Judges xvii. 10, and often elsewhere; sometimes for an indefinite period, as in the phrases, " the day of your calamity," " the day of salvation," " the day of the Lord," " the day of judgment." And in this account of the creation it is used for the period of light in antithesis to night; for the separate periods in the progress of creation; and then, ch. ii. 4, for the whole period: " In the day that the Lord God made the earth and the heavens."

It is of course admitted that, taking this account by itself, it would be most natural to understand the word in its ordinary

[1] *Institutio*, I. xiv. 3; edit. Berlin, 1834, p. 112.

sense ; but if that sense brings the Mosaic account into conflict with facts, and another sense avoids such conflict, then it is obligatory on us to adopt that other. Now it is urged that if the word " day " be taken in the sense of " an indefinite period of time," a sense which it undoubtedly has in other parts of Scripture, there is not only no discrepancy between the Mosaic account of the creation and the assumed facts of geology, but there is a most marvellous coincidence between them.

The cosmogony of modern science teaches that the universe, " the heaven and the earth," was first in a chaotic or gaseous state. The process of its development included the following steps: (1.) " Activity begun, — light an immediate result. (2.) The earth made an independent sphere. (3.) Outlining of the land and water, determining the earth's general configuration. (4.) The idea of life in the lowest plants, and afterwards, if not contemporaneously, in the lowest or systemless animals, or Protozoans. (5.) The energizing light of the sun shining on the earth — an essential preliminary to the display of the systems of life. (6.) Introduction of the systems of life. (7.) Introduction of mammals — the highest order of the vertebrates, — the class afterwards to be dignified by including a being of moral and intellectual nature. (8.) Introduction of man." [1]

Professor Dana further says, " The order of events in the Scripture cosmogony corresponds essentially with that which has been given. There was first a void and formless earth : this was literally true of the ' heavens and the earth,' if they were in the condition of a gaseous fluid. The succession is as follows: —

" 1. Light.

" 2. The dividing of the waters below from the waters above the earth (the word translated waters may mean fluid).

" 3. The dividing of the land and water on the earth.

" 4. Vegetation ; which Moses, appreciating the philosophical characteristic of the new creation distinguishing it from previous inorganic substances, defines as that ' which had seed in itself.'

" 5. The sun, moon, and stars.

" 6. The lower animals, those that swarm in the waters, and the creeping and flying species of the land.

" 7. Beasts of prey (' creeping ' here meaning prowling).

" 8. Man.

---

[1] *Manual of Geology.* By James D. Dana, M. A., LL. D., Silliman Professor of Geology and Natural History in Yale College, p. 743.

" In this succession, we observe not merely an order of events, like that deduced from science ; there is a system in the arrangement, and a far-reaching prophecy, to which philosophy could not have attained, however instructed.

" The account recognizes in creation two great eras of three days each, — an Inorganic and an Organic. Each of these eras opens with the appearance of light; the first, light cosmical ; the second, light from the sun for the special uses of the earth.

" Each era ends in ' a day ' of two great works — the two shown to be distinct by being severally pronounced ' good.' On the third day, that closing the Inorganic Era, there was first the dividing of the land from the waters, and afterwards the creation of vegetation, or the institution of a kingdom of life — a work widely diverse from àll that preceded it in the era. So on the sixth day, terminating the Organic Era, there was first the creation of mammals, and then a second far greater work, totally new in its grandest element, the creation of Man.

" The arrangement is, then, as follows : —

" I. *The Inorganic Era.*

" 1st Day. — Light cosmical.

" 2d Day. — The earth divided from the fluid around it, or individualized.

" 3d Day. — $\begin{cases} 1. \text{ Outlining of the land and water.} \\ 2. \text{ Creation of vegetation.} \end{cases}$

" II. *The Organic Era.*

" 4th Day. — Light from the sun.

" 5th Day. — Creation of the lower order of animals.

" 6th Day. — $\begin{cases} 1. \text{ Creation of mammals.} \\ 2. \text{ Creation of man.''} \end{cases}$

" The record in the Bible," adds Professor Dana,[1] " is therefore profoundly philosophical in the scheme of creation which it presents. It is both true and divine. It is a declaration of authorship, both of creation and the Bible, on the first page of the sacred volume."[2] To the same effect he elsewhere says : " The first thought that strikes the scientific reader [of the Mosaic account of the creation] is the evidence of divinity, not merely in the first verse of the record, and the successive fiats, but in the whole order of creation.

[1] Page 745.   [2] Page 746.

There is so much that the most recent readings of science have for the first time explained, that the idea of man as the author becomes utterly incomprehensible. By proving the record true, science pronounces it divine ; for who could have correctly narrated the secrets of eternity but God himself ? " [1]

The views given in his " Manual of Geology " are more fully elaborated by Professor Dana in two admirable articles in the " Bibliotheca Sacra " (January and July, 1856). He says, in the former of those articles, " The best views we have met with on the harmony between science and the Bible, are those of Professor Arnold Guyot, a philosopher of enlarged comprehension of nature and a truly Christian spirit ; and the following interpretations of the sacred record are, in the main, such as we have gathered from personal intercourse with him." [2]

Professor Dana of Yale and Professor Guyot of Princeton, belong to the first rank of scientific naturalists ; and the friends of the Bible owe them a debt of gratitude for their able vindication of the sacred record.

As the Bible is of God, it is certain that there can be no conflict between the teachings of the Scriptures and the facts of science. It is not with facts, but with theories, believers have to contend. Many such theories have, from time to time, been presented, apparently or really inconsistent with the Bible. But these theories have either proved to be false, or to harmonize with the Word of God, properly interpreted. The Church has been forced more than once to alter her interpretation of the Bible to accommodate the discoveries of science. But this has been done without doing any violence to the Scriptures or in any degree impairing their authority. Such change, however, cannot be effected without a struggle. It is impossible that our mode of understanding the Bible should not be determined by our views of the subjects of which it treats. So long as men believed that the earth was the centre of our system, the sun its satellite, and the stars its ornamentation, they of necessity understood the Bible in accordance with that hypothesis. But when it was discovered that the earth was only one of the smaller satellites of the sun, and that the stars were worlds, then faith, although at first staggered, soon grew strong enough to take it all in, and rejoice to find that the Bible, and the Bible alone of all ancient books, was in full accord with these stupendous revelations

---

[1] *Bibliotheca Sacra* for January, 1856, p. 110.

[2] The views of Professor Guyot are presented at some length by the Rev. J. O. Means, in the numbers of the *Bibliotheca Sacra* for January and April, 1855.

of science.   And so if it should be proved tnat the creation was a process continued through countless ages, and that the Bible alone of all the books of antiquity recognized that fact, then, as Professor Dana says, the idea of its being of human origin would become " utterly incomprehensible."

CHAPTER XI.

§ 1. *Preservation.*

God's works of providence are his most holy, wise, and powerful preserving and governing all his creatures and all their actions. Providence, therefore, includes preservation and government. By preservation is meant that all things out of God owe the continuance of their existence, with all their properties and powers, to the will of God. This is clearly the doctrine of the Scriptures. The passages relating to this subject are very numerous. They are of different kinds. First, some assert in general terms that God does sustain all things by the word of his power, as Heb. i. 3 ; Col. i. 17, where it is said, " By Him all things consist," or continue to be. In Nehem. ix. 6, " Thou, even thou art Lord alone ; thou hast made heaven, the heaven of heavens, with all their hosts, the earth, and all things that are therein, the seas, and all that is therein, and thou preservest them all." Secondly, those which refer to the regular operations or powers of nature, which are declared to be preserved in their efficiency by the power of God. See Psalms civ. and cxlviii. throughout, and many similar passages. Thirdly, those which relate to irrational animals. And Fourthly, those which relate to rational creatures, who are said to live, move, and to have their being in God. These passages clearly teach, (1.) That the universe as a whole does not continue in being of itself. It would cease to exist if unsupported by his power. (2.) That all creatures, whether plants or animals, in their several genera, species, and individuals, are continued in existence not by any inherent principle of life, but by the will of God. (3.) That this preservation extends not only to the substance but also to the form ; not only to the essence, but also to the qualities, properties, and powers of all created things.

The Nature of Preservation.

This doctrine, thus clearly taught in the Scriptures, is so consonant to reason and to the religious nature of man, that it is not de-

nied among Christians. The only question is as to the nature of
the divine efficiency to which the continued existence of all things
is to be referred. On this subject there are three general opinions.

First, That of those who assume that everything is to be referred
to the original purpose of God. He created all things and determined that they should continue in being according to the laws
which He impressed upon them at the beginning. There is no
need, it is said, of supposing his continued intervention for their
preservation. It is enough that He does not will that they should
cease to be. This is the theory adopted by the Remonstrants and
generally by the Deists of modern times. According to this view,
God is seated on his throne in the heavens, a mere spectator of the
world and of its operations, exerting no direct efficiency in sustaining the things which He has made. Thus Limborch [1] describes
preservation, as held by many, to be merely an " actus negativus
. . . . [quo Deus] essentias, vires ac facultates rerum creatarum
non vult destruere ; sed eas vigori suo per creationem indito, quoad
usque ille perdurare potest relinquere." To this view it is to be
objected, —

1. That it is obviously opposed to the representations of the
Bible. According to the uniform and pervading teaching of the
Scriptures, God is not merely a God afar off. He is not a mere
spectator of the universe which He has made, but is everywhere
present in his essence, knowledge, and power. To his sustaining
hand the continuance of all things is constantly referred ; and if
He withdraws his presence they cease to be. This is so plainly the
doctrine of the Bible that it is admitted so to be by many whose
philosophical views constrain them to reject the doctrine for themselves.

2. It is inconsistent with the absolute dependence of all things
on God. It supposes creatures to have within themselves a principle of life, derived originally, indeed, from God, but capable of
continued being and power without his aid. The God of the Bible
is everywhere declared to be the all-sustaining ground of all that
is, so that if not upheld by the word of his power, they would cease
to be. The Scriptures expressly distinguish the power by which
things were created from that by which they are continued. All
things were not only created by Him, says the Apostle, but by
Him all things consist. (Col. i. 17.) This language clearly
teaches that the almighty power of God is as much concerned in
the continued existence, as in the original creation of all things.

[1] *Theologia Christiana*, ii. xxv. 7, edit. Amsterdam, 1700, p. 134.

3. This doctrine does violence to the instinctive religious convictions of all men. Even those the least enlightened live and act
under the conviction of absolute dependence. They recognize
God as everywhere present and everywhere active. If they do
not love and trust Him, they at least fear Him and instinctively
deprecate his wrath. They cannot, without doing violence to the
constitution of their nature, look upon God as a being who is a
mere spectator of the creatures who owe their existence to his will.

Preservation not a Continued Creation.

A second view of the nature of preservation goes to the opposite extreme of confounding creation and preservation. This opinion has been held in different forms, —

1. It is sometimes said that preservation and creation are to be
referred to one and the same divine act. So far, therefore, as God
is concerned, the two are identical. This ground is taken by many
who admit the reality of the world and the efficiency of second
causes. They intend by this mode of representation to deny any
succession in the acts of God. He cannot be viewed as acting in
time, or as doing in time what He has not done from eternity.

2. Others who represent preservation as a continued creation,
only mean that the divine efficiency is as really active in the one
case as in the other. They wish to deny that anything out of God
has the cause of the continuance of its existence in itself; and that
its properties or powers are in any such sense inherent as that they
preserve their efficiency without the continued agency of God.
This is the sense in which most of the Reformed theologians are to
be understood when they speak of preservation as a continuous
creation. Thus Heidegger[1] says, " Conservatio continuata creatio
Dei activa est. Si enim creatio et conservatio duæ actiones dis-
tinctæ forent, creatio primo cessaret, ac tum conservatio vel eodem,
quo creatio cessavit, vel sequenti momento inciperet." This only
means that the world owes its continued existence to the uninterrupted exercise of the divine power. He therefore elsewhere
says, " Conservationi annihilatio opponitur. Cessante actione con-
servante res in nihilum collabitur." In like manner Alsted[2] says,
" Conservatio est quædam continuatio. Quemadmodum creatio est
prima productio rei ex nihilo, ita est conservatio rei continuatio, ne
in nihilum recidat. Deus mundum sustinet." Ryssenius (whose
work is principally from Turrettin),[3] says " Providentia bene altera

---

[1] Heidegger, *Corpus Theologiæ*, loc. vii. 22, Tiguri, 1732, p. 251.
[2] Alsted, *Theol. Didact.*, Hanoviæ, 1627, p. 283.   [3] *Summa Theologiæ*, I. 209 ; *Ibid.*

creatio, dicitur.   Nam eadem voluntate, qua Deus omnia creavit,
omnia conservat, et creatio a conservatione in eo tantum differt,
quod quando voluntatem Dei sequitur rerum existentia, dicitur
creatio ; quando res eadem per eandem voluntatem durat, dicitur
conservatio."   This amounts only to saying that as God created all
things by the word of his power, so also He upholds all things by
the word of his power.

3. There is, however, a third form in which this doctrine is held.
By continued creation is meant that all efficiency is in God ; that
all effects are to be referred to his agency.   As there was no coöperation in calling the world out of nothing, so there is no coöperation of second causes in its continuance and operations.   God
creates, as it were, *de novo* at each instant the universe, as at that
moment it actually is.

Objections to the Doctrine of a Continuous Creation.

All these modes of representation, however, are objectionable.
Creation, preservation, and government are in fact different, and to
identify them leads not only to confusion but to error.   Creation
and preservation differ, first, as the former is the calling into existence what before did not exist; and the latter is continuing, or
causing to continue what already has a being ; and secondly, in
creation there is and can be no coöperation, but in preservation
there is a *concursus* of the first, with second causes.   In the Bible,
therefore, the two things are never confounded.   God created all
things, and by Him all things consist.   As to the first mentioned
of the three forms of the doctrine of a continued creation, it is
enough to remark that it rests on the *à priori* idea of an absolute
Being.   It is not only a gratuitous, but an unscriptural assumption
which denies all difference between will and efficiency, or between
power and act in God.   And as to the idea that God's acts are not
successive ; that He never does in time what He does not do from
eternity, it is obvious that such language has for us no meaning.
We cannot comprehend the relation which the efficiency of God
has to the effects produced successively.   We know, however,
that God acts ; that He does produce successive effects ; and that,
so far as we are concerned, and so far as the representations of
Scripture are concerned, our relation to God and the relation of
the world to Him, are precisely what they would be if his acts were
really successive.   It is the height of presumption in man, on the
mere ground of our speculative ideas, to depart from the plain
representations of Scriptures, and so to conceive of the relation of

God to the world as effectually to make Him an unknown Being, merging all his perfections into the general idea of cause.

The objection to the second form of the doctrine is not to the idea meant to be expressed. It is true that the preservation of the world is as much due to the immediate power of God as its creation, but this does not prove that preservation is creation. Creation is the production of something out of nothing. Preservation is the upholding in existence what already is. This form of the doctrine is therefore a false use of terms. A more serious objection, however, is that this mode of expression tends to error. The natural sense of the words is what those who use them admit to be false, and not only false but dangerous.

To the real doctrine of a continuous creation the objections are far more serious,—

1. It destroys all continuity of existence. If God creates any given thing every moment out of nothing, it ceases to be the same thing. It is something new, however similar to what existed before. It is as much disconnected from what preceded it as the world itself when it arose out of nothing, was disconnected from the previous nothingness.

2. This doctrine effectually destroys all evidence of the existence of an external world. What we so regard, the impressions on our senses which we refer to things out of ourselves, are merely inward states of consciousness produced momentarily by the creating energy of God. Idealism is, therefore, the logical, as it has been the historical consequence of the theory in question. If all necessity for the existence of an external world is done away with, that existence must be discarded as an unphilosophical assumption.

3. This theory of course denies the existence of second causes. God becomes the sole agent and the sole cause in the universe. The heavens and earth with all their changes and with all they contain, are but the pulsations of the universal life of God. If preservation be a continued production out of nothing, of everything that exists, then every material existence, all properties of matter so called, every human soul, and every human thought and feeling, is as much the direct product of divine omnipotence as the original creation. There cannot, therefore, be any causation out of God, or any coöperation of any kind any more than when He said, Let there be light, and there was light. In the same manner He constantly now says, Let men exist with all the thoughts, purposes, and feelings, which constitute their nature and character for the time being, and they are.

4. On this theory there can be no responsibility, no sin and no holiness. If sin exist, it must be referred to God as much as holiness, for all is due to his creating energy.

5. Between this system and Pantheism there is scarcely a dividing line. Pantheism merges the universe in God, but not more effectually than the doctrine of a continuous creation. God in the one case as truly as in the other, is all that lives. There is no power, no cause, no real existence but the efficiency and causality of God. This is obvious, and is generally admitted. Hagenbach [1] says, "Creation out of nothing rests on Theism. It becomes deistic if creation and preservation are violently separated and placed in direct opposition to each other; and pantheistic if creation be made a mere moment in preservation." "In creation," says Strauss, "God works all, the creature which is thus first produced, nothing." If, therefore, preservation is only the continuance of the same relation between God and the creature, it follows that God still effects everything and the creature nothing; hence out of God, or other than God, there are no causes, not even occasional. Leibnitz,[2] quotes Bayle as saying, "Il me semble, qu'il en faut conclure, que Dieu fait tout, et qu'il n'y a point dans toutes les créatures de causes premières, ni secondes, ni même occasionelles." And again, "On ne peut dire que Dieu me crée premièrement, et qu' étant crée, il produise avec moi mes mouvemens et mes déterminations. Cela est insoutenable pour deux raisons : la première est, que quand Dieu me crée ou me conserve à cet instant, il ne me conserve pas comme un être sans forme, comme une espèce ou quelque autre des universaux de logique. Je suis un individu ; il me crée et conserve comme tel, étant tout ce que je suis dans cet instant avec toutes mes dépendances." To make preservation, therefore, a continued creation, leads to conclusions opposed to the essential truths of religion, and at variance with our necessary beliefs. We are forced by the constitution of our nature to believe in the external world and in the reality of second causes. We know from consciousness that we are the responsible authors of our own acts, and that we continue identically the same substance, and consequently are not created out of nothing from moment to moment.

This subject will come up again when treating of President Edwards' theory of identity, and its application to the relation between Adam and his race.

---

[1] *Dogmengeschichte,* II. Zweite Hälfte, p. 288, edit. Leipzig, 1841.
[2] *Théodicée,* III. 386; *Opera,* edit. Berlin, 1840, p. 615.

Scriptural Doctrine on the Subject.

Between the two extremes of representing preservation as a mere negative act, a not willing to destroy, which denies any continued efficiency of God in the world; and the theory which resolves everything into the immediate agency of God, denying the reality of all second causes, is the plain doctrine of the Scriptures, which teaches that the continuance of the world in existence, the preservation of its substance, properties, and forms, is to be referred to the omnipresent power of God. He upholds as He creates all things, by the word of his power. How He does this it is vain to inquire. So long as we cannot tell how we move our lips, or how mind can operate on matter, or in what way the soul is present and operative in the whole body, it requires little humility to suppress the craving curiosity to know how God sustains the universe with all its hosts in being and activity. The theologians of the seventeenth century endeavoured to explain this by a general *concursus*, or, as they called it, influx of God into all his creatures. It is said to be an " Actus positivus et directus, quo Deus in genere in causas efficientes rerum conservandas influxu vero et reali influit, ut in natura, proprietatibus et viribus suis persistant ac permaneant." [1] But what do we gain by saying that the soul by " a true and real influx " operates in every part of the body. The fact is clearly revealed that God's agency is always and everywhere exercised in the preservation of his creatures, but the mode in which his efficiency is exerted, further than that it is consistent with the nature of the creatures themselves and with the holiness and goodness of God, is unrevealed and inscrutable. It is best, therefore, to rest satisfied with the simple statement that preservation is that omnipotent energy of God by which all created things, animate and inanimate, are upheld in existence, with all the properties and powers with which He has endowed them.

§ 2. Government.
Statement of the Doctrine.

Providence includes not only preservation, but government. The latter includes the ideas of design and control. It supposes an end to be attained, and the disposition and direction of means for its accomplishment. If God governs the universe He has some great end, including an indefinite number of subordinate ends, towards which it is directed, and He must control the sequence of

[1] Hollaz, *Examen Theologicum*, edit. Leipzig, 1763, p. 441.

all events, so as to render certain the accomplishment of all his purposes. Of this providential government the Scriptures teach, (1.) That it is universal, including all the creatures of God, and all their actions. The external world, rational and irrational creatures, things great and small, ordinary and extraordinary, are equally and always under the control of God. The doctrine of providence excludes both necessity and chance from the universe, substituting for them the intelligent and universal control of an infinite, omnipresent God. (2.) The Scriptures also teach that this government of God is powerful. It is the universal sway of omnipotence which renders certain the accomplishment of his designs, which embrace in their compass everything that occurs. (3.) That it is wise ; which means not only that the ends which God has in view are consistent with his infinite wisdom, and that the means employed are wisely adapted to their respective objects, but also that his control is suited to the nature of the creatures over which it is exercised. He governs the material world according to fixed laws which He himself has established ; irrational animals by their instincts, and rational creatures agreeably to their nature. (4.) God's providence is holy. That is, there is nothing in the ends proposed, the means adopted, or the agency employed, inconsistent with his infinite holiness, or which the highest moral excellence does not demand. This is all that the Scriptures reveal on this most important and difficult subject. And here it were well could the subject be allowed to rest. It is enough for us to know that God does govern all his creatures and all their actions, and that his government while absolutely efficacious is infinitely wise and good, directed to secure the highest ends, and perfectly consistent with his own perfections and with the nature of his creatures. But men have insisted upon answering the questions, How does God govern the world ? What is the relation between his agency and the efficiency of second causes ? and especially, How can God's absolute control be reconciled with the liberty of rational agents ? These are questions which never can be solved. But as philosophers insist upon answering them, it becomes necessary for theologians to consider those answers, and to show their fallacy when they conflict with the established facts of revelation and experience. Before considering the more important of the theories which have been advanced to explain the nature of God's providential government, and his relation to the world, it will be proper to present a brief outline of the argument, in support of the truth of the doctrine as stated above.

A. *Proof of the Doctrine.*

This doctrine necessarily flows from the Scriptural idea of God. He is declared to be a personal being, infinite in wisdom, goodness, and power; to be the Father of Spirits. From this it follows not only that He acts intelligently, *i. e.*, with a view to an end, and on sufficient reasons, but that He must be concerned for the good of creatures rational and irrational, great and small. The idea that God would create this vast universe teeming with life in all its forms, and exercise no control over it, to secure it from destruction or from working out nothing but evil, is utterly inconsistent with the nature of God. And to suppose that anything is too great to be comprehended in his control, or anything so minute as to escape his notice; or that the infinitude of particulars can distract his attention, is to forget that God is infinite. It cannot require any effort in Him, the omnipresent and infinite intelligence, to comprehend and to direct all things however complicated, numerous, or minute. The sun diffuses its light through all space as easily as upon any one point. God is as much present everywhere, and with everything, as though He were only in one place, and had but one object of attention. The common objection to the doctrine of a universal providence, founded on the idea that it is incompatible with the dignity and majesty of the divine Being to suppose that He concerns himself about trifles, assumes that God is a limited being; that because we can attend to only one thing at a time, it must be so with God. The more exalted are our conceptions of the divine Being, the less shall we be troubled with difficulties of this kind.

Proof from the Evidence of the Operation of Mind everywhere.

The whole universe, so far as it can be subjected to our observation, exhibits evidence of God's omnipresent intelligence and control. Mind is everywhere active. There is everywhere manifest the intelligent adaptation of means to an end; as well in the organization of the animalcule which it requires the microscope to reveal, as in the order of the heavenly bodies. This mind is not in matter. It is not a blind *vis naturæ*. It is, and must be the intelligence of an infinite, omnipresent Being. It is just as much beyond the power of a creature to form an insect, as it is to create the universe. And it is as unreasonable to assume that the organized forms of the vegetable and animal worlds are due to the laws of nature, as it would be to assume that a printing-press could be constructed to compose a poem. There is no adaptation or relation between the means and the end. Wherever there is the intelligent adaptation of means to an end, there is evidence of the presence of mind. And as such evidence of mental activity is found in every part of the universe, we see God ever active and everywhere present in all his works.

Argument from our Religious Nature.

The Scriptural doctrine of a universal providence is demanded by the religious nature of man. It is therefore an instinctive and necessary belief. It is banished from the mind, or overruled only by persistent effort. In the first place, we cannot but regard it as a limitation of God to suppose Him absent either as to knowledge or power from any part of his creation. In the second place, our sense of dependence involves the conviction not only that we owe our existence to his will, but that it is in Him that we and all his creatures live, move, and have our being. In the third place, our sense of responsibility implies that God is cognizant of all our thoughts, words, and actions, and that He controls all our circumstances and our destiny both in this life and in the life to come. This conviction is instinctive and universal. It is found in men of all ages, and under all forms of religion, and in all states of civilization. Men universally believe in the moral government of God; and they universally believe that that moral government is administered at least in part, in this world. They see that God often restrains or punishes the wicked. Did this man sin, or his parents, that he was born blind? was the utterance of a natural feeling; the expression, although erroneous as to its form, of the irrepressible conviction that everything is ordered by God. In the fourth place, our religious nature demands intercourse with God. He must be to us the object of prayer, and the ground of confidence. We must look to Him in trouble and danger; we cannot refrain from calling upon Him for help, or thanking Him for our mercies. Unless the doctrine of a universal providence be true, all this is a delusion. Such, however, is the relation in which the Scriptures and the constitution of our nature assume that we stand to God, and in which He stands to the world. He is ever present, all-controlling, the hearer and answerer of prayer, giving us our daily mercies, and guiding us in all our ways. This doctrine of providence, therefore, is the foundation of all practical religion, and the denial of it is practically atheism, for we are then without God in the world. It may be said that these religious feelings are due to our education; that men educated in the belief of witches and fairies, or supernatural agencies of any kind, refer events actually due to the operations of nature to the intervention of spiritual beings. To this it may be answered, First, that the sense of dependence, of responsibility, of obligation for mercies received, and of the control of outward events by the power of God, is too universal to be accounted for by any peculiar form of education. These are the generic, or fundamental convictions of the human mind, which are manifested in more or less suitable forms, according to the degree of knowledge which different men possess. And secondly, it is to be considered that the argument is founded on the truth and justness of these feelings, and not on their origin. It is in this case as it is with our moral convictions. Because our knowledge of what is right or wrong, and the opinions of men on that point, may be modified by education and circumstances, this does not prove that our moral nature is due to education ; nor does it shake the convictions we entertain of the correctness of our moral judgments. It may be, and doubtless is true that we owe to the Scriptures most of our knowledge of the moral law, but this does not impair our confidence in the authority and truth of our views of duty, and of moral obligation. These religious feelings have a self-evidencing as well as an informing light. We know that they are right, and we know that the doctrine which accords with them and produces them, must be true. It is, therefore, a valid argument for the doctrine of a universal providence that it meets the demands of our moral and religious nature.

Argument from Predictions and Promises.

A fourth general argument on this subject is derived from the predictions, promises, and threatenings recorded in the Word of God. Those predictions are not mere general declarations of the probable or natural consequences of certain courses of action, but specific revelations of the occurrence of events in the future, the futurition of which cannot be secured except in the exercise of an absolutely certain control over causes and agents both natural and moral. God promises to give health, long life, and prosperous seasons ; or He threatens to inflict severe judgments, the desolations of war, famine, drought, and pestilence. Such promises and threatenings suppose a universal providence, a control over all the creatures of God, and over all their actions. As such promises and threatenings abound in the Word of God ; as his people, and as all nations recognize such benefits or calamities as divine dispensations, it is evident that the doctrine of Providence underlies all religion, both natural and revealed.

Argument from Experience.

We may refer confidently on this subject to all experience. Every man can see that his life has been ordered by an intelligence and will not his own. His whole history has been determined by events over which he had no control, events often in themselves apparently fortuitous, so that he must either assume that the most important events are determined by chance, or admit that the providence of God extends to all events, even the most minute. What is true of individuals is true of nations. The Old Testament is a record of God's providential dealings with the Hebrew people. The calling of Abraham, the history of the patriarchs, of Joseph, of the sojourn of the Israelites in Egypt, of their deliverance and journey through the wilderness, of their conquest of the land of Canaan, and their whole subsequent history, is a continuous record of the control of God over all their circumstances, — a control which is represented as extending to all events. In like manner the history of the world reveals to an intelligent eye the all-pervading providence of God, as clearly as the heavens declare his majesty and power.

B. *The Scriptures teach God's Providence over Nature.*

We find that the Bible asserts that the providential agency of God is exercised over all the operations of nature. This is asserted with regard to the ordinary operations of physical laws: the motion of the heavenly bodies, the succession of the seasons, the growth and decay of the productions of the earth ; and the falling of the rain, hail, and snow. It is He who guides Arcturus in his course, who makes the sun to rise, and the grass to grow. These event are represented as due to the omnipresent agency of God and are determined, not by chance, nor by necessity, but by his will. Pau says (Acts xiv. 17), that God " left not himself without witness " even among the heathen, " in that He did good, and gave us rain from heaven, and fruitful seasons, filling our hearts with food and gladness." Our Lord says (Matt. v. 45), God " maketh his sun to rise on the evil and on the good, and sendeth rain on the just and on the unjust." He clothes " the grass of the field, which to-day is, and to-morrow is cast into the oven." (Matt. vi. 30.) In like manner the more unusual and striking operations of natural laws, earthquakes, tempests, and pestilences, are said to be sent, governed, and determined by Him, so that all the effects which they produce are referred to his purpose. He makes the winds his messengers, and the lightnings are his ministering spirits. Even apparently fortuitous events, such as are determined by causes so rapid or so inappreciable as to elude our notice, the falling of the lot; the flight of an arrow; the number of the hairs of our heads, are all controlled by the omnipresent God. " Are not two sparrows sold for a farthing? and one of them shall not fall on the ground without your Father." (Matt. x. 29.)

Providence extends over the Animal World.

The Scriptures teach that irrational animals are the objects of God's providential care. He fashions their bodies, He calls them into the world, sustains them in being, and supplies their wants. In his hand is the life of every living thing. (Job xii. 10.) The Psalmist says (civ. 21), " The young lions roar after their prey, and seek their meat from God." Verses 27, 28, " These wait all upon thee; that thou mayest give them their meat in due season. That thou givest them, they gather: thou openest thy hand, they are filled with good." Matt. vi. 26, " Behold the fowls of the air: for they sow not, neither do they reap, nor gather into barns; yet your heavenly Father feedeth them." Acts xvii. 25, " He giveth to all life and breath, and all things." Such representations are not to be explained away as poetical modes of expressing the idea that the laws of nature, as ordained of God, are so arranged as to meet the necessities of the animal creation, without any special intervention of his providence. It is not the fact, merely, that the world, as created by God, is adapted to meet the wants of his creatures, that is asserted in the Scriptures, but that his creatures depend on the constant exercise of his care. He gives or withholds what they need according to his good pleasure. When our Lord put in the lips of his disciples the petition, " Give us this day our daily bread," He recognized the fact that all living creatures depend on the constant intervention of God for the supply of their daily wants.

Over Nations.

The Bible teaches that the providential government of God extends over nations and communities of men. Ps. lxvi. 7, " He ruleth by his power forever; his eyes behold the nations: let not the rebellious exalt themselves." Dan. iv. 35, " He doeth according to his will in the army of heaven, and among the inhabitants of the earth." Dan. ii. 21, " He changeth the times and the seasons; He removeth kings and setteth up kings." Dan. iv. 25, " The Most High ruleth in the kingdom of men and giveth it to whomsoever He will." Is. x. 5, 6, "O Assyrian, the rod of mine anger, and the staff in their hand is my indignation, I will send him against an hypocritical nation." Verse 7, "Howbeit he meaneth not so, neither doth his heart think so." Verse 15, "Shall the axe boast itself against him that heweth therewith? or shall the saw magnify itself against him that shaketh it? as if the rod should shake itself against them that lift it up, or as if the staff should lift up itself as though it were not wood." The Scriptures are full of this doctrine. God uses the nations with the absolute control that a man uses a rod or a staff. They are in his hands, and He employs them to accomplish his purposes. He breaks them in pieces as a potter's vessel, or He exalts them to greatness, according to his good pleasure.

Over Individuals.

The providence of God extends not only over nations, but also over individuals. The circumstances of every man's birth, life, and death, are ordered by God. Whether we are born in a heathen or in a Christian land, in the Church or out of it; whether weak or strong; with many, or with few talents; whether we are prosperous or afflicted; whether we live a longer or a shorter time, are not matters determined by chance, or by the unintelligent sequence of events, but by the will of God. 1 Sam. ii. 6, 7, "The LORD killeth and maketh alive: He bringeth down to the grave, and bringeth up. The LORD maketh poor and maketh rich, He bringeth low and lifteth up." Is. xlv. 5, "I am the LORD (the absolute ruler), and there is none else; there is no God besides me: I girded thee, though thou hast not known me." Prov. xvi. 9, "A man's heart deviseth his way: but the LORD directeth his steps." Ps. lxxv. 6, 7, "Promotion cometh neither from the east, nor from the west, nor from the south. But God is the judge (ruler): he putteth down one, and setteth up another." Ps. xxxi. 15, "My times (the vicissitudes of life) are in thy hands." Acts xvii. 26, God "hath made of one blood all nations of men for to dwell on all the face of the earth, and hath determined the times before appointed (i. e., the turning points in history) and the bounds of their habitation."

God's Providence in relation to Free Acts.

The Bible no less clearly teaches that God exercises a controlling power over the free acts of men, as well as over their external circumstances. This is true of all their acts, good and evil. It is asserted in general terms, that his dominion extends over their whole inward life, and especially over their good acts. Prov. xvi. 1, " The preparations of the heart in man and the answer of the tongue, is from the LORD." Prov. xxi. 1, " The king's heart is in the hand of the LORD, as the rivers of water : He turneth it whithersoever He will." Ezra vii. 27, " Blessed be the LORD God of our fathers, which hath put such a thing as this in the king's heart, to beautify the house of the LORD." Ex. iii. 21, " I will give this people favour in the sight of the Egyptians." Ps. cxix. 36, " Incline my heart unto thy testimonies." Ps. cxiv. 4, " Incline not my heart to any evil thing." A large part of the predictions, promises, and threatenings of the word of God are founded on the assumption of this absolute control over the free acts of his creatures. Without this there can be no government of the world and no certainty as to its issue. The Bible is filled with prayers founded on this same assumption. All Christians be-lieve that the hearts of men are in the hand of God ; that He works in them both to will and to do according to his good pleasure.

The Relation of God's Providence to Sin.

With regard to the sinful acts of men, the Scriptures teach, (1.) That they are so under the control of God that they can occur only by his permission and in execution of his purposes. He so guides them in the exercise of their wickedness that the particular forms of its manifestation are determined by his will. In 1 Chron. x. 4–14 it is said that Saul slew himself, but it is elsewhere said that the Lord slew him and turned the kingdom unto David. So also it is said, that he hardened the heart of Pha-raoh ; that He hardened the spirit of Sihon the king of Hesh-bon ; that He turned the hearts of the heathen to hate his people ; that He blinds the eyes of men, and sends them strong delusion that they may believe a lie ; that He stirs up the nations to war. " God," it is said, in Rev. xvii. 17, " hath put in their hearts to fulfil his will, and to agree, and give their kingdom unto the beast, until the words of God shall be fulfilled." (2.) The Scriptures teach that the wickedness of men is restrained within prescribed bounds. Ps. lxxvi. 10, " Surely the wrath of man shall praise thee : the remainder of wrath shalt thou restrain." 2 Kings xix. 28, " Because thy rage against me, and thy tumult is come up into mine ears, therefore I will put my hook in thy nose, and my bridle in thy lips, and I will turn thee back by the way by which thou camest.'   (3.) Wicked actions are overruled for good.   The wicked conduct of Joseph's brethren, the obstinacy and disobedience of Pharaoh, the lust of conquest and thirst for plunder by which the heathen rulers were controlled in their invasions of the Holy Land; above all, the crucifixion of Christ, the persecutions of the Church, the revolutions and wars among the nations, have been all so overruled by Him who sitteth as ruler in the heavens, as to fulfil his wise and merciful designs.   (4.) The Scriptures teach that God's providence in relation to the sins of men, is such that the sinfulness thereof proceedeth only from the creature and not from God; who neither is nor can be the author or approver of sin.   1 John ii. 16, " All that is in the world, the lust of the flesh, and the lust of the eyes, and the pride of life, is not of the Father (not from Him as its source or author), but is of the world."   James i. 13, " Let no man say when he is tempted, I am tempted of God : for God cannot be tempted with evil, neither tempteth he any man."   Jer. vii. 9, " Will ye steal, murder, and commit adultery, and swear falsely, and burn incense unto Baal, and walk after other gods whom ye know not ; and come and stand before me in this house, which is called by my name, and say, We are delivered to do all these abominations ? "

Thus the fact that God does govern all his creatures and all their actions, is clearly revealed in the Scriptures.   And that fact is the foundation of all religion.   It is the ground of the consolation of his people in all ages ; and it may be said to be the intuitive conviction of all men, however inconsistent it may be with their philosophical theories, or with their professions.   The fact of this universal providence of God is all the Bible teaches.   It nowhere attempts to inform us how it is that God governs all things, or how his effectual control is to be reconciled with the efficiency of second causes.   All the attempts of philosophers and theologians to explain that point, may be pronounced failures, and worse than failures, for they not only raise more difficulties than they solve, but in almost all instances they include principles or lead to conclusions inconsistent with the plain teachings of the word of God.   These theories are all founded on some *à priori* principle which is assumed on no higher authority than human reason.

§ 3. *Different Theories of the Divine Government.*

A. *The Deistical Theory of God's Relation to the World.*

The first of the general views of God's relation to the world is that which has ever been widely adopted by Rationalists, Deists, and men of the world. It is founded on the assumption that the Supreme Being is too exalted to concern Himself with the trifling concerns of his creatures here on earth. He made the world and impressed upon it certain laws ; endowing matter with its properties, and rational beings with the powers of free agency, and having done this, he leaves the world to the guidance of these general laws. According to this view, the relation which God bears to the universe is that of a mechanist to a machine. When an artist has made a watch it goes of itself, without his intervention. He is never called to interfere with its operation, except to remedy some defect. But as no such defect can be assumed in the works of God, there is no call for his intervention, and He does not interfere. All things come to pass in virtue of the operation of causes which He created and set in motion at the beginning. According to this view God in no wise determines the effects of natural causes, nor controls the acts of free agents. The reason that one season is propitious and the earth produces her fruits in abundance, and that another is the reverse ; that one year pestilence sweeps over the land, and another year is exempted from such desolation ; that of two ships sailing from the same port, the one is wrecked and the other has a prosperous voyage ; that the Spanish Armada was dispersed by a storm and Protestant England saved from papal domination ; that Cromwell and his companions were arrested and prevented from sailing for America, which decided the fate of religious liberty in Great Britain, — that all such events are as they are, must, according to this theory, be referred to chance, or the blind operation of natural causes. God has nothing to do with them. He has abandoned the world to the government of physical laws and the affairs of men to their own control. This view of God's relation to the world is so thoroughly anti-Scriptural and irreligious that it never has been, and never can be adopted by any Christian church. So long as even the simple words of our Lord are remembered and believed, so long must this doctrine be rejected with indignation. " Consider the ravens ; for they neither sow nor reap ; which neither have storehouse nor barn ; and God feedeth them : how much more are ye better than the fowls ? " " Your

Father knoweth that ye have need of these things. But rather
seek ye the kingdom of God ; and all these things shall be added
unto you." Our Lord, therefore, teaches us to confide in the
universal providence of God which supplies the wants and controls
the destiny of all his creatures, so that a hair does not fall from our
heads without his notice.

B. *Theory of Entire Dependence.*

Another theory, the very opposite of the one just mentioned, is
founded on the principle that absolute dependence includes the
idea that God is the only cause. This principle has been widely
adopted, even in the Church. It has been strenuously advocated
by many theists, not only among the schoolmen, but by some of
the Reformers, and by a large class of modern theologians.   There
was a class of the scholastic divines who were virtually pantheistic
in their philosophical views. John Scotus Erigena had taught,
in the ninth century,[1] that " omnis visibilis et invisibilis creatura
theophania, *i. e.*, divina apparitio recte potest appellari." He had
his followers, even in the thirteenth century.[2] Those who did not
go the length of asserting that " Deus est essentia omnium crea-
turarum et esse omnium," still maintained that He so operated in
all as to be the only efficient cause. According to Thomas Aquinas,
they argued, " Nulla insufficientia est Deo attribuenda. Si igitur
Deus operatur in omni operante, sufficienter in quolibet operatur.
Superfluum igitur esset quod agens creatum, aliquid operaretur."
Again, " Quod Deum operari in quolibet operante, aliqui sic in-
tellexerunt, quod nulla virtus creata aliquid operaretur in rebus,
sed solus Deus immediate omnia operaretur : puta quod ignis non
calefaceret, sed Deus in igne. Et similiter de omnibus aliis."[3] Of
all the Reformers, Zwingle was the most inclined to this extreme
view of the dependence of the creature on God. " Omnis virtus,"
he says,[4] " numinis virtus est, nec enim quicquam est quod non ex
illo, in illo et per illud sit, imo illud ipsum sit — creata inquam
virtus dicitur, eo quod in novo subjecto et nova specie, universalis
aut generalis ista virtus exhibetur. Deus est causa rerum universa-
rum, reliqua omnia non sunt vere causæ.[5] Constat causas secundas
non rite causas vocari. . . . . Essentiam, virtutem, et operationem
habent non suam sed numinis. Instrumenta igitur sunt.[6] Vici-

---

1 *De Divisione Naturæ*, lib. iii. 19, edit. Monast. Guestphal., 1838, p. 240.
2 See Rixner's *Geschichte der Philosophie*, vol. ii. § 40, p. 72.
3 *Summa Theologiæ*, part I., quest. cv., art. 5, edit. Cologne, 1640, pp. 192, 193.
4 *De Providentia Dei ; Works*, edit. Turici, 1832, vol. iv. p. 85.
5 *Ibid.* Page 95.   6 *Ibid.* Page 96.

niora ista, quibus causarum nomen damus, non jure causas esse sed
manus et organa, quibus æterna mens operatur."[1] Calvin did
not go so far, although he uses such language as the following,
when speaking of inanimate things, " Sunt nihil aliud quam instrumenta, quibus Deus assidue instillat quantum vult efficaciæ et pro
suo arbitrio ad hanc vel illam actionem flectit et convertit."[2] He
admits, however, that matter has its own properties, and second
causes a real efficiency. The whole tendency of the Cartesian
philosophy, which came into vogue in the seventeenth century, was
to merge second causes into the first cause, and it thus led the way
to idealism and pantheism. Malebranche admitted, on the testimony of Scripture, which declares that God created the heaven and
the earth, that the external world has a real existence. But he
denied that it could produce any effects, or that the soul could in
any way act upon matter. We see all things in God. That is,
when we perceive anything out of ourselves, the perception is not
due to the impression made by the external object, but to the immediate agency of God. And the activity of our own minds is
only a form of the activity of God. The first fruit of this system
was avowed idealism, as all evidence of the existence of an external world was destroyed ; and the second was the pantheism of
Spinoza, which Leibnitz calls Cartesianism *en outre*. It must be
admitted that the devout desire of the Reformed theologians to
vindicate the sovereignty and supremacy of God, in opposition to
all forms of Pelagian and semi-Pelagian doctrine, led many of them
to go to an extreme in depreciating the efficiency of second causes,
and in unduly exalting the omnipresent efficiency of God. Schweizer[3] represents the great body of the Reformed theologians as
teaching that the dependence of creatures on the Creator supersedes all efficiency of second causes. " Die schlechthinige Abhän-
gigkeit des Bestehens und Verlaufes der Welt gestattet keinerlei
andere Ursächlichkeiten als nur die göttliche, so dass Zwischenursachen nur seine Instrumente und Organe sind, er die durch ihre
Gesammtheit wie durch alle einzelnen Zwischenursachen allein
hindurchwirkende Causalität. Dieses ist er vermöge der *præsentia
essentialis numinis* oder doch *divinæ virtutis*, welche das Sein alles
Seins, die Bewegung aller Bewegungen ist." This is Schweizer's
own doctrine, as it is that of the whole school of Schleiermacher,
to which he belongs ; but that it is not the doctrine of the Reformed

---

[1] Zwingle, iv. 97.
[2] *Institutio*, I. xvi. 2, edit. Berlin, 1834, vol. i. p. 135.
[3] *Glaubenslehre der Reformirten Kirche*, p. 318.

theologians is plain from their all teaching the doctrine of *concursus*, which Schweizer admits to be inconsistent with the assumption that God is the sole cause of all things. It was this false assumption that no creature can act; that dependence on God is absolute ; and that all power however manifested is the power of God, which led to the doctrine of a continued creation, as stated when speaking of the efficiency of God in the preservation of the world. It led also to the doctrine of occasional causes; that is, to the theory that what we call second causes have no real efficiency, but are only the occasions on which God manifests his power in a particular way. The world of matter and mind exists indeed, but it is perfectly inert. It is only the instrument or means by which the manifold and everywhere present efficiency of God is manifested. " Consideremus," says Leibnitz, " eorum sententiam, qui rebus creatis veram, et propriam actionem adimunt, ... qui putant non res agere, sed Deum ad rerum præsentiam, et secundum rerum aptitudem; adeoque res occasiones esse, non causas, et recipere, non efficere aut elicere." [1]   The same views of the dependence of creatures on God lies at the foundation of the whole system of Dr. Emmons. He held that if any creature were endowed with activity or power to act, it would be independent of God. " We cannot conceive," he says, " that even Omnipotence itself is able to form independent agents, because this would be to endow them with divinity. And since all men are dependent agents, all their motions, exercises, or actions must originate in a divine efficiency." This is not to be understood as simply asserting the necessity of a divine *concursus* in order to the operation of second causes, for Emmons expressly teaches that God creates all the volitions of the soul, and effects by his almighty power all changes in the material world.

Objections to this Doctrine of Dependence.

To this whole doctrine, which thus denies the existence of second causes, and refers all action both in the material and spiritual world to God, it is to be objected, (1.) That it is founded on an arbitrary assumption. It starts with the *à priori* idea of an absolute and infinite being, and rejects everything inconsistent with that idea. It cannot be proved that it is inconsistent with the nature of God that He should call into existence creatures capable of originating action. It is enough that such creatures should derive all their powers from God, and be subject to his control in all their exercises. (2.) This doctrine contradicts the

---

[1] *De ipsa Natura*, 10 ; *Works*, edit. Berlin, 1840, p. 157.

consciousness of every man. We know, as certainly as we know anything, that we are free agents, and that free agency is the power of self-determination, or of originating our own acts. It contradicts not only our self-consciousness, but the laws of belief which God has impressed upon our nature. It is one of those laws that we should believe in the reality of the objects of our senses; and that belief involves the conviction not only that they really are, but also that they are the causes of the impressions which they make on our sensibility. It is to put philosophy in conflict with common sense, and with the universal convictions of men, to teach that all this is a delusion; that when we see a tree we are mistaken, that God immediately creates that impression in our mind; or that when we will to move the power is not in us, that it is not we that move, but God that moves us; or when we think, that it is God creates the thought. (3.) As has been before remarked, this system naturally leads, and has led to idealism and pantheism, and therefore is utterly inconsistent with all liberty and responsibility, and destroys the possibility of moral distinctions.

C.　*The Doctrine that there is no Efficiency except in Mind.*

According to this view, there are no such things as physical forces. The mind of man is endowed with the power of producing effects; but apart from mind, divine or created, there is no efficiency in the universe. This doctrine finds its way into many theological, as well as philosophical disquisitions. Thus Principal Tulloch says, a cause is "coincident with an agent." It "therefore implies mind. More definitely, and in its full conception, it implies a rational will." [1] Physical causes are therefore regarded as the ever operating will of God. "The idea of causation," he says, "we found to resolve itself into that of the operation of a rational mind or will in nature." [2] Providence is nothing else than a "continued forth-putting of that [originally creative] efficiency." [3] Dr. Tulloch very correctly assumes that a cause is that which has power to produce effects; and that we get our idea of power, and therefore of the nature of causation, from our own consciousness of efficiency. He hence infers that, as mind is the only cause of which we have immediate knowledge, therefore it is the only one that exists. But this is a *non-sequitur*. That mind is a cause, is no proof that electricity may not be a cause. The facts, as understood by the mass

---

[1] *Theism; The Witness of Reason and Nature to an All-Wise and Beneficent Creator.* By the Rev. John Tulloch, D. D., Principal and Primarius Professor of Theology, St. Mary's College, St. Andrews, edit. New York, 1855, p. 43.

[2] *Ibid.* p. 47.　　　　　　　　　　　　　　　[3] *Ibid.* p. 93.

of men are, First, we are conscious of efficiency, or the power to produce effects. Second, the exercise of this power awakens, or gives occasion to the intuition of the universal and necessary truth that every effect must have an appropriate cause. Thirdly, as we see around us effects of different kinds, it is a law of reason that they should be referred to causes of different kinds. The evidence that this is a law of reason, is the fact that men everywhere assume physical causes to account for physical effects, as uniformly as they assume mind for intelligent effects. The theory, however, which resolves all forces into the everywhere operative will of God has great attractions. It makes a way of escape from many of the difficulties which beset the question of God's relation to the world. Even men devoted to the study of nature get so puzzled by such questions, as, What is matter? or What is force? that they are disposed, in many cases, to merge all things into God. The Duke of Argyle says, " Science, in the modern doctrine of Conservation of Energy and the Convertibility of Forces, is already getting something like a firm hold of the idea that all kinds of Force are but forms or manifestations of some one Central Force issuing from some one Fountain-head of Power. Sir John Herschel has not hesitated to say, that 'it is but reasonable to regard the Force of Gravitation as the direct or indirect result of a consciousness or a will existing somewhere.' And even if we cannot certainly identify Force in all its forms with the direct energies of the One Omnipresent and all-pervading Will, it is at least in the highest degree unphilosophical to assume the contrary, — to speak or to think as if the Forces of Nature were either independent of, or even separate from, the Creator's Power." [1]

It was remarked on a previous page that Wallace still more decidedly adopts the same view. In his book on " Natural Selection," after he had defended Darwin's theory on the origin of species (except in its application to man), he comes in the end to start the question, What is matter? This question he answers by saying, " Matter is essentially force, and nothing but force. Matter, as popularly understood, does not exist, and is, in fact, philosophically inconceivable." [2] The next question is, What is force? The ultimate answer to this is, that it is the will of God. " If," says Mr. Wallace, " we have traced one force, however minute, to an origin in our own WILL, while we have no knowledge of any other primary cause of force, it does not seem an improbable con-

---

[1] *Reign of Law*, 5th ed.   London, 1867, p. 123.
[2] *Natural Selection*, pp. 365, 366.

clusion that all force may be will force; and thus the whole universe is not merely dependent on, but actually *is*, the WILL of
higher intelligences or of one Supreme Intelligence."[1]

This theory is substantially the same as that previously mentioned. They differ only as to the extent of their application.
According to the doctrine of " Absolute Dependence," God is the
only agent in the universe ; according to the doctrine just stated,
He is the only agent, or his will is the only energy in the material
world. Matter is nothing. " It does not exist." It is nothing
but force, and force is God; therefore the external world is God.
In other words, all the impressions and sensations made upon us,
as we suppose, by things without us, are in fact made by the immediate power of God : there is no earth ; there are no stars ; no
men or women ; no fathers or mothers. Men cannot believe this.
By the constitution of our nature, which no man can alter, we are
forced to believe in the reality of the external world ; that matter
is, and that it is the proximate cause of the effects which we attribute to its agency.

D. *Theory of Preëstablished Harmony.*

Another assumption made by philosophers is, that one substance
cannot act upon another substance of a different kind ; what is extended cannot act upon what is not extended ; matter cannot act on
mind, nor mind on matter. It is, however, a fact of consciousness
and of daily observation, that, apparently at least, material objects
by which we are surrounded are the causes of certain sensations
and perceptions, that is, they act upon our minds ; and it is no less
a matter of consciousness that our minds do act, at least so it seems,
upon our bodies. We can move, we can control the action of all
our voluntary muscles. This, however, must be a delusion if
matter cannot act on mind nor mind on matter. To account for
the relation in which mind and matter stand to each other in this
world, and for the apparent action of the one on the other, Leibnitz
adopted the theory of a preëstablished harmony. God created two
independent worlds, the one of matter, the other of mind ; each has
its own nature and its own principle of activity. All the changes
in matter, all the actions of our bodies, are determined from a
source within the matter and within our bodies, and would occur
in the same order in which they actually take place if no created
mind were in existence. In like manner, all the varying states of

[1] *Contribution to the Theory of Natural Selection,* by Alfred Russel Wallace. London
1870, p. 368.

the human mind, all its sensations, perceptions, and volitions are determined from within, and would be just what they are though the external world had no existence. We should see the same sights, hear the same sounds, have the same volitions to move this or that muscle, though there were nothing to see, hear, or move. These two worlds, thus automatically moved, coexist, and are made to act in harmony by a prearrangement divinely ordered. Hence the sensation of burning arises in the mind, not because fire acts on the body and the body on the mind, but because, by this preëstablished harmony, these events are made to coincide in time and space. From eternity it was determined that I should have a volition to move my arm at a certain time ; and from eternity it was determined that the arm should move at that time. The two events therefore concur as immediate antecedent and consequent, but the volition stands in no causal relation to the motion. The volition would have been formed had there been no arm to move ; and the arm would have moved, although the volition had never been formed. Leibnitz's hand would have written all his wonderful books, mathematical and philosophical, and conducted all his controversies with Bayle, Clarke, and Newton, though his soul had never been created.[1]

E. Doctrine of Concursus.

A far more widely adopted and permanently influential principle is that no second cause can act until acted upon. Nothing created can originate action. This principle, carried to a greater or less extent, was adopted by Augustine, by the schoolmen, by the Thomists and Dominicans in the Latin Church, and by Protestants, whether Lutherans, Reformed, or Remonstrants. It was assumed as a philosophical axiom, to which all theological doctrines should be conformed. " Ad gubernationem concursus pertinet, quo Deus non solum dat vim agendi causis secundis et eam conservat, sed et easdem movet et applicat ad agendum. Præcursus etiam dicitur, nam causæ secundæ non movent nisi motæ." [2] " Prima causa," says Turrettin, " est primum movens in omni actione, ideo causa secunda non potest movere, nisi moveatur, nec agere, nisi acta a prima ; alioqui erit principium sui motus, et sic non amplius esset causa secunda, sed prima." [3] In the production of every effect, therefore, there is the efficiency of two causes, the first and second. But this is not to be considered as involving two

---

[1] See his *Systeme Nouveau de la Nature ; Works,* edit. Berlin, 1840, p. 124.
[2] Mares, *Collegium Theologicum,* loc. iv. 29; Gröningen, 1659, p. 42, b.
[3] Locus vi. quæstio v. 7, edit. Edinburgh, 1847, vol. i. p. 455.

operations, as when two horses are attached to the same vehicle, which is drawn partly by the one and partly by the other. The efficiency of the first cause is in the second, and not merely with it. Deus "immediate influit in actionem et effectum creaturæ, ita ut idem effectus non a solo Deo, nec a sola creatura, nec partim a Deo, partim a creatura, sed una eademque efficientia totali simul a Deo et creatura producatur, a Deo videlicet ut causa universali et prima, a creatura ut particulari et secunda." [1] " Non est re ipsa alia actio influxus Dei, alia operatio creaturæ, sed una et indivisibilis actio, utrumque respiciens et ab utroque pendens, a Deo ut causa universali, a creatura ut particulari." [2]

This *concursus* is represented, first, as general; an influence of the omnipresent power of God not only sustaining creatures and their properties and powers, but exciting each to act according to its nature. It is analogous to the general influence of the sun which affects different objects in different ways. The same solar ray softens wax and hardens clay. It calls the germinating force of all seeds into action, but does not determine the nature of that action. All seeds are thus quickened; but one develops as wheat, another as barley, not because of the solar force, but because of its own peculiar nature. This is all that the Franciscans and Jesuits among the Romanists, and the Remonstrants among the Protestants allow. The Thomists and Dominicans among the former, and the Augustinian theologians generally, insist that, besides this general *concursus*, there is also a previous, simultaneous, and determining concourse of the first, in all second causes, both in the cause and in the effect; that is, not only exciting to action, but sustaining, guiding, and determining the act; so that its being as it is, and not otherwise, is to be referred to the first, and not to the second cause in every case. On this point, however, the Reformed theologians are not agreed, as Turrettin admits. " Ex nostris," he says, " quidam concursum tantum prævium volunt quoad bona opera gratiæ, sed in aliis omnibus simultaneum sufficere existimant." [3] By previous *concursus* is meant, he says, " Actio Dei, qua in causas earumque principia influendo, creaturas excitat, et agendum præmovet, et ad hoc potius quam ad illud agendum applicat. *Simultaneus* vero est per quam Deus actionem creaturæ, quoad suam entitatem, vel substantiam producit; quo una cum creaturis in earum actiones et effectus influere ponitur, non vero in creaturas ipsas." [4]

[1] Quenstedt, *Theologia*, cap. XIII. i. 15, edit. Leipzig, 1715, vol. i. p. 760.
[2] *Ibid.* cap. XIII. ii. 3, vol. i. p. 782.   [3] Locus VI. quæst. v. 6.
[4] Locus VI. quæst. v. 5.

It is admitted that these do not differ really, " quia concursus simultaneus, nihil aliud est, quam concursus prævius continuatus."
This previous *concursus* is also called predetermining.   " Id ipsum
etiam nomine Prædeterminationis, seu Præmotionis solet designari,
qua Deus ciet et applicat causam secundam ad agendum, adeoque
antecedenter ad omnem operationem creaturæ, seu prius natura et
ratione quam creatura operetur, eam realiter et efficaciter movet ad
agendum in singulis actionibus, adeo ut sine hac præmotione causa
secunda operari non possit, ea vero posita impossibile sit in sensu
composito causam secundam non illud idem agere ad quod a prima
causa præmovetur." [1]

Concursus, therefore, assumes, (1.) That God gives to second
causes the power of acting. (2.) That He preserves them in being
and vigour. (3.) That He excites and determines second causes
to act. (4.) That He directs and governs them to the predetermined end. All this, however, was so understood that —

1. The effect produced or the act performed is to be referred to
the second, and not to the first cause. When the fire burns, it is
to the fire, and not to God that the effect is to be attributed. When
a man speaks, it is the man, and not God who utters the words.
When the moon raises the tidal wave, and the wave dashes a vessel on the shore, the effect is to be attributed, not to the moon, but
to the momentum of the wave. The force of gravity acts uniformly on all ponderable matter, and yet that force may be indefinitely varied in the effects which are produced by intervening
causes, whether necessary or free.

2. The doctrine of *concursus* does not deny the efficiency of second causes. They are real causes, having a *principium agendi* in
themselves.

3. The agency of God neither supersedes, nor in any way interferes with the efficiency of second causes. " Ad providentiam divinam non pertinet, naturam rerum corrumpere, sed servare : unde
omnia movet secundum eorum conditionem : ita quod ex causis
necessariis per motionem divinam consequuntur effectus ex necessitate ; ex causis autem contingentibus sequuntur effectus contin-
gentes. Quia igitur voluntas est activum principium non deter-
minatum ad unum, sed indifferenter se habens ad multa, sic Deus
ipsam movet, quod non ex necessitate ad unum determinat, sed
remanet motus ejus contingens et non necessarius, nisi in his ad
quæ naturaliter movetur." [2] " Concurrit Deus cum naturalibus ad

---

[1] Turrettin, locus VI. quæst. v. 6.
[2] Aquinas, *Summa*, part II. i. quæst. x. art 4, edit. Cologne, 1640, p. 22 of second set.

modum causæ naturalis, cum causis liberis per modum causæ liberæ." [1] "Duo sunt causarum genera, aliæ definitæ et generales, quæ eodem modo semper agunt, ut ignis qui urit, sol qui lucet; aliæ indefinitæ et liberæ, quæ possunt agere vel non agere, hoc vel illo modo agere : ita Deus naturam earum conservat, et cum illis juxta eam in agendo concurrit ; cum definitis, ut ipse eas determinet sine determinatione propria ; cum indefinitis vero et liberis, ut ipsæ quoque se determinent proprio rationis judicio, et libera voluntatis dispositione, quam Deus non aufert homini, quia sic opus suum destrueret, sed relinquit et confirmat." [2] To the same effect the "Westminster Confession" [3] says : God ordereth events "to fall out according to the nature of second causes, either necessarily, freely, or contingently."

4. From this it follows that the efficiency or agency of God is not the same in relation to all kinds of events. It is one thing in coöperating with material causes, another in coöperating with free agents. It is one thing in relation to good acts, and another in relation to evil actions ; one thing in nature, and another in grace.

5. The divine *concursus* is not inconsistent with the liberty of free agents. "Moveri voluntarie est moveri ex se, id est, a principio intrinseco. Sed illud principium intrinsecum potest esse ab alio principio extrinseco. Et sic moveri ex se, non repugnat ei, quod movetur ab alio. — Illud quod movetur ab altero, dicitur cogi, si moveatur contra inclinationem propriam : sed si moveatur ab alio quod sibi dat propriam inclinationem, non dicitur cogi. Sic igitur Deus movendo voluntatem, non cogit ipsam : quia dat ei ejus propriam inclinationem." [4] This is undoubtedly true. Nothing is more certain from Scripture than that God is the author of faith and repentance. They are his gifts. They are blessings for which we pray, and which He promises. Yet nothing is more certain from consciousness, than that faith and repentance are our own free acts. Therefore *moveri ab alio* is not inconsistent with *moveri ex se*. On this point Turrettin [5] says : "Cum providentia non concurrat cum voluntate humana, vel *per* coactionem, cogendo voluntatem invitam, vel determinando physice, ut rem brutam et cæcam absque ullo judicio, sed rationaliter, flectendo voluntatem modo ipsi convenienti, ut seipsam determinet, ut causa proxima actionum suarum proprio rationis judicio, et spontanea voluntatis

---

[1] Quenstedt, cap. XIII. i. 15, vol. i. p. 761.
[2] Turrettin, locus VI. quæst. vi. 6, edit. Edinburgh, 1847, vol. i. p. 460.
[3] Chap. v. sect. 2.
[4] Aquinas, *Summa*, part I. cuæst. cv. art. 4, edit. Cologne, 1640, p. 192.
[5] Locus VI. quæstio VI.

electione ; eam libertati nostræ nullam vim inferre, sed illam potius amice fovere."

6. All the advocates of the doctrine of *concursus* admit that the great difficulty attending it is in reference to sin. The difficulty here is not so much in relation to the responsibility of the sinner. If sin be his own act, and if the divine *concursus* does not interfere with his freedom, it does not interfere with his responsibility. When God by his grace determines the will of his people to holy acts, the holiness is theirs. It constitutes their character. When God gives a man beauty, he is beautiful. And if his coöperation in the sins of men leaves their freedom in sinning unimpaired, they are as truly sinful as though no such coöperation existed. This is not the difficulty. The real question is, how can God's coöperation in sin be reconciled with his own holiness ? We can easily see how God can coöperate in good acts, and rejoice in the goodness which is his gift ; but how can He so concur in sinful acts as not only to preserve the sinner in the exercise of his ability to act, but also to excite to action, and determine his act to be what it is, and not otherwise ? This difficulty was, as has been remarked, freely acknowledged. It was met by defining sin as mere defect. It is a want of conformity to the moral law. As such it requires not an efficient, but only a deficient cause. God is the source immediately or remotely of all efficiency, but is not the source of mere deficiency. In every sinful act, therefore, there was distinguished the act as an act requiring an efficient cause ; and the moral quality of that act, or its want of conformity to law, a mere relation, which is not an *ens*, and therefore is in no way to be referred to God. This is the answer to this objection given by Augustine, and repeated from his day to this. Aquinas[1] says : " Quicquid est entitatis et actionis in actione mala, reducitur in Deum sicut in causam : sed quod est ibi defectus non causatur a Deo, sed ex causa secunda deficiente." Quenstedt[2] says : " Distinguendum inter effectum et defectum, inter actionem et actionis ἀταξίαν. Effectus et actio est a Deo, non vero defectus et ἀταξία sive inordinatio et exorbitatio actionis. Ad effectum Deus concurrit, vitium non causat, non enim in agendo deficit aut errat, sed causa secunda." Bucan[3] says : " Malorum opera quoque decernit et regit. Tamen non est autor mali, quia mali sic aguntur a Deo, ut sponte, libere et sine coactione et impulsu violento agant. Deinde non infundit

---

[1] *Summa*, part I. quest. xlix. art. 2, edit. Cologne, 1640, p. 95.
[2] *Theologia*, cap. XIII. i. 15, vol. i. p. 761.
[3] Bucan, *Institutiones Theologici*, edit. Geneva, 1625, p. 143.

malitiam sicut bonitatem, nec impellit aut allicit ad peccandum." To the same effect Turrettin [1] says : " Cum actus qua talis semper bonus sit quoad entitatem suam, Deus ad illum concurrit effective, et physice. . . . (quoad malitiam) Deus nec causa physica potest ejus dici, quia nec illam inspirat aut infundit, nec facit; nec ethica, qui nec imperat, aut approbat et suadet, sed severissime prohibet et punit." As the same solar influence quickens into life all kinds of plants, whether nutritious or poisonous ; as the same current of water may be guided in one channel or another ; as the same vital force animates the limbs of the sound man and of the cripple; as the same hand may sweep the keys of an instrument when in tune and when out of tune : so it is urged that the same divine effi- ciency sustains and animates all free agents. That they act at all is due to the divine efficiency, but the particular nature of their acts (at least when evil) is to be referred, not to that all-pervading efficiency of God, but to the nature or character of each particular agent. That God controls and governs wicked men, determines their wickedness to take one form, and not another, and guides it to manifestations which will promote good rather than evil, is not inconsistent with the holiness of God. He did not infuse envy and hatred into the hearts of Joseph's brethren, but He guided the ex- ercise of those evil passions, so as to secure the preservation of Jacob and the chosen seed from destruction.

Remarks on the Doctrine of Concursus.

The above statement of the doctrine of *concursus* is designed merely to give the views generally entertained by Augustinians, as to the nature of God's providential government. Whether those views are correct or not, it is important that they should be under- stood. It is very evident that there is a broad distinction between this theory of *concursus* and the theory which resolves all events, whether necessary or free, into the immediate agency of God. The points of difference between the two theories are, (1.) That the one admits and the other denies the reality and efficiency of second causes. (2.) The one makes no distinction between free and necessary events, attributing them equally to the almighty and creative energy of God ; the other admits the validity and un- speakable importance of this distinction. (3.) The one asserts and the other denies that the agency of God is the same in sinful acts that it is in good acts. (4.) The one admits that God is the author of sin, the other repudiates that doctrine with abhorrence.

[1] Locus VI. quæstio vii. 3, 4, edit. Edinburgh, 1847. vol. i. p. 462.

The Reformed theologians protested against the aspersion freely
made by Romanists, and afterwards by the Remonstrants, that
the Augustinian doctrine led by any fair process of reasoning to
the conclusion that God is the cause of sin. They quote from
their opponents admissions which involve all that they themselves
teach in reference to the agency of God in the wicked acts of men.
Thus Bellarmin, who freely brings this objection against the Protestants, himself says, [1] " Deus non solum permittit impios agere
multa mala, nec solum deserit pios ut cogantur pati quæ ab impiis
inferuntur ; sed etiam præsidet ipsis voluntatibus malis, easque
regit et gubernat, torquet ac flectit in eis invisibiliter operando, ut
licet vitio proprio malæ sint, tamen a divina providentia ad unum
potius malum, quam ad aliud, non positive sed permissive ordinen-
tur." As to this passage, Turrettin says, " Quibus verbis nihil
durius apud nostros occurrit." Bellarmin also quotes [2] and adopts
the language of Aquinas when he says, " Deum non solum incli-
nare voluntates malas ad unum potius, quam ad aliud permittendo,
ut ferantur in unum, et non permittendo, ut ferantur in aliud, ut
Hugo recte docuit, sed etiam positive inclinando in unum et aver-
tendo ab alio." It is of importance, not only as a matter of historical truth, but also for its moral influence, that the fact should be
distinctly known and recognized that the Reformed theologians, with
all Augustinians before and after the Reformation, earnestly rejected the doctrine that God is the author or the efficient cause of sin.

The objection to the doctrine of *concursus* is not that it inten-
tionally or really destroys the free agency of man ; or that it
makes God the author of sin, but (1.) That it is founded on an
arbitrary and false assumption. It denies that any creature can
originate action. This does not admit of proof. It is an inference
from the assumed nature of the dependence of the creature upon
the creator ; or from the assumed necessity of the principle in
question, in order to secure the absolute control of God over created beings. It however contradicts the consciousness of men.
That we are free agents means that we have the power to act
freely ; and to act freely implies that we originate our own acts.
This does not mean that it is inconsistent with our liberty that we
should be moved and induced to exert our ability to act by considerations addressed to our reason or inclinations, or by the grace of
God ; but it does mean that we have the power to act. The
power of spontaneous action is essential to the nature of a spirit ;
and God, in creating us in his own nature as spirits, endowed us

<hr>

[1] *De Amissione Gratiæ et Statu Peccati*, II. xiii. edit. Paris, 1608, p. 132.   [2] *Ibid.*

with the power to originate our own acts.   (2.) A second objection to the doctrine is that it is an attempt to explain the inexplicable. Not content with the simple and certain declaration of the Bible, that God does govern all his creatures and all their actions, it undertakes to explain how this is done.   From the nature of the case this is impossible.   We see that material causes act, but we cannot tell how they act. We are conscious of the power to guide our own thoughts, and to determine our own wills ; but how it is we exercise this efficiency, passes our comprehension.   We know that the will has power over certain muscles of the body ; but the point of connection, the *nexus* between volition and muscular action, is altogether inscrutable.   Why then should we attempt to explain how it is that the efficiency of God controls the efficiency of second causes ?   The fact is plain, and the fact alone is important ; but the mode of God's action we cannot possibly understand. (3.) A third objection is that this doctrine multiplies difficulties. By attempting to teach how God governs free agents, that He first excites them to act ; sustains them in action ; determines them to act so, and not otherwise ; that He effectually concurs in the entity, but not necessarily in the moral quality of the act, we raise at every step the most subtle and perplexing metaphysical questions, which no man is able to solve.   And even admitting the theory of *concursus*, as expounded by the schoolmen and scholastic theologians, to be true, what does it amount to ?   What real knowledge does it communicate ?   All we know, and all we need to know, is, (1.) That God does govern all his creatures ; and (2.) That his control over them is consistent with their nature, and with his own infinite purity and excellence.

As this doctrine of Providence involves the question of God's relation to the world, it is confessedly the most comprehensive and difficult in the compass either of theology or of philosophy.   As the world, meaning thereby the universe of created beings, includes the world of matter and the world of mind, the doctrine of providence concerns, first, the relation of God to the external or material universe ; and secondly, his relation to the world of mind, or to his rational creatures.

§ 4. *Principles involved in the Scriptural Doctrine of Providence.*

A. *The Providence of God over the Material Universe.*

So far as concerns the relation of God to the external world, the following facts appear to be either assumed, or clearly taught in the Bible.

1. There is an external world, or material universe. What we call the world is not a phantom, a delusive show. It is not ourselves, our own varying states, however produced. But matter is a real existence. It is a substance; that which is, and continues, and has identity in all its varying states. This is of course opposed to pantheism, which makes the external world an existence form of God; to idealism; and to the dynamic theory which teaches that matter is merely force. This latter doctrine is intelligible, if by force be understood the constantly acting will of God, for that is the energy of the divine substance. But in the way in which the doctrine is commonly presented, force is taken as the ultimate fact. Matter is force, it is not a substance, but simply activity, power. But it is self-evident that nothing cannot act, or cannot produce motion, which force does. It is just as plain that there cannot be action without something acting, as that there cannot be motion without something moving, as has been so often said. Force, therefore, does not exist of itself. It of necessity implies a substance of which it is an affection, or manifestation, or property. The real existence of the external world is one of those common sense and Scriptural facts, vouched for by the very constitution of our nature, and which it is utterly useless to deny.

Matter is Active.

2. The second fact or principle recognized by Scripture, is that matter is active. It has properties or forces, which are the proximate causes of the physical changes which we constantly see and experience. This is considered by scientific men almost an axiomatic truth. "No force without matter, and no matter without force." This is also the general conviction of men. When they take a heavy body in their hand, they attribute its weight to the nature of the body and its relation to the earth. When one substance produces the sensation of sweetness, and another the sensation of acidity, they instinctively refer the difference to the substances themselves. So of all other physical effects; they are always and everywhere referred to physical causes. Such is a law of our nature; and therefore the theory which denies that any physical causes exist, and refers all natural effects or changes to the immediate operation of the divine will, contradicts our nature, and cannot be true. Besides, as we have already seen, that theory logically leads to idealism and pantheism. It merges the universe into God.

These physical forces act of necessity, blindly, and uniformly. They are everywhere and always the same. The law of gravitation is in the remotest regions of space what it is here on our earth. It acts always, and always in the same way. The same is true of all other physical forces. Light, heat, electricity, and chemical affinities are everywhere the same in their mode of operations.

Laws of Nature.

The ambiguity of the words, law and nature, has already been remarked upon. The phrase "Laws of Nature" is, however, generally used in one or the other of two senses. It either means an observed regular sequence of events, without any reference to the cause by which that regularity of sequence is determined; or it means a uniformly acting force in nature. In this last sense we speak of the laws of gravitation, light, heat, electricity, etc. That there are such laws, or such physical forces, acting uniformly, which are not to be resolved into "uniform modes of divine operation," is, as we have seen, an important Scriptural fact.

The chief question is, In what relation does God stand to these laws? The answer to that question, as drawn from the Bible, is, First, that He is their author. He endowed matter with these forces, and ordained that they should be uniform. Secondly, He is independent of them. He can change, annihilate, or suspend them at pleasure. He can operate with them or without them. "The Reign of Law" must not be made to extend over Him who made the laws. Thirdly, As the stability of the universe, and the welfare, and even the existence of organized creatures, depend on the uniformity of the laws of nature, God never does disregard them except for the accomplishment of some high purpose. He, in the ordinary operations of his Providence, operates with and through the laws which He has ordained. He governs the material, as well as the moral world by law.

The relation, therefore, in which God stands to the laws of nature, is, in one important aspect, analogous to that in which we ourselves stand to them. We employ them. Man can do nothing outside of himself without them; yet what marvels of ingenuity, beauty, and utility, has he not accomplished. Dr. Beale, as we have seen, illustrates God's relation to physical forces by a reference to a chemist in his laboratory. The chemicals do not put themselves in the retorts in due proportions, and subject themselves first to one and then to another operation. As mere blind, physical forces, they can accomplish nothing; at least nothing implying purpose or design. The chemical properties of the materials employed have their functions, and the chemist has his, evidently not only different, but diverse; *i. e.*, of a different kind. Professor Henry's illustration was drawn from the relation of the engineer to the engine. The complicated structure of the machine, the composition and combustion of the fuel; the evaporation of the water, are all external to the engineer, and he to them. The locomotive, although instinct with power, stands perfectly still. At a touch of the engineer it starts into life, and yet with all its tremendous energy is perfectly obedient to his will.

These, and any possible illustration, are of necessity very inadequate. The powers of nature of which man avails himself, are not dependent on him, and are only to a very limited extent under his control. He is entirely external to his works. God, however, fills heaven and earth. He is immanent in the world; intimately and always present with every particle of matter. And this presence is not of being only, but also of knowledge and power. It is manifestly inconsistent with the idea of an infinite God, that any part of his works should be absent from Him, out of his view, or independent of his control. Though everywhere thus efficiently present, his efficiency does not supersede that of his creatures. It is by a natural law, or physical force, that vapour arises from the surface of the ocean, is formed into clouds, and condenses and falls in showers upon the earth, yet God so controls the operation of the laws producing these effects, that He sends rain when and where He pleases. The same is true of all the operations of nature, and of all events in the external world. They are due to the efficiency of physical forces; but those forces, which are combined, adjusted, and made to coöperate or to counteract each other, in the greatest complexity, are all under the constant guidance of God, and are made to accomplish his purpose. It is perfectly rational, therefore, in a world where blind, natural forces are the proximate cause of everything that occurs, to pray for health, for protection, for success, for fruitful seasons, and for the peace and prosperity of nations, since all these events are determined by the intelligent agency of God.

The providence of God is thus seen to be universal and extending to all his creatures and all their actions. The distinction usually and properly made between the general, special, and extraordinary providence of God, has reference to the effects produced, and not to his agency in their production; for this is the same in all cases. But if the object to be accomplished be a general one, such as the orderly motion of the heavenly bodies, or the support and regular operation of the laws of nature, then the providence of

God is spoken of as general. Many men are willing to admit of this general superintendence of the world on the part of God, who deny his intervention in the production of definite effects. The Bible, however, clearly teaches, and all men instinctively believe in a special providence. That is, that God uses his control over the laws of nature, to bring about special effects. Men in sickness, in danger, or in any distress, pray to God for help. This is not irrational. It supposes God's relation to the world to be precisely what it is declared to be in the Bible. It does not suppose that God sets aside or counteracts the laws of nature ; but simply that He controls them and causes them to produce whatever effects He sees fit. The Scriptures and the history of the world, and almost every man's experience, bear abundant evidence to such divine interpositions. We should be as helpless orphans were it not for this constant oversight and protection of our heavenly Father. Sometimes the circumstances attending these divine interventions are so unusual, and the evidences which they afford of divine control are so clear, that men cannot refuse to recognize the hand of God. There is, however, nothing extraordinary in the agency of God. It is only that we witness on these occasions more impressive manifestations of the absolute control, which He constantly exercises over the laws which He has ordained.

The Uniformity of the Laws of Nature consistent with the Doctrine of Providence.

It is obvious that the Scriptural doctrine of providence is not inconsistent with the " Reign of Law " in any proper sense of the words. The Scriptures recognize the fact that the laws of nature are immutable ; that they are the ordinances of God; that they are uniform in their operation ; and that they cannot be disregarded with impunity. But as man within his sphere can use these fixed laws to accomplish the most diversified purposes, so God in his unlimited sphere has them always and everywhere under his absolute control, so that, without suspending or violating them, they are ever subservient to his will. Certain philosophers do not admit this. To them the control of mind and the reign of law are incompatible ; one or the other must be denied. " The fundamental character of all theological philosophy," says Lewes, " is the conceiving of phenomena as subjected to supernatural volition, and onsequently as eminently and irregularly variable. Now, these theological conceptions can only be subverted finally by means of these two general processes, whose popular success is infallible in the long run. (1.) The exact and rational prevision of phenomena; and (2.) The possibility of modifying them, so as to promote our own ends and advantages. The former immediately dispels all idea of any ' directing volition;' and the latter leads to the same result, under another point of view, by making us regard this power as subordinated to our own."[1] If the fact that men can use the laws of nature to their "own ends and advantages" is compatible with the uniformity of those laws, the control of God over them for the accomplishment of his purposes cannot be inconsistent with their stability as laws. God rules the creation in accordance with the laws which He himself has ordained.

God's Providence in Relation to Vital Processes.

Life has ever been regarded as one of the most inscrutable of mysteries. However hard it may be to answer the question, What is life? or however diverse and unsatisfactory may be the answers given to that question, or the explanations proposed of its phenomena, there is little difference as to the facts of the case. (1.) It is admitted that there is a great difference between life and death — between the living and the dead. No one who has ever looked upon a dead body has failed to be impressed with the fearful change involved in passing from life to death. (2.) It is very evident that the difference does not consist in anything which can be weighed or measured, or detected by the microscope or by chemical analysis. (3.) Certain processes go on where life is present, and are never seen when it is absent. These processes are organization, growth, and reproduction. (4.) These processes imply the perception of an end; a purpose or will to secure that end; and the intelligent choice and application of means for its attainment. This is the work of mind. If blind physical force can fashion the eye or the ear, and build up the whole animal body, with all its wonderful interdependencies and relations of parts and organs, and its designed adaptations for what is external and future, then there is no evidence of mind in heaven or earth; then all the works of art and of genius with which the world is crowded, may be the productions of dead matter, or of physical forces.

But if life be mind, or, rather, if vital force be mental force, as indicated by the mode in which it acts, where does that mind reside? In the infinitesimally small germ of the plant or animal? or in something exterior to that germ? These are questions which have ever been demanding an answer, and to which different replies

[1] Comte's *Philosophy of the Sciences*, by Lewes, London, 1853, pp. 102, 103.

have been made. First, some say that nature itself is intelligent.
By nature they do not mean the material world, but the *vis in
rebus insita*. The forces which are active in the world, are conceived of as belonging to a substance or animating principle, or
anima mundi. Some who believe in an extramundane personal
God, believe that He has created and rendered immanent in the
world this *natura naturans*, which they hold to be the seat of all
the intelligence manifested in the works of nature. This is the
only God some scientific men are willing to admit. Material nature, it is said, gives no evidence of the existence of a personal
Being. We see in nature a mind, a universal mind, but still a
mind which only operates and expresses itself by law. " Nature
only does and only can inform us of mind *in* nature, the partner
and correlative of organized matter." [1]   Baden Powell, in his
" Order of Nature," says, that the elevated views of a Deity as a
personal God, and Omnipotent Creator, etc., are conceptions which
" can originate only from some other source than physical philosophy." [2]

Secondly, some assume that there is in the germ of every plant
or animal what Agassiz calls " an immaterial principle," to which
its organizing power is to be referred. Some connect this with
the Platonic doctrine of ideas, as spiritual entities, which are the
life and reality of all material organisms.

Thirdly, others refer the intelligence manifested in vital processes to God; not immediately, but remotely. Men can construct
machines to do intellectual work, without the machines themselves
being intelligent. We have orreries, and calculating and type-
setting machines, which, apparently at least, do the work of mind.
If man can make a watch or locomotive engine, why may not God
make watches and engines with the power of reproduction ?   The
analogy, however, between the products of human ingenuity and
living organism is very imperfect.   No product of human art can
think or choose.   A type-setting machine may be made, when the
proper key is touched, to move an arm in the right direction and to
the proper distance to reach the required letter ; but it cannot be
made of itself to select from a confused mass of type the letters
one after another, and arrange them so as to form words and sentences.   In other words, matter cannot be made to do the work
of mind.   It is admitted that everything is possible with God, but
the contradictory is not an object of power.   It is a contradiction

[1] See this doctrine discussed in the *Bampton Lectures* for 1865, by Rev. J. B. Mozley,
p. 96.
[2] Edit. London, 1859, p. 249.

that the extended should be unextended, that the irrational should be rational. It is, therefore, inconceivable that matter with its blind physical forces should perform the mental work exhibited in the processes of organization and growth.

Fourthly, the intelligence required to account for the processes of vegetable and animal life is assumed to be in the everywhere present and everywhere active mind of God himself. This does not imply that physical or second causes have no efficiency, or that those causes are merged into the efficiency of God. It simply means that God uses the chemical, electric, photic, and other forces of nature, in carrying on organization and other vital processes in the vegetable and animal worlds. In such processes there is a combination of two specifically different forces ; physical and mental. The physical are in the matter used ; the mental in God who uses the matter and its forces. Examples of this combination of mental and physical force are familiar. All voluntary motion, on the part of animals, all the works of men, are due to such combination. Walking, speaking, and writing, are possible only so far as mind controls our material organization. In writing, for example, the vital functions are going on in the hand, on which its mobility and susceptibility of nervous impression depend ; and the numerous voluntary muscles are called into action ; but the guiding power is in the mind. It is the mind that determines what letters and sentences the fingers shall form, and what ideas shall be expressed. In like manner, it is the ever-present mind of God that guides the action of physical causes in the processes of animal and vegetable life. And as it would be unreasonable to refer to the physical forces called into activity, when we speak or write, the intelligence indicated in what is uttered or written, so it is unreasonable to refer to the forces of matter the intelligence indicated in the processes of life.

It is because we cannot raise our minds to any proper apprehension of the infinity of God, that we find it so difficult to think of Him as thus everywhere present and everywhere intelligently active. This, however, ceases to be incredible, when we think of the marvellous coöperation of the mind and body which takes place in rapid talking, or, more wonderfully still, in a child before a piano, taking in at a glance the whole score, noticing the power and position of every note, striking eight keys of the instrument at the same time, and moving fifty or sixty voluntary muscles with the rapidity of lightning, and each at the right time, and with the right force. If the mere spark of intelligence in a child can do such wonders, why should it be thought incredible that the Infinite Mind should pervade and govern the universe ?

In support of the view here given, that the intelligence displayed in all vital processes is the intelligence of the everywhere present and everywhere active mind of God, it may be urged, in the first place, that the principle involved in this doctrine is assumed in the simplest truths of natural religion. If God be not thus everywhere present, and everywhere active in the control of secondary causes, there is no propriety or use in prayer, and no ground of confidence in divine protection. In the second place, it seems to be the only way to account for the facts of the case. That the processes of life in vegetables and animals do manifest intelligence cannot be denied. They manifest foresight, purpose, choice, and controlling power. This intelligence cannot be referred to matter, or to physical forces. The most advanced scientific Materialism does not make mind an attribute, or function, or product of all matter, but only of the highly organized matter of the brain. But there is no brain in the vegetable or animal germ. Brain is as much a product of life (and therefore of mind) as sinew or bone.

In the third place, the authority of Scripture may be claimed in support of the doctrine in question. The Bible teaches the omnipresence of God; *i. e.*, the omnipresence of mind. The phrase "God fills heaven and earth," means that mind pervades heaven and earth, that there is no portion of space in which mind is not present and active. The Scriptures also teach that all things, even the most minute, as the number of the hairs of our head, the falling of a sparrow, the flight of an arrow, are all under the control of God. He also is said to cause the grass to grow, which means not only that He so orders physical causes that vegetation is the result, but also, as appears from other representations, that the organization and growth of the plant are determined by his agency. This seems to be clearly taught with regard to the bodies of men in Psalm cxxxix. 15, 16, "My substance was not hid from thee, when I was made in secret, and curiously wrought in the lowest parts of the earth. Thine eyes did see my substance, yet being unperfect; and in thy book all my members were written, which in continuance were fashioned, when as yet there was none of them." However doubtful may be the interpretation of the 16th verse in the original, the general meaning of the passage cannot be mistaken. It clearly teaches that the human body is fashioned in the womb by the intelligence of God, and not by undirected physical causes, acting blindly.

B. *The Providence of God over Rational Creatures.*

God's providence, however, extends over the world of mind, *i. e.*, over rational free agents, as well as over the material universe. The principles involved in the Scriptural doctrine concerning God's providential government of rational creatures are, —

1. That mind is essentially active. It originates its own acts. This is a matter of consciousness. It is essential to liberty and responsibility. It is clearly the doctrine of the Bible which calls on men to act, and regards them as the authors of their own acts. This principle, as we have seen, stands opposed, (*a.*) To the doctrine of a continued creation. (*b.*) To the doctrine which denies the efficiency of second causes and merges all power into the immediate power of God; and (*c.*) To the doctrine that free agents are so dependent that they cannot act unless acted upon, or move unless they are moved *ab extra.*

2. But although free agents have the power to act, and originate their own acts, they are not only upheld in being and efficiency by the power of God, but He controls the use which they make of their ability. (*a.*) He can, and often does, hinder their action. (*b.*) He determines their action to be in one way and not in another; so that it is rational to pray that God would incline the hearts of men to show us favour; that He would change the dispositions and purposes of wicked men; and that He would work in us to will as well as to do. No creature, therefore, is independent of God in the exercise of the powers with which He has endowed it. The hearts of men are in his hands, and He controls their action as effectually as He controls the operations of nature. But his agency in the world of spirits no more interferes with the laws of mind, than his agency in the external world interferes with the efficiency of material causes.

Distinction between the Providential Efficiency of God, and the Influences of the Holy Spirit.

3. The providential agency of God in the government of free agents is not to be confounded with the operations of his grace. These two things are constantly represented in the Bible as distinct. The one is natural, the other supernatural. In the one God acts according to uniform laws, or by his *potentia ordinata*, in the other, according to the good pleasure of his will, or by his *potentia absoluta*. The control which God exercises over the ordinary acts of men, and especially over the wicked, is analogous

to that which He exercises in the guidance of material causes ;
whereas his agency in the operations of his grace is more analogous to his mode of action in prophecy, inspiration, and miracles.
In the former, or in his providential agency over minds, nothing is
effected which transcends the efficiency of second causes.   In the
latter the effects are such as second causes are utterly inadequate
to accomplish.   The most obvious points of difference between the
two cases are, (1.) In the ordinary operations or acts of free
agents, the ability to perform them belongs to the agent and arises
out of his nature as a rational creature, and is inseparable from it ;
whereas the acts of faith, repentance, and other holy affections do
not flow from the ability of men in the present condition of their
nature, but from a new principle of life supernaturally communicated and maintained.   (2.) The ordinary acts of men, and especially their wicked acts, are determined by their own natural inclinations and feelings.   God does not awaken, or infuse those feelings
or dispositions in order to determine sinners to act wickedly.   On
the other hand, all gracious or holy affections are thus infused or
excited by the Spirit of God.   (3.) The providential government
of God over free agents is exercised as much in accordance with
the laws of mind, as his providential government over the material
world is in accordance with the established laws of matter.   Both
belong to the *potentia ordinata*, or ordered efficiency of God.   This
is not the case in the operations of his grace.   Holy affections and
exercises are not due to the mere moral power of the truth, or its
control over our natural affections, but to the indwelling of the
Spirit of God.   So that it is not we that live, but Christ that liveth
in us.   It is indeed our life, but it is a life divine in its origin, and
sustained and guided in all its exercises by a higher influence than
the laws of mind, or an influence which operates merely through
them, and according to their natural operations.   This distinction
between nature and grace, between the providential efficiency of
God and the workings of his Spirit in the hearts of his people is one
of the most important in all theology.   It makes all the difference
between Augustinianism and Pelagianism, between Rationalism
and supernatural, evangelical religion.

Conclusion.

Such are the general principles involved in this most difficult
doctrine of Divine Providence.   We should be equally on our
guard against the extreme which merges all efficiency in God, and
which, in denying all second causes, destroys human liberty and

responsibility, and makes God not only the author of sin, but in reality the only Being in the universe ; and the opposite extreme which banishes God from the world which He has made, and which, by denying that He governs all his creatures and all their actions, destroys the foundation of all religion, and dries up the fountains of piety. If this latter view be correct, there is no God to whom we can look for the supply of our wants, or for protection from evil ; whose favour we can seek, or whose displeasure we need dread. We, and all things else, are in the hands of blindly operating causes. Between these equally fatal extremes lies the Scriptural doctrine that God governs all his creatures and all their actions. This doctrine admits the reality and efficiency of second causes, both material and mental, but denies that they are independent of the Creator and Preserver of the universe. It teaches that an infinitely wise, good, and powerful God is everywhere present, controlling all events great and small, necessary and free, in a way perfectly consistent with the nature of his creatures and with his own infinite excellence, so that everything is ordered by his will and is made to subserve his wise and benevolent designs.

CHAPTER XII.

MIRACLES.

§ 1. *Their Nature. Meaning and Usage of the Word.*

THE word miracle is derived from *miror*, to wonder, and therefore signifies that which excites wonder. In this etymological sense of the word it may be used to designate any extraordinary event adapted to excite surprise and rouse attention. The words used in the Bible in reference to miraculous events do not inform us of their nature. The most common of these are, (1.) פֶּלֶא, something separated, or singular. (2.) אוֹת, *signum, portentum*, something designed to confirm. (3.) מוֹפֵת (of uncertain derivation), used in the sense of τύπος, of persons and things held up as a warning, and for remarkable events confirming the authority of prophets. (4.) גְבוּרָה, *power*, used for any extraordinary manifestation of divine power. (5.) "Works of the Lord." In most cases these terms express the design, rather than the nature of the events to which they are applied.

Such being the indefinite meaning of these Scriptural terms, it is not surprising that the word miracle was used in the Church in a very loose sense. Anything wonderful, anything for which the proximate cause could not be discovered, and anything in which divine agency was specially indicated was called a miracle. Thus Luther says, "Conversion is the greatest of all miracles." "Every day," he says, " witnesses miracle after miracle ; that any village adheres to the Gospel when a hundred thousand devils are arrayed against it, or that the truth is maintained in this wicked world, is a continued miracle to which healing the sick or raising the dead is a mere trifle." As neither the etymology nor the usage of the word leads to a definite idea of the nature of a miracle, we can attain that idea only by the examination of some confessedly miraculous event.

Definition of a Miracle.

According to the "Westminster Confession," "God, in ordinary providence making use of means, yet is free to work without, above, or against them at pleasure." In the first place, there are events therefore due to the ordinary operations of second causes, as upheld and guided by God. To this class belong the common processes of nature ; the growth of plants and animals, the orderly movements of the heavenly bodies ; and the more unusual occurrences, earthquakes, volcanic eruptions, and violent agitations and revolutions in human societies. In the second place, there are events due to the influences of the Holy Spirit upon the hearts of men, such as regeneration, sanctification, spiritual illumination, etc. Thirdly, there are events which belong to neither of these classes, and whose distinguishing characteristics are, First, that they take place in the external world, *i. e.*, in the sphere of the observation of the senses ; and Secondly, that they are produced or caused by the simple volition of God, without the intervention of any subordinate cause. To this class belongs the original act of creation, in which 'all coöperation of second causes was impossible. To the same class belong all events truly miraculous. A miracle, therefore, may be defined to be an event, in the external world, brought about by the immediate efficiency, or simple volition of God.

An examination of any of the great miracles recorded in Scripture will establish the correctness of this definition. The raising of Lazarus from the dead may be taken as an example. This was an event which occurred in the outward world ; one which could be seen and verified by the testimony of the senses. It was not brought about either in whole or in part by the efficiency of natural causes. It was due to the simple word, or volition, or immediate agency of God. The same may be said of the restoration to life of the daughter of the ruler of the synagogue, on Christ's pronouncing the words, *Talitha cumi;* and of his healing the lepers by a word. So when Christ walked upon the sea, when He multiplied the loaves and fishes, when He calmed the winds and the waves by a command ; any coöperation of physical causes is not only ignored, but, by clearest intimation, denied.

Objections to this Definition of a Miracle.

It is objected to this definition of a miracle that it assumes that the laws of nature may be violated or set aside. To this many theologians and men of science object, and declare that it is impossible. If the law of nature be the will of God, that of course cannot be set aside, much less directly violated. This is Augustine's objection, who asks, " Quomodo est contra naturam, quod Dei fit voluntate cum voluntas tanti utique conditoris conditæ rei cujusque natura sit? Portentum ergo fit, non contra naturam, sed contra quam est nota natura."[1] Baden Powell, in behalf of men of science, protests against being called upon to believe in anything " at variance with nature and law." " The enlarged critical and inductive study of the natural world," he says, " cannot but tend powerfully to evince the inconceivableness of imagined interruptions of natural order or supposed suspensions of the laws of matter, and of that vast series of dependent causation which constitutes the legitimate field for the investigation of science, whose constancy is the sole warrant for its generalizations, while it forms the substantial basis for the grand conclusions of natural theology."[2] The question of miracles, he says,[3] is not one " which can be decided by a few trite and commonplace generalities as to the moral government of the world and the belief in the Divine Omnipotence, or as to the validity of human testimony or the limits of human experience. It involves, and is essentially built upon, those grander conceptions of the order of nature, those comprehensive primary elements of all physical knowledge, those ultimate ideas of universal causation, which can only be familiar to those versed in cosmical philosophy in its widest sense." " It is for the most part hazardous ground for any general moral reasoner to take, to discuss subjects of evidence which essentially involve that higher appreciation of *physical truth* which can be attained only from an accurate and comprehensive acquaintance with the connected series of the physical and mathematical sciences. Thus, for example, the simple but grand truth of the law of conservation, and the stability of the heavenly motions, now well understood by all sound cosmical philosophers, is but a type of the universal self-sustaining and self-evolving powers which pervade all nature."[4] Professor Powell's conclusion is, " if miracles were, in the estimation of a former age, among the chief *supports* of Christianity, they are at present among the main *difficulties* and hinderances to its acceptance."[5] His whole argument is this, miracles, as usually defined, involve a suspension, or alteration, or violation of the laws of nature; but those laws are absolutely immutable, therefore that definition must be incorrect, or, in other words, miracles in that sense must be impossible.

---

[1] *De Civitate Dei*, xxi. 8, edit. Benedictines, vol. vii. p. 1006, a.
[2] *Recent Inquiries in Theology, or Essays and Reviews.* By Eminent English Clergymen. Boston, 1860, p. 124.
[3] *Ibid.* p. 1‡0.
[4] *Ibid.* p. 151.   [5] *Ibid.* p. 158.

Answer to the above Objection.

The form in which the objection is presented by those who make nature the will of God, is answered by saying that nature is not the will of God in any other sense than that He ordained the sequence of natural events, and established the laws or physical causes by which that regular sequence is secured. This relation between God and the world, assumes that nature and its laws are subject to Him, and therefore liable at any time to be suspended or counteracted, at his good pleasure.

As to the other form of the objection, which assumes that the laws of nature are in themselves immutable, and therefore that they cannot be suspended, it is enough to say, (1.) That this absolute immutability of natural laws is a gratuitous assumption. That a thing has been is no proof that it must always be. There is no absolute certainty, because no necessity, that the sun will rise to-morrow. We assume with confidence that it will thus rise, but on what ground? What impossibility is there that this night the voice of the angel should be heard, swearing, "That time shall be no longer?" If time began, time may end. If nature began to be, it may cease to be, and all about it must be liable to change. Scientific men have no right to assume that because physical laws are, and, within the limits of our experience, ever have been, regular in their operation, that they are, as Professor Powell says, "self-sustaining and self-evolving." It is a great mistake to suppose that uniformity is inconsistent with voluntary control; that because law reigns, God does not reign. The laws of nature are uniform only because He so wills, and their uniformity continues only so long as He wills.

(2.) It is utterly derogatory to the character of God to assume that He is subject to law, and especially to the laws of matter. If theism be once admitted, then it must be admitted that the whole universe, with all that it contains and all the laws by which it is controlled, must be subject to the will of God. Professor Powell indeed says, that many theists deny the possibility of the suspension or violation of the laws of nature, but then he says that there are many degrees of theism, and he includes under that term theories which others regard as inconsistent with the doctrine of a personal God. It is certain that the objection to the definition of a miracle given above, now under consideration, depends for its validity on the assumption, that God is subject to nature; that He cannot control its laws. J. Müller well says, " Etiamsi

nullus alius miraculorum esset usus, nisi ut absolutam illam divinæ
voluntatis libertatem demonstrent, humanamque arrogantiam, im-
modicæ legis naturalis admirationi junctam, compescant, miracula
haud temere essent edita." [1]

(3.) The authority of Scripture is for Christians decisive on this
point. The Bible everywhere not only asserts the absolute independence of God of all his works, and his absolute control over
them, but is also filled with examples of the actual exercise of this
control. Every miracle recorded in the Scriptures is such an
example. When Christ called Lazarus from the grave, the chemical forces which were working the dissolution of his body ceased
to operate. When He said to the winds, Be still, the physical
causes which produced the storm were arrested in their operation;
when He walked on the sea the law of gravitation was counteracted by a stronger force — even the divine will. In 2 Kings vi.
5, 6, we are told that an " axe head fell into the water," and that
the man of God cut a stick and cast it into the water, " and the
iron did swim." Here an effect was produced which all known
physical laws would tend to prevent. The Scriptures, therefore,
by word and deed, teach that God can act, not only with physical
causes, but without and against them.

(4.) After all, the suspension or violation of the laws of nature
involved in miracles is nothing more than is constantly taking place
around us. One force counteracts another; vital force keeps the
chemical laws of matter in abeyance; and muscular force can control the action of physical force. When a man raises a weight
from the ground, the law of gravity is neither suspended nor violated, but counteracted by a stronger force. The same is true as
to the walking of Christ on the water, and the swimming of the
iron at the command of the prophet. The simple and grand truth
that the universe is not under the exclusive control of physical
forces, but that everywhere and always there is above, separate
from, and superior to all else, an infinite personal will, not superseding, but directing and controlling all physical causes, acting
with or without them. The truth on this subject was beautifully
expressed by Sir Isaac Newton, when he said, " Deum esse ens
summe perfectum concedunt omnes. Entis autem summe perfecti
Idea est ut sit substantia una, simplex, indivisibilis, viva et vivifica,
ubique semper necessario existens, summe intelligens omnia, libere
volens bona, voluntate efficiens possibilia, effectibus nobilioribus
similitudinem propriam quantum fieri potest, communicans, om-

───────────────

[1] *De Miracul. J. C. Nat. et Necess.*, Marburg, 1839, par. i. pp. 41, 42.

nia in se continens, tanquam eorum principium et locus, omnia per
præsentiam substantialem cernens et regens, et cum rebus omnibus, secundum leges accuratas ut naturæ totius fundamentum et
causa constanter coöperans, nisi ubi aliter agere bonum est."[1]
God is the author of nature: He has ordained its laws: He is
everywhere present in his works : He governs all things by
coöperating and using the laws which He has ordained, NISI UBI
ALITER AGERE BONUM EST. He has left Himself free.

Higher Laws.

A second objection to the usual definition of miracles, is that
they should be referred to some higher, occult law of nature and
not to the immediate agency of God. This objection is urged by
two very different classes of writers. First, those who adopt the
mechanical theory of the universe assume that God has given it
up to the government of natural laws, and no more interferes with
its natural operations than a ship-builder with the navigation of the
ships he has constructed. This is the view presented by Babbage
in his " Ninth Bridgewater Treatise." He supposes a man placed
before his calculating machine, which for millions and millions of
times produces square numbers ; then for once produces a cube
number ; and then only squares until the machine wears out.
There are two ways of accounting for the extraordinary cube
number. The one is that the maker of the machine directly
interfered for its production. The other is that he provided for
its appearance in the original construction of the machine. The
latter explanation gives a far higher idea of the skill and wisdom
of the mechanist ; and so, Mr. Babbage argues, it is " more consistent with the attributes of the Deity to look upon miracles not
as deviations from the laws assigned by the Almighty for the government of matter and of mind ; but as the exact fulfilment of
much more extensive laws than those we suppose to exist."[2] In
like manner Professor Baden Powell, contends that every physical
effect must have a physical cause, and therefore that miracles, considered as physical events, must be " referred to physical causes,
possibly to *known* causes ; but, at all events, to some higher cause
or law, if at present unknown."[3]

Secondly, this same ground is taken by many who do not thus
banish God from his works. They admit that He is everywhere

1 Sir David Brewster's *Life of Newton*, vol. ii. p. 154, edit. Edinburgh, 1855.
2 *The Ninth Bridgewater Treatise.* By Charles Babbage, Esq. London, 1838, p. 92.
3 *Essays and Reviews; or Recent Inquiries in Theology*, p. 160. Boston, 1860.

present, and everywhere acting, controlling physical laws so as to accomplish his purposes ; but they insist that He never operates *immediately*, but always acts through the established laws of nature. Thus the Duke of Argyle, whose excellent work on the " Reign of Law " is thoroughly religious, says :[1] " There is nothing in religion incompatible with the belief that all exercises of God's power, whether ordinary or extraordinary, are effected through the instrumentality of means — that is to say, by the instrumentality of natural laws brought out, as it were, and used for a divine purpose." He begins his book with quotations from M. Guizot's work, " L'Eglise et la Société Chrétienne en 1861," to the effect that belief in the supernatural is the special difficulty of our time ; that the denial of it is the form taken by all modern assaults on Christian faith ; and that acceptance of it lies at the root, not only of Christianity, but of all positive religion whatever. By the supernatural, he understood Guizot to mean, what the word does properly and commonly mean, namely, what transcends nature ; and by nature is meant all things out of God. A supernatural event, therefore, in this sense, which is Guizot's sense of the word, is an event which transcends the power of nature, and which is due to the immediate agency of God. M. Guizot is undoubtedly correct in saying that the belief in the supernatural, thus explained, is the great difficulty of the age. The tendency, not only of science, but of speculation in all departments, is, at least for the time being, to merge everything into nature and to admit of no other causes.

Although the Duke of Argyle is a theist, and admits of the constant operation of the Divine will in nature, he is still urgent in insisting that the power of God in nature is always exercised according to law, and in connection with physical causes. Miracles, therefore, differ from ordinary events only in so far as the law according to which they come to pass, or the physical forces acting in their production are unknown. He quotes with approbation from Locke, the following most unsatisfactory definition : " A miracle, then, I take to be a sensible operation, which, being above the comprehension of the spectator, and, *in his opinion*, contrary to the established course of nature, *is taken by him* to be divine." [2] This is the precise view held by Baden Powell, who in the essay repeatedly referred to above, makes a miracle a mere matter of opinion. It is not a matter of fact to be determined by testimony,

---

[1] *Reign of Law.* By the Duke of Argyle. Fifth edition, London, p. 22.
[2] *Reign of Law*, pp. 24. 25.

but a matter of opinion as to the cause of that fact. The fact may be admitted, and one man may say it is due to natural law, known or unknown; and then it is no miracle. Another man says it is due to the immediate power of God. In that case it is a miracle. Which of the two is correct, cannot be decided by testimony. It must be decided by the general views of nature and of God's relation to the world, which men entertain. The doctrine that God works in the external world only through physical force, and even that He can act only in that way, leads, of necessity, to the conclusion that miracles are events in the external world brought about by unknown physical causes. They prove only " the presence of superhuman knowledge and the working of superhuman power." [1]

Objections to the Doctrine of a Higher Law.

(1.) With regard to this theory, it may be remarked in the first place, that it is a perfectly gratuitous hypothesis. It assumes the existence of laws of nature without necessity and without evidence. By laws, in such connections, is usually meant either the ordered sequence of events, or the power by which that sequence is secured. In either case there is this ordered sequence. But where is the evidence that anywhere in the universe the living of the dead, the recovery of the sick, the stilling of the storm, and the swimming of iron, follow as matters of course on a command? The Church doctrine on miracles gives a simple, rational, and satisfactory account of their occurrence, which renders all assumption of unknown laws unnecessary and unjustifiable. It is utterly impossible to prove, as this theory assumes, that every physical effect must have a physical cause. Our own wills are causes in the sphere of nature; and the omnipotent will of God is not tied to any one mode of operation.

(2.) This hypothesis is not only unnecessary, but it is unsatisfactory. There are miracles which transcend not only all known, but all possible laws of nature. Nature cannot create. It cannot originate life; otherwise it would be God, and nothing beyond nature would be necessary to account for the universe and for all that it contains. As, therefore, there are miracles which cannot be accounted for by "a higher law of nature," it is clear that they are to be referred to the immediate power of God, and not to some unknown physical force. All theists are obliged to acknowledge this

---

[1] *Reign of Law*, p. 16, *note*.

immediate agency of God in the original act of creation. Then there were no laws or forces through which his efficiency could be exercised. The fact, therefore, on which the Church doctrine on this subject rests must be admitted.

(3.) The Scriptures not only are silent about any higher law as the cause of miraculous events, but they always refer them to the immediate power of God. Christ said He cast out devils by the finger of God. He never referred to anything but his own will as the efficient antecedent of the effect produced, "I will, be thou clean." He healed by a touch — by a word. When he gave miraculous powers to the Apostles, He did not make them alchemists. They did not claim knowledge of occult laws. Peter, when called to account for the healing of the lame man in the temple, said that it was the name of Christ, faith in his name that had made the man every whit whole. It is moreover plain that, on this theory, miracles must lose their value as proofs of a divine commission. If the Apostles did the wonders which they performed by the knowledge of, or through the efficiency of natural laws, then they are on the level of the experimenter who makes water freeze in a red hot spoon. If God be not the author of the miracle, it does not prove a divine message.

(4.) There is force also in what the Rev. J. B. Mozley says: "To say that the material fact which takes place *in* a miracle admits of being referred to an unknown natural cause, is not to say that the miracle itself does. A miracle is the material fact *as* coinciding with an express announcement or with express supernatural pretensions in the agent. It is this correspondence of two facts which constitutes a miracle. If a person says to a blind man, 'See,' and he sees, it is not the sudden return of sight alone that we have to account for, but its return at that particular moment. For it is morally impossible that this exact agreement of an event with a command or notification could have been by mere chance, or, as we should say, been an extraordinary coincidence, especially if it is repeated in other cases." [1] It is very certain that no one who saw Lazarus rise from the grave, when Jesus said, "Lazarus, come forth," ever thought of any physical law as the cause of that event.

Miracles and Extraordinary Providences.

A third objection urged against the definition above given is, that it is not sufficiently comprehensive. It does not cover a large

---

[1] *Eight Lectures on Miracles;* by J. B. Mozley, B. D. *Bampton Lectures* for 1865. London, 1865, p. 148.

class of miracles recorded in the Scriptures. In the sudden rising of a fog which conceals an army and thus saves it from destruction; in a storm which disperses a hostile fleet and thus saves a nation, — in any such providential intervention, it is said, we have all the elements included in many of the miracles recorded in the Bible. The events occur in the external world; they are not due to mere physical causes, but to such causes guided by the immediate agency of God, and directed to the accomplishment of a particular end. This is all that can be said of many of the plagues inflicted on the Egyptians ; of the flight of quails to supply the wants of the Hebrews in the desert; and of the draught of fishes recorded in the Gospels.

It is true that the strict definition of a miracle does not include events of the kind just mentioned. Such events, therefore, are called by Trench "providential," as distinguished from " absolute miracles." This want of comprehensiveness, however, does not seem to be a sufficient reason for rejecting the common definition of a miracle. Because there certainly is a class of events to which that definition strictly applies ; and it is important that those events on which such stress is laid in Scripture, should have a designation peculiar to themselves, and which expresses their true nature. The importance of what are called providential miracles, is not lessened by their being thrown into a class by themselves. They continue to be clear evidence of divine intervention. As Mr. Mozley says, it is not exclusively on the nature of the event that its value as evidence depends, but on the attending circumstances. The flocks of locusts, or of the quails, would not, of themselves, have been proof of any special divine intervention ; but taken in connection with Moses' threat in the one case, and promise in the other, those events proved as conclusively as the most absolute miracle could have done, that he was the messenger of Him who could control the laws of nature and constrain them to execute his will.

§ 2. *The Possibility of Miracles.*

This is of course denied by all those who do not make any distinction between God and nature. This is done by Spinoza and all his modern disciples. " Existimant," says Spinoza, " Deum tamdiu nihil agere, quamdiu natura solito ordine agit; et contra, potentiam naturæ et causas naturales tamdiu esse otiosas, quam diu Deus agit ; duas itaque potentias numero ab invicem distinctas imaginantur, scilicet, potentiam Dei et potentiam rerum naturalium, a

Deo tamen certo modo determinatam."[1] As he denies that there
is any distinction between the power of God and the power of nature, he of course denies that there is any ground for the distinction
between natural and supernatural events. " Leges naturæ uni-
versales," he says, " mera esse decreta Dei, quæ ex necessitate et
perfectione naturæ divinæ sequuntur. Si quid igitur in natura con-
tingeret, quod ejus universalibus legibus repugnaret, id decreto et
intellectui et naturæ divinæ necessario etiam repugnaret; aut si
quis statueret, Deum aliquid contra leges naturæ agere, is simul
etiam cogeretur statuere, Deum contra suam naturam agere, quo
nihil absurdius.[2] . . . . Ex his—sequitur, nomen miraculi non
nisi respective ad hominum opiniones posse intelligi, et nihil aliud
significare quam opus, cujus causam naturalem exemplo alterius rei
solitæ explicare non possumus.[3] . . . . Per Dei directionem intel-
ligo fixum illum et immutabilem naturæ ordinem, sive rerum naturalium concatenationem.— Sive igitur dicamus, omnia secundum
leges naturæ fieri, sive ex Dei decreto et directione ordinari, idem
dicimus."[4] The Pantheistic theory, therefore, which teaches
" that the government of the world is not the determination of
events by an extramundane intelligence, but by reason as immanent
in the cosmical forces themselves and in their relations,"[5] precludes
the possibility óf a miracle.

It is only a modification of the same general view when it is
said that although the worlds material and mental have a real
existence, there is no causality out of God. Second causes are only
the occasions or the modes in which the divine efficiency is exerted.
This doctrine effectually excludes all distinction between the natural and the supernatural, between what is due to the immediate
power of God and what is due to the efficiency of second causes.
The operations of God, when uniform, we call laws, says Bretschneider; when rare or isolated, we call them miracles. The
only difference is in our mode of viewing them. A third objection of the same general character is that miracles suppose separate,
individual acts of the divine will, which is inconsistent with the
nature of an absolute Being. " A God who performs individual
acts, it is very clear, may be a person, but cannòt be absolute. In
turning Himself from one act to another, or now putting forth a
certain kind of efficiency (the extraordinary), and then resting

---

[1] De Miraculis, Tractatus Theologico-politicus, cap. vi.; Opera, edit. Jena, 1802, vol. i. p.
233.
[2] Ibid. p. 235.   [3] Ibid. p. 236.
[4] Tractatus Theologico-politicus, cap. iii. ut supra, p. 192.
[5] Strauss, Dogmatik. vol. ii. p. 384.

again, He does and is at one moment what He does not and is not at another, and thus falls into the category of the changeable, the temporary, and the finite. If we continue to regard Him as absolute, his working is to be conceived as an eternal act, simple and uniform in its nature as it proceeds from God, and only in the phenomenal world revealing its fulness in a series of various and changing divine operations." [1]

This is an objection which has already been repeatedly considered. All that need be said in answer to it at present, is that it proves too much. If valid against miracles, it is valid against the doctrine of a creation *ex nihilo*, against providence, against revelation, against prophecies, against hearing of prayer, and against all the operations of grace. In all these cases as much as in miracles, there is an assumption of direct agency on the part of God. And if such immediate agency implies separate acts of the divine will in one of these cases, it must in all the rest. So that if the objection be valid against miracles it is valid against the doctrine of a personal God, and the whole system of natural and revealed religion. Whatever evidence, therefore, we have for the being of God and for the reality of religion, we have also to prove that this objection is sophistical, founded on our ignorance of the mode in which the infinite Being reveals and manifests Himself in the finite. Nothing is more certain than that God does act everywhere and always, and nothing is more inscrutable than the mode of his action.

A fourth objection to miracles is founded on the deistical theory that the relation of God to the world is analogous to that of a mechanist to a machine. A mechanist has no occasion to interfere in the working of an engine which he has made, except to correct its irregularities; so if God interferes in the natural order of events as produced by the secondary causes which He has ordained, it can only be because of the imperfection of his work. As this cannot be rationally admitted, neither can the doctrine of miracles, which supposes such special interference, be admitted. This objection is answered by showing that the relation of God to the world is not that of a mechanist to a machine, but of an everywhere-present, all-controlling, intelligent will. The doctrine of miracles, therefore, is founded on the doctrine of theism, that is, of an extramundane personal God, who, being distinct from the world, upholds and governs it according to his own will. It assumes, moreover, that second causes have a real efficiency to which ordinary events are

1 Strauss, *Dogmatik*, vol. i. p. 59.

proximately due; that the divine efficiency does not supersede those causes, but upholds and guides them in their operations. But at the same time this almighty and omnipresent Being is free to act with or without or against those causes, as he sees fit; so that it is just as consistent with his nature and with his relation to the world that the effects of his power should be immediate, *i. e.*, without the intervention of natural causes, as through their instrumentality. That this is the true Scriptural doctrine concerning God and his relation to the world cannot be disputed. It is admitted even by those who deny the truth of the doctrine. "Die ganze christliche Anschauung von dem Verhältniss Gottes zur Welt, von Schöpfung, Vorsehung und Wunder bezeugt diess (namely, that the Absolute is a person). Der Persönlichkeit ist freier Wille wesentlich; die Freiheit verwirklicht sich in einzelnen beliebigen Willensacten: durch einen solchen hat Gott die Welt geschaffen, durch eine Reihe von solchen regiert er sie, durch solche Acte greift er auch ausser der Ordnung seiner continuirlichen weltlenkenden Thätigkeit in die Weltordnung ein."[1]

§ 3. *Can a Miracle be known as such?*

This is denied on various grounds.

1. It is said, if a miracle be an event which transcends the efficiency of second causes we must have a perfect knowledge of the power of such causes, before we can decide that a particular event is miraculous. But as such perfect knowledge is impossible, it must be impossible for us to decide whether it is a miracle or not. It must be admitted that in many cases the mere nature of an event does not afford a certain criterion of its character as natural or supernatural. To savages many effects which to us are easily accountable as the product of natural causes, appear to be miraculous. An adept in the arts of legerdemain, or a man of science, may do many things entirely unaccountable by the uninitiated, which they therefore cannot distinguish from miracles by anything in the mere nature of the effects themselves. But this objection applies only to a certain class of miracles. There are some events which so evidently transcend the power of nature that there can be no rational doubt as to their supernatural origin. No creature can create or originate life, or work without the intervention of means. A large class of the miracles recorded in Scripture imply the exercise of a power which can belong to God alone. The multiplying a few loaves and fishes so as to satisfy the hunger of

[1] Strauss, *Dogmatik*, vol. i. p. 58.

thousands of men, raising the dead, and giving sight to the blind and hearing to the deaf, not by the appliances of art, but by a command, are clearly effects which imply the exercise of almighty power. Besides, it is to be considered that the nature of the event is not the only criterion by which we are to determine its character. To prove an event in the external world to be miraculous, we have only to prove that it is not the effect of any natural cause, and that it is to be referred to the immediate agency of God. To produce this conviction moral evidence is quite as effective as any other. Such an event may be, as far as we can see, supernatural, either in its nature or in the mode of its occurrence, but that alone would not justify us in referring it to God. Much depends on the character of the agent and the design for which the wonder is wrought. If these be evidently bad, we cannot be convinced that God has wrought a miracle. But if both the character of the agent and the design of his work are good, then we are easily and rationally convinced that the wonder is really a miracle.

Lying Wonders.

2. This remark applies equally to another ground on which it is denied that we can certainly determine any event to be miraculous. An effect may transcend all the powers of all material causes and the power of man, and nevertheless be within the compass of the ability of superhuman intelligences. There are rational creatures superior to man, endowed with far higher capacities. These exalted intelligences have access to our world; they do exercise their powers in producing effects in the realm of nature; and therefore, it is said, we cannot tell whether an event, admitted to be supernatural (in the limited sense of that word), is to be referred to God or to these spiritual beings. Such is the latitude with which the words "signs and wonders" are used in the Scriptures, that they apply not only to works due to God's immediate agency, but to those effected by the power of evil spirits. On this account many theologians regard the latter as true miracles. They are called "lying wonders," says Gerhard,[1] not as to their form (or nature), but as to their end, *i. e.*, because designed to promote error. Trench takes the same view; he says it is not a matter of doubt to him that the Scriptures attribute real wonders to Satan. The question is not, Whether the works of the Egyptian Magicians and the predicted wonders of Antichrist are to be regarded as tricks and juggleries. It may be admitted that they were, or are to be,

---

[1] *Loci Theologici*, loc. xxiii. cap. ii. § 274, edit. Tubingen, 1774, vol. xii. p. 102.

the works of Satan and his angels.   But the question is, Are they
to be regarded as true miracles?   The answer to this question
depends on the meaning of the word.   If by a miracle we mean
any event transcending the efficiency of physical causes and the
power of man, then they are miracles.   But if we adhere to the
definition above given, which requires that the event be produced
by the immediate power of God, they of course are not miracles.
They are " lying wonders," not only because intended to sustain
the kingdom of lies, but because they falsely profess to be what
they are not.   Thus Thomas Aquinas says :[1] " Demones possunt
facere miracula : quæ scilicet homines mirantur, in quantum eorum
facultatem et cognitionem excedunt."   They are only wonders in
the sight of men.

The difficulty of discriminating between miracles and these lying
wonders, *i. e.*, between the works of God and the works of Satan,
has been anticipated and provided for by the sacred writers themselves.   In Deut. xiii. 1–3, Moses says, " If there arise among you
a prophet . . . . and giveth thee a sign or a wonder, and the sign
or the wonder come to pass, whereof he spake unto thee, saying,
Let us go after other gods, ... thou shalt not hearken unto the
words of that prophet."   In Matt. vii. 22, 23, our Lord says,
" Many will say to me in that day, Lord, Lord, have we not prophesied in thy name? and in thy name have cast out devils? and in
thy name done many wonderful works?   And then will I profess
unto them, I never knew you : depart from me, ye that work iniquity."   Matt. xxiv. 24, " There shall arise false Christs, and
false prophets, and shall shew great signs and wonders ; insomuch
that, if it were possible, they shall deceive the very elect."   In 2
Thess. ii. 9, the Apostle teaches us that the coming of the man of
sin shall be " after the working of Satan, with all power and signs
and lying wonders."   These passages teach that supernatural
events, *i. e.*, events transcending the power of material causes and
the ability of man, may be brought about by the agency of higher
intelligences ; and that no such supernatural events are to be regarded as of any authority if produced by wicked agents, or for a
wicked purpose.   It was on this principle our Lord answered the
Pharisees who accused Him of casting out devils by Beelzebub the
prince of devils.   He appealed to the design for which his miracles
were wrought to prove that they could not be referred to a Satanic
influence.   Satan will not coöperate to confirm the truth or to promote good.   God cannot coöperate to confirm what is false or to

[1] *Summa*, part I. quest. cxiv. art. 4, edit. Cologne, 1640, p. 208.

promote evil. So that the character of the agent and the design
for which a supernatural event is brought about determine whether
it is truly a miracle, or whether it is one of the lying wonders of
the devil. From the Scriptures this criterion of miracles was
adopted by the Church. Luther says, " Against authenticated
doctrines, no signs or wonders, however great or numerous, are to
be admitted; for we have the command of God, who said from
heaven, ' Hear him,' to listen only unto Christ." Chemnitz [1] says,
" Miracula non debent præferri doctrinæ . . . . neque enim contra
doctrinam a Deo revelatam ulla miracula valere debent." Gerhard [2]
says, " Miracula, si non habeant doctrinæ veritatem conjunctam
nihil probant." Brochmann also says,[3] " Ut opus aliquod sit
verum miraculum duo requiruntur. Unum, est veritas rei; al-
terum, veritas finis."

To this it may be objected, that it is reasoning in a circle to prove
the truth of the doctrine from the miracle, and then the truth of
the miracle from the doctrine. We answer, however, (1.) That
this moral criterion is needed only in the doubtful class of miracles.
There are certain events which from their nature can have no
other author than God. They transcend not only the powers of
matter and of man, but all created power. The efficiency of creatures has known limits, determined, if not by reason, at least by the
Word of God. (2.) It is not unusual nor unreasonable that two
kinds of evidence should be dependent and yet mutually confirmatory. In the case of a historian, we may believe his authorities
to be what he says they are, on account of his character; and we
may believe his statements on account of his authorities. So we
may believe a good man, when he says that the wonders which he
performs are not tricks, or effects produced by the coöperation of
evil spirits, but by the power of God, and we may believe his
teachings to be divine because of the wonders. The Bible assumes
that men have an intuitive perception of what is good; and it
assumes that God is on the side of goodness and Satan on the side
of evil. If a wonder, therefore, be wrought in favour of what is
good, it is from God; if in support of what is evil, it is from Satan.
This is one of the grounds on which Protestants give themselves so
little concern about the pretended miracles of the Romish church.
They do not feel it to be necessary to disprove them by a critical
examination of their nature, or of the circumstances under which

1 *Loci Theologici*, iii. edit. Frankfort and Wittenberg, 1653, p. 121
2 *Ibid*. loc. xxiii. cap. 11, § 276, edit. Tubingen, 1774, vol. ii. p. 107.
' *Theol. Syst.; de Eccles.* ii. vii. dub. 12, Ulm and Frankf., 1658, vol. ii. p. 276, b.

they were performed, or of the evidence by which they are supported. Not one in a thousand of them could stand the test of such an examination; most of them, indeed, are barefaced impostures openly justified by the authorities on the ground of pious frauds. It is a sufficient reason for repudiating, prior to any examination, all such pretended miracles, that they are wrought in support of an antichristian system, that they are part of a complicated mass of deceit and evil.

Insufficiency of Human Testimony.

There is still another ground on which the possibility of a miracle's being known or proved has been denied. It is said that no evidence is adequate to establish the occurrence of a miraculous event. Our faith in miracles must rest on historical testimony. Historical testimony is only the testimony of men liable to be deceived. All confidence in such testimony is founded on experience. Experience, however, teaches that human testimony is not always reliable; whereas our experience, that the course of nature is uniform, is without exception. It will, therefore, always be more probable that the witnesses were mistaken than that the course of nature has been violated. This is Hume's famous argument, of which Babbage says that it, " divested of its less important adjuncts, never has and never will be refuted." [1] He evidently means that it cannot be refuted except mathematically, through the doctrine of probabilities. For he says on a subsequent page, that those who support the prejudice against mathematical pursuits, " must now be compelled to admit that they have endeavoured to discredit a science which alone can furnish an exact refutation of one of the most celebrated arguments against revelation." [2] He endeavours to prove the reverse of Hume's proposition ; that is, that on the doctrine of probabilities, it is unspeakably more probable that there should be a violation of the laws of nature (e. g., that a dead man should come to life) than that six independent witnesses should concur in testifying to the same falsehood. The argument may be valid in the view of mathematicians ; but to ordinary men it seems to be a wrong application of the principles of that venerable science. As we cannot determine by the law of probabilities a question in æsthetics or morals, neither can God's relation to the world, and the use of his power, as involved in the doctrine of miracles, be thus determined. It does not depend on the validity of human testimony. However uncer-

---

[1] *Ninth Bridgewater Treatise*, p. 121.   [2] *Ibid.* 132.

tain or unreliable such testimony may be, such events as miracles may happen, if consistent with the nature of God, and may be rationally believed. There may be proofs of their reality which no man can disregard. It is, however, as just remarked, a false assumption that human testimony is inadequate to produce absolute certainty. Men do not hesitate on the testimony of even two men to consign a fellow-man to death. In order that human testimony should command assent it must, (1.) Be given in proof of a possible event. The impossible cannot be proved by any kind of evidence. Professor Powell asks, How much testimony would be required to prove that two and two had, on a given occasion, made five? As no amount of testimony could prove such an impossibility, the argument is that no amount of evidence can prove a miracle. If miracles be impossible, that is an end of the matter. No man is so foolish as to pretend that the impossible can be proved. (2.) The second condition of the credibility of testimony is that the event admit of easy verification. If a man testify that he saw a ghost, it may be true that he saw something which he took to be a ghost; but the fact cannot be verified. The resurrection of Christ, for example, the miracle on the truth of which our salvation depends, was an event which could be authenticated. The identity between the dead and living Jesus could be established beyond the possibility of any reasonable doubt. (3.) The witnesses must have satisfactory knowledge or evidence of the truth of the facts to which they testify. Had the Apostles seen Christ after his resurrection only on one occasion, at a great distance, in an obscure light, and only for a fleeting moment, the value of their testimony would be greatly impaired. But as they saw Him repeatedly during forty days, conversed with Him, ate with Him, and handled Him, it is out of the question that they should have been mistaken. (4.) The witnesses themselves should be sober-minded, intelligent men. (5.) They should be good men. The testimony of other men, under these conditions, may be as coercive as that of our own senses. And it may be so confirmed by collateral evidence, natural and supernatural, by the nature of effects produced, and by signs and wonders and gifts of the Holy Ghost, as to render unbelief a miracle of folly and wickedness.

The fallacy of Hume's argument has often been pointed out. In the first place, it rests on the false assumption that confidence in human testimony is founded on experience, whereas it is founded on a law of our nature. We cannot help confiding in good men. We know that deceit is inconsistent with goodness; and therefore

know and are forced to believe, that good men will not intention-
ally deceive ; and, therefore, by a law of our nature we are compelled to receive their testimony as to facts within their personal
knowledge. Experience, instead of being the foundation of belief
in testimony, corrects our credulity by teaching us the conditions
under which alone human testimony can be safely trusted. In the
second place, Hume assumes that there is a violent antecedent
improbability against the occurrence of a miracle, which only a
" miraculous " amount of evidence could counterbalance. It is
indeed not only incredible, but inconceivable, that a miracle should
be wrought without an adequate reason. But that God, on great
occasions and for the highest ends, should intervene with the
immediate exercise of his power in the course of events, is what
might be confidently anticipated. Theism being granted, the difficulty about miracles disappears ; but by theism is not meant the
mere admission that something is God, whether nature, force,
motion, or moral order ; but the doctrine of a personal extramundane Being, the Creator and Governor of all things, who does
according to his own will in the army of heaven and among the
inhabitants of the earth ; a God who is untrammelled by cosmical
influences or laws.

In the third place, Hume's argument assumes that our faith in
miracles rests exclusively on human testimony. This is not the
fact. The miracles recorded in the Scriptures are a competent
part of the great system of truth therein revealed. The whole
stands or falls together. Our faith in miracles, therefore, is sustained by all the evidence which authenticates the gospel of Christ.
And that evidence is not to be even touched by a balance of probabilities.

§ 4. *The Value of Miracles as a Proof of a Divine Revelation.*

On this subject extreme opinions have been held. On the one
hand, it has been maintained that miracles are the only satisfactory
evidence of a divine revelation ; on the other, that they are neither
necessary nor available. It is argued by some that, as faith must be
founded on the apprehension of truth as truth, it is impossible that
any amount of external evidence can produce faith, or enable us to
see that to be true which we could not so apprehend without it.
How can a miracle enable us to see a proposition of Euclid to be
true, or a landscape to be beautiful ? Such reasoning is fallacious.
It overlooks the nature of faith as a conviction of things not seen,
on adequate testimony. What the Bible teaches on this subject is

(1.) That the evidence of miracles is important and decisive.
(2.) That it is, nevertheless, subordinate and inferior to that of
the truth itself. Both of these points are abundantly evident from
the language of the Bible and from the facts therein contained.
(1.) That God has confirmed his revelations, whether made by
prophets or Apostles, by these manifestations of his power, is of
itself a sufficient proof of their validity and importance as seals of
a divine mission.   (2.) The sacred writers under both dispensations appealed to these wonders as proofs that they were the messengers of God.   In the New Testament it is said that God confirmed the testimony of his Apostles by signs and wonders and
divers miracles and gifts of the Holy Ghost.   Even our Lord himself, in whom the fulness of the Godhead dwelt bodily, was ap-
proved by miracles, signs, and wonders which God did by Him.
(Acts ii. 22.)   (3.) Christ constantly appealed to his miracles as
a decisive proof of his divine mission. " The works," he says,
" which the Father hath given me to finish, the same works that
I do, bear witness of me, that the Father hath sent me."   (John
v. 20, 36.)   And John x. 25, "The works that I do in my Father's name, they bear witness of me ; " and in verse 38, " Though
ye believe not me, believe the works."   John vii. 17, " If any
man will do his will, he shall know of the doctrine, whether it be
of God, or whether I speak of myself."   Undoubtedly the highest
evidence of the truth is the truth itself; as the highest evidence
of goodness is goodness itself.   Christ is his own witness.   His
glory reveals Him, as the Son of God, to all whose eyes the God
of this world has not blinded.   The point which miracles are designed to prove is not so much the truth of the doctrines taught as
the divine mission of the teacher.   The latter, indeed, is in order
to the former.   What a man teaches may be true, although not
divine as to its origin.   But when a man presents himself as a
messenger of God, whether he is to be received as such or not
depends first on the doctrines which he teaches, and, secondly,
upon the works which he performs.   If he not only teaches doctrines conformed to the nature of God and consistent with the laws
of our own constitution, but also performs works which evince
divine power, then we know not only that the doctrines are true,
but also that the teacher is sent of God.

CHAPTER XIII.

ANGELS.

So much is said in the Scriptures of good and evil angels, and such important functions are ascribed to them both in the providence of God over the world, and especially in the experience of his people and of his Church, that the doctrine of the Bible concerning them should not be overlooked. That there are intelligent creatures higher than man, has been a general belief. It is so consonant with the analogy of nature as to be in the highest degree probable, apart from any direct revelation on the subject. In all departments of nature there is a regular gradation from the lower to the higher forms of life; from the almost invisible vegetable fungus in plants to the cedar of Lebanon; from the minutest animalcule to the gigantic mammoth. In man we meet with the first, and to all appearances the lowest of rational creatures. That he should be the only creature of his order is, *à priori*, as improbable as that insects should be the only class of irrational animals. There is every reason to presume that the scale of being among rational creatures is as extensive as that in the animal world. The modern philosophy which deifies man leaves no room for any order of beings above him. But if the distance between God and man be infinite, all analogy would prove that the orders of rational creatures between us and God must be inconceivably numerous. As this is in itself probable, it is clearly revealed in the Bible to be true.

§ 1. *Their Nature.*

As to the nature of angels, they are described, (1.) As pure spirits, *i. e.*, immaterial and incorporeal beings. The Scriptures do not attribute bodies of any kind to them. On the assumption that spirit unconnected with matter cannot act out itself, that it can neither communicate with other spirits nor operate on the external world, it was maintained by many, and so decided in the council held at Nice, A. D. 784, that angels had bodies composed of ether or light; an opinion which was thought to be favoured by such passages as Matt. xxviii. 3, Luke ii. 9, and other passages in

which their luminous appearance and the glory attending their
presence are spoken of. The Council of Lateran, a. d. 1215,
decided that they were incorporeal, and this has been the common
opinion in the Church. They are declared to be "substantiæ
spirituales, omnis corporeæ molis expertes." As such, therefore,
they are invisible, incorruptible, and immortal. Their relation to
space is described as an *illocalitas ;* not ubiquity or omnipresence,
as they are always somewhere and not everywhere at any given
moment, but they are not confined to space circumscriptively as
bodies are, and can move from one portion of space to another. As
spirits they are possessed of intelligence, will, and power. With
regard to their knowledge, whether as to its modes or objects,
nothing special is revealed. All that is clear is that in their intellectual faculties and in the extent of their knowledge they are far
superior to man. Their power also is very great, and extends
over mind and matter. They have the power to communicate one
with another and with other minds, and to produce effects in the
natural world. The greatness of their power is manifest, (*a.*) From
the names and titles given to them, as principalities, powers, dominions, and world-rulers. (*b.*) From the direct assertions of Scripture, as they are said to "excel in strength ; " and (*c.*) From the
effects attributed to their agency. However great their power may
be, it is nevertheless subject to all the limitations which belong to
creatures. Angels, therefore, cannot create, they cannot change
substances, they cannot alter the laws of nature, they cannot perform miracles, they cannot act without means, and they cannot
search the heart; for all these are, in Scripture, declared to be
prerogatives peculiar to God. The power of angels is, therefore,
(1.) Dependent and derived. (2.) It must be exercised in accordance with the laws of the material and spiritual world. (3.) Their
intervention is not optional, but permitted or commanded by God,
and at his pleasure, and, so far as the external world is concerned,
it would seem to be only occasional and exceptional. These limitations are of the greatest practical importance. We are not to
regard angels as intervening between us and God, or to attribute
to them the effects which the Bible everywhere refers to the providential agency of God.

Wrong Views on the Subject.

This Scriptural doctrine, universally received in the Church,
stands opposed, (1.) To the theory that they were transient emanations from the Deity. (2.) To the Gnostic view that they were

permanent emanations or æons ; and (3.) To the rationalistic view, which denies them any real existence, and refers the Scriptural statements either to popular superstitions adopted by the sacred writers in accommodation to the opinions of the age, or to poetical personifications of the powers of nature. The grounds on which the modern philosophy denies the existence of angels have no force in opposition to the explicit statements of the Bible, which cannot be rejected without rejecting the authority of Scripture altogether, or adopting such principles of interpretation as destroys its value as a rule of faith.

§ 2.   *Their State.*

As to the state of the angels, it is clearly taught that they were all originally holy. It is also plainly to be inferred from the statements of the Bible that they were subjected to a period of probation, and that some kept and some did not keep their first estate. Those who maintained their integrity are represented as confirmed in a state of holiness and glory. This condition, although one of complete security, is one of perfect liberty ; for the most absolute freedom in action is, according to the Bible, consistent with absolute certainty as to the character of that action. These holy angels are evidently not all of the same rank. This appears from the terms by which they are designated ; terms which imply diversity of order and authority. Some are princes, others potentates, others rulers of the world. Beyond this the Scriptures reveal nothing, and the speculations of schoolmen and theologians as to the hierarchy of the angelic hosts, have neither authority nor value.

§ 3.   *Their Employments.*

The Scriptures teach that the holy angels are employed, (1.) In the worship of God. (2.) In executing the will of God. (3.) And especially in ministering to the heirs of salvation. They are represented as surrounding Christ, and as ever ready to perform any service in the advancement of his kingdom that may be assigned to them. Under the Old Testament they repeatedly appeared to the servants of God to reveal to them his will. They smote the Egyptians ; were employed in the giving of the law at Mount Sinai ; attended the Israelites during their journey ; destroyed their enemies ; and encamped around the people of God as a defence in hours of danger. They predicted and celebrated the birth of Christ (Matt. i. 20 ; Luke i. 11) ; they ministered to Him in his temptation and sufferings (Matt. iv. 11 ; Luke xxii. 43) ; and they announced his resurrection and ascension (Matt. xxviii. 2 ; John

xx. 12; Acts i. 10, 11). They are still ministering spirits to believers (Heb. i. 14) ; they delivered Peter from prison ; they watch over children (Matt. xviii. 10) ; they bear the souls of the departed to Abraham's bosom (Luke xvi. 22) ; they are to attend Christ at his second coming, and gather his people into his kingdom (Matt. xiii. 39 ; xvi. 27 ; xxiv. 31). Such are the general statements of the Scriptures on this subject, and with these we should be content. We know that they are the messengers of God; that they are now and ever have been employed in executing his commissions, but further than this nothing is positively revealed. Whether each individual believer has a guardian angel is not declared with any clearness in the Bible. The expression used in Matt. xviii. 10, in reference to the little children, "whose angels" are said to behold the face of God in heaven, is understood by many to favour this assumption. So also is the passage in Acts xii. 7, where Peter's angel is spoken of (verse 15). This latter passage, however, no more proves that Peter had a guardian angel than if the servant maid had said it was Peter's ghost it would prove the popular superstition on that subject. The language recorded is not of an inspired person, but of an uneducated servant, and can have no didactic authority. It only goes to prove that the Jews of that day believed in spiritual apparitions. The passage in Matthew has more pertinency. It does teach that children have guardian angels; that is, that angels watch over their welfare. But it does not prove that each child, or each believer, has his own guardian angel. In Daniel, ch. x., mention is made of the Prince of Persia, the Prince of Grecia, and, speaking to the Hebrews, of Michael your Prince, in such a way as to lead the great majority of commentators and theologians in all ages of the Church to adopt the opinion that certain angels are intrusted with the special oversight of particular kingdoms. As Michael, who is called the Prince of the Hebrews, was not the uncreated angel of the covenant, nor a human prince, but an archangel, the inference seems natural that the Prince of Persia and the Prince of Grecia were also angels. This opinion, however, has been controverted on various grounds. (1.) On the silence of Scripture elsewhere on the subject. Neither in the Old nor in the New Testament do we find any intimation that the heathen nations have or had either a guardian angel or an evil spirit set over them. (2.) In verse 13 of the tenth chapter of Daniel the powers who were arrayed against Michael the angel who appeared to the prophet, are called "the kings of Persia;" at least, according to one interpretation of that passage. (3.) In the following chapter earthly sovereigns are introduced in such a way as to show that they, and not angels good or bad, are the contending powers indicated by the prophet.[1] It is certainly unadvisable to adopt on the authority of a doubtful passage in a single book of Scripture a doctrine unsupported by other parts of the Word of God. While this must be admitted, yet it is nevertheless true that the ordinary interpretation of the language of the prophet is altogether the most natural one; and that there is nothing in the doctrine thus taught out of analogy with the clear teaching of the Scriptures. It is plain from what is elsewhere taught that spiritual beings higher than man, both good and evil, do exist; that they are exceedingly numerous; that they are very powerful; that they have access to our world, and are occupied in its affairs; that they are of different ranks or orders; and that their names and titles indicate that they exercise dominion and act as rulers. This is true of evil, as well as of good angels; and, being true, there is nothing in the opinion that one particular angel should have special control over one nation, and another over another nation, that is in conflict with the analogy of Scripture.

So far, however, as the good angels are concerned, it is clear,—

1. That they can and do produce effects in the natural or external world. The Scriptures everywhere assume that matter and mind are two distinct substances, and that the one can act upon the other. We know that our minds act upon our bodies, and that our minds are acted upon by material causes. There is nothing, therefore, beyond even the teaching of experience, in the doctrine that spirits may act on the material world. The extent of their agency is limited by the principles above stated; and yet from their exalted nature the effects which they are able to produce may far exceed our comprehension. An angel slew all the first-born of the Egyptians in a single night; the thunder and lightning attending the giving of the law on Mount Sinai were produced by angelic agency. The ancient theologians, in many cases, drew from the admitted fact that angels do thus operate in the external world, the conclusion that all natural effects were produced by their agency, and that the stars were moved in their courses by the power of angels. But this is in violation of two obvious and important principles: First, that no cause for an effect should be assumed without evidence; and Second, that no more causes should be assumed than are necessary to account for the effect. We are not authorized, therefore, to attribute any event to angelic

---

[1] See Hävernick on Daniel x. 13.

interference except on the authority of Scripture, nor when other causes are adequate to account for it.

2. The angels not only execute the will of God in the natural world, but they also act on the minds of men. They have access to our minds and can influence them for good in accordance with the laws of our nature and in the use of appropriate means. They do not act by that direct operation, which is the peculiar prerogative of God and his Spirit, but by the suggestion of truth and guidance of thought and feeling, much as one man may act upon another. If the angels may communicate one with another, there is no reason why they may not, in like manner, communicate with our spirits. In the Scriptures, therefore, the angels are represented as not only affording general guidance and protection, but also as giving inward strength and consolation. If an angel strengthened our Lord himself after his agony in the garden, his people also may experience the support of angels; and if evil angels tempt to sin, good angels may allure to holiness. Certain it is that a wide influence and operation are attributed to them in Scripture in furthering the welfare of the children of God, and in protecting them from evil and defending them from their enemies. The use which our Lord makes of the promise, " He shall give his angels charge over thee, to keep thee in all thy ways. They shall bear thee up in their hands, lest thou dash thy foot against a stone " (Ps. xci. 11, 12), shows that it is not to be taken as a mere poetic form of promising divine protection. They watch over infants (Matt. xviii. 10); they aid those of mature age (Ps. xxxiv. 7), and are present with the dying (Luke xvi. 22).

3. A special agency is also attributed to them as the servants of Christ in the advancement of his Church. As the law was given through their ministry, as they had charge of the theocratic people under the old economy, so they are spoken of as being still present in the assembly of the saints (1 Cor. xi. 10), and as constantly warring against the dragon and his angels.

This Scriptural doctrine of the ministry of angels is full of consolation for the people of God. They may rejoice in the assurance that these holy beings encamp round about them ; defending them day and night from unseen enemies and unapprehended dangers. At the same time they must not come between us and God. We are not to look to them nor to invoke their aid. They are in the hands of God and exercise his will; He uses them as He does the winds and the lightning (Heb. i. 7), and we are not to look to the instruments in the one case more than in the other.

§ 4. *Evil Angels.*

The Scriptures inform us that certain of the angels kept not their first estate. They are spoken of as the angels that sinned. They are called evil, or unclean spirits; principalities; powers; rulers of this world; and spiritual wickednesses (*i. e.*, wicked spirits) in high places. The most common designation given to them is δαίμονες, or more commonly δαιμόνια, which our translators unfortunately render devils. The Scriptures make a distinction between διάβολος and δαίμων, which is not observed in the English version. In the spiritual world there is only one διάβολος (devil), but there are many δαιμόνια (demons). These evil spirits are represented as belonging to the same order of beings as the good angels. All the names and titles, expressive of their nature and powers, given to the one are also given to the others. Their original condition was holy. When they fell or what was the nature of their sin is not revealed. The general opinion is that it was pride, founded on 1 Tim. iii. 6. A bishop, the Apostle says, must not be " a novice, lest being lifted up with pride he fall into the condemnation of the devil ; " which is commonly understood to mean the condemnation which the devil incurred for the same sin. Some have conjectured that Satan was moved to rebel against God and to seduce our race from its allegiance, by the desire to rule over our globe and the race of man. Of this, however, there is no intimation in Scripture. His first appearance in the sacred history is in the character of an apostate angel. That there is one fallen angel exalted in rank and power above all his associates is clearly taught in the Bible. He is called Satan (the adversary), διάβολος, the traducer, ὁ πονηρός, the evil one; the prince of the power of the air; the prince of darkness; the God of this world; Beelzebub; Belial; the tempter; the old serpent; and the dragon. These, and similar titles set him forth as the great enemy of God and man, the opposer of all that is good and the promoter of all that is evil. He is so constantly represented as a personal being, that the rationalistic notion that he is only a personification of evil, is irreconcilable with the authority of Scripture and inconsistent with the faith of the Church. The opinion that the doctrine of Satan was introduced among the Hebrews after the Exile, and from a heathen source, is no less contrary to the plain teachings of the Bible. He is represented as the tempter of our first parents, and is distinctly mentioned in the book of Job written long before the Babylonish captivity. Besides this representation of Satan in

general terms as the enemy of God, he is specially set forth in
Scripture, as the head of the kingdom of darkness, which embraces all evil beings. Man by his apostasy fell under the dominion
of Satan, and his salvation consists in his being translated from
Satan's kingdom into the kingdom of God's dear Son. That the
δαιμόνια who are represented as subject to Satan, are not the spirits
of wicked men who have departed this life, as some have maintained, is clear. (1.) Because they are distinguished from the
elect angels. (2.) From its being said that they kept not their
first state (Jude 6). (3.) From the language of 2 Pet. ii. 4,
where it is said God spared not the angels that sinned. (4.)
From the application to them of the titles " principalities " and
" powers," which are appropriate only to beings belonging to the
order of angels.

Power and Agency of Evil Spirits.

As to the power and agency of these evil spirits, they are represented as being exceedingly numerous, as everywhere efficient, as
having access to our world, and as operating in nature and in the
minds of men. The same limitations, of course, belong to their
agency as belong to that of the holy angels. (1.) They are
dependent on God, and can act only under his control and by his
permission. (2.) Their operations must be according to the laws
of nature, and, (3.) They cannot interfere with the freedom and
responsibility of men. Augustine says of Satan : " Consentientes
tenet, non invitos cogit." Nevertheless, his power is very great.
Men are said to be led captive by him ; evil spirits are said to
work in the hearts of the disobedient. Christians are warned
against their devices, and called upon to resist them, not in their
own strength, but in the strength of the Lord and armed with the
whole panoply of God.

Great evils, however, have arisen from exaggerated views of the
agency of evil spirits. To them have been referred, not only all
natural calamities, as storms, conflagrations, pestilences, etc., but
what was far more lamentable, they have been regarded as entering
into covenant with men. It was thought that any person could
enter into a contract with Satan and be invested for a season with
supernatural power upon condition that the person thus endowed
yielded his soul to perdition. On this foundation rested the numerous prosecutions for witchcraft and sorcery which disgraced the
annals of all Christian nations during the seventeenth and eighteenth centuries. The most enlightened men of Europe yielded

themselves to this delusion, under which thousands of men and women, and even children, were put to the most cruel deaths. It is not necessary to go to the opposite extreme and deny all agency of evil spirits in nature or over the bodies and minds of men, in order to free ourselves from such evils. It is enough to adhere to the plain teaching of the Bible. These spirits can only act, as before stated, in accordance with the laws of nature and the free agency of man ; and their influence and operations can no more be detected and judicially proved than the influence and operations of holy angels for good. Both classes are efficient ; we are to be thankful to God for the unseen and unknowable ministry of the angels of light, and be on our guard and seek divine protection from the machinations of the spirits of evil. But of neither are we directly conscious, and to the agency of neither can we with certainty refer any specific effect ; if its occurrence admits of any other explanation.

Demoniacal Possessions.

The most marked exhibition of the power of evil spirits over the bodies and minds of men, is afforded by the demoniacs so often mentioned in the evangelical history. These demoniacal possessions were of two kinds. First, those in which the soul alone was the subject of the diabolic influence, as in the case of the " damsel possessed with a spirit of divination," mentioned in Acts xvi. 16. Perhaps in some instances false prophets and magicians were examples of the same kind of possession. Secondly, those in which the bodies alone, or as was more frequently the case, both the body and mind were the subjects of this spiritual influence. By possession is meant the inhabitation of an evil spirit in such relation to the body and soul as to exert a controlling influence, producing violent agitations and great suffering, both mental and corporeal. That the demoniacs mentioned in the New Testament were not mere lunatics or the subjects of epilepsy or other analogous diseases, but cases of real possession, is plain, First, because this was the prevailing belief of the Jews at that time ; and secondly, because Christ and his Apostles evidently adopted and sanctioned that belief. They not only called those thus affected demoniacs, but addressed the spirits as persons, commanded them, disposed of them, and in every way spoke and acted as they would have done had the popular belief been well founded. It is certain that all who heard Christ thus speak would and did conclude that he regarded the demoniacs as really possessed by evil spirits. This conclusion he

nowhere contradicts; but on the contrary, in his most private con-
ferences with the disciples abundantly confirmed. He promised to
give them power to cast out demons; and referred to his possession
of this power, and his ability to delegate its exercise to his disciples as one of the most convincing proofs of his Messiahship and
divinity. He came to destroy the works of the devil; and that
He did thus triumph over him and his angels, proved that He was
what He claimed to be, the promised almighty king and conqueror,
who was to found that kingdom of God of which there is to be no
end. To explain all this on the principle of accommodation would
destroy the authority of Scripture. On the same principle the doctrine of atonement, inspiration, divine influence, and every other
distinctive doctrine of the Bible, may be, and has been explained
away. We must take the Scriptures in their plain historical sense
— in that sense in which they were designed to be understood by
those to whom they were addressed, or we do thereby reject them
as a rule of faith.

There is no special improbability in the doctrine of demoniacal
possessions. Evil spirits do exist. They have access to the minds
and bodies of men. Why should we refuse to believe, on the authority of Christ, that they were allowed to have special power
over some men? The world, since the apostasy, belongs to the
kingdom of Satan; and to redeem it from his dominion was the
special object of the mission of the Son of God. It is not surprising, therefore, that the time of his advent, was Satan's hour; the
time when, to a greater degree than before or after, he manifested
his power, thus making the fact of his overthrow the more conspicuous and glorious.

The objections to the common doctrine on this subject are, —

1. That calling certain persons demoniacs no more proves that
they were possessed by evil spirits, than calling others lunatics,
proves that they were under the influence of the moon. This is
true; and if the argument rested only on the use of the word de-
moniac, it would be altogether insufficient to establish the doctrine.
But this is only a collateral and subordinate argument, without
force in itself, but deriving force from other sources. If the sacred
writers, besides designating the deranged as lunatics, had spoken
of the moon as the source of their derangement, and had referred
to its different phases as increasing or lessening the force of their
mental disorder, there would be some analogy between the cases.
It is readily admitted that the use of a word is often very different
from its primary signification, and therefore that its meaning can-

not always be determined by its etymology.   But when its signification is the same with its usage ; when those called demoniacs
are said to be possessed with evil spirits; when those spirits are
addressed as persons, and commanded to depart; and when this
power over them is appealed to as proof of Christ's power over
Satan, the prince of these fallen angels ; then it is unreasonable to
deny that the word is to be understood in its literal and proper
sense.

A second objection is that the phenomena exhibited by those
called demoniacs are those of known bodily or mental diseases, and
therefore that no other cause can rationally be assumed to account
for them.   It is not, however, true that all the phenomena in question can be thus accounted for.   Some of the symptoms are those
of lunacy and epilepsy, but others are of a different character.
These demoniacs often exhibited supernatural power or knowledge.   Besides this, the Scriptures teach that evil spirits have
power to produce bodily disease.   And therefore the presence of
such disease is no proof that the agency of evil spirits was not
active in its production and its consequences.

3. It is further objected that such cases do not now occur.   This
is by no means certain.   The evil spirits do now work in the children of disobedience, and for what we know they may now work
in some men as effectually as in the ancient demoniacs.   But admitting the fact to be as assumed, it would prove nothing to the
point.   There may have been special reasons for allowing such displays of Satanic power when Christ was on earth, which no longer
exist.   That miracles are not wrought in the Church now, is no
proof that they were not wrought during the apostolic age.

We are not to deny what is   plainly recorded in the Scriptures
as facts on this subject; we have no right to assert that Satan and
his angels do not now in any cases produce similar effects ; but we
should abstain from asserting the fact of Satanic or demoniacal influence or possession in any case where the phenomena can be
otherwise accounted for.   The difference between believing whatever is possible, and believing only what is certain is strikingly illustrated in the case of Luther and Calvin.   The former was disposed to refer all evil to the spirits of darkness; the latter referred
nothing to their agency that could not be proved to be actually
their work.   Luther [1] says : " Die Heiden wissen nicht, woher das
Unglück so plötzlich kommt ; aber wir wissen es, dass es eitel
Teufels Arbeit ist, der hat solche Helleparten, Bleikugeln und

[1] *Werke*, edit. Walch, vol. xiii. p. 2850.

Büchsen, solche Spiesse und Schwerter, damit er unter uns schiesst, wirft und sticht, wenn Gott es ihm erlaubt. Darum zweifle nur Niemand dran, wo ein Feuer aufgehet, dass ein Dorf oder ein Haus abbrennet, da sitzt allewege ein Teufelein dabei, das bläset immer in das Feuer, dass es soll grosser werden." " Ein Christ soll das wissen, dass er mitten unter den Teufeln sitze, und dass ihm der Teufel näher sei denn sein Rock oder Hemde, ja näher denn seine eigene Haut, dass er rings um uns her sei, und wir also stets mit ihm zu Haare liegen und uns mit ihm schlagen müssen."[1] " The heathen know not whence evil so suddenly comes. But we know. It is the pure work of the devil ; who has fire-brands, bullets, torches, spears, and swords, with which he shoots, casts, or pierces, when God permits. Therefore let no man doubt when a fire breaks out which consumes a village or a house, that a little devil is sitting there blowing the fire to make it greater." Again, " Let a Christian know that he sits among devils : that the devil is nearer to him than his coat or his shirt, or even his skin ; that he is all about us, and that we must always grapple with and fight him." Calvin's view of the subject is,[2] " Quæ de diabolis Scriptura tradit, eo fere tendunt omnia, ut solliciti simus ad præcavendas eorum insidias et molitiones : tum iis armis nos instruamus, quæ ad propulsandos potentissimos hostes satis firma sint ac valida." And he asks,[3] " Quid nostra refert vel plura, vel in alium finem de diabolis scire ? "

[1] Edit. Walch, vol. x. p. 1234; edit. Erlangen. 1828, vol. xvii. p. 178.
[2] Institutio, I. xii. 13.   [3] Ibid. 16.